Harvey's Wallbangers
The 1982 Milwaukee Brewers

EDITED BY GREGORY H. WOLF

Associate Editors

Len Levin, Bill Nowlin, and Carl Riechers

Society for American Baseball Research, Inc.
Phoenix, AZ

Harvey's Wallbangers: The 1982 Milwaukee Brewers
Copyright © 2020 Society for American Baseball Research, Inc.

Edited by Gregory H. Wolf
Associate Editors: Len Levin, Bill Nowlin, and Carl Riechers

Cover Photo:
Cover photos courtesy of the Milwaukee Brewers Baseball Club

All photos in this book are courtesy of
the Milwaukee Brewers Baseball Club
to which SABR expresses thanks and gratitude.

ISBN 978-1-970159-27-1
(Ebook ISBN 978-1-970159-26-4)

Book design: David Peng

Society for American Baseball Research
Cronkite School at ASU
555 N. Central Ave. #416
Phoenix, AZ 85004
Phone: (602) 496-1460
Web: www.sabr.org
Facebook: Society for American Baseball Research
Twitter: @SABR

TABLE OF CONTENTS

1 .... **Introduction and Acknowledgements**
By Gregory H. Wolf

4 .... **County Stadium, Milwaukee, Wisconsin**
By Gregg Hoffmann

9 .... **The Fingers-Simmons-Vuckovich Deal**
By Rory Costello

14 .... **The Final Puzzle Piece: Harvey Kuenn**
By Dennis D. Degenhardt

17 .... **How the 1982 Brewers Were Built**
By Rod Nelson

OWNER AND GENERAL MANAGER

20 .... **Allan Huber (Bud) Selig**
By Mario Ziino

32 .... **Harry Dalton**
By Dale Voiss

MANAGER AND COACHING STAFF

36 .... **Harvey Kuenn**
By Dale Voiss

45 .... **Buck Rodgers**
By Maxwell Kates

49 .... **Pat Dobson**
By Bill Bishop

57 .... **Larry Haney**
By Austin Gisriel

63 .... **Ron Hansen**
By Jimmy Keenan

70 .... **Cal McLish**
By Joe Wancho

75 .... **Harry Warner**
By Richard Bogovich

1982 BREWERS PLAYERS

81 .... **Jerry Augustine**
By Rick Schabowski

87 .... **Kevin Bass**
By Phillip Bolda

92 .... **Dwight Bernard**
By J.G. Preston

99 .... **Mark Brouhard**
By Isaac Buttke

104 .... **Mike Caldwell**
By Isaac Buttke

111 .... **Cecil Cooper**
By Eric Aron

116 .... **Jamie Easterly**
By Gregory H. Wolf

121 .... **Marshall Edwards**
By Rick Schabowski

125 .... **Rollie Fingers**
By Dale Voiss

131 .... **Jim Gantner**
By Gregg Hoffmann

137 .... **Moose Haas**
By Dennis D. Degenhardt

143 .... **Larry Hisle**
By David E. Skelton

152 .... **Roy Howell**
By Maxwell Kates

159 .... **Doug Jones**
By Richard Riis

163 .... **Pete Ladd**
By Gordon Gattie

170 .... **Randy Lerch**
By Alan Cohen

177 .... **Bob McClure**
        By Chris Rainey

184 .... **Doc Medich**
        By Gregory H. Wolf

192 .... **Paul Molitor**
        By Daniel R. Levitt and Doug Skipper

207 .... **Don Money**
        By Steve Kuehl

213 .... **Charlie Moore**
        By Phillip Bolda

218 .... **Ben Oglivie**
        By Jay Hurd

224 .... **Rob Picciolo**
        By John Gabcik

230 .... **Chuck Porter**
        By Mike Huber and Bill Mortell

234 .... **Ed Romero**
        By Bill Nowlin

240 .... **Ted Simmons**
        By Gregory H. Wolf

250 .... **Bob Skube**
        By Clayton Trutor

253 .... **Jim Slaton**
        By Isaac Buttke

262 .... **Don Sutton**
        By Gregory H. Wolf

274 .... **Gorman Thomas**
        By Dennis D. Degenhardt

282 .... **Pete Vuckovich**
        By Rory Costello

290 .... **Ned Yost**
        By Ken Carrano

298 .... **Robin Yount**
        By Gregory H. Wolf

BROADCASTER

311   **Bob Uecker**
        By Eric Aron

GAME STORIES

THE REGULAR SEASON

319 .... **April 9, 1982**
        **Brewers Shake Off Winter Blues
        With Opening Day Onslaught**
        By Isaac Buttke

322 .... **May 12, 1982**
        **Molitor Slams Three Homers For
        Only Time In Career**
        By Gregory H. Wolf

325 .... **June 20, 1982**
        **Ben Oglivie Wallops Three Homers
        As Harvey's Wallbangers Roll**
        By Gregory H. Wolf

328 .... **September 8, 1982**
        **Sutton Tosses Shutout For First Win
        In AL To Keep Brewers In The Hunt**
        By Gregory H. Wolf

331 .... **September 17, 1982**
        **Caldwell's Shutout Against Yankees
        Eases Brewers' Worries**
        By Phillip Bolda

334 .... **September 20, 1982**
        **Vuckovich Hurls 11-Inning Complete Game
        As Brewers Rally To Win**
        By Joel Rippel

336 .... **October 3, 1982**
        **Harvey's Wallbangers Clinch Division
        In Season Finale**
        By Lee Kluck

THE AMERICAN LEAGUE CHAMPIONSHIP SERIES

338 .... **October 5, 1982**
        Baylor Concentrates, Drives In Five
        By Ken Carrano

341 .... **October 6, 1982**
        **Kison's Complete Game Shuts Down
        Harvey's Wallbangers**
        By Gregory H. Wolf

344 .... **October 8, 1982**
        Sutton Hurls A Gem
        By Rick Schabowski

347......... **October 9, 1982**
Harvey's Wallbangers Have
A New Member
By Gregg Hoffmann

350......... **October 10, 1982**
Cecil Cooper's Two-Run Single
In 7th Propels Brewers To Victory In
The ALCS
By Frederick C. Bush

THE WORLD SERIES

353......... **The Opponent:**
The 1982 St. Louis Cardinals
By Russ Lake

360......... **October 12, 1982**
Mike Caldwell Tosses Three-Hitter As
Brew Crew Demolishes Redbirds In
Series Opener
By Gregory H. Wolf

363......... **October 13, 1982**
Rookie Reliever Walks In Winning Run
By Dennis D. Degenhardt

366......... **October 15, 1982**
Willie Mcgee's Two Homers Sink Brewers
By Stew Thornley

369......... **October 16, 1982**
Harvey's Wallbangers Explode
By Stew Thornley

371......... **October 17, 1982**
Robin Yount Collects Four Hits,
Mike Caldwell Notches Second Victory As
Brewers Win To Take 3-2 Advantage In
World Series
By Stew Thornley

373......... **October 19, 1982**
Stuper Was Stupefying In Complete
Game Win To Force Game Seven
By Gregory H. Wolf

376......... **October 20, 1982**
Cardinals Capture Ninth World Series
Championship
By Joseph Wancho

379......... **The Parade**
By Rick Schabowski

THE FINAL TALLY

381 .... **By The Numbers:**
The 1982 Milwaukee Brewers
By Dan Fields

391 .... **A Hall of Fame**
Roster of Contributors

INTRODUCTION AND ACKNOWLEDGEMENTS
HARVEY'S WALLBANGERS
THE 1982 MILWAUKEE BREWERS

By Gregory H. Wolf

Harvey's Wallbangers. What a moniker for the 1982 Milwaukee Brewers, who captured the hearts and imagination of baseball fans not just in Wisconsin, but around the country. Following the strike-shortened 1981 season, big-league baseball needed a feel-good narrative to rekindle fan interest. Harvey's Wallbangers were one of those stories. The club was filled with a memorable cast of characters, future Hall of Famers, and All-Stars: from Robin Yount, the former Boy Wonder who at age 26 was playing in his ninth full season with the Brewers; the Fu Manchu-wearing and prodigious slugger Gorman Thomas; Ted Simmons, whose shoulder-length mane of hair resulted in the nickname Simba; and Rollie Fingers, with his famous groomed twirling handlebar 'stache, to the criminally underrated, perennial .300 hitter and RBI machine Cecil Cooper; former HR champ Ben Oglivie; and emerging superstar Paul Molitor. Aiming for the fences, Harvey's Wallbangers led the majors with 216 home runs, 30 more than any other big-league team. Three of the top five home-run hitters in the AL were Brewers, including Stormin' Gorman, who tied the California Angels' Reggie Jackson for the league lead with 39. Harvey's Wallbangers weren't just sluggers. They were a close-knit and resilient group that weathered controversies and slumps to capture the AL East crown on the last day of the season, overcome a two-games-to-none deficit to win the best-of-five League Championship Series, and move to within one game of winning the World Series.

The Brewers did not begin the 1982 season as Harvey's Wallbangers. Their manager was Buck Rodgers, who had guided the club to its first postseason berth in franchise history a year earlier. Many predicted that the Brewers would challenge the Baltimore Orioles, Boston Red Sox, and New York Yankees for the AL East crown. The Brewers, however, started the season sluggishly, losing five straight games in early April, and then slumped in May, losing 14 of 20 games during a woeful stretch. On June 1 the Brewers were languishing with a losing record (23-24), tied with the Baltimore Orioles for fifth place in the seven-team division. Team owner Bud Selig and GM Harry Dalton acted decisively and replaced Rodgers with longtime coach and former 10-time All-Star Harvey Kuenn. Harvey's Wallbangers were born. The Brewers immediately responded to the first-time skipper's laid-back and let's-have-some-fun attitude. With the offense firing on all cylinders, the Brewers won 21 of their first 29 games under Kuenn's guidance to move into a tie with the Red Sox on July 3. They began September in first place, 4½ games ahead of the Red Sox and 5 in front of the Orioles. The outlook looked even more promising as the team acquired future Hall of Famer Don Sutton in a trade with the Houston Astros for the final month. However, the situation grew tense. Reigning AL MVP and Cy Young Award winner Rollie Fingers was sidelined with an arm injury and ultimately missed the last month of the regular season and the entire postseason, putting pressure on a pitching staff generally regarded as mediocre.

As well as the Brewers played in September (17-11), the Orioles were even hotter, winning 30 of 40 games, to pull to within one game of the Brewers and set up a dream scenario: a season-concluding four-game, winner-take-all series between the two teams in Baltimore. The Orioles trounced the Brewers in the first three contests, outscoring them 26-7, to pull into a tie. In the season's final game, the Brewers' stars led them to victory and the team's first divisional crown, in a crushing 10-2 victory. Robin Yount slugged two home runs and beat out a triple to cement his MVP season, Cecil Cooper and Ted Simmons bashed round-trippers, and 37-year-old graybeard Don Sutton pitched the most important game of his career to that point, tossing eight strong innings.

The Brewers experienced a roller-coaster postseason. After losing the first two games of the ALCS to the California Angels in Anaheim, Harvey's Wallbangers returned to County Stadium in Milwaukee and won three straight, led by pitching, to take the pennant. The World Series pitted two philosophies: the Brewers' prodigious power against the St. Louis Cardinals' Whitey Ball, so named for manager Whitey Herzog's emphasis on speed, defense, and pitching. After winning Game Five at County Stadium, 6-4, once again led by Yount's four hits, including a home run and double, Harvey's Wallbangers were on the precipice of the title. In agonizing fashion, the Brewers lost Games Six and Seven in St. Louis, their bats quieted by excellent pitching, scoring just four runs.

Despite the loss, the Brewers were still champions, at least in the hearts of their fans. Upon returning to Milwaukee, the team was feted by a grand parade. Four decades later, Harvey's Wallbangers still hold a special place in Milwaukee sports lore.

This book is the result of the tireless work of more than 40 members of the Society for American Baseball Research. SABR members researched and wrote all of the biographies, game accounts, and essays in this volume. These uncompensated volunteers are united by their shared interest in baseball history and a resolute commitment to preserving its history. Without their unwavering dedication, this volume would not have been possible.

I am indebted to the associate editors and extend to them my sincerest appreciation. Bill Nowlin, the second reader; fact-checker Carl Riechers; and copy editor Len Levin each read every word of all the contributions and made numerous corrections to language, style, and content. Their attention to detail has been invaluable. It has been a pleasure to once again work on a book project with such professionals, with whom I corresponded practically every day, and typically more than once. What a team we have!

I thank all of the authors for their contributions, meticulous research, cooperation through the revising and editing process, and finally their patience. It was a long journey from the day the book was launched to its completion, and we've finally reached our destination. We did it! Please refer to the list of contributors at the end of the book for more information.

This book would not have been possible without the generous support of the staff and Board of Directors of SABR, SABR Publications Director Cecilia Tan, and designer David Peng.

We express our sincere thanks and heartfelt gratitude to the Milwaukee Brewers Baseball Club and Robbin Barnes, publications assistant, for providing every photo for this book, including those on the cover. The Brewers' support of SABR's nonprofit mission is greatly appreciated. Without their generosity, this book would not have been possible.

And finally, I wish to thank my wife, Margaret, and daughter, Gabriela, for their support of and endless patience with my baseball pursuits. They're accustomed to me working on my "SABR stuff." We're looking forward to seeing the Brewers this season and enjoying their wonderful ballpark.

As the Brewers and Major League Baseball celebrate the 50th anniversary of the club in Milwaukee in 2020, we invite you to sit back, relax for a few minutes, and enjoy reading about Harvey's Wallbangers — the 1982 Milwaukee Brewers!

Gregory H. Wolf
Editor
May 2020

COUNTY STADIUM
MILWAUKEE, WISCONSIN

By Gregg Hoffmann

Milwaukee was ready for major-league baseball in 1953.

More than 10,000 people turned out for an open house at the ballpark on March 15, three days before the Braves' move to Milwaukee was approved by the National League owners.

Another large crowd turned out on April 6 and braved sleet and cold just to watch an exhibition game against the Boston Red Sox which lasted two innings. When County Stadium opened for the first Milwaukee Braves regular-season game on Tuesday afternoon, April 14, fans lined up hours before the gates opened in order to be among the first to get inside.

Fans that Opening Day started tailgating, a tradition that continues in Milwaukee, while bands played and dignitaries flocked to the new ballpark. A crowd of 34,357 packed the stadium and thousands more listened on radios outside and in homes and pubs around the town. Fans cheered wildly for every hit, every strike, and everything else. It was all new and exciting.

The game lived up to the excitement the day promised, with center fielder Billy Bruton winning the 3-2 contest on a disputed tenth-inning home run that bounced off the glove of a leaping Enos Slaughter, the Cardinals' right fielder.

It had been a long journey to that opener. County officials and others had talked about building a "major league" ballpark in Milwaukee since the 19-teens. Several locations were bandied about over the years, according to Milwaukee County records. Local politicians had differing opinions about where best to situate the stadium. Transportation, parking, and the demolition of existing buildings all factored in, delaying the project by decades.

Officials originally planned to build the stadium for the Milwaukee Brewers of the Triple-A American Association, an affiliate of the Boston Braves. In September 1948, they finally focused on Story Quarry, an abandoned landfill on the west side of the city.

Construction began in October 1950. Officials had to scramble to get materials, in part due to the demands of the Korean War. They were able to convince federal officials that construction had begun before the war rationing was imposed and were thus able to get the necessary steel. Between the material shortage and a required land swap with the adjacent Soldiers Home, the creation of Milwaukee's new ballpark literally required an act of Congress.

The ballpark, whose cost was initially put at $5 million, was the first in the country to be paid for by public funds. The funds came from a combination of city and County of Milwaukee bonds. As for the site, the US Congress in 1949 approved the leasing of 22 acres of federally-owned land for $1 a year and the county bought another 98 acres. A federal agency, the National Production Authority, also had to approve the construction after it had banned any new recreational facilities because of the need for steel and other materials for the Korean War. The stadium project was approved because groundbreaking had taken place a week before the ban was put into effect.

Osborn Engineering was the architect. Hunzinger Construction was the general contractor on the project. The stadium was built primarily for baseball, but was intended to be multipurpose, like Exhibition Stadium in Toronto and Municipal Stadium in Cleveland. (In 1988 home-game scenes for the movie Major League, which dealt with the Cleveland Indians, were shot at County Stadium during the summer of 1988, in part because it resembled Municipal Stadium, which was undergoing work at the time.)

The new stadium featured a double-decked grandstand and mezzanine that ran from first base to third base. The lower grandstand extended down the right-field line and to the foul pole. Temporary bleachers occupied the space down the left-field line, as well as several bleacher sections in the outfield. Over the years, a picnic area in left field became a popular feature of the ballpark. So did a grove of fir and spruce trees planted in March 1954, which acquired the name Perini's Woods. Throughout its history, County Stadium was expanded piecemeal, and eventually reached a capacity of 55,000-plus.

It was considered state-of-the-art in its early days and helped to lure the Braves from Boston. The franchise shift also paved the way for other teams, notably the Dodgers and Giants, to join the westward migration.

County Stadium was ready to go by spring 1953, but the Brewers, the Braves' top minor-league team, never played there. Instead, the Boston Braves owners, who had struggled for years at the gate as the second team to the Red Sox, applied for permission to move to Milwaukee.

Lou Perini, principal owner of the Braves, had blocked the St. Louis Browns from moving to Milwaukee earlier. Perini was able to persuade the National League owners to allow his club to move, only three weeks before the season was to start.

With Charlie Grimm, who had piloted the Brewers, as the Braves manager, the club immediately became competitive. Eddie Mathews, Johnny Logan, and others who had come through Milwaukee as minor leaguers, became fan favorites. The 1953 Braves finished 92-62, good for second place, in their first season and set a National League attendance record of 1,826,397.

The Braves continued to contend in their early years in Milwaukee; in fact, they never had a losing season in their 13 years there. Their fewest wins up to the 1957 championship season was 85 in 1955. They finished no worse than third place from 1953 through 1960.

In 1956 the Braves finished only one game behind the Brooklyn Dodgers. They seemed poised to make the move to the top after that season. Fred Haney, a contrast in managing style to the affable Grimm, took over as the skipper in mid-June of 1956 and meant business from the beginning.

The Braves made the move to first in 1957 when they won 95 games. One of the biggest moments in County Stadium history came on September 23, 1957. Henry Aaron, who was the Most Valuable Player that season, homered in the 11th inning off the St. Louis Cardinals' Billy Muffett to give the Braves a 4-2 victory that clinched the pennant. Aaron has often said that that blast against St. Louis was the biggest of his career, even surpassing the homer in Atlanta that broke Babe Ruth's record of 714.

County Stadium was decked out in red, white, and blue for the World Series. One member of the Yankees — reported to be manager Casey Stengel — referred to Milwaukee as "bush," and the fans took that up as their rallying cry, with signs "Bushville Wins" once the Braves won.

Opened in 1953, County Stadium was the home ballpark of the Milwaukee Braves (1953-1965) and Milwaukee Brewers (1970-2000).

The Braves clinched the World Series in New York in Game Seven behind Lew Burdette's third win of the Series. Game Five goes down as one of the great games in the stadium's history. Each team had won two games. Burdette, who had beaten the Yankees 4-2 in Game Two, was opposed by Whitey Ford, who had defeated the Braves 3-1 in Game One. In the sixth inning of a scoreless battle, the Braves broke through with a run. With two out and nobody on base, Mathews bounced a chopper toward second baseman Jerry Coleman. Hustling down the line, Mathews narrowly beat the throw to first. Aaron blooped a single to right-center, sending Mathews to third base. Then Joe Adcock smacked a line-drive single to right that scored Mathews. The single tally was all Burdette needed. He shut out the Yankees, 1-0, on seven hits.

From 1954 through 1957 the Braves drew more than two million fans each season. On June 12, 1954, journeyman Braves pitcher Jim Wilson fired the first major-league no-hitter in Milwaukee, against the Philadelphia Phillies. The cover of the inaugural issue of Sports Illustrated, on August 16, 1954, displayed a photo of Eddie Mathews batting in County Stadium. On July 12, 1955, the stadium hosted its first All-Star Game. More than 45,000 fans saw the National League roar back from a 5-0 deficit to win 6-5 in 12 innings. Attendance peaked at 2,215,404 in 1957 but slipped to 1,971,101 in 1958. In 1959, the year the Braves lost the pennant to the Los Angeles Dodgers in two games during a best-of-three playoff, attendance dropped to 1,749,112.

The subsequent years still had winning seasons and historic events, including two no-hitters by Spahn and one by Burdette, Pittsburgh's Harvey Haddix hurling 12 perfect innings in 1959 only to lose to the Braves in the 13th, San Francisco's Willie Mays hitting four home runs in a game in 1961 and many other thrills. But the magical team that won the championship gradually broke up. The Miracle in Milwaukee had run its course.

From 1960 through 1965, their last season in Milwaukee, the Braves never won fewer than 83 games. Even so, attendance continued to decline, dipping under a million for the first time in 1962. Rumors of the club moving already were circulating.

The 1964 season was marred by rumors about the Braves' status in Milwaukee, and outright feuding began between the ballclub and members of the community. County Board Chairman Eugene Grobschmidt intimated that he thought the Braves weren't making an all-out effort on the field. "I don't think the players or somebody isn't doing something right here," Grobschmidt said with more passion than grammar.[1]

Manager Bobby Bragan, who never caught on with the Milwaukee fans, snapped back at Grobschmidt. Club president John McHale said, "Grobschmidt had better have proof… or be prepared to retract the statement." McHale said the team would even consider a lawsuit.[2]

Congressman Henry Reuss, who represented a Milwaukee district, talked about trying to keep the club in Milwaukee through an antitrust suit against Major League Baseball. Milwaukee County officials indicated a willingness to force the team to stay through the end of 1965 through legal maneuvering.

The final parting of the Braves from Milwaukee was a bitter one. Both sides took legal action and hurled verbal hardballs. Warren Spahn, who was sold to the Mets in November 1964, and Oshkosh native Billy Hoeft, who was released in the spring of 1965, both said the Braves had tried not to win in 1964.[3]

"We should have won the pennant," Hoeft said. "But they didn't want to win."[4] Bragan, a Southerner who supposedly wanted the team below the Mason-Dixon Line, was looked at as the guy who did management's dirty work on the field.

Because of a judge's ruling regarding the County Stadium lease, the Braves had to play the 1965 season in Milwaukee. By July 28 of that season, however, corporation papers were filed for the Milwaukee Brewers Baseball Club, and the search for a new team was on. That served as an admission that the Braves were gone. From 1966 through 1969 Milwaukee was a city in search of a ballclub to call its own.

Perhaps the saddest day in County Stadium's history came when the Braves played their last game there, on September 22, 1965. Mathews recalled his last at-bat. A crowd of 12,577 gave him a standing ovation, and Mathews admitted his eyes teared up. "The fans gave me about a two-minute standing ovation," he recalled. "I was overwhelmed. I tried to bat, but I had to step out of the batter's box three or four times."[5]

Some legal action still took place after the season. Judge Elmer Roller ruled in the spring of 1966 that the Braves and the National League had violated Wisconsin's antitrust laws and must either give Milwaukee a new franchise or return to play in County Stadium. To that verdict, Braves executive William Bartholomay said, "There is as much chance of the Braves playing in Milwaukee this summer as there is the New York Yankees."[6] The Wisconsin Supreme Court overruled Roller.

County Stadium was without baseball. Officials tried to keep some revenue coming in with religious revivals, tractor pulls, wrestling matches, concerts, and other events. The Green Bay Packers, who had played some of their games in the stadium since 1953, continued to play there. But without baseball, the ballpark seemed like a home without a family.

Allan "Bud" Selig, who owned a car-leasing business in Milwaukee, organized a group to get baseball back to Milwaukee and the stadium. They almost bought the Chicago White Sox, who played 20 games at the stadium in 1968 and 1969. But that deal fell through. Selig's group eventually bought the bankrupt Seattle Pilots of the American League, in a move that had almost eerie similarities to the Braves move in 1953, coming only weeks before the opening of the 1970 season.

Milwaukee fans were excited to have baseball back in town, but they warmed up to the Brewers more slowly than they did the Braves; home attendance did not top one million until 1973. The Brewers also struggled on the field in the early years, and even the acquisition of Henry Aaron before the 1975 season didn't move the Brewers out of last place. Aaron hit the final home run (No. 755) of his 23-year career on July 20, 1976, at County Stadium. The Brewers finally built a winning team from the 1978 through the 1982 seasons with Harry Dalton as general manager. In 1982, the World Series returned to County Stadium, and the franchise drew over two million in home attendance in 1983.

The Brewers continued in the stadium for almost two more decades, but by the early 1990s it was clear that the ballpark had become outdated. Selig started talking about the need for a new stadium to keep baseball viable in Milwaukee.

After a contentious political debate about financing, Miller Park was eventually approved. For a couple of seasons, fans could watch the modern facility being built beyond the center-field wall of County Stadium.

The old ballpark had to work overtime after a construction accident killed three workers and delayed the opening of Miller Park for a year. Eventually County Stadium was closed, with its last game on September 28, 2000. Some of the greats who had played there came back for an emotional ceremony to say goodbye to what announcer Bob Uecker called an "old friend." Uecker read a short goodbye for the old park as the lights were turned off, standard by standard. He closed with "So long, old friend, and goodnight everybody."[7]

County Stadium's demolition was completed on February 21, 2001. However, the infield portion of the field was transformed into a youth playing field under the name of Helfaer Park.

SOURCES

Buege, Bob, *Milwaukee Braves: A Baseball Eulogy* (Milwaukee: Douglas American Sports Publications, 1988).

Gershman, Michael, *Diamonds: The Evolution of the Ballpark* (New York: Mariner Books, 1995).

Hoffmann, Gregg, *Down in the Valley: The History of Milwaukee County Stadium* (Holt, Michigan: Partners Publishers Group, 2000).

Lowry, Philip J., *Green Cathedrals: Ultimate Celebration of All 273 Major League and Negro League Ballparks* (New York: Walker and Company, 2006).

Milwaukee Journal (various issues ranging from 1948 until 2001).

Milwaukee Journal (various issues ranging from 1948 to 2001).

Milwaukee County Historical Association documents (1948-53 and 1964-66).

Povletich, William, *Milwaukee Braves: Heroes and Heartbreak* (Madison, Wisconsin: Wisconsin Historical Society Press, 2009).

Wisconsin State Historical Society documents (1948-53).

Interviews (done from 1994 to 1999 for *Down in the Valley*) with baseball commissioner and former Brewers owner Bud Selig, former Milwaukee Mayor Frank Zeidler, former Braves players Eddie Mathews, Henry Aaron, Warren Spahn, Bob Uecker, and Johnny Logan, former Brewers players Robin Yount, and Jim Gantner, and others.

NOTES

1. Lou Chapman, "Braves 'Call Off' Suit," *Milwaukee Sentinel*, July 10, 1964: II, 4.

2. Ibid.

3. Milton Gross, "Spahn Wonders What Mets Paid," *Milwaukee Journal*, November 24, 1964: II, 10.

4. Bob Wolf, "'Bragan Tried to Lose' – Hoeft," *Milwaukee Journal*, April 1, 1965: II, 17.

5. Eddie Mathews and Bob Buege, *Eddie Mathews and the National Pastime* (Milwaukee: Douglas American Sports Publications, 1988, 253).

6. Raymond E. McBride, "Braves Say They Won't Return Despite Judge Roller's Decision," *Milwaukee Journal*, April 14, 1966: 1.

7. Crocker Stephenson, "So Long, Old Friend, Crowd Says to Ballpark," *Milwaukee Journal Sentinel*, September 29, 2000: 7A.

THE FINGERS–SIMMONS–VUCKOVICH DEAL

By Rory Costello

On December 12, 1980, the Brewers and the St. Louis Cardinals made a seven-player trade. Three central figures on the 1982 AL pennant-winners came to Milwaukee: closer Rollie Fingers, starting catcher Ted Simmons, and frontline starter Pete Vuckovich. In return, St. Louis received two starters, Dave LaPoint and Lary Sorensen; outfielder Sixto Lezcano; and another outfielder, touted prospect David Green. Two years later, Dave Anderson of the *New York Times* wrote, "Some trades hurt both teams, but the best trades help both teams. That trade between the Brewers and the Cardinals not only helped both teams, but it also helped both teams get to this 79th World Series."[1]

Let's take a look back at how the complex blockbuster deal developed — and the value that each team got from it. The bottom line:

The Brewers benefited more directly in the short term…: The trade is viewed by many as the best the franchise has ever made. It brought back-to-back Cy Young Award winners, helped get Milwaukee into the playoffs for the first time ever in 1981, and nearly paid off with a World Series championship the next year. However, injuries curtailed the careers of Fingers and Vuckovich, and Simmons was in decline after 1982. Unlike the Cardinals, Milwaukee got almost no value from subsequent transactions.

… but the Cardinals won big through secondary deals and beyond: The players obtained from Milwaukee didn't make the same kind of direct impact — but subsequently, they were involved in other very important trades. Lezcano was part of the deal that brought the brilliant shortstop Ozzie Smith. Sorensen was part of a three-way trade that provided another key member of the '82 champs, Lonnie Smith. Even though Green didn't fulfill his vast potential, he and LaPoint helped net Jack Clark, the big bopper on the pennant winners of 1985 and 1987. What's more, when Clark left as a free agent, the Cardinals got a draft pick who turned out to be a star: Brian Jordan. Thus, they were still benefiting from this deal as late as 1998. It might have gone on even longer had Chance Caple, the pick received when Jordan too became a free agent, reached the majors.

HOW THE DEAL DEVELOPED

According to Daniel Okrent in *Nine Innings*, the Brewers and Cardinals started to feel each other out in October with a simple even-up proposal: Vuckovich for Sorensen. Cardinals manager/general manager Whitey Herzog wasn't willing to give Vuckovich a long-term contract. Brewers GM Harry Dalton turned down the offer then and again in

November, but he got scout Dee Fondy to check out Vuckovich — his ability, the condition of his arm, his alleged love of nightlife. The reports all came back positive. Ray Scarborough, then a special-assignment scout for the Brewers, seconded Fondy.[2]

Milwaukee's primary goal that offseason was to obtain a high-quality relief pitcher. They wanted either Fingers, then with the San Diego Padres, or Bruce Sutter, then a Chicago Cub. But on December 8, 1980, the Cardinals obtained Fingers in an 11-player trade with San Diego. The very next day, St. Louis got Sutter too.

The Brewers had also been looking into another Cubs reliever, Dick Tidrow, who was capable but not in the same echelon. "As soon as Whitey got Sutter, we figured he wouldn't want to keep Fingers, too," Harry Dalton said. "That's when we started talking about Fingers, and we also knew that Vuckovich and Simmons might be available."[3]

Indeed, the St. Louis makeover started on December 7 with the signing of free-agent catcher Darrell Porter from the Kansas City Royals. The idea was to move Simmons (somewhat suspect defensively) to first base and put Keith Hernandez in left field. Both players expressed their doubts. "You're taking a Gold Glove and putting him at a position other than where he might win it," Simmons said of Hernandez, one of the best-fielding first basemen ever to play the game. After mulling it over, Simmons asked to be traded.[4]

It's also notable that Milwaukee's plans for the 1981 season included shifting Paul Molitor from the infield to center field and Gorman Thomas from center to right. "The Brewers decided to gamble on putting Lezcano up for barter," *Sports Illustrated* wrote in March 1981. "Sixto became expendable," said Buck Rodgers, then the team's manager. "We knew we had to give up quality to get quality. We had to decide what good player to give up."[5]

Surrendering Vuckovich meant that the Cardinals "needed depth on the staff," said Herzog. "So we traded for Lary Sorensen."[6] LaPoint was still just a prospect then. He was in the mix for a spot on the St. Louis staff in 1981 but did not play with the big club until that September.

As negotiations progressed, the sticking point was Green. The gifted but troubled Nicaraguan was off the table at first. Brewers scout Ray Poitevint, who'd signed Green in 1978, argued vehemently against including him. Former Brewers PR director Tom Skibosh recalled, "It got so heated that Ray Poitevint and Ray Scarborough almost came to fisticuffs in a meeting. Poitevint was saying, 'David Green is the future of this organization,' and Scarborough was saying, 'Forget the future. We have a chance to get these guys; we want to win now.' They almost went at it. They had to separate them."[7]

But as Herzog said, "We think so much of Green that we would not have made the deal if he had not been in it."[8] Poitevint — and Dalton — relented.

Green's potential outweighed Herzog's reservations. In 1995 he said that he'd heard from a Milwaukee scout that Green had a problem with alcohol *before* the trade was made.[9] Players' substance-abuse history was an undercurrent in Herzog's decision-making. Darrell Porter had gone through rehab in the spring of 1980 and had to battle problems throughout his life (cocaine use contributed to his death in 2002). Sorensen also developed severe alcoholism, though it is not clear whether it had come to a head during his time in Milwaukee and St. Louis.

There was one final hurdle to clear, though: Simmons's agent, Larue Harcourt, demanded payment before the catcher would waive his "10-and-five" rights (i.e., as a veteran of 10 years' standing, the last five with the same club, Simmons could block a trade).[10] Originally Harcourt wanted $1 million, his estimate of the market value then for Simmons.

Dalton had reconciled himself to the idea of a payment, but he also was still considering a smaller-scale deal with St. Louis. He also was in talks with the Philadelphia Phillies about a deal involving Lezcano, who'd been disappointing in 1980 after a career year in 1979. Herzog had a good fallback option too — the New York Yankees had offered a deal that included their best pitcher, Ron Guidry. He was willing to take it if Milwaukee couldn't sign Simmons.[11]

In December 1980 the Brewers completed a blockbuster, franchise-altering trade with the St. Louis Cardinals, acquiring Ted Simmons (pictured), Rollie Fingers, and Pete Vuckovich. In 1981 the Brewers made their first postseason appearance and captured the AL pennant in 1982.

Milwaukee didn't want the deal to blow up; they'd heard the Yankees were also very interested in Vuckovich as well as Simmons. Also, because of New York's offer, the smaller trade with St. Louis was no longer an option. So the Brewers' president/owner, Bud Selig, authorized Dalton to go up to a $750,000 payment to get Simmons.[12] "We decided to wrap it up and we did," said Dalton in 1982.[13]

With the benefit of hindsight, how did the big trade work out?

Let's first look at it from Milwaukee's side.

Fingers: The mustachioed closer paid immediate dividends for the Brewers, winning the AL Cy Young Award in 1981. Alas, injury in September 1982 ended his season early; who knows how the World Series might have turned out had he been available? He missed all of 1983 and the second half of 1984. Milwaukee released him after 1985 and his big-league career was finished.

Simmons: The catcher had a down year in 1981 but rebounded strongly in '82. The 1983 season was the last in which he played a significant amount behind the plate. Milwaukee traded him to the Atlanta Braves in March 1986 for catcher Rick Cerone and two other players who never made it to the majors (pitcher David Clay and infielder Flavio Alfaro). Cerone played just one season with the Brewers and then joined the Yankees as a free agent. The Brewers received a second-round draft pick as compensation. That player, pitcher Curt Krippner, never advanced beyond Class A.

Vuckovich: The menacing mound psychologist had two good years in Milwaukee, including a Cy Young Award in 1982. Subsequent arm problems may well have been caused by overuse down the stretch in '82, though the ultra-competitive Vuke always wanted the ball. From 1983 on, he pitched in just 31 games; he retired after spring training 1987.

The following table quantifies Milwaukee's benefits in terms of Wins Above Replacement (WAR) at the primary and secondary level.

MILWAUKEE	PRIMARY WAR	SECONDAR WAR	TOTAL
Fingers	7.9	-	7.9
Simmons	5.9	1.9	7.8
Vuckovich	5.1	-	5.1
Total	18.9	1.9	20.8

Primary: Total WAR for Fingers, Simmons, and Vuckovich during their time in Milwaukee.

Secondary: Cerone's WAR of 1.3 for his season in Milwaukee minus Simmons's total WAR of -0.6 in Atlanta (1986 until his career ended in 1988). The Brewers were right to part with Simmons when they did.

Tertiary: Nil because Clay, Alfaro, and Krippner didn't make it.

Source: Baseball-Reference.com.

And now let's turn to the value the Cardinals received. This is trickier to analyze because the "trade tree" has a lot more branches.

LaPoint: During the trade talks in 1980, Harry Dalton thought that the lefty prospect might develop into a 15-game winner. George Bamberger, who'd managed the Brewers for part of that season and who was renowned for his knowledge of pitching, said, "Good luck to him. Don't look back."[14] LaPoint played in St. Louis from 1981 through 1984 after the trade with Milwaukee. He was then part of the five-player deal in February 1985 that brought Jack Clark from the San Francisco Giants. As it developed, the most valuable player the Giants got from St. Louis was shortstop José Uribe. Uribe was not an impact player like Clark, though, which shows a limitation of the WAR analysis here.

LaPoint actually did wind up winning as many as 14 games in 1988. His major-league career lasted through 1991.

Sorensen: The righty pitched just one year in St. Louis, going 7-7 with a 3.27 ERA during the strike season of 1981. He then went to the Cleveland Indians as part of the three-way deal in November 1981 that brought Lonnie Smith to St. Louis from the Phillies. As Whitey Herzog recalled in 2016, Smith was a risk, because of a known cocaine habit (which landed him in rehab in 1983) and an apparent fight he'd had with the Phillies' mascot, the Phanatic.[15] Yet when Herzog heard that Indians GM Phil Seghi said the Tribe needed pitching more than Smith, and that the price was Sorensen and Silvio Martinez, Herzog said, "Get [Seghi] on the phone and make that deal right now."[16]

Smith was the Cardinals' starting left fielder from 1982 — when he was runner-up for National League MVP — until he was traded in May 1985. Sorensen spent two seasons with the Indians — the first subpar, the second pretty good — and then left as a free agent. His major-league career lasted through 1988 and was hampered by alcohol and cocaine use. Later in life, Sorensen's alcohol problem became especially severe.[17]

Lezcano: Like Sorensen, the Puerto Rican was in St. Louis only for 1981. He didn't do all that much. In December 1981, Ozzie Smith — "The Wizard" — came to St. Louis in the trade that featured shortstop Garry Templeton, often labeled "talented but moody." Smith stayed with the Redbirds for 15 years and then retired; six years later, he entered the Hall of Fame. Lezcano was out of the majors after 1985.

Green: David Green is one of baseball's big "what if?" stories. But as Harry Dalton put it, "Not every phenom phenominates."[18] Nagging injuries as well as his personal troubles kept Green from realizing his "five-tool" promise. Green spent one unimpressive season with the Giants, and after that, his only other time in the majors was 14 games for the Cardinals in late 1987.

The following table quantifies the Cardinals' benefits from the deal in terms of WAR at the primary, secondary, and tertiary levels.

ST. LOUIS	PRIMARY WAR	SECONDARY WAR	TERTIARY WAR	TOTAL
LaPoint	3.2	-0.2	17.2	20.2
Sorensen	1.0	8.8	-3.1	6.7
Lezcano	0.5	46.6	—	47.1
Green	4.5	*	*	4.5
Total	9.2	55.2	14.1	78.5

Primary: Total WAR for LaPoint, Sorensen, Lezcano, and Green during their time in St. Louis.

Secondary:
From LaPoint and Green:
Jack Clark's total WAR as a Cardinal (1985-87): 9.7.
Subtract total WAR for the Giants of LaPoint (1985): 1.9, and Green (1985): -0.3, as well as that of the other players in that trade – Uribe (1985-1992): 8.9, and Gary Rajsich (1985): -0.6.

From Sorensen:
Lonnie Smith's total WAR as a Cardinal (1982-85): 11.6.
Subtract total WAR for the Indians of Sorensen (1982-83): 2.8, and pitcher Silvio Martinez, the other player St. Louis gave up in that trade: nil.

From Lezcano:
Ozzie Smith's total WAR as a Cardinal (1982-96): 65.6.
Add total WAR for the Cardinals of pitchers Steve Mura and Al Olmsted, the other players St. Louis received in that trade – Mura (1982): 0.4. Olmsted: nil.
Subtract total WAR for the Padres of Lezcano (1982-83): 6.2, Templeton (1982-1991): 10.0, and pitcher Luis de León (1982-85): 3.2.

Tertiary:
From LaPoint and Green: After Clark joined the Yankees as a free agent, the Cardinals obtained Brian Jordan as a supplemental pick in the June 1988 draft. Jordan's total WAR as a Cardinal (1992-98) was 20.0. Clark's as a Yankee (1988) was 2.8.

From Sorensen: After Lonnie Smith was traded to the Kansas City Royals, his total WAR from 1985 through 1987 was 3.3. The Cardinals got 0.2 total WAR from reserve outfielder John Morris, who played for them from 1986 through 1990 and then became a free agent. Based on his statistical ranking, the Cardinals did not receive a compensatory draft pick.

* Double counting with LaPoint avoided.

Source: Baseball-Reference.com.

NOTES

1. Dave Anderson, "Trade That Brewed the 6-Pack Series," *New York Times*, October 12, 1982.
2. Daniel Okrent, *Nine Innings* (Boston: Houghton Miflin Company, 1985), 206-207.
3. Anderson, "Trade That Brewed the 6-Pack Series."
4. Rick Hummel, "Cards Do a Quick-Change Routine," *The Sporting News*, December 27, 1980: 41.
5. Ron Fimrite, "The Trade That Made Milwaukee Famous," *Sports Illustrated*, March 16, 1981.
6. Joseph Durso, "It's Experimental, but Cards Beat Mets, 5-3," *New York Times*, March 15, 1981.
7. Dennis Punzel, "Brewers' Trade Dilemma Has Familiar Ring," *Capital Times* (Madison, Wisconsin), July 6, 2008.
8. "Cardinals Trade Simmons, Fingers to Milwaukee." *United Press International*, December 13, 1980.
9. Rick Hummel, "Herzog Laments Wasted Potential of David Green," *St. Louis Post-Dispatch*, February 5, 1995: 7F.
10. Hummel, "Cards Do a Quick-Change Routine."
11. Okrent, *Nine Innings*, 210-212.
12. Okrent, *Nine Innings*, 212-213.
13. Anderson, "Trade That Brewed the 6-Pack Series."
14. Okrent, *Nine Innings*, 206.
15. Todd Eschman, "Whitey Herzog Revisits the Year He Rebuilt the Redbirds," *Belleville* (Illinois) *News-Democrat*, January 24, 2016.
16. Whitey Herzog and Kevin Horrigan, *White Rat* (New York: Harper & Row, 1987), 139.
17. "The Successes, Demons, and Trials of Lary Sorensen," *Yes! Weekly*, July 16, 2014.
18. Okrent, *Nine Innings*, 210.

THE FINAL PUZZLE PIECE
HARVEY KUENN

By Dennis D. Degenhardt

On June 2, 1982, general manager Harry Dalton's firing of second-year manager Buck Rodgers and appointing longtime hitting coach Harvey Keunn as the interim manager was the final piece in the Milwaukee Brewers' only World Series appearance. As Bob Wolf, sports columnist with the Milwaukee Journal, succinctly stated, "Kuenn lost no time in proving that he was the right man for the job. He ran a loose ship and just let the players play, and they reacted so well to the change from Rodgers' tight rein that they began winning immediately."[1]

Buck Rodgers, Milwaukee's third-base coach since 1978, replaced popular and charismatic manager George Bamberger, who retired for health reasons after the 1980 season. After enduring ups and downs, the Brewers rallied to make the franchise's first postseason appearance, in another playoff level caused by the first midseason strike. They battled the New York Yankees to Game Five before losing. Owner Bud Selig and Dalton felt they owed the only manager to lead them to the playoffs by rehiring him with a one-year contract although concerned with his management style. In September, the *Milwaukee Journal* published an article quoting undisclosed players' very critical comments about Rodgers because he overmanaged, didn't communicate, and didn't relate to the players. "If they win, it was in spite of their manager. I don't think anyone on the club likes him," one said.[2]

Entering the spring of 1982, Rodgers admitted that his managerial style, playing the percentages by the book, caused questioning the previous year. Unlike his beloved predecessor who made out the lineup and let his players compete, he preferred making moves, removing pitchers quickly, and changing lineups, which caused second-guessing and accusations of over-managing. Rodgers said, "Maybe I'm too blunt but I don't think so. As much as I can, I let them know where they stand."[3]

The Brewers were struggling, falling below .500 and dissension was growing to a boiling point on Monday, May 31, when closer Rollie Fingers loudly complained about Rodgers' using matchups instead of his closer, with Mike Caldwell giving up the tying run in the ninth in a game lost in extra innings. After the game, Fingers proclaimed, "That's the nail in the coffin."[4] Others wondered why not use your best pitcher. Change was needed. It was the fourth time in eight games that the Brewers lost a late lead and their 14th defeat in 20 games, dropping them from second place to fifth, 7½ games out of first. After contemplating a change for two weeks, Dalton deciding on the afternoon of Tuesday, June 2, to fire Rodgers and notified him on Wednesday morning.[5] Monday's blowup wasn't the last straw, he said, adding, "I don't consider it a question of respect. I consider it a matter of responding to the manager. Whether they respect him, or defy him doesn't matter. But they were not responding. We were not getting a performance up to their capabilities."[6]

Rodgers wasn't surprised, saying he had been expecting to be fired for two weeks. "If I did wrong, I did wrong. But I did it according to what I believe was right," he said. "I'd do the same thing all over again."[7] Dalton's action had immediate effect. The *Milwaukee Journal* reported, "The mood in the Brewers' clubhouse was lighter and happier than it had been in some time, but very few players were blaming Rodgers for the recent failures."[8] Mike Caldwell, who battled with Rodgers' quick pitching hook, said, "Buck to me, just didn't interject the personality into the club that was needed." Ted Simmons, who also had issues was conciliatory, saying, "This may sound strange, but it always a little saddening. I don't like to see people fired. Cecil Cooper responded, "I think we needed a change. We are not a .500 team."[9]

The new manager fostered a relaxed atmosphere, reminding the players often that it wasn't life or death but a ballgame. Kuenn said his primary point to the players was: "I like the club to have a good time, be loose, and have a laugh. Go out and play the game and have fun. But I can be tough if I have to. They all know it."[10] His message was well received. Gorman Thomas, who praised Kuenn for helping him become a major-league hitter, said, "I don't think you can find a better choice. He's got the total respect of the players."[11] He showed he was different in his first game when Caldwell struggled in the sixth inning. Unlike Rodgers, he showed confidence in his starter, giving him an opportunity to work out of trouble, and Caldwell did, turning in a complete-game victory.

The fun-loving Brewers went on a rampage, becoming Harvey's Wallbangers with their nightly power displays. They won 21 of 30 games, returned to the top of the AL East on July 3, and took permanent ownership of first place on August 1. Kuenn's record was 72-43, a .626 winning percentage, and at season's end Milwaukee had baseball's best record, 95-67. With his calm demeanor, he led the team with big must-win games, all the way to Game Seven of the World Series, losing to the St. Louis Cardinals. Kuenn finished second for *The Sporting News* Manager of the Year Award and was named the Associated Press AL Manager of the Year.[12]

The players' respect for Kuenn was captured in an article by Mario Ziino in the *Brewers Game Day* in 2007, the 25th anniversary of the pennant year. Jim Ganter told Ziino, "It was like playing for your dad. No monkey business. Once the game started he was serious. But he'd always tell us to have fun playing the game." Gorman Thomas said, "You'd look at him and say this man has given his heart and soul to the game and us. How could I not run through a wall for him?" And the 1982 MVP, Robin Yount, fondly recalled, "Harvey Keunn was my hitting coach when I first came up. We hit it off from the start. He saw something in me. We became very close and he was the biggest influence in my career."[13] Said Bud Selig, "Harvey was the perfect manager for that club. Just let the club play was his philosophy. These guys knew how to play. Harvey was so unassuming and didn't overmanage. He did a brilliant job"[14]

After the World Series Caldwell said, "I think more than anything else in the world, I wanted to win it for Harvey Kuenn. Even above getting a ring, getting the money, getting all that stuff in the winter."[15]

And the feelings were mutual. Kuenn said after the World Series, "Every player on this team is like a son of mine and they gave it all they had."[16]

NOTES

1. Bob Wolf, "Kuenn Is a Champion ... Even in Defeat," *Milwaukee Journal*, October 21, 1982: Part 3, 3.

2. Tom Flaherty, "Players Not Happy with Buck," *Milwaukee Journal*, September 13, 1981: Sports, 1.

3. Vic Feuerherd, "Rodgers and Players Working on Understanding Each Other," *Milwaukee Sentinel*, April 6, 1982: Part 2, 1.

4. Vic Feuerherd, "Dalton Will Avoid Quick Decision About Rodgers," *Milwaukee Sentinel*, June 2, 1982: Part 2, 1.

5. The Brewers 2-1 victory that evening gave Rodgers a 124-102 record, a .549 winning percentage. Of the 19 Brewers managers as of 2018, only Kuenn's .575 was better (minimum 20 games).

6. Vic Feuerherd, "Rodgers Fired; Kuenn at Helm," *Milwaukee Sentinel*, June 3, 1982: 1.

7. "Rodgers: A Sense of Failure," *Milwaukee Sentinel*, June 3, 1982: Part 3, 1.

8. "Kuenn Starts New Job with Brewers," *Milwaukee Journal*, June 3, 1982: Part 3, 1.

9. "Brewer Players Speak on Managerial Switch," *Milwaukee Journal*, June 3, 1982: Part 3, 1.

10. Tom Flaherty, "Kuehn Manages to Win," *Milwaukee Journal*, June 3, 1982: Part 3, 1.

11. "Kuenn Starts New Job with Brewers," *Milwaukee Journal*, June 3, 1982: Part 3, 1.

12. Tom Flaherty, "Kuenn Wants '83 One Game Better," *The Sporting News*, November 8, 1982: 30.

13. Mario Ziino, "Like a Father, Harvey Kuenn Got the Most from His Boys, *Brewers Game Day*, Issue 10-2007.

14. Ibid.

15. Tom Flaherty, "A Dream Ends for Caldwell," *The Sporting News*, November 1, 1982: 29.

16. Wolf.

HOW THEY WERE BUILT

By Rod Nelson

AMATEUR SIGNINGS AND DRAFTS

DATE	PLAYER	TRANSACTION
June 8, 1971	Charlie Moore	DRAFTED by the BREWERS in the 5th ROUND of the 1971 AMATEUR DRAFT. Scouted/Signed by Jack Sanford.
June 5, 1973	Robin Yount	DRAFTED by the BREWERS in the 1st ROUND (#3) of the 1973 AMATEUR DRAFT. Scouted/Signed by Gordon Goldsberry and Roland LeBlanc
June 5, 1974	Moose Haas	DRAFTED by the BREWERS in the 2nd ROUND of the 1974 AMATEUR DRAFT. Scouted/Signed by Brad Kohler
June 5, 1974	Jim Ganter	DRAFTED by the BREWERS in the 12th ROUND of the 1974 AMATEUR DRAFT. Scouted/Signed by Emil Belich.
June 5, 1974	Jerry Augustine	DRAFTED by the BREWERS in the 15th ROUND of the 1974 AMATEUR DRAFT. Scouted/Signed by Emil Belich.
November 14, 1975	Ed Romero	SIGNED by the BREWERS as an AMATEUR FREE AGENT. Scouted/Signed by Felix Delgado.
June 7, 1977	Paul Molitor	DRAFTED by the BREWERS in the 1st ROUND (#3) of the 1977 AMATEUR DRAFT. Player SIGNED June 24, 1977. Scouted/Signed by Emil Belich and Dee Fondy.
June 7, 1977	Kevin Bass	DRAFTED by the BREWERS in the 2nd ROUND of the 1977 AMATEUR DRAFT. Scouted/Signed by Dee Fondy.
January 10, 1978	Doug Jones	DRAFTED by the BREWERS in the 3rd ROUND of the 1978 AMATEUR DRAFT (January). Player SIGNED May 18, 1978. Scouted/Signed by Roy PoitevintScouted/Signed by Ray Poitevint.
June 5, 1979	Bob Skube	DRAFTED by the BREWERS in the 13th ROUND of the 1979 AMATEUR DRAFT.

TRADES AND FREE AGENT SIGNINGS

DATE	PLAYER	TRANSACTION
October 31, 1972	Don Money	TRADED by the Philadelphia Phillies with Bill Champion and John Vukovich to the BREWERS for Ken Brett, Jim Lonborg, Ken Sanders and Earl Stephenson.
December 6, 1976	Cecil Cooper	TRADED by the Boston Red Sox to the BREWERS for Bernie Carbo and George Scott.
December 6, 1976	Marshall Edwards	DRAFTED by the BREWERS from the Baltimore Orioles in the 1976 RULE 5 DRAFT.
March 15, 1977	Bob McClure	The Kansas City Royals sent Bob McClure to the BREWERS to complete an earlier deal made on December 6, 1976. December 6, 1976: The Kansas City Royals sent a player to be named later, Jamie Quirk and Jim Wohlford to the BREWERS for Jim Colborn and Darrell Porter.
June 15, 1977	Mike Caldwell	TRADED by the Cincinnati Reds to the BREWERS for Rick O'Keeffe (minors) and Garry Pyka (minors).
November 17, 1977	Larry Hisle	SIGNED as a FREE AGENT with the BREWERS.
December 5, 1977	Ned Yost	DRAFTED by the BREWERS from the New York Mets in the 1977 RULE 5 DRAFT.
December 9, 1977	Ben Oglivie	TRADED by the Detroit Tigers to the BREWERS for Rich Folkers and Jim Slaton.
February 8, 1978	Gorman Thomas	PURCHASED by the BREWERS from the Texas Rangers.
November 28, 1978	Jim Slaton	SIGNED as a FREE AGENT with the BREWERS.
October 26, 1979	Dwight Bernard	TRADED by the New York Mets to the BREWERS for Mark Bomback.
December 3, 1979	Mark Brouhard	DRAFTED by the BREWERS from the California Angels in the 1979 RULE 5 DRAFT.
May 16, 1980	Chuck Porter	SIGNED as a FREE AGENT with the BREWERS.
September 22, 1980	Jamie Easterly	PURCHASED by the BREWERS from the Montreal Expos.
December 12, 1980	Rollie Fingers	TRADED by the St. Louis Cardinals to the BREWERS for David Green, Dave LaPoint, Sixto Lezcano and Lary Sorensen.
December 12, 1980	Ted Simmons	TRADED by the St. Louis Cardinals to the BREWERS for David Green, Dave LaPoint, Sixto Lezcano and Lary Sorensen.
December 12, 1980	Pete Vuckovich	TRADED by the St. Louis Cardinals to the BREWERS for David Green, Dave LaPoint, Sixto Lezcano and Lary Sorensen.
December 20, 1980	Roy Howell	SIGNED as a FREE AGENT with the BREWERS.

TRADES AND FREE AGENT SIGNINGS

DATE	PLAYER	TRANSACTION
March 1, 1981	**Randy Lerch**	TRADED by the Philadelphia Phillies to the BREWERS for Dick Davis.
October 23, 1981	**Pete Ladd**	TRADED by the Houston Astros to the BREWERS for Rickey Keeton.
May 14, 1982	**Rob Picciolo**	TRADED by the Oakland Athletics to the BREWERS for Johnny Evans (minors) and Mike Warren.
August 11, 1982	**Doc Medich**	PURCHASED by the BREWERS from the Texas Rangers.
August 30, 1982	**Don Sutton**	TRADED by the Houston Astros to the BREWERS for players to be named later and cash. The BREWERS sent Kevin Bass (September 3, 1982), Frank DiPino (September 3, 1982) and Mike Madden (September 3, 1982) to the Houston Astros to complete the trade.

*Compiled by Rod Nelson, SABR Scouts Committee; Transactions data courtesy of Retrosheet

ALLAN HUBER (BUD) SELIG

By Maria Ziino

It is often said that those who focus only on the destination tend to forget and appreciate the ride. Not Allan H. "Bud" Selig. He often said his life was an incredible journey — a dream come true.

For Selig, who began his voyage with the childlike attitude that he'd someday accomplish something meaningful in life, having major-league baseball in Milwaukee was a driving force. True to his courage and vision, his mission was rooted in that conviction, which cemented his lasting legacy, not only in his hometown but throughout the industry. Selig's passion for sports, particularly baseball, was inspired by his mother and it became quite evident from the outset. He didn't envision himself as a celebrated athlete as most youngsters romanticized, but rather as a prolific owner, one who could influence the game itself. History documented his course in the sport as a leader and inspiration, and as one who modernized the game for generations to come.

Born on July 30, 1934, at Milwaukee's Mount Sinai Hospital, Selig grew up in the predominantly Jewish neighborhood on 52nd Street. His parents immigrated to the United States shortly after the turn of the century as youngsters from Eastern Europe. His father, Benjamin, was from Romania, and his mother, Marie (Huber) Selig, was born in the Ukraine. They married in 1929 and raised two sons, Jerome and Allan.

Ben was a car salesman for the Mertz-Knippel Co., owned by Otto Mertz and Ray Knippel, before partnering with Ray to form Knippel-Selig Ford. Marie taught third and fourth grades at Lee Street School (later renamed Sherman School), which her sons attended. She was an avid baseball fan and took Allan, whom she called Bud, to watch the local minor-league Brewers at nearby Borchert Field or to Chicago to watch White Sox games, especially when the New York Yankees were in town. Joe DiMaggio was Bud's boyhood idol. After attending Steuben Junior High School and Washington High School on Milwaukee's West Side, Selig attended the University of Wisconsin/Madison.

With aspirations of becoming a college professor, Selig went on to earn a degree in history before serving a brief stint in the Army and going on to postgraduate school for an accounting degree. Instead of pursuing a career in academia, Selig worked for his father, whose business expanded and became known as the largest Ford dealership in Wisconsin.

"My father said to me at the time, "Give me a year," Selig shared. "I was very close to both my parents, and when your father asks you to give him a year, you give it. And I did it with some trepidation. But in all honesty, he did me a great favor; though I often wondered how different my life would have been had I stayed in Madison as a history professor."

BRAVES MOVE TO MILWAUKEE

While Selig was in college, the Boston Braves, under the ownership of Lou Perini, moved to Milwaukee where a new stadium, built to attract a major-league franchise, awaited its arrival in 1953.

As a college sophomore, Selig made a point of attending the very first Braves National League game at County Stadium, driving the 80 miles to Milwaukee from Madison. He was thrilled that his hometown had finally landed a major-league team — some 50 years after the last big-league franchise left the city for St. Louis following just one season as a charter member of the original American League.

Like many fans in Milwaukee, Selig understood what the Braves meant to the community. In 13 years in the city, the team never had a losing season, winning back-to-back National League championships in 1957 and 1958, and narrowly missing pennants in 1956 and 1959. At County Stadium the Braves were the first National League franchise to top 2 million in attendance, surpassing that number four straight seasons in the 1950s. The night the Braves clinched the National League pennant in 1957, Selig was there. He watched as Henry Aaron hit a walk-off ninth-inning home run to defeat pitcher Billy Muffett and the St. Louis Cardinals. He watched with tears in his eyes as Aaron was carried off the field on the shoulders of his teammates in celebration.

In 1963 rumors of a move became fact when the Braves announced plans to shift the franchise to the greener pastures of Atlanta. By then, Selig had become the largest public shareholder, and, together with other local business and political influences, they tried to block the move. To no avail: They couldn't control the fate of the Braves, who opened the 1966 season in Atlanta.

"I remember the last night the Braves played in Milwaukee," Selig said. "They played the Los Angeles Dodgers at County Stadium. I was sitting (in the stands) with Ed Fitzgerald, one of my partners who was the president of Cutler Hammer, and a woman came up to us with tears streaming down her face. She said, 'Don't fail. You're all we have.' With that she walked away. I never forgot that."

In the mid-'60s, Selig took over as owner of the dealership when his father retired, and in 1971 changed the company name to Selig Ford. He eventually switched to the Chevrolet brand while adding an automobile-leasing company.

With the Braves' departure, Selig stood in the forefront of a seemingly improbable crusade to keep Milwaukee relevant in the eyes of major-league baseball. At the age of 30, he embarked on a new mission, organizing a group of local businessmen known as Teams, Inc. in an effort to convince the major leagues that Milwaukee was still interested in a big-league franchise. It wasn't easy. Over a grueling five-year period, he attended every baseball function, pleaded with every executive willing to listen and debated Milwaukee's worthiness as a potential future expansion or relocation city; his efforts resulted in nothing more than disappointment and frustration.

When expansion was finally brokered in 1968, Milwaukee's proposal was rejected twice. Instead, Kansas City, Seattle, San Diego, and Montreal were given franchises. Refusing to accept abandonment of his dream, Selig continued to pursue other options, even the possibility of taking on an existing franchise on the brink of insolvency. That attempt was quashed, too, despite Selig and Milwaukee bailing out the Chicago White Sox organization. Teams, Inc. granted the White Sox an opportunity to play a series of games at County Stadium. Those games boosted Chicago's overall attendance figures and helped its bottom line. Selig believed he had forged an agreement with White Sox owner Arthur Allyn to buy the struggling franchise. But Commissioner Bowie Kuhn refused to allow the deal, instead accepting a last-minute offer from Allyn's brother, John, to purchase the franchise.

BIG LEAGUE AGAIN

At the same time, after only one season the expansion Seattle Pilots were in financial trouble. Rumors had it that baseball was looking to move the franchise. Selig and his group focused its efforts on acquiring the team, admitting that this bid would be the last gasp for the Milwaukee group. It was a long negotiating winter. Finally, at the eleventh hour, his mission, his dream, was fulfilled.

It was punctuated by a resolution of the gavel. At 10:20 P.M. on Tuesday, March 31, 1970, Sidney Vohnn, a federal bankruptcy court referee in Seattle, ruled that Teams Inc.'s offer of $10.8 million for the Pilots "should be and is approved."

The decision cleared the way for the new Milwaukee Brewers, a name adopted to honor the American Association team that thrived for 50 years in the community. Assuming the Pilots' schedule and position in the American League West, the Brewers were slated to open the 1970 season on Tuesday, April 7, 1970, at 1:30 P.M. against the California Angels at County Stadium. The night before the bankruptcy ruling, moving trucks had started a trek from the Pilots' spring training site in Tempe, Arizona, to Seattle. When the news became official, the trucks set a new course for Milwaukee. With less than a week to prepare for a major-league opener, and no time to order new uniforms and equipment, the name Pilots was stripped from every jersey and replaced with Brewers, and the "S" on every cap was replaced with an "M." On Opening Day, sunshine and cold temperatures greeted 36,107 fans. For the first time in 1,647 days, a team came strutting out of the dugout sporting a Milwaukee uniform. Behind a complete-game effort by pitcher Andy Messersmith and a 14-hit attack, the Angels blanked the Brewers, 12-0, spoiling the debut but not the enthusiasm.

"It was the only game the Brewers ever played that I didn't care who won," Selig said. "That changed by the next day."

Winning would be a tough road to navigate. In the early years, Selig realized he needed patience and guidance. Dealing with losing and trying to maintain the viability of baseball in a small market was difficult.

"My mentor in baseball was a man named John Fetzer, who was the owner of the Detroit Tigers for many years. He was a great man, a visionary," Selig said. "He took me under his wing in 1970. He taught me the basic lesson that so many in baseball and sports never learn: that sport transcends all of us. The only way you should ever decide anything is on what's in the best interest of baseball."

The early years were quite lean. Even with well-known players like Ken Sanders, Dave May, and George Scott, who was the Brewers' first $100,000 player, the best the team could do was a 76-86 finish in 1974. The following year, Selig added a legend from the Braves' glory years.

"Through thick and thin, we had the most loyal fan base," Selig said. "We brought back Henry Aaron to finish out his illustrious career where it started — in Milwaukee."

While Aaron was in the twilight of his career, the Brewers introduced an 18-year-old shortstop by the name of Robin Yount, who would go on to become the longest-tenured player in franchise history and the first inducted into the Hall of Fame. After the 1977 campaign, Selig made one of the boldest moves he had ever made. In the media, it was called the "Saturday Night Massacre." In a front-office housecleaning, Selig fired manager Alex Grammas and player development director Al Widmar, and accepted the resignation of general manager Jim Baumer. Selig then hired general manager Harry Dalton who in turn hired new manager George Bamberger. In just the first season together, what was termed the "Dalton Gang" turned the franchise from a 95-game loser into a 93-game winner that finished a strong third in the American League East.

"I remember in 1978, our first winning season, and how the fans soaked it all in with George Bamberger and the whole cast of players, who earned the nickname Bambi's Bombers," Selig said.

Bud Selig purchased the bankrupt Seattle Pilots and relocated them to his hometown, Milwaukee, in 1970. The longtime Brewers president served as acting commissioner of baseball (1992-1998) and then commissioner (1998-2015). He was elected to the Baseball Hall of Fame in 2017.

Looking to improve the Brewers' chances at a pennant, Dalton pulled off what may be considered the greatest trade in franchise history. During the 1980 Winter Meetings in Dallas, vDalton acquired Pete Vuckovich, Rollie Fingers, and Ted Simmons. The next season, 1981, the Brewers qualified for the playoffs, though it came during a strike-shortened season.

BREWERS WIN A PENNANT

Winning had become contagious, and expected, and in 1982 the Brewers reached the pinnacle of success led by hometown hero Harvey Kuenn, who took the managerial reins in June, after the team struggled out of the gate, and guided it to the American League pennant and birth in their first and only World Series appearance. Known as 'Harvey's Wallbangers,' the Brewers won a major-league-best 95 games.

But the Brewers had to survive a shaky final month of the season. Entering September, they had a seemingly comfortable six-game lead in the East. But Selig knew all too well that that could quickly evaporate, especially after Rollie Fingers, the best closer in baseball, was lost for the rest of the season with a forearm injury. On top of that, Milwaukee had to play New York, Boston, and Baltimore exclusively down the stretch.

"That was a tough month," Selig said. "We played Baltimore at County Stadium before going on that last road trip to end the season. They took two of three games and crept to within two games. The team headed to Boston but I stayed home and watched the games on television."

One of those games from Fenway Park featured a dramatic performance by the Brewers' backup catcher.

"In a pivotal game at Fenway, Harvey sent Ned Yost to pinch-hit in the ninth inning with the score tied and he hit the only home run he had all year," Selig said [Yost actually entered the game in the bottom of the eighth as catcher]. "He won the game. And to this day, I remember it as if it happened yesterday. Little did Ned realize at the time that it would be a big part of Brewers lore."

Heading into a four-game series at Baltimore's Memorial Stadium, the Brewers needed to win just once to clinch the AL East flag. Anyone who knew Selig in those days realized that he could never sit still, pacing constantly as he chain-smoked Tiparillo cigars. History will show that the Sunday showdown was a classic. No fewer than 10 future Hall of Famers played in the game, including Sutton and Palmer (who went toe-to-toe), Robin Yount and Paul Molitor for the Brewers and Cal Ripken and Eddie Murray for the O's. In addition, Earl Weaver and Fingers were in their respective dugouts and Ford Frick Award winners Chuck Thompson and Bob Uecker handled the broadcast for their respective teams. Once at the ballpark, Selig felt compelled to visit his players in the clubhouse.

"It was the only time I spoke to the team before a ballgame," Selig said. "I simply told them how much I loved them and admired them. We had been through a lot. That was it. Very short visit."

But for Selig, it gave him a chance to look into their eyes. There was no fear. No signs of feeling the pressure of the magnitude of the contest. Instead, he sensed his team was as loose as one could expect before a defining moment. Selig watched the game from the owner's box on the first-base side near the visiting dugout.

"And even though we never trailed in the game, I was nervous," Selig said. "I'd get up and start walking in the concourse. The tension was unbelievable."

But the Brewers prevailed, claiming the pennant by a convincing 10-2 score. And it was off to Anaheim to open the ALCS against the California Angels — the same team that had rudely welcomed the Brewers to the American League 12 years earlier. Perhaps because of a letdown after the grueling series in Baltimore, the Brewers dropped the first two games in Anaheim before returning to County Stadium, one loss away from elimination in the best-of-five series.

To Milwaukee fans, it didn't matter. They were ready to support their team, period.

"I drove to the ballpark on that Friday and you would've thought we were up two games," Selig said. "Fans were filling the parking lot, waving and having a good time. I guess that carried over to the game because we won behind Don Sutton."

It came down to another Sunday. Another showdown. Could it be déjà vu? The stakes were high as the winner would go on to the World Series — the first for either team.

"Here we go again," Selig said. "This time we had our crowd behind us. I think it may have been the most emotional crowd I had ever seen. From the fifth inning on you couldn't hear yourself think. Everything you had ever hoped for was about to unfold. The Angels are very good. Don Baylor. Reggie Jackson. Brian Downing. Tommy John. So we battle. Back and forth. In the seventh inning, Cecil (Cooper) gets the big hit to put us ahead. The place is rocking. I can still see Charlie Moore and Jim Gantner sliding across the plate. We're up one. We get through the eighth. My heart is pounding out of my chest. I think I had three cigars lit at one time. I don't think I knew what I was doing."

The Angels were down to their last batter in the game. Selig felt destiny was on the Brewers' side until the announced batter strolled to the plate.

"To this day," Selig said, "I remember thinking to myself, 'Why does it have to be Rod Carew?' After all these years of dreaming for this moment, why does it have to be the greatest hitter in baseball? Why couldn't it be some stiff who can't hit?'"

Carew hit a sharp one-hop grounder right at short. Selig thought just two or three feet either side of the fielder and the game would've been tied. Instead, Yount handled it cleanly, threw across the diamond to Cooper at first base and the game was over.

"What a feeling," Selig added. "Oh my God."

The players were mobbed by fans who rushed the field. Selig stood on the overhang in front of the press box with his fist held high as he cheered his team's triumph.

"Here we are champions of the American League," Selig said. "After celebrating in the clubhouse, I drive home drained and exhausted. I sit in the den with a little black radio tuned to CBS News, and the announcement is broadcasted, 'The 79th World Series will be between the St. Louis Cardinals and the Milwaukee Brewers.' I began to cry."

It was the first fall classic for the Brewers — the first for Milwaukee in 25 years. The Brewers opened on the road with a convincing 10-0 win before dropping Game Two, 5-4.

Back in Milwaukee, the Brewers won two of the three games to forge ahead 3 games to 2. The team needed one more victory to clinch the championship but had to do it in St. Louis. However, there was no magic. The Cardinals won a rain-soaked Game Six, and rallied from a 3-1 deficit in the seventh inning of Game Seven to win the championship. Clearly, the plane ride back to Milwaukee was quite somber. Brewers' Vice President Dick Hackett received a telephone call from the Chamber of Commerce during the flight. He approached Selig with a request from city leaders to stage a parade through the streets of downtown.

"We pulled out and it was unbelievable," Selig said. "We crawled along Wisconsin Avenue. People walked up to every car to shake hands with everyone. It took us forever to get to County Stadium. And once we got there it was if there was a ballgame going on. People filled the lower grandstands. It was a very emotional day. That's when it hit me. It said a lot about Milwaukee and what the Brewers meant to the fans."

PLAYERS' LOCKOUT

Selig learned a long time ago that the strife and skepticism that triggered work stoppages in the past did more harm than good to the national pastime. In 1990 something extraordinary happened when two envoys from opposite sides of the negotiating table came together to foster peace. After the seventh stoppage in 18 years, the ownership group turned to Selig to foster an accord for the good of the game. As the owner of the Brewers for 20 years, Selig gained firsthand knowledge of what he would eventually endure when he became commissioner of baseball.

Paul Molitor, the Brewers veteran third baseman who was the team's Players Association representative, was the American League player representative at the negotiations. Weeks earlier, owner and player were able to amicably collaborate on a new contract for the future Hall of Famer to stay in one of the smallest markets in baseball. Molitor's contract was reportedly worth $9.1 million over three years, similar to the one agreed upon months earlier by another future Hall of Famer, Robin Yount. It may have seemed odd at the time, but Selig and Molitor were back at it representing more than their own interests. Molitor sat across from Selig during the negotiations.

"To begin with, I had a great relationship with Paul," Selig said. "The Union knew that. We were trying to find a solution to our problems."

With both sides far apart, the lockout which began in February and lasted 32 days, wiping out virtually all of spring training. Opening Day had to be moved back a week to April 9, and because of that, the season had to be extended three additional days to accommodate a full 162-game schedule. At issue was the five-year Basic Agreement between the players and owners, which had expired entering 1990. During the buildup to the lockout, both sides spent months trying to iron out long-standing disagreements over free agency and arbitration. Player salaries had already surpassed the $3 million-a-year level as evident by the Brewers superstar players' salaries. Understanding the seriousness of the matter, Selig and Molitor met several times privately to resolve the differences. These were thoughtful discussions behind the scenes. Afterward, many in the industry believed their deliberations were instrumental in ending the discord.

A new Basic Agreement was reached on March 19. The minimum major-league salary was raised from $68,000 to $100,000. (As of 2019 the minimum had climbed to $555,000.) The new deal wasn't permanent but it bridged the gap for a while. Four years later, in 1994, the players went on strike. That one devastated the game. Small-market teams like the Brewers were drowning in debt with little hope of competing on a yearly basis. Yet, the union refused to budge on a salary cap.

TAKING THE REINS

September 9, 1992, would become a momentous day in Selig's career.

The Brewers' Robin Yount was on the threshold of becoming only the 17th major leaguer to reach the magical 3,000-hit plateau. He needed one hit and had only one chance to accomplish the feat at home before heading on a long road trip. Some 375 miles to the south, another significant announcement was about to be made. Baseball owners had gathered in St. Louis to appoint a head to their newly formed

Executive Council following the dismissal of Commissioner Fay Vincent just days earlier.

Smack-dab in the middle of both developments was Selig. The face of his franchise was on the brink of making history and he was about to become the most powerful authority in the sport.

"I'm hearing from other owners, 'Bud, you've got to take over,'" Selig said. "I had no intention of becoming commissioner. I was part of a group that was trying to help us move on."

Selig and his daughter, Wendy Selig-Prieb, the team's general counsel, attended the meeting, hoping to wrap things up early so that they could fly back to Milwaukee to be on hand for Yount's triumph.

"At the meeting, everyone agreed, whether or not I did, that I should become chairman of the Executive Council," Selig said. "That was it. A vote was taken and it was unanimous. (Cardinals owner) Gussie Busch had a big party planned for everyone that evening but I told him that I had to get back to Milwaukee."

Selig made arrangements for a private jet to whisk him away at a moment's notice. Accompanying Selig and his daughter on the flight were American League President Bobby Brown and Tom Werner, managing partner of the San Diego Padres, who eventually became an owner of the Boston Red Sox and Liverpool FC of Britain's Premier Soccer League. Just before departing St. Louis, Selig picked up another hitchhiker.

"Well, I couldn't say no when he asked me, 'Can I come with you to see Yount get his hit tonight,'" said Selig of Texas Rangers owner George W. Bush, who in less than three years would be governor of Texas and eventually the 43rd president of the United States. "He loved those special moments in the game."

As Selig's unmarked white van pulled up to County Stadium, home-plate umpire Rocky Roe yelled play ball. Selig and his entourage were escorted from the service level to the owner's box adjacent to the press box on the loge level just as the Brewers came to bat in the home half of the first inning.

In the seventh inning the inevitable happened — Yount lined a single to right-center field off Indians pitcher Jose Mesa. And with that, Yount's mission was completed and Selig's was about to begin.

"What a day," Selig said. "It was quite an historic day."

WORLD SERIES CANCELED

By the summer of 1994, baseball had hit rock bottom. The players strike, which began on August 12, stopped play for 232 days — the longest ever — and it forced the cancellation of the remainder of the season. Even the fall classic was lost, the first time that had happened since 1904 when John T. Brush, president of the National League champion New York Giants, refused to allow his team to compete against the Boston Americans, the representative of the American League. Selig felt the pain of his decision on September 14 to cancel the World Series. But the strike also affected the start of the 1995 season.

"That was part of my history," Selig acknowledged. "The way I look at it is that in my career in baseball we had had eight work stoppages, and this one was the worst. I was getting slaughtered. The owners and players were getting slaughtered. Everyone."

At the heart of the matter was the rampant increase in salaries, which jeopardized the future of many small-market franchises. The stalemate lasted right into the winter. On January 13, 1995, baseball's Executive Council approved the use of replacement players in an attempt to salvage the 1995 season. But in March, the US District Court and the National Labor Relations Board interceded. Judge Sonia Sotomayor forced both sides to find an agreement. On March 28 the players voted to return, and three days later, Judge Sotomayor issued a preliminary injunction blocking the owners from using replacement players. According to the terms of the injunction, both sides were bound to the expired collective-bargaining agreement until a new one could be reached. The season began on April

26, and the schedule was revamped to include 144 games instead of the scheduled 162.

As a sacrificial lamb, Selig was thrown to the wolves twice, first during the 1990 lockout and then with the 1994 strike. He acknowledged it for what it did to the game and vowed to never let it happen again under his watch. And true to his word, it didn't.

"As tough as it was and it truly did break my heart, I believe history will show that we had to go through something like that to get to where the game is today," Selig said. "The heartbreaking pain of '94 produced two-plus decades of labor peace which led to the greatest resurgence and growth in major-league baseball history."

GROUNDBREAKING DECISION

As a ramification of the gap between large- and small-market economics, franchises labeled as "fragile" had to look to the future with creative strategies in hopes of finding other revenue streams if they wanted to survive. Their options were simple: build modern ballparks that offered amenities or move to new markets. Selig was not about to move his team. For years, he lobbied for a new ballpark. County Stadium had outlived its usefulness and renovating it was not viable.

"It was such a difficult political process," Selig said. "It was painful at times. We fought to bring a team back to Milwaukee against insurmountable odds but nothing compared to getting the new ballpark built. I don't think people to this day understand it."

Selig had to convince the populace and politicians alike that survival in modern major-league baseball depended on the amenities of a new stadium that would generate additional revenue streams necessary for the franchise to stay viable and competitive. By 1989, after countless discussions about where to build a new facility — with many politicians weighing in on a downtown location — a task force of the Greater Milwaukee Committee concluded that the best site remained in the Menomonee Valley, where County Stadium was situated.

"The fact of the matter is, and let the record show, there never was a downtown site," Selig said. "That was all demagogy. But I must say, I was resolute. We were not going to fail. We got a team. We kept a team. And we were going to get a new ballpark."

In 1992, the first true obstacles surfaced. A 400-million-year-old rock formation was discovered on the former Soldiers Home property owned by the US Department of Veterans Affairs. To compound matters, a wildflower on the state's endangered-species list was detected in clumps near the site. Resolution took nearly two years. Finally, in 1995 the Brewers made a presentation to the Milwaukee Stadium Commission, in which they committed $90 million to help build the new ballpark. That same year the Brewers, together with Wisconsin Governor Tommy Thompson, Milwaukee County Executive Tom Ament, and Milwaukee Mayor John Norquist formally presented an agreement that included a 30-year lease commitment.

That moved the process to Madison, where on September 28, 1995, the State Assembly voted 52 to 47 to accept the new stadium plan. In essence, the plan called for a five-county sales tax of 0.1% or roughly one penny for every $10 to help pay for the new ballpark. The five counties were Milwaukee, Racine, Ozaukee, Washington, and Waukesha. The tax would begin in 1996. It was on to the State Senate, where the deliberation bogged down. Rumors began circulating that if the Brewers couldn't win the necessary vote, the franchise would move. Nothing was further from the truth, though it angered many politicians who thought the Brewers were trying to hold the state hostage. Despite Selig and an entourage that included Hall of Famers Henry Aaron and Robin Yount, lobbying efforts at the State Capitol twice failed to secure the necessary support in the Senate chambers. In the wee hours of the morning of October 7, a new amendment to the referendum was added and a new vote was called for. This time, with the backing of Racine Senator George Petak, who cast the deciding vote, the Senate approved the new ballpark package by a 16-to-15 count.

"Every day was a battle," Selig said. "We finally won at 5 o'clock in the morning after an all-night session. A lot of criticism of the Brewers and its leadership was unfair. As opposed to so many other places, here was a team and an ownership desperately trying to stay."

A week later, Governor Thompson signed legislation providing financing to help build a new ballpark and safeguard the Brewers' future in Wisconsin.

In March of 1996, Miller Brewing Company jumped on board with a 20-year, $41.2 million pact for the naming rights. However, in June the project hit another snag when the Stadium District Board rejected the proposed financing plan. Local business leaders were upset and disappointed, fearing the Brewers would now be forced to go elsewhere. On the night of June 14, before a Brewers game against the Oakland A's, Selig in an emotional press conference at County Stadium blamed "a polluted political environment" for creating the impasse. Truly upset with the stalemate, Selig believed it marked a significant turning point in the dialogue. In essence, it woke a sleeping giant.

"That was the day, politically, it turned around," Selig said. "We staged the press conference in front of the ballpark. After dealing with the media following the press conference, I finally got up to my box to watch the game. The next thing I know something's going on. I couldn't figure it out. The crowd slowly rose and cheered but the action on the field had stopped. I finally realized, they stood and cheered me on. It must have lasted eight or nine minutes."

Before the homestand ended, an estimated gathering of 10,000 fans attended a "We Love Ya, Bud" pep rally in the stadium parking lot. The rally called for action on construction as fans waved signs that read: "Build It Now." The chants followed fans into County Stadium.

"It was amazing," Selig said. "I went through the stands shaking hands and talking to fans. It took me most of the game to do so. I believe the fans helped turn things around."

Soon after, a new financing plan was drafted and approved unanimously by the Stadium District Board, paving the way for shovels to meet dirt. Nearly 20,000 supporters looked on as Aaron and Yount joined a number of dignitaries in the official Miller Park groundbreaking ceremony on November 9, 1996. The future of major-league baseball in Milwaukee was back on schedule for a 2000 opener.

Miller Park was the largest construction project ever undertaken in Wisconsin. The initial cost to build the ballpark was nearly $400 million, with $290 million generated by the five-county sales tax. Over the next three years, construction on the new retractable-roof ballpark went seamlessly according to the timetable until tragedy struck on the sunny but windy afternoon of July 14, 1999.

It was the worst possible news. Three ironworkers were killed in a freak crane accident. The Lampson Trans-lift crane, known as "Big Blue," collapsed attempting to position a 400-ton right-field roof panel into place. The workmen, observing and directing the "pick" from a nearby hoist bucket, were struck by the crumpled winch.

"My heart sank," Selig said. "As quickly as I could, I drove out to the site. I didn't know it at the time, but after spending hours at the scene, a county sheriff followed me home because he noticed how distraught I was over the death of those workers."

The catastrophe and cleanup of the site lasted a full year. With no further incidents, the ballpark finally opened on April 6, 2001. The Brewers honored the three fallen men. A plaque and statue dedicated to them and all the workers was erected on the main plaza. And Miller Park became a jewel in Milwaukee's economic landscape.

Selig and President George W. Bush participated in the pregame ceremony, each tossing out a first ball. The Brewers went on to earn a 5-4 victory over the Cincinnati Reds in front of 42,024 fans — the first of 17 sellouts that inaugural season. During the campaign, the Brewers drew 2,811,041 fans, an average of 34,704 per game.

With Miller Park, the Brewers have been able to surpass attendance goals never deemed possible — topping 3 million in three different seasons, and averaging nearly 2.8 million per season since its opening.

NINTH COMMISSIONER OF BASEBALL

As Miller Park was being built, Selig made a historic announcement involving the Brewers. As part of Phase One of Major League Baseball's realignment plan, on November 9, 1997, the Brewers became the first team in over a century to switch leagues. The dramatic shift was part of MLB's expansion which involved the Arizona Diamondbacks. The Brewers joined the revamped 16-team National League, slotting into the Central Division, along with new rivals in the Chicago Cubs, Cincinnati Reds, Houston Astros, Pittsburgh Pirates, and St. Louis Cardinals.

"The Milwaukee Brewers, mindful of the city's National League heritage, volunteered to make the switch," Selig said. "In the end, it was so right and so logical that history will record it and ensure a brighter future."

As the acting commissioner, Selig's vision modernized and diversified the game. Baseball prospered. And because of that, and after a six-year search for a permanent commissioner, the owners unanimously named Selig as the ninth commissioner on July 9, 1998. He was the first owner ever elected to the post. While serving, Selig was allowed to maintain a satellite office in downtown Milwaukee at the U.S. Bank Building. He occasionally traveled to the main office on Park Avenue in New York but carried out most of his duties right at home. A month after his appointment, Wendy Selig-Prieb was officially named the Brewers new president and chief executive officer. She had previously served as the team's vice president and general counsel. Selig's interest in the team was placed in trust, ending his 33-year reign as president, which began with Teams, Inc.

Under Selig, the major leagues went through a number of advancements, including the introduction of interleague play, three-division leagues and the wild-card format, which added a divisional round to the playoffs. These changes spiked attendance and revenue throughout the major leagues.

In 2003 Selig changed the All-Star Game format by expanding rosters after an embarrassing conclusion to the 2002 midsummer classic, which took place, in all places, Miller Park. That game ended in a 7-7 tie because both managers, Bob Brenly and Joe Torre, had exhausted their rosters, forcing Selig to call the game after 11 innings. Not only did Selig expand future rosters, he added an incentive by which home-field advantage in the World Series would be awarded to the league that won the All-Star Game. It was a novel idea that lasted until 2017.

In his first term as commissioner, Selig guided baseball through two major expansions and spearheaded a renaissance that included several new ballparks. In addition, he prioritized the need to give baseball a more global presence, and in 2006 introduced the World Baseball Classic, in which teams from every corner of the world compete during the spring.

"It's one of the game's priorities to internationalize baseball," Selig said. "We're doing everything we can to move the sport in an international direction. I think it's absolutely spectacular."

By 2005 Selig had to endure another dark period in the game's history. Anabolic steroids had polluted all sports with grave consequences. Many players in many sports were accused of using, affecting the integrity and long-standing legitimacy of the games' records. Selig commissioned US Senator George Mitchell to conduct a 20-month investigation into the use of anabolic steroids and human growth hormones (HGH). On December 13, 2007, the 409-page Mitchell Report outlined the abuse of performance enhancing drugs by players, which outed several well-known stars.

"People say we were slow to react," Selig said. "No we weren't. This is a subject collectively bargained with the union. Even through the cocaine era of the 1980s, and the Pittsburgh trials, the union never agreed to testing. In 2001 we were able to put testing in the minor leagues because I could unilaterally do so and it worked. Now baseball has the toughest testing program, not only in American sports but WADA (World Anti-Doping Agency) is one of the toughest anti-doping agencies ever. I'm proud of what we did. We are a social institution. Yes, I felt badly about it, but steroids wasn't a baseball problem, it was a societal problem. But who could have ever believed that we would wind up with this kind of drug-testing program?"

The Mitchell Report provided baseball with the tools to better understand and deal with enforcing regulations on banned substances.

Despite all the trials and tribulations, Selig's resolve to improve baseball's bottom line was unprecedented. He inherited a $1.2 billion industry and took it to a $9 billion business. Selig was able to transform America's pastime from its grassroots traditions into a contemporary and energized sport of the future. His accomplishments over his 23-year tenure were many, putting his stamp on the following initiatives:

- Interleague play
- Three divisions in the American and National Leagues.
- The institution of divisional play, first with one wild-card entrant, then later a second for each league.
- Team realignment in phases, first moving Milwaukee to the National League in 1998, followed by Houston switching to the American League in 2013, creating 15-team leagues.
- Consolidating the umpires into the commissioner's office.
- Launching MLB.com and the MLB Network.
- The opening of 22 new ballparks.
- Revenue-sharing among teams and a competitive-balance tax.
- The expansion of All-Star Game rosters and the incentive of home-field advantage for the World Series to the league that won the game.
- Instant replay.
- An unprecedented and comprehensive drug-testing program.
- Record attendance in both leagues.
- A global attraction with the introduction of the World Baseball Classic and season openers played in Mexico, Japan, Puerto Rico, and Australia.
- Championing diversity and inclusion in all phases of the sport.
- Servicing as an outreach to major charities.
- And perhaps his greatest accomplishment, nearly a generation-long uninterrupted labor peace.

RETIREMENT AND BEYOND

For all that he accomplished as commissioner over a two-decade reign, Selig was most proud that the game he loved thrived in his hometown. In 2010 the Brewers showed their appreciation by dedicating a statue of Selig's likeness on the Miller Park Plaza alongside bronze sculptures of Henry Aaron and Robin Yount that had stood like sentries since the ballpark opened.

The statue was not the first or last recognition Selig received for his lifetime in baseball. In 2002 his name was added to a plaque on the Miller Park Walk of Fame. In 2014, he joined 57 other former players, coaches, and executives of the Brewers to be enshrined on the Miller Park Wall of Honor.

After serving four terms as commissioner, Selig retired on January 25, 2015. He had served for 23 years –second longest only to Judge Kenesaw Mountain Landis, the first commissioner (1920-1944). In essence, Selig had spent 51 of his 80 years in the game. Baseball rewarded Selig by naming him the first commissioner emeritus.

"When I made the decision in October of 2013, I said, 'You're going to be 80' — I never dreamed that

I'd work until 80 — I wanted to have a good normal transition," Selig said. "I wanted to do what was best for baseball. And quite frankly, I was ready."

In 2015 the Brewers invited Selig back to Miller Park to officially retire uniform number 1 in his honor. He joined the likes of Henry Aaron, Rollie Fingers, Robin Yount, Paul Molitor, Bob Uecker, and Jackie Robinson on the Miller Park Ring of Honor. Later that season, the Brewers unveiled Selig Experience, an exhibit at Miller Park that highlighted his career in baseball.

"It means a great deal to me," Selig said. "It's where I started and how I started. I never believed something like this would happen. I'm a history buff, and to share this history with all our fans, so that they can understand how this all happened, I can't tell you how much it means to me."

Not to be outdone, baseball had one more honor to bestow upon Selig. In 2017 a special 16-member panel of the Today's Game Era Committee (formerly the Veterans Committee) of the National Baseball Hall of Fame voted to induct Selig and former Kansas City and Atlanta general manager John Schuerholz into the Hall of Fame. Selig was the fifth former commissioner to be voted into the Hall of Fame — the first since Happy Chandler in 1982 to actually participate in the ceremony. Other commissioners honored over the years were Kenesaw Mountain Landis, Ford C. Frick, and Bowie Kuhn.

"(It) was a high honor, to say the least," Selig said. "I've looked forward to this day for a long time and I'm really honored. I consider myself to be very fortunate to have had a career in a sport that I love."

Selig moved into a downtown Milwaukee office, decorated in memorabilia collected over a lifetime as one of the most influential figures in the history of sport. He began to fill his days doing what he initially wanted to do — teach. Selig accepted an adjunct faculty position at Marquette University Law School as a distinguished lecturer in sports law and policy. His emphasis was on the history of collective bargaining and free agency, underscoring revenue-sharing and antitrust exemptions. At the University of Wisconsin at Madison, Selig endowed the Allan H. Selig Chair in the History of Sport and Society, and lectured in a course called Baseball and American Society since World War II. Besides having a home in Milwaukee, Selig and his wife, Sue, acquired a residence in the Phoenix area. As a way to maximize his time there, he added a third academic position to his itinerary, joining the Sandra Day O'Connor College of Law on the campus of Arizona State University.

Selig also started work on his memoirs. "It's true, I'm working on a book," Selig said. "I'm going to replay this by the year. It'll be a great history of baseball over the last 50 years. So, I guess I'm going to stay busy for a while."

With the help of longtime baseball writer Phil Rogers, Selig's book entitled, *For the Good of the Game* was released in July, 2019. The foreword was written by renowned historian Doris Kearns Goodwin.

Selig shaped his own retirement with dignity and grace — just as he nurtured his Brewers and guided the industry to new heights.

"You know, this all started in 1964," he said. "As I look back I never could have dreamed my career would take me to the places I went to. I was fortunate and I'm truly grateful. It has been the highest privilege to lead our national pastime, a sport that links generations, buffers the passage of time and continues to reflect the spirt of our great country. I've often said this is one of those rare times in this incredible journey that I've been on, that a little boy's dreams did come true. Oh, I still hear from a lot of people — players and owners alike — who just want to know how I am. I tell them, 'I'm fine.'"

NOTES

All quotes and personal background material contained in this biography were collected by the author during interviews with Selig from 1979 to 2017.

Mario Ziino is the director of sports publications at Delzer Lithograph Co. He spent 25 years with the Milwaukee Brewers as the director of publications and assistant director of public relations. He also writes for the Brewers Gameday Magazine.

HARRY DALTON

By Dale Voiss

He was born Harry I. Dalton on August 23, 1928, in West Springfield, Massachusetts, the same hometown as Leo Durocher. He graduated as an English major from Amherst College in Amherst, Massachusetts. Historically, Amherst faced Williams in the world's first intercollegiate baseball game in 1859. He had been accepted to the Columbia University School of Journalism, but was drafted into the military; Dalton joined the Air Force and fought in Korea where he earned a Bronze Star.

After leaving the military he had a brief stint as a sportswriter in Springfield. After the 1953 season, the St. Louis Browns franchise relocated to Baltimore. Coincidentally, Harry's parents had moved there earlier, and in early 1954, while in Baltimore to visit his parents, Dalton phoned the Orioles and asked for an interview and was hired by scouting director Jim McLaughlin as a gofer in the Orioles organization. The job paid so little that Dalton had to drive a taxicab at night just to make ends meet.

McLaughlin was so impressed with the young man's intelligence and work ethic that he moved him over to the baseball operations side to become his assistant. During his stint as farm assistant, Dalton was put in charge of the Birds' minor-league spring camp in Thomasville, Georgia.

Just prior to the two major-league All-Star Games in 1960, he married Pat Booker on July 9, 1960. The couple had originally met on a blind date. They had three daughters — Kimberly (1962), Cynthia (1965), and Debbie (1967).

Before the 1961 season, McLaughlin left the Orioles after a dispute with manager Paul Richards over the signing of pitcher Dave McNally. Ironically, Richards left the Orioles late in the 1961 season to accept the general managership of the expansion Houston Colt .45s.

General manager Lee MacPhail replaced McLaughlin with the 32-year-old Dalton, who assumed his new position on February 1, 1961. Dalton, having spent seven years under McLaughlin, had developed a reputation as a man with good baseball sense and a wonderful memory for names and maintained the work ethic which had first secured him the job. The Orioles farm system had been magnificently successful under McLaughlin so Dalton decided in the early days to maintain the status quo. Dalton later credited McLaughlin with training him well. That training led to a smooth transition from assistant to farm director.

Among the things Dalton did in his first year on the job was to name Cal Ripken, Sr., a 25-year-old catcher in the Orioles farm system, as player-manager of the Class D farm club at Leesburg, Florida. Ripken would manage the major-league team a quarter of a century later.

Dalton was very proud of his scouts and gave them a lot of credit for the success of the team's minor-league system. In the minor-league draft of December 1962 the Orioles lost an astounding 18 players to other organizations. While disappointed in losing so many players, Dalton also noted that the losses were a credit to the scouts who had signed so many talented players. Dalton gave his scouts a lot of leeway in negotiating with potential signees. He asked only that they call him in the cases where a particular signee might require a large bonus.

During his nearly five years in the position of farm director, the Orioles produced such talent as Jim Palmer, Dave McNally, Boog Powell, and Dave Johnson.

In the autumn of 1965, new Commissioner of Major League Baseball Spike Eckert brought Oriole president and general manager Lee MacPhail aboard to assist him in baseball matters. MacPhail's departure led to a reorganization of the Orioles' front office. Chairman of the Board Jerry Hoffberger assumed MacPhail's former role as team president with Frank Cashen assuming the executive vice presidency. Cashen was put in charge of improving the club's public image and increasing ticket sales. While Dalton would be reporting to Cashen, Cashen was given no power in player moves. This power was vested entirely in the 37-year-old Dalton.

Dalton was named to replace MacPhail in his role as director of player personnel. At the time of his appointment, MacPhail had been working on a trade with the Reds to bring outfielder Frank Robinson into the fold. Dalton's first move was to try and get an additional player out of the Reds.

In what is still considered one of the most lopsided trades in baseball history, Dalton obtained the future Hall of Famer for pitchers Milt Pappas and Jack Baldschun and minor-league outfielder Dick Simpson. The trade was finalized on Dalton's third day in his new job. Robinson had recently reached his 30th birthday and the Reds were concerned that he was about to enter the downside of his career. As it turned out, nothing could have been further from the truth. All Robinson did in his first year in

Harry Dalton (on left with George Bamberger) served as GM for the Baltimore Orioles (1966-1971), the California Angels (1971-1977), and the Milwaukee Brewers (1977-1991). He was twice named Major League Executive of the Year (1970 and 1982).

Baltimore was to win the American League Triple Crown and the league's MVP award.

Dalton immediately divided the team's minor-league operation into two separate arms. Lou Gorman was put in charge of player development while Walter Shannon was put in charge of scouting. Shannon had spent 27 years as a scout with the Cardinals during which he was involved in the signings of players such as Bob Gibson and Tim McCarver. Gorman was a minor-league general manager before Dalton hired him.

In 1966, Dalton's first year at the helm, the Orioles, managed by Hank Bauer, won the American League pennant with a 97-63 record, finishing nine games ahead of the second-place Twins. As they were coming down the stretch, Dalton tried to make a trade for additional pitching but found the price was too high. Teams wanted some Triple A talent and Dalton was unwilling to mortgage the team's future. It was the first pennant the team had won in their 13 seasons in Baltimore. The Orioles were led by the bat of Robinson, who won the league's MVP award, and second-year pitcher Jim Palmer who led the team with 15 wins.

During their pennant-winning season, Dalton proposed cutting the major-league schedule from 162 games to 144. He cited three reasons for the proposal. One: fans feel the season is too long; two, players get tired and their performances suffer as a result; three: a shorter season would lengthen the career of most players. Dalton's plan called for the season to begin in late April and run until mid-September. This, other league executives noted, would not help ease the problem of fatigue as the schedule would require the same number of trips. The proposal was not accepted, and the schedule remained at 162 games.

In 1967 the Orioles fell from the top of the league standings to sixth. This was due in part to a sore shoulder suffered by Jim Palmer that limited him to nine starts and a 3-1 record. The Orioles quickly proved the 1967 season was an anomaly by rising to a second-place finish in 1968.

After Bauer got the team off to a 43-37 record at the All-Star break in 1968, he was fired by Dalton. The firing took place less than two years after Bauer led the team to their first World Series title. He was replaced by Earl Weaver who had been a longtime manager in the Orioles chain. Weaver took the team to a second-place finish in the league.

In his first three full seasons at the helm, 1969-71, Weaver led the team not only to the AL East title but to the World Series as well. This was a great credit to Dalton who as farm director and director of player personnel had led the Orioles in their development of such players as Jim Palmer, Dave McNally, and Boog Powell. In those three seasons, the Orioles won one World Series (in 1970) and lost two. The World Series title led to Dalton being named Major League Executive of the Year for 1970.

In late October 1971, Dalton accepted an offer from Angels owner Gene Autry to leave Baltimore and become executive vice-president and general manager in Anaheim. The five-year deal, at a reported $60,000 per year, included stock options. Oriole President Jerry Hoffberger originally charged Autry with tampering for stealing Dalton away from Baltimore but later stated that he only asked Commissioner Bowie Kuhn to prevent teams from talking directly with personnel from another organization in the future.

One of Dalton's first moves as Angels general manager was to swap longtime Angels shortstop Jim Fregosi to the Mets for four players, one of whom was future Hall of Famer Nolan Ryan. The trade, which took place three months after Dalton assumed his new position, reaffirmed his reputation as a shrewd trader and a keen judge of talent.

Despite the emergence of Ryan as one of the American League's best starting pitchers, Dalton was unable to duplicate the success he had had in Baltimore. In six seasons at the helm of the Angels he failed to produce a winning season and was never able to rise above fourth place in the AL West. At the end of the six years, Autry decided to replace Dalton with former Padres President Buzzie Bavasi. Autry announced that Dalton would remain with the Angels and left in charge of player trades and free agent negotiations while Bavasi would oversee baseball operations.

On November 21, 1977, Milwaukee Brewers president Bud Selig fired both GM Jim Baumer and field manager Alex Grammas. After receiving Autry's permission to talk with Dalton, Selig hired Harry as his GM.

Dalton took over a Brewers team that had finished sixth in 1977 and had never had a winning season in the franchise's nine-year history. But all was not bad. Four days before hiring Dalton, Selig had managed to lure defending AL RBI leader Larry Hisle from the Twins by signing him as a free agent.

Selig granted Dalton full power in all player moves. Coming to Milwaukee along with Dalton were Walter Shannon, Walter Youse, and Roy Poitevint. This group became known as Dalton's Gang as they loyally followed him from Baltimore to the Angels and then to the Brewers.

With just weeks to go before the start of his first spring training in Milwaukee, Dalton named George Bamberger as his manager. Bamberger had been the pitching coach in Baltimore when Dalton was there and continued in that role until Dalton lured him away. Milwaukee was pitching-poor and Dalton valued Bamberger's work in Baltimore.

It turned out to be a good move; the 1978 Brewers turned in the first winning season in franchise history going 93-69, good for third place in the AL East. They were spurred on by the emergence of Rookie of the Year candidate Paul Molitor and pitcher Mike Caldwell who won 22 games in '78. Molitor finished second to Lou Whitaker in ROY voting.

The Brewers continued to win going into the early 1980s. In 1979 they won a franchise-record 95 games finishing second in the AL East — behind the Orioles. After posting a third-straight winning season in 1980 the Brewers made the first postseason appearance in franchise history in 1981. In that strike-ravaged season, the Brewers won the second-half title in the AL Eastern Division but lost the playoff to first-half champion New York Yankees. The Brewers were led by Cy Young Award-winning reliever Rollie Fingers, who also won the League's MVP that year.

The Brewers entered the 1982 season with high hopes of winning a division title. The team got off to a slow start and manager Buck Rodgers found himself fired after a 23-24 start; he was replaced by hitting coach Harvey Kuenn, who took over the reins and led the team to their first-ever World Series appearance. They took it to the seventh game before losing to the Cardinals. Dalton's accomplishment was recognized with his second Major League Executive of The Year honor.

Dalton was never able to return his team to that level of success, and team owner Bud Selig was forced to release him following the 1991 season. Selig replaced Dalton with assistant GM Sal Bando. Bando was hired in the hopes that his business acumen would help the financially-strapped franchise rebound. Dalton remained as a consultant in the team's front office through the 1994 season at which time he retired.

Dalton's contributions to the franchise were recognized when he was inducted into the Brewers Walk of Fame outside Miller Park in July of 2003. Dalton retired to Scottsdale, Arizona, and died there of complications from Lewy body disease, misdiagnosed as Parkinson's disease, on October 23, 2005. Dalton was 77 years old.

SOURCES

Baseball.Reference.com

Telephone interview with Pat Dalton, May 23, 2012.

Daniel Okrent, *Nine Innings* (New York: McGraw-Hill, 1989)

The Sporting News, January 25, 1961.

The Sporting News, June 12, 1961.

The Sporting News, November 1, 1961.

The Sporting News, December 6, 1965.

The Sporting News, December 18, 1965.

The Sporting News, January 29, 1966.

The Sporting News, August 13, 1966.

The Sporting News, September 17, 1966.

The Sporting News, November 5, 1977.

The Sporting News, November 12, 1977.

The Sporting News, December 3, 1977.

HARVEY KUENN

By Dale Vaiss

Picture this: You are standing in a dugout in St Louis. It is the seventh game of the World Series. The team you have managed for most of the year is nursing a 3-2 lead over the home Cardinals as you enter the bottom half of the sixth inning. Your ace pitcher, the eventual Cy Young Award winner, Pete Vuckovich is on the mound.

This is the position Harvey Kuenn found himself in one October night in 1982. While his team went on to lose that game, and the Series, that night did not reflect poorly on Kuenn in the eyes of his team's fans. In their eyes Harvey was a hero, the man who had pulled their team out of a funk in mid-June and led them to this grand stage. This power-hitting team had taken on the freewheeling personality of its manager. Because of their power and Kuenn's name, the team was nicknamed "Harvey's Wallbangers."

This was not just any team. These were the Milwaukee Brewers. This team represented the town where Kuenn grew up. He was an All-American shortstop for his home-state University of Wisconsin Badgers. He married a former Miss Wisconsin. He won the American League Rookie of the Year Award in 1953 and the American League batting title in 1959. Oh, and he had a leg amputated below the knee.

Harvey Edward Kuenn Jr. was born on December 12, 1930, in the Milwaukee suburb of West Allis, Wisconsin. He was the only child born to Harvey and Dorothy (Wrensch) Kuenn. The Kuenns were the typical German-American blue-collar family that so heavily populated Milwaukee. Both of Harvey's parents worked for a paper and packaging processing firm in Milwaukee. Harvey Sr. worked on the dock as a shipping clerk while Dorothy ran the company's credit union.

Kuenn grew up on Milwaukee's south side, where his father would work with him almost daily on his baseball skills. Harvey Sr. had been a talented third baseman on some of the top area teams in Milwaukee. He once got a tryout with the minor-league Milwaukee Brewers but did not make the club. He began teaching his son how to hit at a very early age and vowed that one day Harvey Jr. would be a major league-hitter.

Eventually, Kuenn developed into a baseball-obsessed child. He played baseball from sunup to sundown. When it rained, he would take a ball to the basement and throw it around down there.

Among Harvey Jr.'s early influences were some people who had major-league experience themselves. At the age of 12, he played for Jack Kloza's team. Kloza had a cup of coffee with the

St. Louis Browns in the early 1930s. He appeared in 25 games as an outfielder for the Browns in 1931 and 1932. Kloza ended his career as a member of the minor-league Brewers and settled in Milwaukee.

Harvey also attended a baseball camp run by Bunny Brief. Brief had been a major league outfielder with the Browns, Chicago White Sox and Pittsburgh Pirates from 1912 to 1917. Like Kloza, he ended his career with the Brewers and settled in Milwaukee. During Harvey's childhood, Brief had run a baseball camp on the city's south side.

Kuenn attended Milwaukee Lutheran High School, where he was a standout three-sport athlete who became the first athlete in school history to earn 10 letters. He earned four letters in baseball and three each in basketball and football.

Among his accomplishments at Lutheran was a 52-yard dropkick field goal in October 1948 while playing for the Lutheran football team. He was named all-conference at quarterback his junior and senior years and received honorable mention all-state as a quarterback his senior year

In basketball, he led his team to three straight Wisconsin Prep Conference titles. He led the conference in scoring in basketball in both his junior and senior seasons and was named all conference at forward all three years.

It was in high school where Kuenn first began to attract the attention of major-league scouts. His .425 batting average over his three-year career there was the highest in school history. Several scouts wanted to sign him right out of high school but Kuenn decided to continue his education.

While in high school, Kuenn spent his summers playing baseball for the Highway Beer Depot team, sponsored by a Milwaukee-area liquor store. A teammate of his with the Depot team, Ron Unke, was also a teammate of his at Milwaukee Lutheran.

Because both Kuenn and Unke, a right-handed pitcher, were believed to be asking for $50,000 from major league scouts, the Highway Depot team became known as "the $100,000 team." Unke and Kuenn were also teammates at Wisconsin. Unke eventually signed with the Cardinals and spent four years in their minor league system.

"Tex" Belich ran the Highway Beer Depot team. Tex and his brother Emil, who was a scout for the Philadelphia Phillies and Boston Braves, were very influential in Harvey's further development as a player. Kuenn developed a brother-like relationship with Emil, who had a brief minor-league career in the early 1940s, never rising above Class D Ball. Harvey often sought the advice of the Belich brothers not only on baseball matters but on life matters as well.

After graduating from high school in 1949, he opted to go to Luther College in Decorah, Iowa, to play football and baseball. After a week at Luther, he decided he did not like it there so he hitchhiked home. After returning to Milwaukee, he decided to accept a scholarship offer from the University of Wisconsin to play baseball for the Badgers.

Kuenn enrolled at Wisconsin for the second semester in January 1950. Kuenn, who stood 6-foot-2 and weighed 190 pounds, played junior varsity basketball for the Badgers in the 1950-51 season. He made the varsity team as a forward in the fall of 1951 but left the team in February to focus on baseball. While attending school in Madison he was a member of the Delta Upsilon fraternity.

As a member of the Badgers' baseball team, Kuenn quickly established himself as a top hitter. He captained the freshman team in 1950. He moved to varsity his sophomore year and became the starting shortstop. In his junior year, he served as team captain and led the Badgers to a third-place finish in the Big Ten. After leading the conference in six offensive categories, he was named the first team All-Big Ten shortstop. He also became the first Badger in the program's history to be named first team All-American. His .436 batting average was the highest of any member of the All-American team. His career average of .382 ranks as the second highest in the program's history.

His coach at Wisconsin was Arthur "Dynie" Mansfield, who had played collegiate baseball for the Badgers and minor league ball in the New York Giants organization in the 1930s. He coached the Badgers' baseball team from 1940 to 1970 and Kuenn developed a great deal of respect for him during his time in Madison. After signing his first pro contract, Harvey gave Mansfield a lot of credit for his success.

While attending school in Madison, Harvey met Dixie Sarchet, who won the Miss Wisconsin-USA beauty pageant in 1954. She and Harvey married in October 1955. Together they had two children. A daughter, Robin, was born in the summer of 1956 and a son, Harvey III, was born in December 1958.

As an amateur, the right-handed-hitting Kuenn had developed a reputation as a solid line drive hitter. He did not have much power. Kuenn, most thought, could have hit for power, but that was not his strong suit. He could hit about any pitch to any part of the field that he wanted. That is what made him so valuable. He once said that he did not like to hit home runs because they tended to throw off his hitting rhythm.

After completing his junior year there was a lot of speculation that Kuenn would opt to give up his final year of college eligibility to sign a pro contract. Teams were offering $50,000 and more for him to sign. After the season, he sat around a table with the Belich brothers and Mansfield and opened up the 12 sealed bids that he received. From there Kuenn narrowed his choices down to the Detroit Tigers and another team. After discussing it with his parents, he chose the $55,000 bonus offered by the Tigers. Kuenn signed the contract on June 9, 1952. While it was called a bonus, the $55,000 served as his first three years' salary. Kuenn used some of the money to buy a new home for his parents in Milwaukee.

Tiger assistant farm director John McHale had, at the urging of scout George Moriarity, watched Kuenn play in his final college game. After that game, the Tigers decided to make the $55,000 offer. There had been some concern from some organizations that a knee injury from his prep football days would prevent Kuenn from realizing his potential. Word of the knee injury had caused the Boston

The 1953 AL Rookie of the Year with the Detroit Tigers, Harvey Kuenn was a 10-time All-Star and led the AL in hits four times. He took over as skipper of the Brewers after 47 games in 1982, and Harvey's Wallbangers were born.

Red Sox to drop out of the bidding. This injury had caused the military give him 4-F status and kept him out of the service.

McHale, who became the Tigers' general manager in 1957, said he hoped Kuenn is "half as good as the last guy who came into this league with a bad knee — Joe DiMaggio."

Upon signing Kuenn, the Tigers sent him to Davenport (Iowa), their Class B team in the old Three-I League. In the summer of 1952, Kuenn hit .340 in 63 games with Davenport. One of the highlights of his time there came on July 29 against Burlington. That day he broke up a no-hitter with two out in the ninth. That single allowed Kuenn to extend his hitting streak to 18 games. Because of his success, Kuenn finished second in the MVP balloting for the Three-I League that year and earned a call-up to the Tigers on September 6.

When Kuenn made his major-league debut in September of 1952, the shortstop position was manned by veteran Johnny Pesky. Pesky, a Boston legend, had come over to Detroit in a nine-player deal between the Red Sox and the Tigers that June. When Kuenn arrived, Pesky took him under his wing and assisted him in his transition to the majors.

When Kuenn arrived in Detroit Fred Hutchinson managed the Tigers. "Hutch," as he was known, was an All-Star pitcher with the Tigers in the 1940s and '50s. The Tigers named him player-manager in the middle of the 1952 season, replacing Red Rolfe.

Hutchinson was a big Kuenn supporter from the start. In 85 plate appearances in September 1952 Kuenn hit .325. Maybe the most amazing stat to come out of that month was the fact that he only struck out once in those 85 plate appearances. That was to the Indians' Bob Lemon, a future Hall of Famer. For the next nine years, Kuenn never finished worse than fifth in the AL in number of at bats per strikeout.

After the 1952 season, Kuenn returned to Madison to continue to work on his degree. Even so, he never did graduate from college.

Kuenn arrived in Florida for spring training in 1953 as the starting shortstop. Kuenn did not disappoint. As a 22-year-old rookie batting out of the leadoff spot most of the season, he led the league in plate appearances, at-bats, and hits. His 679 at bats were a new American League record. He made the AL All-Star team and won the Rookie of the Year Award. In the rookie voting, he received 23 of 24 votes.

Kuenn had established himself, at the age of 22, as one of the game's best hitters. However, Kuenn was not the only young Tiger making noise. In June of 1953, an 18-year-old kid from Baltimore by the name of Al Kaline made his big-league debut in a Tiger uniform. For the remainder of the decade, the "K & K Boys," gave the Tigers one of the best one two punches in baseball.

While they got along and clicked well as teammates Kaline and Kuenn were quite different. Kaline, who never played a single inning of minor-league ball, was quiet and shy. He was the son of a Baltimore preacher. Kuenn, meanwhile, was rarely seen on the field without a mouth full of chewing tobacco and was known to like his beer. He claimed the tobacco made him drink less water during the game.

The next three seasons saw Kuenn continue to build his reputation as one of the game's best hitters. He finished no lower than seventh in the AL batting race in any of those years. Over his career Kuenn led the league in doubles three times ('55, '58, '59) and in hits four times ('53, '54, '56, '59).

In the off-seasons, Kuenn returned to Milwaukee. He spent his winters staying in shape by bowling. Kuenn maintained good winter conditioning by bowling three times a week. His league averages ranged from 181 to 195. He posted one 671 series. His father, Harvey Sr., was the captain of one of the teams.

In one offseason Kuenn went to work at the West Allis Bank in his hometown of West Allis, Wisconsin. He later opened a pro shop in Milwaukee that sold sporting equipment of all types. It was while spending time in Milwaukee that Kuenn developed a close friendship with Milwaukee Braves third baseman Eddie Matthews.

During spring training 1957, Kuenn flew to Washington State to be the best man at the wedding of teammate, pitcher Billy Hoeft. Hoeft was another Wisconsin native from Oshkosh who married a woman from Lakeland, Washington, on February 25. Both Hoeft and Kuenn had been signed by scout George Moriarity, the former Tigers third baseman and manager and AL umpire. Hoeft returned the favor by serving as Harvey III's godfather.

In 1957, suffering through defensive problems, Kuenn slipped to a .277 batting average. Kuenn had become too big to play shortstop and had lost a step. The Tigers decided to move him to third base for the 1958 season. The Tigers later changed their mind and moved Kuenn to center field. There he would join Kaline in right and Charley Maxwell in left. Because Kuenn was the Tigers' team captain, the poor season was even more disappointing.

Coming off a poor year in 1957, Kuenn was forced to take a $3,000 pay cut for the 1958 season. In 1958, Kuenn returned to his old self. He hit .319 to finish third in the league behind Boston Red Sox teammates Ted Williams and Pete Runnels. He also led the league with 39 doubles. Kuenn also received heavy praise from several for his play in center field. None other than Leo Durocher, who had said Kuenn would never make it in the outfield, said Kuenn had adapted well to his new position. After watching Kuenn on television make a great play at Comiskey Park, Durocher said that only Willie Mays could make a play like that. In his first year in center, he led the league's outfielders with 358 putouts.

In 1958, Kuenn and Jim Smilgoff collaborated to write a book, Big League Batting Secrets. Kuenn's teammate Kaline wrote the book's introduction. Smilgoff was a minor-league catcher from 1933 to 1936 who had befriended Kuenn. He was also a legendary high school coach at Taft High School in Chicago. Two years earlier Smilgoff had written his own book, Winning High School Baseball.

The 1959 season came with much optimism for Kuenn. His hitting had returned to its pre-1957 level and he had become comfortable in a new position. His performance in 1958 proved that the 1957 season was an aberration. Kuenn ran away with the 1959 AL batting championship. His .353 batting average was 27 points higher than that of teammate Kaline, the second-place finisher. The .353 batting average included a career-high 22-game hitting streak in midsummer.

As the 1960 season approached, trade rumors swirled around Kuenn. It was rumored that Kuenn would be traded to the Cleveland Indians for reigning AL home run king Rocky Colavito. Cleveland GM Frank Lane had been trying to pry Kuenn from the Tigers since before the 1957 season.

In January 1958, Lane went on NBC's Today show and announced that he had offered pitcher Hank Aguirre, catcher Jim Hegan, first baseman Vic Wertz and outfielder Gene Woodling to Detroit for Kuenn. The Tigers rejected the offer; all but Woodling eventually made their way to Detroit later.

After winning the batting crown in 1959, Kuenn, who had developed a reputation as a tough negotiator, asked the Tigers for a $10,000 raise for 1960. This would bring his pay to near $50,000, making him one of the highest-paid Tigers ever. The Tigers merely laughed at the suggestion. Meanwhile, Colavito had asked the Tribe for a raise from $28,000 to $45,000. He got no better reaction than Kuenn did. This further fueled the trade rumors.

Kuenn, who did not want to leave Detroit, became nervous when the rumors surfaced and settled with the Tigers for $42,000. Colavito settled for $35,000 in the first week of March. After they signed, the two teams announced the trade was dead. On April 17, two days before Opening Day, the trade was made and Kuenn was now an Indian. This was the only time in baseball history that a league batting champion had been traded for a home run champion.

The reaction in Cleveland was swift and extremely negative. Calls to the Indians ran 7 to 1 against the trade. Colavito was a hero in Cleveland and the fans were not happy to see him go. Many threatened to boycott Indians games. Despite this, Lane said that in acquiring Kuenn he had traded "hamburger for steak." The reaction in Detroit was surprisingly positive given how popular Kuenn was there. However, it was clear that the Tigers needed more power.

The Indians and Tigers opened the season against each other just two days after the trade. Colavito had what he called the worst day of his career, striking out four times in his Tigers debut.

During his eight years in Detroit, Kuenn had played six different positions. He had played everywhere except second base, catcher and pitcher. With the Indians he was an outfielder. He was placed in the second spot in the order after second baseman Johnny Temple. Kuenn hit .308 for the Indians in 1960 and made the All-Star team for the eighth straight year. This was his last appearance on an All-Star team. He played mostly in right field with an occasional game in left or at third base. In December of that year, the Tribe traded Kuenn to the San Francisco Giants for veteran pitcher Johnny Antonelli and outfielder Willie Kirkland.

Kuenn got off to a bad start in his first season in the National League. He hit .265 in 1961. At the time, that was a career low for him. Despite that, the Giants did not cut his pay. Entering spring training in 1962, he vowed to bat .300. He kept his word and hit .304 as the Giants won the NL pennant and Kuenn made his first postseason appearance. He went 1-for-12 in the 1962 World Series as the Giants lost to the New York Yankees in seven games. His son later said that Harvey played the series with a broken pinkie finger.

Harvey's father died in May 1962, and Harvey missed four days with the team to attend the funeral in Milwaukee.

The Giants traded Kuenn to the Chicago Cubs in May 1965. The Cubs sold Kuenn to the Phillies in April 1966, three games into the season. As a result, Kuenn's tenure under new Cubs manager Leo Durocher was cut short. He played the 1966 season with the Phillies under Gene Mauch.

On September 9, 1965, Kuenn struck out in the bottom of the ninth to become the final out in Sandy Koufax's perfect game. Kuenn had also been the final out in the Dodgers ace's no-hit triumph over the Giants in May 1963.

The Phillies left Kuenn off the roster during the offseason leading up to the 1967 season. He did receive an invitation to spring training in the hopes he might be able to fill in for injured first baseman Bill White, who was expected to miss the start of the season with a torn Achilles tendon. However, just as spring training was about to begin, Kuenn suddenly announced his retirement from baseball. He had accepted a job at a Milwaukee television station.

Throughout his playing career Kuenn had been very active in the Players Association. As Tigers team representative, Harvey took an active role in the players' move to abolish the reserve clause. In 1959, he was elected head player rep for the American League. He, along with Phillies pitcher Robin Roberts and Los Angeles Angels third baseman Ed Yost, were the driving force behind the union's growth in the early 1960s. Kuenn was a member of the four-man committee that hired Marvin Miller as head of the union in 1965.

He served as the ten o'clock sports anchor at WVTV in Milwaukee for a couple of years. Eventually WVTV dropped its sports programming and Harvey took a job as a sales representative with a local printing company.

In 1969, when the expansion Montreal Expos named Mauch their manager, Mauch offered Kuenn a job on his coaching staff. Kuenn, after discovering that his children did not want to move to Montreal, turned down the offer.

In 1971 the Milwaukee Brewers, who had moved from Seattle for the 1970 season, named Kuenn as their new batting coach. In this role, Kuenn mentored some of the game's top young hitters. Among them were future Hall of Famers Robin Yount and Paul Molitor. Ironically, the Brewers general manager who hired Kuenn was none other than "Trader" Frank Lane, who as Indians GM in 1960, made the trade that brought Kuenn to Cleveland.

During the 1971 season, the Brewers put Kuenn on the active roster for the last month of the season. The Brewers did this so he would be able to add service time in order to improve his players' pension. Kuenn never got into a game. In fact, on September 17 he left Milwaukee to help coach the Brewers Instructional League team in Arizona.

Harvey and Dixie divorced in 1971. In October 1974 he married Audrey Cesar, a native of the Milwaukee area. Audrey's parents owned a bar near County Stadium. Several baseball people patronized the bar. Harvey met Audrey at the bar. Brewers announcer Bob Uecker served as best man at the wedding.

Audrey eventually took over the bar from her parents, and she and Harvey moved into a place behind the bar. The Kuenns would spend their summers in Milwaukee but wintered in Arizona.

Kuenn served as interim manager of the Brewers following the firing of Del Crandall with two games remaining in the 1975 season. Kuenn was hopeful that the Brewers would offer him the job for the 1976 season. The Brewers decided to give the job to Alex Grammas, a longtime protégé of Cincinnati Reds manager Sparky Anderson who had served for years as Sparky's third base coach in Cincinnati. Other than his brief stint as interim manager, Kuenn served as Brewers hitting coach from 1971 to 1982.

In 1976, Kuenn underwent open-heart surgery and had a quadruple bypass. The bypass was the result of poor circulation, a condition that would plague him the rest of his life. In 1977, Crohn's disease, a stomach ailment, kept him hospitalized for four months during the season.

The Expos took Kuenn's son, 18-year-old Harvey III, in the 20th round of the June 1977 amateur draft as a first baseman. Kuenn the younger had played high school ball for Milwaukee Central High School. He hit .215 for the Expos' Rookie League team in 1977. Following that season the Expos released him, and he was signed by the Brewers. He hit .214 in 23 games for Newark of the New York-Penn League in 1978. That ended his professional baseball career as a player. In January 1990, he took a scouting job with the Brewers and remains with that organization to this day, currently as a Midwest area scout for the Brewers.

In 1978, the Brewers hired Harry Dalton as their new general manager. Dalton, who had built the Angels and the Baltimore Orioles into contenders, was named to replace Jim Baumer, who had been fired by team president Bud Selig.

Dalton immediately began turning things around in Milwaukee. He hired Orioles pitching coach George Bamberger as the team's new manager. In spring training, he released outfielder Von Joshua. Joshua had been the team's best hitter a season earlier but Dalton thought he did not hustle enough. Because of these and other moves and others, the Brewers had the first winning season in franchise history in 1978, much to Selig's delight.

Over the years, Kuenn had developed a good relationship with Selig. Both had grown up in Milwaukee around the same time and thus had a lot in common. Kuenn always felt a lot of gratitude to Selig for sticking with him through all his health problems.

In 1980, Kuenn faced the toughest health battle of his life. He had been complaining about a foot problem that had been bothering him. He told his son that whenever he put the foot on the ground it would turn white. The problem resulted from the poor circulation that had led to his quadruple bypass four years earlier.

After four operations to repair the leg, one day the doctor walked in and told him he would have to take the leg off below the knee. The operation took place on February 16, 1980. He was just 49 years old. Three days after the operation he began therapy. According to Audrey, the doctors "couldn't believe the strength of this guy."

In 1981, the Brewers, under manager Bob "Buck" Rodgers, made their first postseason appearance. Spurred on by the hitting of Yount, Molitor and Cecil Cooper and the pitching of newly acquired relief ace Rollie Fingers, the Brewers captured the second-half title in the American League East Division. (The major leagues played a split season in 1981 because a bitter players' strike interrupted the season.) They lost to the first-half champion New York Yankees three games to two in the AL Championship Series.

The 1982 season started with much optimism in Milwaukee. After four straight winning seasons, the Brewers were in a position to make a run for the AL East flag. However, that optimism quickly turned sour.

On June 2, with the team struggling to a 23-24 record to start the season, Dalton fired Rodgers and named Kuenn to replace him. Kuenn would finally get the opportunity he had dreamed of since the 1958 Tigers considered him as a possible player-manager.

After the firing, Rodgers was quoted as saying his firing was the result of some cancers on the team. Several players on the club did not like Rodgers' managerial style. Some of his biggest critics were thought to be Fingers, catcher Ted Simmons, and center fielder Gorman Thomas.

Immediately after his hiring, Kuenn held a team meeting and told the players just to go out and have fun. The team seemed to loosen up. He set the batting order and rarely changed it. He seemed to trust his pitchers more than Rodgers did. As a result, the team began to play better baseball.

After going 23-24 under Rodgers, the team suddenly took off and went 20-7 in June, hitting an unbelievable .294 as a team. They also hit 47 home runs in those 27 games and averaged over six and a half runs a game.

Some believed the respect Kuenn had built up among the players over his years as the hitting coach made the players want to play well for him. It is known that Yount had a deep respect for Kuenn. Yount had come to the majors at age 18 and Kuenn was the only major league batting coach he had ever known. In 1982, Yount was named AL MVP after batting .332 and hitting 29 homers.

Whatever the reason, the players responded to Kuenn the way Dalton had hoped they would when he hired him. The Brewers went 72-43 under Kuenn to finish with 95 wins.

However, even with that, the season's outcome came down to the final series of the season. The Brewers were three games up on the Orioles for the AL East lead with four games to play. Those four games consisted of a four-game weekend series in Baltimore. There was a doubleheader scheduled for Friday and single games on Saturday and Sunday.

Baltimore swept Friday's doubleheader to move within one game of Milwaukee with two to play. They also won Saturday's game to move into a tie for first. Therefore, the season came down to one game on Sunday to win the division title. The game featured two future Hall of Fame pitchers going against each other.

Jim Palmer, Baltimore's perennial Cy Young contender, faced Don Sutton, whom the Brewers had acquired from the Houston Astros in a trade barely a month earlier. On Sunday, Yount hit a pair of homers, and Sutton allowed just two runs over eight innings as the Brewers won the game, and the division, by a score of 10-2.

Kuenn had taken his team to the postseason. Along the way, his team hit 216 home runs. That was the most that any major league team had hit since the Minnesota Twins hit 225 in 1963.

There was power throughout this lineup. Led by Thomas' league-leading 39 home runs, the Brewers had five players finish with 20 or more home runs. The team also featured four future Hall of Famers: Yount, Molitor, Sutton, and Fingers.

In the ALCS, the Brewers faced the California Angels for the right to advance to the World Series. Kuenn's former manager, Gene Mauch, managed California. The Brewers got a big base hit from Cooper in the bottom of the seventh in Game Five to take the series 3 games to 2 when the ALCS was a best-of-five playoff. Milwaukee became the first team ever to come back from a two-games-to-none deficit to win a five-game series. They advanced to the World Series but lost to the Cardinals in seven games.

According to Kuenn's wife Audrey, the Brewers were like a family while Kuenn was managing. In spring training the players would often eat at the Kuenn house in Arizona. During the summer they would go to the bar that the Kuenns owned.

Kuenn returned to manage the team in 1983. This time, however, he would have to do it without two big arms. Starting pitcher Pete Vuckovich was out with an injury until late August. Rollie Fingers missed the entire season due to injury. The two of them had combined to win the last two AL Cy Young Awards, Fingers in 1981 and Vuckovich in 1982 thanks to an 18-win campaign.

In addition to this, at midseason, Dalton traded local hero Gorman Thomas to the Indians for veteran centerfielder Rick Manning and pitcher Rick Waits. This ripped a big power producer out of the middle of the Brewers lineup.

Despite that, the team managed to keep the division lead in their sights nearly all year. However, a 10-game losing streak in mid-September sealed their fate. The streak, brought on by a horrendous hitting slump, was part of a stretch that saw them lose 18 of 24 games. The Brewers limped home with an 87-75 record to finish 11 games behind the eventual world champion Orioles.

On October 3, the day after Harvey Kuenn finished his only full season as a major league manager, Dalton fired him. The Brewers notified Kuenn of the move on October 1, the day before the team's final game. Bud Selig offered Kuenn a job as a scout and minor-league hitting instructor with the Brewers.

Kuenn was replaced by Rene Lachemann. In 1984, under Lachemann, the Brewers went 67-94 to finish last in the AL's Eastern Division. Following the season Dalton fired Lachemann.

Kuenn spent the remainder of his life in his new role as scout and minor-league hitting instructor for the Brewers. He and his wife continued to winter in Arizona. During the summer months, Harvey would travel from Wisconsin, mostly to Chicago, as an advance scout for the Brewers.

On February 28, 1988, Harvey and Audrey were preparing to play golf when Harvey went to use the restroom. When he did not come out for a while, Audrey went to check on him and found him dead. He died of a heart problem that resulted from the poor circulation that had caused him so much trouble over the last twelve years of his life. He was two months past his 57th birthday.

Bob Uecker read the eulogy at Kuenn's funeral. Six players from the 1982 Brewers served as his pallbearers.

The University of Wisconsin inducted Kuenn into their Sports Hall of Fame in 1991. He also had his name placed on the Brewer Walk of Fame at Miller Park in 2005.

Kuenn was eligible to have his name placed on the Hall of Fame ballot in 1972. However, when the Brewers activated him in 1971, his appearance on the ballot was delayed by five years. In the 15 years that his name appeared on the ballot, Kuenn never received the necessary 75 percent of the vote needed for enshrinement.

SOURCES

In addition to Baseball-Reference.com and SABR.org, the author also consulted:

Okrent, Daniel. *Nine Innings*. New York: Houghton Mifflin Company, 1985.

Pluto, Terry. *The Curse of Rocky Colavito: A Loving Look at a Thirty-Year Slump*. New York: Simon & Schuster, 1994.

Okrent, Daniel & Steve Wulf. *Baseball Anecdotes*. New York: Harper Collins, 1989

Dolson, Frank. "The Homer that Made Kuenn Blush." *Baseball Digest*, January 1963.

"Garner Wins Three-I VP Prize" *The Sporting News*, September 10, 1952: 44.

"Mark Big Week in Kid Roundup" *The Sporting News*, June 18, 1952: 36.

The Sporting News, January 30, 1957; February 27, 1957; March 6, 1957; May 1, 1957; April 30, 1958; January 7, 1959; May 20, 1959; April 10, 1971; September 18, 1971; and January 1, 1972

Interview with Audrey Kuenn, January 24, 2010.

Interview with Harvey Kuenn III, December 31, 2009.

Milwaukee Sentinel, June 15, 1952.

Racine (Wisconsin) *Journal Times*, December 9, 1948.

Rhinelander (Wisconsin) *Daily News*, October 27, 1948.

Wisconsin State Journal (Madison), August 2, 1949; May 15, 1952; and December 10, 1952.

BUCK RODGERS

By Maxwell Kates

Millions of Californians were not born there but chose the Golden State as the epicenter of their career and family lives. Two of them, London's Bob Hope and Tacoma's Bing Crosby, won fame and glory in Hollywood with a series of "Road" movies. The subject of this article, however, is a baseball personality whose life has followed a unique road from the heartland of America to the state of California.

Even as a rookie with the 1961 Los Angeles Angels, Buck Rodgers demonstrated leadership qualities and the ability to motivate his teammates. After injuries prevented him from reaching his full potential as a player, Rodgers was frequently mentioned as a possible Angels manager. After a coaching and managing odyssey that took him to Minnesota, San Francisco, Milwaukee, and Montreal, he achieved that goal. Rodgers described himself as "a teacher, a motivator, someone who's fair but who will never take fairness for weakness."[1]

His openness, honesty, and willingness to communicate made him a popular figure with the fans and the media despite periodic clashes with some of his players and general managers. The road that Rodgers traveled, however, was not always a safe one, and on more than one occasion, it proved calamitous for the Rodgers family.

Rex and Winifred Rodgers of Delaware County, Ohio welcomed a son, Robert Leroy, on August 16, 1938. A naturally gifted athlete who was nicknamed Buck, Rodgers won letters in basketball and track in addition to baseball at Prospect High School, where he pitched six no-hitters. He also played American Legion baseball in nearby Marion, Ohio.[2] Converted to a catcher at Ohio Wesleyan University, he was studying towards a liberal arts degree when, in 1956, he signed as a free agent with the Detroit Tigers. Rodgers soon found himself caught in a logjam of catchers, including Dick Brown, Mike Roarke, and rising star Bill Freehan. The Tigers deemed him expendable, and he was selected by the Los Angeles Angels in the 1960 expansion draft. Years later, Rodgers credited Angels' owner Gene Autry with "[saving him] from having to find a real job."[3] Meanwhile, Rodgers had married his high school sweetheart, the former Judy Long, on January 18, 1958.

Rodgers, a 6-foot-2, 195-pound switch hitter, played for Walker Cooper at Dallas-Ft. Worth, where he was honored by *Look* magazine as the American Association's top catcher of 1961. A scouting report describes him as having "excellent speed for a catcher, good accurate arm, line drive power, [and a] fine handler of pitchers."[4] That September, the Angels brought him up, where he batted .321 in 16 games, including a grand slam off the Indians' Barry Latman.

After watching that performance, manager Bill Rigney lauded Rodgers as "an imaginative catcher who can go on to become one of the game's best."[5] Meanwhile, Rodgers was learning from Rigney that "the competitive edge lay in guile, cunning, and courage to make the right moves at the right time."[6] Cerebral and bumptious, Rigney was constantly challenged by both his young catcher and his shortstop Jim Fregosi. In reference to Rodgers and Fregosi, Rigney noted that "you wouldn't have had to look very far" in predicting future big-league managers on the team."[7]

A country image fused with urban charm served Buck Rodgers well in Tinseltown: "Rodgers was a tall man, broad shoulders, blessed with bright eyes and a movie star's face. He wore cowboy boots, well cut sports coats, and open collared shirts… he had chewed tobacco all of his adult life, yet always took care to use whitening drops on his teeth to combat the inevitable staining. *Playgirl* magazine even featured Rodgers in an article on baseball's sexiest men."[8]

The season of 1962 was a banner year for both the fledgling Angels and Rodgers: Rodgers disappointed nobody in the Angels' home opener when he drove in five runs in a 12-5 victory over the Minnesota Twins.[9] A month later, on May 5, he caught Bo Belinsky's no-hitter at Chavez Ravine. After sweeping the Washington Senators in a July 4 doubleheader, the Angels led the American League, in this, their sophomore season. On August 28, Rodgers hit one of three consecutive fourth-inning home runs as part of 10-5 decimation at Kansas City, and went on to hit .440 during a two-week span in September. Although the Angels finished the season in a third-place tie with Detroit, their young catcher shattered the record for games caught by a rookie with 150 while turning a club-record 14 double plays.[10] He displayed marksmanship with his bat, leading the Angels with eight sacrifice flies and 34 doubles while tying Albie Pearson with six triples. Rodgers finished second to Tom Tresh as Rookie of the Year.

The 1962 offseason marked the first of several in which Rodgers' name was suggested by the Angels in trades. One winter, rumors had him going to Chicago, the next winter he was headed for Baltimore, and the third time, he and Bob Lee were to be packaged to Minnesota for Jimmie Hall and Earl Battey. Rodgers was candid in telling sportswriter Ross Newhan, "[I]f I worried every time I heard my name involved in a trade, I'd be a nervous wreck." General manager Fred Haney routinely tried to ease Rodgers' apprehensions by declaring that his catcher was "not for sale."[11]

A finger injury curtailed Rodgers' effectiveness in 1963, but he continued to show flashes of brilliance.[12] In 1964, he tied his record of 14 double plays, and batted .387 during the club's 18-game-winning streak, along the way touching Dick Radatz for an inside-the-park home run. An ankle injury among other ailments limited Rodgers to a .209 average and 32 RBIs in 1965. After a stellar defensive season in 1966, Rodgers was developing a reputation as one of the better callers of pitches in the game. He complimented pitchers George Brunet and Marcelino Lopez on "never having better control of [their] breaking stuff" in spring training 1967.[13] Of course, there was no love lost with pitchers who ignored Rodgers' advice — he once called Dean Chance "the dumbest I've caught." As the vice president of Pacific Bus Lines, Rodgers was only too pleased to offer Dean Chance a one-way ticket to Minnesota when traded to the Twins. Chance "shook him off" and rode Greyhound.[14]

Another injury in 1967, a lingering blood infection, limited Rodgers to six home runs with 41 RBIs in 139 games.[15] Having recovered by August 18, he caught Jack Hamilton the night Red Sox outfielder Tony Conigliaro was beaned. Rodgers compared the horrific incident to "taking a bat to a pumpkin."[16] By the end of the decade, Rodgers moved his family, including daughters Lori, Lisa, and twins Jan and Jill, from his home state of Ohio to Yorba Linda, California.

After Rigney was fired in 1969, the Angels released Rodgers. In 1970, he followed Rigney to Minnesota as one of his coaches (Dean Chance

Skipper Buck Rodgers led the Brewers to their first postseason berth in franchise history, in the strike-shortened 1981 season. Replaced by Harvey Kuenn during the 1982 season, Rodgers subsequently piloted the Montreal Expos (1985-1991) and California Angels (1991-1994).

had since been traded to Cleveland). Sandwiched around another Rigney coaching assignment in San Francisco were two managerial postings in the Angels' organization: Salinas in 1975 and El Paso in 1977. By then, the name "Buck Rodgers" was synonymous with "Angels' manager of the future" — but it would prove a circuitous route for Rodgers' return to Anaheim.

After the Milwaukee Brewers hired Angels general manager Harry Dalton, other Angels personnel moved to new positions with the Brewers in 1978, among them Milwaukee's new third-base coach Buck Rodgers. Two years later, he was promoted to replace the ailing George Bamberger as manager. Rodgers won a division title in 1981 but a slow start in 1982 could not save his job. After a successful campaign managing Indianapolis in 1984, he was hired to manage the Montreal Expos beginning in 1985. During most of his tenure in Montreal, he kept the Expos in contention despite operating on a shoestring budget. The apex of his career occurred in 1987, when his club won 91 games and he was honored as Manager of the Year. Falling out of favor with a new regime in Montreal, he accepted his release early in the 1991 season.

Meanwhile, the Angels were imploding under manager Doug Rader. Was it time for a change? General manager Whitey Herzog thought so and brought Rodgers back to Anaheim. The Angels did not improve in the standings under Rodgers, finishing in last place in 1991 despite a .500 record. Off the field, Rodgers endured the fright of his life on May 21, 1992, when the Angels' team bus crashed into a ravine alongside the New Jersey Turnpike. Rodgers recalled the incident a few years later: "I saw a big tree limb coming and I ducked. Fortunately I missed it because it would have taken my head off. Then I got hit in the right side of the head... My right ribs were hit by the trees that crashed into the right side of the bus and I had a crushed elbow."[17]

After a long convalescence — he also had a broken leg — Rodgers returned to the Angels' dugout on August 28. Piloted in his absence by interim managers John Wathan and Marcel Lachemann, the Angels ended the 1992 season with a losing record. The following year, the Halos won only 71 games in 1993, and after butting heads with new general manager Bill Bavasi, Rodgers knew the team had to contend in 1994 in order for him to keep his job. The team did not, and after calling Angels president Rich Brown a "cancer," he was fired from his final managing position.[18]

Rodgers went to work for his friend Jim Fregosi as a West Coast scout for the Philadelphia Phillies.[19] In 1997, he was hired as the manager and director of baseball operations the Mission Viejo Vigilantes, a team that represented Orange County in the independent Western Baseball League. But Rodgers' 1997 season ended suddenly in June when his family was rocked by another highway tragedy: His mother Winifred was killed and his father was seriously injured in a car accident in Ohio.[20] Rex Rodgers died from injury-related illness six months later.[21] After returning to Mission Viejo in 1998, Rodgers was able to retire that year when he was awarded an insurance settlement of approximately $1 million from the 1992 bus accident.[22]

After many years in Yorba Linda, Buck and Judy Rodgers moved to the seaside village of Corona Del Mar, where they reside, 20 miles from Angel Stadium. He remains active in the community, conducting golf tournaments and other charitable events with Mike Witt and other Angel alumni. In the half-century he has spent here, Buck Rodgers has represented Southern California well. Those who have followed his career closely would agree with his family in recognizing him as "a man, a gentleman, and a baseball manager — in that order." *Les Expos, Nos Amours.*

SOURCES

In addition to the sources cited in the Notes, the author consulted Baseball-Reference.com, and Goodale, George, and Irv Kaze. *Los Angeles Angels 1965 Yearbook* (Los Angeles: Petersen Publishing Company, 1965).

NOTES

1. *Les Expos, Nos Amours*, English ed., produced by Brian Schecter (Montreal: TV Labatt, 1989).
2. *Los Angeles Angels 1962 Year Book* (Los Angeles: Los Angeles Angels, 1962), 19.
3. Daniel Okrent, *Nine Innings: The Anatomy of a Baseball Game* (New York: Ticknor & Fields, 1985), 6.
4. *Angels 1962 Year Book*, 19.
5. *Los Angeles Angels 1963 Year Book* (Los Angeles: Los Angeles Angels, 1963), 23.
6. Okrent, 115.
7. Ibid, 6.
8. Ibid, 5.
9. *Angels 1963 Year Book*, 3.
10. Ibid, 23.
11. Ross Newhan, "Rodgers Wrecks 'For Sale' Tag – He's Avenging Angel With a Bat," *The Sporting News*, May 28, 1966: 17.
12. Braven Dyer, "Rig Raids Bullpen for Seraph Starters," *The Sporting News*, June 1, 1963: 23.
13. Ross Newhan, "'Dean Dumbest Pitcher I've Caught' Says Rodgers," *The Sporting News*, April 8, 1967: 12.
14. Ibid.
15. Ibid.
16. Danny Gallagher, *Angels' Halo Haunted: Baseball Tragedies Revisited* (Toronto: Scoop Press, 1998), 26.
17. Gallagher, 16.
18. Rev Halofan, "Top 100 Angels: Bob Rodgers #46" on Halos Heaven, http://www.halosheaven.com/2009/1/11/716939/top-100-angelsbob-rodgers; Accessed May 24, 2010.
19. Gallagher, 25.
20. "Mother of Vigilantes' Rodgers Dies in Crash," *Los Angeles Times*. http://articles.latimes.com/1997-06-08/sports/sp-1491_1_ohio-state-highway-patrol; accessed May 24, 2010.
21. "Rex Rodgers" in Social Security Death Index: retrieved June 7, 2009.
22. Gallagher, 24.

PAT DOBSON

By Bill Bishop

Patrick Edward Dobson Jr. was born February 12, 1942, in Depew, New York, a small village ten miles east of Buffalo. In his youth, Pat often took the bus there to watch his heroes Joe Caffie and Luke Easter, stars of the Buffalo Bisons of the International League. Pat attended Lancaster Central High School, where he was the star pitcher, amassing an impressive 19–1 record. His high school buddies gave him the nickname "The Cobra." A lanky, hard-throwing right-hander, Pat stood 6-foot-3. Scouts from Boston, Detroit, and San Francisco pursued him, and he eventually was signed by Tigers scout Cy Williams. At the age of 17 he received an impressive $25,000 signing bonus. Pat would later say, "I blew my money on cars and good living, but I enjoyed it and I'd do it again."

In 1960, Pat made his professional debut with the Durham Bulls, at that time a Class A Detroit affiliate. He compiled a 7–9 record, striking out 137 batters in 157 innings, but he also walked 98. The following year was split between Knoxville and Durham. His 4–10 record was reflected by his elevated WHIP (walks plus hits per innings pitched) of 2.01 over 119 innings. In 1962, Pat pitched for Montgomery, going 8–7. He significantly lowered his WHIP to 1.39 and struck out better than a batter per inning. He finished the year with Duluth-Superior in the Northern League, appearing in four games and being treated rather roughly by opposing teams.

The 1963 season found Pat still toiling in the lower minors, starting with Jamestown in the New York-Penn League and finishing in Knoxville of the Double A South Atlantic League. He showed some promise by year's end, winning five and losing one at Knoxville with an impressive 1.33 ERA. Dobson began 1964 in Knoxville, reclassified a Double A club, and in midseason was promoted to the Tigers' Triple A farm team in Syracuse. He struggled a bit with the top minor league talent and was demoted to Double A Montgomery in 1965. There he appeared in only 17 games, going 4–1. He finished the year back in Syracuse, pitching four times in relief. Pat spent the winter playing ball in Puerto Rico. He said later that his success there was instrumental in rebuilding his confidence.

Dobson was at a crossroads in 1966. He didn't believe he was getting a real chance in the Detroit organization. He found himself on loan to Cleveland's Portland team in the Triple A Pacific Coast League. Dobson started slowly, not getting into the starting rotation until the third week of the season. Despite missing a week to bursitis, he ended up becoming one of the top pitchers in the league. Pat finished with a record of 12–9 and a 3.45 ERA. His manager, John Lipon, remarked, "Pat's got a good fast ball and slider, and at times a good curve. In fact, when he gets his big curve working effectively, he reminds me of Tommy Bridges." Pat played winter ball that year in the Dominican League and was one of the most impressive American pitchers, jumping out to a 3–0 record.

Dobson started 1967 with the Triple A Toledo Mud Hens, by then the Tigers' top farm team. After an impressive 4–1 start, he was called up to the parent club. He made his major league debut May 31, 1967, against Cleveland. He came into the game in the sixth inning with a runner on second and promptly surrendered a run-scoring single. He settled down and got the next two batters. In the seventh inning he surrendered a two-run home run to Leon Wagner. In his inning and two-thirds, Pat gave up two runs on four hits, but did not walk a batter and recorded three strikeouts. He was in the major leagues to stay.

Dobson appeared in 28 games in his rookie season. Initially, he was used only in Detroit blowout losses. But on August 2 Pat came in and pitched three strong innings against the Orioles to preserve a 1–0 lead. Manager Mayo Smith showed great confidence in the rookie by leaving Dobson in to start the ninth inning. But disaster struck when Pat walked Frank Robinson and then gave up a game-ending home run to Brooks Robinson. Still, his strong showing earned him his only start of the 1967 season on August 6 in the nightcap of a doubleheader against Cleveland. He surrendered four runs in the first inning, three of them coming on a Duke Sims homer. He left for a pinch-hitter in the top of the third, trailing 4–0. Dobson ended up with the loss as the Tigers fell 6–3. Then, from August 16 through September 15, Pat strung together eight appearances with 18.1 innings of shutout relief. Mayo Smith called him "the most improved pitcher on the staff." Dobson earned his first major league victory September 9 against the Chicago White Sox when the Tigers overcame a 3–0 deficit by scoring seven runs in the ninth inning. His scoreless string ended abruptly September 17 against Washington as he surrendered a three-run home run to the Senators' Hank Allen that turned a close game into a rout. Smith didn't use Dobson again until the final game of the season when he faced two California Angels, walking the first and giving up a sacrifice before being pulled in favor of Mickey Lolich in a Detroit defeat. The Tigers saw the 1967 pennant go to the Boston Red Sox.

Pat spent the winter playing ball in Puerto Rico. He impressed a lot of baseball men when he rewrote the record books December 10, 1967, by striking out 21 batters, eclipsing Juan Pizzaro's old league mark of 19.

Dobson entered 1968 full of confidence. He developed a strong working relationship with pitching coach Johnny Sain. Pat said Sain told him that he gripped the ball too tight and was teaching him to relax. As Dobson explained, "This gives my pitches better movement, better everything." Sain also taught him a different grip for his slider; it became his best pitch. Dobson commented, "I can throw it anytime I want to for a strike. I used to have a slider that was flat. It broke away from a right-handed hitter. The one Sain gave me is better because it dips."

Dobson worked a couple of innings in relief of Earl Wilson during the April 10 opening day loss to Boston. He contributed two scoreless innings in each of two Tigers come-from-behind victories in April. He then had a bad outing against the Yankees, allowing three batters to reach base without recording an out; he also threw two wild pitches. But the Tigers once again rallied for the victory. Pat got little work from manager Smith the first two months. He appeared in only 10 games, working 12 innings. On June 1, he was called upon to relieve Les Cain, who had been knocked around by the Yankees for four runs in the first inning. Pat shut the Yankees down for 5.2 innings, and the Tigers came back to win the game.

Following an injury to Earl Wilson, Dobson and John Hiller undertook several starts in his place. Pat hurled a complete-game shutout at Boston June 4. Coach Wally Moses called it the Tigers' most important victory of the season. A week later he earned a victory against the Minnesota Twins, allowing just one run in 7.2 innings, while striking out 10 batters. He had a string of 25 scoreless innings snapped by a Tony Oliva home run. Three days later he pitched five scoreless innings in relief as the Tigers went on to beat the White Sox in 14 innings. Pat saved the second game of a doubleheader against Chicago June 16. Over the next eight days he racked up two more saves. On June 21, Dobson came on to start the tenth inning and shut the Indians down through the twelfth. When the Tigers took the lead in the top of the thirteenth, Pat was in line for another victory. But he surrendered a single to Duke Sims and a home run to Tony Horton. Pat bounced back to save three more games before the All-Star break. In a string of 13 games won by the Tigers, Dobson won one and saved five.

Dobson's contributions weren't limited to the ball field. He had a flair for having fun with his teammates. He coined nicknames for many of them, including "Pizza" for Tom Matchick in honor of his red hair. He also hung the name "Ratso" on his roommate John Hiller, naming him after the Dustin Hoffman character in the movie *Midnight Cowboy*. He said, "When I fool around in the bullpen, I do it for a purpose. I stay relaxed and so do the guys around me." Pat was known simply as "Dobber," a nickname he carried the rest of his life. Bill Freehan emphasized Pat's competitiveness. "He goes after the hitters now and really challenges them. The pressure is on them, not him."

The Tigers appeared sluggish after the All-Star break. They dropped five out of eight games heading into a big four-game series with the Baltimore Orioles. In the first game, the Tigers trailed 4–2 in the ninth inning as Dobson came in to retire the side. When Matchick hit a dramatic two-run homer with two out and a 3–2 count on him, Dobson ended up with his third win of the season. Two days later Mayo needed a starter for the second game of a doubleheader against the O's. Dobson only lasted 2.1 innings, giving up two runs on four hits and a walk to suffer his second loss of the season. He started once again in Washington on August 1 and was handed another defeat as he gave up a grand slam to light-hitting Ron Hansen. Pat got five more starts in August, losing two and getting no decisions in the other three games. He pitched well in the games he lost, falling 5–3 and 1–0. Twice the bullpen cost him victories. Eventually, however, Joe Sparma was returned to the starting rotation, and Pat was sent back to the bullpen.

Dobson started September off with a bang, winning back-to-back games against the Oakland A's in relief, then saving the third game of the series. He was given another starting assignment against the Twins. Dobson pitched brilliantly except for two pitches to rookie Graig Nettles that were lined into the seats. The second one proved to be the winner in a 2–1 loss for the Tigers. Pat appeared in only four of the last 19 games, for a total of six innings. He got a save and took two losses in those four games. His final numbers for the pennant-winning Detroit Tigers were 5–8, a 2.66 ERA, and seven saves. He pitched in 125 innings and had an impressive WHIP of 1.10. He led the staff with 47 appearances.

Dobson appeared in the three games the Tigers lost in the 1968 World Series. He mopped up for Denny McLain in Game 1, allowing a home run to Lou Brock. In the third game, he came on for an injured Earl Wilson with the Tigers up 2–1 and two runners on. He got Orlando Cepeda out, but gave up a three-run home run to Tim McCarver as the Cardinals went on to win the game 7–3. His final appearance was in Game 4, in which he shut down the Cards for two innings on one hit.

In 1969 Pat appeared in 49 games, winning five games, losing ten, and saving nine. As in 1968, he worked as both a starter and reliever. He had one complete-game victory on July 1 against the Red Sox. He appeared in his last game as a Tiger on September 16, pitching two scoreless innings against the Yankees. His season ended prematurely when Wayne Redmond jumped on the little toe of his left foot after being startled by a mouse in the dugout.

Dobson once again went to Puerto Rico for winter ball. While down there he railed against

Pat Dobson won 122 games in his 11-year big-league career (1967-77), including 20 for the Baltimore Orioles in 1971. In 1982 he began his second career as a longtime pitching coach, joining the Brewers.

Detroit management for firing pitching coach Johnny Sain and not making any moves during the season. He criticized the Tigers' aging infield and declared that General Manager Jim Campbell had "no guts to make the trades we need to make." On December 4, 1969, Campbell promptly made a trade, sending Pat Dobson and Dave Campbell to the San Diego Padres for Joe Niekro.

Despite going from a perennial contender to a second-year expansion team, Dobson was excited to finally get a chance to be a full-time starter. He beat the Atlanta Braves 8–3 on opening day in San Diego. He struck out six batters, including Hank Aaron. For the season, Dobson compiled a 14-15 record for the worst team in the National League. He was a workhorse for the Padres, starting 34 games and even picking up a save in six relief appearances. Despite pitching on a bad knee all year, Pat was not about to give up his spot in the rotation now that he was a starting pitcher. "I waited three years to become a regular starter. They can have the bullpen" Dobson said. He said being in the rotation allowed him to work on his control. "It was excellent discipline. And I learned that control pitchers get the corners from the umpires," he said. Dobson established single season records for wins and strikeouts for the young franchise.

Dobson's stay in San Diego was limited to one season. On December 1, 1970, he was traded to the Orioles along with Tom Dukes for Tom Phoebus, Al Severinsen, Fred Beene, and Enzo Hernandez. Earl Weaver, the Orioles manager, was elated. He had been a fan of Dobson "ever since the night I saw him strike out 21 guys in a game in Puerto Rico." His first start of the season was against his old team, the Tigers. He gave up three runs in the first inning, then shut Detroit out for the next seven. He was pulled for a pinch-hitter, and the Tigers went on to win in extra innings. Pat won his next start against the Yankees, only allowing one run in the complete-game victory. But he won one of his next nine starts. Before his June 17 start, his record stood at 3–4 with an ERA of 3.70. Starting with a victory over the Yankees that day, Pat would win 12 starts in a row. Eleven of the twelve victories were complete games. Then, starting with a loss to the Yankees, Pat slumped, winning only two of nine starts. He finished strong, however, winning his last three starts to reach the coveted twenty-win level. Dobson and teammates Mike Cuellar, Dave McNally, and Jim Palmer all won 20 or more games, and the 1971 Orioles were only the second team in major league history to boast four twenty-game winners.

Baltimore swept the Oakland A's in the American League playoffs, and went into the 1971 World

Series as the favorite over the Pittsburgh Pirates. Pat at first was the odd man out as Weaver decided to go with a three-man rotation for the postseason. Pat did not appear in the AL Championship Series but finally got a chance to start Game 4 of the World Series. The O's staked him to a 3-0 lead in the first, but Pittsburgh came back with two runs in the bottom of the inning. They tied it up in the third, and Pat was pulled in the sixth inning with the score 3-3. The Pirates went on to win, 4-3. Pat made another Series appearance in Game 6, coming on to start the 10th inning. He retired the first batter, but then gave up a single to Dave Cash, who stole second on a strike-three pitch to Richie Hebner. Dobson intentionally walked Roberto Clemente and then was replaced by lefty Dave McNally to face the left-handed batting Willie Stargell. McNally ended up with the win when the Orioles scored in the bottom of the tenth. In Game 7, Dobson came on to start the ninth inning with the Orioles down 2-1. He retired the first two batters, striking out Clemente. But he gave up back-to-back singles, and McNally was once again summoned to face Stargell, whom he retired for the final out. The Orioles went down meekly in the ninth, and the Pirates were world champions.

After the Series, the Orioles and Dobson were scheduled for an exhibition tour of Japan. On November 2, 1971, in Toyama, Japan, Pat hurled a no-hit, no-run game against the Tokyo Yomiuri Giants, winning 2-0.

The Oriole dynasty slipped in 1972, finishing five games behind the Tigers. Dobson's record fell to 16-18 despite his posting a lower ERA and WHIP than he had in his 20-win season. He made the All-Star team, although he did not appear in the game. Pat stirred up a little controversy in Detroit when he suggested that Billy Martin was misusing Tom Timmerman, saying he made a better relief pitcher than a starter. When Baltimore came into Detroit for a four-game set, they were trailing the Tigers by two games. Dobson was scheduled to pitch the opener for the O's. Martin suggested Dobson would tremble and flee under the Tiger Stadium long ball hex. Instead, Pat threw a complete-game four-hitter, winning 3-2.

Dobson loved it in Baltimore and was shocked when the Orioles traded him to Atlanta on November 30, 1972. Along with Dobson, Atlanta got Davey Johnson, Roric Harrison, and Johnny Oates while sending Earl Williams and Taylor Duncan to Baltimore. Dobson's debut for Atlanta was inauspicious as he was bombed by the Astros 10-3. He beat San Diego in his next start, then went 1-6 in his next nine starts. After beating the Cubs to raise his record to 3-7, he was traded to the Yankees on June 7, 1973. He had hated it in Atlanta. He complained, "I went from the best defensive team to the worst. I throw ground balls. I need defense. Their whole game is tailored to offense—the park, the wind, and the grass." He was happy to be in New York and compiled a 9-8 record for the Yankees. He enjoyed playing for Ralph Houk, and the Yankees were in contention up until late August.

Dobson was a little concerned when manager Ralph Houk was replaced by Bill Virdon. He felt Houk had been forced out by management. Pat won his first game in 1974, but lost eight of his next ten decisions. At that point, he started butting heads with Virdon over the pitching rotation. Virdon was experimenting with a five-man rotation, while Dobson insisted he needed to work every fourth day. The manager relented and went back to the four-man rotation. Dobson suddenly got hot and went on a 16-7 run the rest of the way. The Yankees were in first place on September 23, but wound up two games behind Baltimore as the Orioles won their last eight games while New York was winning five and losing three. Pat ended up 19-15 with a 3.07 ERA.

The Yankees believed that 1975 would be the year they returned to their former glory. Dobson started slowly, but he won six games in a row to raise his record to 8-5. He complained to the press after being pulled with two out in the seventh inning in a game against the Twins. At the time the Yankees were trailing 1-0, and there were two outs. Sparky Lyle came in and gave up a two-run single to Lyman

Bostock. Virdon held a clubhouse meeting the next day and said, "One guy is causing dissension on the club." When the manager reinstituted the five-man rotation, Dobson went into a tailspin, winning only three more games all year. Virdon was fired in August and replaced by Billy Martin. But Martin and Dobson didn't get along well, either. Pat said Billy "had a habit of second-guessing what you threw, too."

In November, Dobson found himself traded once more, this to Cleveland in exchange for Oscar Gamble. Dobson's outspokenness didn't always sit well with management. But he said, "I have never regretted one word I've said. 'Course, there have been repercussions, but if you're right you have to take the consequences."

His manager with the Indians was Frank Robinson, his old Orioles teammate. Dobson respected Robinson, calling him the finest player he'd ever teamed with. Pat was considered the "elder statesman" of a young Indians staff that also included a rookie named Dennis Eckersley. Dobson had a fine season with the Indians, posting a 16–12 record with a 3.48 ERA. Cleveland finished above .500 for the first time since 1968. But in 1977, his record plummeted to 3–12, and his ERA soared to 6.14. He didn't get his first victory until June, after losing his first five decisions. His last victory came early in July against the Kansas City Royals. Shortly after that he lost his spot in the rotation and was relegated to the bullpen. What would be his final major league appearance came on September 19, 1977 — fittingly, at Tiger Stadium. Dobson came on in relief in the seventh inning, getting the final two outs. He gave up a leadoff single in the eighth and was pulled from the game. The runner eventually scored, and Pat ended up taking the loss. He was released by the Indians on April 14, 1978, without making an appearance that year.

Pat Dobson won 122 games while losing 129 in the major leagues and saved an additional 19 games. His ERA for his career was a solid 3.54, and his WHIP was 1.28. In 17 seasons of professional ball, he played for 15 different teams.

Dobson developed a second career as a pitching coach. He summed up the logic behind the move: "Who knows more about pitching than me? Just take a look at the crap I'm getting away with out there [on the mound]. I rest my case." He was working for Triple A Nashville in 1982 when he was summoned to the parent club, the Milwaukee Brewers. Their pitching coach, Cal McLish, had become ill, and Pat was asked to fill in. This was the year of Harvey's Wallbangers, and the Brewers advanced to the World Series, losing to the St. Louis Cardinals in seven games. Pat's son Chris fondly remembers the days in Milwaukee. His dad would work his charts, chug coffee, chain smoke his menthol cigarettes, and complete the crossword puzzle in the New York Times. "I never saw a crossword puzzle my father couldn't finish," Chris said. After the Brewers fell to last place in 1984, Dobson and all the coaches were let go. He returned to coaching in the minor leagues before returning to the majors with San Diego from 1988 to 1990.

Dobson managed of the Fort Myers Sun Sox in the Senior League in 1989 and 1990. The Senior League was a new winter ball league set in Florida for players 35 and older. There were eight teams in two divisions. Pat's team finished second and was eliminated in the first round of the playoffs. The league folded halfway through its second season.

In 1991, Dobson became the Royals' pitching coach. He was considered a key man on the team, trying to restore the confidence of reliever Mark Davis. He had handled the star pitcher before at San Diego. Another project was Mark Gubicza, coming back from shoulder surgery. Pat was considered as a possible replacement for manager John Wathan, who was fired in May 1991. The job went instead to Hal McRae. Dobson's relationship with the new manager was rocky, and Pat resigned on September 9 when he could not get assurance that he would be asked to return the next year. Later that year, Pat attended the final-day ceremonies at Memorial Stadium in Baltimore and reunited with his fellow 20-game winners, Jim Palmer, Dave McNally, and Mike Cuellar.

Dobson joined the Colorado Rockies expansion team as an advance scout in December 1992, serving in that capacity until 1995. He left the Rockies to take the Baltimore pitching coach job in 1996, working with his close friend, manager Davey Johnson.

Despite the Orioles finishing a close second to the New York Yankees, Dobson was fired at the end of 1996 by owner Peter Angelos. Pat and the Orioles' young ace, Mike Mussina, did not see eye to eye and after a shouting match at the mound during a crucial September game, the writing was on the wall. Over the objections of General Manager Pat Gillick and manager Johnson, Ray Miller was hired as the new pitching coach.

Dobson next took a position as an advance scout with the San Francisco Giants in 1997, eventually becoming a special assistant to General Manager Brian Sabean. He was one of Sabean's top talent evaluators and scouted many of the players the Giants acquired, particularly pitchers. In 1998, Dobson was elected to the Greater Buffalo Sports Hall of Fame. His induction notice credited him with enlivening every clubhouse he entered. One writer even suggested that Pat may have been the funniest man who ever wore a baseball uniform.

Dobson played a key role in persuading Bruce Bochy to take the manager's position with the Giants in 2006, even jetting to San Francisco with Bochy when he went for an interview. Shortly afterward, Pat began to feel ill. After two weeks, he went to a hospital for tests and was diagnosed with leukemia. One night after checking in to the hospital, Pat Dobson died on November, 22, 2006, in San Diego. He was survived by his wife Kathe, and six children, Pat III, Nancy, Stacy, Chris, Shannon, and Stephanie.

SOURCES

Baggerly, Andrew. "Dobson played role in Bochy's decision." *Oakland Tribune*, December 6, 2006.

Cour, Paul. "Bulldog Dobson–Padre Workhouse and Battler." *The Sporting News*, September 19, 1970: 20.

Flaherty, Tom. "McLish Loses Out In Coaching Change." *The Sporting News*, November 29, 1982: 60.

Frau, Miguel. "Dobson Eclipses Pizarro's Strikeout Record, Fans 21." *The Sporting News*, December 23, 1967: 47.

Hatter, Lou. "Dobson Turns Detroit Into Bengal Snakepit." *The Sporting News*, July 22, 1972: 9.

Jackman, Phil. "Pat Dobson Acquired to Fill No. 4 Spot on Oriole Staff." *The Sporting News*, December 19, 1970: 38.

Jackman, Phil. "O's Thank Their Lucky Stars for New Ace Dobson." *The Sporting News*, August 14, 1971: 10.

Jackman, Phil. "O's Boast Four 20-Win Aces, Equal Feat of '20 Chisox Stars." *The Sporting News*, October 9, 1971: 11.

Kaegel, Dick. "Kansas City Royals." *The Sporting News*, September 23, 1991: 26.

Kubatko, Roch. "O's 'gamer' won 20 in '71." *Baltimore Sun*, November 24, 2006, p. D11.

McKean, Dale. "'All I Needed Was a Chance'–Beaver Ace Dobson Proving It." *The Sporting News*, July 29, 1966: 38.

Nightengale, Bob. "Orioles Functioning Like a Dysfunctional Family." *The Sporting News*, October 28, 1996: 15.

Nightengale, Dave. "1991: Hello to Odd Ball." *The Sporting News*, April 1, 1991: 12.

Pepe, Phil. "Sleight of Hand Provides Dobson Toehold on Wins." *The Sporting News*, September 14, 1974: 29.

Powers, Roger. "Sports of All Sorts." *Grit*, (Williamsport, Pa.), November 14, 1971: 43.

Reidenbaugh, Lowell. "Cardinals Flash Muscle, Speed in a 7-3 Triumph." *The Sporting News*, October 19, 1968: 9.

Spoelstra, Watson. "Winter Loop Whiff Feats Mark Dobson as '58 Bengalani to Watch." *The Sporting News*, January 6, 1968: 50.

Spoelstra, Watson. "Unheralded Dobson and Hiller Win Tiger Headlines." *The Sporting News*, June 29, 1968: 11.

Spoelstra, Watson. "Tiger Jokester Dobson Wipes Grin Off Batters' Faces." *The Sporting News*, June 21, 1969: 12.

Spoelstra, Watson. "Kilkenny Is Tough Pitcher In a Paradise for Swingers." *The Sporting News*, October 11, 1969: 17.

Sudyk, Bob. "The Travels and Travails of Pat Dobson." *Baseball Digest*, Vol. 36, No.1 1977: 74-78.

Vicioso, Fernando. "Dobson Helps Tigers Bare Sharp Teeth." *The Sporting News*, November 26, 1966: 43.

www.buffalosportshallfame.com

www.espn.com

www.sfgate.com

www.thebaseballcube.com

www.thebaseballpage.com

NOTE

This article originally appeared in the book *Sock It To 'Em Tigers – The Incredible Story of the 1968 Detroit Tigers*, published by Maple Street Press in 2008.

LARRY HANEY

By Austin Gisriel

A backup catcher who amassed only 984 plate appearances in 12 seasons, Wallace Larry Haney nevertheless was a member of some historic teams, including the 1974 Oakland Athletics. Upon retiring as an active player, the right-handed hitting Haney spent an additional 34 years in professional baseball as a coach and scout, and his dedication to the game is exceeded only by his love of family. In fact, when asked to recount his most cherished moment in the game, it is not the home run he hit in his first major-league contest or being a member of two world championship teams or playing with Hall of Famers. "The biggest thrill I had was getting to see my son Chris pitch at [the big league] level," said Haney in his mild Southern drawl.[1]

Haney, who was born on November 19, 1942 (he was christened Wallace Larry Haney), and his two older brothers, George and Wayne, grew up on a farm in Barboursville, Virginia, near Charlottesville, along with their sister, Jeanette. George, who pitched as high as Triple-A in the Yankees' system before hurting his elbow, was the superior athlete, according to Haney, who himself played four sports at Orange County High School. "Probably because I didn't want to work on the farm," he joked.

"Without the support my mom and dad gave us as young kids and the support they gave our baseball habits, I wouldn't have had the opportunity to do what I did over 46 years in the game," said Haney, who helped repay that support immediately upon embarking on his pro career when he bought his parents, George and Janice, a house with part of the $60,000 bonus money he received from the Baltimore Orioles upon graduation.

Haney, who considered himself a better football player than a baseball player, had accepted a full scholarship to play quarterback at Virginia Tech, but several baseball clubs came calling. "My parents didn't have a lot of money, of course, growing up on a farm, and a number of clubs called me the day after I got out of high school. I had made up my mind that if I didn't get a certain amount of money, that I was going to go to Virginia Tech and play football. Obviously, I got [the amount I was looking for] and maybe a little more. It was something I was able to help my parents out with and buy a house for them and do some things for them that they wouldn't have been able to do on their own."

The Orioles sent Haney, who as an amateur played primarily third base and shortstop and caught occasionally, to Bluefield in the Appalachian League, where he was immediately converted into a full-time catcher. "I guess they thought I couldn't play anywhere else! I had good hands and a plus arm, so maybe they thought that was my best opportunity to play at a higher level."

Two years later Haney was already playing regularly at Double-A Elmira for an incredibly talented team that included infielders Davey Johnson and Curt Blefary, as well as pitchers Tom Phoebus, Darold Knowles, and Frank Bertaina. The pitching staff also included a couple of interesting left-handers: Pat Gillick and Steve Dalkowski.

"I used to tell Pat later on when I'd run into him in Toronto or Philadelphia or wherever, that the best thing about his pitching was he'd walk a guy and pick him off first! He had a great move; plus the fact that Pat Gillick was one of the sharpest guys I think I ever met in baseball. He's very intelligent. He would get on the bus and read *The Sporting News* from cover to cover and remember everything in it."

As for Dalkowski, "Steve was Steve." The legendary fireballer hurt his arm late in spring training in 1963 while pitching against the Yankees in a game Haney recalled clearly. "He was going through the Yankees, who had Mantle and Maris and Elston Howard and Boyer and all those guys, and he was pitching great when all of a sudden he just threw one up on the screen; and the next pitch he threw up on the screen, and he walked off the mound holding his elbow."

Dalkowski's arm was never the same. According to Haney, he was "down to 94 [mph]. There's no telling how many pitches he threw back then. He would have to go to the bullpen and warm up for half an hour just to try to wear his arm down a little bit to where they thought he could come in and throw strikes."

In addition to Elmira's talent on the field, prowling the dugout was future Hall of Fame manager Earl Weaver.

"Earl was very fiery in the minor leagues; one of the most knowledgeable baseball managers as far as matchups. I think his game management was as good as anybody I've ever seen. He was able to maximize ability and get the most out of players. He did it a little differently maybe; he intimidated some players, but he knew the right buttons to push."

Five years into his pro career, Haney married Connie Deane in 1965. "I've known her family and I've known her ever since we were 10 or 11 years old, I guess. We went to the same church, the same high school, but didn't really start dating until I was a few years into pro ball. I don't know why she chose me, because she had a lot of opportunities!" The Haneys had three sons, Chris, Kevin, and Keith.

By 1966, Haney and Weaver were at Triple-A Rochester as the Orioles were beginning a reign that would see them win four pennants in the next six years. Haney's former roommate Andy Etchebarren established himself as Baltimore's primary catcher that year, but the Birds used several backups, including Charlie Lau, who missed the rest of the season after undergoing elbow surgery in May, Camilo Carreon, and Vic Roznovsky. When Etchebarren suffered a broken bone in his right hand, Haney was summoned to Baltimore and made his major-league debut on July 27. He actually took Wally Bunker's spot on the roster, as the Orioles were suffering from a slew of injuries to the pitching staff as well.[2]

Haney started that night and in his second at-bat, the right-handed hitter drove a John O'Donohue pitch into the left-field stands at Memorial Stadium for a two-run homer in what proved to be a 7-1 victory over the Cleveland Indians. Haney would hit only 11 more homers in his big-league career, but he remained the only Oriole to homer in his first game until 2013, when Jonathan Schoop did it.

Haney got into 20 games for the Orioles that year and made the World Series roster, but didn't play in the Series. Of course, many Orioles never played in Baltimore's four-game sweep of the Los Angeles Dodgers, as the Birds used only one extra position player (Russ Snyder and Paul Blair platooned in center field) for the entire series. In fact, Haney never had much of a chance to even catch anyone in the bullpen because Baltimore used only one reliever, Moe Drabowsky, in Game One and none in the next three games.

"To have the opportunity to go the World Series and play the Dodgers and see Koufax and Drysdale and Wills and all those guys. I mean, I was a big fan of a lot of those guys, and I was a fan during the Series because that's all I did was sit there and cheer for our club!"

Haney made the Orioles coming out of spring training in 1967, and on April 30 found himself involved in one of the strangest no-hitters in major-league history. Baltimore lefty Steve Barber had held the Detroit Tigers hitless through eight innings in the first game of a doubleheader, but had walked seven and hit two batters. He entered the ninth with a 1-0 lead thanks to a Luis Aparicio sacrifice fly in the bottom of the eighth, but promptly walked Norm Cash and Ray Oyler. After a sacrifice bunt and a foul out to Haney, who had entered the game in the ninth, the southpaw got ahead of Mickey Stanley 0 and 2. Barber then "bounced the ball four feet in front of the plate and over catcher Larry Haney's head, enabling the tying run to score."[3]

When Barber walked Stanley to reload the bases, manager Hank Bauer brought in Stu Miller, who induced a groundball to shortstop Aparicio. He flipped to Mark Belanger at second. In keeping with the absurdity of the game, Belanger, who would win eight Gold Gloves at shortstop, dropped the ball.

The Orioles lost the combined no-hitter, 2-1, and then lost the second game as well, 6-4. It was a portent of a disastrous season following Baltimore's first world championship, although Haney's .268 average in 164 at-bats was the highest of his career.

Haney got into only 38 games in 1968 and the Orioles were shopping him around.[4] A trade became a moot point when Haney was selected as the 32nd pick in the expansion draft by the Seattle Pilots.

"I was happy to go somewhere to get an opportunity to play," said Haney. "Not that I wanted to leave Baltimore, but I knew it wasn't going to happen there."

The opportunity to play never materialized in Seattle either. Haney found himself backing up once again, this time for Jerry McNertney. Just 2½ months into the season, the Pilots traded

Baseball lifer Larry Haney amassed only 984 plate appearances as a backup catcher in parts of 12 big-league seasons (1966-1970; 1972-1978), but worked for 34 more years in professional baseball as coach and scout.

Haney to Oakland on June 14 for second baseman John Donaldson. Haney received regular playing time under former Oriole manager Hank Bauer, who was now in Oakland, but an injury derailed this opportunity.

"Got a foul tip that broke my right toe and really never had a chance to catch a whole lot after that. We were winning and Bauer says, 'Even with a broken toe, you're going to play!' and I tried, but it didn't work. I ended up hurting my arm a little bit trying to play with a broken toe."

Haney did find himself taking part in another Baltimore no-hitter that year, however, when on August 13 he was the final out in Jim Palmer's no-hitter.

"Palmer reminds me of that all the time," laughed Haney. "He said he walked the bases loaded to get to me because he knew I'd hit a groundball to the shortstop." [Haney did, resulting in a fielder's choice.]

Apparently, the Baseball Gods were listening to the prayers of a certain Oriole fan in Barboursville.

"It's tough to get a hit when your mother roots against you," recounted Haney. "My mom told me later on: 'I'll have to be honest with you. I was hoping you wouldn't get a hit because Jimmy needed a no-hitter worse than you needed a base hit.' I said, 'I don't think you've been reading the papers, Mom!'"

Appearing in only two games for Oakland in 1970, Haney was loaned out to Montreal's Triple-A affiliate which began the year in Buffalo, but ended in Winnipeg. "Gene Tenace was catching at Des Moines, and they didn't want both of us to be on the same club to split catching time," Haney explained.

Haney spent the entire 1971 season at Iowa (Des Moines), Oakland's Triple-A affiliate, and the vast majority of 1972 at Honolulu, San Diego's Triple-A affiliate, after the A's sold his contract to the Padres on May 30. Oakland bought him back in September of that year, but he did not appear on the postseason roster. It was back to Triple-A in 1973, this time in Tucson, Oakland's latest Triple-A affiliate, and once again Oakland sold the soon-to-be 31-year-old backstop, to St. Louis on September 1.

"They wanted someone that could back up Ted Simmons in case they needed a body because [Tim] McCarver couldn't throw at that time. I was there the last month of the season, and I got in two ballgames. Simmons caught probably 157 games that year in that heat in St. Louis; Simmons was an animal, really. [Simmons appeared in 161 games for the Cardinals in 1973, starting 151 games at catcher.]

"I went to spring training with the Cardinals the next year, and they basically told Jeff Torborg and myself that 'One of you is going to be the backup catcher; whichever one has the best spring.' At the end of spring training, they let Jeff Torborg go, and a couple of days later they sold me back to Oakland, which was a blessing in disguise because that was the '74 season when we beat the Dodgers in the World Series in Oakland." [Tim McCarver was the primary backup for St. Louis in 1974, as Simmons caught in "only" 141 games.]

Haney remained on Oakland's roster for the entire season in 1974, appearing in 76 games while sharing the catching duties with Ray Fosse and Gene Tenace. During the World Series, he appeared in two games defensively, but never got an at-bat.

"A great pitching staff," recalled Haney of the A's that year. "One of the best and most competitive pitchers I caught at [the major-league] level was Catfish Hunter. He had great command of the strike zone with all pitches. Also on that staff was another Hall of Famer, Rollie Fingers. Ken Holtzman and Blue Moon Odom were two other starters, and with Bando, Campaneris, Green, Tenace, Fosse, Rudi, North, and Jackson, this club from '72 to '75 was one of the best in the game.

"They had speed, defense, pitching, and a Hall of Fame manager in Dick Williams, followed by Alvin Dark in '74-75 who, along with Earl Weaver, I consider one of the better managers I played for."[5]

Haney spent two more seasons in Oakland, catching in 47 games while garnering only 27 plate appearances in 1975, as Oakland won its fifth consecutive AL West crown, and playing in 88 games in 1976. On December 6 of that year, his contract was sold to Milwaukee. He appeared in 63 games for the Brewers in 1977. Released by Milwaukee on March 30, 1978, he remained with the team as the bullpen coach, but was activated when rosters expanded on September 1, appearing in another four games before retiring as an active player for good. As a Brewers coach, Haney again went to the World Series, this time in 1982, when future Hall of Famers Robin Yount and Paul Molitor, along with Haney's former St. Louis teammate Ted Simmons, led Milwaukee against the Cardinals, ultimately losing in seven games.

Haney remained with the Brewers as the bullpen coach until 1990, when he was named Milwaukee's pitching coach. The next year, 1991, Chris Haney made his major-league debut for the Montreal Expos on June 21. Like any parent, Larry Haney found it nerve-wracking when it came to watching his child play.

"Oh yeah, without a doubt. I had control over what I did; I had no control over what he did. All you can do is sit there and hope for the best!

"His first start was in Cincinnati, who had won the World Series the year before. I couldn't go because I was the pitching coach in Milwaukee. It was really tough on me, sitting there watching my pitcher and watching the scoreboard trying to figure out what was going on. [Chris started the game, gave up four runs in four innings, and took the loss.] I did get to see him pitch a number of times in pro ball when I was doing pro scouting."

Sal Bando became Milwaukee's general manager after the 1991 season, hiring Phil Garner to manage the club. Naturally, Garner brought with him an entirely new coaching staff, and Haney was relieved of his coaching duties. Bando, however, had an assignment for his former Oakland teammate, and named Haney a major-league scout. With no big-league players to evaluate during the 1994 strike season, Haney was asked to look at amateur talent around the country. He continued to scout both major leaguers and amateurs until his retirement in 2006.

Haney said he felt very fortunate for the support that his wife, Connie, gave him throughout his career.

"Without Connie and her ability to handle the needs of the family and moving around the country, none of my baseball ventures would have been possible," he said. "She would film [our sons'] games and keep me updated on what was going on with the boys. She is one strong lady and someone I will be forever thankful for."[6]

The Haneys celebrated their 48th wedding anniversary in 2013.

"I didn't get a chance to see [any of our three boys] play in Little League, high school, or college; they all played at [each of] those levels. Chris had a little boy, and I decided I wanted to watch him play. I decided it was time to pack it in and watch Jake play all of his sports," said Haney, explaining the reason for his retirement.

Jake, Larry and Connie's only grandchild, attended Orange County High School, as did his father and grandfather. Although he had retired from professional baseball, Larry remained in the game, helping Chris coach Little League, and also starting an American Legion team, which the father-son duo coached for three years.

Larry and Chris continued to coach through their business, Old School Academy, which offered private lessons and clinics. As of 2013 the academy sponsored four travel teams. Chris took on most of the teaching duties. Larry said in 2013 "I still go up to the building in the afternoons if Chris is teaching some kids up there. I just sit there and second-guess him now!"

Larry was honored by his alma mater when the Orange County Hornets inducted him into its Hall of Fame on May 10, 2013. His Milwaukee jersey was hung next to Chris's Kansas City jersey in the Hornets' Sports Center.

Living about a mile from where he grew up, Haney said he still wondered if he could have successfully quarterbacked Virginia Tech. "I miss the fact that I didn't get a chance to play football in college, to find out whether I could have played at that level. Just having that competitive nature, you always want to find out if you could have done it.

"[However] being in baseball for 40-some years, meeting all the people that I've met … I was very fortunate; I wasn't a good player, but [had] the opportunity to play on clubs that had great players. Not good players, but great players. You look at Baltimore, you look at Oakland; I was with St. Louis for a month, the Hall of Famers, Bob Gibson, Lou Brock, guys like that. And I even look at Ted Simmons, who should have a shot at the Hall of Fame, when you look at his numbers. To have an opportunity to play with guys like that … and to play against the great players … guys you admired from afar, and you get a chance to see them up close and personal. I had a chance to play against Mickey Mantle. It was his last two years in New York, and he was just a shell of himself, but … guys that I idolized as a little kid and to see those guys …"

Haney recalled a play by Willie Mays, not from his own playing days, however, but from his childhood, in a game that he and his dad attended.

"Willie Mays was in the Army, I think during the Korean War. He was playing for one of the forts, either Fort Lee or Fort Eustis, but they played a local team in a tournament. … There was a fence that ran kind of parallel along the highway on an angle. Willie was playing center field. Some guy hit a ball up over the fence. Willie went up over the fence with his back to the infield, caught the ball, turned, and threw a seed to second base. I see highlights of the play that he made in the Polo Grounds and all these others, but that to me … when I was 10 years old, or whatever I was. My dad had taken me to the game, but it stuck out all these years as one of the greatest catches I've ever seen a guy make in the outfield."

From seeing Willie Mays with his dad to coaching his grandson, Larry Haney could lay claim to one of baseball's best numbers: part of four successive generations who have passed the love of the game and the encouragement to play from father to son.

SOURCES

Beard, Gordon, *Birds on the Wing: The Story of the Baltimore Orioles* (New York: Doubleday & Co., 1967).

Eisenberg, John, *From 33rd Street to Camden Yards: An Oral History of the Baltimore Orioles* (Chicago: Contemporary Books, 2001).

Weaver, Earl, *Winning*. Edited by John Sammis (New York: William Morrow & Co, Inc., 1972).

baltimoresun.com

Baseball-Reference.com

dailyprogress.com (Orange County, Virginia)

Personal correspondence:

Telephone interview with Larry Haney, October 16, 2013

E-mail from Larry Haney, October 25, 2013

NOTES

1   All quotations are from October 16, 2013 telephone interview with Larry Haney, unless otherwise noted.

2   Gordon Beard, *Birds on the Wing: The Story of the Baltimore Orioles* (Doubleday & Co., New York, 1967), 73.

3   Doug Brown, "No-hitter ruined by walks, Barber now drives a bus," *The Sun* online, August 17, 1995.

4   Earl Weaver, edited by John Sammis. *Winning* (William Morrow & Co, Inc., New York, 1972), 70.

5   Email, October 25, 2013.

6   Email, October 25, 2013.

RON HANSEN

By Jimmy Keenan

On July 30, 1968, Washington Senators shortstop Ron Hansen pulled off one of baseball's rarest and most difficult feats when he turned an unassisted triple play against the Cleveland Indians. This diamond rarity took place at Municipal Stadium in Cleveland during the bottom of the first inning after leadoff hitter Dave Nelson singled and Russ Snyder followed that up with a walk. The next batter, catcher Joe Azcue, worked the count to three balls and two strikes off Senators pitcher Bruce Howard. With both runners moving on the pitch, Howard delivered the ball to Azcue, who laced a line drive between Hansen and second base. Ron took a step to his left and snagged the ball out of the air. With his momentum carrying him toward second, he stepped on the bag to double up Nelson. Hansen then ran towards Snyder, who was caught in no man's land between first and second base, tagging him for the third out. It was the first unassisted triple play in the major leagues in 41 years. Hansen later donated his glove and the ball from that historic play to the Hall of Fame.

When speaking to a reporter after the game, the modest Hansen remarked, "It was one of the best plays I've ever made in terms of all of the putouts, but it wasn't that difficult, in fact it was made to order. I just happened to be in the right place at the right time."

Ronald Lavern Hansen was born on April 5, 1938, in Oxford, Nebraska. His father Audrey and his mother, the former Edna Wolfe moved from Nebraska to Albany, California, when Ron was two years old.[1] When the Hansens arrived in Albany, Audrey took a job as a moulder at a local foundry.

Hansen attended Albany High, where he played football, baseball and basketball. In addition to his gridiron exploits, he was the school's star third baseman and the Most Valuable Player on the basketball squad during his senior year. Ron graduated from high school in 1955, and after turning down a scholarship to the University of California, signed a professional baseball contract with the Baltimore Orioles on April 7, 1956.

Don McShane, the Orioles chief scout on the West Coast, discovered and recommended Hanson, but it was actually Oakland Oaks owner C.L. "Brick" Laws who took care of the signing. At that time, the Orioles had a working agreement with Oakland, so Laws, who was adept at handling player contracts, orchestrated the deal, complete with a $4000 signing bonus.

Thirteen major league teams were interested in signing the young infielder, but Ron chose the Orioles. In a 1960 interview with *Baseball Digest*, Hansen gave his reasons for picking the

Birds, "I decided to sign with Baltimore because I had the best chance of advancing with them and I had read a lot about Mr. Richards [Orioles manager Paul Richards] although I had never actually met him."

A short time later, Laws relocated his Oakland franchise to Vancouver, British Columbia, and Hansen went with him. Ron played a few games for the Vancouver Mounties under the watchful eye of manager Lefty O'Doul before being sent down to the Class C Stockton Ports at the beginning of the season.

Hansen started out playing third base for the Ports but was moved over to shortstop after an injury to starter Gary Robin. Ron ended up playing thirty games at short that year, hitting .289 with 20 doubles.

That winter, Hansen played for the Pueblo team in the Mexican League. Under the tutelage of manager Jimmy Adair, who hit Ron hundreds of grounders, the young shortstop began to show marked improvement on balls that were hit to his right side in the hole.

In 1957, Ron was invited to the Orioles spring training camp in Scottsdale, Arizona. After the first few days of practice, baseball insiders were beginning to compare him to St. Louis Cardinal shortstop Marty Marion. The scouting report on Hansen read: "He has sure hands; moves beautifully to either side; can throw from the hole; he has a strong cross body throw; a perfect infielder's arm.

When asked about Hansen, Baltimore manager Paul Richards replied, "There is no doubt in my mind that this kid has big league ability."

Hansen, who stood 6'3" and weighed nearly 200 pounds, was one of the first big men to play the shortstop position. In addition to being a great defensive player, he also had power at the plate, which made him an even more valuable prospect. Ron was well on his way to making the Baltimore team in 1957 when he hurt his back during an exhibition game against the Chicago Cubs. Ron tried to downplay the injury, but over the next few weeks he started experiencing severe back pain

The 1960 AL Rookie of the Year for the Baltimore Orioles, Ron Hansen fashioned a 15-year big-league career (1958-1972) as a shortstop and utility infielder. From 1980 to 1983 he served as first-base coach for the Brewers.

and weakness in his left leg. Despite the best efforts of Oriole trainer Eddie Weidner, Hansen's health issues continued to escalate.

Baltimore management, not wanting to take any chances with their shortstop of the future, sent him to team physician Dr. Erwin Mayer. From there Hanson was sent to the Mayo Clinic for a more thorough examination. Unfortunately for Ron, the prognosis was not good as he was diagnosed with a ruptured disc in his back along the sciatic nerve that controls the upper part of the legs.

In an interview in *Boys Life* magazine, Hanson spoke about waiting so long to seek medical help. "I know I should have gone to the doctor right off but here I was an eighteen year old and in the big leagues. I wasn't about to give that up for a Charlie Horse."

On May 17, 1957, the Oriole infielder underwent spinal surgery at Union Memorial Hospital in Baltimore. The operation was a success, and from there he began the long rehabilitation process. Through a vigorous regimen of exercises, he slowly began to regain his strength and dexterity.

After missing all of the 1957 season, Ron started out the following year with Vancouver. On April 15, the Orioles placed him on their major league roster. To make room for Hansen, the Orioles optioned catcher Frank Zupo to their farm club in Nashville.

Unfortunately, Ron was not fully recovered from the surgery. When asked about his back by a local sports writer, Hansen replied, "When it's cold, windy and damp it does stiffen up a little. It doesn't keep me from making the plays but it does give me a little trouble."

After going hitless in 12 games with the Orioles, he was sent down to Knoxville to regain his stroke at the plate. A short time later, Ron experienced another setback when a broken hand sidelined him for part of the season.

Due to his injuries, Hansen did not hit much at Knoxville and was sent to Nicaragua to play winter ball for former major leaguer Earl Torgeson's Boer team. Ron belted 17 home runs for Torgeson's ballclub and was hitting around .300 when he tweaked his back during the league playoffs and had to be sent back to the States. Fortunately, the injury was diagnosed as a muscle spasm, and he was given a clean bill of health for the upcoming season.

In 1959, the Orioles had veterans Chico Carrasquel and Willy Miranda playing shortstop, so Ron was sent to Vancouver, where he would play every day. There, he teamed up with another highly touted Oriole prospect, second baseman Marv Breeding, the two making a formidable keystone combination.

Hansen went on lead the Pacific Coast League with 321 putouts, 496 assists, and 96 double plays. He had a solid year with the bat too, clubbing 18 home runs to go along with 61 RBI and a .256 batting average. Ron was called up to the Birds at the end of the year, appearing in two games.

In 1960, everything came together for Hansen and the Orioles. Ron, playing his usual outstanding defense, coupled with his ability to hit the long ball, earned the starting job at shortstop for Baltimore that spring.

On April 19, Ron garnered his first major league hit off the Washington Senators Pedro Ramos. Hansen and second baseman Marv Breeding also turned three double plays that day, helping the Orioles edge out the Senators 3-2.

By early May, the Birds' rookie shortstop was on a torrid hot streak. At one point he went 7-for-17, raising his average to .363, which was second best in the loop, just five points behind league leader Roger Maris.

On July 2, Hansen was named the starting shortstop for the American League All-Star team. The squads were selected by the players, coaches and managers in their respective leagues. Hansen, who was hitting .255 with 51 RBI, received 165 out of 208 possible votes, 124 more than Hall of Fame shortstop Luis Aparicio, who had been the starter the previous two seasons.

There were two All-Star games played that year, one in Kansas City and the other in New York. The American League lost both contests, but Hansen acquitted himself well, going 1-for-2 in the first game and 2-for-4 in the second while accepting a total of six chances in the field.

Yankee manager Casey Stengel, after watching Hansen play, commented to the press, "That kid looks like he was born at shortstop."

The Baltimore Orioles played first-rate ball in 1960, winning 89 games and finishing in second place, eight games behind the New York Yankees. It was the first time the Birds had a winning record since the team came over from St. Louis in 1954.

The Orioles pitching staff, mostly made up of

players under the age of 23, led the loop in complete games and tied for the league lead in earned run average. The Orioles' youthful, yet extremely talented infield, made up of Brooks Robinson at third, Hansen at shortstop, Marv Breeding at second, and Jim Gentile at first, turned an amazing 172 double plays.

In addition, veterans Gus Triandos, Gene Woodling, and Jackie Brandt performed well, keeping the Birds near the top of the standings for most of the season. The Orioles were in the thick of the pennant race until a four-game sweep by Yankees in mid-September effectively knocked them out of contention.

Defensively, the twenty-two-year-old Hansen had an outstanding year, leading the junior circuit in putouts by a shortstop with 325. At the plate, Ron hit .255 with 22 home runs while driving in 86 runs. His outstanding all-round play earned him the American League's Rookie of the Year Award, as he received 22 out of 24 possible votes from the Baseball Writers of America. The other two votes went to his Oriole teammates, pitcher Chuck Estrada and first baseman Jim Gentile.

Cleveland Indians colorful and outspoken general manager Frank Lane told members of the press that he felt that the Orioles' success in 1960 was mainly due to Hansen's contributions. "In my book, he's not just the rookie of the year; he's the player of the year. He's the main reason that the Orioles were challenging for the lead in the last two months."

Ron was called into the Army Reserves in October of 1960 so he learned of the award while stationed at Fort Knox, Kentucky. When asked how he felt about being named Rookie of the Year, Hansen replied to a reporter, "I can't believe it. It's just unbelievable. This is something every ballplayer dreams of but never believes will happen." *The Sporting News* also gave the nod to Hansen for its American League Rookie of the Year.

After serving for six months in the Army Reserve, Hansen reported to the Orioles, but he was only able to get in 10 days of spring training before the season started.

On April 30, 1961, Jim Gentile, Gus Triandos, and Hansen blasted consecutive home runs off the Detroit Tigers' Paul Foytack, helping lead the Orioles to a 4-2 victory. The three home runs in a row tied a major league record at that time.

Ron put together a decent year in 1961 although his home runs, doubles and triples fell off a bit from the previous season. At shortstop, he was still a strong defensive presence in the middle of the Baltimore infield.

Uncle Sam came calling again in October of 1961, and once more Ron was summoned for Army Reserve duty. Stationed at nearby Fort Meade, Maryland, he was able to fulfill his military obligations and still commute to Memorial Stadium to get his work in with the team before the start of the 1962 campaign. In April, the Army granted Hansen a month's leave, and in May he received another 30-day extension. The Pentagon would later allow men with seasonal occupations to report to their jobs 90 days in advance of their scheduled discharge. This ruling allowed Ron to re-join the Orioles for good later in the season.

Unfortunately, the injury bug bit Hansen once again in late August when he sustained a broken hand after being hit by White Sox pitcher John Buzhardt. Ron had his usual outstanding year with the glove in 1962, but offensively his batting average dropped 75 points and his power numbers slipped as well.

In January of 1963, the Orioles traded Hansen, outfielder Dave Nicholson and third baseman Pete Ward along with pitcher Hoyt Wilhelm to the Chicago White Sox for shortstop Luis Aparicio and outfielder Al Smith.

Chicago was managed by Al Lopez, who took an immediate liking to the 25-year-old shortstop, eventually naming him co-captain of the team. Ron adapted well to his surroundings in Chicago, teaming up with Hall of Fame second baseman Nellie Fox. When asked by a reporter about his new double play partner, Fox replied, "Aparicio was great, no question, but I get along real well with Ron. Hansen covers as much ground as Luis, although he does it with the longer strides of a Marty Marion rather than with Aparicio's speed."

On June 21, 1963, Ron connected for a two-run home run off Cleveland Indians pitcher Early Wynn with two outs in the top of the ninth inning. The White Sox and the Indians were knotted in a scoreless tie at the time, the game-winning blast spoiling the future Hall of Famer's bid for his 300th win.

The White Sox finished second in the American League in 1963, winning 94 games, and Ron led all American League infielders in assists. He would accomplish this feat two other times during his career. At the plate, he knocked in 67 runs.

The hard-charging Sox finished the 1964 season one game behind the first place New York Yankees. Chicago's tall rangy shortstop hit for a .261 batting average to go along with 20 home runs and 68 RBIs. He also posted career highs in doubles (25) and hits (150). Ron also led the loop in putouts for the second time.

The following season, Hansen set the major league mark for the most chances by a shortstop in a doubleheader on August 29, 1965. Chicago swept Boston in the twinbill, and Ron recorded 19 chances in the first game, which went 14 innings, and 10 more in the nightcap. He also hit a double in the 14th inning of the first tilt that put the eventual winning run on third base. Hansen's 28 chances eclipsed the old mark of 26 set by Pittsburgh Pirates shortstop Arky Vaughn in 1940.

Hansen played all 162 games for the White Sox in 1965 while continuing to establish himself as one of the most consistent infielders in the game. That season, he led all American League shortstops in assists for the second year in a row.

In early May of 1966, Ron re-injured his back during pre-game batting practice. The injury occurred when Hansen stepped back and came down on a baseball that someone had thrown into the infield. He tried to play through the pain but was eventually removed from the White Sox lineup on May 14.

A short time later, he underwent a myelogram[2] at Mercy Hospital in Chicago that showed a defect between the fifth lumbar vertebrae and sacrum. The injury required a second back operation, and he missed the rest of the season. After losing Hansen's services, the White Sox used infielders Al Weis, Lee Elia, and newly acquired Wayne Causey to help fill the gap at shortstop.

Hansen, who was fully recovered from the surgery, came back to play in 157 games for the White Sox in 1967. He also led all American League shortstops in assists for the third time in his career. On September 10, he was involved in another baseball milestone when he handled the final out of teammate Joel Horlen's no-hitter.

On February 13, 1968, the White Sox traded Hansen along with pitchers Dennis Higgins and Steve Jones to the Washington Senators for second baseman Tim Cullen plus pitchers Bob Priddy and Buster Narum.

On July 30, 1968, Hansen turned an unassisted triple play in the first inning of a 10–1 loss to the Cleveland Indians.

Two days later, Washington traded Hansen back to the White Sox for Tim Cullen. It was the first time in baseball history where the same two players were traded for each other twice in the same season.

When Hansen returned to Chicago, the White Sox had Luis Aparicio (who had re-joined the team in a trade the previous November) at shortstop so Ron played third base for the remainder of the 1968 season.

The following year, the versatile infielder took on the role of utility man for the Sox, playing every infield position, and hitting .259 with 2 home runs and 22 RBI.

Ron went through prolonged contract negotiations with Chicago management in the off-season. Figuring he would practice with the team until an agreement could be reached, he left his home in Maryland and drove to the White Sox spring training facility in Sarasota, Florida. While he was en route, the Chicago front office sold his contract to the New York Yankees for $5000.

New York used Ron as a utility infielder in 1970, and despite a trip to the disabled list in late August, he had a good year, compiling a solid .297 batting average. The Yankees won 93 games and finished in second place behind the Baltimore Orioles. Hansen's hot bat allowed manager Ralph Houk the luxury of going with an all right-handed hitting lineup against some of the tougher left-handed pitchers in the league.

Ron continued in the same infield back-up role with the Yankees in 1971, but his batting average dropped off from the previous season.

In February of 1972, the Yankees released Hansen, and two months later he was picked up by the Kansas City Royals. His stay with the Royals was brief, as he was let go after appearing in only 16 games.

Hansen finished his 15-year major league career with 1007 hits, 106 home runs and 501 RBIs. Defensively, he had a stellar .968 lifetime fielding percentage to go along with a 4.82 range factor at shortstop [95th all-time].

Ron would go on to serve as the first base coach for the Milwaukee Brewers from 1980 through 1983. In 1984, he managed the Paintsville team (Brewers minor league affiliate) in the Appalachian League. The following year, the Montreal Expos hired him as their first base coach and infield instructor. He also saw duty as the Expos' hitting coach under manager Felipe Alou. Hansen remained with the Expos through the 1989 season.

A keen judge of baseball talent, Hansen signed on as an advance scout with the New York Yankees in 1991 and later worked in that same capacity with the Philadelphia Phillies.

Always fond of his days spent with Washington, Hansen appeared in the 1995 Television program *DC Baseball: You Gotta Have Heart* that chronicled baseball in the nation's capital.

The former Senator shortstop and a number of other Washington players, including Frank Howard, Roy Sievers, and Mickey Vernon were in attendance for the final baseball game at RFK Stadium on September 23, 2007.

On May 12, 2008, Cleveland Indians second baseman Asdrubal Cabrera made an unassisted triple play against the Toronto Blue Jays. Coincidentally, Hansen was in the stands at Progressive Field in Cleveland that night working as an advance scout for the Philadelphia Phillies. When asked about witnessing the triple play, Hansen told a reporter, "First one I've ever seen from the stands. This kid is a real good fielder and has a great future. On a play like that it's just reaction, and he reacted right."

Hansen retired from his scouting duties in 2010.

Ron and his wife Dale were married in 1960 and currently reside in the rural community of Baldwin, Maryland. They have two daughters and three grandchildren.

SOURCES

In addition to Baseball-Reference.com and SABR.org, the author consulted:

Ellis, Jim. "Big Hunk of Man at Short," *Baseball Digest*, September 1960.

The Spokesman-Review

Spokane Daily Chronicle

The 1959 Baltimore Orioles, presented by Phillies Cigars and prepared by Sports Illustrated.

Sporting News

Boys Life Magazine, December 1962.

The Times – News

Reading Eagle

Daytona Beach Morning – Journal

Lawrence Journal-World

Lodi News Sentinel

St. Joseph Gazette

Schenectady Gazette

The Whig Standard

WSI News – White Sox Interview by Mark Liptak

MASN interview by Pete Kerzel, September 11, 2011.

Baseball Todd's Dugout article and interview of Ron Hansen by Todd Newville

Thorn, John, Phil Birnbaum, Bill Deane, et al. eds. *Total Baseball: The Ultimate Baseball Encyclopedia*. 8th ed. Toronto: Sport Media Publishing, Inc., 2004.

A special thanks to SABR member Cappy Gagnon for contacting the BioProject Committee to suggest that someone write a biography of Mr. Hansen.

NOTES

1. An article in the September 1960 *Baseball Digest* gives the names of Ron Hansen's parents as Audrey and Edna.
2. A myelogram is a test that uses x-rays and a special dye to make images of the back and the fluid-filled spaces between the bones of the spine.

CAL MCLISH

By Joe Wancho

Indians fans in Cleveland awoke the morning of May 23, 1957, to the musings of columnist James E. Doyle of the *Cleveland Plain Dealer*. Doyle often wrote a small poem at the beginning of his column, and this spring day was no exception.

> *Soxcess with Cal*
> *"That stuff served up by Cal McLish,"*
> *The Red Sox say "was quite a dish."*
> *From homer hunger were the Sox –*
> *And then they gave poor Cal his knocks.*

McLish indeed received his knocks, as Boston went deep against the Cleveland right-hander four times in the sixth inning at Fenway Park. With Cleveland trailing 3-0 and McLish pitching in relief, Gene Mauch homered, Ted Williams went deep to right field, Jackie Jensen walked, Dick Gernert smacked one to the screen atop the Green Monster, and Frank Malzone capped the barrage with a solo shot to left field. 8-0 Red Sox.

"I wasn't even supposed to be pitching that day," McLish recalled years later. "I had been pitching a lot. The writers asked our manager, Kerby Farrell, how come McLish wasn't starting in Fenway Park. Farrell said, 'I can't start McLish because I've been using him too much.'"

Farrell started Bud Daley, a left-hander. McLish relieved Daley in the fifth inning, after the starter surrendered three runs. "I threw a changeup, a fastball, a curve and a slider and they all went out."[1]

In a career that spanned 20 years of professional baseball, McLish had his share of setbacks, ups and downs, and just plain bad luck. But through perseverance and resiliency, McLish was able to carve out quite a career for himself, both as a pitcher (with a half-season on the 1964 Phillies) and as a top-notch pitching coach.

Calvin Coolidge Julius Caesar Tuskahoma McLish was born on December 1, 1925, in Anadarko, Oklahoma, a small agricultural city. He was the seventh of eight children born to John and Lulu McLish. Of his unique name, McLish said, "Until I came along, my dad never got to name any of the kids. So I suppose he was into the firewater and he named me."[2] John McLish, who worked as a farmer, was part Choctaw and Lulu was part Cherokee. Cal's name has always been a bit of a mystery. Even though his father was a staunch Democrat and Calvin Coolidge was a Republican from Vermont, Cal took pride in being named after the 30th president. The reason behind the Julius Caesar portion of his name is unknown, at least to Cal. Tuskahoma, a Choctaw word meaning "red warrior," is also the name of a tiny community in the southeast part of Oklahoma.

Cal McLish won 92 games in his 15 years in the majors, including 19 as an All-Star with the Cleveland Indians in 1959. He had a long career as a pitching coach, including with the Brewers (1976-1982).

While at Central High School in Oklahoma City, McLish mostly played shortstop. In 1944 he was signed by Brooklyn Dodgers scout Tom Greenwade, who saw that the youngster had speed on his throws. Cal had made a pact with two of his high-school teammates: Any scout who wanted to sign one of them had to sign all three. So Greenwade signed McLish's teammate Bobby Jarvis, but conveniently forgot to sign Bobby Morgan. McLish and Jarvis didn't realize this until they got to the Dodgers' 1944 spring-training camp in Bear Mountain, New York. Learning that they'd been duped, they refused to play until all three returned to Oklahoma so they could see Greenwade actually sign Morgan.[3] McLish reported to the varsity as an 18-year-old, fresh out of high school with virtually no pitching experience. He received a bonus of $1,500 and was paid $150 a month.

Without any minor-league experience, the teenage McLish was on the Dodgers' roster to start the season. With the shortage of players because of World War II, the 1944 version of "Dem Bums" was a mix of players from opposite ends of their baseball careers. There were young, unproven players like McLish and Gene Mauch, and players whose better years were in the rear-view mirror, like Paul Waner and Johnny Cooney.

McLish won his first major-league game on May 31, beating the Pittsburgh Pirates 8-4. He hit a double and drove in a run to aid his own cause. As the season wore on, the possibility grew that McLish might be drafted into the military at any time. While the Dodgers were in St. Louis, he got the call and reported for active duty on August 21. At that point he had a 3-10 record with a 7.82 earned-run average. He served in the 3rd Infantry Division in Europe, earning two battle stars, before the Germans surrendered in May 1945. During that summer McLish pitched for the division baseball team in Czechoslovakia. He was discharged in August 1946. He had missed the equivalent of two seasons of major-league baseball.

McLish returned to baseball, pitching in one game for the Dodgers against the Cardinals in St. Louis on August 25, and facing just two batters. He didn't retire either, and allowed two earned runs. That was his only appearance in 1946, and after the season, he was part of a five-for-one deal when he was sent with four other players to Pittsburgh for outfielder Al Gionfriddo and $100,000.

When a player returned from the service in those days, he had to be kept on a major-league roster for one year. McLish pitched one inning for the Pirates on May 25, 1947, against the Cardinals and allowed two earned runs. After the year was up, McLish was optioned to the Kansas City Blues of the American Association, a Yankees Triple-A team, as part of a deal that sent pitcher Mel Queen to the Pirates from the Yankees.

McLish compiled a 6-7 record in Kansas City, pitching 92 innings.

The next season, McLish pitched one inning in a game against the Cincinnati Reds on April 25 before he was sent down to the American Association, where he posted a 12-9 record for the Indianapolis Indians. Pittsburgh's top farm team, managed by Al Lopez, won the league pennant with a 100-54 record, but lost to the St. Paul Saints in the playoffs. McLish was called up by the Pirates in September and started a game on the 25th against the Reds in Pittsburgh. He pitched four innings and allowed five runs, seven hits, and a wild pitch, and didn't get the decision as the Pirates won, 8-6.

McLish changed addresses again in December 1948 when he was dealt to the Chicago Cubs. He pitched sparingly for the Cubs — 23 innings in 1949, with a 1-1 record — instead spending most of his days toiling on the mound for their top farm team, the Los Angeles Angels of the Pacific Coast League. Because of control problems (he issued more than six walks per game), McLish compiled an 8-11 record. Cutting his bases-on-balls almost in half in 1950, he won 20 games (20-11), while also leading the team in ERA (3.60) and innings pitched (260). McLish, a switch-hitter, proved to be adept at the plate as well as the mound; he hit .317. He found the time to exchange "I dos" with his hometown girlfriend, Ruth Iris Lamer. They had five children: Cal Jr., John, Luanne, Ruth Ann, and Thomas.

McLish gained experience in 1951 at the back end of the starting rotation for the last-place Cubs (62-92). His only real highlight of the season occurred on May 5, when he pitched Chicago to a 2-0 victory over Johnny Sain and the Boston Braves. Though he struck out only one, McLish yielded just five singles and two walks. It was one of his four victories that season against ten losses.

Back in Triple-A pitching for a mediocre (87-93) PCL Angels team again in 1952, he had a so-so, 10-15 year, but he began to turn things around by limiting his walks to 2.7 per game, thus giving himself a better chance for success. He won 16 games (16-11) in 1953, trailing Joe Hatten's 17 for the Angels' team lead. In 1954, he compiled a 13-15 record. Early in the 1955 season McLish was sold to San Diego, a Cleveland affiliate, for $5,000. There he blossomed under manager Bob Elliot, cutting his ERA to 2.86 with the Padres and winning 16 games (16-11), again finishing second for the team lead. "I was in Venezuela (playing winter ball) when I heard I had been bought by a big-league club. When I found out it was Cleveland, I couldn't believe it," he said in 1979. "Of all the places to try and make a ballclub! They had superstar pitchers."[4]

McLish was not only a switch-hitter at the dish, but he was also ambidextrous throwing the ball. Though he never threw left-handed in the major leagues, "There was one time in Venezuela [when] we were winning by six or seven runs," Cal recalled, "and we had one out to go. A left-handed batter was up, and all the guys had been trying to get me to throw left-handed. So I switched the glove to my other hand and threw one pitch left-handed. The manager of the other team came running out and argued for 15 minutes. Finally I said, 'Hell, it's not worth it.' [So] I went back to the other hand."[5]

McLish landed a spot in Cleveland. Though the Tribe boasted four solid starters in Herb Score, Bob Lemon, Early Wynn, and Mike Garcia. "Buster," or "Bus," as many teammates referred to McLish, competed for playing time with Art Houtteman, Bob Feller, Ray Narleski, and Hank Aguirre. He increasingly earned manager Al Lopez's trust as the Tribe finished in second place, nine games behind the Yankees. His record of 2-4 and his 4.96 ERA wasn't really indicative of his value to the team.

Lopez departed Cleveland after the 1956 season, and the front office promoted Kerby Farrell to replace him. The change of skippers did not much alter McLish's role on the staff, as he was again used mainly in middle relief, though his starts increased from two games to seven, and his innings from 61⅔ to 144⅓. He compiled a 9-7 record but more importantly he lowered his ERA to 2.97.

In 1958 Farrell was replaced by Bobby Bragan, who in turn was replaced by Joe Gordon on June 27. General manager Frank Lane was anything but patient, changing managers and trading players at a brisk pace. Gordon, the former Yankees and Indians great, continued what Bragan had started — that is, keeping McLish in the starting rotation. At the age of 32, McLish had finally found a steady spot and responded to Gordon's confidence by winning the first five games he started for Gordon. After losing a game to the Senators, McLish strung four straight victories together. "Probably the best move I made all season," Gordon said.[6]

McLish ended the year with a 16-8 record and a 2.99 ERA. He led the team in wins, innings pitched (225 ⅔) and complete games (13). He was grateful to Gordon for the opportunity. "Joe Gordon is an ideal manager," McLish said. "He showed he had confidence in me after I won my first game for him. He didn't say so. He just kept starting me regularly and giving me a chance to prove that I could win. It was wonderful to know that I'd finally found a guy who didn't look at statistics. Joe saw me work, liked what I did and proved it by sending me to the box in my regular turn."[7]

The Indians' pitching staff had undergone a metamorphosis by 1959. Gone were Wynn, Lemon, and Bob Feller, and Mike Garcia was in the twilight of his career. McLish soon found himself as the ace of a staff that included youngsters Jim Perry, Mudcat Grant, and Gary Bell. Herb Score was trying to come back from various injuries, principally the effect of being struck in the eye by a line drive hit by the Yankees' Gil McDougald in 1957. McLish led the mound staff. He was 13-4 at the midseason break and was rewarded by being named to the All-Star Game on August 3 at the Los Angeles Coliseum. He pitched one-hit ball over the final two innings to earn the save as the American League topped the National League 5-3. The Indians fielded a good hitting team as well, and went toe-to-toe with Chicago for much of the season. The "Go-Go" Sox came into Cleveland in late August, nursing a 1½-game lead. The Tribe had won eight straight, but were swept in the critical four-game series. They never recovered, finishing in second place behind the White Sox. McLish led the team with 19 victories.

Yankees manager Casey Stengel had an answer for the sudden success of McLish: "Take this here McLish, which when he is a lot younger and stronger with the Dodgers, he doesn't make it. How do you figure that? Well, I will tell you. McLish has a slider and a sinker, which he does not have with Brooklyn. He still is called Cal McLish, but he ain't the same pitcher."[8]

McLish lost his chance for the magical 20 wins when it was decided that Score would pitch the season finale. "They wanted him to pitch without any pressure after coming back from his injury when he was hit in the eye. I said, 'That's okay with me.' I figured I wasn't going to set any records on winning 20 games."[9]

Despite having led Cleveland pitchers in victories over the last two seasons, McLish was dealt with Billy Martin and first baseman Gordon Coleman to Cincinnati for second baseman Johnny Temple after the 1959 season. "I was hoping I wouldn't be traded and I didn't want to leave the league," McLish said after the trade. "After you get used to it, it's like starting all over again to pitch someplace else. But since I'm going to have to go over to the National, I'm kind of glad it's Cincinnati because they've got a pretty good ball club."[10]

But McLish's season in the Queen City was horrendous. He posted a 4-14 record for the sixth-place Reds. He struck out a paltry 56 batters over 151⅓ innings pitched. McLish did not enjoy the same run support he had backing him in Cleveland. The Tribe had supported him with 5.57 runs per game in 1958 and 4.94 in 1959. The Reds mustered only 3.38 runs an outing for McLish in 1960.

Again Cal was on the move after the season, this time traded to the White Sox with pitcher Juan Pizarro for infielder Gene Freese. On Chicago's South Side he was reunited with Al Lopez. Their new teammate, veteran Roy Sievers, was very pleased with the deal for the two pitchers, saying, "I believe that Juan Pizarro and Cal McLish will strengthen our pitching staff and that we'll win the pennant. … It was pitching that prevented us from winning the flag last year and I think McLish and Pizarro will give us enough of a lift to make the difference."[11]

Sievers was half-right in his assessment: Pizarro led Chicago in wins in 1961, while McLish scuffled in mediocrity with a 10-13 mark. It was later learned that he had been suffering from a double hernia, which required surgery at the end of the season.

For the third straight season, McLish was swapped to another team. On March 24, 1962, he headed to Philadelphia, to complete a trade between the two clubs from the previous December. Again he was reunited with a familiar face, Phillies skipper Gene Mauch. "I don't know exactly how much Cal can help us, but he should be pretty good insurance in case some of [our] kids get off badly," said Mauch. "He's been a winning pitcher in the past, and I like that. I know on good days he can throw 25 or 30 curveballs or breaking balls in succession and get them over the plate."[12]

On the surface, it appeared that McLish pitched well for the Phillies, going 11-5 in 1962. But Mauch picked the spots for him to pitch, and of those 11 victories, six came at the expense of the two expansion teams, the Houston Colt .45s and the New York Mets.

McLish pitched well in 1963, winning 13 games with 11 losses and enjoying separate streaks of five and four games. But soreness at the top of his right shoulder ended his season two weeks early. The same soreness, which was later diagnosed as tendinitis, developed again the following season. After two appearances in 1964, the 38-year-old McLish ended his playing career when he was released by the Phillies in July.

But he did not stray far from the game of baseball, or the city of Philadelphia, for that matter. Mauch added McLish to his coaching staff, naming him as the Phillies' pitching coach, replacing Al Widmar. "Widmar and McLish are both real good men," said Mauch. "But we think the organization will benefit more with Cal working with the Phillies and Al with the kids in the minors."[13]

McLish's second career took hold as he followed Mauch to Montreal after Philadelphia, serving as pitching coach from 1969 to 1975. He joined the staff of Alex Grammas in Milwaukee in 1976, and served under managers Grammas, George Bamberger, Buck Rodgers, and Harvey Kuenn. In 1982, McLish's last season as pitching coach, the Brewers won the American League pennant, besting Mauch's California Angels three wins to two in the American League Championship Series. Under McLish's tutelage, Milwaukee had two Cy Young Award winners, Rollie Fingers in 1981 and Pete Vuckovich in 1982.

In his retirement, Cal enjoyed playing golf and writing poetry. In 2009 he was inducted into the Jim Thorpe Oklahoma Sports Hall of Fame.

McLish died on August 26, 2010 in Edmond, Oklahoma after a long battle with leukemia. He was preceded in death by his daughter Ruth Ann, who had been killed in an automobile accident in 1972.

SOURCES

This biography is included in the book *The Year of the Blue Snow: The 1964 Philadelphia Phillies* (SABR, 2013), edited by Mel Marmer and Bill Nowlin.

NOTES

In addition to BaseballReference.com and SABR.org, the author also consulted the following:

1   Rich Marazzi, *Sports Collectors Digest*, March 13, 1988: 90-91.
2   Ibid.
3   Stan Baumgartner, "Morgan Shifts Into High Gear at Second for Phils," *The Sporting News*, April 20, 1955, 27.
4   *New York Times*, April 16, 1979.
5   *The Sporting News*, May 13, 1959.
6   *Baseball Digest*, July, 1959.
7   *The Sporting News*, June 10, 1959.
8   Marazzi.
9   *Cleveland Press*, December 16, 1959.
10 *The Sporting News*, February 1, 1961.
11 Marazzi.
12 *The Sporting News*, April 4, 1959.
13 *Philadelphia Bulletin*, December 1, 1964.

HARRY WARNER

By Richard Bogovich

"There are a lot of men like Harry Warner at the fringes of the game," observed *Minneapolis Tribune* columnist Doug Grow shortly after the 1982 World Series. "The game grabs them young and holds on forever. And it doesn't give them a whole bunch in return."

Be that as it may, Warner certainly appreciated what he did receive. "It's something you can't put into words," he told Grow. "We were playing that big series in Baltimore at the end of the season and I was standing by (pitcher) Doc Medich during the national anthem. He looks to me and says, 'I've been waiting 10 years for this.' I said, 'Try 37 on for size.'"[1]

Warner was 53 years old at that time. Harry Clinton Warner was born on December 11, 1928, in Reeders, an unincorporated community in Pennsylvania's Poconos, and though Warner worked all over North America, Reeders was always his home.

He was the third child of four born to the former Alice E. Butz and Milo Norman Warner. Brother Max was the oldest, and Harry was born between sisters Betty and Nita. However, the three youngest almost weren't born at all. On the morning of September 20, 1919, Alice was working in the family's general store when she was robbed at gunpoint by a robber later identified as Steve Lepaske. The robber took $76 and fled into the dense woods. State police searched in vain for the robber. Meanwhile, Norman Warner and a few friends had formed a posse, which found the gunman at an abandoned huckleberry picker's cabin and exchanged shots with him. Lepaske escaped into a large swamp, and a group of troopers later captured him. He soon confessed to robbing a store in Bear Creek as well, and to holding up people in a car nearby. He was sentenced to nine years in the Eastern Penitentiary.[2]

Happily, when Harry made a big splash in the news at the age of 9, it was all good. In early September of 1938 he was fishing at the Reeders Trout Lake Pond and reeled in a bullhead catfish plus a 20-inch pickerel weighing about three pounds. *Pennsylvania Angler* magazine was so impressed by Harry's haul that it reported on it in two different issues.[3]

Harry was a basketball and baseball star at Pocono High School.[4] He attended Muhlenberg College in nearby Allentown for one year, but in mid-1946 he informed his father that he wouldn't return to school. He was working that summer and playing for the Reeders team on Sundays when he was persuaded to try minor-league baseball by Marty Baldwin, president of the Stroudsburg Poconos of the Class D North Atlantic League.[5] He'd be playing about 10 miles from home.

Warner's batting average was above .290 each year with Stroudsburg from 1947 through 1949, but when he started with the team in 1946 he hit only .255 in 24 games. Luckily for him, he made a great first impression as a newcomer: In his very first game he smacked two homers and a double.[6] His manager that season was Joe Antolick, whose major-league career consisted of four games for the Phillies in 1944. Only one of the Poconos would later play major-league ball: fellow novice Harry Schaeffer, who pitched in five games for the Yankees in 1952.

At the start of Warner's minor-league career he was taking home $48.02 every two weeks. He played mostly at second base that first season but for the rest of his career was primarily a first baseman. In 1947 Stroudsburg became a Yankees affiliate for one season and in 1949 it was an Indians affiliate. In 1949 Warner hit a staggering .347 and drove in 125 runs in 127 games. Boston Braves scout Honey Russell persuaded his bosses to purchase Warner's contract from the Poconos.[7] The Braves were one of the two major-league franchises Warner was associated with during his playing days. He did well for Wisconsin's Eau Claire Bears in the Class C Northern League, batting .285 with 12 homers in 112 games, but success with his new team at a higher level was overshadowed by the death of his mother in 1950.

Warner was promoted to Boston's Class B team in Evansville, Indiana, for 1951 and 1952. Despite low batting averages, for 1953 he was promoted again by the now Milwaukee Braves, to the Class A team in Jacksonville, Florida. Reminiscing more than 20 years later, he said a highlight that year was playing with Hank Aaron just before the future Hall of Famer broke into the majors.[8]

For 1954 Warner played the farthest from home, in Oregon, when he was assigned to the Class A Salem Senators, a Phillies affiliate. He made *The Sporting News* when the league suspended him for "allegedly" pushing umpire Lowell Fulk during a home game on August 12.[9] Regardless, his batting average rebounded very nicely that season. In fact, 1954 was the only year among his seven at the Class A level in which he batted above .300 and had a slugging percentage above .500 (.315 and .535).

Warner returned to the Jacksonville Braves for 1955, batted .274, and for 1956 Milwaukee promoted him to the Austin Senators in the Double-A Texas League. His 29 games with Austin constituted his only playing time at the Double-A level. Back home in the Stroudsburg area, *Daily Record* sports editor Bob Clark commented cryptically on Warner's departure from Austin, and Milwaukee's organization, during May of that year. Warner switched to the Class A Charlotte Hornets in the Washington Senators' farm system and received a new contract "with a substantial cash agreement," according to Clark, who credited Warner with "showing major league diplomacy in financial problems."[10] By mid-August, new manager Rollie Hemsley was crediting Charlotte's dramatic improvement to the arrival of Warner, Harmon Killebrew, and veteran minor-league catcher José "Joe" Montalvo. Clark noted that Hemsley had Warner "batting in the No. 3 spot ahead of Killebrew, the Senators hope for future stardom."[11]

Warner spent the rest of his playing career in Washington's organization, and continued in it when the Senators became the Minnesota Twins. After his second year with Charlotte, his life baseball entered a brand-new phase: On December 22, 1957, he married Betty J. Bost of Rock Hill, North Carolina, an Eastern Airlines stewardess, at St. Luke's Evangelical Lutheran Church in Charlotte. His best man was Hornets teammate Glenn Zimmerman.[12] The Warners celebrated the birth of their daughter Cynthia Louise on September 17, 1958. They had two other daughters, Dina Lynn and Beth Alice, born in 1962 and 1965, respectively.[13]

Warner played for Charlotte through 1959 but by the dawn of the 1960s he had turned 31 years old. He transitioned to player-manager for three seasons, two at Class D Erie and one with the Class B Wilson Tobs in the Carolina League. All told, he played 17 years in the minors and batted .279; seven

Baseball lifer Harry Warner (on left, followed by coaches Cal McLish, Ron Hansen, and Larry Haney, and skipper Harvey Kuenn) was the Brewers' third-base coach in 1981 and 1982.

of those seasons were at the Class A level, and in those he batted .272.

Midway through his last season before managing, an article drawing from an interview with Warner appeared in the *Charlotte Observer*. It stressed that he hadn't come very close to playing in the majors after more than 13 seasons of pro ball, and Bob Clark said the writer "attempted to reveal to his reading public a sort of dejected figure." Clark continued:

"Harry is far from a person who is down in the dumps. He has a right to be, especially since the year the Washington Senators purchased his contract and then never gave him a chance to work out with the Nats in spring training. … In our conversation with Harry we never heard him complain once about his missed opportunities. Always it was good words for those who he worked under. While the feature bit by the *Charlotte Observer* newsman was the tear-jerking type piece, we know for certain Harry would never want it that way. He's not that type of a man."[14]

Warner's winning percentage as Erie's manager in 1960 was an impressive .643, and he followed that up with a mark of .544 in 1961. Though his 1962 Tobs had a losing record, when Warner became a manager exclusively for 1963, he was promoted to Class A Orlando. He led them through 1965 and again in 1969. With the exception of the latter year, he spent 1966 through 1971 managing Charlotte, now at the Double-A level. His peak winning percentage managing each of those teams was .606 with Orlando in 1969 and .648 with Charlotte in 1971.

During that final season at Orlando, Warner was asked about the stresses of managing a successful club. "I don't let it get the best of me," he asserted. "My philosophy is to leave the game at the ballpark. If you take it home with you and start figuring out what might have happened if you'd done this or that, then it starts eating at you."[15]

Warner's .648 winning percentage with Charlotte in 1971 was his best ever as a manager, and it earned him a year leading the Triple-A Tacoma

Twins. That team had a record of 65-83 in 1972 under Warner, and through 1976 he bounced around the nation with four more single-season managing assignments, though he led three of his teams to winning records.

After more than three decades in the minor leagues, the previous 21 in the same franchise's system, Warner's concern that he would never get to work in a major-league dugout was understandable. Suddenly, in mid-October of 1976, that dream came true when Roy Hartsfield offered him a coaching job with the expansion Toronto Blue Jays. Hartsfield and Warner had managed against each other in 1963 and 1964 in the Florida State League. "I wanted to coach badly in the big leagues," Warner admitted at the time. "There was nowhere for me to go in the Twins organization."[16]

Warner was the bullpen coach for the Blue Jays during their first three years of existence. In 1978 he subbed for his boss toward the end of May while Hartsfield's wife underwent surgery. Though the Jays lost nine games and won only three under Warner, his first game managing was a win over the Yankees. The game ball was one of the few mementos he kept 20 years later, when he expressed some regret about not having more. "I was never one to get autographs, but when I look back I could have gotten a lot from prominent people who attended games," he said. He recalled President Richard Nixon and Hollywood legend Bob Hope among the famous people he encountered.[17]

Like almost all expansion teams, the Blue Jays struggled early on. They lost more than 100 games in the three years Hartsfield managed them, and maintaining morale can be tricky under such circumstances. Ken Carson, who was the trainer for Toronto for a decade, recalled that Warner and first-base coach Don Leppert helped by playing frequent practical jokes. Warner and Leppert were both in Milwaukee's farm system in 1955 and may have met during spring training before or after that season.

Carson recalled two pranks in particular that played out publicly, and both times the target was Doug Passmore, the team's kitchen attendant. Once Warner and Leppert "hired a moving firm to take his stove and refrigerator and set them along the third-base line." Carson said Passmore himself "really kept the clubhouse loose" but was also known for yelling at umpires during games. As a solo prank, Warner conspired with AL umpire Bill Deegan before a game to eject Passmore as his screaming peaked that day. Carson said Passmore was permanently cured of the habit afterward. Carson was also the victim of a scheme at least once, though more behind-the-scenes:

"After our first road tip, we came into the clubhouse and the grounds crew had put up some shelving in my trainer's room. I was upset because I never asked them to do it and I didn't want the shelves. I insisted they take them down. It took them a long time to do it, having to patch holes and paint. Harry and Don knew I was upset so they just had to do another prank. They arrived at the ballpark early the next morning and took about five hours to put the shelves back up again before I got there. I walked in, saw it and couldn't help but laugh."[18]

Carson wasn't alone in appreciating Warner's unofficial role on the staff. "Harry kept us sane, never a dull moment," said third-base coach Jackie Moore.[19]

Hartsfield was fired after the 1979 season, and hitting coach Bobby Doerr was the only prominent member of Hartsfield's staff retained by new manager Bobby Mattick. For Warner, 1979 became sad for a second reason: His father died that year.

However, on December 4, a week before Warner's 51st birthday, the Blue Jays announced that he would manage the Syracuse Chiefs in the Triple-A International League. He spoke candidly when interviewed by Syracuse sportswriter Rick Burton. "I've only managed in the minors for 17 years, so I'm not overly enthused that I'm managing again," Warner said. Burton characterized Warner's reaction as understandable. "A coach (or manager) needs four years in the major leagues to qualify for the fairly lucrative pension program," Burton noted. "Warner, with three years under his belt, is short by one baseball season." Burton said Warner faced a paradox: If he succeeded at Syracuse, he might be stuck managing in the minors again. Burton then spoke to the likelihood that Warner's work at Syracuse would be valued. "He is credited with having done so much to recognize and establish the potentials of such baseball stars as Rod Carew, Graig Nettles, and Butch Wynegar — all of whom he managed while working in the Minnesota Twins organization," Burton wrote. "Carew even reportedly said that Warner is the reason he stayed in baseball when he seriously considered quitting in 1964."[20]

Syracuse had a losing record under Warner, but he was invited back to the Twins for the final month of the 1980 season. Two reasons for the decision were announced. One was that 11 players on Toronto's roster at the time played for Warner at Syracuse, and the parent club's front office wanted him to provide insights about them firsthand. The other reason was kindness, stemming from awareness of his pension situation. Warner was quite happy.[21]

On October 13, 1980, Brewers manager Buck Rodgers hired Harry Warner to coach third base the following season. "I've known him for quite a while," Rodgers said at the time, while heaping praise on Warner.[22] They had played against one another in the South Atlantic League during 1959 and both managed in the California League during 1975. That was Rodgers' first season as a manager, and Warner's Reno Silver Sox walked away with the pennant.

Warner was the third-base coach of the Brewers in 1981 and 1982. Not surprisingly, he was still glowing about the 1982 World Series when interviewed by a reporter back home in 1998. "It made all the time I put in the minor leagues worthwhile," he said. "When you think of all the good players, managers and coaches who never got to the World Series, all in all it was quite an experience."[23]

Warner returned to Minnesota's organization for a final year of minor-league managing in 1983, for the Visalia Oaks of the Class A California League. He proved that he still had that managerial magic by leading the Oaks to a .621 winning percentage. In 19 seasons as a minor-league manager he achieved a winning percentage of .529, and his mark at the Double-A level for six of those seasons was .520.

From 1984 to 1990 Warner maintained his connection to major-league baseball as a scout for the Twins and the San Diego Padres. His wife, Betty, died on January 8, 1994, and he was a widower for more than a decade.[24]

In that 1998 interview, Warner acknowledged that his managerial career was tough on his family. Though they always kept a house in Reeders, Betty would take the three girls to whatever minor-league city Harry was assigned to. In a way, Betty may have perceived her husband as the head of a very large extended family that included the young men he was guiding. "It's their first time away from home," Harry noted, "and you have to be Mommy, Daddy and a psychologist."

Warner's obituary, composed by his daughters after he died on April 11, 2015, seemed to dovetail with his own perception of his role from 1960 into the 1980s. "Harry will always be remembered as a great coach and mentor to many baseball players and helped mold their careers," it read. "He touched many lives and was full of encouragement."[25]

SOURCES

In addition to the sources cited in the Notes, the author also accessed Baseball-Reference.com.

NOTES

1. Doug Grow, "Little Man Hopes to Find Baseball Life after World Series," *Minneapolis Tribune*, December 5, 1982: 2C.
2. *Commonwealth of Pennsylvania Biennial Report of the Department of State Police for the Years 1918-1919*, 1920, 135. The genealogical information is primarily from the 1930 and 1940 federal censuses, plus Warner's obituary at wmhclarkfuneralhome.com/obituary/3033502.

3   "Here and There in Anglerdom," Pennsylvania Angler, February 1939: 24; "Nice Pickerel," *Pennsylvania Angler*, January 1940: 23.

4   Jim Riley, "Life of Riley," *Daily Record* (Stroudsburg, Pennsylvania), June 11, 1953: 12.

5   Marta Lindenmoyer, "44 Seasons in the Sun," *Pocono Record* (Stroudsburg, Pennsylvania), July 13, 1998: poconorecord.com/article/19980713/Features/307139991.

6   Lindenmoyer; "Harry Warner Gives Talk on Baseball," *Pocono Record*, September 26, 1968: 15.

7   Joe DeVivo, "Harry Warner Finally Gets His Major League Chance," Pocono Record, December 17, 1976: 19. Despite Warner's gaudy numbers, it wasn't easy to stand out on that team. The 1949 Stroudsburg Poconos, with a record of 101-36, are ranked as one of the top 100 minor-league teams of all time. See milb.com/milb/history/top100.jsp?idx=64, with commentary by Bill Weiss and Marshall Wright. Warner's detailed statistics for 1949 and three later seasons are provided by Jamie Selko in *Minor League All-Star Teams, 1922-1962* (Jefferson, North Carolina: McFarland & Company, Inc., 2007). See Warner's name in the book's index.

8   DeVivo.

9   "Chiefs Upset Bronc Cart," *The Sporting News*, September 1, 1954: 33.

10 Bob Clark, "Off the Record," *Stroudsburg Daily Record*, May 29, 1956: 12.

11 Bob Clark, "Off the Record," *Stroudsburg Daily Record*, August 15, 1956: 12.

12 "Harry Warner Married in Charlotte, N.C., Church," *Stroudsburg Daily Record*, January 2, 1958: 10.

13 "Warner Baby Baptized," Pocono Record, November 19, 1958: 26, "Hospital Notes," *Stroudsburg Daily Record*, March 13, 1962: 3; "The Baby's Named," *Pocono Record*, March 23, 1965: 5.

14 Bob Clark, "Off the Record," *Stroudsburg Daily Record*, July 23, 1959: 13.

15 Jim Haynes, "Now Let's Settle Down," *Orlando Sentinel*, July 21, 1969: 17.

16 DeVivo.

17 Lindenmoyer.

18 Ken Carson with Larry Millson, *From Hockey to Baseball: I Kept Them in Stitches* (Victoria, British Columbia: FriesenPress, 2016), 98-99.

19 Bob Elliott, "Rangers Coach Has Canadian Roots," *Sudbury* (Ontario) *Star*, April 23, 2009: B2.

20 Rick Burton, "Chiefs' New Chief Has Vast Experience in Minors," *Syracuse Post-Standard*, December 5, 1979: C1.

21 "Warner Gets Call to Help Blue Jays," *Medicine Hat* (Alberta) *News*, September 6, 1980: 15.

22 "Warner Is Picked as Brewer Coach," *Milwaukee Sentinel*, October 14, 1890: Part 2, Page 2.

23 Lindenmoyer.

24 Obituary, Harry C. Warner, wmhclarkfuneralhome.com/obituary/3033502.

25 Ibid.

JERRY AUGUSTINE

By Rick Schabowski

It's very rare when an athlete plays high school, college, and professionally in his native state, but Jerry Augustine, a left-handed pitcher for the Brewers for a decade, went even further by being a baseball coach for an NCAA Division I school (University of Wisconsin-Milwaukee), and in 2009 he has been a TV analyst for the major-league team he played for, the Milwaukee Brewers.

Gerald Lee Augustine was born to Donald and Elerene Augustine on July 24, 1952, at old St. Mary's hospital in Green Bay, Wisconsin. The family lived in nearby Kewaunee. He was part of a big family, with brothers and sisters Dale, David, Susan, Joe, Mark, and Randy, as well as half-brothers Donald and Orville, the latter two half-brothers were instrumental in Jerry becoming a left-hander. Donald, who was right-handed, and Orville, who was left-handed, debated on how Jerry should throw. Orville settled the debate by giving Jerry a left-hander's glove.

At Kewaunee High School Gerald starred in baseball, football, and basketball. His high-school classmates included Jack Novak, who played in the NFL, and Dale Koehler, who played basketball at the University of Wisconsin.

Augustine played baseball at the University of Wisconsin-La Crosse. While in La Crosse he and his high-school sweetheart, Nancy Flaherty, were married and had their first child, Tammy. They later added Todd, Ted, Matthew, and Melanie to their family.

Augustine helped the UWL Eagles win back-to-back conference championships in 1972 and 1973. He was selected to the All-Wisconsin State University Conference first team. As a starter, he posted 14 wins with 186 strikeouts. Many years later he looked back fondly on his college days: "As you go through life, you go through different areas. When I look back at La Crosse, I was given the opportunity to not only grow as a baseball player, but to grow as a person and get my education. La Crosse is very special to me because of that."[1] Augustine also praised his baseball coach, saying, "Bill Terry was the right coach for me. It was Bill's way of handling people that really made me grow up as a person. I don't think I would be able to go on and play and achieve the things the way I did without that. He helped me become a better baseball player and a better person."[2] Augustine graduated with a degree in physical education and health, and later he taught during the offseason.

Augustine was drafted by the Brewers in the 15th round of the June 1974 free-agent draft and was signed for what he described as "a small bonus" by Brewers scout Emil Belich, who also signed Paul Molitor and Jim Gantner.[3]

The Brewers sent Augustine to Danville (Illinois) of the Class A Midwest League, where he started 12 games, completed 6, and posted a 7-4 record with a 2.56 ERA. Danville, was the winner of the second half of the league's split season, then won the league championship in the playoffs. During the playoffs Augustine pitched a two-hitter against Quad Cities, striking out 14 in the 1-0 win. He had a no-hitter going until the eighth inning.

Augustine reported to the Brewers' 1975 spring-training camp at Sun City, Arizona, on March 3 and in the first hour of the camp he injured his knee so severely during pitcher's fielding practice covering first base that he needed surgery. He was out of action until June 28, when he joined the Sacramento Solons, the Brewers' Triple-A affiliate in the Pacific Coast League. After pitching in short stints, Augustine moved into the starting rotation in July.[4]

The Solons played their games at Hughes Stadium, a football field located on the campus of Sacramento City College. The park favored hitters, with a left-field dimension of 251 feet, with a screen erected. In 15 games (11 starts) Augustine posted a 4-3 record with a 4.78 ERA and three complete games. When the major-league roster limits were raised to 40 on September 1, Augustine joined the Brewers and made his major-league debut on September 9 against Baltimore, coming into the game in the eighth inning with two out in relief of Larry Anderson. The first batter he faced, Mark Belanger, doubled. Ken Singleton singled to center field, driving in Belanger. Augustine ended the inning on a fly out by Paul Blair.

After a three-inning, no-hit performance against the New York Yankees the next day, Augustine got his first start on September 16, against the Yankees at County Stadium. He wasn't informed that he would be the starter until the morning of the game when the Brewers were boarding a bus at Boston's Logan Airport for the flight to Milwaukee. "Ken McBride (the Brewers pitching coach) told me about it," Augustine said after the game. "I got nervous, of course, but I was determined to do

Jerry Augustine played his entire 10-year big-league career with the Brewers (1975-1984), going 55-59 as a starter and reliever.

well."[5] Augustine picked up his first major-league victory, 5-2, going 8⅓ innings and giving up two runs on nine hits. Brewers catcher Darrell Porter was impressed with Augustine's performance, saying, "He's aggressive and he is a competitor."[6] Augustine, obviously, was very happy, "It's everybody's dream come true."[7]

Because of the short notice, none of Augustine's family could attend the game, including his wife and their three-year-old daughter, Tammy, who had a cold. Augustine wasn't upset, explaining, "My wife and I have a thing going. It's a superstition.

Every time she watched me pitch for the first time I didn't do well. This was my first start in the majors, so it was best she didn't watch me, but there'll be other times."[8]

Augustine pitched his first complete game on September 27 against the Tigers, a seven-hit, 5-2 victory. Brewers manager Del Crandall was impressed, commenting, "He's got to figure in this club's plans. He's had very little experience, but he takes it to 'em. He's not a nibbler. His ball is very alive, he works hard and he has good aptitude. Kenny McBride has worked with him on his curveball, and it has really come along."[9] Reflecting on his one month with the Brewers, Augustine said, "It's been really exciting. I really enjoyed it. Something super."[10]

During the offseason Augustine pitched winter ball in the Dominican Republic.

Augustine began the 1976 season in the bullpen. He didn't make his first start until June 10. After five straight losses he was 2-7 on July 16. But between July 20 and September 3 he went 6-2 with a 2.18 ERA.

On July 24, Augustine's 24th birthday, he pitched his first major-league shutout, a four-hit, eight-strikeout, 5-0 win over the Orioles.

In his next starting assignment, against the Tigers on July 28 at County Stadium, Augustine lost a heartbreaker. His 21-scoreless-innings streak ended when Pedro Garcia hit a sacrifice fly scoring Alex Johnson in the top of ninth, giving the Tigers a 1-0 win. After the game, manager Alex Grammas said of Augustine, "I think he's reached the point where he's much more relaxed. Just from looking at him before the game tonight, I got the feeling that he had arrived. I think he knows what he has to do, and he pitched one hell of a game tonight. Damn, he pitched a good game."[11]

Augustine got revenge against Detroit at Tiger Stadium on September 3 with a complete-game, five-hit, 11-2 win over Mark Fidrych.

Augustine ended the season with a 9-12 record with a 3.30 earned-run average, his major-league best. He was named to the Topps American League Rookie All-Star Team, took second to Mark Fidrych as *The Sporting News* Rookie Pitcher of the Year in the American League, and was voted the Brewers' Rookie of the Year by the Wisconsin Baseball Writers' Association. After the season he signed a two-year contract, worked in the Brewers ticket office, and took a real-estate course.

In 1977 Augustine started 33 games and led the 68-94 Brewers in victories with 12, defeats (18), and complete games (10), and pitched a career-high 209 innings, second best on the team to Jim Slaton. He pitched seven complete games in May, his best month, compiling a 4-3 record with a 3.10 ERA. Two of the three losses in May were tough ones. On May 11, Augustine lost a 4-3 five-hitter against Cleveland with three of the runs unearned, and on May 24, he lost at Baltimore, 2-1, a game in which he pitched another five-hitter. After Mike Hegan was released, Augustine was elected the Brewers' player representative and assumed his duties after the All-Star Game.

Augustine set a personal high in 1978 with 13 wins. He lost 12 games, ranked third on the team with 188⅓ innings pitched, and had nine complete games. His finest stretch as a starter was in June when he allowed three runs in 32⅓ innings in victories over the Blue Jays, Mariners, Indians, and Yankees. His 4-1 record and 2.48 ERA earned him the Brewer Pitcher of the Month Award for June.

On August 28 Augustine pitched a two-hit, 10-1 victory over the Tigers. He also pitched two three-hitters and two five-hitters during the season. He was 3-1 against the World Series champion Yankees.

A game against the Blue Jays on September 7 was his final start of the 1978 season. He was sent to the bullpen and rookie Mark Bomback, a call-up from Spokane, took his spot in the starting rotation. Brewers manager George Bamberger said the switch to the bullpen was not a demotion. "From here on in, the bullpen will play an important part for us," Bamberger said. "Augie gives us two left-handers (along with Bob McClure) in the bullpen."[12] In his last four relief appearances, he didn't allow a run in 4⅓ innings. Bamberger was pleased with Augustine's performance out of the bullpen as a short man, saying after the season, "I liked the way he handled himself. He took charge. Maybe that's the right situation for him next season."[13]

In 1979 Augustine pitched out of the bullpen except for two starts. He appeared in 43 games and posted a 9-6 record with a 3.47 ERA, with five saves. (He was 1-1 in his starts.) He had a 5-1 record at County Stadium. In his longest relief appearance, on September 25, he worked eight innings in a 7-6 win over the Mariners. Between May 9 and July 23, during a span of 20 appearances, he didn't allow a home run. He finished the season on a high note, posting a 5-1 record, with a 0.92 ERA from August 15 to September 25. He was named the Brewers' Rolaids Relief Pitcher of the Year.

In midseason Augustine spoke about his new role: "I kind of miss being a starter and yet, I've been having just as much fun out of the bullpen. I'm able to pitch in more games. That's what I really enjoy about the bullpen. The toughest thing when you're in the bullpen is that you have to be mentally ready every day."[14]

Augustine pitched in 39 games for the Brewers in 1980, posting a 4-3 record with two saves and a 4.52 ERA. His only start came on May 9, when he lost to the Orioles, 5-2.

Augustine was excused the last two weeks of the season to go to the Arizona Instructional League and work on his delivery with George Bamberger. Bamberger had resigned as the Brewers manager on September 7, 1980, and was hired as a special consultant to Harry Dalton, who sent him to Arizona. The Brewers wanted to see if it would be helpful if Augustine shortened his stride and kept his body back. Of this experience, Augustine said, "I think it had a positive influence on me. When you change your delivery almost completely the way I did, it's quite a change."[15]

In the strike-shortened 1981 season, Augustine appeared in 27 games, posting a 2-2 record in 61⅓ innings with two saves. He started two games, one on April 30 when he substituted for Pete Vuckovich, who was out with tightness in his right shoulder, and defeated the Angels, 12-1. Augustine pitched seven innings, allowing just two hits. In his other start, on May 25, Augustine went just two innings and lost to the Tigers, 12-3. August was an especially good month. He had eight appearances, earning a win and a save.

In 1982 Augustine pitched in 20 games and had a 1-3 record. June was a good month as he went 1-0 with a 1.08 ERA. On June 20, he pitched 4⅓ scoreless innings against Detroit, allowing only one hit and getting the victory in relief of Jim Slaton. He threw his first complete game in four years on July 19, against the Twins, allowing two earned runs in a 6-4 loss. After the Brewers acquired Don Sutton from the Astros on August 30 in a trade to help them make the playoffs, Augustine was designated assignment.

It was difficult not being on the roster for the 1982 postseason. Twenty-five years later, Augustine said, "I was replaced on the roster by Don Sutton, not a bad guy to be replaced with."[16] Still, it was a difficult adjustment for Augustine. "At the time I didn't handle it very well. I really struggled with it. It was a real tough time for me personally. I had some good, long talks with Jamie (Easterly).Teddy Simmons took me aside and had a really good perspective. He said, 'You know, Augie, if you weren't here, we would not be here.' You learn from those things and put it in perspective. It did take 25 guys, and with us, probably 30 guys."[17]

Even though not on the roster, Augustine was given permission to suit up and sit next to manager Harvey Kuenn in the dugout. He loved the experience. "I really learned a lot about baseball because I sat there next to Harvey," he said in 2007. "I listened to everything they did. Harvey would turn to me every now and then and say, 'Augie, what do you think here?' He made you feel like you were part of it, no matter what was going on."[18]

Even before the 1983 regular season began, the Brewers had issues with their starting pitching. An arthogram of Pete Vuckovich taken in March revealed a tear in his rotator cuff sending him to the disabled list. After Dwight Bernard was released, Augustine was expected to fill the gap as the Brewers' fifth starter. The Brewers started the season with three complete games by Sutton, Mike Caldwell, and Augustine. Augustine pitched 8⅓ innings of scoreless ball against the Angels until Bobby Grich hit a three-run homer as the Brewers won 5-3. It was the first time the Brewers had three complete games in a row since August 1980, and the first time they had ever opened the season with three complete games.

In his next start, against the Blue Jays on April 14, Augustine had to leave the game when he strained knee ligaments fielding a bunt by Willie Upshaw. He was out for two weeks, and in his next start against the White Sox, on April 27, Carlton Fisk hit a line drive off Augustine's forearm. The injury was so severe that Augustine went on the disabled list until May 20. Augustine joked about the incident: "I always said that the Lord would tell me when it's time to retire. This time he told me to become a better defensive pitcher."[19]

Pitching coach Pat Dobson commented on the injury: "He can't catch a break. He gets over one injury and he gets another. He was really starting to get his feet on the ground. He pitched well both times out. Now he'll have to wait and start all over again. That's tough."[20] Augustine started seven games and then went to the bullpen for the remainder of the season.

Augustine pitched in four games for the Brewers in 1984, the last one on April 11, working 3⅔ innings against the Angels, allowing no earned runs. When the Brewers took Rick Waits off the disabled list, Augustine was designated for assignment. He was sent to Vancouver (Pacific Coast League). On June 6 versus Salt Lake City, he allowed one hit in 7⅓ innings. He posted a 3-8 record with a 4.55 ERA. At the end of the season he declared himself a free agent but was not picked up by any team.

In 1985 Augustine pitched for the Rochester Red Wings, the Orioles' Triple-A team, and had a 0.92 ERA through early June. He pitched 17⅓ innings before allowing an earned run. He picked up his fifth victory of the season on August 6, throwing 3⅓ scoreless innings in relief against Columbus. He posted a 6-3 record and had six saves and a 3.96 ERA.

After appearing in five games for Rochester and 34 for Columbus posting a 3-6 record, with six saves and a 4.14 ERA, Augustine retired from baseball in 1986. It was obviously a tough decision. Augustine commented in 2007, "I don't know if I'd say it was hard going back to the minors. I was actually throwing the ball better at the end than I did with Milwaukee. I was throwing harder, I had a better breaking ball, and I adopted a changeup that I could throw for strikes. If I had gone back the next year, I think I could have made it back. But we had twins and I made a family decision. I just missed my family too much. I had five kids, and it was time to spend time with them."[21]

After deciding against a teaching career, in November 1986 Augustine opened an insurance agency in West Allis, Wisconsin, a suburb of Milwaukee, which as of 2019 was still in business. He implemented lessons learned from playing professional baseball: "When managers come to the mound to talk to a pitcher, every eye in the stadium is on that conversation. Your words need to be direct and to the point. The same is true when I talk to clients. I learned to be direct and always be honest. It helped me learn as a player, and it has helped me succeed in business." Did it help that he was a former major leaguer? "Name recognition was important when I started, and it remains important today. If people do not recall my name from my days with the Brewers, they'll be reminded the moment they walk through the door."[22]

In 1995 Augustine was named the baseball coach at the University of Wisconsin-Milwaukee. In 12 seasons the team posted a 347-297-1 record and made three NCAA tournaments. In the 1999 tournament, UWM defeated top-ranked Rice.

The University of Wisconsin-La Crosse inducted Augustine into its Wall of Fame in 1984, and the Milwaukee Brewers put him on their Wall of Honor in 2014.

In 2009 he began working as a Brewers' Live Color Analyst for Fox Sports Wisconsin for the pre- and postgame shows and filled in as a radio broadcaster in 2014.

SOURCES

In addition to the sources cited in the Notes, the author had a personal conversation with Jerry Augustine, and accessed Retrosheet.org, Baseball-Reference.com, Newspapers.com, Paper of Record, the 2018 Milwaukee Brewers Media Guide, and SABR.org.

NOTES

1. Alex Vandenhouten, "Former Brewer Jerry Augustine: La Crosse Is a Baseball Town," *La Crosse Tribune*, March 2, 2017.
2. Jeff Brown, "La Crosse Instrumental in Jerry Augustine's Formative Years – On and Off the Field," *La Crosse Tribune*, March 1, 2017.
3. Lou Chapman, "Brewers Happy Over List to Portside," *The Sporting News*, September 18, 1976: 15.
4. Lou Chapman, "Yankees Tee Off on New Brewers," *Milwaukee Sentinel*, September 11, 1975: 2, 1.
5. Lou Chapman, "Brewers Find Rookie Hero," *Milwaukee Sentinel*, September 17, 1975: 2, 1.
6. Ibid.
7. Ibid.
8. Ibid.
9. Mike Gonring, "A Promotional Dream – State Pitcher Wins," *Milwaukee Journal*, September 28, 19752, 1.
10. Ibid.
11. Mike Gonring, "Even a 1-0 Defeat Fails to Ruffle New Augustine," *Milwaukee Journal*, July 29, 1976: 2, 12.
12. "Augustine Is Back in Bullpen," *Milwaukee Sentinel*, September 9, 1978: 2, 6.
13. Mike Gonring, "Can Augustine Cure Brewer Bullpen Woe?" *The Sporting News*, November 4, 1978: 47.
14. Mike Gonring, "Ex-Starter Augustine Brewers' New Stopper," *The Sporting News*, June 30, 1979: 18.
15. Tom Flaherty, "Augustine Has a Super Tutor," *The Sporting News*, November 15, 1980: 50.
16. Tom Haudricourt, "Where Have You Gone, '82 Brewers?" *KCI Sports*, 2007: 9.
17. Haudricourt: 80.
18. Ibid.
19. Peter Gammons, "A.L. Beat," *The Sporting News*, May 23, 1983: 25.
20. Tom Flaherty, "Hard Luck Hounds Hurler Augustine," *The Sporting News*, May 16, 1983: 24.
21. Haudricourt.
22. Dan Aznoff, "Ex-Players Turn Discipline Into Pay Dirt with 2nd Careers," *Property Casualty 360*, July 30, 2003

KEVIN BASS

By Phillip Balda

Trading a promising young outfielder — a future All-Star — for a pitcher with a large contract at the end of his career may be the worst trade Harry Dalton ever made. But the pitcher was future Hall of Famer Don Sutton. The arrival of the 37-year-old Sutton wowed Brewers fans and was the final piece in the Milwaukee Brewers successful run to the 1982 World Series. Sending 23-year-old outfielder Kevin Bass to the Astros was necessary to complete the August 30, 1982, deadline deal.

Four years later, Bass made the All-Star team and was a key member of the 1986 NL West champion Houston Astros, hitting .311, his finest season, with 20 homers and 79 RBIs in 157 games. He made the final out in the 16th inning of Game Six of the 1986 NL playoffs, striking out against Jesse Orosco. The game sent the New York Mets to the World Series.

Bass played 14 years in the majors, 10 of them in two stints with the Astros. He played in 1,571 major-league games, winding up with a .270 lifetime batting average, 611 runs batted in, and 118 home runs.

Kevin Charles Bass was born on May 12, 1959, in Redwood City, California and raised in Menlo Park, on San Francisco Bay. Nine-year-old Kevin was a shortstop on a Menlo Park Little League team coached by his father; his older sister kept score.[1]

Chris Haft, a high-school teammate, remembered that Kevin spoke about his determination to be a major-league baseball player as early as his freshman year.[2]

The Bass family had roots in baseball and sports. Kevin's brother, Richard, was a minor-league outfielder in 1976 and 1977, and his cousin is NFL Hall of Fame receiver James Lofton. His uncle Stan "Lefty" Johnson received the first baseball scholarship offered to an African-American at the University of San Francisco; he went on to play briefly for the 1960 Chicago White Sox and the 1961 Kansas City Athletics and played 10 years in Triple A for four major-league teams before ending his career in Japan with the Taiyo Whales. After retiring in 1970 he became a West Coast scout for the Boston Red Sox.[3]

In Menlo Park High School Bass was an all-league player in football and baseball, and also played basketball. His hopes of playing college football waned when baseball scouts began coming to see him play. They had reason to make the trip: At the end of the 1977 season, Bass was named a first-team All-American high-school player by the High School Division of the American College of Baseball Coaches.

The Brewers selected the high-school senior in the second round of the June 1977 free-agent draft.

(They used their first-round pick to select Paul Molitor.) "He's got a good arm, good speed, and he has an excellent instinct about going after the ball," said Brewers scout Roland LeBlanc of the 18-year-old switch-hitting outfielder.[4]

After signing with the Brewers, Bass was sent to Newark (New York) of the New York-Penn League In his first 44 at-bats he hit .182. By the time he accumulated 96 at-bats his average had improved to .313.

The next season Bass was invited to major-league spring training. He later said that Cecil Cooper became a mentor to him, watching him take batting practice and offering batting tips.[5] He saw his own assets as his speed, power, and his strong arm — in addition to being a switch-hitter. After his retirement he said his faults were technical weaknesses as a left-handed hitter and a base stealer.

The 6-foot Bass, listed at 183 pounds, started as the leadoff man for Burlington of the Class A Midwest League in 1978, and after showing power he was moved to the middle of the lineup. He was named to the league all-star team, both at midseason and at yearend, after batting .265 average with 18 home runs, 69 RBIs, and 36 steals.

In 1979 Bass was promoted to Holyoke of the Double-A Eastern League and started slowly, the surged in June. "The difference is confidence," he said. "When I get down on myself, I can't do the job. When I'm loose and relaxed, I'm okay."[6] In 1980 he returned to Holyoke and in June, the month of his 21st birthday, he hit safely in 25 of 27 games.

Holyoke won the Eastern League title and Bass was again an all-star. He and his manager, Lee Sigman, were rewarded by promotions to Triple-A Vancouver (Pacific Coast League), where in 1981 he batted .257 in 97 games.

Bass was named in 1982 spring training as one of four rookies (along with Bob Skube, Thad Bosley, and Marshall Edwards) considered for the starting role in right field, which eventually went to Charlie Moore. He made the Opening Day roster but was sent back to Vancouver in May after going hitless in his first nine major-league at-bats. (He started only one game.) In Vancouver he hit .315 with 17 home runs, 65 RBIs, and 23 stolen bases in 102 games.

Bass was traded by the Brewers with Frank DiPino and Mike Madden to the Houston Astros on September 3, 1982, to complete a trade for pitcher Don Sutton.

Bass went 0-for-8 with the Astros in September after being added to the roster along with second baseman Bill Doran. He got his first major-league hit on September 8 — an RBI single against Atlee Hammaker of the San Francisco Giants, and said, "I've had trouble seeing the ball. I don't think the pitchers I'll face are that much better than the ones I've seen in Triple A, I mean consistently. I just have to get used to playing inside (the Astrodome) I guess, even in center field."[7]

In July 1983 Bass married Elaine Bell on the campus of Mills College in Oakland, California. On the field that year, he was a part-time player, appearing in only 88 games with 195 at-bats. Bass played in the winter leagues that winter and throughout the early years of his major-league career. His friend Gary Haft asked him that year why he just did not relax in the offseason. Bass's reply was, "Have you ever tried to hit off Lavelle?" referring the San Francisco relief pitcher Gary Lavelle.[8]

Bass began the 1984 season on the disabled list with a severely pulled right thigh muscle and then came off the bench, starting only 64 games in the outfield. He was splitting time with Terry Puhl and Tim Tolman in right field and Jerry Mumphrey in center. He was a reliable pinch-hitter, getting 13 hits in 44 attempts, and put together a 12-game hitting streak from September 14 to September 25 as he got a chance to play in the outfield every day.

The Astros moved the Astrodome's outfield fence in before the 1985 season, Bass's first as a starting outfielder. He batted .269 with 16 homers, 68 RBIs, and 19 stolen bases in 539 at-bats. As he did for most of his career, he hit for a higher average from the right side (.311) than the left (.241), but his power numbers were more equally distributed.

In 1986 the Astros came together as a contender under the fiery first-year manager Hal Lanier with young talent and strong pitching led by Mike Scott, Bob Knepper, and Nolan Ryan. They also added Billy Hatcher and Tony Walker, eliminating their need to use Bass in center field. Lanier saw Bass's speed as an asset and installed him as the starter in right.

During that year Bass's trademark consistency was highlighted by long hitting streaks including one of 20 games, and his selection to the 1986 National League All-Star team. He joked, however, that his nickname the team had become "Rodney" (for comedian Rodney Dangerfield) as he was still largely an unknown and not yet an established star. The lack of respect was so pervasive that writer Bill Conlin, in a preview of the All-Star Game, confused him with Randy Bass, a former major leaguer who won the Triple Crown in Japan.[9]

The 1986 season was Bass's best. He batted .311 with a career-high 20 home runs and finished seventh in the voting for the NL Most Valuable Player Award. But he would be remembered most for his game-ending strikeout in the deciding game of the NCLS against the New York Mets. "My adrenaline was so high for the whole series, most of it was like a blur, except for that last at-bat," he said in a 2002 interview.[10]

In 1987 Bass batted .284 and had 31 doubles, 19 home runs, 85 RBIs, and 21 stolen bases. During a 10-1 Astros win over the Cubs on September 2, he became the first National League player to homer from both sides of the plate twice in one season. Chili Davis of the San Francisco Giants accomplished the feat 13 days later, on September 15.

In 1988 Bass's average dropped to .255, but he had 72 RBIs and 31 steals. On July 23 he flied out to left field against Steve Bedrosian of the Philadelphia Phillies in the eighth inning after fouling off 15 pitches, which stood for many years as the record for foul pitches in a single at-bat.

In 1989 Bass batted .300 in 87 games for the Astros, but missed nearly half the season with a broken right shinbone after fouling a pitch from Bill Landrum of the Pittsburgh Pirates on May 27. He played for four weeks before an x-ray revealed that a stress fracture had developed. He returned to the lineup on August 11.

After the season Bass was a free agent and he signed a three-year contract with the San Francisco Giants. He received a $500,000 signing bonus and the first no-trade clause general manager Al Rosen had ever included in a player contract. The deal was worth $5.25 million and made Bass the highest-paid player on the Giants.

Bass had been involved in Astros trade rumors over several years — he had once been all but traded to the New York Yankees for Dave Winfield before Winfield refused to go to Houston. And he was perplexed by moves the Astros had made under general manager Dick Wagner, including firing manager Lanier after the 1988 season and their recent decision to let Nolan Ryan sign with the Texas Rangers as a free agent. "It was tough leaving Houston," he said in 1990 spring training. "I had been there for so long, and they treated me pretty good. But the offer came up and it was a chance to come back home."[11]

The Astros had refused to include a no-trade clause in their offer to Bass. "That ended up being the key factor," he said in a conference call for Bay Area media from his home in Sugarland, Texas. "I think the Astros were pretty serious about signing me, but the Giants were more serious."[12]

Rosen knew Bass's talent well. He was with the Astros in 1982, and responsible for prying him away from the Brewers.

Bass had been batting fifth with Houston and admitted he might have been trying to do too much to lead the Astros' offense. With the Giants he was slated to bat second between Brett Butler and Will Clark.

He was especially excited about returning to the Bay area. His wife had grown up in Palo Alto, and both their parents still lived there. Bass said his agent had also received calls from Montreal, Cleveland, Detroit, and Milwaukee — along with a call from Japan. They were also attempting to

Kevin Bass made his major-league debut with the Brewers in 1982. Part of the blockbuster trade to the Houston Astros for Don Sutton in September 1982, Bass was an All-Star in 1986 and batted .270 in 14 seasons.

gain interest from the San Diego Padres and Los Angeles Dodgers.

But an injury to his left knee on May 27, 1990, limited Bass's impact with the Giants. Although he was able to return after surgery that September, he later admitted that it took almost three years for his injury to heal. Dogged by the creaky knee and unable to provide the solid defense and consistency he had become known for, he hit .252 and .233 in his first two seasons with San Francisco. "I didn't realize how important (speed) was to me," he said at spring training in March 1992. "Man, if you can't run you can't hit. If you can't run you can't play defense."[13]

The Giants traded Bass to the New York Mets near the end of the 1992 season and after the season, a free agent, again, he re-signed with the Astros. He said later that it took until the 1993 season until his knee to fully heal, and by that time he had lost any legitimate chance to remain a starting outfielder in Houston.

The players strike in 1994 very much hurt Bass's career. On July 31, 1994 the Astros obtained veteran outfielder Milt Thompson from the Phillies with the idea of platooning him with Bass, who was struggling with right-handed pitching. On August 12 the season ended with the players strike, and didn't resume until April 1995.

During the strike-bound offseason Bass was again a free agent, and he signed with the Orioles. Baltimore released him after a season in which he hit .244 with five home runs. He spent 1996 at home in Sugarland. He later said he was "just being a dad to my kids and husband to my wife."[14] He became a 5-handicap golfer with a powerful drive. As his own father had done, he coached the little league team for his two older sons. Just before he decided to attempt a comeback with the Angels, he had been offered a job hosting a radio talk show. The general manager agreed to hold the job open for six weeks.

Before the 1997 season Bass signed a minor-league contract with the Anaheim Angels. He had been offered a job hosting a radio talk show, and the station manager agreed to hold the job open for six weeks. Bass arrived at spring training two months short of his 38th birthday but taut and slim and hoping to make a comeback. In the Angels camp he remembered that the years with the Giants had been hard and were a turning point in the way he looked at his career. "The funny thing is that it doesn't matter how much money you have. My wife and I, we're financially stable. We can do whatever we want, and go wherever we want. But you realize that is not really the answer. Your financial needs are met, but you need something to care about, to care about and that you can get some fulfillment out of."[15]

Bass was unable to return to the major leagues. Hampered by an Achilles' tendon injury, he announced his retirement on May 20, 1997, after playing in four games with the Angels' Triple-A team at Vancouver.

Bass and his wife, Elaine, have four children. In 2007 two of his sons were selected in the major-league draft. Garrett was selected by the Washington Nationals in the 42nd round from Jacksonville State University and played four minor league seasons, including the 2010 season an independent league playing for his father's former manager Hal Lanier. Justin, a 21st-round pick by the Angels, played for seven seasons after high school, and also ended his career in independent ball.

Bass and his wife founded a real-estate investment business in Texas in 1993, and he continued to attend events on behalf of the Astros, as well as taking part in old-timers' games, fantasy baseball camps and other events.

"It's a fraternity," Bass said. "It's a time in the players' lives that basically is probably the best time of our lives. Ten, fifteen years, however long you played, you just meet some of the best guys ever. It's always great to be able to come back, just get together and just reminisce, talk about the good old days and watch these [current Astros] out there do the stuff that we used to be able to do."[16]

SOURCES

The addition to the works cited in the Notes, the author consulted Baseball-Reference.com, Retrosheet.org, and The Sporting News, as well as the following:

Stone, Larry. "Baseball Goes Shopping," *Santa Rosa* (California) *Press Democrat*, December 6, 1987: 37.

Krell, David. "Hal Lanier," SABR BioProject, sabr.org/bioproj/person/2bd24617.

Briley, Ron. "The Greatest Game Ever Played? October 15. 1986," *SABR: The National Pastime*, 2014. sabr.org/research/greatest-game-ever-played-october-15-1986.

Costello, Rory. "October 15, 1986: Mets Win NLCS Thriller in 16 Innings," SABR Games Project, sabr.org/gamesproj/game/october-15-1986-mets-win-thriller-16-innings.

NOTES

1. Buster Olney, "Getting Started; Remembering Roots, New O's Look Back Fondly," *Baltimore Sun*, May 1, 1995: 31, 41.
2. Chris Haft, "Motivation Stands Out Most When Recalling a Major Leaguer," *Twin Falls* (Idaho) *Times-News*, June 26, 1984: 17.
3. Stanley Johnson Obituary, Duggan's Serra Mortuary, Daly City, California, April 2012. duggans-serra.com/obituary/Stanley-Lucius-Johnson/Daly-City-CA/1062910.
4. Associated Press, "Molitor May Succeed Yount," *Chippewa Falls* (Wisconsin) *Herald Telegram*, June 8, 1977: 12.
5. "Kevin Bass Career File," *Baltimore Sun*, May 19,1995 p 173
6. "Eastern League," *The Sporting News*, June 23, 1979: 44.
7. Terrence Moore, "Blown Out Giants Try to Regroup," *San Francisco Examiner*, September 9, 1982: 63-66.
8. Steve Sneddon, "Everything Right for Bass This Spring," *Reno Gazette-Journal*, March 17, 1992: 25.
9. "Voice of the Fan/Conlin Confused," *The Sporting News*, August 11, 1986: 6.
10. Ray Kerby, An Interview with Kevin Bass, January 14, 2002, Astros-Daily.com. astrosdaily.com/players/interviews/Bass_Kevin.html.
11. Richard Obert, "To Improve Cast, Giants Catch Bass, Throw Him in Right," *Arizona Republic* (Phoenix), April 8, 1990: 49.
12. Larry Stone, "Giants Hook Bass," *Santa Rosa* (California) *Press Democrat*, November 17, 1989: 37.
13. Sneddon.
14. Gwen Knapp, "Bass Among Old Vets Trying to Come Back." *Daily Oklahoman* (Oklahoma City), March 9, 1997: 253.
15. Ibid.
16. Alyson Footer, "Astros Host Ex-players for Legends Weekend, MLB.com, August 11, 2018. mlb.com/astros/news/astros-host-annual-legends-weekend/c-289917276.

DWIGHT BERNARD

By J.G. Preston

Dwight Bernard took an unusual path to the major leagues. He played one year of high-school baseball, in which he pitched just a few games and won only one, then went to a tiny Baptist college that did not offer intercollegiate sports. He transferred to another small college that had a baseball team but to that point had only three alumni who had moved on to professional ball. But Bernard became a second-round draft pick in June 1974 and made the big leagues, pitching in the 1982 World Series before launching a career of more than 30 years as a pitching coach in pro ball.

Dwight Vern Bernard (accent on the last syllable) was born on May 31, 1952, in Mount Vernon, Illinois, to Murrel and LaVerne (Adams) Bernard. He was the second oldest of eight siblings: four boys and four girls.[1] Mount Vernon is the seat of Jefferson County in the southern part of the state with a population of about 15,000. Dwight grew up on the family farm near the small village of Belle Rive (rhymes with "five"), about 10 miles southeast.

Murrel Bernard opened a grain elevator on the farm in 1959 and established a business, M. Bernard & Sons Grain Co. He hauled grain until he was 92 and was driving a combine the evening before he suffered a stroke at the age of 94.[2] He died in October 2017. The farm and the grain business remained in the family.

"We have about 400 acres, mostly soybeans and sometimes corn," Bernard said in 2018.[3] "Three of us brothers work at the grain elevator, the other two are there year round. Whenever I get done with baseball I'm heading back that way also. My brothers and I will keep it going as long as health and everything works out good. We all live just right around there close. Mom and dad's house is not an eighth of a mile away from mine." Bernard's mother was still living on the farm when this was written in July 2018.

"We enjoyed baseball," Bernard said. "Dad would take us over to St. Louis (about 90 miles northwest) and we'd watch the Cardinals. Back in the fourth grade, I believe it was, I had a teacher that had us write down what we wanted to be, and I had professional baseball player on the top of the list, I don't know why. Mom's still got that paper, too. I don't even remember doing that."

Bernard played church league basketball and summer Khoury League baseball for high-school boys, but he didn't play at Mount Vernon Township High School until his senior year, when he played basketball and baseball. "I had to work on the farm and really didn't have transportation," he said by way of explanation. When he finally did put on a high-school baseball uniform, it didn't take long for him to make an impression. In his first start on the mound, he pitched a no-hitter, striking out the first six batters he faced and a total of 15 in the seven-inning game.[4] Yet that would be his only win as a high-school pitcher. He played center field when he didn't pitch.

Playing professional baseball would seem to have been the furthest thing from Bernard's mind when he graduated from high school in 1970. That fall he enrolled at Free Will Baptist Bible College in Nashville, where his older brother, Gil, was already a student.[5] Free Will had only about 300 students and did not offer intercollegiate athletics, although there was an active sports program organized by the campus fraternities. "They had basketball, baseball, and football," Bernard said. "I just enjoyed playing them all; being competitive was probably the biggest thing."

Bernard left Free Will after his first semester when he was declared ineligible to play. "I flunked a two-hour course, and somebody else at another fraternity who was pretty good flunked a three-hour course, and it was decided that I couldn't play sports and he could," is how Bernard remembered it. Upset about what seemed an injustice, Bernard transferred to another small (but slightly larger) Baptist school in Nashville, one that did have an intercollegiate baseball team.

That school is now known as Belmont University. It has grown in recent years to have about 8,000 students. Its teams compete in the NCAA Division I Ohio Valley Conference; the men's basketball team has played in the NCAA tournament, and a number of its baseball players have gone on to the pro ranks in recent years. But when Bernard arrived on campus in January 1971, the school was known as Belmont College. It had about 1,000 students and its teams belonged to the National Association of Intercollegiate Athletics (NAIA), playing other small Tennessee schools in the Volunteer State Athletic Conference.

Bernard walked on to the baseball team at Belmont. "Their coach didn't know me at all," he said. He made the team as a freshman and pitched four seasons at Belmont while majoring in physical education.[6]

"My freshman and sophomore years, I didn't know where the ball was going," Bernard said in 1974. "All I did was throw hard because that's all I knew how to do. Coach Dave Whitten did so much for me. He taught me techniques, taught me not to roll my head from side to side in my delivery. He made me concentrate on pitching to a spot, made me concentrate on what I was doing. I realized control was the key to success I might have as a pitcher."[7]

As a junior in 1973 he was the team's most valuable pitcher and made the Nashville all-city team, posting a 2.17 ERA in 68 innings, including seven shutout innings against Belmont's much bigger crosstown rival, Vanderbilt.[8] His performance that season gave him hopes of possibly playing professionally.

Bernard married a fellow Belmont College student, Barbara Lankford, on August 25, 1973. They were still married as this was written in 2018 and had three children, son Jason (born in 1974) and daughters Jamie (1978) and Kelley (1982). Jason played baseball at Belmont, as did Dwight's younger brother Tom. Dwight's older brother, Gil (who finished his college education at Belmont), never played high-school or college baseball, but he was a very successful high-school baseball coach and administrator, and he was inducted into the Illinois High School Baseball Coaches Association Hall of Fame in 2007.

As a senior in 1974, Bernard drew attention from pro scouts around the country. He went 8-0 with a 1.39 ERA and struck out 97 batters in 84⅓ innings to earn NAIA All-District 24 first-team honors. He struck out 16 in his final college appearance, against Millikin, and his 234 career strikeouts were a school record at the time (and as of 2018 ranked fourth in school history).[9]

In June 1974 Bernard became the first Belmont player ever drafted, when the New York Mets made him their second-round selection, the 41st player chosen overall. (Jerry Bell, who was drafted by the Seattle Pilots in January 1969 and pitched for the Brewers from 1971 to 1974, pitched for Belmont in 1966 and '67 before transferring to Rhodes College, where he finished his collegiate career. As of 2018, Bernard and Bell were the only major leaguers who played at Belmont. Prior to Bell, two other Belmont alumni had played in the minors, but neither was drafted.)

Mets scout Paul Tretiak signed Bernard the day after the draft (for a bonus of "a little over $20,000," Bernard said at the time).[10] Bernard was assigned to Victoria (Texas) in the Double-A Texas League, and his pro career began with a bang. In his second start he pitched a five-hit shutout.[11] A three-hit shutout followed two weeks later,[12] and in August he went 12 innings to get a 2-1 win.[13] Bernard finished his half-season at Victoria with a 7-4 record and a 3.06 ERA in 14 starts, then earned a 4-1 victory in the second game of the playoffs as Victoria won the league championship.[14]

Bernard was invited to major-league spring training in 1975, to throw batting practice, and was promoted to Triple-A Tidewater. He got off to a great start: through June 11 he had a record of 6-3 (the Tides were shut out in two of his losses) with an ERA of 2.05.[15] But he struggled at times after that, and his final season record was 9-9 with a 3.29 ERA in 126 innings, with more walks than strikeouts. For the second straight year he was on a championship team, as the Tides had the International League's best regular-season record and then won the league playoffs, although Bernard missed the playoffs with tendinitis in his pitching shoulder.

"Toward the end of 1975, probably the last month and a half, I had a little soreness that couldn't let go," he recalled in 2018. "Of course you never tell anybody. I had heard horror stories from some of the older guys, so I wasn't sayin' nothin'. I was just hoping that I could get through it."

At the time he blamed his injuries on bad coaching. "I got fouled up because some people in the Mets organization tried to change my pitching style," he said as he prepared to head to spring training in 1976.[16] He elaborated in 2018: "With Tom Seaver and Jerry Koosman and those guys there [with the Mets], they wanted to try to mold guys a little bit after them."

Back at Tidewater in 1976, Bernard lost his first seven decisions[17] and had a 1-9 record with a 6.40 ERA when he asked to be sent down to Jackson (Mississippi) in the Texas League. "They wanted to make me a reliever at Tidewater and I didn't want that," he said. "I asked to go to Jackson because I wanted to be a starter. I felt I started coming around once I got to Jackson."[18] It went a little bit better for him at Jackson, as he went 2-5 with a 4.17 ERA in nine starts.

After going to spring training with the Mets in 1977, Bernard was sent back to Tidewater and had another undistinguished season as a starter, finishing with a 9-13 record and a 4.32 ERA. He started only four more games in pro ball after that, as the Mets made the decision in the spring of 1978 to move him to the bullpen.

"At first I wasn't very happy, because I'd seen some of the relief pitchers sat for two or three weeks sometimes and didn't pitch," Bernard remembered. "I had a very good spring as a starter and right at the very end they decided to make that move. I wasn't very happy, I stayed home for a day or two before I decided to try it and see."

"I had a very good spring as a starter and right at the very end they decided to make that move," Bernard remembered. "I wasn't very happy, because I'd seen some of the relief pitchers sat for two or three weeks sometimes and didn't pitch. I stayed home for a day or two before I decided to try it and see."

Bernard thrived in the bullpen at Tidewater, going 5-3 with two saves and a 1.64 ERA, before making his major-league debut with the Mets on June 29. He spent the rest of the season in the Mets' bullpen, posting a record of 1-4 with a 4.31 ERA.

He went north with the Mets in 1979 and didn't allow an earned run in 14 of his first 17 appearances, but he was hit hard enough in the other three games that he had a 4.50 ERA when he was sent back to Tidewater in late May. "I thought I was better than at least four guys they kept," he said. "I was surprised when I was sent down — and so were the other guys on the team."[19]

Again Bernard pitched well in the International League, this time as the Tides' closer, with a 1.95 ERA and 13 saves in two months before he was recalled by the Mets on July 27.[20] Bernard said general manager Joe McDonald, manager Joe Torre, and pitching coach Rube Walker made promises when he was recalled that weren't kept.

"They called me into the office for a meeting," Bernard said. "They said I had proved myself at Tidewater, that no one else was doing the job and that the bullpen was mine. But it never happened. I never got a chance to save a game."[21]

He was sent back to Tidewater a few weeks later before returning to New York after the International League season. His final Tidewater numbers were great — 16 saves and a 1.77 ERA (he was second in the league in saves despite spending less than half the season there) — but with the Mets he was 0-3 with a 4.70 ERA.

After the season the Mets moved on, trading Bernard to the Milwaukee Brewers for Mark Bomback, who had just earned Minor League Player of the Year honors from The Sporting News by going 22-7 with Vancouver in the Pacific Coast League. "When you get traded, you gotta feel like somebody wants you," Bernard said. "I thought that would be a pretty good opportunity."

But 1980 was basically a lost season for Bernard; he pitched just 33 innings between Triple-A Vancouver and Double-A Holyoke (Massachusetts), with an ERA above 7.00 at both stops. Surgery on the thumb of his pitching hand caused him to miss a chunk of the season. "They said it was some sort of a tumor, on the right-hand side of my thumb beside my thumbnail, it was a big knot," he remembered. "My control had come around pretty good, and then it left me because I couldn't grip the baseball the way I needed to. They took it out and everything was good after that."

Going into 1981, Bernard's career was on the line. "When I went to spring training, I knew if I didn't do well, I'd be sent home," he said. "I was realistic about it."[22] But Brewers manager Buck Rodgers liked what he saw in the spring enough to

In his last of four seasons in the majors, reliever Dwight Bernard appeared in 47 games for the Brewers in 1982, which trailed only Rollie Fingers' 50.

send Bernard to Vancouver, where he saved 11 games with a 3.35 ERA and had the best strikeout rate of his pro career (7.4 per nine innings). That earned him a return to the major leagues when the rosters expanded in September, and he had a 3.60 ERA in six outings for the Brewers.

That was the year of the players strike, and a playoff was held in each major-league division pitting the team with the best record before the strike against the team with the best record after play resumed. The Brewers went 31-22 after the strike for the best record in the American League East and advanced to the playoff against the Yankees, who had the division's best pre-strike record. When Reggie Cleveland developed tendinitis, the Brewers chose Bernard to take Cleveland's place in the bullpen for the postseason.

Bernard got into two games against the Yankees, both games that the Brewers lost (they lost the best-of-five series in five games), and retired all seven batters he faced. "It looks like we might have found a pitcher," general manager Harry Dalton said.[23]

Bernard spent all of 1982 with the Brewers, the only year of his career he spent entirely in the major leagues. His 47 pitching appearances were second-most on the team, behind Hall of Famer Rollie Fingers, and his six saves were tied with Jim Slaton for second on the team behind Fingers. He finished the year with a 3-1 record and a 3.76 ERA, helping the Brewers win the AL East and advance to the World Series.

Asked in 2018 about his memories of the championship season, Bernard said, "Probably the number-one thing was I got my first major-league save against Minnesota [on May 2]. And I struck out Gary Gaetti from Centralia, Illinois [about 40 miles from Bernard's home in Belle Rive], three times, that was a pretty good feeling." (Gaetti was 0-for-4 against Bernard that year, with a walk and a sacrifice bunt.)

The Brewers' bullpen was thrown into chaos when Fingers tore a muscle in his right (pitching) forearm on September 2, an injury that caused him to miss the entire 1983 season.[24] From that point on, Bernard and rookie Pete Ladd each had two saves in the regular season, Slaton one and Moose Haas (who had been used mostly as a starter) one. But when the postseason came around, Bernard was all but forgotten by Harvey Kuenn, who had replaced Rodgers as manager in June.

Ladd got two saves and Slaton one in the American League Championship Series against the Angels. Bernard made just one appearance, entering Game One with Milwaukee trailing by five runs and pitching a perfect inning. In the World Series the Brewers' two saves were by Bob McClure, who made only eight of his 34 regular-season appearances in relief and did not save a game. McClure pitched in relief five times in the seven-game series and was the losing pitcher twice. Haas, Mike Caldwell, and Doc Medich, who were all primarily starters during the regular season, also were used in relief in the World Series, against St. Louis.

"When you start bringing starters in out of the bullpen, guys who are out of their realm, they didn't have the proper time to warm up, they didn't go through their normal routines… it's a lot different," Bernard said. "It was the bullpen that got us there, and then all of a sudden it changes, and that was an aggravating thing. But I was a team guy and I just wanted to win, and if those guys could do it, then that was fine. I felt like there were a couple of times in there where I had been used in those situations, and it didn't happen."

Bernard took the mound once in the World Series, entering Game Six with the Brewers trailing 13-0, and pitched a scoreless inning. In his four career postseason appearances he retired 13 of the 14 batters he faced, the other one reaching on an error.

Little did Bernard know that his World Series appearance would be his last in the major leagues. After a rough spring training in 1983, when he had a 10.13 ERA in five appearances, Bernard was released.[25] A month later he signed a minor-league contract with the Astros[26] and spent two seasons with their Triple-A Tucson team before pitching for the Orioles' Double-A team at Charlotte in 1985.

Bernard pitched well at Charlotte, but when the season ended without his getting a chance to return to the majors, he decided to end his playing career. "I was still throwing the ball pretty good, that's for sure," he remembered, "but I was 33 years old and everybody kind of went with youth in the minor-league free-agent deal. It really gave you no choice but to figure out something else to do."

What that "something else" turned out to be stemmed from his experience after he had surgery in 1980 and was rehabbing at Double-A Holyoke. "They didn't have a pitching coach," Bernard said. "Well, I was down in the bullpen working with those kids. Me being a guy who had some major-league experience, they were all younger guys, why wouldn't they listen? And they did, they listened. It was fun, and we ended up winning the Eastern League championship."

That made an impression on team owner Tom Kayser, who in 1986 was the Pittsburgh Pirates' assistant minor-league director. Kayser gave Bernard a job as pitching coach of the Pirates' Class-A affiliate in Macon (Georgia) that year, and as of 2018 Bernard has been a pitching coach ever since. He coached at the minor-league level in all those years except for one he spent in the Alaska summer league.

Asked what he liked about coaching, Bernard said, "Working with the kids and watching them improve and be successful, that's the biggest thing. Even the guys who didn't make it to the big leagues, those are the guys you're going to help the most, trying to make their careers last as long as you can and making them better ballplayers as organizational-type guys. It's fun, I have a lot of good memories from young men that I hear from here and there."

SOURCES

Newspaper articles were accessed via newspapers.com and newspaperarchive.com. Thanks to Bill Francis of the National Baseball Hall of Fame Library for sharing Bernard's player file there, and thanks to April Szarek of the C.E. Brehm Memorial Library in Mount Vernon, Illinois, for sharing pages from the 1970 Mount Vernon Township High School yearbook.

NOTES

1. Murrel Bernard's obituary with names of all the family members is online at obituaries.commercial-news.com/obituary/murrel-bernard-1923-2017-995741311.
2. Ibid.
3. Telephone interview with Dwight Bernard, February 16, 2018. Unless otherwise attributed, all quotes from Dwight in this article are from this interview.
4. "Bernard No-Hits Tamaroa," *Mt. Vernon* (Illinois) *Register-News*, May 1, 1970: 9. The Register-News is available on newspapers.com, and a search finds only three games in which Bernard pitched. In what appears to be his only other start he pitched a two-hitter and lost, with both the runs he allowed unearned. In a July 1974 interview, Bernard said he pitched four times in high school. Cecil Parker, "Bernard Hopes Wild Days Gone Forever," *Victoria* (Texas) *Advocate*, July 13, 1974: 1B. But a 1978 story said Bernard pitched only three games in high school with a 1-2 record. Alan Freedman, "Mt. Vernon's Bernard (P)itching to Stay in Majors," *Southern Illinoisan* (Carbondale, Illinois), September 19, 1978: 13.
5. The campus moved 30 miles northeast to Gallatin, Tennessee, in 2008, and the school's name was changed to Welch College in 2012.
6. Team media guides from his playing days (Mets 1979, Brewers 1982, Brewers 1983) show Bernard as having a B.S. in physical education from Belmont, but a check with school officials in July 1978 through studentclearinghouse.org showed Bernard did not earn a degree.
7. Bob Forbes, "Dwight Bernard Enjoying Success With Texas Club," *Mt. Vernon Register-News*, July 19, 1974: 1-B.
8. Jeff Hanna, "Rebels Clip Vandy 1-0," *Tennessean* (Nashville), April 25, 1973: 25. The game was scheduled for seven innings as part of a doubleheader; Bernard was replaced after seven innings because of a foot injury, with the game tied 0-0. Belmont scored in the bottom of the eighth to win the game.
9. Bernard's 1974 ERA was a school season record at the time and ranks fourth in school history as of 2018. His strikeout total that year was also a school season record at the time and ranked fifth in school history as of 2018. His career ERA at Belmont of 2.18 was tied for second in school history as of 2018.
10. David Climer, "Belmont Grad Still Learning," *Tennessean*, August 9, 1974: 54.
11. "Bernard Hurls Shutout," *The Sporting News*, July 13, 1974: 36.
12. *The Sporting News*, Jtuly 27, 1974: 57.
13. "Iron-Man Bernard Wins, 2-1," *Mt. Vernon Register-News*, August 19, 1974: 1-B.
14. Dwight Rowin, "Victoria Tops El Paso in Texas Series," *The Sporting News*, September 21, 1974: 38.
15. Bob Forbes, "Fine Year for Bernard," *Mt. Vernon Register-News*, June 13, 1975: 1-B; "International league Batting and Pitching Records," *The Sporting News*, July 5, 1975: 34.

16   Bob Forbes, "In Sports It's Wise Not to Assume," *Mt. Vernon Register-News*, March 5, 1976: 1-B.

17   Bob Forbes, "Sideline Watching," *Mt. Vernon Register-News*, July 1, 1976: 1-B.

18   Bob Forbes, "Bernard to South America," *Mt. Vernon Register-News*, November 16, 1976: 1-B.

19   Mike Chamness, "Mt. Vernon's Bernard Glad to Leave 'Big Apple.'" *Southern Illinoisan*, October 31, 1979: 15.

20   "Mets Recall Mt. Vernon's Bernard," *Southern Illinoisan*, July 29, 1979: 14.

21   Chamness, "Mt. Vernon's Bernard Glad to Leave 'Big Apple.'"

22   Tom Flaherty, "Brewers' Bernard Makes a Big Leap," *The Sporting News*, November 7, 1981: 26.

23   Ibid.

24   Dale Voiss, "Rollie Fingers," Society for American Baseball Research BioProject, sabr.org/bioproj/person/4e17d265.

25   Mike Estel, "Bernard Cut by Milwaukee," *Southern Illinoisan*, March 29, 1983: 13.

26   "Bernard Joins Astros System," *Southern Illinoisan*, May 18, 1983: 12.

MARK BROUHARD

By Isaac Buttke

Mark Brouhard isn't one of the names people think of when they discuss the 1982 Brewers. Many other players who were a part of Harvey's Wallbangers went on for storied, even Hall of Fame-worthy careers. Paul Molitor, Robin Yount, Rollie Fingers, Don Sutton, Cecil Cooper… this team was a who's who of great Brewers, and may have arguably been the greatest Brewers roster ever assembled. With that in mind, Brouhard's presence is easy to overlook at first. However, Milwaukee's World Series run may not have come to fruition had it not been for Brouhard's contributions in his lone playoff appearance during that fateful 1982 season.

Mark Steven Brouhard was born on May 22, 1956, in Burbank, California. Despite his father's wishes that he take up hunting or fishing, Brouhard's mother persuaded him to play baseball. "She liked the sport and she urged me to play in a park league," he recalled in a 1979 interview with *The Sporting News*.[1] "She always wanted me out of the house. I guess I caused too much trouble. She encouraged me to play sandlot ball. I liked hunting and fishing, but I liked baseball better."

He remained in the Burbank area for much of his pre-professional life, ultimately attending El Camino Real High School in Woodland Hills, California, where he garnered all-conference honors after batting .395 for the season. He played at Los Angeles Pierce College in 1974 and 1975, batting over .300 both seasons as a catcher, and was named to the all-conference team. (Fellow major leaguers Greg Garrett, Rick Auerbach, and Doug DeCinces also played for Pierce, a junior college.)

After two years at Pierce, Brouhard entered the January 1976 amateur draft. (At this draft session, teams would select from junior-college players and those whose eligibility had expired.) The California Angels selected Brouhard with their fourth-round pick.

Brouhard felt he was overlooked as a draft prospect. "I wasn't drafted very high and I wasn't even signed as a draftee," he told *The Sporting News* in 1979. "I thought about giving up baseball."[2] This was before Angels scout Joe Carpenter took him to a team workout camp. "I went there every single Sunday for about five or six months," Broussard said. "I guess I improved and I was signed."[3]

Although Brouhard was primarily a catcher during his prep days, the Angels seemed intent on using him as an outfielder, and he primarily acted as a designated hitter in his first pro season (44 of 69 games). Commenting on his defense, Brouhard was relatively bearish. "There's no doubt about it. My batting is better than my fielding. Even though I was signed as a catcher, I've never played a game as a catcher. I don't think they're too high on my arm," he said in 1979.[4]

Assigned to the Idaho Fall Angels of the rookie-level Pioneer League, Broussard batted .314 in 291 plate appearances with 7 home runs and 57 RBIs. (His BA was only third-best on the team but sixth in the league.)

Brouhard's next stop was in the Arizona Instructional League. This isn't the same as today's Arizona Fall League, where the most prestigious prospects gather to tout their talents before major-league scouts. Brouhard earned league all-star honors.[5]

Brouhard's next assignment was a full-season league. In 1977 he spent the entire year with the Salinas Angels in the Class-A California League. In 136 games (which would prove to be the highest number of games he'd ever play in a single season), he batted .278 with 16 homers. Since the 21-year-old Brouhard was younger than the average player at the level, the Angels had him repeat the level the following year.

Before heading back to Salinas, however, Brouhard took another tour of the Arizona Instructional League. This proved to be a good move, as he finished with an unofficial .400 batting average and another all-star selection.[6]

In his second year in the California League, Brouhard improved markedly. His batting average jumped up 32 points to .310, and his OPS skyrocketed nearly 100 points. A home run he hit in the Salinas ballpark in June was touted as having traveled an improbable 600 feet, and spurred this item in *The Sporting News*:

Managers Stan Wasiak of Lodi (California) and Chuck Cottier of Salinas were in agreement on one thing June 26: the homer hit by the Angels' Mark Brouhard was the longest either of the veteran pilots had ever seen. The ball was estimated to have traveled 600 feet in the air. It cleared the left field fence, the stadium parking lot and a row of houses beyond, landing in the parking lot of a market.[7]

The team later measured the drive at 533 feet. Real or not, and other long home runs Broussard hit during the season earned the nickname "Mad Bomber."[8]

After this strong showing, Brouhard was moved up to the Double-A El Paso Diablos of the Texas League for 1979, and posted an MVP and all-star season. Brouhard batted a league-leading .350 with 28 home runs, 107 RBIs, and 97 runs scored en route to winning the league's first Triple Crown since 1927… it seemed. But a recheck of the statistics showed that Jim Tracy of Midland had accumulated enough plate appearances to qualify for the batting title, outhitting Brouhard by five points.[9]

That wasn't enough to earn him a spot on the Angels' roster just yet, and Brouhard was eligible to be taken in the Rule 5 draft at the 1979 Winter Meetings in Toronto. He was plucked from the Angels organization by the Milwaukee Brewers.

Many people were surprised, as the Brewers already had their fair share of right-handed power bats in the lineup. But Brewers general manager Harry Dalton thought Brouhard's bat was simply too good to pass up. "We didn't think he would still be available," Dalton said. "His bat was just too attractive not to take a chance."[10]

Brewers farm director Ray Poitevint was also high on Brouhard. "We tried to make a trade for him [in 1979] on the minor-league level," Poitevint said. "He's a hitting fool."[11] But the outlook for Brouhard wasn't as good as it might have been had he remained with California. If the Brewers wanted to keep him in the organization, they would have to keep him on the major-league roster for all of the 1980 season. Otherwise, they'd have to offer him back to the Angels for half his draft price of $25,000. This was a daunting task considering that the Brewers already had outfielders Gorman Thomas, Sixto Lezcano, Ben Oglivie, and Larry Hisle. The expectation was that Brouhard would likely only contribute as a pinch-hitter with an occasional start in the outfield or as the designated hitter.[12]

This expectation did indeed become reality. Brouhard played in only 45 games (13 starts in the field) for Milwaukee in 1980. He batted .232 with 5 home runs. This was the first time Brouhard was ever relegated to the bench full-time in his playing career. "I've never sat in my life, not even in Little League," he said. "It's been a little bit of an adjustment for me. … Sometimes it gets depressing, sitting a lot. At least I'm here, and that's been my goal. Basically, I think I prefer being here instead of in Triple A, but sometimes I wish I could play more."[13]

The Brewers felt the same way at the time. "Naturally, the ideal situation would be to put him where he can play every day," commented Buck Rodgers, the Brewers' acting manager while George Bamberger was sidelined after heart bypass surgery. "In absence of that, he's getting a lot of work." The work Rodgers was discussing included not only fielding drills and batting practice, but also workouts at first base to increase his versatility off the bench.[14]

Broussard did manage to make some impact during his first major-league season. He collected his first major-league hit after replacing an ejected Sixto Lezcano against the Twins on May 24, then followed that up with a diving catch in right field. He hit his first big-league homer the next day.

With full control of Brouhard heading into the 1981 season, the Brewers were finally able to send him to the minors for more seasoning. He started the season with the Vancouver Canadians of the Triple-A Pacific Coast League. He got into only 16 games with Vancouver before an injury to Paul Molitor led to his being summoned back to Milwaukee. He had 199 plate appearances with the Brewers and batted .274.

Manager Buck Rodgers praised Broussard's defense. "Everything he does isn't pretty out there," Rodgers said. "Everything he gets to, he catches. He's not a bad outfielder, in fact, he's better than average. He just doesn't always look good doing it."[15]

Brouhard wasn't able to stick with the Brewers for their 1981 playoff run. Shortly before the American League Division Series against the Yankees, he pulled a calf muscle and was unable to play in the series, in which the Yankees ousted the Brewers from the postseason.

Heading into the 1982 campaign, the Brewers thought of getting Brouhard more playing time by moving Molitor to third base. This would create a chain reaction in the lineup that would move Gorman Thomas back into center field and open up right field for Brouhard. "I would like that," Brouhard said. "But they haven't committed themselves in any way. I think I have to go to spring training and do the job and try to earn the position. I don't think anything is guaranteed in this game, especially for me."[16]

Most expected Brouhard to win the job out of the gate, and he did just that. Brouhard showed up to spring training "about 20 pounds lighter than [1981], worked hard and had a good spring."[17] He started in right field on Opening Day. Things changed quickly, however, as he wound up ceding much of his playing time to Charlie Moore, who got off to a torrid start to begin the season. Although Brouhard did his job, the man affectionately known by Brewers fans as "Big Bro" was forced to wait on the bench even more.[18]

Even though it was simply a "hot bat" that had Moore playing over Brouhard in right field, it seemed as if Brouhard was largely passed over for the remainder of the season. The Californian wound up playing in just 40 games for Milwaukee, batting a modest .269 with 4 home runs and 10 RBIs. He was demoted to Triple-A Vancouver for a bit, producing a .282 batting average in 17 contests for the Canadians. Brouhard was included on the big-league playoff roster, although he played in only one game. What a single game it was, though.

Brouhard started Game Four of the American League Championship Series against the Angels, the team that drafted him. This was because of a rib injury suffered by Ben Oglivie. It was said that Brouhard didn't even learn about the start from coach Sal Bando until a half-hour before the game. "I went over and looked at the lineup card and

Backup outfielder Mark Brouhard played six seasons in the majors (1980-1985), all with the Brewers, batting .259 with 25 home runs.

there I was," Brouhard commented.[19] Although the circumstances of his start were less than ideal, the result was well needed. The team was down two games to one in the series, and Brouhard provided the spark needed to create a Game Five.

Brouhard opened the scoring with an RBI single. The Brewers cruised to a 7-0 lead behind a stellar outing from Moose Haas, but the Angels crept back and made things interesting thanks to a grand slam by Don Baylor. Brouhard slammed the door shut after that, though, bashing a two-run homer to bring Milwaukee a 9-5 victory. He closed the day at 3-for-4 with a double, a home run, three RBIs, and four runs scored (the latter tying a playoff record).

This performance wasn't enough to land Brouhard any more playing time, though. He sat on the bench for the remainder of the playoffs and watched as the Brewers lost the World Series to the Cardinals. "That's just the way things worked out," Brouhard said in 1991. "I had my ups and downs during my career, but I have no regrets. It was a great experience."[20]

Brouhard was never able to live up to the potential the Brewers thought he had. He split time between the big leagues and Triple-A Vancouver over the following three seasons, hitting just .257 with 14 homers for Milwaukee in that span. He also lost the speed component of his game, as he went 0-for-7 on stolen-base attempts during that timeframe.

After those three disappointing seasons, Brouhard took his talents to Japan. He agreed to play for the Yakult Swallows in 1986 and stayed there into the next season, 140 games altogether with 23 home runs and 69 RBIs. His most interesting memory from Japan came during a rain delay in which he donned the mascot's head, pretended to hit home runs and slid across the rain-soaked tarp to the fans' great amusement.[21]

Brouhard briefly returned Stateside for an attempted comeback with the Angels organization, but opted to retire after the 1987 season in order to spend more time with his family. He bounced around from job to job before founding a painting business with a neighbor.[22] In 2016 he was inducted into the Texas League Hall of Fame.[23]

Brouhard was one of the biggest "what if's?" in Brewers history. Despite much potential given his success in the minor-leagues, he never got a full chance to prove his worth in the big leagues. Could he have made a big enough difference in that 1982 World Series to push Milwaukee over the hump? It's something we can never know.

SOURCES

In addition to the sources cited in the Notes, the author consulted Baseball-Reference.com (baseball-reference.com/players/b/brouhma01.shtml) and Baseball-Almanac.com,

NOTES

1. Jim Thomas, "Brouhard Mother's Gift to Angels," *The Sporting News*, September 1, 1979: 62.
2. Ibid.
3. Ibid.
4. Ibid.
5. Ed Prell, "Leonard Unanimous Pick on Cactus Loop All-Stars," *The Sporting News*, December 4, 1976: 71.
6. Ed Prell, "Three Cub Pitchers All-Stars," *The Sporting News*, November 19, 1977: 63.
7. *The Sporting News*, July 22, 1978: 48.
8. *The Sporting News*, August 12, 1978: 42.
9. Kim Brazell, "Triple Crown Vanishes," *The Sporting News*, September 29, 1979: 40.
10. Tom Flaherty, "Brewers Surprised, Elated to Get Brouhard's Big Bat," *The Sporting News*, December 22, 1979: 53.
11. Ibid.
12. Ibid.
13. Tom Flaherty, "Brewers Like Brouhard's Future," *The Sporting News*, May 24, 1980: 5.
14. Ibid.
15. Tom Flaherty, "Brouhard Fills Brewer Bill," *The Sporting News*, June 20, 1981: 33.
16. Tom Flaherty, "Brewers' Brouhard May Win Steady Job," *The Sporting News*, January 30, 1982: 59.
17. Tom Flaherty, "A Mighty Long Wait for Mark Brouhard," *The Sporting News*, May 17, 1982: 27.
18. "A Mighty Long Wait for Mark Brouhard," 33.
19. "Braves 2 Down, Brewers Even Up," *Daytona Beach* (Florida) *News-Journal*, October 9, 1982: 1C.
20. John Ortega, "Career Remembered for a Game Effort: Hero in Game 4 of '82 American League Playoffs Against Angels Adjusting to Life After Baseball," *Los Angeles Times*, August 17, 1991.
21. Wayne Graczyk, "Keys to Success as a Foreign Ballplayer in Japan," *Japan Times*, November 21, 2015.
22. "Braves 2 Down, Brewers Even Up."
23. "Contingent of RockHounds Executives Elected to TL Hall of Fame," *Midland* (Texas) *Reporter-Telegram*, June 1, 2016.

MIKE CALDWELL

By Isaac Buttke

Baseball is no stranger to big personalities. The game has seen colorful characters ranging from Mark Fidrych and his strange mound antics in the 1970s to Adrian Beltre simply being his ridiculous self after the turn of the century. On the opposite end of the spectrum, players like Nolan Ryan and Roger Clemens are better known for their relatively hot heads. One can find Mike Caldwell, known by many as "Mr. Warmth," in the latter group. The nickname was partly due to his fiery demeanor on the mound. "He's one of the most fierce competitors you'll find in this business," former Padres manager Don Zimmer said.[1] Vic Feuerherd of Madison.com commented that Caldwell was "ornery, obnoxious, nasty and sometimes downright mean."[2] Even so, the passion Caldwell brought to the mound helped make him an instrumental part of the Milwaukee Brewers' run to the World Series in 1982.

Ralph Michael Caldwell was born on January 22, 1949, in Tarboro, North Carolina, to Ralph Franklin and Annie Bruce (Holland) Caldwell. He attended Tarboro High School, then enrolled at North Carolina State University in 1968.

At NC State, Caldwell was expected to be one of the Wolfpack's top pitchers as a freshman thanks to "good control" and "a sneaky fastball," according to the team's preseason outlook booklet.[3] The left-hander's talent was certainly evident at Tarboro High, where he threw three straight shutouts and two consecutive no-hitters.[4] Wolfpack head coach Sam Esposito had tempered optimism regarding Caldwell's standing, saying, "Our young boys like [fellow freshman Joe] Frye and Caldwell have talent, but we just don't know how they'll react in tight situations."[5]

Not only did Caldwell manage to meet those high expectations, but he was a major cog in one of NC State's best seasons ever. The southpaw led the Atlantic Coast Conference with nine complete games, and tied for the conference lead among freshmen with eight victories in 1968. The Wolfpack won the ACC championship with a 25-9 record and made it to the College World Series, where they finished in third place.

Although the team's performance never got back to that exemplary level, Caldwell continued to dominate collegiate hitters. He led the ACC in complete games the next two seasons, led the league in shutouts during his junior and senior years and finished his collegiate career with a 32-10 record and a 2.30 ERA. As of 2019 he remained the ACC's career complete-game (32) and shutout (10) leader. He earned first-team All-ACC honors in 1970 and 1971, and won the ACC Player of the Year award in 1971.[6] He graduated from the university in four years with a degree in sociology.⁷

Coming out of college, Caldwell wasn't a major draft prospect. He wound up falling all the way to the 12th round, where the San Diego Padres selected him with the 273rd overall pick. Caldwell seemed to be disappointed by being selected this low in the draft. In response to the perceived slight, he began hunting for other work and lined up a position with a phone company in Tarboro.⁸ But the Padres increased their signing bonus offer and signed him. In hindsight, the lefty fared much better than the Padres' top draft pick, right-handed pitcher Jay Franklin, who appeared in just three major-league games.

Caldwell began his professional career in the lower levels of the minors and immediately proved his worth. With the short-season Tri-City Padres, he overwhelmed the young hitters, striking out 19 batters and allowing just two runs in 11 innings of work. He was promoted to Class-A Lodi, where he continued his strong showing with a 3.66 ERA and 38 strikeouts in 32 innings.

The Padres, in the midst of what would become a 100-loss season, decided to energize the fan base by calling up three young prospects for the final month of the season: 1971 first-round pick Jay Franklin, 1970 first-round pick Mike Ivie, and Caldwell.⁹ While Franklin and Ivie were more highly regarded because of their more prominent draft position and their relative youth (both were teenagers, forming the youngest battery in the majors that season[10]), Caldwell held his own in his first taste of the majors, pitching a scoreless inning in relief on September 4, 1971. Afterward manager Preston Gomez said, "Caldwell showed me a great sinker and kept the ball down."¹¹ Scouting director Bob Fontaine said, "We're very encouraged the way Franklin, Ivie, and Caldwell broke in. This certainly bodes well for the future of the Padres."¹² Caldwell pitched five more times that September, keeping the opposition scoreless in each instance.

Mr. Warmth's stock kept rising, with many in the organization beginning to take notice. Pitching coach Johnny Podres likened Caldwell to his former teammate Ron Perranoski, who pieced together several good seasons as a starter and a reliever for the Dodgers and the Twins. Podres said, "Mike has Perranoski's poise and the same kind of equipment — a great sinker, a sharp curve and control. And he throws harder than Ron did in his prime."¹³ Caldwell paired this newfound high standing in the organization with a strong spring performance in 1972, and earned a major-league roster spot. He split time between the rotation and the bullpen, producing a 7-11 record and a 4.01 ERA in 163⅔ innings. The 5.6 strikeouts per nine innings he posted were a far cry from Tri-City and Lodi, but the figure wound up being the best mark of his career in the majors.

After proving to be a versatile and durable pitching option for San Diego in 1972, Caldwell was expected to be a major cog in the Padres' pitching plans in 1973, whether as a starter or as a reliever.¹⁴ In some respects, he did take a step forward. In 13 starts and 42 relief appearances, Caldwell improved his ERA to 3.74 and earned 10 saves. But he had just a 5-14 won-lost record and walked batters at a higher rate than the season prior.

After the season Caldwell's tenure with the Padres came to an abrupt end. The Padres jumped at a chance to acquire Willie McCovey from the Giants, sending Caldwell to San Francisco in exchange for the slugging first baseman and outfielder Bernie Williams.¹⁵ Gaining a power bat was a positive for the Padres, but they still seemed sad to part with Caldwell. General manager Peter Bavasi said, "We hated to lose Mike."¹⁶ But Bavasi said the team had a pair of young pitchers who could fill the void, right-handers Dave Freisleben and Mike Johnston.¹⁷

San Francisco's fans weren't thrilled about losing McCovey, but the decision-makers seemed excited about their return. Manager Charlie Fox said, "Caldwell pitched very effectively against us. He's a left-hander who can throw strikes. He can be either a starter or a reliever, long or short. From all our reports, he has great promise."¹⁸

With a new team came a new role: Caldwell was expected to start the season as a member of the starting

A tough-as-nails competitor, Mike Caldwell won 102 games as a Brewer (1977-1984). In 1978 he was the AL Cy Young Award runner-up after winning 22 games and completing 23, both of which were still Brewers records as of 2020.

rotation. Fox put it firmly: "Caldwell is a sound big-league pitcher, definitely a starter."[19] He said Caldwell would be the number-four starter behind Ron Bryant, Tom Bradley, and John D'Acquisto.[20] Caldwell responded well, posting a 14-5 record and a 2.95 ERA for the season. However, things deteriorated quickly. Caldwell had to have surgery after the season to remove bone spurs from his elbow, and as a result he wasn't the same pitcher the next two seasons.[21] He produced 7-13 and 1-7 records with ERAs of 4.79 and 4.86 in 1975 and 1976 and was transitioned into more of a bullpen role for the Giants.

The Giants opted to deal Caldwell. Soon after the 1976 season they swung a trade with the St. Louis Cardinals, sending Caldwell, D'Acquisto, and catcher Dave Rader to St. Louis for outfielder Willie Crawford, left-handed pitcher John Curtis and utilityman Vic Harris.[22] Whether Caldwell was included for on-field or off-field reasons, he was certainly happy to be out of the Giants' clubhouse. For one thing, he didn't think he was used enough in San Francisco.[23] And there were some internal issues Caldwell was fine leaving in the past: "I didn't get along with a couple of the coaches, and they took it personally," he said. ..." I'm glad to get away from Candlestick. Not because of the ballpark. I'm just glad to get away from a bad situation."[24]

One of the staff members in San Francisco was pitching coach Buck Rodgers, who later became the manager of the Milwaukee Brewers. Rodgers wasn't specifically named by Caldwell as one of the coaches who drew his ire, though there's a good chance he was, based on later events in Milwaukee.

For the time being, though, Caldwell had to carve out a role in St. Louis. The Cardinals planned to use him in middle relief, but then dealt him again at the tail end of spring training. This time, Caldwell went to Cincinnati in exchange for Pat Darcy. Caldwell was used sparingly with the Reds, appearing in just 14 games and logging a 4.01 ERA in the first 2½ months of the season. Despite what seemed to be a downturn in his career, the southpaw caught a break that resurrected his career.

On June 15, 1977, the Reds traded Caldwell to the Brewers for minor leaguers Rick O'Keeffe and Garry Pyka.[25] The initial reaction in Milwaukee wasn't favorable. *Milwaukee Journal* columnist Bob Wolf called Caldwell a "longshot" to produce anything for Milwaukee.[26] "Caldwell hasn't done a thing since his one big year, 1974," Wolf wrote, even calling him "an anonymous member" of the Reds' bullpen.[27]

Wolf also noted that the price the Brewers paid to get Caldwell seemed a bit steep. Pyka had shown little promise in the minors, but O'Keeffe was considered the team's top pitching prospect.

Wolf questioned why a club in need of pitching help would trade away one of its brightest youngsters in exchange for a seemingly broken-down hurler. Manager Alex Grammas went as far as to say "[O'Keeffe]'s a cinch major-leaguer of the future."[28] But few could argue that Caldwell's presence would at least add some depth to a bullpen in need of just that. Caldwell wound up splitting time between the bullpen and the starting rotation, notching a 5-8 record with a 4.58 ERA in his first half-season with Milwaukee.

In 1978 Caldwell was thrust into the starting rotation because of injuries to two starters: an elbow injury to Bill Travers at the end of 1977, the other an elbow injury to Moose Haas in April. Caldwell produced the best season of his career: a 22-9 record, a 2.36 ERA, and a league-leading 23 complete games en route to a second-place finish in Cy Young Award voting, while also earning American League Comeback Player of the Year honors by a wide margin over Ferguson Jenkins.[29]

Caldwell attributed part of this massive upswing to his naysayers: "Lots of people had given up on me. Maybe the people who gave up on me were responsible in an indirect way for my coming back. I knew I could pitch, and I hope those who gave up on me will say now, 'Well, he had the guts to battle back and win.'"[30]

Others thought something else was the reason for this unexpected bounceback. Many American League hitters believed his sinker had evolved into more of a "spitter."[31] In his book *Nine Innings*, Daniel Okrent suggested that manager George Bamberger even helped Caldwell perfect the pitch.[32] The New York Yankees were the main accuser of the left-hander, and for good reason: Caldwell shut them out three times and concluded the season with a 0.64 ERA in five starts against them. Yankees owner George Steinbrenner vowed to place cameras all over Yankee Stadium during the 1979 season in an attempt to catch Caldwell in the act. However, the Brewers fought back. Brewers owner Bud Selig recalled, "I told George we had filed a spitter complaint on his Ron Guidry."[33]

Caldwell's strong 1978 campaign effectively assured him a spot in the Brewers' rotation for 1979. Things started out well, as Mr. Warmth shut down the Yankees once again on Opening Day in a 5-1 victory. However, he got off to what some considered to be a slow start: a 6-5 record with a 3.18 ERA by the beginning of July. This was nowhere near as good as his breakout 1978 campaign, but it was still a solid line. It was also close to the same line he held around that time the year before, so few in the Brewers front office were worried about Caldwell. But he was unable to fully recapture the magic that won him the Comeback Player of the Year Award, and he finished the year with a 3.29 ERA in 30 starts, though he went 16-6.

The 1980 season also started poorly for Caldwell. Before he even took the mound at spring training, the southpaw injured his ankle on a shopping trip in Milwaukee and ended up in a walking cast for a couple of months. Caldwell explained, "I had just bought some T-shirts to take to some kids in North Carolina. I was carrying a box, and I hit some concrete that was uneven and turned my ankle."[34] He called the issue a minor one despite the need for the cast. "I usually start working out in December, so I didn't miss anything. ... By spring training, I should be the same as always."[35]

Perhaps he was fine in terms of health, but in terms of performance, things continued to trend downward. Caldwell was 13-11, but his ERA rose to 4.03, the first time it had exceeded 4.00 since his brutal 1977 campaign. His 11 complete games were his fewest since that same year. The 1981 season wasn't much better, either, as he wound up winning just 11 games (9 losses) and throwing a mere three complete games to go with his 3.93 ERA. The frustration also seemed to be getting to him: He went as far as to flip a table at a reporter after the reporter had written something he didn't like.[36] He struggled in his two appearances during the Brewers' American League Division Series matchup with the Yankees. After dominating the team during his best years, Caldwell gave up four runs and two home runs in 8⅓ innings. It appeared that Caldwell's best years were behind him.

The Brewers were nearly persuaded to deal the left-hander before the 1982 season. They reportedly talked with Philadelphia that offseason, with the Phillies offering Ryne Sandberg, Jon Reelhorn, and Don McCormack in exchange for Caldwell.[37] Despite his recent struggles, the Brewers were content with keeping Caldwell and declined the trade. Having Sandberg, a future Hall of Famer, on the roster could have altered the history of the franchise, but keeping Caldwell around wound up working in the Brewers' favor in the short term.

The Brewers started off the 1982 campaign slowly, ending May with a 22-24 record. Caldwell was struggling, holding a 5.04 ERA into mid-June, after a stretch in which he allowed 38 runs in 42⅔ innings. Something had to be done. General manager Harry Dalton fired manager Buck Rodgers in an effort to improve the clubhouse dynamic. This development was music to Caldwell's ears. As Daniel Okrent wrote in *Nine Innings*, "Caldwell had hated Bob Rodgers and Bob Rodgers had hated him, and there was no one else on the team as happy to see Rodgers gone."[38] Caldwell even lashed out on a team flight during the rough month of May, exclaiming, "I hope we lose 10 in a row and get his [butt] fired."[39] The feeling between the player and manager appeared to be mutual: Rodgers reportedly considered Caldwell a "cancer," and even speculated that Caldwell "tried to stab [him] in the back" during his tenure as manager.[40] Still, Rodgers was out and Harvey Kuenn was in as the skipper, marking the start of a summer filled with Brewers wins.

Caldwell nearly wasn't a part of the team for the entire season. According to Vic Feuerherd, then of the *Milwaukee Journal*, the Brewers were considering a trade that would have sent him to the Texas Rangers for Doc Medich.[41] In the end, the Brewers did not pull the trigger. Caldwell did his best to help the team's cause down the stretch, finishing the regular season with a 3.91 ERA in 258 innings, his highest workload since his outstanding 1978 campaign.

At the onset of the postseason, Caldwell appeared to still be on his way out the door. In his lone start in the American League Championship Series against the California Angels, he lasted just three innings, allowing six runs (five earned) on seven hits and a walk. However, the Brewers won the series and trusted Mr. Warmth enough to let him take the hill for Game One of the World Series against the St. Louis Cardinals. Caldwell rewarded their confidence in him with a shutout, allowing just three hits and a walk. He got the ball again for Game Five and managed to scrape out a victory despite allowing 14 hits in 8⅓ innings. His luck ran out by the end of the Series as he was called upon to get the final out of the eighth inning in Game Seven and wound up giving up two run-scoring hits as the Cardinals took the Series.

Caldwell was dismayed by the end result, but was grateful to even be put in the position to win. He said, "I think more than anything else in the world, I wanted to win it for Harvey Kuenn. Even above getting a ring, getting the money, getting all that stuff in the winter, I wanted to win it for Harvey. Just below that, for Bud Selig and Harry Dalton and the Brewers organization. It's the finest organization I've ever played for and I don't think I'll ever get a chance to play for a better one."[42]

Caldwell's strong performance in the World Series didn't carry over to the next couple of seasons. The 1983 season started off well enough: He was one of three Brewers pitchers to open the season with complete games. However, he soon fell off and concluded the season with a 12-11 record and a 4.53 ERA, his worst ERA since his time in the National League. He got off to a hot start in 1984, but an ankle injury sidelined him for a bit in May. This problem seemingly hampered him the rest of the year, leading to a demotion to the bullpen, a 6-13 record and a 4.64 ERA in 126 innings pitched.

Adding to the list of issues was an ongoing drug probe by the commissioner's office that accused Caldwell and fellow Brewer Paul Molitor of using cocaine. The two-year investigation concluded with no action being taken against the pair.[43]

Between the decline in performance and the off-field allegations, it seemed that Caldwell's time in Milwaukee was coming to an end. The Brewers made that notion a reality before the 1985 season, waiving the nearly 36-year-old hurler in order to make room on the roster for Rollie Fingers, who returned to the team on a two-year pact.[44] Caldwell remained optimistic despite being cut, stating, "I'm glad they did it now instead of two, three weeks into spring training. This way, I'll have a chance to catch on with someone."[45] That chance didn't come, though, effectively ending Caldwell's big-league playing career.

Although he left the game with little more than a murmur, Caldwell was heralded for his bountiful pitching career. He was inducted into the North Carolina State University Hall of Fame in 2013 on the basis of his collegiate and professional accomplishments.[46] In 2014 the Brewers inducted him into the Wall of Honor, which honors "Brewers players, coaches and executives (for their) service to the organization and/or career accomplishments."[47] While it's not the Walk of Fame, which is more akin to other teams' Hall of Fame, it's still a prestigious honor.

Caldwell finished his career with a 3.81 ERA and a 137-130 record in 475 appearances (307 of which were starts). While his hot demeanor sometimes spoke louder than his performance, there's no denying that Mr. Warmth has a prominent place in Brewer lore for nearly helping to deliver a World Series title to Milwaukee.

SOURCES

In addition to the sources cited in the Notes, the author also relied upon Baseball-Reference.com.

NOTES

1. Phil Collier, "Padres Lift Eyes to Caldwell for Pitching Help," *The Sporting News*, March 3, 1973: 22.
2. Vic Feuerherd, "Trade Winds Start to Blow/Fiery Starter Mike Caldwell Was One Brewer on the Trading Block in the Summer of 1982." Madison.com, August 12, 2007.
3. "1968 Wolfpack Baseball," North Carolina State Library, accessed April 29, 2019.
4. Ibid.
5. Ibid.
6. Mike Caldwell NC State Athletic Hall of Fame bio, accessed April 1, 2019. gopack.com/hof.aspx?hof=12.
7. Daniel Okrent, *Nine Innings* (New York: Book Sales, 1985), 111-112.
8. Phil Collier, "Meteoric Rise by Padres' Caldwell," *The Sporting News*, April 1, 1972: 36.
9. Paul Cour, "Padres' Farms Produce Trio of Future Phenoms," *The Sporting News*, September 25, 1971: 29.
10. Ibid.
11. Ibid.
12. Ibid.
13. Phil Collier, "Meteoric Rise by Padres' Caldwell."
14. Phil Collier, "Padres Lift Eyes to Caldwell for Pitching Help."
15. Phil Collier, "Padres Unzip Their Wallet, Pocket Big Mac and Matty," *The Sporting News*, November 10, 1973: 26.
16. Ibid.
17. Ibid.
18. Pat Frizzell, "McCovey Trade Irks Giants' Fans," *The Sporting News*, November 10, 1973: 38.
19. Pat Frizzell, "Only Giants' Hill in Air as Fox Selects a Lineup," *The Sporting News*, March 9, 1974: 39.
20. Ibid.
21. Neal Russo, "Cards Swing 3-for-3 Deal – And They're Not Through," *The Sporting News*, November 6, 1976: 21.
22. Ibid.
23. Ibid.
24. Ibid.
25. "Brewers Get Lefty from Reds," *Milwaukee Journal*, June 16, 1977: 21.
26. Bob Wolf, "Brewers Still Lack Pitching," *Milwaukee Journal*, June 16, 1977: 21.
27. Ibid.
28. Ibid.

29 Mike Gonring, "Caldwell Battles Back to Gain A.L. Honors," *The Sporting News*, November 25, 1978: 39.

30 Ibid.

31 Ibid.

32 Okrent, 111-112.

33 "Caldwell Under Scrutiny," *The Sporting News*, April 28, 1979: 36.

34 Tom Flaherty, "Injury Fails to Shake Caldwell," *The Sporting News*, December 15, 1979: 54.

35 Ibid.

36 Feuerherd.

37 Hal Bodley, "Phils Disgusted; Deals Collapse," *The Sporting News*, January 2, 1982: 38.

38 Okrent.

39 Feuerherd.

40 Tom Flaherty, "Fired Rodgers 'Saw It Coming,'" *The Sporting News*, June 14, 1982: 25.

41 Feuerherd.

42 Tom Flaherty, "A Dream Ends for Caldwell," *The Sporting News*, November 1, 1982: 29.

43 Stan Isle, "No Action in Brewers' Drug Probe," *The Sporting News*, November 19, 1984: 57.

44 Tom Flaherty, "Fingers Is Sticking With Brewers," *The Sporting News*, January 21, 1985: 38.

45 Ibid.

46 Mike Caldwell NC State Athletic Hall of Fame bio, accessed April 1, 2019. gopack.com/hof.aspx?hof=12.

47 "Wall of Honor," Brewers.com, accessed April 15, 2019. mlb.com/brewers/ballpark/attractions/wall-of-honor.

CECIL COOPER

By Eric Aron

Once described by *Baseball Digest* as the "Rodney Dangerfield of baseball," Cecil Cooper was a great player who didn't get the respect he deserved.[1] An introverted Texan, Cecil Cooper remained in the shadows for much of his 17-year playing career. The left-handed first baseman spent his major-league years with Boston and Milwaukee from 1971 to 1987, appearing in two World Series. "Coooop!" — as his fans would cheer when he stepped up to the plate — was a lifetime .298 hitter, two-time Gold Glove Winner, and five-time All-Star.

Cecil Cooper was born on December 20, 1949, in Brenham, Texas, a city of 13,000 located 70 miles northwest of Houston. Raised in nearby Independence, Cooper was the youngest of 13 children — seven boys and six girls. Cooper's mother, Ocie, died when he was just 10. His ball-playing father, Roy, worked with a nearby Department of Public Works. A left-hander who grew to 6-feet-2, Cecil was taught baseball by his brothers John, Sylvester, and Jessie. John and Sylvester later played with the barnstorming Indianapolis Clowns.[2] John was a pitcher while Sylvester was a catcher who, according to Cecil, once caught Satchel Paige. According to the 1980 *Sports Illustrated* story, Cecil's father, Roy, also played in the Negro Leagues.

Cooper followed his brothers, playing ball for three years at the all-black Pickard High School, and transferring his senior year to the integrated Brenham High School. At Pickard High, he won two state championships under coach Henry Rogers. Intending to go to college after his graduation, Cecil was spotted by Boston Red Sox scout Dave Philley and was drafted by Boston in the sixth round of the 1968 amateur draft. He opted to take courses at Blinn Junior College and Prairie View A&M during the offseason. St. Louis took Cooper in the Rule 5 draft in November 1970, but returned Cooper to the Red Sox on April 5, 1971. He spent five seasons in the minor leagues (in Jamestown, Greenville, Danville, Winston-Salem, Louisville, and Pawtucket), hitting a combined .327 with 45 home runs and 298 RBIs.

Called up from Double-A Pawtucket after batting .343, Cooper made his major-league debut with the Red Sox on September 8, 1971, pinch-hitting for Roger Moret and grounding to second against Yankees pitcher Jack Aker. He got his first hit three days later, a pinch single off the Tigers' Joe Coleman. He hit .310 in 42 at-bats that month.

It was thought that Cooper had a shot at the starting job in 1972, but just before the start of the season, the Red Sox acquired Danny Cater from the Yankees and sent Cooper to Triple-A Louisville.

Another fine campaign in the minors produced a .315 average, thanks to a league-leading 162 hits, Cooper returned to Boston in September, but got just 17 at-bats during the tight pennant race that saw the Red Sox fall a half-game short.

Despite Cater's shortcomings, Cooper again failed to stick with the Red Sox in 1973, as the team elected to move Carl Yastrzemski back to first base. Cecil was sent to Pawtucket, now the Triple-A affiliate, where he hit .293 with 15 home runs. This time he was recalled before the rosters expanded, first playing on August 24 and playing nearly full-time the rest of the season. In 30 games and 101 at-bats, Cooper hit .238 with his first three major-league home runs. His first round-tripper was struck on September 7 at Fenway Park off the Tigers' Bob Miller.

In 1974 Cooper was the team's Opening Day first baseman, hitting third in the lineup. New manager Darrell Johnson used a lot of lineups, trying to divide playing time at first base, left field, and designated hitter among Cooper, Yastrzemski, Cater, Tommy Harper, and Bernie Carbo. Cooper ended up playing 74 games at first and 41 more as the designated hitter, getting most of the starts when facing right-handed pitchers. He hit .275 in 414 at-bats.

Cooper did not have a good defensive reputation early in his career, which is why he spent a lot of time as a designated hitter. For 1975, the Red Sox had two rookie outfielders (Jim Rice and Fred Lynn), plus the comebacking Tony Conigliaro, who initially won the DH job. Cooper would have to beat out a lot of people in order to get a chance to play. At the end of May, he was the odd man out, getting just six hits in 24 at-bats. He persevered, and by late June he was platooning against right-handed pitchers. He ended up hitting .311 with 14 home runs in 305 at-bats.

One of the team's hottest hitters in August and September, Cecil had a scary moment on September 7. In the second game of a doubleheader against the Milwaukee Brewers, he was hit in the face by future teammate Bill Travers. Cooper was carried off on a

One of the most underrated hitters of his generation, Cecil Cooper batted .302 during his 11 years with the Brewers (1977-1987), including a career-high .352 in 1980. He led the AL in RBIs twice (1980 and 1983).

stretcher and was bleeding from his nose and mouth. The incident hampered his performance the rest of the season. With Jim Rice's wrist injury requiring Carl Yastrzemski to play left field, Cooper had first base to himself for most of the postseason. He was 4-for-10 in the ALCS against Oakland but just 1-for-19 in the World Series against Cincinnati.

Playing in 123 games in 1976 while again splitting time between first base and designated hitter, Cooper hit .282 with 15 homers and 78 RBIs. After the season manager Don Zimmer told Cooper that he would become Boston's regular first baseman.

This was not to be the case, as on December 6, 1976, Cooper was traded to the Milwaukee Brewers for two former Red Sox, first baseman George Scott and outfielder Bernie Carbo.

The trade was not particularly popular in either Boston or Milwaukee. Brewers owner Bud Selig was told by other AL East clubs that if you "keep making trades like that you will be in last place forever."[3] In 1976 the Brewers finished last in the American League East with a record of 66-95. The extremely popular Scott had first played in a Red Sox uniform from 1966 to 1971 and had posted several good seasons for the Brewers. But neither Scott nor Carbo ever again had the kind of success they had achieved in earlier seasons. And Cecil Cooper would become a legend in Milwaukee.

Cooper was a clutch contact hitter who could hit for both average and power. He kept putting up such solidly consistent numbers year after year that it was easy to overlook his achievements. In his first year in Milwaukee, he hit .300; in his second year he hit .312; and in 1979 Cooper hit .308. He had a league-leading 44 doubles in 1979. Former Milwaukee player-coach Sal Bando once said of him, "Cecil Cooper can beat you with a home run or a flare to left or a bunt. And he can field his position. You have guys who can hit home runs and guys who can hit singles. But not many can do both. Cecil can."[4]

Playing for a small-market team in the Midwest allowed Cooper to thrive, and in 1980 he did just that. He hit better than .300 in every month of the season finishing with a .352 average, 25 home runs, 219 hits, and an American League-leading 122 RBIs. His season was largely overlooked because Kansas Royals third baseman George Brett flirted with a .400 batting average, settling for .390. The unassuming Cooper said, "With Brett hitting close to .400 all year, I didn't expect to get much publicity, and I didn't have any trouble living with that."[5]

Cooper was part of a record game in 1980. On April 12, in an 18-1 Brewers rout of the Red Sox, he and infielder/DH Don Money connected for two grand slams in the same inning. It was only the fourth time the feat had been accomplished in the major leagues. (There have been two since, most recently in 1999, when Fernando Tatis of the St. Cardinals hit two grand slams in one inning.) In the late 1970s and early 1980s, the Brewers franchise was moving up in the standings, finishing with 93 wins in 1978 and 95 wins in 1979. In 1981, in a strike-shortened split season, the New York Yankees won the first half in the AL East while the Brewers finished first in the second half. This set the stage for a best-of-five divisional playoff between the two clubs, which the Yankees won in five games. Cooper hit .320 with 12 home runs in the abbreviated campaign.

In 1982 first baseman Cooper was at the heart of the one of the era's great lineups, batting third behind Paul Molitor and Robin Yount, and in front of Ted Simmons, Gorman Thomas, and Charlie Moore. Cooper hit .313 with 32 home runs and 121 runs batted in. On October 3, 1982, in a game deciding the American League East championship, the Brewers defeated the Baltimore Orioles 10-2, closing out the season with a mark of 95-67. They eliminated the California Angels in five games in the American League Championship Series, becoming the first team to come back from a two-games-to-none deficit and win a best-of-five postseason series. In the decisive Game Five, Jim Gantner and Charlie Moore scored on Cooper's seventh-inning bases-loaded single. In a gesture reminiscent of former teammate Carlton Fisk, who waved his arms to keep the ball fair in Game Six of the '75 Series, Cooper motioned for the ball to get down. "I remember thinking, 'Get down ball, get down.' The crowd was so loud I couldn't really hear myself saying anything, but I just wanted to keep waving so that ball would fall in there."[6] Overall he hit just 3-for-20 in the League Championship Series.

The 1982 World Series was called the Suds Series because it pitted the two of America's largest beer-brewing cities against each other. The National League champion St. Louis Cardinals featured first baseman Keith Hernandez and future Hall of Fame shortstop Ozzie Smith. Cooper homered in a losing effort in Game Three, and his 8-for-28 record was not enough, as his team lost in seven games.

Cooper's teammate Robin Yount won the American League MVP award, and just as in 1980 when he lost to George Brett, Cooper finished fifth in the voting. Yount hit .331 with 29 home runs and 114 RBIs. "Maybe I'm the Lou Gehrig of my time … always in the shadows of someone else," Cooper said. "He's a pretty good role model, though."[7]

While in Milwaukee, Cooper wrote a column for the Brewers' magazine, *What's Brewing?* He wrote about everything from his baseball experiences to how youngsters could get autographs from their favorite players. In 1983 Cooper won baseball's coveted Roberto Clemente Award for his community service. Cooper worked with Athletes for Youth, a Milwaukee inner-city program, teaching children about baseball, and was honorary chairman of both the Kidney Foundation of Wisconsin and the 1982 Food for Families Project. Bud Selig said of Cooper, "I think Cecil does a lot more than any of us know. Cecil is shy. What he does, he prefers to do in anonymity."[8]

Cooper played for the Brewers until 1987, and as he passed through the mid-30s his batting average and power numbers fell off, although he did make the AL All-Star squads in 1983 and 1985. Named as a reserve for both games, he did make appearances as a pinch-hitter in both Midsummer Classics. He retired from major-league baseball in 1987 but did play a month in the Senior Professional Baseball Association in 1989. Appearing in 16 games with the Winter Haven Super Sox, Cooper hit .407 with three home runs and 15 RBIs. During this time he also served as a player agent for CSMG International.

In 1996 he became farm director for the Brewers. In 2002 Cooper returned to the dugout as the Brewers bench coach. In 2005 and 2004 Cooper managed the Brewers' Triple-A affiliate Indianapolis Indians. In 2005, he took advantage of an opportunity to return to his native Texas and served as the bench coach for Houston Astros manager Phil Garner.

On August 27, 2007, Cooper was named interim manager after Garner was fired, becoming the team's first African-American skipper. On September 28 the interim tag was removed and Cooper was signed to a two-year contract as the Astros' manager. In 2008 the Astros (86-75) finished in third place in the National League Central Division.

On September 21, 2009, though they had picked up Cooper's option for 2010, the Astros fired him with 13 games left in the season and the club at 70-79. Fairly or unfairly, he was dismissed from a team had a high payroll and aging stars who weren't performing to expectations. Overall, Cooper's record as a manager was 171-170.

Through 2014, Cooper held the Brewers' season record for hits (219 in 1980) and singles (157, also 1980), and was second in RBIs (126 in 1983). He was ranked fourth in Brewers career batting average (.302), third in hits (1,815) and doubles (345), and fourth in at-bats (6019) and games played (1490). He was second in RBIs with 994. His single-season average of .352 in 1980 was the team's second best, just behind Paul Molitor's .353 in 1987.

In his hometown of Brenham, a field was dedicated in Cooper's honor and his number was retired at Brenham High School. In 2002 he was inducted into the Walk of Fame at the Brewers' Miller Park. That same year he was inducted into the Wisconsin Athletic Hall of Fame.

In 2014 Cooper was among 58 former Brewers who were inducted into the Wall of Honor outside Miller Park.

As of 2014 Cooper lived in Katy, Texas with his wife, Octavia. There are three daughters: Kelly (born in 1978), Brittany (1987), and Tori (1993).

SOURCES

Chass, Murray, "What Cecil Cooper Can Do," *New York Times*, June 27, 1982.

Cotton, Anthony, "No Condolences, please," *Sports Illustrated*, September 22, 1980. Although there is no record by SABR's Negro Leagues Committee, this SI issue and Cooper himself in a June 2005 interview said that his brothers played for the Indianapolis Clowns.

Elderkin, Phil, "Brewer Who Chased Brett: Milwaukee's Cecil Cooper Hits Anything," *Christian Science Monitor*, October 7, 1980.

Fimrite, Ron, "I'm the Lou Gehrig of My Time," *Sports Illustrated*, September 19, 1983.

Flaherty, Tom, "Cooper Earns Clemente Prize," *The Sporting News*, February 28. 1983.

Gammons, Peter, "Cooper groggy, but in one piece," *Boston Globe*, September 8, 1975.

Guiliotti, Joe, "Cecil Cooper: He Would Rather be No. 1!" *Baseball Digest*, June 1981.

Hoffmann, Gregg, *Down in the Valley: The History of Milwaukee County Stadium* (Milwaukee: The Milwaukee Brewers Baseball Club and the Milwaukee Journal-Sentinel, 2000).

Leerhsen, Charles, "Harvey's Wallbangers," *Newsweek*, August 2, 1982.

Astros.com

BaseballLibrary.com

Baseball-Reference.com

MilwaukeeBrewers.com

Thanks to Tom Skibosh, Jim Long, Howard Bryant, Cecil Cooper (June 2005), and the late Merle Harmon for their contributions.

NOTES

1   *Baseball Digest*, June 1981.
2   *Sports Illustrated*, September 22, 1980.
3   *Sports Illustrated*, September 19, 1983.
4   *New York Times*, June 27, 1982.
5   *Christian Science Monitor*, October 1980.
6   Gregg Hoffmann, *Down in the Valley: The History of Milwaukee County Stadium*, 97.
7   *Sports Illustrated*, September 19, 1983.
8   *The Sporting News*, February 28. 1983.

JAMIE EASTERLY

By Gregory H. Wolf

After several trials as a starter with the Atlanta Braves in the 1970s and out of the big leagues in 1980, southpaw Jamie Easterly emerged as a dependable reliever for the Milwaukee Brewers in 1981, helping them to their first-ever postseason berth. He suffered a strained knee in 1982 and was not on the pennant-winning Brewers postseason roster. Plagued by injuries for much of his 13-year big-league career, Easterly was forced into retirement by a torn rotator cuff.

James Morris Easterly was born on February 17, 1953, in Houston, but grew up 115 miles north in Crockett, a small town of about 6,000 people. His parents were Morris Elan Easterly, a rural mail carrier, and Arie Bernice (Corbitt) Easterly. An athletic youngster, Jamie played Little League and Pony League baseball, and lettered in all three varsity years at Crockett High School in five sports — a guard in basketball, an all-district quarterback in football, golf, track, and baseball. Standing just 5-feet-9, the left-handed pitcher dazzled on the mound in his senior year in 1971, posting an 11-3 record, fanning 231 in 111 innings with a 0.40 ERA.[1] Easterly also pitched American Legion ball for nearby Nacogdoches. Austin sportswriter Tom Rice reported that Easterly was the "No. 1 baseballer in Texas on pro draft lists."[2] According to Rice, it appeared that Easterly might accept a scholarship offer to Texas A&M University, owing to his father's friendship with baseball coach Tom Chandler. Based on scout Al LaMacchia's recommendation, the Atlanta Braves selected Easterly in the second round, with the 34th overall pick in the 1971 amateur draft.

Assigned to Greenwood (South Carolina) in the Class-A Western Carolinas League, Easterly made a big splash, posting an 0.62 ERA in 29 innings and striking out more than a batter an inning. Team manager Clint Courtney raved that Easterly was "the best prospect" he had seen in the organization.[3] The 18-year-old's future looked bright. Bill Lucas, the Braves' assistant farm director, cooed in the offseason, "I know it's a big jump from Class A to the majors, but this kid … has the stuff to make it."[4]

Easterly impressed Braves brass at spring training in 1972 as a nonroster invitee, but fractured a rib in early March and was sidelined for six weeks.[5] That began a series of physical setbacks that limited to Easterly to just 95 innings over the next two seasons. Back with Greenwood in 1972, he came down with arm trouble and pain between his elbow and shoulder.[6] After another spring camp with the Braves, Easterly spent the entire '73 campaign with Savannah in the Double-A Southern League, making 13 starts among his 15 appearances and posting a 5-3 slate.

Easterly arrived at Braves spring training in 1974 apparently in the best shape of his life. He had pitched for six weeks for Mazatlan in the Mexican League and participated in instructional camp in February. "Jamie just might have the best arm in the Braves organization," gushed VP Eddie Robinson.[7] On March 11 he combined with three other hurlers to no-hit the New York Yankees in West Palm Beach.[8] "He throws strikes," said Braves pitching coach Herm Starrette of Easterly, who made the 25-man roster.[9] Easterly made his big-league debut, hurling a 1-2-3 ninth against the Cincinnati Reds at Riverfront Stadium on April 6. He was hit hard in his next two outings, victimized for five earned runs in 1⅔ innings, and was subsequently optioned to Triple-A Richmond in the International League. He raised his stock once again, posting a 2.54 ERA in 138 innings and a 9-6 record, earning a September call-up. He was scheduled to make a late-season start, but his campaign ended when he required knee surgery due to a lingering injury.[10] While in Mexico the previous year, Easterly had suffered a "freak injury" when he was accidentally hit on the knee by a fungo bat, eventually causing bone chips to develop and necessitating the operation.[11]

After right-handers started every game for the Braves in 1974, the club desperately hoped that the 22-year-old Easterly could take a big step forward in '75. That looked to be the case when he led the team with three wins in the Grapefruit League and secured a spot on the staff. Relegated to mop-up duty when the season started, Easterly rusted on the bench, making four appearances in the first six weeks of the season, and was shipped to Richmond. Recalled in mid-June, he was collared with the loss in his first start, yielding four runs in 2⅔ innings against the Big Red Machine on June 23. Four days later he picked up his maiden victory, hurling seven frames in front of friends and family in the Astrodome. It was otherwise a long season for Easterly (2-9, 4.98 ERA in 68⅔ innings) and the Braves (67-94), who completed their worst season since 1942 when they were the Boston Braves.

Southpaw Jamie Easterly battled all sorts of injuries throughout his 13-year big-league career (1974-1979; 1981-1987), to fashion a 23-33 slate with a 4.62 ERA in 321 appearances.

Easterly spent the 1976 season under the tutelage of pitching instructor Johnny Sain with Richmond, where he occasionally flashed the potential the Braves thought he could consistently show. His pitching arsenal consisted of a fastball, sinking fastball, curve, slider, and changeup. He struggled with control, walking 88 in 137 innings, but still produced a stellar 2.96 ERA while splitting his time as a starter and reliever. He earned another September call-up and made four starts, winning one. His sole loss was in his last appearance, when the San Francisco Giants' John Montefusco tossed a no-hitter.

Easterly prepared for the 1977 season by pitching for the first of three times for Navegantes des Magallanes in the Venezuela Winter League in 1976-1977.[12] Arriving early at the Braves camp out of options, he was relegated to mop-up duty when the season started and had an ERA of 10.50 in his first 18 innings (over 10 appearances). Suddenly pressed into a starting assignment, Easterly "literally arose from the depths of the bullpen to give the staff a shot in the arm," wrote Braves beat reporter Frank Hyland after the southpaw tossed the "best game" of his career, eight shutout innings against the St. Louis Cardinals on May 13, but getting a no-decision.[13] That outing earned Easterly another shot, and he responded by picking up wins in his next two starts. On June 5 he injured himself swinging a bat against the Giants. Diagnosed as an "inflamed ulnar nerve," the injury landed him on the disabled list, and ultimately ended his season after several poor relief appearances in July.[14] On July 21 he underwent surgery on his left elbow to remove bone chips and was lost for the season.[15]

Addressing what seemed like the Braves' annual need of southpaw starters, first-year skipper Bobby Cox tabbed Easterly early in spring training as one in his quintet in 1978, if the 25-year-old's arm was healthy — and that was a big if. Due to scheduling quirks and rainouts, however, Easterly was pushed to the pen, and then bypassed in favor of another left-hander, Mickey Mahler. Later in the season, left-handed rookie Larry McWilliams emerged to win nine games. The Braves once again finished in the cellar of the NL West, while Easterly's future with the Braves looked cloudy. Over the previous two seasons, he made just 11 starts among his 59 appearances, and posted a dismal 5.86 ERA in 136⅔ innings while battling injuries. In one of those starts (the first game of a doubleheader against the San Francisco Giants on June 30, 1978), he made history by surrendering Willie McCovey's 500th home run, the 12th major leaguer to reach that milestone.

Despite a productive stint with Magallanes in Venezuela in the offseason (7-3, 2.71 ERA in 73 innings) Easterly did not make the Braves' Opening Day roster in 1979 and was assigned to Richmond.[16] He was recalled in late May when McWilliams came down with a bum arm, but struggled in his four relief outings. Returned to Richmond, Easterly was later loaned to the Denver Bears, the Montreal Expos' affiliate in the Triple-A International League. Under skipper Jack McKeon, the club attempted to give the 26-year-old Easterly one last chance to make it as a starter. He started 13 of his 20 games, one of which was a seven-inning perfect game in the first contest of a doubleheader against Iowa on July 14.[17] "It's one of my top thrills in baseball," said Easterly, looking back on his accomplishment years later.[18]

Easterly's career was at a crossroads when he was sold in a waiver deal to the Expos on October 22, 1979. Following his final stint with Magallanes in Venezuela in the offseason,[19] Easterly was given just an "outside chance" to make the Expos staff in 1980.[20] The Expos already had two graybeard southpaw relievers, productive 40-year-old closer Woodie Fryman and 37-year-old Fred Norman, acquired in the offseason. Easterly was optioned to Denver, where he spent the entire season.

In his 10th big-league season but just 27 years old, Easterly was converted into a full-time reliever and prospered. He made the second-most appearances (56) in the American Association and finished tied for second in saves (15) and third in strikeouts (105) with a respectable 3.63 ERA in 134 innings.

Easterly fell into an ideal situation when the Milwaukee Brewers acquired him in a waiver transaction on September 22, 1980. The club was coming off three consecutive winning seasons in the highly competitive AL East, but one of skipper Buck Rodgers' top priorities was looking for a southpaw reliever to complement offseason acquisition Rollie Fingers. Easterly debuted in the season opener on April 11 against the Indians, retiring all seven batters he faced, followed by a 3⅓-inning save the next day. Easterly "looked like a rejuvenated Sparkly Lyle," quipped Rodgers.[21] Pitching more often and more consistently than at any other time during his big-league career, Easterly strung together two impressive streaks: he tossed 16⅓ consecutive innings in May, allowing just one unearned run; and then topped it with 17⅔ straight scoreless innings in August-September.[22] "He doesn't have a trick pitch," said batterymate Ted Simmons. "He just comes in and throws strikes.[23] The season was marked by the players strike, which wiped out about one-third of the games, resulting in a split-season format for the playoffs. During the September push that which catapulted the Brewers into contention for the second-half divisional crown, Easterly pitched in some of the highest-leverage games in his career. On September 25 he hurled 2⅓ scoreless, one-hit innings against the Tigers in Detroit, emerging as the victor, 8-6, when Robin Yount hit a dramatic three-run home run in the ninth to pull the club to within a half-game of the lead. In the Brewers' clinching victory, on October 3 at County Stadium against the Tigers, Easterly hurled an inning of scoreless relief. "It was a special moment for Jamie Easterly, the little lefthander whose effective relief pitching has been overshadowed by Fingers," praised the AP.[24] While Fingers was named both the AL Cy Young Award and MVP winner, Easterly logged 62 innings over 44 appearances (3.19 ERA) and did not yield a home run. In the Brewers' ALDS loss to the Yankees in five games, Easterly made the only two postseason appearances in his career, yielding a run and two hits in 1⅓ innings.

Easterly arrived in the Brewers camp in 1982 with a new feeling — job security. The club got off to a poor start, resulting in Harvey Kuenn replacing Rodgers. Harvey's Wallbangers were born, and the home-run-bashing club captured its first-ever AL East crown. However, it was a frustrating season for Easterly, who strained his right knee in July, and missed more than eight weeks of the season. Upon his return on September 11, he struggled in his first two outings and never gained Kuenn's confidence. With a 4.70 ERA in 30⅔ innings, Easterly was not on the Brewers' postseason roster.

Back in his customary position of competing for a job in spring training in 1983, Easterly landed the last spot of a 10-man staff, but didn't last long with the club. On June 6 GM Harry Dalton shook up the struggling team, sending Gorman Thomas, who had tied Reggie Jackson for the AL lead in home runs the previous season, to the Indians in exchange for Rick Manning and Rick Waits. Easterly and prospect Ernie Camacho were toss-ins. Indians pitching coach Don McMahon admitted the club wasn't "counting on" Easterly, who emerged as the staff's biggest surprise.[25] Appearing in more games than any other member of the staff after his arrival (41), Easterly went on a tear beginning July 18, posting a 1.74 ERA over his next 27 outings (and 31 innings).

Easterly closed out his career with the Indians, who had a losing record in four of the five seasons he was on the club and finished no better than fifth in the competitive AL East. Easterly's stint was characterized by all sorts of injuries. He missed most of spring training in 1984 after injuring his back at home in Texas prior to camp. Tensions rose between Easterly and the Tribe's front office when he refused to report for a rehab assignment in the minors.[26] Relegated to mop-up duty when he returned in mid-June, Easterly (3.38 ERA in 69⅓ innings) proved to be dependable. While the Indians lost an AL-most 102 games and had the majors' highest team ERA (4.91) in 1985, Easterly "was perhaps the Tribe's most consistent pitcher."[27] He posted a stellar 2.25 ERA as a reliever in 43 appearances, but was hit hard when pressed into a starter's role, evidenced by a 7.01 ERA. After logging a career-high 98⅔ innings in '85, Easterly was limited to 29 appearances and 49⅓ innings over the next two seasons, plagued by arm and shoulder problems. He eventually had arthroscopic surgery on his rotator cuff in 1987, which effectively ended his career. He attempted an abbreviated comeback in 1988, signing a minor-league deal with the Twins, but persistent shoulder pain forced him to announce his retirement before the end of camp.

In parts of 13 big-league seasons, Easterly appeared in 321 games with a 4.62 ERA in 611⅓ innings, and posted a 23-33 slate.

Easterly retired to his hometown, and offseason home, in Crockett. In November 1982 he had married Stacy Wood. In 1989-1990, Easterly played with the Orlando Juice, one of the eight teams in the inaugural season of the Senior Professional Baseball Association.

As of 2019, Easterly still resided in Crockett.

SOURCES

In addition to the sources cited in the Notes, the author also accessed Retrosheet.org, Baseball-Reference.com, SABR.org, The Sporting News archive via Paper of Record, and Ancestry.com.

ACKNOWLEDGEMENTS

Thanks for Richard Cuicchi, Kellen Nielson, Rick Schabowski, and Joe Wancho for providing information about Jamie Easterly from various team media guides.

NOTES

1 United Press International, "Braves Sign Young Pitcher," *Bonham (Texas) Daily Favorite*, June 28, 1971: 10.

2 Tom Rice, "Sports Tom-Tom," *Austin American*, May 28, 1971: 34.

3 "S.L. All Stars Face Easterly," *Atlanta Constitution*, July 8, 1971: 6-D.

4 Wayne Minshew, "Braves Have Hope on Farm," *Atlanta Constitution*, November 4, 1971: 3-D.

5 Wayne Minshew, "Upshaw Gets $7,000 Raise," *Atlanta Constitution*, March 8, 1972: 1D.

6 Jim Joyce, "Doubleheaders Picking Up," *Index-Journal* (Greenwood, South Carolina), May 24, 1972: 9.

7 Charles Roberts, "Non-Roster Lefty May Boost Braves," *Atlanta Constitution*, March 1, 1974: 6E.

8 The other hurlers were Ron Reed, Dave Cheadle, and Joe Grzenda. "Wayne Minshew, "Braves Throw No-Hitter at Yankees," *Atlanta Constitution*, March 12, 1974: 1-D.

9 Wayne Minshew, "Several New Faces Likely," *Atlanta Constitution*, March 21, 1974: 1H.

10 Wayne Minshew, "Braves to Name King 1975 Manager," *Atlanta Constitution*, September 30, 1974: 3-D.

11 Wayne Minshew, "Easterly Aims to Be a Starter," *Atlanta Constitution*, February 28, 1975: 4-D.

12 Easterly posted a 4-5 slate and 4.71 ERA in 72⅔ innings in 1976-1977; see pelotabinaria.com.ve/beisbol/mostrar.php?ID=eastjam001.

13 Frank Hyland, "Braves Lose; Bristol Wins," *Atlanta Constitution*, May 14, 1977: 1C.

14 Wayne Minshew, "Braves Draft Pitchers, But Present Ones Ailing," *Atlanta Constitution*, June 8, 1977: 6-D.

15 Wayne Minshew, "Astros Put Woeful Braves in Orbit, 15-3," *Atlanta Constitution*, August 16, 1977: 3-D.

16 Easterly's statistics courtesy of pelotabinaria.com.ve/beisbol/mostrar.php?ID=eastjam001.

17 Gene Raffensperg, "Easterly's Perfect Pitches Stun Cubs," *Des Moines Register*, July 15, 1979: 27.

18 Jim Ingraham, "Easterly Has Fond Memories of Perfect Game," *News-Journal* (Mansfield, Ohio), June 14, 1985: 20.

19 Easterly went 1-1 with 5.89 ERA in 36⅔ innings for Magallanes. pelotabinaria.com.ve/beisbol/mostrar.php?ID=eastjam001.

20 "Jackson Absent from Camp Again," *Palm Beach* (Florida) *Post*, March 2, 1980: E2.

21 Bill Brophy, "Easterly Offers a Bit of Early Relief," *Wisconsin State Journal* (Madison), April 14, 1981: 13.

22 The first streak covered 10 appearances between May 1 and May 24; the second, 12 appearances from August 18 to September 12.

23 Tom Flaherty, " 'Too Small' Edwards Tattles Odds, Wins Brewer Job," *The Sporting News*, May 2, 1981: 21.

24 Associated Press, "Thomas settles for champagne," *Journal-Times* (Racine), October 4, 1981: 5E.

25 AP, "Indians Pitching Coach Pleased with Progress," *The Tribune* (Coshocton, Ohio), September 7, 1983: 7.

26 "Streaking Tribe Wins 4 in a Row, *The Sporting News*, June 25, 1984: 21.

27 *1986 Cleveland Indians Media Guide*.

MARSHALL EDWARDS

By Rick Schabowski

Marshall Lynn Edwards, a fleet outfielder and one of three brothers who played in the major leagues, was with the Milwaukee Brewers in parts of three seasons, 1981, 1982, and 1983. He was on the postseason roster in 1981 and 1982.

Edwards was born on August 27, 1952, in Fort Lewis, Washington. He had two brothers who also played in the major leagues. His twin brother, Michael, played second base for the Pittsburgh Pirates and the Oakland A's, and a younger brother, Dave, was an outfielder for the San Diego Padres and the Minnesota Twins.

The family moved to Los Angeles, and Edwards graduated from Jefferson High School in 1970. Besides playing baseball in high school, he ran track. He played American Legion baseball, and his Joe DiMaggio sandlot team won a national title in 1971.

After high school, Edwards attended Los Angeles Community College and then UCLA, graduating in 1974. In his senior year Edwards stole 19 bases for the Bruins, tying the school record. (It had since been broken.)

Marshall hoped he'd be selected in the amateur draft. Both of his brothers had been drafted. Mike was selected four times, and Dave, once. But Marshall was not drafted. Reflecting on that later in his career, he said, "It hurt inside, but it just gave me more motivation. Not being drafted made me work harder. When I finally got into pro ball, with all the good coaching, I was able to develop as a player."[1]

Edwards was signed as a free agent by the Baltimore Orioles on June 24, 1974, by scout Ray Poitevint. In 74 games with the Ogden Spikers of the Rookie-level Pioneer League, he batted .291 and stole 33 bases.

Edwards spent the next two seasons with the Miami Orioles of the Class A Florida State League. He had decent seasons there, batting .279 with 38 stolen bases in 1975 and .296 with a league-leading 57 steals in 1976.

He began the 1977 season with Miami, where after 94 games he was batting a league-leading .334 with 31 stolen bases. He was promoted to Charlotte of the Double-A Southern League, where he struggled in the higher competition, batting .171 in 36 games with eight steals.

During the winter league meetings on December 6, 1977, the Brewers selected Edwards in the Rule 5 draft from Baltimore.

The Brewers assigned Edwards to the Holyoke (Massachusetts) Millers of the Double-A Eastern League for 1978. He got off to a hot start and had a 14-game hitting streak, during which he batted .346. He tied for the league lead with 11 triples and batted .285 with 31 stolen bases.

Edwards was involved in a controversial play

on August 8 against the Jersey City A's. With Jersey City pitcher Rick Lysander tossing a no-hitter, Edwards bunted down the third-base line and reached base when LeRoy Robbins's low throw pulled to first baseman Kelvin Moore off the base. The official scorer ruled the play a hit, not an error. It was the only hit of the game off Lysander.

The Brewers assigned Edwards to Vancouver of the Triple-A Pacific Coast League for 1979. In 111 games he batted .273 and led the team with 19 stolen bases. With his two brothers already in the majors, Edwards thought he had a decent shot to make the big leagues. His belief was, "If the heart's there, the body has to follow."[2]

In 1980 Edwards batted .291 for Vancouver, led the PCL league with 17 triples, stole 68 bases. After he stole his 50th base on July 25, Vancouver manager Bob Didier said. "His best assets are his legs. For Marshall to get to the big leagues, he has to steal bases. He's been a big plus for us with his running and it's amazing the runs he has driven in. If he stole 70 bases and had 70 RBIs, it would be a big feather in his cap."[3]

The Brewers invited Edwards to major-league spring training in 1981. He played well, and with the Brewers needing speed and defense, he made the Opening Day roster. Brewers manager Buck Rodgers was happy to have Edwards on the team. "Marshall gives us speed as well as defensive ability in the outfield," the manager said. "One thing we won't have to do much is pinch-hit. That's why pinch-running is as important as pinch-hitting to us. His biggest asset is his speed. Plus, he can play all three outfield positions."[4]

Edwards was elated to make it to the big leagues, calling it "a dream come true." He added, "From Little League through college, to when you go into the minor leagues, you want to be a major-league player. This is the highest any player can go. So now it's time to show what you can do. However the Brewers decide to use me, I have to keep myself ready. So I try to do a lot of little extra things off the field to keep ready. Doing extra exercises and doing a little more thinking to keep myself mentally sharp."[5]

Marshall Edwards played parts of three seasons in the majors (1981-1983), all with the Brewers, batting .258 with two home runs. His brothers Dave and Mike Edwards were also big leaguers.

Edwards made his major-league debut on April 11, 1981. In the top of the ninth inning, with the Brewers leading the Indians 5-3, Edwards ran for Gorman Thomas, who had walked. In the bottom of the inning he replaced Thomas in right field. On April 22, he got his first major-league hit, a ninth-inning pinch-hit single off Toronto pitcher Jerry Garvin.

Outfielder Paul Molitor suffered an ankle injury on May 3 and needed surgery, so Edwards continued as an outfield backup. On June 12 the players struck and the season didn't resume until August 9. By that time Molitor was activated and Edwards was sent back to Vancouver. He was called back up on September 1 and made the playoff roster against the Yankees, replacing Mark Brouhard, who had a pulled calf muscle. He ran for Charlie Moore in Game Three and stayed in the game and struck out against Rudy May. He ran for Roy Howell in the eighth inning in Game Five.

After posting a .485 batting average in 1982 spring training, Edwards thought he was a lock to make the major-league roster. When manager Buck Rodgers told Edwards he was starting the season in Vancouver, it was difficult to accept. Edwards recalled, "It was a jolt. I tried to accept it. I think that was the turning point of my career. I knew I had to forget it and play as hard as I could. Feeling down like I did, and being able to go out and play, by the grace of God, I did it."[6]

After Larry Hisle was placed on the 15-day disabled list on May 7 with a tear in his right rotator cuff, Edwards, who was hitting .380 at Vancouver, was called up. He hit his first major-league home run on May 12, in the fifth inning off Royals pitcher Dennis Leonard. In early June Edwards was briefly hospitalized with a bleeding ulcer.

After leaving the hospital, Edwards platooned with Charlie Moore in right field and saw playing time. His speed and baserunning were assets for the Brewers, and he was confident he would improve his hitting. "I believe I can be a good hitter if I work at it, hitting to the opposite field," Edwards told a reporter. "The guys have helped me a lot. Cecil Cooper, Ben Oglivie, and Roy Howell have helped me a lot. Ed Romero, Don Money, and Ted Simmons. These are the guys I go to if I need help."[7]

In 178 at-bats for the Brewers in 1982, Edwards posted a .247 batting average and stole 10 bases. The Brewers won the AL East with a 95-67 record and faced the California Angels for the American League pennant. Edwards ran for Don Money in the seventh inning of Game Three, scoring on Paul Molitor's home run, and it seemed like déjà vu when he ran for Money in the eighth inning of Game Four, this time scoring on a home run by Mark Brouhard. There were bigger things ahead in the fifth and deciding game, played at Milwaukee County Stadium on Sunday, October 10, 1982.

In the top of the seventh inning, with the Brewers leading 4-3, Edwards replaced Gorman Thomas in center field for defensive purposes. With one out in the eighth inning, Don Baylor hit a ball to deep center field. It looked as though the game would be tied, but Edwards had other thoughts.

"I knew Don Baylor," he said years later. "I was playing a little deeper than normal. He was trying to make his name, too, trying to produce in that situation. When the ball came off the bat, I knew he had hit it well. It was like everything was in slow motion, like you always hear in moments like that. I said, 'This is a nice dream.' I saw it in the last five feet. There it was. I saw it plain as day. I remember losing my balance after the catch and going down. I tossed the ball to Benjie (Oglivie) and he threw it back in. That was my moment."[8] It is also an indelible moment for Brewers fans everywhere as the catch helped make a Brewers World Series appearance a reality.

The Brewers lost the Series to the St. Louis Cardinals in seven games. Edwards' only appearance in the Series was in the eighth inning of Game Six, when he ran for Gorman Thomas.

There would be no trip to Vancouver in 1983 as Edwards spent the entire season with the Brewers. He batted .297 in 74 at-bats and stole five bases.

After the season Edwards was removed from the Brewers' major-league roster, but he was invited to their 1984 spring training camp. He was the final cut and was sent to Vancouver. In a book published in 2019 Edwards reflected about that moment and his last season playing in the minor leagues:

"I was kind of shocked when they sent me down. They said my time was up. They decided to go another way. I had a split contract (meaning lower pay for the minors), so they sent me down. After that, all of the air went out of me. That whole year, I was looking at the transition in my life. I figured my major-league time was up. I decided to retire. Cincinnati wanted

me and so did a couple of teams in Japan, but I decided that was enough. I was grateful for what God gave me. I had 10 years in professional baseball."[9]

Edwards returned home to Southern California and worked in home construction and real estate. His wife, Alice, was from Anniston, Alabama; she and Edwards pulled up stakes and he relocated his business ventures there.

As of 2019 Edwards was a minister at the World Changes International Church in College Park, Georgia, near Atlanta. He and his wife have three children: a daughter Adrienne, who is a math teacher, and Casey and Justin, who, as of 2019, attended Jacksonville State University in Jacksonville, Alabama.

SOURCES

In addition to the sources cited in the Notes, the author also accessed Retrosheet.org, Baseball-Reference.com, and SABR.org.

NOTES

1. Tom Flaherty, "'Too Small' Edwards Battles Odds, Wins Brewer Job," *The Sporting News*, May 2, 1981: 21.
2. "Brother Act," *The Sporting News*, June 16, 1979: 43.
3. "Base Bandit," *The Sporting News*, August 23, 1980: 38.
4. Flaherty, "'Too Small Edwards."
5. Ibid.
6. Flaherty, "Edwards' Success Keyed to Patience," *The Sporting News*, August 30, 1982: 26.
7. Ibid.
8. Tom Haudricourt, *Where Have You Gone '82 Brewers?* (Stevens Point, Wisconsin, KCI Sports, 2019) 100.
9. Ibid.

ROLLIE FINGERS

By Dale Voiss

Rollie Fingers was clearly excited as he caught a leaping Ted Simmons, his catcher, after Fingers struck out Detroit's Lou Whitaker to nail down the victory and the second-half American League East title for his Milwaukee Brewers in 1981. (The unprecedented split season was devised after the players' two-month strike was settled.) The Brewers were in the postseason for the first time in their 13-year history. They lost in the first round to the first-half champion New York Yankees, three games to two, but Fingers, whose 28 saves that season preserved 45 percent of the Brewers' 62 victories, won not just the Cy Young Award but the American League Most Valuable Player award as well. Only four pitchers (Don Newcombe, Sandy Koufax, Bob Gibson, and Vida Blue) had done that before Fingers, and only three (Willie Hernandez, Roger Clemens, Dennis Eckersley, and Clayton Kershaw) did it after him, as of the end of the 2019 season.

Roland Glen Fingers developed his mustache, perhaps the most colorful in major-league baseball, on his own. But he credited his father with teaching him how to pitch. Roland was born on August 25, 1946, in Steubenville, Ohio, to George and Pearl (Stafford) Fingers. His father, a steelworker, had pitched in the St. Louis Cardinals farm system for four years and had been a roommate of Stan Musial.

One day, after returning home from a tough day in the steel mill, George Fingers said, "That's it, we're moving to California," Roland Fingers recalled in a TV appearance with Tim McCarver in August 2010. He sold his house for $1,500, bought a car, and moved the family to Cucamonga, California, where he went to work in yet another steel mill. On the drive west, the family couldn't afford to stay in hotels, and they were forced to sleep in sleeping bags by the side of the road.

At Upland High School (Upland and adjoining Cucamonga are east of Los Angeles), Fingers played left field and pitched on the baseball team. He also played American Legion baseball for the Upland Post. In August 1964, after graduating from high school, Fingers pitched his Legion team to the national American Legion title and was named the tournament's player of the year. After winning local and regional tournaments, Upland went to the national tournament in Little Rock, Arkansas. Playing the outfield, Fingers belted three hits and made two running catches in Upland's victory over a Detroit team in the opener of the round robin. He pitched a three-hitter against a team from Charlotte, North Carolina, to wrap up the title. For the Legion season he finished with an 11-2 record, a 0.67 earned-run average, and 102 strikeouts in 81 innings. In the regional and national tournaments, he batted .450 (18-for-40).

After the tournament Fingers returned home to California to discuss his baseball future with his parents. The free-agent draft hadn't been instituted yet, and Fingers had already received offers from more than a dozen major-league organizations. He was prepared to turn them all down to attend Chaffey Junior College at Alta Loma, California.

The Los Angeles Dodgers offered Fingers a $20,000 bonus to sign a contract. But because they already had a solid pitching staff, led by Fingers' boyhood heroes Sandy Koufax and Don Drysdale, he felt it would take him years to make the majors with the Dodgers. Instead, he accepted a $13,000 offer from the Kansas City Athletics, signing the contract on Christmas Eve of 1964.

The Athletics originally wanted Fingers as an outfielder but decided in his first spring training to have him pitch. At Leesburg, in the Class A Florida State League in 1985, he won 8 games and lost 15, with a 2.98 ERA. In late August he went to Cooperstown, where in a ceremony at the Baseball Hall of Fame he received the American Legion player of the year award from the previous summer.

Fingers spent the 1966 season with the Modesto Reds of the Class A California League. Still a starter, he went 11-6 in 22 games with a 2.77 ERA. Among his teammates that season were future Hall of Famers Reggie Jackson and Tony La Russa.

In the spring of 1967, Fingers married his high-school sweetheart, Jill Cutler, who had been the statistician for the Upland High School baseball team. He moved up the A's ladder again, to Birmingham of the Double-A Southern League. Pitching on Opening Day, he suffered a fractured cheekbone and jawbone, and lost some teeth when he was hit by a line drive off the bat of Fred Kovner of Evansville. Fingers' jaw was wired shut for five weeks. He returned to the mound in two months and finished the season with a 6-5 record and a 2.21 ERA. After Birmingham's season ended, to get in some more work, Fingers pitched for the Athletics' entry in the Arizona Fall Instructional League.

The Athletics moved from Kansas City to Oakland after the 1967 season, but Fingers stayed in Birmingham in 1968 for a second straight year. He started the season with eight straight victories, including a two-hit, 5-0 shutout of Evansville, and ended the season with a 10-4 record and a 3.00 ERA. This performance earned him a call-up to Oakland in September, and Fingers would never again pitch in a minor-league game. He pitched just once for the A's after his call-up, allowing four runs on four hits in relief in a 13-0 loss to the World Series-bound Detroit Tigers on September 15. The four hits included a home run by Tigers catcher Bill Freehan.

In the winter of 1968-69, Fingers pitched for the La Guaira club of the Venezuelan Winter League, and worked on developing a slider to supplement his "out" pitch, the fastball.

In 1969 the Athletics' new manager, Hank Bauer, installed a four-man starting rotation Blue Moon Odom, Chuck Dobson, Catfish Hunter, and Jim Nash — and said that to keep the starters on four days' rest, Fingers would start when the A's played more than four straight days. Fingers made his first start of the season on April 22 in Minnesota. He shut out the Twins on five hits, 7-0, facing just 32 batters. He made his next start five days later in Seattle, going 8⅓ innings and allowing five runs on six hits in a 13-5 win over the Pilots. Seven days later he started against Seattle again, this time at Oakland, and lost, 6-4, giving up 11 hits in six-plus innings. He didn't start again until May 30, when he was shelled by the Cleveland Indians, lasting just one-third of an inning in a 9-2 loss. For the next 3½ months, Fingers worked out of the bullpen; he did not start again until September 15, when he lost to the Twins. In the remaining two weeks of the season he made three more appearances as a starter. In 60 games, including eight starts, Fingers was 6-7 with 12 saves.

Hank Bauer was fired in September and replaced by third-base coach John McNamara, who had been Fingers' manager at Birmingham in 1967. Under McNamara in 1970, Fingers got 19 starts and made 26 relief appearances, posting a 7-9 record.

Dick Williams replaced McNamara for 1971.

Fingers began the season in the rotation and started eight games, winning one and losing three. His last start of the season came on May 15, after which Williams made Fingers the closer. Except for two starts early in the 1973 season, Fingers was a closer for the next 15 years. In that 1971 season he earned 17 saves in 20 opportunities, the fourth highest saves total in the American League.

The A's won 101 games that year to win the American League's West Division by 16 games over the Kansas City Royals, but were swept by the Baltimore Orioles in the American League Championship Series. Fingers pitched in two games in the series, allowing two runs in 2⅓ innings.

The division championship in 1971 was the first of five straight for the A's. Their rise to the top was fueled by the talent they got out of their minor-league system in the 1960s, players like Fingers, Reggie Jackson, Bert Campaneris, Joe Rudi, Sal Bando, Catfish Hunter, Blue Moon Odom, and Vida Blue. As these players came together, they jelled as a team and brought success to Oakland. The A's appearance in the 1971 ALCS was the first postseason play for the franchise and its predecessors since the Philadelphia Athletics lost the 1931 World Series to the St. Louis Cardinals.

In 1972-74 the A's won three straight World Series. Over that span, in a time when the semi-automatic ninth-inning closer was not as much of a fixture as it became two decades later, Fingers had 61 saves and a 27-22 won-lost record with an ERA of 2.34. In each of those seasons he pitched between 111 and 126 innings — numbers unheard of among closers of the 21st century. He made the American League All-Star team in 1973 and 1974. (He was also an All-Star in 1975, 1976, 1978, 1981, and 1982.)

Reggie Jackson, Oakland's star outfielder, showed up for spring training in 1972 with a mustache. His teammates did not like the idea of Jackson with a mustache so they all started growing facial hair to protest. Team owner Charles Finley, instead of making everyone shave, as the players hoped he would, offered a cash prize to the player who could grow the best facial hair by Opening Day. Finley felt the look would help sell tickets. Fingers grew a handlebar mustache that curled at the tips. It won the contest, and the mustache became his trademark look.

After the 1972 season Finley sent Fingers a contract calling for a $1,000 raise for 1973. Fingers phoned Finley to argue about the contract. Finley would not budge, so Fingers slammed down the receiver and vowed never to talk to Finley again. He hired agent Jerry Kapstein to represent him in negotiations with Finley and kept his word never to speak to Finley again.

In each of the three seasons from 1974 to 1976, Fingers pitched in at least 70 games, leading the league in appearances in 1974 and 1975. During that span, he saved 62 games for Oakland and had a better than 3-to-1 strikeout-to-walk ratio.

In June 1976, anticipating that he might lose them to free agency after the season, Finley sold Fingers and Joe Rudi to the Boston Red Sox, and Vida Blue to the New York Yankees for a total of $3.5 million ($1 million each for Fingers and Rudi and $1.5 million for Blue). Baseball Commissioner Bowie Kuhn rescinded the deals, saying they were not in the best interests of baseball. Finley's argument had been that if the three became free agents at the end of the season, he would not get anything in return if they signed elsewhere. Kuhn, on the other hand, said that if he allowed the sale to go through, "the door would be opened wide to the buying of success by the more affluent clubs." Finley sued Kuhn for restraint of trade but lost the suit.

After the 1976 season, with Fingers and several teammates eligible for free agency, Finley chose not to sign them and they all went their separate ways. In an attempt to prevent teams from making offers to Fingers, Finley stated that he was washed up, but the San Diego Padres signed Fingers anyway, for a salary of slightly over $250,000, almost triple his highest salary as an Athletic. (The Dodgers, Cardinals, Giants, and Pirates had also wooed Fingers.) Among the players leaving Oakland that winter were Don Baylor, Joe Rudi, Sal Bando, Bert

Campaneris, and Gene Tenace, who also signed with the Padres. In signing, Fingers said he was glad to move to the National League because he was a low-ball pitcher and NL umpires were more likely to call the low-ball strike. Fingers' signing with the Padres came shortly after his wedding to the former Danielle Lamar on November 14. (His first marriage had ended in divorce in 1974, and this one would, too.) A former A's teammate, pitcher Ken Holtzman, was Fingers' best man at the ceremony in the Oakland suburb of Lafayette.

On the Padres, Fingers was reunited with former Athletics manager John McNamara. But McNamara, who took over the Padres in 1974, was fired 48 games into the 1977 season and was replaced by Alvin Dark. At the time Fingers signed, many believed that McNamara would move him into the rotation. This would leave the closer role to Butch Metzger, who had saved 16 games for the Padres in 1976 and earned the NL Rookie of the Year Award. McNamara surprised many by giving the closer job to Fingers and using Metzger in middle relief.

In San Diego, Fingers joined a staff anchored by 1976 Cy Young Award winner Randy Jones. Jones had won 22 games for the Padres in 1976, but an arm injury in September threatened his 1977 season. Jones recovered enough to start the season but went a disappointing 6-12 in 27 games. Meanwhile, Fingers saved 35 games, more than half of the Padres' 69 wins.

Fingers spent four years in San Diego as the Padres' closer, going 34-40 while earning 108 saves in 265 outings. The Padres had just one winning season in the four years and never finished higher than fourth in the six-team National League Western Division. Fingers could hardly be blamed; during his stay in San Diego he won the unofficial National League Fireman of the Year Award three times, in 1977, 1978, and 1980. In his final year in San Diego, Fingers surpassed Hoyt Wilhelm's career record for saves. (As an indication of how the use of closers has changed over the years, Fingers' career total of 341 put him, as of the beginning of the 2014 season, only 11th among closers; the leader as of that year was Mariano Rivera, with 652.)

After the 1980 season Fingers returned to the American League. The Padres traded him, Tenace, and pitcher Bob Shirley to the St Louis Cardinals for seven players; then the Cardinals sent Fingers, catcher Ted Simmons, and pitcher Pete Vuckovich to the Milwaukee Brewers for outfielders Sixto Lezcano and David Green and pitchers Lary Sorensen and Dave LaPoint. When Fingers arrived in Milwaukee, the Brewers were coming off three straight winning seasons. They were led by an explosive offense that included future Hall of Famers Robin Yount and Paul Molitor. But they struggled to find a consistent closer. Fingers was seen by many as the final piece of the puzzle that could send the team to their first postseason appearance. Fingers did not disappoint. In what was regarded as one of the greatest seasons a relief pitcher had up to then, he saved 28 of the team's 62 victories as the Brewers sailed to the second-half American League East title in the strike-shortened 1981 season. Fingers' dominating performance, which included a minuscule 1.04 earned-run average, landed him not only the Cy Young Award but the MVP award as well. Fingers had one victory and one save as the Brewers fell to the Yankees three games to two in the divisional playoffs.

In 1982 Fingers saved 29 games through late August as the Brewers led the American League East for most of the season. The team had really taken off when hitting coach Harvey Kuenn replaced Buck Rodgers as manager in early June. Rodgers' removal had been precipitated by the team's poor play (the Brewers were 23-24 when he was fired) along with criticism of Rodgers by several players, including Fingers.

On August 30 the Brewers obtained right-handed pitcher Don Sutton from the Houston Astros in exchange for three prospects. Sutton, a future Cooperstown inductee, joined the team the next day and started the second game of a doubleheader September 2 against the Cleveland Indians. The Brewers lost the game, 4-2. The loss, however, was

Acquired in a blockbuster trade with the St. Louis Cardinals prior to the 1981 season, Rollie Fingers led the Brewers to their first postseason berth that season and won both the AL Cy Young Award and the MVP award. He missed the entire 1982 postseason with a forearm injury.

not the worst news the team received that night. In the first game of the doubleheader Fingers tore a muscle in his right forearm. The injury kept him out of action for the remainder of the season. Rookie Pete Ladd replaced him as the closer, and the Brewers, without Fingers, advanced to the World Series, which they lost to the Cardinals in seven games.

This tendinitis injury left Fingers sidelined for the entire 1983 season. He returned to form for the Brewers in 1984, saving 23 games for a team that disappointed nearly everyone by finishing 67-94, last in the American League East, under manager Rene Lachemann.

In 1985 Fingers, now 38 years old, returned to the Milwaukee bullpen but clearly wasn't his old self. He saved 17 games but had eight blown saves and finished with a 1-6 record and a 5.04 ERA. The Brewers released him after the season. He received overtures from the Cincinnati Reds, but a team rule against facial hair would have forced him to shave his trademark handlebar mustache, so he declined the Reds' offer and retired.

Fingers went to work for a communications company in the San Diego area, where he worked for about a dozen years. He followed that with a short stint at a printing company, also in the San Diego area.

In January 1992, on just his second appearance on the ballot, Fingers was elected to the Baseball Hall of Fame, along with pitcher Tom Seaver. Before his induction the Brewers retired his uniform number, 34. The following year the Athletics followed suit by also retiring number 34.

Golf became a major passion for Fingers in retirement. He carried a handicap of 2 to 3 for most of his adult life. Fingers played over a decade, with several other pro athletes, on the Celebrity Golf Tour, where he was known to finish as high as third.

In 1999 Fingers moved from his home in California to Las Vegas, where he took a job with Billy Walters, who owned several golf courses in the area. After less than a year he left Walters Golf and later got involved with a golf company that developed a product which helps clean up lakes.

In January 2007 the state of Wisconsin listed Fingers as number eight on its list of tax delinquents. The state Department of Revenue alleged that he owed nearly $1.5 million in income tax from his days as a pitcher for the Brewers. In July the state filed documents saying that two of the three cases it had filed against Fingers had been satisfied, with the third case, for more than $58,000, still pending. The next month Fingers said that his name had been cleared and he had never been delinquent.

As of 2014 Fingers still resided in Las Vegas. Of his five children, a son, Jason, was drafted by the

Kansas City Royals in the tenth round of the June 2000 amateur draft. He pitched for Spokane of the Class A Northwest League in 2000 and Burlington in the Class A Midwest League in 2001 before ending his baseball career. During the summer of 1970 Fingers' younger brother, Gordon, pitched in eight games for Coos Bay-North Bend, Oakland's entry in the Northwest League

SOURCES

Wisconsin State Journal (Madison, Wisconsin), November 4, 1981.

The Sporting News, September 12, 1964, August 7, 1965, April 27, 1967, November 25, 1967, November 16, 1968, January 11, 1969, February 8, 1969, April 19, 1969, July 3, 1976, December 11, 1976, March 12, 1977.

Armour, Mark, Charles Finley biography at SABR BioProject website.

Fingers' Hall of Fame induction speech, 1992

Online interview with Fingers by Jimmy Scott, at jimmyscottshighandtight.com/node/824

"Fingers still takes pioneer route," at lasvegasgolf.com/departments/features/rollie-fingers-golf-326.htm

JIM GANTNER

By Gregg Hoffmann

Jim Gantner played 17 years in the big leagues, all with the Milwaukee Brewers In many ways, he was considered the "heart and soul" of the 1982 Brewers, bringing a competitive spirit and hard-nosed approach to the game.

The image of Gantner and Charlie Moore embracing each other at home plate in County Stadium after scoring the go-ahead runs in the fifth game of the 1982 American League Championship Series against the Angels will always be etched in the history of the Brewers.

Gantner's ties to the Brewers, baseball, and the state of Wisconsin started very, very early. While living in tiny Eden, he was introduced to the game by his father, Elmer.

"I was very, very young. You know, five years old, six years-old," recalled Gantner in a July 19, 2008, interview with the author.[1] "First thing I ever remember doing was playing catch with my dad. We used one of his old gloves. He was a semipro player. He'd throw me the ball, throw me groundballs all the time.

"I remember always taking a rubber ball and throwing it off the garage and catching it. I pretended I was one of the Milwaukee Braves players.

"Nine kids in the family. I was the first son born. [My father] was at Cupie Canning Company. Mom worked too. She worked in Fond du Lac at different jobs. With nine kids, both had to work. Being poor, you don't take anything for granted. Nothing will be given to you."

Gantner was born James Elmer Gantner on January 5, 1953, in Fond du Lac, Wisconsin, to Elmer and Erma Gantner, and was one of nine children. They are brothers Jerry, Mike and Tom and sisters. Linda (Mike) Meissner, Lisa (Bob) Schommer, Patty (Ken) Rickert and (deceased) Shirley Strom and Judy Lee. Both of Gantner's parents are deceased.

The Milwaukee Braves seemed a million miles away for Gantner as a kid, but they were an influence on him. "I heard the Braves on the radio. They were never on TV then. I used to play with that rubber ball against the barn, and make it like groundballs, then throw it to first. I'd pretend to be Eddie Mathews, Hank Aaron, Johnny Logan. Eddie was my number 1."[2]

Gantner played Little League in Eden, amateur baseball in Campbellsport, and then high-school ball at Campbellsport High School. He played four years of baseball at the school and led the basketball team in scoring his senior season.[3]

"Hubie Diekfuss was my coach," Gantner recalled. "He was there forever. He had to do everything. One coach. He had to take care of the field. He was a big influence on my life, very big influence.

"I still wasn't very big, probably 5-10, 5-11. We

had some good baseball players at Campbellsport. They didn't have divisions then, so we had to play against everybody."

Gantner knew he would likely play at UW-Oshkosh, then a small-college power in the NAIA. "I remember visiting Oshkosh and seeing all the plaques," he said. "They were the elite team in the state school system. I remember seeing all the pictures and them guys going to the World Series."

Oshkosh coach Russ Tiedemann saw the potential in Gantner. Tiedemann "was another big influence in my life," Gantner said. "He was another father figure to me. He had to put me in my place at times. Sometimes, you're not that responsible at that age. He had to set me down a few times and say, 'Hey, be responsible, be on time.'"

While Gantner was at Oshkosh in 1973-74, the Titans made it to the NAIA tournament, finishing third in 1973 and fifth in 1974. Gantner accumulated enough hits to rank fourth on the school's all-time list and fifth in runs.[4]

"In my freshman year, we got to the World Series in Phoenix, Arizona," Gantner said. "Oh man, that was the first time I ever flew on an airplane. It was a 747, the big one. I had never been on one. It was an incredible experience. I think we finished third that year.

"That's the first time I could compare. How good are we? How good am I? Can I play with these guys? Did I have a chance to play pro ball? Playing in that tournament gave me the confidence that I could play with these guys. A lot of our players, hey, we could play at this level."

One of Gantner's opponents in college would become a teammate with the Brewers. "I faced Jerry Augustine my freshman year," Gantner said. "He was at La Crosse. He was very good. He was probably one of the best pitchers in the conference. Once we were teammates with the Brewers, we laughed and talked about those days.

"One episode, we were playing at Oshkosh. It was a cold day, and Augie was pitching outstanding. He had 2-and-2 on me and threw me a nasty curveball. It was strike 3. The umpire called it a ball. I remember I said, "Oh my gosh." Some relation to Tiedemann was the home-plate umpire. Augie always kidded me about that. It was 3-and-2, and the next pitch I hit a home run, after he had me struck out. We kidded about that for years."

The Brewers picked Gantner in the 1974 draft. "I got picked though in the 12th round of the draft after my sophomore season," Gantner said. "I didn't know the Brewers were going to draft me. I thought Pittsburgh or Cincinnati were going to draft me."[5]

Gantner recalled some the early time in the minors. "I bought a bike to get around. It had a banana seat and high handlebars. That's what I drove all summer. Couldn't afford a car. I rode that bike back and forth to the ballpark. That was a lonely time. It was my first time away from home and you can't hitchhike back. You get homesick. At least it was a short season — June, July, and August.

"John Felske was my manager. He was my manager at every level of the minor leagues. We got to know each other real well."[6]

Gantner played shortstop originally, but knew Yount was going to hold down that position for quite some time. So he became as versatile as he could, playing second and third base too.

He moved to Double A in his second year and played at Thetford Mines (which he said was worse than Newark). The Brewers moved that franchise to Pittsfield, Massachusetts, and Gantner enjoyed playing there much more. He was then called up from Double A after the Brewers' Don Money was injured.

"I remember coming to the park and Felske called me into the office," Gantner said. "He was kind of secretive. He kind of started slow, you know, and said, 'I got a call today. You're going to the big leagues.'" When he first shook my hand, I thought he was going to tell me I was going to Triple-A, but it was the big leagues. That was even better.

"I was married to my first wife by then. I remember packing up the car. We had a big Pontiac. I had to drive to Detroit, to meet the team in Detroit. I got picked up for speeding on that trip.

"I'm cruising along. I don't even remember

what state I was in. The State Patrol pulls me over. I'm going with the traffic, but I get pulled over. I'm not even leading the pack. So I said to the police officer, 'Man, I was just going with the traffic.'

"He said, 'I know. Are you a hunter? I said, 'Yeah, I'm a hunter.' He said, 'When a flock of ducks go over, I can't shoot them all. I can only shoot one. You happen to be that duck.' I had Wisconsin plates on the car and I think he pulled me over because I was from out of state."

Gantner started as soon as he reported to the Brewers. "I remember I was in the lineup that first night, playing third base because Money had been injured. Fidrych was pitching. My first big league at-bat was against Mark 'The Bird' Fidrych. That's the year he won 19 games.

"Ron LeFlore was the leadoff hitter. Remember they got him out of prison. He could fly. My first play with the first batter was a bunt play. I was playing in. They said he's probably going to bunt to test the new kid. I got him out.

"Jerry Augustine pitched that night. That was the night Hegan hit for the cycle. There was forty-some thousand people there. We beat Fidrych pretty bad that night. My first hit was off Fidrych."

Hank Aaron was Gantner's teammate in Milwaukee. "[He] was one of my childhood idols. As a kid, I pretended to be Hank Aaron and Eddie Mathews when I was throwing the ball off the garage and catching it. Here I am on the same team with him."

Gantner suffered through those early years with the Brewers, but in 1978 things began to change, and change rapidly.

Harry Dalton had been brought in as general manager, and he hired George Bamberger, who had been pitching coach with the Baltimore Orioles, as manager. Few knew who Bamberger was. Many joked about his name resembling hamburger.

But Bamberger set a different tone in the Brewers' clubhouse immediately. He made some lineup changes, including giving Gantner more playing time, and suddenly "Bambi's Bombers" were born.

Gantner and the other Brewers loved Bamberger's folksy, almost grandfatherly way. The fans also loved him, especially when he would join them in the parking lot for tailgating after the game. The Brewers were on their way up. So was the young infielder from Eden.

"When they brought in Bamberger, I didn't even know who he was. He was the pitching coach from Baltimore is all I knew. Harry Dalton hired him because of his Baltimore ties. But a lot of us were like the average fan and didn't know who he was.

"Once I got to spring training, I remember he called me into the office. Like I said, Grammas never really communicated. But George told me, 'You can't make this team as a regular, but I'm going to give you a chance to make this team as a utility ballplayer.' By that time, we had Molitor, Yount, Bando, Cooper, Money. I understood that. That's fine. He played me almost every game."

Gantner became a valuable player on the up-and-coming club, but wanted to play every day. "I was having a lot of fun, but still wanted to play every day. So I asked to be traded.

"I almost got traded, to Kansas City for Larry Gura. I remember Jim Colburn was at Kansas City and he told me I might be going there. But I would have been utility there too. It never happened."

Gantner ended up being very happy about not going to KC. The Brewers just kept improving and got to the Series in 1982.

"We came so close in that split season of 1981," Gantner said. "Then we started the '82 season with Buck Rodgers as manager and a lot of optimism, but we just couldn't get it going.

"I remember we were in Seattle, and Buck called me into the office and told me, 'You're not going to play tomorrow.' We were struggling overall. I remember saying, 'I don't want to sit out.' He told me he had to sit me out because he was going to sit Cecil [Cooper], who had been struggling, and I would have been the only left-hander in the lineup.

"He got fired that night, and Cecil and I were in the lineup the next day. We thought it might happen, but we didn't expect it that night. I guess Harvey [Kuenn] was already at the hotel. Nobody knew it. He was our manager the next day. We won the game. That was the start of our good streak."⁷

The Brewers went on under Kuenn to the Division title, but it had to go down to the last weekend of the regular season for them to clinch it. They went to Baltimore and lost the first three games of the series. That brought it down to the final game, pitting Don Sutton against the Orioles' Jim Palmer.

"The final series in Baltimore was incredible," Gantner recalled. "We wanted to go in there and take care of business early. We knew we had to win one out of four. We wanted to get it out of the way quick.

"We lost the first night, then had a doubleheader. We figured if we'd win one of those it would be over. I never (saw) such excitement as there was in Baltimore then. I remember going on the bus from the hotel to the ballpark, and the streets were already packed. We'd be going down the streets in the bus, and the people would be yelling at us — we're going to beat you again today. The sidewalks were just full of people.

"I remember taking infield. The stands were already filled up. They were standing and yelling during infield. (I've) never seen anything like that. That was Earl Weaver's last year, so everything was coming together. They were like World Series games."⁸

The game is etched in Brewers lore. Robin Yount had key hits, Ben Oglivie made a clutch catch, Sutton was superb and the Brewers won.

"One of the biggest things I remember about that game was (Ben Oglivie's) catch. He dove and made a great catch. There wasn't much room there in left field, and he dove and caught it. They would have scored a couple runs right there. He made that catch and you could see it took something out of them. We scored a bunch of runs then. Robin [Yount] hit two home runs. But that catch kind of slammed the door on them. …"⁹

The Brewers flew to the West Coast to meet the Angels in the Championship Series. They lost the first two games, but came back to win the next three.

Jim Gantner was a fixture at second base and third base during his 17-year major-league career (1976-1992), played entirely with the Brewers. "Gumby" batted .274 and collected 1,696 hits.

"I remember we thought after we lost the first two games, 'Hey, we did it in Baltimore, we can to it again.' We knew we had to get back here to County Stadium and get a win. Just that one win, and then we'd be ready to take off. We had to get that first win."

The Brewers did get that first win, then another, and brought it to Game Five. "That fifth game was a great one. I was on base when Cecil got his famous big hit. I remember being on second base and seeing that little line shot Cecil hit to left. I can remember Cecil leaving the home-plate area and saying, 'Get down, get down' with his arms.

"It wasn't that deep. I remember sliding across home plate, and Charlie (Moore), who had scored before me tackled me. Charlie was really excited. I remember saying, 'Hey, let me up. We got two innings to go yet.'"[10]

The Brewers were in the World Series for the first time in their history. It would not come out well, with the Cardinals beating them in seven games. "The World Series was incredible, but the outcome was very disappointing. I still think we had a better team, but the difference was they had (Bruce) Sutter and we didn't have Rollie (Fingers).[11] (Fingers had torn a muscle in his forearm in early September and was lost for the season and the postseason.)

"I remember after we had lost, we came home. We had to wake up and have that parade. It was cold that day. Nobody really wanted to do. We thought for sure nobody was going to be there. We got in the cars and we saw the streets were just packed. I said, 'Holy man. Just think if we had won what would have happened.' It was incredible the response we got. It was fun riding in those cars through that crowd. You forgot about the fact you lost. The people were cheering for you and yelling your name.

"Then getting into the stadium. It was a very, very special day. Then Robin coming in on that motorcycle. That topped it off. It was an incredible homecoming for us. If we had won that last game, it might have lasted for a week."

Gantner and the Brewers would never get to the Series again during his career, but he did play until 1992 for the club. A highlight came in 1987, when the team won 13 straight to start the season.

"That Easter Sunday game that kept the streak alive was incredible. It was 77 degrees; I remember that. I remember (Rob) Deer Hunter hitting that three-pointer to tie it up. I batted after him and walked. It was a 3-and-2 pitch when Dale (Sveum) hit that home run. Those were incredible games. They had to delay the start of games because traffic was on the highway yet."[12]

Another highlight was Yount's 3,000th hit in 1992. Gantner and Molitor, who with Yount had played together longer than any trio in history to that point, were the first to greet him at first base.

"It really became well known when Robin got his 3,000th hit. Paulie and I were the first ones out there. I respected our teammates for that. They told us, 'We want you and Paulie out there first.' It meant a lot."[13]

Gantner had a torn rotator cuff in his latter years and retired in 1994. He continued to be linked with the Brewers, making personal appearances as sort an ambassador for the club, and coaching for manager Phil Garner in 1996-97. He later managed Wausau in the Northwoods League for a couple of seasons.

Gantner picked up the nickname Gumby, allegedly from Gorman Thomas, and became known for his Yogi Berra-type misuse of the language at times. These things, his unpretentious personality and friendliness, and the way he played baseball for the home state team endured him to fans. He has been inducted into the Wisconsin Athletic Hall of Fame.

"I have always felt lucky and privileged to have been able to play in the state where I was born, and remain a Wisconsin guy," Gantner said. "The people, the fans have been great to me."[14]

SOURCES

In addition to the sources cited in the Notes, the author also accessed Retrosheet.org, Baseball-Reference.com, the SABR Minor Leagues Database, accessed online at Baseball-Reference.com, and SABR.org.

NOTES

1. Interview with Gregg Hoffmann, June 19, 2008, La Crosse, Wisconsin.
2. Unless otherwise noted, all quotations from Gantner are from interviews with Gregg Hoffmann (2008-9) for a project called "Gumby of Eden," to be published as part of a series to be called "Immortalized in Bronze: An-Depth Story."
3. University of Wisconsin-Oshkosh Athletic Department Archives.
4. uwoshkoshtitans.com.
5. *Wisconsin Athlete Magazine*, May 1982: 19-20.
6. *Wisconsin Athlete Magazine*, May 1982: 21.
7. Interview with Gregg Hoffmann, July 30, 2008, Wausau, Wisconsin. Weaver came back to manage the Orioles in 1985 and 1986.
8. Gantner conflates the dates. The Brewers lost a doubleheader to the Orioles on Friday, October 1, then lost on Saturday. They won on Sunday to clinch the division.
9. Interview with Gregg Hoffmann, July 27, 2009, Wausau, Wisconsin.
10. Interview with Sean Callahan, *Wisconsin Sportsvue*, August 1984: 5
11. Ibid, 6-7.
12. Interview with Gregg Hoffmann, July 27, 2009, Wausau, Wisconsin.
13. Ibid.
14. Interview with Gregg Hoffmann, August 28, 2009, Milwaukee.

MOOSE HAAS

By Dennis D. Degenhardt

When his parents wanted him to have a backup plan in case the baseball thing didn't work, his father taught him to be a locksmith. He was the second youngest starting pitcher[1] to make his debut for the Brewers (20 years, 139 days), started second most games, and saw his career cut short while still young, only 31. Welcome to Moose Haas.

Bryan Edmund Haas was born on April 22, 1956, to George Edmund "Bud" Haas, a Baltimore police officer and Dorothy M. (Hailey) Haas, a florist in Baltimore, Maryland. Bud nicknamed him Moose as a baby because he thought he was going to as big as a moose with his broad shoulders. This did not happen and Haas played major-league baseball at 6 feet, 180 pounds.[2] But the name stuck. He was the second of three children with an older brother, George Michael Haas and a younger sister, Dawn Renee Hass-Dauer.

In high school, Haas earned four letters in baseball and basketball playing for Franklin High School in Reisterstown, a suburb of Baltimore. He excelled on the diamond as a pitcher, starting for three years and earning all-county honors once and all-metro twice. With scouts in attendance, the team captain threw a 1-0 no-hitter[3] in his senior year. He also played sandlot baseball for renowned coach Sterling Fowble, who sent a number of players to the major leagues including Hall of Famer Al Kaline, Dave Boswell, Phil Linz, Jim Spencer, Tim Nordbrook, and Ron Swoboda.[4]

Considered the best pitcher in Maryland, Haas was selected by the Brewers in the second round of the June 1974 amateur draft.[5] Preferring baseball over college, he signed and reported to the Newark (New York) Co-Pilots of the short-season New York-Penn League. As one of the younger players, he started 13 games, completing six and going 5-5 with a 3.19 ERA. He was promoted to the Burlington (Iowa) Bees in the Class A Midwest League for 1975; he was nearly two years younger than the league-average player. A league all-star, he struck out nearly three batters for every walk and was 11-8 with a 2.05 ERA. In his only professional opportunity to bat, he got 15 hits for a .250 batting average with three home runs.

Although Haas was pegged for promotion to the Double-A Berkshire Brewers for the 1976 season, Frank Howard, managing the Brewers Triple-A team in Spokane, needed pitching, persuaded the front office that Haas could make the move, and then named him the Opening Day starter.[6] Haas threw seven innings while yielding two earned runs with no decision as the Indians lost.[7] Competing with players averaging age 25, Haas won his first Pacific Coast League game while still 19, the day before his birthday.[8] He led the Indians in wins, finishing 13-9 on a team 13 games below .500. Only six PCL pitchers had more wins.

When major-league rosters expanded in September, Haas was promoted to Milwaukee; he never spent another day in the minors. Wearing the number 30,[9] the 20-year-old rookie joined the team on September 8 in New York and was thrown into the fray, making his debut in the fifth inning with runners on the corners and no outs with the division-leading Yankees leading 4-0. The first batter he faced was Thurman Munson, who grounded out, driving in the fifth run. He then struck out Lou Piniella and got Chris Chambliss to ground out. In three innings, he allowed three hits and one run. His manager, Alex Grammas, said Haas "showed a lot of poise."[10] Haas admitted he was "nervous, but nothing about Yankee Stadium. I just wanted to do well."[11] He pitched in four more games, including two starts, with only one poor outing, a three-inning start in his hometown, Baltimore, where he walked six and yielded four earned runs. In 16 innings, he was 0-1 with a 3.94 ERA.

After a great spring, Haas was one of three rookies[12] making the Brewers rotation in 1977 and opened his 1977 season where he debuted, Yankee Stadium. He hurled a strong 7⅔ innings, allowing a run in the second inning, then retiring 17 of 20 in a no-decision. His first major-league win came at Toronto, 3-1 on May 2. Through his first seven games, Haas's ERA was 2.65 with a 3-1 record and six quality starts.[13] He then slumped through June, seeing his ERA climb to 4.55 before reversing course with a strong July and being named the Brewers pitcher of the month, winning three of five decisions with two complete games. He finished the season 10-12 with a 4.33 ERA. The Milwaukee baseball writers named Haas the Brewers Rookie of the Year.[14]

Just before the season ended, Haas married Diana Landgrebe of Milwaukee on October 1. They would have one son, Joshua Ryan, born in 1984.

With the Brewers trading their oldest starter, Jim Slaton (age 27), and another out injured, new manager George Bamberger expected Haas to help pick up the slack in 1978. He pitched complete-game victories over the Orioles and Yankees to start the season. In defeating the New Yorkers, he fanned 14 batters,[15] establishing a franchise record that held until 2004. Bamberger said, "It looks to me like this is the guy who might be the stopper on this club."[16] But those were his only victories, and his season stopped in the second inning of his fourth start, on April 20, when he heard a pop throwing a curveball. He went on the disabled list, diagnosed with a partial tear of the flexor muscle near the elbow.[17] An attempted return in June didn't work, and he returned to the DL with elbow tendinitis. Bamberger wanted Haas to pitch again, saying, "I want him to go home with a clear mind."[18] And he did, tossing three scoreless innings in the last game of the season. Haas felt good. "Now I can rest a little easier this winter knowing I can pitch and get somebody out," he said. "The important thing was how my arm would feel, and it felt great."[19]

Haas spent the offseason preparing for the 1979 campaign, strengthening the injured elbow, and it paid off as Haas played the entire season. Early in spring training he initially felt stiffness but no pain and stayed behind in Arizona to get in extra work before making his first start two weeks into the season. He tossed his first complete game and first win on May 2, his fourth outing, giving up one run in Cleveland. He continued to have success against the Indians, defeating them three times including his first major-league shutout on July 21, his second victory during the Brewers' record-tying 10-game winning streak. One of Haas's challenges returning from the injury was inconsistency. When he struggled, he was bad, his ERA topped at 6.24 and he lost 11 times. When he was good, he was great. In his 11 wins, he had a 2.34 ERA with seven complete games. Bamberger blamed it on missing nearly a year.[20] Haas improved after the All-Star break and finished strong in September, a harbinger of the future, with a 3.29 ERA and three complete games. By season end, he had lowered his ERA to 4.78 in 184⅔ innings with his 95 strikeouts again leading the team. The improving Brewers finished second in the AL East.

A year removed from injury, Haas was optimistic about the 1980 season, being more consistent to win the pennant after finishing third then second. Although he started 1-3, he had only one poor outing. He reeled off six wins in his next 10 starts. In Baltimore, before friends and family, he tossed a five-hit shutout, winning in his hometown for the first time after three losses. His father was "tickled to death," saying, "He idolized the Orioles as a kid. It's nice to beat them right on their home grounds."[21] He was the American League Player of the Week through August 3 after allowing only one run in 16 innings. Haas was the needed stopper, shutting out the first-place Yankees on three hits to avoid a four-game sweep. He ended the season slumping, losing four of six with one exception, a two-hit 7-1 victory in Seattle. Haas led the Brewers with a 16-15 record, both career highs. He also set career highs by leading the team with 252⅓ innings pitched, 14 complete games, 3 shutouts, and 146 strikeouts.[22] In Haas's 15 losses the Brewers were shut out four times, and they scored two or fewer runs in 11 games. With better run support he would have easily been a 20-game winner.

After Haas's best year, the Brewers added needed pitching in a blockbuster trade with St. Louis, acquiring starter Pete Vuckovich, closer Rollie Fingers, and All-Star catcher Ted Simmons in December.[23] But the 1981 season was interrupted by a midseason players strike that wiped out all games from June 12 until August 10. There was a new division playoff format with each half's winners meeting in a best-of-five series and the winner advancing to the league championships. Haas was not as consistent as in 1980, with his ERA remaining above 4.00 after May, topping at 4.97. He finished the first half with a 5-4 record, his team finished third and needing a second-half turnaround to make the playoffs. Haas saved his best for his last two starts, throwing a new split-finger fastball. At Detroit versus the contending Tigers, his eight-inning five-hit win returned the Brewers to first place. He was even better in a must-win game against the Tigers at home with a complete-game victory. Opposing manager Sparky Anderson said, "He was super tonight."[24] The excited fans called Haas out for a curtain call as the Brewers needed one win with two games remaining to clinch their first postseason berth; they won that the next night. Haas finished with an 11-7 record, leading the team in complete games.

Haas started Game One of the Division Series against the New York Yankees[25] but didn't last long, surrendering eight hits and four runs in 3⅓ innings and losing 5-3 at County Stadium. Haas had an opportunity to redeem himself in the decisive Game Five. As in Game One, he did not get out of the fourth inning, giving up back-to-back home runs to Reggie Jackson and Oscar Gamble as the Brewers lost 7-3. The Yankees got to him for 13 hits and seven earned runs in 6⅔ innings.

Like his teammates, Haas spent more time looking forward to the next season than backward. Getting going was delayed when an 8.7-inch snowstorm wiped out the 1982 home opener and first series. Through May, Haas had nine starts and one relief appearance but only a 2-2 record, often due to poor run support and arm soreness. His first complete game, on May 20, an important 4-1 victory, prevented the struggling Brewers from slipping to .500. On June 2, GM Harry Dalton fired manager Buck Rodgers and named Harvey Kuenn interim manager, because the team was not playing up to his expectations. That move became the catalyst to winning the pennant. Haas won the second game under Kuenn, and six before August, including four straight in July. But he struggled in six August starts and became the odd man out when the Brewers acquired starter Don Sutton at the trading deadline. After Haas's start on September 2, his 10th win, he went to the bullpen as he admitted, "I haven't been pitching as well as I can. I know that."[26] Haas made only five appearances the remainder of the season. He earned his 11th win in relief on September 8 and had a three-inning scoreless save[27] on September 28 to protect the Brewers' three-game lead entering the final weekend in Baltimore when the Brewers won the finale and advanced to the ALCS. Haas repeated with 11 wins, with a 4.47 ERA.

Haas again pitched in the postseason, making his first start in nearly a month in the must-win ALCS Game Four, earning a big 9-5 win over the Angels. The Brewers won the biggest game in franchise history the next day, 4-3, to advance to the World Series against the St. Louis Cardinals. Haas was unsure of his Series role until he was notified before Game Two that he would start Game Four. His response: "I'm excited, I've dreamed about it."[28] In 5⅓ innings he allowed five runs, falling behind 5-1, but the Brewers' six-run seventh-inning rally clinched a 7-5 victory, tying the Series at two games each. He relieved in the sixth inning of Game Seven with the Brewers trailing, 4-3, two men on base, with two outs, and coaxed an inning-ending groundball. But the Brewers could not score again, and the Cardinals won their ninth championship, 6-3.[29] Haas's postseason experience was very disappointing with a 7.17 ERA over the past two years.

After a disappointing season and playoff experience, Haas went from "power pitcher to reliable pitcher," adding a changeup in spring training.[30] He struggled with consistency and bad luck in his first six starts with four no-decisions and a 1-1 record with a 5.03 ERA. His first complete game wasn't until May 31, a 5-2 victory in Oakland, and he said, "I can feel it's turning. These things usually even out."[31] He was right on; a victory over the Tigers on June 21 dropped his ERA to 4.06. On July 2, he won his sixth game but had to leave after five innings with a tender elbow. In 11 starts after the All-Star break, Haas had a 7-1 record with four complete games and three shutouts, including a five-game winning streak. During this stretch he tossed 28 scoreless innings in August, a franchise record until 1987.[32] And then the train left the tracks, with a sore arm ending his season the week of Labor Day. After he skipped a start due to soreness, Haas's last game, on September 9, was an eight-inning 2-1 win in Detroit. Haas went on the DL and the Brewers went on a 10-game losing streak resulting in their elimination from the playoffs. Still the 1983 season was one of Haas's best, his fifth in a row (and last) with double-digit wins, 13. With only three losses, his .813 winning percentage was the league best.

Coming into spring training in 1984, Haas was not concerned after having a clean November examination and resting his arm. But it was a bad season for the Brewers: They were below .500 for the first time since 1978, winning only 67 games with poor offense and bullpen performance, both of which cost Haas opportunities for victories. After losing his first two starts on the road with poor mechanics, he earned his first win starting his first home opener.[33] He pitched well, but was unable to run a winning streak longer than two games. Haas pitched well on a poor team, deserving better than a 9-11 record with a 3.99 ERA. His four complete games matched Mike Caldwell for the team lead and with only 13 the Brewers set the AL record for futility.[34] During the season he fought through some arm soreness and dealt with a divorce from Diana.[35] Diana and Moose had one son, Joshua born in 1984.

In 1985, Haas started his first-ever season opener, at home with the familiar lack of offensive support plus poor defense, three unearned runs, for a 4-1 defeat. But he was 5-2 with a 2.62 ERA over his first 10 starts, yielding more than three earned runs only once. On June 29 he hurled the best game of his career, with only Don Mattingly's one-out double in the seventh ending Haas's no-hit bid. He finished with an 84-pitch, one-hit shutout at Yankee Stadium.

After the All-Star break, Haas struggled going deeper than five innings, leaving his start on July 30 because of shoulder stiffness diagnosed as tendinitis and not pitching until a relief appearance on August 17. Returning to the rotation, he wasn't very sharp, finally earning a win on August 30. It was his first since his June gem and his last "W" as a Brewer. He left his final start on September 26 with a loss and with sore triceps. After starting with a 7-3 record through June with a 2.38 ERA, he finished at .500, 8-8, with his ERA rising to 3.84 as he struggled with injuries. With another poor year for the Brewers, changes were anticipated, with Haas high on the trade list.

With too many young arms, Haas became expendable at age 29, traded to Oakland on Easter

Moose Haas overcame a serious elbow injury in 1978 to notch at least 11 wins in five straight seasons (1979-1983) for the Brewers, including 16 victories in 1980, though none were as important as his victory in Game Four of the 1982 ALCS against the California Angels.

Sunday, March 30, 1986, for four minor leaguers.[36] After many rumors, Haas was relieved. "There's some sadness in leaving," he commented. "I'm leaving some guys I played with a long time, and the city of Milwaukee was great to me. But I'm happy to go somewhere I'm wanted."[37]

Haas repaid the welcome, winning his first six games, allowing two or fewer runs in each, and receiving strong offensive support with the A's averaging 9.2 runs per game.[38] His streak ended the next game when he lost to Boston, tying a career high with six walks. He won his next start, in Baltimore, thanks to an early seven-run lead. Then, at New York on May 21, he left after two innings because of stiffness in his shoulder. Haas made two attempts to return, in June and July, but experienced pain and was shut down with bursitis. As he did with 1978's injury, he made an encouraging start on October 1, allowing no runs with two hits in five innings. What started with a bang, ended in a whimper: He missed over half of the season, making 12 starts, going 7-2 with a 2.74 ERA.

Although concerned with his health but encouraged by his end-of-season start, the A's signed Haas as a free agent for the 1987 season. Their fears were well founded. Haas started the season on the 21-day disabled list with a pulled rotator-cuff muscle[39] and didn't make his first start until May 1. He made only nine starts in all, getting his 100th and last win on May 27. On June 19 he left his start with a sore elbow and did not pitch again. His 2-2 mark and 5.75 ERA were an unfortunate end to a good 12-year career. Once a strikeout pitcher he had only 13. The A's released Haas on November 9, 1987.

Haas wasn't ready to call it quits in 1988, trying out with the San Francisco Giants and working out with Phoenix during the summer. He tried out with the California Angels the following season, but his arm was not up to the task.

After his baseball career, while pursuing his interest in fitness and conditioning, Haas developed a relationship with the Brewers' one-time aerobics instructor and left his wife for her. Together they raised thoroughbred race horses in Arizona and California for 12 years before breaking up in the mid-1990s.[40] Haas became a strength and conditioning coach with certification from the National Strength and Conditioning Association and continues doing so part-time with figure skaters while residing in Arizona. He was inducted into the Maryland Athletic Hall of Fame in 1992 and the Milwaukee Brewers Wall of Fame in 2014. In December, 2002, he married Julie Patterson, a Canadian professional skater who spent 14 years with the Ice Capades. Haas was also an active participant in the annual Brewers Fantasy Camp, traditionally tossing the first inning of the first game versus the campers.[41]

ACKNOWLEDGMENT

Special thanks to SABR member Bill Mortell of Maryland, whose knowledge of Ancestry.com and research skills have proven invaluable in finding information on Haas. Tracking down his family history was a true challenge for Bill.

SOURCES

In addition to the sources cited in the Notes, the author also accessed Retrosheet.org, Baseball-Reference.com, SABR.org, and The Sporting News archive via Paper of Record.

NOTES

1. The youngest starting pitcher was Kevin Kobel, 19, who pitched in two games June 1973. Dave LaPoint is listed as pitching at age 20 with his debut on September 10, 1980, but his birthday is listed as July 29, 1959, making him 21.
2. Chuck Stewart, "Haas Answers Moose Calls With Victories at Spokane," *The Sporting News*, August 7, 1976: 31.
3. National Baseball Hall of Fame, Moose Haas file.
4. The Sun, Obit for Virginia E.K. Foble, 87, baseball scorekeeper, GenealogyBank.com. *The Baltimore Sun*, June 23, 2005.
5. The second-round draft choice was signed by Brewers scout Brad Kohler.
6. Stewart.
7. Ibid.
8. "Coast Toasties," *The Sporting News*, May 8, 1976: 33.
9. Haas wore the number 30 with both major-league teams, the Brewers and Oakland A's.
10. Lou Chapman. "Brewer Rookie Stars but His Mates Don't," *Milwaukee Sentinel*, September 9, 1976: Part 2, 1.
11. Ibid.
12. Lou Chapman, "Brewers Put Their Money on 2nd Base," *The Sporting News*, April 23, 1977: 24. In addition to Haas, the rookies included Barry Cort and Gary Beare.
13. For a quality start a starting pitcher must complete at least six innings while yielding three or fewer earned runs.
14. Lou Chapman, "Augustine Is Dean of Brewers Pitchers at 25," *The Sporting News*, January 21, 1978: 57.
15. Included in the 14 K's was future Hall of Famer Reggie Jackson, who whiffed four times.
16. Mike Gonring, "Haas's Pitching on the Money," *Milwaukee Journal*, April 21, 1978: Part 2, 1.
17. Mike Gonring, "Haas' Injury, Then Red Sox, Jolt Brewers," *Milwaukee Journal*, April 21, 1978: Part 2, 1.
18. Mike Gonring, "Brewers' Season Ends Up Smashingly," *Milwaukee Journal*, October 1, 1978: Part 2, 11.
19. Ibid.
20. Mike Gonring, "Davis Jumps Off Bench to Fuel Brewer Attack," *The Sporting News*, June 23, 1979: 7.
21. Tom Flaherty, "Haas Junks Baltimore Jinx with a Sentimental Shutout," *Milwaukee Journal*, June 4, 1980: 14.
22. This was the only time Haas exceeded 200 innings pitched.
23. The future Hall of Famer Rollie Fingers and Pete Vuckovich would win the next two Cy Young Awards with Fingers adding MVP to his 1981 Cy Young.
24. Tom Flaherty, "Haas Stands as a Hero Among Brewer Heroes," *Milwaukee Journal*, October 3, 1982: 10.
25. The Yankees were a familiar playoff foe for Milwaukee fans who recalled their Braves playing them in the 1957 (win) and 1958 (loss) World Series.
26. Tom Flaherty, "Great Debut for Sutton … Until the End," *Milwaukee Journal*, September 3, 1982: Part 2, 10.
27. This was the second of two career saves.
28. "Molitor's Hits Tie a World Series Record," *Milwaukee Journal*, October 14, 1982: Part 3, 2.
29. The Cardinals won in 1926, 1931, 1934, 1942, 1944, 1946, 1964, 1967 and 1982.
30. Peter Gammons, "Brewers Win Without Power," *The Sporting News*, August 29, 1983: 29.
31. Tom Flaherty, "Pieces Finally Fall in Place for Haas, Brewers," *Milwaukee Journal*, June 1, 1983: Part 2, 9.
32. Haas pitched shutouts on August 5 and 10 and eight innings on the 15th. On August 21 he stretched the streak two more innings, then gave up a run in the third.
33. "Notes & Quotes," *Milwaukee Sentinel*, April 18, 1984: Part 2, 2. Pitching coach Pat Dobson said Haas was throwing across his body.
34. Tom Flaherty, "Bamberger Counting on Stars," *The Sporting News*, October 29, 1984: 48. The record does not include strike-shortened years. For a twenty-first-century perspective on how the game has changed, the 2018 Milwaukee Brewers had zero complete games.
35. Vic Feuerherd, "Haas Evolved as a Pitcher," *Milwaukee Sentinel*, April 9, 1985: Part 2, 1.
36. The players received in the trade with Oakland were Mike Fulmer, Pete Kendrick, infielder Mike Kiefer and catcher Charlie O'Brien.
37. Tom Haudricourt, "Moose Is Dealt to A's," *Milwaukee Sentinel*, March 31, 1986: Part 2, 1.
38. "A.L. West," *The Sporting News*, May 19, 1986: 21.
39. "A.L. West," *The Sporting News*, April 13, 1987: 22.
40. Tom Haudricourt, *Where Have You Gone, '82 Brewers?* (Stevens Point, Wisconsin: KCI Sports Publishing, 2007), 59-62.
41. I had the pleasure of having Moose as my fantasy camp coach in 2005 and I am eternally grateful he allowed me to turn a triple into a double with the old wheels struggling to run the bases.

LARRY HISLE

By David E. Skelton

Consider the two nearly identical rookie seasons below:

	AB	R	H	2B	3B	HR	RBI	AVG
Player #1	464	59	127	22	5	20	68	.274
Player #2	482	75	128	23	5	20	56	.266

These highly acclaimed prospects started 18 years apart. Both were center fielders, blessed with power and speed. Player #1 was the runaway choice for National League Rookie of the Year and had one of the greatest careers in major-league history. Player #2 finished a distant fourth in the N.L. Rookie of the Year voting, suffered a "sophomore jinx" that nearly ended his career, rebounded with some excellent seasons, but was derailed by injury. Though they were playing for different teams, Player #1 offered batting tips to Player #2 at one point during the latter's rookie season.[1]

Player #1 is Hall of Famer Willie Mays.

Player #2 is Larry Hisle.[2]

Hisle, an Ohio native, grew up playing sports alongside fellow major-league star Al Oliver. He was also a fine basketball player but passed up a possible NBA career to sign with the Philadelphia Phillies in 1965. His most productive seasons came more than a decade later for the Minnesota Twins and Milwaukee Brewers. He made two All-Star appearances and received Most Valuable Player consideration in two of his 14 major-league seasons. Yet, in the course of attaining this suctcess, his career encountered various detours.

Larry Eugene Hisle (pronounced HY-sul) was born on May 5, 1947, in Portsmouth, Ohio. This municipality along the northern banks of the Ohio River has been home to other baseball notables such as Branch Rickey and Al Bridwell. Gene Tenace, who grew up and went to high school in nearby Lucasville, played American Legion ball in Portsmouth with Hisle and Oliver. Hisle's life echoes the 19th century rags-to-riches stories of Horatio Alger. After a childhood of want and pain, Hisle's determination and continued hard work eventually made him wealthy — though family and friendship were what made him happiest.

After baseball, Hisle's message of endurance has resonated. His memory of personal hardship and generous spirit have motivated him to help numerous children in need. This calls baseball's foremost legend to mind: Babe Ruth.

Larry Hisle was the only child of Hubert and Claudine Hisle. Claudine, a big baseball fan, named her son after Lawrence Eugene "Larry" Doby, the African-American baseball star who made his debut with the Cleveland Indians just two months later.[3] Alas, Larry lost both parents at an early age.

When he was just 10 years old, his father suffered a devastating brain hemorrhage "Jupiter" Hisle never again recognized his son (he eventually died in 1962).[4] Single mother Claudine struggled to keep basic utilities running. "We were on welfare and things were tough," Larry recalled in 1978. "We used to get checks around the fourth of each month and around the last week of the month things became extremely difficult."[5] Yet even though they were poor, Hisle called himself "the happiest kid on the planet" thanks to his mother. However, several months after her husband was stricken, Claudine Hisle died from a kidney infection — it was even more poignant because she hadn't been able to afford earlier treatment.[6]

Hisle lived for several years with his mother's sister and then was adopted by Orville Ferguson, a successful construction contractor, and his wife Kathleen. The foster parents "treated me better than any son could be treated."[7] Yet his mother had a lasting impact, instilling "a will to settle for nothing less than the absolute best that life had to offer."[8] Hisle channeled his grief by throwing himself into sports with a self-imposed goal of making his beloved mother proud. "I lived in a housing project adjacent to a park and I'd go out there every morning and practice," Hisle said. "When I'd begin to get tired and think of going home, I would ask myself, 'What would my mother do if she were in my shoes?' She would do her absolute best to be the best she could be. I'd stay out there and work harder."[9]

The hard work paid off handsomely; Hisle became a high school All-American in both baseball and basketball. He was also an honor student. Before long, colleges were furiously bidding for his talents, with some notable recruiters. NBA superstar Oscar Robertson called on behalf of the University of Cincinnati.[10] Hisle visited Ohio State University many times, meeting with the state's Governor, Jim Rhodes, plus Buckeye basketball greats John Havlicek and Jerry Lucas.[11]

Hisle signed a letter of intent with Ohio State — but the Phillies, led by scout Tony Lucadello, had also been pursuing him weekly. Lucadello later described what impressed him while scouting Hisle in an American Legion tournament game. "Portsmouth was playing in Athens on the diamond of Ohio University… Larry put three home runs out of the park, one to left that bounced off the gymnasium, one to center and a third to right… Larry's awesome display of power was like nothing I had ever witnessed."[12]

Lucadello — joined by Phillies owner Bob Carpenter, general manager John Quinn, and farm director Paul Owens — convinced Hisle that baseball was the way to go. A hefty signing bonus, reportedly in the $40,000 — $60,000 range, got the young man to sign with the Phillies in August 1965.[13] He had been chosen in the second round (38th pick overall) in the major leagues' first-ever amateur draft. Hisle attended Ohio State that fall (he eventually continued his education there during the baseball off-seasons) but was ineligible to play basketball.

By the following summer, the 19-year-old found himself nearly 1,000 miles away from home playing for the Huron (South Dakota) Phillies in the Northern League (short-season Class A). The schedule was short — 70 games — and curtailed even more by the discovery of Hisle's previously unknown spinal defect (which kept him out of military service). Still, a .433 batting average and .667 slugging percentage in 60 at-bats showed the Phillies why the large signing bonus was warranted.

Hisle started the following spring with the Tidewater (Virginia) Tides of the Carolina League (Class A). He got off to a strong start, with two home runs and four RBIs on April 19, and made the league's All-Star Game. He "topped the East [squad's] win with three straight hits and two RBIs before being lifted."[14] By season's end, Hisle ranked among the league leaders in every offensive category (including .302-23-78 in the major three). He fell just short of winning the Most Valuable Player award in what was reported to be the closest voting in the league's 22-year history to that point.

The winner was his future teammate with both the Phillies and Brewers, Don Money (then a shortstop).

On December 15, 1967, the Phillies traded Jim Bunning, their mound ace and future Hall of Famer, to the Pittsburgh Pirates for a package of youngsters that included Money. Hisle and Money were considered key components in the parent team's future, even though they had played fewer than 500 pro games between them, and none above Single-A ball. The prospects, both just 20 years old, appeared destined for further minor league development — but instead they both made the Phillies' starting lineup on Opening Day 1968. A strong spring, combined with nagging injuries to the Phillies' veteran shortstop and center fielder, contributed to this startling maneuver. Yet as Manager Gene Mauch said, "I've got to see what [Hisle and Money] can do… They're exceptional young men, and exceptional young men do exceptional things."[15]

Hisle started three times, pinch-hit once, and appeared in three more games as a late-inning defensive replacement. He was 4 for 11 (.364) in his limited duty. Both he and Money were optioned to the team's Triple-A affiliate in San Diego in late April, and both continued to do well, finishing 1968 with identical .303 batting averages. Hisle's season ended in July, however, after he was diagnosed with hepatitis.

Meanwhile, the Phillies plummeted to a distant seventh-place finish, and the club evaluated its older veterans amid rebuilding. As part of this process, they left Tony González, their starting centerfielder for most of the 1960s, unprotected in the expansion draft. The San Diego Padres claimed González, and the door was fully open for Hisle to step into the centerfield position.

Hisle was again in the Opening Day lineup when the Phillies opened their 1969 season in Chicago. He hit just .159 in April, though that included his first big-league homer. It came on April 21 at Shea Stadium off Gary Gentry of the Mets. Hisle got his first four-hit game in the majors on May 2 and another on May 18. He continued to heat up as the

After leading the AL with 119 RBIs with the Minnesota Twins in 1977, Larry Hisle signed with the Brewers as a free agent. In 1978 he clubbed 34 HRs with 115 RBIs, but suffered a torn rotator cuff that limited him to just 79 games in his last four seasons (1979-1982).

summer went on and finished the season batting .266, with 20 homers (second on the team behind Dick Allen) and 56 RBIs. It would likely have been more except for a thumb injury — later determined to be a hairline fracture — that limited Larry to 23 at-bats after September 1. Had he sustained his output over the full year, Hisle would likely have placed higher in the Rookie of the Year voting, or won outright. As consolation, he was eventually selected to the Topps Rookie All-Star Team, along with teammate Don Money and childhood competitor Al Oliver.

The Phillies opened 1970 with a largely new cast. Gone were such long-time notables as Allen, Johnny Callison, and Cookie Rojas. Rookies Larry Bowa and Denny Doyle came in, along with manager Frank Lucchesi, finally getting his shot in the majors. For the second straight season, the Phillies avoided a last-place finish in the NL East division only thanks to the Montreal Expos, the league's other expansion team. Hisle fared even worse than his team. He had a good spring and a strong start, but then went into a severe and extended slump. He was below the Mendoza Line for nearly half his season, and strikeouts — a concern dating back to his minor-league days — were again a problem (more than one in every three at bats). A flurry in late September lifted him over .200, but by that point Hisle was a platoon player. He appeared in only 126 games with 405 at-bats overall. He was deemed vulnerable to high, inside fastballs, and Lucchesi offered that in "some way, we've got to get Larry started [again]."[16]

Intense training in the Florida Instructional League was the perceived solution, and Hisle responded positively. The Phillies were confident that the slugger who had displayed such early promise would return. Indeed, when the Pittsburgh Pirates dangled former batting champ Matty Alou in trade for a package that included Hisle, the Phillies declined. Unfortunately, management's confidence did not extend past spring training. The Phillies again platooned Hisle, starting him only against lefty pitchers. A mere 14 at-bats in April further indicated the team's lost confidence; in early June, they optioned Hisle to Triple-A Eugene. He did well there and was recalled in September, but finished the year at just .197-0-3 in 36 games.

Less than a month later, Hisle's ties to the Phillies were severed. He was traded even-up to the Los Angeles Dodgers for first baseman Tommy Hutton. The deal required the approval of Bob Carpenter — showing that certain circles of the organization still held Hisle in high regard. Yet the trade also reopened an ugly, lingering side of the Philadelphia franchise: its race relations.

Over the years, Hisle had been variously described in the oft-critical Philadelphia press as "polite [and] soft-spoken,"[17] "modest [and] unassuming,"[18] and "mild-mannered."[19] So when this genuinely nice, honest athlete opened up about his perception of the Phillies' negative treatment of African-American players, his opinions made news. Long-respected columnist Allen Lewis latched on and issued a withering appraisal of both the checkered history — the Phils were the last National League team to employ an African-American player — and the problems the club had in retaining once-budding stars such as Richie Allen, Grant Jackson and Johnny Briggs. Uncited, but certainly relevant, was the team's lack of patience with African-Canadian Ferguson Jenkins, who became a Hall of Famer with the Chicago Cubs. Bob Carpenter admitted, "Our track record hasn't been good", and club officials stated their commitment toward resolving the situation.[20]

Hisle was moving on to the team renowned for breaking the color barrier with Jackie Robinson — but he never played a big-league game in Dodger blue. Los Angeles was on the verge of becoing one of the most successful teams of the decade. A lot of young talent was on the way up, especially in the infield — but in 1972 the starting outfielders were all veterans: Willie Davis in center, flanked by Manny Mota and Frank Robinson. Bill Buckner and Willie Crawford were their backups. Hisle could not break through and was assigned to Triple-A Albuquerque. There he mounted the comeback that defined the rest of his professional career. His numbers — .325-23-91 — ranked him with teammate Ron Cey, Gary Matthews, and Mike Schmidt among the Pacific Coast League's leaders. It was reported that "Hisle [was] probably the most scouted player in the Pacific Coast League… [with] no fewer than nine major league scouts watching him nightly."[21]

The Dodgers shipped him to St. Louis for two minor-league hurlers. Yet just over a month later, the Cardinals flipped Hisle to Minnesota for veteran reliever Wayne Granger.

In Hisle, the Twins were perceived to be filling various needs going into the 1973 season — greater defensive range in the outfield, plus a combination of speed and power from the leadoff position. Aside from his continued propensity to strike out, Hisle filled those needs well over a very successful five-year run with the Twins. As it developed, though, he seldom led off after 1973.

There were a couple of interesting side notes to the 1973 season. After a freak accident, Hisle became the Twins' designated hitter in the opening game of spring training — the first big-league DH ever, albeit in exhibition play. He made the new rule look good — though baseball purists will never agree — by hitting two home runs (including a grand slam) while driving in seven runs. Also, the Twins had an odd number of African-American players, so Hisle had a white roommate on the road. It's amusing in retrospect, but this was called "one of the most progressive moves in the franchise's history."[22]

Hisle took a modest step up in 1974, lifting his basic batting line from .272-15-74 to .286-19-79. His OPS rose from .773 to .818. His club did not improve quite so much, though; the Twins finished 82-80, one game better than the prior season.

Minnesota had not been truly competitive since winning the AL West in 1970, but Hisle — now batting in the middle of the lineup — was a big contributor to a team that hoped to be on the rise. "I was having the best season of my career," he said that October.[23] He may have had additional incentive because he was not listed on the computerized All-Star ballots.

Unfortunately, a bone spur in his elbow (and subsequent surgery) limited Hisle to just 35 at-bats after June 17. In his absence, the team fell below .500 and finished 20 1/2 games behind the division champion Oakland Athletics. Manager Frank Quilici was fired, and Hisle was reunited with his first major-league skipper, Gene Mauch.

Shortly after taking the helm, Mauch expressed a need to improve the Twins' defense and run production.[24] The club did score slightly more in 1976, leading the AL in runs with a small-ball approach that emphasized sacrifice bunts and stolen bases. Unfortunately, they were also third in the AL in runs allowed, fueled by a league-leading 172 errors. Still, by closing the season with a 21-8 run, the Twins finished third in the division, just five games behind Kansas City.

Hisle's season mirrored the team's offense. He led the Twins in RBIs with 96, while hitting 14 homers and batting .272. On June 4, he became the third player in Twins' history to hit for the cycle. Yet he also laid down 11 sacrifice bunts and stole 31 bases, both career highs.[25] Speed had always been part of Hisle's arsenal, but Mauch gave him the green light. For example, on June 30, Hisle stole four bases against the Royals, a team record that he still held alone as of 2012. Small ball seemed to agree with Hisle — but he would come to flourish as a power hitter.

The Twins spent much of 1977 in first place but collapsed down the stretch (something Mauch could remember most painfully from his 1964 Phillies). Their distant fourth-place finish disappointed fans, team, and Hisle himself, despite his personal success. Hisle started strongly and stayed consistent –his batting average never dipped below .290 after May 13. He finished at .302– the only time he hit .300 over a full season in the majors — and led the AL with 119 RBIs. His 28 home runs also placed him among the league's top 10. He made the American League All-Star squad for the first time and got some votes for Most Valuable Player.

His performance also came against a backdrop of long and sometimes bitter contract negotiations. The tone was actually set after Hisle won in arbitration before the 1974 season. In response, Twins owner Calvin Griffith — a noted tightwad — allegedly said that "he would get back the money... even if [the team] had to trade" Hisle.[26] The Twins submitted a two-year pact before the 1977 season, but Hisle discovered that the amount "wasn't [nearly] as flattering" as the period.[27] Considering that other star outfielders such as Reggie Jackson, Joe Rudi and Gary Matthews had signed attractive free-agent deals, Hisle contemplated playing out his contract and exploring the market himself.

Negotiations continued throughout the 1977 season, and despite hopeful indications of closure, terms could not be reached. Time ran out and Hisle became a free agent. He was courted aggressively by numerous clubs — including the Texas Rangers, whose owner was fined on charges of tampering. Hisle eventually signed with the Milwaukee Brewers for a structured six-year contract exceeding $3 million, a vast increase over the reported $47,200 he'd earned the year before.

The Brewers (formerly the Seattle Pilots) had never finished above .500 in nine seasons. The perceived route to success was free agency. The club had already made a splash by signing Oakland's slugging third baseman Sal Bando a year earlier. The lineup also included Cecil Cooper, future Hall of Famers Robin Yount and Paul Molitor, and Hisle's former teammate Don Money. The team looked like a contender in the AL East.

Hisle immediately contributed to this powerful squad — he became the AL's first Player of the Week in 1978 and was second runner-up for Player of the Month for April. Though he missed the second half of May, Hisle returned and had his strongest season overall. He hit .290, with a personal best of 34 homers (second in the league behind Jim Rice) and 115 RBIs (third after Rice and Rusty Staub). His OPS of .906 was a career high. Milwaukee won 93 games, but still finished third, behind the New York Yankees — the eventual world champions — and Boston. Yet Hisle's efforts were recognized; he became an AL All-Star for the second time, and he finished third in the MVP voting behind Rice and Ron Guidry. The Milwaukee chapter of the Baseball Writers' Association of America named him team MVP. Hisle was still just 31, and a league MVP award seemed within his grasp.

Yet after an excellent start in 1979 — .341, 3 home runs and 10 RBIs in 10 games — Hisle suffered a devastating injury in a game at Baltimore on April 20. That summer he said, "I was playing left field… and had six balls hit out to me… I had to make hard throws on all six of them, and on the last one, I felt something snap in my shoulder."[28] The diagnosis was a torn rotator cuff — the severity was the fourth degree out of five.[29]

Determined to play through the pain, Hisle served as Milwaukee's designated hitter over the next two weeks, but he eventually was forced to yield and went on the disabled list. An exercise program to strengthen the shoulder — in lieu of surgery — took longer than expected, and Hisle did not make another appearance until early September. Even then, he was limited to eight at-bats before he was shut down.

Hisle continued his hard exercise over the off-season — he was reluctant to undergo surgery, in part because he saw that other victims of rotator-cuff tears weren't the same after their operations. He pointed to pitchers Don Gullett and Wayne Garland, as well as fellow outfielder Hal McRae.[30]

On Opening Day 1980, he was back in uniform and ready to play. Milwaukee used him strictly as a DH, bringing him along slowly to avoid aggravating the injury. He hit two homers on May 17 — the last of eight times he achieved this feat — but two days later, he hurt the shoulder again while sliding into second base. Initially, it was thought that rest would suffice, but subsequent tests "revealed another tear in the rotator cuff…[and] surgery was performed by Dr. Frank Jobe," innovator of the Tommy John procedure.[31]

A second, related procedure — the removal of a bone spur from Hisle's right shoulder — was required in July 1981. Along with the players' strike, that limited Hisle to just 87 at-bats for the season. He doggedly pursued his comeback against long odds — he later said, "[It] took more guts, work and determination than everything else I accomplished in life," ranking it right along with overcoming the death of his mother.[32] However, he fared no better in 1982. He made a total of just nine appearances and 31 at-bats before another disabled list assignment. His last of 166 major-league homers came as a pinch-hitter off Kansas City's Paul Splittorff on May 3 — his final game in the majors was just three days later.

Hisle still held out hope of coming back that fall, but he said that the variety of surgical procedures — five areas of his shoulder had been worked on — and rehabilitation had damaged the shoulder enough. "The team doctor [Paul Jacobs] said any part of the body can take only so much."[33] He announced his retirement that off-season. The same report stated that he would "become a special instructor in the Brewers' minor league system and a scout… work[ing] with the Brewers' Class A and rookie league teams."[34]

Over the next 15-plus years, Hisle served in a similar capacity with his first pro organization, the Phillies. He also had brief coaching stints in the minors with the Houston Astros (1989), Toronto Blue Jays (1990-91), and the Brewers again (1997). From 1992 through 1995, Hisle was with the Blue Jays' parent team as batting coach. He won a strong review after the 1992 season, the first of back-to-back World Series championships for Toronto. "The team's improved hitting… benefited from Hisle's emphasis on patience and discipline."[35] In 1993 a trio of Blue Jays, John Olerud, old teammate Paul Molitor, and Roberto Alomar finished one-two-three in the American League batting race. That feat had been accomplished only once before, by three Phillies players exactly 100 years earlier.

Hisle and his wife, the former Sheila Sanford, were married on September 28, 1970. She was a secretary for a law firm that handled some Phillies affairs. They had one child, a son named Larry Jr.[36] The Hisles had always extended themselves in charitable efforts throughout his baseball career. But after he retired to his home outside Milwaukee, this endeavor went into overdrive. The man once dubbed the "honorary captain of the major league Nice Guy Team"[37] demonstrated an even deeper meaning of nice-guy.

Rather than plush, multi-million-dollar stadiums and the adulation of thousands of sports fans, Hisle sought out community group homes, detention centers, and public schools. He assisted youngsters of little means, with the profound appreciation of social workers, teachers and judges. In addition to his status as the Brewers' Manager of Youth Outreach, he has joined forces with his son, Larry Jr., a strong basketball player who also performed in independent baseball leagues from 1995 through 1997. Larry Jr. founded Directors of Continuing Services, a firm that provides psychological, educational and mentoring services to children and families. His father, the orphan who had once longed for such assistance, stepped into a mentoring role himself. He has often taken on round-the-clock responsibilities to help those most at risk.

"I'm only doing something for these kids that should be done for every kid in the country," says the ever-humble ex-athlete renowned for never turning down a request for help. His expressed goal is to "manufacture dreams" for those that "society has written off," and in this capacity, Hisle has been described as "one of the best things happening in Milwaukee."[38]

This man with the infectious smile had never been forgotten in his native Portsmouth either. Around 2,000 of his hometown fans celebrated "Larry Hisle Day" at Cincinnati's old Crosley Field in August 1969. Portsmouth held another such day in October 1977, dedicating a city park in Hisle's name. The affection ran both ways, as a Twins teammate, the late Lyman Bostock, remembered. "When I met this fellow, all he would do is talk about Portsmouth."[39]

People readily respond to Hisle in the most positive ways, as these descriptions demonstrate:

"The kind of player kids should look up to… without a doubt, one of the nicest men I've ever known."
— George Bamberger, former Brewers manager.[40]

"A wonderful human being…he is one of the nicest human beings I've ever met in my life."
– Bud Selig, former Brewers owner/ Commissioner of Major League Baseball.[41]

"No matter what good things have been written about him, he's even better…one of the nicest ballplayers ever to come in here."
– Jim Ksicinski, former Milwaukee clubhouse attendant.[42]

ACKNOWLEDGMENTS

Thanks for assistance from Jan Larson, Jim Baker, Rory Costello, and the unknown sportswriter who originally came up with the Mays/Hisle comparison that I never forgot.

SOURCES

Jael Ealey Richardson, The Stone Thrower, Markham, Ontario: Thomas Allen Publishers, 2012, This book is by the daughter of Chuck Ealey, a former pro football player in Canada who was a close friend of Larry Hisle's as they grew up in Portsmouth.

www.Baseball-Reference.com

www.Ancestry.com

www.Retrosheet.org

www.MLB.com

Adam McCalvy, "Where have you gone, Larry Hisle?" MLB.com, June 12, 2002 (http://mlb.mlb.com/news/article.jsp?ymd=20020612&content_id=51295&vkey=news_mil&fext=.jsp&c_id=mil)

Aaron Gleeman, "Top 40 Minnesota Twins: # 27 Larry Hisle," December 28, 2010, http://aarongleeman.com/2010/12/28/top-40-minnesota-twins-27-larry-hisle/

http://www.baseballlibrary.com/ballplayers/player.php?name=Larry_Hisle_1947

NOTES

1. *Associated Press*, May 19, 1969. The San Francisco Giants visited Connie Mack Stadium in Philadelphia for a weekend series.
2. "Larry Hisle Strives for Improvement Over 1969 Despite Good Statistics," *Associated Press*, March 7, 1970. This may not be the exact story that the author remembers, but it is very similar.
3. Jael Ealey Richardson, *The Stone Thrower*, Markham, Ontario: Thomas Allen Publishers, 2012.
4. Richardson, *The Stone Thrower*. Hubert Hisle's death record – ancestry.com
5. Lou Chapman, "Welfare to Well Off Is Story of Hisle's Life," *Milwaukee Sentinel*, March 1, 1978: Part 2, Page 2.
6. Gary D'Amato, "Ex-Brewer Hisle goes to bat for troubled youth," *Milwaukee Journal-Sentinel*, November 8, 2011.
7. D'Amato, "Ex-Brewer Hisle goes to bat for troubled youth."
8. Richardson, *The Stone Thrower*.
9. D'Amato, "Ex-Brewer Hisle goes to bat for troubled youth."
10. Allen Lewis, "Hisle Looks Like Money In Bank," The Sporting News, April 13, 1968: 21.
11. Lee Caryer, "The Buckeye Who Never Played A Game," Bucknuts.com website, December 27, 2010 (http://ohiostate.247sports.com/Article/OSU-Hoops-Becomes-Black-and-White-35287
12. David V. Hanneman, *Diamonds in the Rough: The Legend and Legacy of Tony Lucadello*, Austin, Texas: Eakin Press, 1990. Quoted in Steve Triplett, "Lucadello Book 'Real Diamond,'" *Portsmouth Times*, February 26, 1990: 11.
13. Lewis, "Hisle Looks Like Money In Bank."
14. Tom Northington, "Slugger Walton Hero of Carolina All-Star Game," *The Sporting News*, July 29, 1967: 39.
15. Allen Lewis, "Frosh Hisle, Money Spring Surprises – Earn Phillies Jobs," *The Sporting News*, April 20, 1968: 24.
16. Allen Lewis, "Phils Sink Outfield Bundle on Gamble," *The Sporting News*, October 31, 1970: 48.
17. Allen Lewis, "Phils Figure on Hisle in Center, Despite Mini-Mini Experience," *The Sporting News*, November 9, 1968: 52.
18. Allen Lewis, "Hisle Severe Self-Critic…But Phils Say He's Great," *The Sporting News*, April 5, 1969: 20.
19. Allen Lewis, "Phils Attack Old Problem: Handling of Negro Players," *The Sporting News*, November 20, 1971, 48.
20. Lewis, "Phils Attack Old Problem: Handling of Negro Players."
21. "Pacific Coast League," *The Sporting News*, July 8, 1972: 32.
22. Bob Fowler, "Possum, Bam-Bam Strike Terror for Twins," *The Sporting News*, April 21, 1973: 19.
23. Bob Fowler, "Twins' Fortunes Faded Following Hisle's Injury," *The Sporting News*, October 4, 1975: 19.
24. Bob Fowler, "A New Twist for the Twins: Mauch Will Stress Defense," *The Sporting News*, January 31, 1976: 35.
25. Both Hisle and Rod Carew had 30-plus stolen bases, the only time in Twins history (through 2012) that two players achieved that threshold in the same season. Indeed, only six other Twins players have ever had 30 or more steals in a season.
26. Bob Fowler, "Consultation With Rowe Bolsters Brye," The Sporting News, July 27, 1974: 28.
27. Bob Fowler, "Twins' Low-Ball Pay Pitch Jolts Hisle," *The Sporting News*, January 15, 1977: 31.
28. "Portsmouth native roots for team," *Pomeroy* (Ohio) *Daily Sentinel*, July 19, 1979: 4
29. Don Willman, "Hisle Faces Probable End of Career," *Portsmouth Times*, September 10, 1982, 10.
30. Bob Wolf, "Hisle getting himself armed for 1980," *Milwaukee Journal*, February 15, 1980: Part 2, page 1.
31. "Brewers' Larry Hisle Undergoes Surgery," *The Sporting News*, August 2, 1980: 12.
32. Willman, "Hisle Faces Probable End of Career," D'Amato,

"Ex-Brewer Hisle goes to bat for troubled youth."

33 Willman, "Hisle Faces Probable End of Career."

34 Tom Flaherty, "Good Health Meant Success for Money," *The Sporting News*, January 24, 1983: 47.

35 Neil MacCarl, "Toronto Blue Jays," *The Sporting News*, October 5, 1992: 23.

36 "Sheila Hisle Enjoys Pro Baseball Life," *Portsmouth Times*, October 27, 1977. Online obituary of Sheila Sanford's mother, Dorothy (http://www.krausefuneralhome.com/obituary.php?id=2631)

37 Mike Gonring, "Hisle a Brewer Money Player in All Respects," *The Sporting News*, July 29, 1978: 16.

38 D'Amato, "Ex-Brewer Hisle goes to bat for troubled youth"

39 Don Lundy, "Portsmouth Area Fans Treat Hisle to Big Day," *Portsmouth Times*, August 11, 1969: 1.

40 Dan Montgomery, "Area Pays Tribute to Larry Hisle," *Portsmouth Times*, October 28, 1977: 1, 6.

41 D'Amato, "Ex-Brewer Hisle goes to bat for troubled youth."

42 Ibid.

43 Mike Gonring, "Realtor Clubhouse King to Brewer Visitors," *The Sporting News*, June 30, 1979: 18a

ROY HOWELL

By Maxwell Kates

He was a hardnosed player whose blue-collar work ethic maximized his talent and inspired his teammates. His red hair and true grit made him the most recognizable Blue Jay as their starting third baseman for nearly four years. Josh Donaldson? No, Roy Howell, whose career included stops with the Texas Rangers and the Milwaukee Brewers in addition to Toronto. In fact, Howell hung up his spikes even before the Bringer of Rain was born.

"I go out there to play the game hard," he told Tom Flaherty of the *Milwaukee Journal*. "I play the game aggressively. That's all I know how to do. I'll go out there, I'll give you my best shot, I'll swing the bat, and I'll get dirty for you."[1]

Roy Lee Howell was born on December 18, 1953, in Lompoc, California, 120 miles northwest of Los Angeles. He had an upbringing that left him with insurmountable physical and mental toughness:

"I grew up farming and ranching and digging ditches," Howell told Jim Seip of the *York* (Pennsylvania) *Daily Record*.[2] Physical conditioning gave young Roy a 200-pound frame by the time he attended Lompoc High School, where he starred in baseball and football. In 1972, Howell's senior year, he attracted the attention of scouts from several organizations, including the San Diego Padres and the Texas Rangers. Milwaukee Brewers scout Harry Smith even described him as "a 25-year-old playing with a bunch of kids."[3] The Padres had the first draft choice; if they signed Howell, they intended to promote him directly to San Diego. Howell was nonplussed by their intention:

"I'm 18 years old. I love playing the game. But you would be doing me a big disservice to take me out of high school and… take me right to the major leagues."[4] Instead, he signed with the Rangers for $40,000 and was assigned to Double-A Pittsfield. Howell batted .250 in 116 official at-bats with 2 home runs and 9 RBIs. A gruesome incident that offseason left him lucky to be alive.

On the final day of deer-hunting season, Howell and a friend waited by the side of a mountain road for friends to pick them up, their guns unloaded. A pickup truck stopped 50 yards away before the driver extinguished his headlights. Then he turned on the brights, blinding Howell and his friend. That was when he started to shoot indiscriminately. Roy was hit in the left arm, the limb exploding on contact. Somehow both young men, covered in blood, managed to hitch a ride with a woman who soon became as terrified as they were. Ultimately, the California Highway Patrol drove Howell to a hospital in Santa Ynez, where he was admitted. Howell said of the ordeal:

"[The doctor] took a look at my arm and he said, 'I'm going to put it back together.' With no anesthesia… he threw about four hundred stitches into it… When he took all the strings and pulled it straight up, everything in my arm came back together."[5] Howell was discharged the next day and the cast came off three weeks later. The experience left him with the nickname "Target" that stuck for the rest of his career.

"About two weeks after," Howell remembered, "I went duck hunting… and some guy shot me in the back. But that's another story."[6] Then he went to spring training.

Howell's bat improved during his second season in Pittsfield as he hit 15 home runs with 47 RBIs. Off the field, he married the former Karla Gilman in Santa Barbara on January 26, 1974. Promoted to Spokane, Howell ripped through Pacific Coast League pitching as he hit .338 in his first 19 games. His performance did not go unnoticed by Rangers manager Billy Martin.

"The kid doesn't swing at bad pitches and he knows the strike zone. And that's rare in someone so young," Martin said.[7] Howell's understanding of fundamentals as a 20-year-old earned Martin's respect, a manager rarely impressed by rookies. He also earned high praise from Del Wilber, his own manager in Spokane, who compared the third baseman to fellow Santa Barbaran Eddie Mathews. Howell credited his father, Bob, for his success in the game thus far. Bob Howell taught him to play every position and to bat left-handed. "He figured I'd have a better chance from that side because there are more right-handed pitchers."[8]

By the end of the season, Howell's batting average had cooled to .281, albeit with 22 home runs and 80 RBIs as the Spokane Indians won the Pacific Coast League championship. While celebrating on the road in Albuquerque, Howell received instructions from Billy Martin to "meet us in Texas."[9]

It was a baptism by fire. Howell flew to Arlington to await his teammates' return from a California road trip. In his motel, the phone rang. It was Martin. "We want you in Anaheim tonight." Howell chartered another plane and upon arrival received word that "Billy wants to see you in his office." Martin showed him the lineup card, exclaiming "We're playing a doubleheader, and you're playing in both of them!" Howell had not slept in two days at this point. Unfazed, he replied "All right, let's go!" Later, he recalled that that was "Billy instilling confidence in me. He wanted to see what I was made of."[10]

Howell notched his first major-league hit off Chuck Dobson in the opener while touching Ed Figueroa for a home run in the second game of the doubleheader, September 9, 1974. He appeared in 11 more games for the Rangers, winners of 84 games after finishing in last place in both 1972 and 1973. Howell looked forward to a long career playing for Billy Martin:

"He would test you tremendously," Howell remembered. "There would be no explanation for what he did. … Billy always wanted to know about a player 'Will you stand and fight or turn and run?'"[11] Expectations were high for Billy Martin's "Turn-Around Gang" in 1975 with Howell installed as the regular at the hot corner. After a slow start, Billy was fired, replaced by Frank Lucchesi. Initially, relations between Howell and Lucchesi were cordial.

"When I see a swing like [Howell's] with that kind of power," Lucchesi told Randy Galloway of the *Dallas Morning News*, "when I see all that potential, I don't think Roy should have to prove he can play. He's got to prove he can't play."[12] There had been discussions to move Howell to first base or the outfield in order to make room for Mike Cubbage, but Lucchesi assured him that he "was going to play a lot of third" in 1975 as well as 1976 and "to go out there and be relaxed."[13]

For the season, he batted .251 with 10 home runs and 51 RBIs. On August 7, 1976, Howell broke up a no-hitter by the Twins' Steve Luebber with two outs in the ninth inning:

"I was getting my breaking stuff over… then we throw kind of a waste pitch," Luebber recalled. "And then we throw the pitch we thought was strike three, and it didn't get called." For five pitches, Luebber was sitting on strike two, one pitch away from a no-hitter. "Then he got the single up the middle."[14]

Howell's offense in 1976 was nearly a carbon copy of 1975 as he hit .253 with 8 home runs and 53 RBIs. By now, Lucchesi had soured on Howell, deeming his output "a disappointment," compounded by his league-leading 28 errors at third base."[15] The Rangers sent him to the Florida Winter Instructional League to master a new position.

"The reason I went to Florida was because both Eddie Robinson and Frank told me they wanted me to learn about left field so I could play it next season," Howell told Randy Galloway.[16] It was a reasonable request, considering that when the Rangers signed free-agent shortstop Bert Campaneris, Toby Harrah was forced to move to third base. Imagine Howell's surprise when upon arriving at spring training 1977, he was told that Tom Grieve had won the left-field position.

"Frank came up to Lenny Randle and me, and he said, 'I don't care if you guys hit a thousand in spring training and make every play. You're not gonna play.'"[17] All the Rangers could offer Howell was the opportunity to platoon as a designated hitter. Howell was outraged: "Let me put it this way — I will not DH. If they aren't going to play me at a position, then I want to go someplace else and play."[18] Howell was without a contract, which exposed the risk that he could walk away from the Rangers as a free agent at the end of the season. When the Rangers offered Howell three-year deal, he replied that he would sign only if the team traded him.

Meanwhile, any contract squabbles between Howell and the Rangers were dwarfed on April 3 when a tragedy took place during an exhibition game at Driller Park in Tulsa. During a second-inning rain delay, the Rangers and the Houston Astros witnessed a grandstand walkway collapse. The cataclysm became known as "Black Sunday" in Tulsa. According to Barry Lewis of the *Tulsa World*, fans fell more than 20 feet to the pavement, and 18 were sent to the hospital.[19] Astros reliever Joe Sambito was in the clubhouse on the side of the collapse when it occurred.

"I heard a big crash and a lot of screams," he said.[20] Howell and Sambito were two of the players who rose to the occasion, treating victims and providing whatever help they could. No matter. Howell was still in Texas when the season opened. Coming off the bench, he went hitless in 17 at-bats.[21]

"I won't sit here. I'm history. I've got to play."[22] On May 10, 1977, Howell got his wish. He was traded, along with an undisclosed amount of cash, to the Toronto Blue Jays for pitcher Steve Hargan and infielder Jim Mason. According to Blue Jays manager Roy Hartsfield, "I don't care what the price tag is, because Howell is worth every buck."[23]

A change of scenery brought an immediate improvement in results. Howell drove in a run in his first Toronto appearance against Seattle in what stated a 15-game hitting streak. By May 23, his batting average had improved to .302. The Blue Jays soon visited Arlington, where Howell went 7-for-12, including a game-winning home run against future Hall of Famer Bert Blyleven. Blue Jays general manager Peter Bavasi said, "We are very pleased with the deal. He's a proven major leaguer at the age of 23 and now that he has a lock on a position, he can concentrate on the other aspects of the game. He's going to be with us for a long time."[24]

On September 10, 1977, Howell enjoyed a career day at Yankee Stadium. He went 5-for-5 with a single, two doubles, and two home runs and drove in nine runs, a Stadium record, as the Blue Jays demolished the Yankees, 19-3. (Howell's mentor in Texas, Billy Martin, was now managing the Yankees.)

"I enjoy playing in this ballpark," Howell told Neil MacCarl of the *Toronto Star*.

For the season, Howell batted .302 with 10 home runs and 44 RBIs despite missing 41 games to hand and ankle injuries. As he was now under contract through the 1979 season, Howell could focus expressly on his game:

"Now that I've hit .300, I hope to do it again. I think I improved my fielding last year after making the adjustment from grass to artificial turf. I know I have a long way to go and I'll never stop working hard at that."[25]

Howell fell short of his goal in 1978, as he batted .270 with 8 home runs and 61 RBIs. Still, his numbers were solid enough to merit an invitation to represent the Blue Jays at the All-Star Game in San Diego. Called upon to pinch-hit, he grounded out against Montreal's Steve Rogers to end the fourth inning. Howell's bat, glove, and presence were so highly valued by the Blue Jays that Peter Bavasi offered to extend his contract, complete with a pay increase. The third baseman was grateful but unimpressed.

"Thank you, I appreciate it, but I'll live up to my contract," Howell told Bavasi. "I'll wait until after the third year, and then we can renegotiate the option."[26] It was the beginning of the undoing of any relationship between Howell and the Blue Jays management. When Bavasi stated audaciously in 1978 that "I wouldn't want my daughter dating a Blue Jay," the situation with Howell only became more tenuous.[27]

Any budding acrimony between Howell and the front office was not evident to watch the third baseman's performance on the field in 1979. On May 26 he touched Boston's Bill Campbell for a three-run home run in a mesmerizing come-from-behind 7-6 victory.[28] Meanwhile, his fielding continued to improve. An acrobatic dive to rob Butch Hobson of a base hit while making two great plays against Jim Rice drew rave comparisons to Graig Nettles for his defensive excellence. Manager Roy Hartsfield offered the following report:

"He is probably playing as well right now as he has ever played. He is scorching the ball."[29] For the season, Howell batted .247 with 15 home runs and 72 RBIs, earning him the Blue Jays' Player of the Year Award. However, when he inquired about his trophy, it was sent to him in the mail. The derision only intensified from there. The Blue Jays did not offer Howell a contract for 1980. He took the team to arbitration and won before hitting 10 home runs while driving in 57 and batting .269. With third-base prospect Danny Ainge waiting in the wings, the Blue Jays were content to allow Howell to file for free agency.

Having played his entire career with losing teams, Howell instructed agent George Kalifatis that he was resolved to sign only with a contender. Although five teams drafted him, the only winner among them was the Milwaukee Brewers. When general manager Harry Dalton and manager Buck Rodgers promised Howell the opportunity to play every day, he signed a five-year, $1.825 million contract with the Brewers on December 20, 1980.[30]

After languishing in the second division since their inception in 1970, the Brewers won 93 games in 1978, challenging the Yankees and the Red Sox in the American League East. Winners of 95 in 1979 and 86 in 1980, the Brewers appeared poised to capture their first division title. Harry Dalton was busy that winter, adding Ted Simmons, Rollie Fingers, and Pete Vuckovich to a roster that already included Cecil Cooper, Gorman Thomas, Mike Caldwell, and future Hall of Famers Paul Molitor and Robin Yount. Randy Lerch, who joined the Brewers the same year, retained fond memories of playing in Milwaukee:

"Milwaukee wasn't a media center. It was just a lot of blue-collar people who would have their tailgate parties. It was a super town to play in, real low key. … We put on a uniform and played hardball."[31]

It might not have occurred to Howell that he was joining a team already stocked with two third basemen of All-Star caliber. Team captain Sal Bando, 36, was understood to be retiring while Don Money, 33, plagued by a collection of injuries, did not seem far off. According to rotisserie baseball pioneer Daniel Okrent, "Roy Howell at third base was an adventure [Rodgers and his coaches] didn't particularly enjoy."[32] His fielding had regressed to an "atrocious" level to the point that Bando held off retirement for another year. Even with Money out of commission for most of the second half of the strike-shortened 1981 season, Howell played in only 53 games at third base. By the end of the season, "the spectre of ground balls clanging off Howell's chest horrified Rodgers and Dalton" enough to

An All-Star third baseman with the Toronto Blue Jays in 1978, Roy Howell played his final four of 11 big-league seasons (1974-84) with the Brewers. In 1982 he platooned as DH, batting .260 with four home runs.

make them award his position to Molitor for 1982.[33] Once again Howell demanded a trade.

"No words are going to change it," Howell protested to the *Milwaukee Journal*. "What am I going to do, tell [Rodgers] I can play? I guess I have as much respect for him as a manager as he has for me as a player."[34] Howell appeared visibly upset during spring training to the point that Dalton was compelled to inform him that the less interested he was in playing for Milwaukee, the less attractive he would become to general managers as trade material. Any attempt to trade Howell fell on deaf ears and when the regular season began, he remained in Milwaukee, riding the lonesome pine.

The Brewers won their first playoff berth in 1981, only to lose the American League Division Series to the Yankees in five games. In 1982 they won the American League pennant and fell to the St. Louis Cardinals in seven games in the World Series. Although Howell was limited to part-time duties during those seasons, he did display flashes of brilliance.

On August 10, 1981, the Brewers' first game back from the strike, they were deadlocked with the Indians through 13 innings of a rain-delayed game. With Marshall Edwards on first base, Howell attempted a sacrifice bunt. When Cleveland catcher Bo Diaz attempted to nail Edwards at second base, the slippery ball landed in center field. Once Howell realized he had reached first base safely, he kept on running.

"I was going to make [Rick] Manning make the play," he reported. "Even if he gets me, Marshall's on third with one out."[35] What Howell did not expect was for Manning to execute a perfect throw to shortstop Jerry Dybzinski. He knew he was out if he did not improvise, so he "tried to do something to surprise them."[36] Howell went into a slide, jumped up, and somersaulted over Dybzinski to reach base. His sleight of hand led to a three-run inning, which proved to be the winning margin for Milwaukee. The next night, Howell hit a home run and a double as part of a doubleheader sweep.

Howell batted .400 in the 1981 postseason, going 2-for-5 against the Yankees. He was hitless in 14 at-bats in the ALCS and the World Series in 1982. Howell continued to see diminished playing time, batting .278 in 1983 and only .232 in 1984. With one year left on his contract, the Brewers released him on October 1, 1984. Howell signed a minor-league contract with the San Francisco Giants in 1985. Failing to make the team, he signed with the Philadelphia Phillies, reaching Triple-A Portland. When Howell was cut by the Pittsburgh Pirates in spring training 1986, he decided to call it a career. Philosophical, he said, "You have to be able to walk away; if you take it, they've got you."[37]

In 1989 Howell attempted a comeback with the St. Petersburg Pelicans of the Senior Professional Baseball Association. The league had a 72-game winter schedule and many players hoped, no doubt, to use the league as an entrée back to the major leagues. Howell was installed as the Pelicans' regular third baseman, despite battling ankle and leg injuries throughout the season. The Pelicans went wire-to-wire, finishing the regular season 42-30 before defeating the West Palm Beach Tropics for the league championship.[38] On November 26, 1989, Howell became a father for the third time; Troy and Lindsay Howell welcomed baby brother Daniel to the family.

While playing in the Senior League, Howell and Joe Sambito, now teammates on the Pelicans, expressed their philosophy on autographs to author Peter Golenbock. At the time, two well-known former Mets refused to participate in a team sponsored autograph signing for the fans.

"'You know, there are players who haven't even made it to the big show who won't sign autographs,' said Sambito. 'I heard [Robin] Ventura won't sign autographs because he didn't want to lessen the value.'

"Howell laughed, 'He didn't want to flood the market?'

"Sambito said, 'The value of his autograph has only one determination: performance.'

'You got that right,' Howell replied."[39]

Howell spent the final decade of the twentieth century out of professional baseball, working in insurance.[40] In 2000 he returned to the game when former teammate Ted Simmons offered him a coaching position in the Padres' farm system. He began at Mobile and was promoted in 2001 to Portland. From 2003 to 2005, Howell managed the Padres' affiliate in Eugene. After a year out of baseball, he managed San Luis Potosi of the California Collegiate League from 2007 to 2010. In 2011 he managed the Pennsylvania Road Warriors, a travel team in the independent Atlantic League. The following year Howell joined the Seattle Mariners' organization. After two years as the hitting coach at High Desert, he was promoted in 2014 to manage Tacoma. Howell began the 2015 season as a coach for Jackson and was promoted to manager in midseason. As of 2018, he was the hitting coach for the Arkansas Travelers.

Roy Howell brought the work ethic of a California farmer to the baseball diamond. When given the chance to play, he excelled both in the field and at the plate. Ultimately he wanted to win, and fell within two games of baseball's most coveted prize as a member of the 1982 Milwaukee Brewers. True to his word, he swung the bat, he got dirty, and he gave baseball his best shot.

ACKNOWLEDGMENTS

Marty Appel, Peter Bavasi, Bill Carle, Louis Cauz, Pat Gillick, Peter Golenbock, Lee Kluck, Dave McKay, Joey McLaughlin, Bill Nowlin, Jim Prime, Harvey Sahker, Howard Starkman, Elliott Wahle, Eric Zweig

SOURCES

Besides the sources cited in the Notes, the author consulted the following:

MacCarl, Neil. "Jays' Roy-and-Ron Show Rates Fine N.Y. Notices," *The Sporting News*: October 1, 1977: 16.

Prime, Jim. *Tales from the Blue Jays Dugout* (New York: Sports Publishing Inc.), 2014.

NOTES

1 Tom Flaherty, "Brewers: Hustlin' Howell," *The Sporting News*, August 29, 1981: 37.

2 Jim Seip, "Howell Prepared to Lead Road Warriors," York (Pennsylvania) *Daily Record*, April 2, 2011, ydr.com; accessed December 28, 2017.

3 Daniel Okrent, *Nine Innings* (New York: Ticknor & Fields, 1985), 86.

4 Peter Golenbock, *The Forever Boys* (New York: Birch Lane Press, 1991), 188.

5 Golenbock, 187.

6 Ibid.

7 Chuck Stewart, "Spokane's Hitting Howell Proves Father Knew Best," *The Sporting News*, June 1, 1974: 33.

8 Ibid.

9 Golenbock, 190.

10 Golenbock, 190-191.

11 Golenbock, 191-192.

12   Randy Galloway, "Howell Fires Homer Barrage to Grab Rainier 3rd Base Job," *The Sporting News*, August 30, 1975: 16.

13   Ibid.

14   Brad Myers, "Luebber's Long Ride: 29 Years in Minor League Ball," Wilmington (Delaware) News Journal, July 13, 2015. delawareonline.com, accessed December 28, 2017.

15   Randy Galloway, "Roy Howell Howls Over Ranger Job," *The Sporting News*, March 5, 1977: 28.

16   Ibid.

17   Golenbock, 194.

18   Galloway, "Roy Howell Howls"

19   Barry Lewis, "Pro Baseball: 'Black Sunday' Preceded Drillers' First Season" Tulsa World, April 2, 2017, tulsaworld.com; accessed December 28, 2017.

20   Lewis. 3

21   Neil MacCarl, "Swap to Blue Jays Sets Off Big Bat Barrage by Howell," *The Sporting News*, June 11, 1977: 14.

22   Golenbock, 195.

23   MacCarl, "Swap to Blue Jays.

24   Ibid.

25   Neil MacCarl, "Happy Howell a Rare Bird in Blue Jays' Nest," *The Sporting News*, February 4, 1978: 57.

26   Golenbock, 198.

27   Bob Elliott, *Blue Jays Trivia Quiz Book* (Toronto: McClelland and Stewart Inc., 1993), 36.

28   Neil MacCarl, "Meek Jays Boast a Big Bat: Howell's," *The Sporting News*, June 16, 1979: 20.

29   Ibid.

30   Okrent, 218.

31   Golenbock, 122-123.

32   Ibid.

33   Ibid.

34   Okrent, 87.

35   Flaherty.

36   Ibid.

37   Golenbock, 132.

38   William Schneider, "One Last Season in the Sun: The Saga of the Senior Professional Baseball Assocation," in Cecilia Tan, ed., *The National Pastime: Baseball in the Sunshine State* (Phoenix: SABR, 2016), 75-77.

39   Golenbock, 90-91.

40   Charles Faber, *Major League Careers Cut Short: Leading Players Gone by 30* (Jefferson, North Carolina: McFarland & Company Inc., 2011), 130.

DOUG JONES

By Richard Riis

Doug Jones grew up listening to the roar of the 650-horsepower engines and watching as the drivers raced their cars around the dusty dirt tracks of the Indiana sprint-car circuit. Jones's father was a part-time racer, and young Doug hoped to follow in his father's tire tracks some day. When the elder Jones thought his son ready for his first taste of competitive driving, he allowed the 18-year-old to get behind the wheel in a qualifying heat at Lebanon's Paragon Raceway. On the second lap, the rookie racer clipped the retaining wall, spun out of control, and crashed. Doug was unhurt but made up his mind to pursue a career in the somewhat safer sport of baseball.[1]

Douglas Reid Jones was born on June 24, 1957, in the town of Covina, in the San Gabriel Valley about 20 miles northeast of Los Angeles. His parents, Rex, a sheet-metal worker, and Hazel (Hale) Jones, relocated the family to Lebanon, Indiana, when Doug was very young. Distinguishing himself on the mound and playing center field for the Lebanon High School Tigers, Jones made the four-county Sagamore All-Conference Baseball Team as a junior in 1974.[2] He pitched for a year at Butler University in Indianapolis before transferring to Central Arizona College. When he won second-team junior college All-America honors in 1977, the 6-foot-2 right-hander caught the eye of major-league scouts, and in the 1978 January draft he was selected in the third round by the Milwaukee Brewers.[3] He responded by earning All-America honors again[4] while pitching Central Arizona into the Arizona Community College Athletic Conference tournament with a 10-2 won-lost record in the regular season, including a six-inning, 11-0 no-hitter against Pima College.[5]

After the college season, the Brewers assigned Jones to their New York-Penn League farm club in Newark, New York, where he pitched 38 innings, primarily in relief, compiling a 2-4 record and a 5.21 ERA. Given a chance to start in 1979 at Class A Burlington of the Midwest League, Jones put together a so-so 10-10 record, but coupled it with a league-leading 1.75 ERA and 16 complete games in 20 starts. Jones was selected for the league's in-season and postseason All-Star teams.

Jones worked his way up the minor-league ladder in 1980, from Stockton (Class A) to Holyoke (Double A) to Vancouver (Triple A), pitching well at each level and combing for a 14-7 won-lost record and a 2.97 ERA. His performance earned him a trip to spring training with the Brewers in 1981. He failed to make the major-league roster and split the 1981 season between Vancouver and Double-A El Paso. Jones's 10-10 record and 4.50 ERA were

After a cup of coffee with the Brewers in 1982, Doug Jones waited four more years for his next big-league appearance. But the wait was worth it as he developed into a five-time All-Star reliever with the Cleveland Indians and Houston Astros.

deemed worthy of another look at the Brewers' training camp in 1982.

Again Jones failed to earn a spot on the major-league roster and was returned to Vancouver, but he was almost immediately recalled when pitcher Jim Slaton was put on the 21-day disabled list with back spasms on April 3.[6] Jones made his major-league debut on April 9, hurling a hitless inning of relief against the Toronto Blue Jays, but after three more games and an ERA of 10.12 he was sent back to Vancouver. Pitching most often in long relief, Jones' posted a decent 2.97 ERA for the Brewers' top farm club while but his won-lost record was a poor 5-8.

Amid signs that the Brewers' were souring on his prospects, Jones spent 1983 and 1984 in Vancouver and El Paso, with little to show but a combined 7-9 record and a 4.99 ERA, mostly as a starter. In October 1984, the Brewers gave him his release.[7]

At 27, now married and a father, it seemed a good probability that Jones was done as a professional player. But the Cleveland Indians were desperate for pitching, and they accepted Jones's offer to come to their spring-training camp at his own expense. After a few poor outings, Jones realized he had little to lose by experimenting with a new pitch he'd learned from former Vancouver teammate Willie Mueller, an offspeed pitch thrown without the use of his forefinger, the ball held between his thumb and remaining three fingers.[8] Jones could always hit his spots with his fastball, curve, and occasional knuckleball, but the new pitch gave him a devastating changeup that threw opposing hitters off balance. In his next outing, Jones pitched three scoreless innings, and the Indians were impressed enough to sign him to a minor-league contract.

In 39 games and 116 innings at Double-A Waterbury, Jones went 9-4 with a 3.65 ERA and seven saves, and struck out 113, the fourth highest total in the Eastern League. Promoted to Triple-A Maine for 1986, Jones turned in an outstanding season. "The scouts will tell you everything Jones can't do," observed sportswriter Terry Pluto. "But in this, Jones' 29th year, he … is doing a Mike Marshall imitation. Now Jones is the best reliever in the International League."[9]

Nine saves and a league-best 2.09 ERA earned Jones a call-up to Cleveland on September 1. Against the Toronto Blue Jays on September 14, he relieved starter Ken Schrom with the bases loaded and one out in the ninth. Jones walked in a run but got the final two outs for his first major-league save. Twelve days later he won his first major-league game, pitching the final two innings of a 12-inning Cleveland win over the Seattle Mariners.

Jones made the Cleveland roster out of spring training in 1987, but after a disappointing April, he was again assigned to the minors. He was recalled in June and finished the season with a team-high eight saves and a 3.15 ERA.

In his first full season with Cleveland, 1988, Jones emerged as one of the league's best closers, allowing just 69 hits (only one home run) and 16 walks in 83⅓ innings. His 37 saves, third most in the American League, for a club that won only 78 games, broke the Indians' record of 23, set by Ernie Camacho in 1984, and his 14 consecutive saves surpassed the major-league mark of 13 just a year before by the Phillies' Steve Bedrosian. That summer Jones was named the Indians' lone representative to the AL All-Star team, and at season's end placed 15th in voting for the MVP.

As he moved into the ranks of elite closers with a fastball that seldom topped the mid-80s, some nicknamed Jones "The Sultan of Slow."[10] He made the All-Star team in each of the next two seasons, saving 32 games in 1989 and a club-record 43 in 1990. His 112 saves from 1988 to 1990 for a bad Indians team trailed only the 126 gathered by Dennis Eckersley for the perennial AL champion Oakland A's and Chicago White Sox closer Bobby Thigpen's 125.

Jones suffered a major reversal of fortune in 1991. Starting with a game on April 24 in which he gave up a two-out, two-run, ninth-inning home run to Detroit's Kirk Gibson in what became a 4-2 Cleveland loss, Jones went 1-4 over a stretch of 12 games with five blown saves and a 12.66 ERA. "Yes, I'm concerned," said Cleveland skipper John McNamara. "He's leaving the ball up over the plate and they're not missing it."[11] "I understand what managers don't like," Jones responded. "They'd much rather have someone who can throw it by people and get it over with, one way or another. Those kind of pitchers will get the strikeout but be vulnerable to the home run. Someone like me, who doesn't throw hard, can give up cheap hits and drag things out. Meanwhile the manager's heart rate is about 100 miles per hour and his blood pressure's going up."[12]

Jones's troubles mirrored that of the rest of the team, which lost 20 of 44 after the Gibson home run, costing McNamara his job. New manager Mike Hargrove installed Shawn Hillegas as the closer, then Steve Olin when Hillegas proved inconsistent. By July there were rumors that Jones might be traded to the Dodgers,[13] but despite continuing to pitch poorly, he remained with the Indians through the rest of the season. In 36 games in 1991, Jones went 4-8 with only seven saves and a bloated 5.54 ERA.

Cleveland opted not to offer Jones a contract for 1992, making him a free agent, and he found a willing taker in the Houston Astros, who signed the 34-year-old to a three-year deal. Pitching for the first time in the National League, Jones returned to his old form and delivered one of his finest seasons. He pitched in 80 games, finishing an NL-best 70. He won a club-leading 11 games against 8 losses, saved 36, and posted an ERA of 1.85. His control was as precise as ever: He struck out 93 in 111⅔ innings while walking only 17. He made the NL All-Star team and finished 14th in MVP balloting at season's end. He received *The Sporting News'* Fireman of the Year Award.

Despite 26 saves, Jones struggled again in 1993, going 4-10, his ERA ballooning to 4.54, prompting a trade with pitcher Jeff Juden to the Phillies for World Series goat Mitch Williams. Jones made a comeback for the Phillies, saving 27 with an ERA of 2.17 in 47 games, and earning his fifth and final All-Star berth. Perhaps the highlight of his season came in Pittsburgh on May 12 when manager Jim Fregosi allowed Jones to come to the plate against the Pirates in the bottom of the eighth with the Phillies ahead by two runs. Jones lined a single to short right field for his first ML hit. Jones played six more years in the major leagues but never got another hit.

Granted his free agency for 1995, Jones signed with Baltimore and saved 22 games but with a disappointing 5.01 ERA. Again granted free agency, he was signed for 1996 by the Chicago Cubs, who released him in June after he pitched in 28 games with only two saves. Finishing the season with the Milwaukee Brewers, who had given up on him more than a decade before, Jones then enjoyed a resurgence at age 40 in 1997. After reliever Mike Fetters missed the first month of the season will a strained hamstring,[14] Jones took his place as the team's closer and never gave it up. He finished an AL-best 73 games for the season, saving 36 in 38 opportunities and pitching to a 2.02 ERA.

Halfway through 1998, Jones was traded to the Indians for Eric Plunk, and that fall pitched in his first postseason game, the first matchup of the ALDS, throwing 2⅔ innings against the Boston Red Sox. The Indians advanced to the ALCS, but Jones was left off the roster, and after the season signed as a free agent with the Oakland A's, for whom he pitched two seasons to close out his career at age 43, at the time the oldest player in the AL.

At the time of his retirement, Jones's 303 career saves, all but one earned after he turned 30, ranked 12th in major-league history, and his 846 games pitched ranked 21st. His 129 saves for Cleveland, at one time the club's all-time top total, was still good enough for third place as of 2019. Upon his eligibility for the Hall of Fame in 2006, Jones received two votes, failing to qualify for subsequent ballots.

After working as a minor-league assistant for the Arizona Diamondbacks for three seasons, Jones spent five years as the pitching coach for San Diego Christian College, helping lead the team to its first season and regional championships, plus its first trip to the NAIA World Series in 2014. In 2015 Jones was named pitching coach for the Boise Hawks, a minor-league affiliate of the Colorado Rockies. Jones and his wife, Caty, also run a Christian music recording label, His Heart Music.

SOURCES

In addition to the sources cited in the Notes, the author also accessed Retrosheet.org, Baseball-Reference.com, and SABR.org.

NOTES

1. "Ex-Lebanon Athlete Finds Success in Phillies' Pen," *Muncie (Indiana) Evening Press*, July 12, 1994: 11.
2. "Time Out," *Noblesville (Indiana) Ledger*, July 17, 1974: 10.
3. "Lebo Drafted First, 7 Go from State," *Arizona Republic (Phoenix)*, January 11, 1978: 18.
4. "'Riders' Soesbe Honored," *Arizona Daily Sun (Flagstaff)*, June 4, 1978: 13.
5. "Central Rips Pima Twice, 11-0, 14-4," *Arizona Republic*, May 6, 1978: 81.
6. "Expos Trim to One Over Limit," *Vancouver (British Columbia) Sun*, April 3, 1982: 24.
7. "Waddell Hurting," *Mansfield (Ohio) News-Journal*, April 29, 1986: 2B.
8. "Movie 'Star' Leads Doug Jones to Major Leagues," *Mansfield (Ohio) News-Journal*, June 8, 1989: 18.
9. "Experts Foresee Bountiful Harvest on Indians' Farms," *Akron Beacon Journal*, August 9, 1986: B5.
10. "Doug Jones: The 'Sultan of Slow,'" Lebanon Indiana Fun City Finder, lebanon-indiana.funcityfinder.com/2010/12/01/doug-jones/, Accessed June 30, 2018.
11. "McNamara Not Concerned About Jones," *Coshocton (Ohio) Tribune*, May 3, 1991: 8.
12. "Jones' Troubles Continue to Build," *Newark (Ohio) Advocate*, May 5, 1991: 22.
13. "Notebook," *Akron Beacon Journal*, July 27, 1991: 28.
14. "Unfettered, Jones Remains the Closer," *The Sporting News*, June 2, 1997: 48.

PETE LADD

By Gordon Gattie

Milwaukee fans anxiously awaited the outcome of rookie Pete Ladd's duel with future Hall of Famer Rod Carew. With one more out, the Brewers would earn the franchise's first trip to the World Series.

The 1982 American League Championship Series between the California Angels and Milwaukee Brewers was knotted at two games apiece. The Angels won the first two games at Anaheim Stadium, and the Brewers rallied back to win Games Three and Four at County Stadium in Milwaukee. As the unexpected late-innings replacement for injured closer Rollie Fingers, the rookie right-hander Ladd had saved Game Three with two groundouts and two strikeouts to preserve Milwaukee's 5-3 margin, providing the Brewers an opportunity to fight another day.[1] Two nights later, in the ninth inning with two outs and pinch-runner Rob Wilfong representing the tying run on second base, Ladd faced Carew with the AL pennant hanging in the balance. In the on-deck circle stood another future Hall of Famer, Mr. October, Reggie Jackson, who had struggled all series but was famous for his postseason home runs.

On a 1-and-2 count with 54,968 fans in hushed anticipation, Ladd fired a fastball across the plate. Carew hit a one-hop grounder directly at shortstop Robin Yount, who threw a perfect strike to first baseman Cecil Cooper and the ensuing pennant-winning celebration began. After the game Ladd commented, "When I saw the umpire raise his arm, that's when I lost my mind."[2]

Peter Linwood Ladd was born on July 17, 1956, in Portland, Maine. His parents, William E. and Ruth Ladd, were high-school sweethearts who were married in 1941. Ladd spent his early childhood years in Portland, listening to the Boston Red Sox on his transistor radio. "I was like any kid who listened to the Red Sox a little bit past my bedtime," he commented in a post-career interview.[3] His family moved to Atlanta when his parents were transferred there during his high-school years.[4] Ladd graduated from Henderson High School in Atlanta, where former Yankees catcher Jake Gibbs recruited him to join the NCAA Division I ballclub at the University of Mississippi in Oxford.

Ladd pitched three seasons (1975-1977) at the University of Mississippi. Ole Miss finished the 1977 season with a 39-19 record, establishing the school record for most wins in a season.[5] The 1977 Rebels were Southeastern Conference Champions, and advanced to the NCAA Southern Regional tournament in Miami, Florida. During the season, Ladd finished with a 4-3 record as the number 3 starter in the rotation. Ladd took the loss during the Rebels' 5-2 defeat to Miami (Florida), the game that ended the Rebels' tournament participation.⁶ A starting pitcher while playing at Ole Miss, he compiled a 10-7 record during his collegiate career and attained a 1.74 ERA as a sophomore.⁷

In June 1977 the 6-foot-3 Ladd was drafted in the 25th round of the free-agent draft by the Red Sox. The 20-year-old Ladd made his professional debut with the Winter Haven Red Sox of the Class A Florida State League. He finished the season with a 4-1 record, 5 saves, 27 strikeouts in 27 innings, and a 1.67 ERA as he transitioned from a starting pitcher to a reliever. Ladd returned to Winter Haven the next year for a full season, and led the league with 18 saves.

In 1979 Ladd was promoted to the Double-A Bristol (Connecticut) Red Sox, who won the 1978 Eastern League title despite finishing third during the regular season.⁸ Ladd joined future major leaguers Wade Boggs, Bruce Hurst, and Mike Smithson on the talent-laden roster. People took notice of his hulking frame and 15EEE shoe size; as one sportswriter commented, "His appearance is intimidating. He's burly and he peers down at the batter through glasses that look to be too small for him. His mustache and whiskers are reddish brown. He brings his head with a snapping arm and the big body behind it."⁹ Ladd's large shoes also provided fodder for the "Big Foot" nickname that followed him throughout his career. The intimidating reliever had compiled a 3-1 record with 9 saves and a microscopic 0.62 ERA over 29 innings when he was traded to the Houston Astros with a player to be named and cash for Bob Watson on June 13.¹⁰ After the trade announcement, Bristol's manager, Tony Torchia, complimented Ladd on his future prospects: "Houston knew what it was doing when it grabbed Peter Ladd. He's an outstanding prospect, definitely a big leaguer. He's got an overpowering fastball."¹¹ Ladd reported to the Columbus (Georgia) of the Double-A Southern League. Though he continued pitching in relief, he won two games and saved four others in his first six appearances,¹³ Ladd also started four games — the first games he started since pitching at Ole Miss — which included the only shutout he recorded in professional baseball.

In August, when Columbus teammate and fellow Mainer Bert Roberge was injured while pitching for the parent club, the 23-year-old Ladd received his call to big leagues. The Astros were leading the NL West Division, ahead of the Cincinnati Reds, and Ladd immediately jumped into a pennant race. On August 17 the Astros were trailing the Philadelphia Phillies 5-2 going into the ninth inning when manager Bill Virdon summoned Ladd from the bullpen.¹⁴ The first batter Ladd faced, Bake McBride, lined out to center field. Then Pete Rose grounded out, Mike Schmidt walked, and Greg Luzinski flied out as Ladd didn't allow a run against the heart of Philadelphia's order. He threw two scoreless innings four days later against the New York Mets. The reliever won his first major-league game on August 26, when he pitched the seventh and eighth innings of an Astros late-inning victory against the Phillies. Ladd finished his first big-league season with a 1-1 record and 2.92 ERA in 10 appearances totaling 12⅓ innings. Houston faltered down the stretch, while Cincinnati surged ahead and won the NL West title by 1½ games.

Ladd returned to the minor leagues the following April, splitting time between Columbus and the Triple-A Tucson Toros (Pacific Coast League). Over the next two seasons, Ladd pitched well but couldn't crack the Astros' star-studded staff. The Astros compiled the best NL team ERA during the 1980 and 1981 seasons, with a starting rotation anchored by Joe Niekro, Nolan Ryan, and Vern Ruhle, complemented by a powerful 1-2 bullpen punch in Dave Smith and Joe Sambito. In 1980 the unheralded Ladd went 6-5 with 5 saves and a 3.44 ERA at Columbus before his July promotion to Tucson.¹⁵ With his fastball and intimidating presence, he tied a Tucson team record by striking out five consecutive batters against the Ogden Athletics.¹⁶ Both Ladd and Roberge returned to the Toros for the 1981 season.¹⁷ By now, Ladd was fiercely intimidating and nurtured the image; he entered a 1981 exhibition game in the ninth inning with the go-ahead run on third base and missed the strike zone on all six warm-up pitches, then commented after the game, "A big part of my game is intimidation. I get the catcher going all over the place. Then when I get 'em in a situation, I'll do my real warm-ups. I'm not out there for no purpose."[18]

His intimidating image was useful for other reasons. During the offseasons, Ladd worked as a probation and parole officer at the Cumberland County Jail in Portland, Maine. Working as a parole officer provided a unique perspective to playing baseball, providing extra motivation to earn a spot on a major-league roster.

On October 23, 1981, Ladd was traded from Houston to Milwaukee for pitcher Rickey Keeton.[19] The Brewers assigned Ladd to their Triple-A affiliate, the PCL's Vancouver Canadians. The 25-year-old Ladd was now with his third organization though the Brewers didn't have nearly as much pitching depth as the Astros. As the 1982 season approached, *Baseball Digest* placed Milwaukee in the middle of the AL East Division with an outlook of "better pitching could move up" based on "great power, good bullpen, fair defense, balanced starting staff, and some speed."[20] Although Ladd was a welcome addition to the Canadians' bullpen, he wasn't mentioned in either *Baseball Digest*'s rookie report, which listed pitchers Frank DiPino, Charles Porter, Willie Mueller, and Rich Olsen,[21] or in a later local interview that focused on Vancouver's starting rotation.[22]

As the 1982 All-Star break approached, the 48-35 Milwaukee Brewers stood atop the AL East, slightly ahead of Boston. After Milwaukee's staff ace, Pete Vuckovich, and reliever Jamie Easterly were placed on the disabled list, Ladd received his second call-up to the majors. He had compiled a 10-2 record with 8 saves and a 2.91 ERA for Vancouver. On July 17 Ladd celebrated his 26th birthday by debuting in the AL and pitching 1⅔ scoreless innings and getting the win against the Chicago White Sox in front of more 52,000 spectators in Milwaukee. Harvey Kuenn, Milwaukee's manager, said of Ladd's performance, "He did an outstanding job. He came in and did everything

With All-Star closer Rollie Fingers injured, reliever Peter Ladd emerged as an unsung hero in the 1982 ALCS, tossing 3 1/3 innings of scoreless relief and picking up two saves against the California Angels.

they told us he could do." Ladd said, "Being my birthday and one of the largest crowds here, you could feel the tension. That was nice. I don't get nervous. I was very excited. More excited than when I was first called up with Houston."[24] Ladd credited Eli Grba, Vancouver's pitching coach, and adviser Pat Dobson with improving the consistency of his slider, which helped him return to the majors.[25]

Ladd earned his first career save on August 20 when he entered in the ninth inning of a 6-4 contest against the Seattle Mariners, with no outs and runners on first and third. Ladd struck out Dave Revering looking, then Rick Sweet delivered a sacrifice fly to bring Seattle within a run. Manny Castillo flied out to end the game as Ladd preserved the victory.[26] His first blown save occurred when he allowed three runs against the Oakland Athletics on August 28 after not pitching for over a week.[27]

Ladd's importance to Milwaukee's playoff dreams would quickly change. During the first game of a September 2 doubleheader, when Rollie Fingers exited the ninth inning of a 2-1 matchup against the Cleveland Indians with an 0-and-2 count on Andre Thornton, Ladd entered the game without warming up and struck out Thornton on a sinking fastball, then struck out Von Hayes, ending the game.[28] That game turned out to be Fingers' last appearance of the 1982 season; he had suffered a muscle tear in his right arm. Ladd inherited closer duties for the September stretch run and playoffs. Fingers complimented Ladd's response: "That was outstanding. If he can handle that kind of pressure, he can handle anything."[29]

Though Ladd struggled in his new role during the month, Milwaukee successfully fended off the Baltimore Orioles, who compiled a 22-10 record starting September 1, coming from five games behind to pulling even with the Brewers on October 2 for Game 162, which Milwaukee won, 10-2, to clinch the AL East title.[30]

The ALCS pitted two teams each seeking their first pennant. The California Angels, who started play in 1961, had reached the playoffs only once before — in 1979, when they lost in four games to the Orioles. The Brewers, who started play in 1969, also played in one postseason — in 1981, when they lost the AL Division Series to the Yankees in five games. California won Game One, 8-3, in which Ladd pitched a scoreless eighth inning, striking out all three Angels hitters he faced. California won Game Two, 4-2, and the Brewers now had their backs to the wall. The Brewers rebounded in Game Three. They built a 5-0 lead behind Don Sutton's seven shutout innings. However, Sutton experienced trouble in the eighth inning as a home run and consecutive doubles by the Angels made it 5-3. Ladd relieved Sutton and induced a groundout to end the threat. In the ninth inning, Ladd needed 11 pitches to retire California on a groundout and two swinging strikeouts to the end the game. When asked by reporters if he ever faced a more challenging situation, Ladd drew upon his law-enforcement experience and responded, "Yeah, I got punched by a triple murderer this year."[31] Milwaukee evened the series by winning Game Four, though Ladd didn't appear. Ladd was unstoppable in the deciding game: He replaced Milwaukee starter Bob McClure in the ninth with no outs and the tying run on first base. After Bob Boone sacrificed Wilfong to second base, Brian Downing and Carew grounded out to end the series. Ladd delivered on expectations; he saved two games, pitched to 10 batters and retired all 10, striking out five. He was the runner-up to Darrell Porter in the voting for the Championship Series MVP.

Ladd pitched in only one game of the seven-game World Series against the St. Louis Cardinals. He entered Game Two in St. Louis in the bottom of the eighth inning with the score tied, runners on first and second, and Lonnie Smith at the plate. He walked Smith on a questionable 3-and-2 call to load the bases and then walked Steve Braun on four pitches to force in the winning run.[32] After Game Two, Kuenn relied on McClure as his closer throughout the Series while awaiting Fingers' potential return that never materialized.[33] St. Louis won the Series in seven games.

As Milwaukee prepared to defend its AL pennant in 1983, the Brewers' toughest question centered on Fingers' status; versatile Milwaukee pitcher Jim Slaton noted, "I'm not sure how (Fingers' situation) will influence me because we have Pete Ladd who specializes in short relief."[34] Throughout spring training, Ladd was slated to serve as the number-two short reliever behind Fingers. Even as the regular season approached, Fingers' status was unclear, which left the relievers' roles up in the air.[35] Milwaukee's fortunes dimmed when reigning AL Cy Young Award winner Vuckovich developed a torn rotator cuff that kept him from pitching until late August.[36] Fingers didn't return in time for the regular season, and Kuenn named Ladd as the closer. Confident in his abilities, Ladd commented, "I'm not trying to be Rollie Fingers. I'm just trying to make a name for myself. Time and again I've said it, I'm not Rollie Fingers' replacement."[37] In Ladd's first two games, he kept his opponents off the scoreboard, and then he absorbed two losses in late April. His ineffectiveness continued into early May and he apparently lost the good technical habits he had developed.[38] After going 0-2 with a 7.11 ERA in eight appearances, Ladd was sent down to Vancouver to focus on regaining his skills.[39] At Vancouver, he quickly bounced back, was recalled on June 21, and returned to the closer role.[40] Ladd didn't allow a hit or run during his first four return appearances, and on July 18 he earned saves in both ends of a doubleheader against the Texas Rangers. Ladd pitched effectively for the rest of the season, with 23 saves and a 1.88 ERA after he returned from Vancouver. He finished fifth in the AL with 25 saves as Fingers was on the shelf all year. Milwaukee dropped to fifth place in the AL East with an 87-75 record, 11 games behind Baltimore. Recognizing Ladd's effectiveness, the Brewers selected him as their Most Valuable Pitcher for the 1983 season.

Fingers returned for the 1984 season, and Ladd returned to the number-two spot, where he established career highs with 54 appearances, 91 innings, and 75 strikeouts. His 4-9 record, 3 saves, and 5.24 ERA reflected the Brewers' difficult season, as they slipped to last place in the AL East. "It was a bad, long dream. I don't want to think about this season," Ladd commented after the season.[41] He made his sole career start that season, on June 4, when no starting pitchers were available after three starters were injured in successive days; Ladd volunteered to start the game, and manager Rene Lachemann agreed.[42] Ladd pitched four innings against the Orioles in Baltimore, and allowed five earned runs while taking the loss.[43] Off the field, Ladd was recognized for his sportsmanship, character, and community involvement as the Milwaukee Brewers' nomination for the Roberto Clemente Award.[44]

Neither Ladd nor the Brewers fared much better in 1985. After enduring a tough season, Ladd wasn't guaranteed a roster spot heading into spring training,[45] and he had to prove himself to a new coaching staff. Throughout spring training, he worked on his delivery and also took a different approach to camp. With his trademark determination, Ladd commented, "I had to come here and do everything all over again and let them know last year was a fluke and that I could help this ballclub."[46] After posting a 1.50 ERA in spring training, he was one of 10 Milwaukee pitchers when the season started.[47]

Ladd finished the season without a decision, two saves, and a 4.53 ERA in 45⅔ innings, while Milwaukee ended the year sixth in the AL East with a 71-90 record. He pitched well during the first half of the season, with a 3.41 ERA in 29 innings, though his strikeout rate fell noticeably from the previous year and his batting average against was .322. He struggled throughout July, and was sent down to Vancouver in August. Ladd returned to the Brewers in September, but he endured his worst month that season. In November, per request to Milwaukee general manager Harry Dalton, he was designated for assignment and later released by the Brewers.

On January 18, 1986, Ladd found new life when he signed as a free agent with the Seattle Mariners. They had struggled in the AL West's second division since their inception in 1977, and were rebuilding their bullpen. At the end of spring training, Ladd was sent to Seattle's Triple-A farm club in Calgary, but was quickly recalled when reliever Karl Best was placed on the disabled list. Ladd started the season in the closer's role, earning three relief wins and four saves through late May, but was eventually replaced by Matt Young, who was converted from a starter to reliever. Ladd stayed with Seattle all season, pitching consistently and effectively, and enjoyed his best season since 1983.

He pitched in his last major-league game on October 3, 1986, against Cleveland, when he struck out Cory Snyder, the only batter he faced after relieving starter Mike Morgan in the seventh inning. Just before Ladd entered the game, Morgan allowed a run-scoring double that reduced Seattle's lead to

5-3. Immediately after Ladd left the game, reliever Ed Nunez gave up a game-tying two-run homer. As he had done so many times throughout his career, the burly reliever quietly and effectively did his job.

Ladd finished second on the Mariners with six saves, second with 52 appearances, and tied for second with a 3.82 ERA. He won a career-high eight games; his 70⅔ innings pitched and 53 strikeouts were the second-highest totals in his career. The following January, Ladd signed a one-year deal with Seattle, but at the end of spring training he was released. Two weeks later, Ladd signed with the Los Angeles Dodgers as a free agent. He spent the entire season with the Albuquerque Dukes, the Dodgers' Triple-A affiliate. Experiencing arm trouble throughout the season, Ladd had shoulder surgery during the offseason.

Adding to his aura of determination, Ladd wasn't finished playing baseball when the 1987 season ended. In February 1988, Ladd's agent contacted every major-league club to land his services. When none responded with an offer, Ladd purchased a full-page advertisement in USA Today with the catch phrase, "Have Fastball Will Travel."[48] The ad didn't help him land a spot on a big-league roster.

In 205 appearances over six major-league seasons, Ladd compiled a 17-23 record with 39 saves and a 4.14 ERA. He struck out 209 batters in 287 innings, and had a 2.18 strikeout-to-walk ratio. In addition to his major-league time, Ladd pitched for parts of nine seasons in the minor leagues. Throughout his career, he was known for his determination as much as his stature.[49] Ladd was inducted into the Maine Baseball Hall of Fame in 2009.[50]

SOURCES

Besides the sources cited in the Notes, the author consulted Baseball-Almanac.com, Baseball-Reference.com, Retrosheet.org, TheBaseballCube.com, and the following:

James, Bill. *The New Bill James Historical Abstract* (New York: The Free Press, 2001).

Okrent, Daniel. *Nine Innings* (New York: McGraw-Hill Book Company, 1985).

Thorn, John, and Pete Palmer, et al. *Total Baseball: The Official Encyclopedia of Major League Baseball* (New York: Viking Press, 2004).

NOTES

1 Bill Brophy, "Brewers Find Way Home," *Wisconsin State Journal* (Madison), October 9, 1982: 9.

2 Gannett News Service, "Ladd New Brewers' Savior," *Green Bay Press-Gazette*, October 11, 1982: 17.

3 Kalle Oakes, "Ladd's Career Touched Greatness," *Lewiston* (Maine) *Sun Journal*, July 12, 2009. sunjournal.com/2009/07/12/ladds-career-touched-greatness/. Accessed November 15, 2018.

4 Owen Canfield, "He's Goin' Like Balls o' Fire," *Hartford Courant*, May 11, 1979: 84.

5 University of Mississippi Athletics Communications Office, *2019 Ole Miss Baseball Media Guide* (Oxford: University of Mississippi, 2011), 10.

6 *2019 Ole Miss Baseball Media Guide*, 97.

7 Jerry Potter, "Hurricane Blows Out Rebs' Fire," *Jackson* (Mississippi) *Clarion-Ledger*, May 22, 1977: 53.

8 United Press International, "Rebs' Ladd Goes Pro," *Delta Democrat-Times* (Greenville, Mississippi), July 6, 1977: 27.

9 Associated Press, "Bristol Red Sox Eastern League Champs for 1978," *Hanover* (Pennsylvania) *Evening Sun*, September 5, 1978: 13.

10 Canfield, 84.

11 United Press International, "Red Sox Trade Scott to KC, Acquire Watson from Houston," *Berkshire Eagle* (Pittsfield, Massachusetts), June 14, 1979: 31.

12 Peter Gammons, "Watson Could Best Deal," *Boston Globe*, June 17, 1979: 74.

13 Ron Coons, "Astros in Different Orbit," *Louisville Courier-Journal*, July 8, 1979: 43.

14 Michael O'Connor, "Phils Gain 1," *Pottsville* (Pennsylvania) *Republican*, August 18, 1979: 6.

15 Associated Press, "Toros Win 8th Straight," *Arizona Daily Star* (Tucson), July 18, 1980: 58.

16 Dave Adam, "Toros Find Relief, Victory with Ladd," *Arizona Daily Star*, August 8, 1980: 61.

17 Dave Adam, "Toros' Manager Happy After Astros Make Final Cuts," *Arizona Daily Star*, April 4, 1981: 10.

18 Dave Adam, "Toros Intimidate Cats, 6-5," *Arizona Daily Star*, April 14, 1981: 25.

19 "Pete Ladd Traded to Brewers," *Arizona Daily Star*, October 24, 1981: 3.

20 George Vass, "How Major League Pennant Races Shape Up for 1982," *Baseball Digest*, April 1982: 29-31.

21 "1982 American League Rookie Scouting Report," *Baseball Digest*, March 1982: 29.

22 Dennis Feser, "C's Not Counting on a Mound of Trouble," *Vancouver* (British Columbia) *Sun*, April 10, 1982: 21.

23 "Ladd Gone, Is DiPino Far Behind?" *Vancouver Province*, July 16, 1982: 20.

24 Tom Flaherty, "Ladd Stands Tall on His Big Night," *The Sporting News*, August 23, 1982: 23.

25 John Hughes, "Milwaukee's Ladd Slides Back Into Major Leagues," *Wisconsin State Journal*, July 18, 1982: 56.

26 Associated Press, "Ladd Puts His Big Foot Down on Mariners," *Racine* (Wisconsin) *Journal Times*, August 21, 1982: 11.

27 Bill Brophy, "Brewers Come Up Short," *Wisconsin State Journal*, August 29, 1982: 25.

28 Associated Press, "Ladd Provides Fingers' Relief," *Racine Journal Times*, September 3, 1982: 15.

29 Ibid.

30 Bill Brophy, "Brewers Win AL East," *Wisconsin State Journal*, October 4, 1982: 18.

31 Bill Brophy, "Ladd Handcuff Angels? It's Not an Idle Threat," *Wisconsin State Journal*, October 9, 1982: 13.

32 Mike O'Brien, "Brewers Bemoan a 'Bad Call'," *Wisconsin Rapids Daily Tribune*, October 14, 1982: 5.

33 Bill Brophy, "Fingers' Availability Still a Question Mark," *Wisconsin State Journal*, October 17, 1982: 27.

34 Bill Brophy, "Spotlights Find Kuenn," *Wisconsin State Journal*, January 26, 1983: 14.

35 Associated Press, "Complete Brewer Pitching Staff Won't Be Decided Until April 1," *Marshfield* (Wisconsin) *News-Herald*, March 15, 1983: 12.

36 Associated Press, "Vuckovich Has a Torn Rotator Cuff," *Wisconsin State Journal*, March 16, 1983: 21.

37 Bill Brophy, "New Ways to Spell Relief," *Wisconsin State Journal*, March 31, 1983: 15.

38 Tom Flaherty, "Stout Ladd Gets on Beam," *The Sporting News*, August 22, 1983: 19.

39 Malcolm Moran, "Players; Ladd Finds Consistency After Glory," *New York Times*, September 15, 1983: 16.

40 Associated Press, "Ladd Gets Second Chance," *Racine Journal Times*, June 21, 1983: 11.

41 Moran, 15.

42 Associated Press, "Brewers Promise to Forget 1984," *Wisconsin State Journal*, October 1, 1984: 13.

43 Tom Flaherty, "Injuries Decimate Pitching Staff," *The Sporting News*, June 18, 1984: 14.

44 Associated Press, "Pitcherless Brewers Flop," *Capital Times*, June 5, 1984: 13.

45 Associated Press, "Ladd Up for Award," *Wisconsin Rapids Daily Tribune*, January 31, 1985: 9.

45 John Hughes, "Searage Leaving Nothing to Be Desired," *Wisconsin State Journal*, March 28, 1985: 16.

46 Associated Press, "Ladd Gets Chance to Prove He's Back," *La Crosse* (Wisconsin) *Tribune*, April 6, 1985: 7.

47 Dennis Punzel, "Brewers Release Enatsu," *Capital Times*, April 3, 1985: 21.

48 Tony Kornheiser, "Former Reliever Pete Ladd Making a Final Pitch with an Ad," *Los Angeles Times*, March 1, 1988. latimes.com/archives/la-xpm-1988-03-01-sp-61-story.html. Accessed November 17, 2018,

48 Denny Moyer, "If Determination Were the Deciding Factor, Pete Ladd Would Win the Cy Young Award," *Sheboygan Press*, February 1, 1985: 19.

49 Michael Hoffer, "Deering Coach, Former Major Leaguer Ladd Named to Maine Baseball Hall of Fame," *The Forecaster* (Portland, Maine), April 24, 2009. theforecaster.net/deering-coach-former-major-leaguer-ladd-named-to-maine-baseball-hall-of-fame/. Accessed November 13, 2018. Maine Baseball Hall of Fame. sites.google.com/site/mebhof/home/members-h-n. Accessed November 13, 2018.

50 Michael Hoffer, "Deering Coach, Former Major Leaguer Ladd Named to Maine Baseball Hall of Fame," *The Forecaster* (Portland, Maine), April 24, 2009. theforecaster.net/deering-coach-former-major-leaguer-ladd-named-to-maine-baseball-hall-of-fame/. Accessed November 13, 2018. Maine Baseball Hall of Fame. sites.google.com/site/mebhof/home/members-h-n. Accessed November 13, 2018.

RANDY LERCH

By Alan Cohen

There is nothing quite like one's first view of a big-league ballpark. From a distance you see the light standards rising high into the sky and as you get closer the rest of the building comes into focus. The car ride that Gordon Tillett took his grandson on in 1962 was to a relatively new ballpark. Candlestick Park had opened in 1960 and it was time for Gordon to take his 8-year-old Randy to his first big-league game.

> "It was that day I made up my mind someday I would pitch in Candlestick Park. Making it to the majors became an obsession with me. It was my dream, the only thing I ever wanted to do."[1]

Randy Lerch would, on April 30, 1977, return to Candlestick Park as a member of the Philadelphia Phillies. The rookie left-hander was making his fourth start of the season and going for his third straight win. Grandpa was there along with Randy's parents and sister, not to mention more than 100 supporters.

By that time, Lerch was 6-feet-5 and 190 pounds and had a fastball that rivaled those of his more experienced teammates. The Phillies gave the youngster a 6-1 lead on that Saturday afternoon. But the Giants chipped away with a run in the seventh inning and two in the eighth before Ron Reed relieved Lerch and put out the fire. Randy Lerch had realized his childhood dream.

Randy Louis Lerch was born on October 9, 1954, in Sacramento, California. His parents were Robert and Barbara Lerch. Robert was born in 1934, Barbara was born on 1935. They had been married on January 16, 1953, Barbara's 18th birthday. Randy was the oldest of four children. After Randy came Steve (1956), Sandy (1958), and Jeffrey (1961). Robert had pitched semipro ball in the Sacramento area and was the fire chief in Rancho Cordova, a Sacramento suburb.

Randy's teammates at Cordova High School in Rancho Cordova included two players who were drafted in the first round in 1972, Jerry Manuel and Mike Ondina. Manuel reached the major leagues and managed the White Sox and Mets; Ondina got as far as Triple A in the White Sox organization. As a high-school junior in 1972, Lerch went 13-0 but he was overused by his coach and his senior year was not as good, resulting in his not being chosen as high as initially expected in the June 1973 amateur draft. He was picked in the eighth round by the Philadelphia Phillies.

Lerch made a steady climb up the Phillies organization, beginning in 1973 with the Auburn Phillies in the short-season Class A New York Penn League, where he went 9-2 with a 2.91 ERA. He led the team in wins and pitched two shutouts.

He married Janet Margaret Brown on December 15, 1973. They had two children, Kristy (born 1977) and Randy Jr. (1978). They were subsequently divorced.

In 1974 Lerch played with the Rocky Mount Phillies in the Class A Carolina League. Suffering from elbow problems, he was limited to 21 starts, posting a 7-6 record with a 3.60 ERA. It was then on to the Reading Phillies in the Double-A Eastern League where he played for manager Bob Wellman and was helped greatly by the presence of coach Tony Gonzalez and roommate Dane Iorg.[2] The 20-year-old youngster led the league with 16 wins (against 6 losses) and had a 2.69 ERA. He had an opportunity to impress the Phillies in an exhibition game on July 10. That day, he pitched for the Phillies, allowing four hits in six innings as Philadelphia defeated its Toledo Triple-A farm club, 3-0.[3] His control improved from the year before with 45 walks in 177 innings.

He was called up to Philadelphia in September and made three relief appearances. In this first brief tour with the Phillies, Lerch had yet to grow to his full height and weight. He was 6-feet-3 and weighed 175 pounds. Teammate Larry Bowa said he was "thin as a blade but sharp as a razor." Thenceforth, Lerch was called Blade by his teammates.[4] In his debut he pitched the ninth inning of a game in which the Phillies were leading the Cubs by 11 runs. Lerch allowed five runs on four hits and a walk but finished the game. He was more effective in his next two games, pitching three scoreless innings each time.

Lerch's hopes of making the jump to the big leagues after his big year at Reading were stymied when the Phillies obtained left-hander Jim Kaat (one of Lerch's heroes) after the season. Lerch pitched with the Oklahoma City 89ers in the Triple-A American Association in 1976. He got off to a good start when he defeated Evansville, 5-1, on May 1 and pitched a 5-0 shutout against Indianapolis on May 6. This prompted coach Ruben Amaro to say, "He's probably the closest we have to a big-league pitcher."[5] Working under manager Jim Bunning, Lerch was 13-11 with a 3.35 ERA in 29 starts. He struck out 152 batters in 207 innings. He pitched one game for the Phillies in September, getting a save with a three-inning outing in a 9-1 win against the St. Louis Cardinals.

But making his way to the majors for a longer stint would prove difficult, especially as the Phillies had nine veterans on the staff. Steve Carlton, Jim Lonborg, Larry Christenson, Tommy Underwood, Jim Kaat, and Wayne Twitchell were accomplished starters and the bullpen was secure with Ron Reed, Tug McGraw, and Gene Garber. But Lerch felt, "I can count. I know what's going on. I also know that all I need is a chance to get my foot in the door. I'll take it from there. I'll run somebody out of a job."[6] True to his word, in 1977 spring training he won the number-four spot in the rotation.

Lerch lost his first start, at home, to the Cubs on April 13. In his next start, five days later at Wrigley Field, he got his first big-league win with one of the best performances of his career. He took a no-hitter into the seventh inning in a 3-1 victory.

Lerch was 5-2 with a 3.02 ERA through May 16. Then he went into a slump that extended through August and saw his ERA increase to 5.58. In September, he pitched well enough to win three of five decisions, but he did not start after a disappointing two-inning stint against the Cubs on September 21. He finished the season with a 10-6 record and a 5.07 ERA. He didn't appear in the postseason as the Phillies went with Carlton, Lonborg, and Christenson and were defeated in four games by the Los Angeles Dodgers in the best-of-five National League Championship Series.

The disappointing finish to Lerch's 1977 season led to a determination to show improvement in 1978. During the offseason, he returned to Philadelphia to train with strength and flexibility expert Gus Hoefling, with whom teammate Steve Carlton had found success.

The 1978 season was an improvement and ranked among the best of Lerch's career. He won a career-high 11 games, lost 8 and had a 3.96 ERA.

He was especially good in the second half of the season, going 7-2 in his last 15 starts with an ERA of 3.19. (The team was 11-5 in games he pitched during the second half, including a one-inning relief appearance.) He also got to show off his skills as a batter. On April 24 against the Cubs, in a 12-2 win, his third-inning two-run homer against Woodie Fryman gave the Phillies a 2-1 lead, and his RBI double two innings later made the score 3-1. The Phillies broke the game open with a nine-run sixth inning, and the crowed gave Lerch a standing ovation when he came to bat in the seventh inning.[7]

"I made up my mind I wasn't going to give in to these guys."
— Randy Lerch, August 1978.[8]

The Phillies were contending for the NL East championship. They led the division by 5½ games on August 12, but then lost five straight and nine of their next 12 games. Philadelphia still led the division when Lerch took the mound on August 26, but they had lost the first two games of their series at Los Angeles and needed him to stop the bleeding. With the Phillies leading 3-1, the Dodgers put runners on second and third with one out in the seventh and sent up pinch-hitter Reggie Smith, one of the more dangerous bats in their lineup. Lerch struck out Smith and went on to record the last seven outs for the victory.

"I kept myself busy thinking about everything except baseball until I got to the park that night. But doing a job made me feel pretty good."
— Randy Lerch, September 1978.[9]

The Phillies won five in a row, but had trouble closing the deal as the Pirates were able to pull within one game of the division lead on September 19. Lerch took the mound at Montreal on September 20 in a must-win situation and allowed two runs in eight innings as the Phils won 4-2.

"The game was nerve-wracking," Lerch recalled a couple of years later. "It was amazing just because we went into Pittsburgh for a makeup doubleheader and we lost both games, giving us a 1½-game lead over the Pirates with two left to play in the season. We had to win one game to clinch and I was scheduled to start that September 30 game.

The race for the division championship went down to the last weekend of the season, and the Phillies traveled to Pittsburgh for four games with the second-place Bucs. Pittsburgh swept a doubleheader on September 29 to pull within 1½ games of Philadelphia and extend their home winning streak against the Phillies to 24 games. Lerch was given the ball on September 30 and yielded a first-inning grand slam to Willie Stargell that gave Pittsburgh a 4-1 lead. The Phillies mounted a comeback and Lerch's second-inning homer off Don Robinson made the score 4-2. Next time up, in the fourth inning, he homered again off Robinson to make the score 4-3. He left the game for a pinch-hitter in the top of the sixth inning, and the Phillies took the lead. They held on to win 10-8, giving Lerch his 11th win of the season and the Phillies the division championship.

"I remember this, I knew Willie and it was one of those days in batting practice when I was really hitting a lot of balls out of the park and Willie told me later on that he told Robinson to be careful pitching to me because I was swinging the bat good in BP. Robinson responded by saying, 'Forget it, he can't hit.' And Willie told me that after the first home run he went to the mound to talk to Robinson and said, 'You know what, I told you, this guy can hit so be careful.' Then after the second home run, Willie went up to Don again and Robinson said, "That ----- can hit."[10]

Once again the Phillies faced the Dodgers in the NLCS. Los Angeles took a 2-games-to-1 lead and Lerch was given the ball in the fourth game of the series. He left the game with one out in the sixth inning and the Dodgers leading 3-2. The Phillies came back to tie the game and take Lerch off the hook, but the Dodgers won the game with a run in the 10th inning and moved on to the World Series.

Lerch pitched the second highest innings total on the Phillies' staff in 1979 as he finished under .500 (10-13) for the first time in his career, though his ERA was lower than it had been the season before.

"Our pitching so far has kept us up there, and when we start hitting — which we will — we'll be awesome."
— Randy Lerch May 4, 1979.[11]

On May 17 the bats came alive. Lerch was the starting pitcher at Chicago when the Phillies used three-run homers by Mike Schmidt and Bob Boone and a solo shot by Lerch (his fourth and final major-league homer) to take a 7-0 first-inning lead against the Cubs. On his way to his position at shortstop, Larry Bowa shouted to Lerch, "Is that enough runs for you?" Turns out it wasn't. Each of the first four Cubs batters scored, the last three coming on a three-run homer off the bat of Dave Kingman. Lerch then got one out, but after a double by Jerry Martin, he was yanked by manager Danny Ozark. The game became a sluggers' duel, and after nine innings, the score was 22-22. The Phillies pushed across a run in the 10th inning to win. By that point, Lerch was at the airport, as the team was flying to Montreal to begin a series the next day.

The team went through injuries to key players, including the double-play combination of Bowa and Manny Trillo, and Lerch wasn't immune to the injury epidemic that, in early July, shelved three of the team's starting pitchers. He and his wife went out to dinner with another couple after the game on July 3 and had encountered a group of delinquents when they left the restaurant at 12:45 A.M. They attacked Lerch, who wound up with a broken bone in his right wrist and was out of the lineup until July 11.[12] At the time of the injury, he was 4-7 with a 3.61 ERA and had pitched in some bad luck. In five of his seven losses, the Phillies had scored two runs or fewer. The team finished in fourth place.

The 1980 season didn't start well for Lerch. He lost his first six decisions. Still, he showed spurts of brilliance. He lost a 1-0 decision to Montreal on June 26 and followed that up on July 1, again against the Expos, when he pitched the first 10 innings and

Randy Lerch notched 15 of his 60 big-league wins for the Brewers in 1981 and 1982 before he was sold to the Montreal Expos during the pennant race in August 1982.

received credit for the win when Philadelphia won in the 11th. The win was Lerch's third of the season. The Phillies removed him from the rotation at the end of July.

He had two starts in August, but they were necessitated by the team's scheduling of doubleheaders to make up for rainouts. His last win of the season, also his last start, came on August 17 in the second game of a doubleheader against the Mets at Shea Stadium. He pitched into the seventh inning, allowing one run and four hits, as Philadelphia won 4-1 and moved its record to 62-53. They were in third place, 3½ games behind the division-leading Pirates, and primed for a stretch run. Lerch was not a meaningful factor in the season's last weeks. The Phillies were 29-18 in their last 47 games and won the division title by one game over Montreal. Lerch's record for the year was an unimpressive 4-14, with an ERA of 5.16.

"They want me to go along (with the team to Houston). They want me to sit on the bench the way a disabled person would. I've got more pride than that. I don't want to go anywhere I'm not wanted. All we've gone through in the last few years, it would be nice to be part of the Phillies winning the championship."

— Randy Lerch, October 7, 1980.[13]

Lerch was not on the postseason roster. He was replaced by Kevin Saucier, a middle reliever who had gone 7-3 with an ERA of 3.42. The Phillies went on to win the World Series for the first time since they entered the National League in 1883.

Drug scandals were ongoing during the time Lerch was in the majors and his name and those of several other Phillies players were mentioned during an investigation of doctors who were accused of illegally dispensing amphetamines to the players.[14] In February 1981 Lerch, under subpoena, testified that he had twice obtained the antidepressant drug Preludin.[15] He was the only player to testify.

Charges against the accused doctors were dismissed and Lerch knew that his time with the Phillies was over. In early March of 1981, he was traded to the Milwaukee Brewers for outfielder Dick Davis. At the time of the trade, Lerch's career batting average was .207 with four homers and 22 RBIs. Lerch had batted .267 in 1980. He would not bat during his time with the Brewers.

With the Brewers in 1981, Lerch went 7-9 with a 4.31 ERA in 23 appearances, of which 18 were starts. He was uneven in the early part of the season with a periodic good start. His first win came in relief on April 20 when he entered the game against Toronto in the 11th inning with the score tied 4-4. After the Brewers scored the lead run in the top of the 12th, he struck out the side for the win, and was given a spot in the starting rotation. On April 26 he pitched eight innings as the Brewers shellacked Kansas City, 11-1, and a month later he had his first complete game of the season, defeating Detroit 5-1. On June 1 he went 10 innings, allowing three runs, in a game the Brewers would lose in 12 innings. The players strike shut down the season from June 12 through August 9. Lerch's first post-strike win came on August 16 when he pitched into the eighth inning in a 2-0 shutout at Toronto.

As Milwaukee contended for the second-half championship in the AL East, Lerch won back-to-back starts on September 12 and 16, which brought his record for the season to 6-8. On September 30 Lerch entered the game in the fourth inning with the score tied 3-3. The Brewers took the lead in the fourth inning and broke the game open with four runs in the fifth inning. They ended the night in a virtual tie with the Tigers and traveled to Detroit, where they won two of three games to win the AL East second-half title.

Lerch started Game Three of the best-of-five American League Divisional Series at Yankee Stadium with the Yankees leading the series 2 games to none. Fighting off a pregame illness, he allowed only three hits in six innings, coming out of the game in the seventh inning with the Brewers leading 3-1. He was not involved in the decision as the Brewers relinquished the lead before coming back to win 5-3. The series went the full five games with the Yankees winning and advancing to the American League Championship Series.

In 1982 the Brewers found it tough in the early part of the season and finished May in sixth place. Lerch was 3-4 and 5.24 at that point. Harvey Kuenn replaced Buck Rodgers as manager and the Brewers began to jell. By July, the Brewers were in first place and Lerch, winning each of his four decisions from June 13 through July 18, was contributing. On July 10 he shut out Kansas City 7-0, and the Brewers were within a game of the division-leading Red Sox. After the Brewers went into first place, Lerch's 9-3 win at Chicago on July 18 extended the team's division lead to 1½ games. But then Lerch had three ineffective outings.

Lerch came back on August 12 with a win at Toronto, but he would not be with the Brewers for the stretch run. He was sold to the Montreal Expos on August 14. Although he went 2-0 with a 3.42 ERA in six appearances (four starts) with the Expos, Lerch was unhappy with the deal that sent him from a possible postseason appearance to a team that, despite some great talent and three future Hall of Famers, was destined to finish in third place.

Lerch's role with the Expos in 1983 was as a middle-inning reliever. In his scant opportunities as a starter, he had only one success, a 5-2 win at New York on June 11, in which he pitched the first six innings. In 19 appearances (five starts), he was 1-3 with a 6.75 ERA when he was released on July 28. He signed with the Giants on August 9 and was sent to their Triple-A affiliate in Phoenix. He returned to the big leagues in September and made seven relief appearances, registering a 3.38 ERA in 10⅔ innings and winning his only decision in his final appearance of the season, on September 29.

Lerch played the entire 1984 season with the Giants, his last full season in the majors. He missed most of July due to injury but was valuable as the lefty long man in the bullpen. His record was 5-3 with two saves. He appeared in 37 games, pitched 72⅓ innings, and had a 4.23 ERA.

Lerch became a free agent after the season but there was little interest in his services. He signed with the Phillies on May 21, 1985, and was assigned to Portland in the Triple-A Pacific Coast League. In 20 appearances, 17 of which were starts, he was 6-6 with a 2.75 ERA, best among starters on the Portland staff. Back with Portland in 1986, he was 6-5 with a 3.01 ERA when he was called up by the Phillies in June. The team's roster was in a state of turbulence and Lerch was the 33rd man to play for the Phillies thus far in the season. He was largely ineffective in four June relief appearances, getting his last major-league win with a scoreless one-third-inning relief stint against Montreal on June 14. He was 1-1 with a 7.88 ERA when he was released on June 26. He finished his season and his career with the Louisville Redbirds in the Triple-A American Association, going 4-2 in eight starts with a 3.89 ERA.

Lerch's major-league career won-lost record was 60-64 with a 4.53 ERA in 253 games.

Immediately after retiring, he was in the restaurant business in California, but grew restless.

In 1989 Lerch played for the St. Petersburg Pelicans of the Senior Professional Baseball Association. The following spring he was in the spring-training camp of the Baltimore Orioles, but knew his playing days were over.

Lerch relocated to New Jersey, worked in construction with the Kline Construction Company, opened a pitching school in Absecon, and played with the Pleasantville team in the Atlantic County (New Jersey) League in 1991.

On August 17, 2000, Lerch was inducted into the Reading Baseball Hall of Fame in consideration of his spectacular season there in 1975.

Lerch relocated to California in 1994 and headed a construction company. He retired from the construction industry in 2014. He remarried in 2008, and he and his wife, Maria, as of 2018 lived about an hour west of Lake Tahoe and visit frequently with Randy's four grandchildren. His children from his first marriage, Kristy and Randy Jr., lived close by. Kristy has two sons and Randy Jr. has a boy and a girl. In 2015 Lerch was inducted into the Rancho Cordova Sports Hall of Fame.

SOURCES

In addition to the sources cited in the Notes, the author used Baseball-Reference.com, the Randy Lerch file at the National Baseball Hall of Fame and Museum Library, and the following:

Author interview with Randy Lerch, June 6, 2018.

Conlin, Bill. "Starting Over – Lerch Counting on Maturity to Help Him Stay with Phils," *Philadelphia Daily News*, February 28, 1986.

Hilt, Ed. "Playoff Exclusion Hurt Lerch – Phils' Left Hander Dropped from Roster for 1980 Postseason," *Atlantic City* (New Jersey) *Press*, July 17, 1990: D1.

NOTES

1. Ray Kelly, "Family, Friends Cheer Phils' Lerch to Victory," *The Sporting News*, May 21, 1977: 13.

2. Mike Drago, "Lerch: Reading Was So Natural," *Reading Eagle*, August 6, 2000: D4.

3. "Reading Loses Lerch," *The Sporting News*, August 2, 1975: 39.

4. Guy Gargan, "Remember the Phillies' Randy Lerch? He's Playing for Pleasantville Now," *Atlantic City* (New Jersey) *Press*, June 30, 1991: B1.

5. "A.A. Day by Day," *The Sporting News*, May 22, 1976: 39.

6. Ray Kelly, "All Arm-Strong Lerch Asks Is Foot in Door," *The Sporting News*, April 2, 1977: 15, 26.

7. Kelly, "Lerch Swings Bat in Phillies' Style," *The Sporting News*, May 13, 1978: 9.

8. Kelly, "Kid Lerch Old Smoothie in Phils' Crisis," *The Sporting News*, September 16, 1978: 15.

9. Kelly, "Clutch Hurler Lerch Takes Heat Off Phils," *The Sporting News*, October 7, 1978: 31.

10. Bob Kuenster, "Pitchers Recall Two-HR Games," *Baseball Digest*, May-June 2010: 26-31.

11. Associated Press, "Lerch Stops Dodgers on Six Hits," *Gettysburg* (Pennsylvania) *Times*, May 5, 1979: 9.

12. *Associated Press*, "Three Starting Pitchers Lost to Phillies," July 5, 1979 (From Randy Lerch File at National Baseball Hall of Fame).

13. Frank Dolson, "Phillies Shaft Two Pitchers," *Boca Raton* (Florida) *News*, October 8, 1980: 2C.

14. United Press International, "Phils Farm's Doctor Accused," *New York Times*, November 22, 1980: 18.

15. Thom Greer, "Will Champion Phillies Be Big Enough to Apologize to Trenton Sportswriter?" *Philadelphia Daily News*, February 7, 1981.

BOB McCLURE

By Chris Rainey

A steady, left-handed pitcher can always find employment in baseball. Bob McClure was armed with a tremendous competitive spirit and a deceptive curveball. He turned his talent into 19 major-league seasons. "Bob Uecker told me that if I were right-handed I would have been digging ditches 10 years ago," McClure said.[1] After his playing days, McClure became a coach and has put in over two decades guiding and developing pitching talent.

Robert Craig McClure was born on April 29, 1952, at the US Naval Base in Oakland, California.[2] His parents were Thomas R. and Muriel (Riley) McClure. Bob grew up in the city of Pacifica, south of San Francisco. His proximity to the Bay Area made him a Giants fan. He had the pleasure of watching Willie Mays, Willie McCovey, and Orlando Cepeda at Candlestick Park. His own baseball career began in the Linda Mar neighborhood Little League, where a teammate was future major leaguer Keith Hernandez.

Sources often said that McClure and Hernandez played together in high school. In fact, Hernandez played at Capuchino High School in the Middle Peninsula League. McClure attended Terra Nova High School, which played in the Northern Peninsula League (NPL). At 5-feet-11 and 170 pounds, he played guard in basketball. On the diamond, he played outfield until a need for pitching arose his junior year. Armed with a heavy fastball that could reach 90 mph and an excellent curve, he found his true calling.

The Terra Nova Tigers baseball team took the NPL title in 1969 and 1970 thanks to McClure's arm. He hurled a no-hitter during a string of 33 consecutive shutout innings in 1970.[3] After high school, McClure joined Hernandez at the College of San Mateo, the local community college. McClure was the ace of the team for two seasons while posting a career mark of 21-3, which earned him All-American recognition.

The Dodgers drafted McClure in the third round of the January draft in 1973, but terms could not be worked out. The Kansas City Royals drafted him in the third round of the June draft secondary phase. This time he was able to come to a contract agreement thanks to the help of scout Dick Hager.

McClure began his professional career with the Royals' rookie farm club in Billings, Montana. His manager in the Pioneer League was Gary Blaylock, who had pitched professionally in 15 seasons. McClure paired with fellow 21-year-old lefty Bob Falcon to anchor the pitching staff. They both started 13 games with McClure leading the circuit with 10 wins and Falcon adding 8. McClure led the league with three shutouts as the Mustangs easily won the pennant. He also batted .289 and homered twice in the same game. His .658 slugging percentage was the best on the team.

McClure's performance and development earned him a jump all the way to Omaha in the Triple-A American Association for the 1974 season. Farm director John Schuerholz explained why McClure was chosen to make an unprecedented leap: He "could throw a breaking ball for a strike behind in the count or at any time." In addition, the brass figured that McClure had the makeup of a fighter and that if the leap turned out a failure, he would not be adversely affected.[4]

McClure joined the rotation, featuring future major leaguers Dennis Leonard and Mark Littell, as the only lefty. Omaha struggled to 54 wins with McClure posting a 5-8 record in 136 innings. His ERA of 3.84 was second on the team to Leonard.

McClure's best weapon, a lethal pickoff move, was perfected during the 1974 season. By early August he had already "wiped out 14 runners."[5] Opposing teams were curtailing their running games and not using the hit and run as often against McClure.

He was invited to spring training with Kansas City in 1975 but suffered a broken wrist at home. It was originally reported that the injury came while conditioning, but it is more likely to have occurred when he tried to dunk a basketball by jumping from a chair. McClure remarked that he would go "incognito on that one."[6]

Originally ticketed for Omaha in 1975, McClure ended up in the Double-A Southern League with the Jacksonville Suns. In May he joined the staff as a starter and turned in two complete games, including a shutout. He was shagging balls in the outfield before a game when a collision led to a broken left wrist. This injury kept him out of action until August 1.

When McClure returned to action, he was used as a reliever. On August 11 he was brought up by the Royals, who were desperate for some left-handed bullpen help because Steve Mingori was ill. McClure made his major-league debut on August 13 in Baltimore. He took the mound in the eighth with the Royals down 3-0. The game had been delayed by rain and it was after midnight when he took the hill. He coaxed Lee May into a grounder to short that Freddie Patek misplayed. A balk moved the runner to second and forced McClure to walk Bobby Grich intentionally. The uneven start did not ruffle McClure as he retired the side without further incident.

McClure's reaction to his debut was typical for him. When asked if he was scared or nervous, he replied, "Didn't you hear my knees shaking?" Manager Whitey Herzog said, "How about that for a debut? Pitching in the mud at 12:30 in the morning."[7]

His next action came on August 16 at home versus the Yankees. The Royals had a 4-2 lead in the eighth when the Yankees rallied and plated a run. McClure was summoned to face Graig Nettles with two outs and two on. Nettles grounded out to first base. In the ninth, McClure set the side down in order for his first major-league save.

In his next nine appearances McClure tossed only seven innings, all of them scoreless. On September 23 against the Texas Rangers, he relieved Doug Bird with one out in the second. He hurled no-hit ball until one out in the eighth, when Roy Smalley poked a single to center. The Royals were up 4-0 when Whitey Herzog replaced him. Behind the relief twirling of Mingori and Marty Pattin, they won by the same score. McClure earned his first major-league victory and finished the season with a 0.00 ERA in 12 appearances.

McClure became a favorite of the beat writers. He was open, honest, straightforward, and funny. When quizzed about his broken wrists, he quipped, "I guess my ankles are next." Quick repartee like that made him a favorite of writers. As a lefty, the scribes were quick to label him "quirky," "unconventional," and "flaky" as they had done with so many southpaws before him.[8]

Newspapermen pointed to his early attempt to sneak his girlfriend onto a team flight as proof of his uniqueness.[9] McClure never did develop the character of a Rube Waddell or Al Hrabosky. He did develop a funky pitching style with a

Tiantesque back-to-the-batter windup. His most notable unconventional contribution was a humorous book written with his friend Dave Downing entitled *Rotting: The Craze of the 90's*. In it the two authors poked fun at the art or science of doing nothing as a couch potato.

The girlfriend from the plane incident was Jody D. Smith. They were wed on October 11, 1975, in Contra Costa, California. They would have three children (Jessica, Jacob, Adam) together. The family would join McClure only for a visit or two in the summers. The California home was their base and they did not move to whatever city Bob was playing in.[10] They divorced in January 1999.

McClure joined teammates John Wathan and Dennis Leonard for winter ball with Arecibo in the Puerto Rican League. The experience he gained cemented his place in the Royals bullpen for 1976. McClure joined Mingori and Ray Sadecki as left-handed relievers on the roster for Opening Day. He extended his scoreless streak on April 9. On April 14 McClure entered the game against the Angels and walked both batters he faced. They came around to score to help the Angels to a 7-6 win. In his next outing, he again walked two and surrendered a run. On May 7 the Royals acquired veteran lefty Tom Hall and sent McClure back to Omaha.

In Omaha McClure returned to the starting rotation. He threw nine complete games, including two shutouts, and struck out 91 batters. All those figures led the team. His nine wins were tied for third on the squad. Omaha lost the playoffs to the Denver Bears and McClure rejoined the Royals. He made three relief appearances in the last four weeks of the season for the division champion Royals.

In December 1976 McClure became the "player to be named later" in a deal between the Royals and Brewers that sent Darrell Porter to Kansas City. He put together a strong season as the only lefty in the Brewers bullpen. He led the team in appearances (68) and ERA (2.52). His six saves were second to Bill Castro's 13.

George Bamberger took over as manager in 1978 and used both Castro and McClure as closers. Bob had more saves and Castro had the better ERA and WHIP for the third-place club. The following season, McClure was joined by Jerry Augustine in the bullpen, giving the Brewers two lefties. Bamberger employed a closer-by-committee approach and McClure's five saves were second to Castro's six. The Brewers improved to finish in second place.

Despite a tremendous season at the plate from Cecil Cooper, the Brewers dropped in the standings in 1980. McClure led the bullpen staff in innings and saves (10). In September he was given a chance to show what he could do as a starter. His first outing was a complete-game 6-1 win over the Royals. The Rangers sent him to the showers in the third inning of his next start. Undaunted, he took the hill for three more starts and won them all. The best performance came against the Mariners on September 19, when he shut them out on five hits.

Manager Buck Rodgers expected McClure to join Mike Caldwell as the lefties in a five-man rotation for 1981. Early in training camp, McClure experienced arm pain that was diagnosed as tendinitis. He did some light tossing and mound work but saw no action in spring-training games. On March 30 he was placed on the disabled list. McClure finally returned to action in September, making four relief appearances. The tendinitis was actually a rotator-cuff issue. With rest and treatment, he was able to return to form.

The Brewers faced the Yankees in the American League Division Series in 1981. McClure had shown enough to be on the roster. He made three appearances in the series and held the Yanks scoreless in each outing. He set the stage for Rollie Fingers' save in Game Four by striking out Reggie Jackson in the eighth and then setting down Lou Piniella and Graig Nettles in the ninth. The Yankees captured the series with a 7-3 win in the fifth game.

McClure went into training camp in 1982 earmarked for the starting rotation. His arm was rejuvenated and with some help from pitching coach Cal McLish he came up with his funky delivery that hid the ball from the batters. It also gave his curve better break. He was a three-pitch pitcher (curve, fastball, changeup) in 1982. A few years later he

A converted reliever, Bob McClure was thrust into the starting rotation in 1982, setting career highs with 12 wins, 26 starts, and 172⅔ innings pitched. He posted a 68-57 record and appeared in 698 games in his 19-year big-league career (1975-1993).

added a knuckleball to his repertoire.

McClure opened the season with a long relief stint against Toronto that earned him the win. His first start came on April 17 when he was on the losing end of a 5-3 game against the Rangers. Two no-decisions followed before he took the hill against Minnesota on May 9. Ron Washington lined the first pitch off McClure's arm just above the left elbow. The swelling forced him to miss a start, but on April 21 he beat the Mariners.

June was McClure's best month of the summer. He won four games without a loss. He beat the Red Sox on June 27 in Boston, then hurled a complete-game victory against them in Milwaukee on July 2. That cut the Red Sox lead to one game. His record was 7-2 at that point. He finished the year at 12-7. Following the acquisition of Doc Medich and Don Sutton, he found himself being readied for postseason relief duty.

McClure had filled a vital role in the Brewers rotation as the sole lefty. He made 17 appearances against Eastern Division rivals and posted a stellar 8-1 record. He posted a career high in wins and innings pitched. At the close of the 1982 season, he was listed on the Brewers' all-time Top 10 in appearances (fourth with 238), saves (fifth with 30) and ERA (eighth at 3.61).[11]

Facing California in the Championship Series, the Brewers dropped the first two games. They battled back and found themselves down by a run in the fifth and final game. McClure came on in the seventh with one out and a man on first. Facing Reggie Jackson, he coaxed a grounder to second that resulted in a double play. In the bottom of the inning, Cecil Cooper drove home two runs. McClure pitched into the ninth, but after a single he gave way to Pete Ladd, who set the Angels down in order for the save. McClure earned the win.

The Brewers took on the St. Louis Cardinals in the World Series. McClure suffered the loss in Game Two. He relieved Sutton to open the seventh and escaped after a single and a walk. In the eighth he walked Keith Hernandez and then with one out surrendered a single to Darrell Porter. Ladd came in and walked the bases full and then walked in the winning run.

McClure faced a single batter in the Game Three loss. In Game Four he came in with two runners on in the eighth. The Brewers were up 7-5. He got Willie McGee to hit into a double play to close out the inning. He then set the side down in the ninth for the save. The series was now tied at two games each.

Game Five was the Brewers' last home game. Mike Caldwell took the hill for Milwaukee and entered the ninth up 6-2. He got an out, but then surrendered two doubles and a single. With the Brewers now ahead 6-4, McClure was brought in to face Darrell Porter and Willie McGee. Porter singled, but McGee went down on strikes. A fly ball to left closed out the game and gave McClure a second save.

In Game Seven the Brewers were up 3-1 in the sixth. Pete Vuckovich gave up a single and double before McClure was summoned. A walk loaded the bases before Keith Hernandez and George Hendrick plated three runs with a pair of singles. Down 4-3, the Brewers could get nothing going. The Cardinals added two runs for the 6-3 win. The loss went to McClure.

Over the winter McClure signed a four-year, $1.95 million deal with the Brewers. With a strong spring training, he opened the 1983 season as the number-four man in the starting rotation. He struggled, dropping his first five starts. Three of them were one-run losses. He tossed a complete game against Minnesota on May 11 for his first win, but then lost his next two outings. He finished May a dismal 1-7. In June and July his fortunes took a 180-degree turn. He won seven and had three no-decisions.

On August 20, after facing two batters McClure felt a pain in his back and was pulled from the game. He was placed on the 21-day disabled list. After his activation, he pitched in relief on September 16. After just 11 pitches the pain returned; he was done for the season.[12]

New manager Rene Lachemann used McClure in relief to open the 1984 season. He made his first start on May 9 without getting the decision in a loss to Chicago. On June 7 he beat Boston for his first win. He made six more starts before returning to the bullpen for most of July. In August he rejoined the rotation and closed out the season with 10 consecutive starts and a 4-8 overall record.

In 1985 McCLure made a start in May and then settled into being a full-time reliever for the duration of his career. On June 8, 1986, he was sent to Montreal for a player to be named later (Kent Bachman). He was the last pitcher from 1982 left on the Brewers' roster. In Montreal he was reunited with manager Buck Rodgers, who saw to it that he had plenty of work. His 65 combined appearances in 1986 were the most of his career. In 1987 he made another 52 trips to the hill for the Expos, posting a 6-1 record with five saves.

Did the two seasons take a toll on McClure's arm? He was awarded a half-million-dollar contract for 1988, but early in training camp he seemed to have lost some velocity and movement. His issues persisted into the regular season and he posted a 1-3 record with a dismal 6.16 ERA in 19 games. The Expos released him on July 2. There is always a market for left-handed pitchers and the Mets signed McClure on July 13 as part of the retooling of their middle relief. He contributed 11 innings of work with a win and a save to the Mets pennant drive. They released him on October 27.

The young and inexperienced California Angels closed out the 1988 season winless in the final two weeks. The front office spent the winter bringing in veteran talent for manager Doug Rader. McClure joined Bert Blyleven, Lance Parrish, and Claudell Washington as new veteran influences. He signed for $200,000.

McClure took the hill in the ninth inning of the season opener with the Angels trailing 4-2. Two hits, a fielder's choice, and an error plated a run and put two men on. After a single and an out, Harold Baines launched a home run and "applauded himself" as he circled the bases.[13] McClure had been in baseball long enough to know the unwritten rules. He meant to brush back the next hitter, Ivan Calderon, but caught him on the hand. A typical baseball donnybrook ensued; McClure was ejected from the game.

Four of those Opening Day runs were unearned, but McClure still had a 13.50 ERA. From then until June 20, he made 16 appearances without allowing a run. His ERA dropped to 0.52 and he had two wins and three saves. The Angels had arguably the best pitching in the league in 1989 but could not catch the Oakland A's for the pennant. McClure finished with a 6-1 record and a sparkling 1.55 ERA.

Eligible for salary arbitration, McClure settled with the club for $825,000. He had asked for $880,000 in his filing. McClure went to camp as a respected and important piece of the pitching staff. But tendinitis developed in his elbow, making the year a painful struggle. He rested most of the summer until a rehab stint in Palm Springs. In late August he rejoined the Angels and made six consecutive scoreless appearances from August 18 to September 6. That start was followed by five consecutive games where he was scored upon. He closed the season with two wins and a 6.43 ERA. He proved that he was healthy enough to be considered for 1991 and signed an incentive-laden contract.

The 1991 season was feast or famine for McClure. He made 13 appearances. Nine of them were scoreless. In the other four outings he was touched up for 12 hits and 11 runs. The Angels released him on June 16.

The Cardinals signed McClure a week later and he gave them a season and a half of fine pitching. He pitched 103 games for St. Louis and posted an ERA of 3.16. On August 24, 1991, McClure entered the game against the Dodgers and closed out the seventh inning. He led off the bottom of the frame with his second major-league hit, a single to left. He rode home on a Ray Lankford home run, but not without incident as he tripped over second base. "It was really strange out there. I had never been all the way around before," he joked.[14] He was a free agent after the 1992 season and signed with the Florida Marlins.

The Marlins used McClure as a left-handed specialist. In 14 appearances he pitched only 6⅓ innings. The Marlins released him on May 18 after 698 major-league games, and he took the job as bullpen catcher for Florida. When the Marlins made some personnel changes in 1994, he became the bullpen coach.

McClure stepped away from the professional game for a couple of seasons. He helped coach his son in high school and summer ball. In the summer of 1998 he coached a DiMaggio League contingent from San Mateo. He returned to the professional game the next season, joining the Colorado Rockies franchise in Salem, Virginia, as pitching coach. He stayed with the Rockies organization through the 2005 season; his last stint was in Triple A at Colorado Springs.

The Kansas City Royals had gone through eight pitching coaches from 1998 to 2005. McClure was hired in October 2005 when the Royals cleaned house. Buddy Bell was brought in as manager. McClure guided the Royals staff through 2011. The team never contended but that was more a lack of talent than of guidance. In his own way, McClure got Zack Greinke to add a changeup to his pitch collection and it led to his 2009 Cy Young Award.[15]

When the young Greinke first met McClure, he informed his coach that he would "never throw a changeup" and that he "did not listen to pitching coaches."[16] McClure avoided confrontation by saying the last comment was fine. It took four seasons, but Greinke learned to throw the changeup under McClure's guidance.

McClure developed his own approach to coaching, based upon all the mentors he had played for. He chose not to be a lecturer and took a simplistic approach: "My philosophy is pretty simple. Get guys out with a minimum of pitches."[17] Because McClure never had overpowering pitches, he had to concentrate on his delivery. "The better you can repeat your delivery, the easier it is for you to command a baseball."[18]

McClure guided the Royals staff through the 2011 season. During that time, he remarried and in 2011 his twins Brock and Teddy were born. The Boston Red Sox hired him as pitching coach to join newly appointed manager Bobby Valentine. The two had never worked together. The Red Sox also had a new general manager as the Theo Epstein/Terry Francona era came to a close. McClure and Valentine never developed the chemistry necessary for a good working relationship. When Brock McClure had an urgent medical crisis, Bob took two weeks off to be with his son. In an August 1 radio interview, Valentine characterized the absence as a "vacation." Within three weeks McClure was fired. He was ready to move on because "that (the 'vacation' remark) was the final straw for me. That was very unprofessional, very uncalled for."[19]

McClure stayed out of coaching for a while. He turned down an offer from the Padres before taking the Phillies' pitching-coach position in November 2013. He worked with the team for four seasons. Youngster Aaron Nola made great strides during his tenure, but otherwise the seasons were a struggle for the pitching staff. Bob became the target of media and boo-birds after he left outfielder Jeff Francoeur on the mound for a 50-pitch inning.

In 2018 McClure was reunited with Brewers teammate Paul Molitor. Molitor was the Twins manager and McClure was hired by the organization as a senior pitching adviser. Essentially his job was to see that all the coaches in the organization were on the same page. His experience was valued because the Twins had a new major-league pitching coach and a rookie minor-league pitching coordinator.

ACKNOWLEDGMENTS

Thank you to SABR member Stew Thornley for his assistance. Also to Cassidy Lent at the Giamatti Research Library in Cooperstown. They were invaluable.

NOTES

1. Rick Hummel, "St. Louis Cardinals," *The Sporting News*, August 24, 1992: 18.
2. The information comes from a questionnaire McClure filled out for the Baseball Hall of Fame, probably in 1975 or 1976 because he mentioned being in winter ball. It is uncertain whether his father was in the Marines or the Navy.
3. Jerry Littrell, "Terra Nova Hurler Gets No-Hitter," *The Times* (San Mateo, California), April 11, 1970: 15.
4. Al Figone, "The Origins of Bob McClure's Pitching Backward Mentality and Punch Out Pickup Move to First Base: Application to Coaching," October 28, 2015. academia.edu/18646962/The_Origins_of_Bob_McClures_Pitching_Backwards_Mentality_And_Punch_Out_Move_To_First_Base.
5. Larry Porter, "0-2 Autry Will Pitch for Royals," *Omaha World-Herald*, August 6, 1974: 17.
6. Steve Cameron, "Flaky Bob McClure Already a Legend," *Maryville (Missouri) Daily Forum*, September 27, 1975: 2.
7. "Royal's Notes," *Kansas City Star*, August 14, 1975: 17.
8. Sid Bordman, "McClure Admits Only to Being Left-Handed," *Kansas City Star*, March 2, 1976: 22.
9. Cameron.
10. "Meet Jacob McClure: Back in Baseball After Growing up in Ballpark," missoulian.com/sports/osprey/meet-jacob-mcclure-back-in-baseball-after-growing-up-in/article_0260a90c-175a-11e3-b347-0019bb2963f4.html. Accessed September 15, 2018.
11. *1983 Milwaukee Brewers Media Guide*, 61.
12. "Baseball," *Boston Herald*, September 17, 1983: 7.
13. Tom Singer, "Is Squared Circle Next for Angels?," *The Sporting News*, April 17, 1989: 16.
14. Hummel: 16.
15. Ken Rosenthal, "Meet Bob McClure, the Phillies' Mad Scientist," FoxSports.com, May 4, 2016. foxsports.com/mlb/story/bob-mcclure-philadelphia-phillies-pitching-coach-mad-scientist-050416. Accessed August 6, 2018.
16. Ibid.
17. Bob Dutton, "Experience Talks for Pitching Coach," Kansas City Star, March 2, 2006. Posted on Kansas City.com.
18. Rosenthal.
19. Ibid.

DOC MEDICH

By Gregory H. Wolf

[He] **is what every boy wants** to become and every mother dreams their daughter will bring home," gushed sportswriter Phil Musick. "Tall, blond, handsome. Bright, articulate and personable. ... He is Everyman's vision of himself if he had been a little stronger, taller, handsomer, luckier, whatever."[1] Add to that list big-league pitcher and surgeon, too. His name was George "Doc" Medich, winner of 124 games in an 11-year career (1972-1982), and likely the last major-leaguer to be simultaneously a doctor. Here's his story.

George Francis Medich was born on December 9, 1948, in Aliquippa, Pennsylvania. He was the only child of David and Esther (Mason) Medich. Nestled on the Ohio River about 25 miles northwest of Pittsburgh, Aliquippa of the post-World War II years was a booming industrial town, where an estimated 8,000 of the 27,000 residents worked in the steel industry.[2] The elder Medich, a native Ohioan, settled in Aliquippa after serving in World War II, and soon found a job as a carpenter at the Jones & Laughlin steel mill, one of the world's largest. George's childhood was a microcosm of the baby-boomer idyll. His father's job afforded the family a sturdy middle-class lifestyle; the Mediches were active members of St. Elijah Serbian Orthodox Church, and they loved sports. By the time George was 8, he was playing Little League baseball while attending Five Points Elementary School. At Hopewell High School, George's size (about 6-feet-4 as a senior) made him a three-sport star in football, basketball, and baseball as the seasons progressed. Upon graduation in 1966, he accepted a football scholarship to attend the University of Pittsburgh, where Aliquippa's most famous son, Mike Ditka, had starred on the gridiron a few years earlier.

Given his size and speed, Medich played tight end and split end on Pitt's football team from 1967 to 1969, during some of the leanest years (a combined 6-24 record) of the storied program's existence. Smoky City sportswriter Russ Franke considered Medich an "excellent pass receiver" who had a good shot to be selected in the 1970 NFL draft.[3] However, Medich's interests had already drifted away from football by that time. He joined the varsity baseball team in 1969, and posted a 4-2 record (1.64 ERA), followed by another strong campaign (5-2, 2.43) in 1970 to earn consecutive berths on the Tri-State College All-Star team.[4]

Despite his passion for sports, Medich never let athletics define his identity. He was a pre-med student and let it be known that he wanted to attend medical school after graduation. Medich's insistence on education and his career undoubtedly scared prospective baseball suitors. He was summarily dismissed by the Pirates at a tryout during his college years, but he wasn't deterred. Instead, he sought advice from baseball's most famous player-turned-physician, Bobby Brown, the New York Yankees former infielder who retired at the age of 29 in 1954 to pursue medicine full-time. "The scouts all assumed I wouldn't play, but never bothered to ask me," recalled Medich. "I wrote to Dr. Bobby Brown prior to the draft about the possibility of combining the two careers and he discouraged me."[5] The Yankees, however, were intrigued. Based on scout Randy Gumpert's recommendation, they selected Medich in the 30th round, with the 700th overall pick, of the 1970 amateur draft, just weeks after he graduated with a degree in chemistry.[6]

Medich began his professional baseball career with a clear focus on medical school as his top priority. After making 12 combined starts with Oneonta in the in the Class-A New York-Penn League and Manchester (New Hampshire) in the Double-A Eastern League, Medich cut his season short to begin medical school at the University of Pittsburgh at the end of August. For the next two seasons, he missed spring training completely and reported late to his respective minor-league teams, raising questions about his commitment to baseball. "I knew that missing spring training would slow down my baseball a little," he said, "but I was willing to make the sacrifice and so were the Yankees. I have no regrets."[7]

The Yankees had a good reason to be flexible. Medich posted a 7-4 record and spiffy 2.43 ERA in just about two months of work with Kinston in the Class-A Carolina League in 1971. After the season, Medich organized a meeting between Yankees GM Lee MacPhail and Dr. Alvin Shapiro, associate dean of Pitt's medical school. With a detailed plan, Medich convinced them that he could pursue both careers at once. "Everybody told me how it couldn't be done, but they had blinders on," recalled Medich. "It seemed like I was the only on who knew it could be done."[8]

While Medich was finishing his second year of med school, MacPhail worked out a deal with the Pirates GM Joe L. Brown allowing Medich to pitch

An orthopedic surgeon in the offseason, Doc Medich compiled a 124-105 record and logged 1,996⅔ innings in 11 big-league seasons (1972-1982). He was acquired by the Brewers in August 1982 and made his final 10 starts in the pennant race, winning five of them.

batting practice to the Pirates in April and May.[9] The extra conditioning helped. Medich set the Eastern League on fire in his abbreviated stint with West Haven (Connecticut) in 1972, going 11-3 (1.44 ERA in 119 innings). Many wondered how good he could become if he had a spring training. The Yankees called him up to pitch in the 10th annual Mayor's Trophy exhibition game against the New York Mets on August 24, at Yankee Stadium. Medich dazzled everyone by tossing a complete-game four-hitter to win, 2-1, and sealed his fate.[10] On September 5, Medich made his big-league debut. Starting against the Orioles in Baltimore, he faced only four batters, yielding two walks and two singles, and was charged with two runs without retiring a batter. Any anxiety Medich had was justifiable — he had to report to medical school the next day.

For the first time in his baseball career, Medich participated in spring training, in 1973, at the Yankees facility in Fort Lauderdale. Given the moniker Doc even though he had not yet completed his MD. Medich was a breath of fresh air on a stale club in the last vestiges of the so-called "Horace Clarke Years," a period from 1965 to 1973 when the team floundered in the standings and at the gate searching for an identity after an unprecedented four-decade run of success. "Medicine has helped me to mature faster as a pitcher," once said Medich. "In pursuing both careers simultaneously I had to be very careful in evaluating myself."[11] Medich never doubted his athletic ability, but also had a trump card few players had. Said Medich, "If I fail to make it as a pitcher, my life won't be shattered."[12] He shouldn't have worried. Medich emerged as the most effective rookie hurler and one of the brightest stars in baseball. For a sub-.500 club Medich went 14-9, completed 11 of 32 starts, and posted the fifth best ERA in the AL (2.95) in 235 innings. He finished with a flurry in September, hurling a three-hitter, a five-hit shutout, and an 11-inning no-decision, en route to a 1.51 ERA and 4-1 record in his final six starts. He finished tied with the Kansas City Royals' Steve Busby for third in the AL Rookie of the Year voting, behind Baltimore's Al Bumbry and the Milwaukee Brewers' Pedro Garcia.

The Yankees' baseball world was in chaos as the 1974 season got underway. Skipper Ralph Houk had resigned on the last day of the previous season, the same day Yankee Stadium saw its final home game for two years during which it underwent massive renovation. Home games were played at the Mets' Shea Stadium. George Steinbrenner, who had purchased the Yankees in early 1973, was involved in offseason legal battles with the Oakland A's because of his attempt to hire their former manager, Dick Williams, who was still under contract. Unable to secure Williams from the A's, Steinbrenner hired no nonsense Bill Virdon, the Pirates' ex-pilot, instead. Medich took in the drama with the detachment of an outsider aggravating baseball's old guard who wanted players to fit the mold of a rah-rah jock, which Medich never was. "I have an advantage over most of these fellas because baseball is not the only thing that matters to me," he said. "But this doesn't mean I have a cavalier attitude toward the game. I hate to lose as much as anybody. But I can temper losing because I know I have a career in medicine."[13]

After a shaky spring, Medich got off to a hot start, winning five of his first six decisions. When the longtime stalwart and last remnant of the Yankees glory years, Mel Stottlemyre, injured his shoulder on June 11, 25-year-old Medich assumed the mantle of staff ace. At 6-foot-5 and 225 pounds, Medich cut an imposing physical presence on the mound, but was not an overpowering pitcher (he fanned 10 or more in a game only once in his career); instead, he depended on ball movement and control for his success, and never shied away from pitching to contact. On July 20, he held the Royals hitless for eight innings before yielding a single on his first pitch of the ninth to Fran Healy, eventually settling for a 6-2 win. It was closest Medich ever came to a no-no in the majors, though he did throw one for Kinston, "where the lights were bad," he said.[14] Snubbed for All-Star Game despite his 12-7 record, Medich continued his torrid July in his first start after the midsummer classic by hurling a five-hit shutout to conclude a five-start stretch with five complete-game victories (1.20 ERA) and was named the AL Pitcher of the Month. His most important victory of the season, described as an "extraordinary effort" by *Times* sportswriter Gerald Eskenazi, was a five-hit shutout against the Brewers in New York on September 4 to put the Yankees in first place, tied with Boston.[15] It was first time since October 1, 1964, that the team had occupied the top position so late in the season. The Yankees finished in second place in the AL East, two games behind the Orioles, but their future looked bright. Matching teammate Pat Dobson's

19-15 slate, Medich completed 17 of 38 starts with a 3.60 ERA in 279⅔ innings.

The Yankees' success and the offseason acquisitions of free agent Catfish Hunter, and Bobby Bonds in a trade with the San Francisco Giants for clubhouse leader Bobby Murcer led to elevated expectations in 1975; however, the season was anything smooth sailing. Honored as Opening Day starter, Medich was shelled for five runs in 5⅔ innings in a 5-3 loss to the Indians in Cleveland on April 8. That game marked the debut of the first African-American manager in baseball history, Frank Robinson, who belted a home run in his first at-bat. Medich rebounded with three consecutive complete-game victories, including a two-hit and a three-hit shutout, only to lose six straight starts while his teammates provided seven total runs of support. The Yankees' offense, featuring Graig Nettles, Chris Chambliss, Thurman Munson and Bonds, was thought to be among the league best, but it underperformed all season, while the Yankees struggled to play .500 ball. On August 1, Steinbrenner, who had been suspended by Commissioner Bowie Kuhn in late November 1974 for two years for illegal contributions to President Richard Nixon's political campaigns, replaced Virdon with Billy Martin. That move only exacerbated tension in the clubhouse that seemed at times to border on open mutiny. "Everything's been falling apart," said Medich, who expressed his sympathy for Virdon. "The attitude is really bad.… We [don't] have any enthusiasm.… It seems like nobody's really concentrating and I don't think everybody's putting out. We're just going through the actions."[16] Medich won five times in September to finish the campaign with a 16-16 slate and 3.50 ERA in 272⅓ innings for the third-place club.

On December 11 Medich was shipped to the Pittsburgh Pirates in a blockbuster deal for pitchers Dock Ellis and Ken Brett and highly-touted second-base prospect Willie Randolph. The trade proved to be one of the worst in Pirates history. While Randolph emerged as a perennial All-Star and the disgruntled Ellis won 17 games, Medich failed to live up to expectation as an innings-eater capable of winning 20 games. A day after his no-decision as the Opening Day starter against the Phillies in Philadelphia on April 10, Medich's other professional instincts took over when he rushed into the stands at Veterans Stadium to administer CPR to an elderly man having a heart attack. [A similar scene occurred two years later when Medich performed life-saving CPR on a heart-attack victim at Municipal Stadium in Baltimore.[17]] In his debut at Three Rivers Stadium on April 16, Medich tossed a complete game against the Mets for his first Bucs victory. "Pitching in my hometown for the first time meant an awful lot to me," said Medich. "I felt a lot of pressure to pitch well and did."[18] Perhaps the pressure was too much. From May 31 to August 15, Medich won only one time. That stretch, however, included one of the best games in his career, 10 innings of scoreless five-hit ball against Tom Seaver and the Mets that ended in a Pirates 1-0 win in 13 innings. Pitching coach Dave Osborn thought Medich nibbled too much, "trying to hit spots," leading to poor control and inconsistency.[19] Medich rejected that diagnosis. "I'm not an overpowering pitcher," he declared. "I don't have a fastball like Nolan Ryan or a breaking pitch like Bert Blyleven. I have to pitch to spots."[20] Frustrated with his hurler, manager Danny Murtaugh shunted him to the bullpen in mid-August, and Medich made only one start over a four-week stretch. Medich concluded his lackluster campaign with an 8-11 record and 3.51 ERA in 179⅓ innings for the second-place Bucs.

Just weeks after completing his medical degree at the University of Pittsburgh, Medich was unexpectedly sent along with five other players (notably young slugger Tony Armas and pitcher Rick Langford) to the Oakland A's in exchange for Phil Garner and two others on March 15. Medich, who had not signed his 1977 contract in order to become a free agent at the end of the season, was livid. "I'm really kind of fed up with the Pirates. I've burned my bridges," he vented. "They demand loyalty from the players, but it's a two-way street.

If they can't respect you, I can't respect them. They really screwed up my life."²¹ Set to begin his medical residency in Pittsburgh that fall, Medich threatened to quit baseball rather than move across the county, but ultimately reported to the A's.

Medich desired stability; instead, he found himself in five different baseball uniforms in less than 12 months. As to be expected, the cerebral and ofttimes outspoken Medich clashed with the A's owner Charlie Finley, who had the hurler on the trading block as soon as the season commenced. Pitching inconsistently for the eventual last-place club, Medich won five straight decisions from August 22 to September 10 to improve his record to 10-6. When it became clear that he would not sign a contact with the A's, Finley sold him on September 13 to the Seattle Mariners, but Medich barely had time to unpack his bags. He was with the club only two weeks, long enough to win his only two decisions. In his Mariners debut on September 16, he tossed a complete-game seven-hitter to snap the Kansas City Royals' 16-game winning streak, the majors' longest in 24 seasons. "After I pitched my last game for Seattle," said Medich about yet another twist to his weird season, "I headed home to Pittsburgh when a guy from the Mets called and said they had claimed me on waivers (on September 26)."²² As fate would have it, the Mets were playing in Pittsburgh. In his only appearance as a Met, Medich hurled seven innings and yielded three runs, but picked up the loss. "I got $12,000 in moving expenses from (the Mets) and never set foot in New York," joked Medich.²³ His combined 12-7 slate was offset by the ninth-highest ERA among qualified starters (4.53 in 177 innings) in both leagues.

On November 11, free agent Medich signed a lucrative four-year deal worth $1 million with the Texas Rangers. Coming off a second-place finish in the West Division, the Rangers had also added All-Star pitchers John Matlack and Fergie Jenkins in trades and slugger Richie Zisk via free agency and were predicted to compete for divisional crown in 1978. Medich had a "disappointing" spring training,

according to beat reporter Randy Galloway, casting doubts on his spot in the rotation.²⁴ After he was clobbered in his first two regular-season starts, he was relegated to the bullpen, making only one start in a seven-week period. He subsequently tossed a few gems, such as a seven-hit shutout against the California Angels on June 25 to increase the Rangers' divisional lead to one game; and blanked the Boston Red Sox on two hits on July 26, ending the club's eight-game skid. The Rangers staff finished with the second lowest ERA in the league (3.36), but their offense lacked the firepower to compete with Royals, who captured their third straight crown. Medich posted a 9-8 record and logged 171 innings with a 3.74 ERA, just below the league average of 3.76.

Described as the "perennial forgotten man" by sportswriter Galloway, Medich was relegated by manager Pat Corrales to mop-up duty for the first 2½ months of the 1979 season.²⁵ With an 8.27 ERA in 20⅔ innings, his spot on the team was in jeopardy. Making his first start on June 24, in the second game of a twin bill against the A's, Medich pitched seven effective innings to pick up his initial victory of the season and moved back into the rotation. He won four of five starts in July, and then kicked off a four-start winning streak on August 30 with a two-hit shutout against the Red Sox. Going against Boston in Fenway Park is "like pitching in a shower stall where you reach out and touch four walls," he quipped.²⁶ Medich's turnaround and final line (10-7, 4.17 ERA in 149 innings) offered the Rangers a ray of hope for 1980.

Medich overcame pain in his elbow during spring training in 1980 to have his most productive season since he was a Yankee. After tossing a complete-game six-hitter to beat the Milwaukee Brewers, 8-1, on June 18 for his third straight victory, improving his record to 7-3, Medich was described by Galloway as the "best pitcher" on the club.²⁷ The now 31-year-old reached a personal milestone on September 7 when he collected his 100th victory, securing all but the final out against the Brewers in a 7-2 win at County Stadium. Medich (14-11), reached the 200-inning plateau for the fourth and final time in his career, posting a 3.92 ERA in 204⅓ innings for a sub-.500 team.

On June 12, 1981, major-league baseball experienced its first work stoppage since 1972, following a unanimous vote by the players union, the Major League Baseball Players Association, to strike. While many players enjoyed their time off or worried about their future, Medich returned to Pittsburgh to continue his medical residency. Medich, who had pitched consistently before the strike, showed no signs of rust when the season resumed on August 9, yielding just a single earned run in his first three starts (and 22⅓ innings), including a six-hit shutout against the Toronto Blue Jays in Canada on August 24. On September 24, he flirted with a no-hitter for 7⅔ innings against the Twins in the Texas heat before surrendering a single to Sal Butera. Medich settled for his fourth career-two-hit shutout. It also proved to be his last of 16 whitewashings. He lost a heartbreaker to the Mariners, 2-1, in his next start, yielding an RBI single in the 11th. Medich finished the campaign with a 10-6 record and a robust 3.08 ERA in 143⅓ innings, and tied three other hurlers for the AL lead with four shutouts.

Prior to arriving at spring training, Medich announced that 1982 would be his 11th and final big-league season. At 33, he was ready to turn attention full-time to his medical career. The last chapter of Medich's baseball life was a difficult one. In late February, he was diagnosed with hepatitis, which cast doubt on his readiness for Opening Day. Defying expectations, he was on the mound three weeks later for an exhibition game, but came down with elbow and then shoulder pain. Laboring through an arduous campaign, Medich lost four straight starts, culminating with a shellacking on August 9 in Milwaukee in which he yielded six runs in five innings, to drop his record to 7-11 with a 5.06 ERA. Two days later Medich went from last place to first place when he was sold in a waiver transaction to those same Brewers. "It's nice to be with a team that's in first place for a change rather than chasing somebody," said Medich. "I've been in that situation throughout my career."[28] In his second start for the "Brew Crew," Medich tossed three-hit ball over seven scoreless innings against the Mariners. His first Brewers victory was also a significant milestone for Rollie Fingers, who hurled two innings, becoming the first reliever to record 300 saves. Medich went 5-4 (5.00 ERA) as the fourth starter for skipper Harvey Kuenn's explosive club, affectionately known as "Harvey's Wallbangers," who captured their first division crown.

Medich was relegated to the bullpen in the playoffs in favor of Moose Haas, whose place in the rotation he had originally taken. Medich did not see action in the Brewers' exciting ALCS victory in five games against the California Angels, and made just one appearance in the World Series against the St. Louis Cardinals. With the Brew Crew trailing, 7-0, in Game Six, Medich entered in mop-up duty in the sixth inning, which might be the longest inning in World Series history. In what proved to be his last big-league game, Medich unraveled on the biggest stage in baseball. He yielded a double and two singles, walked one, and threw two wild pitches resulting in one run before he retired a batter. After Ozzie Smith grounded out, the game was delayed by rain for 2 hours and 13 minutes. When it resumed, Doc was back on the mound, but it didn't get any better. By the time the inning was over Medich had been tagged for five hits and six runs (four earned). Medich set down the side in order in the seventh and then stepped off the mound for the last time. The Brewers lost Game Seven, in St. Louis, 6-3.

Medich announced his retirement after the Brewers' defeat in the fall classic and returned to Pittsburgh and his family. "It was the travel more than anything," he said. "I had played 10 years and planned on playing five, I wasn't one of those guys who they had to tear the uniform off of."[29] While an undergraduate at Pitt, he had met Donna Lynn Creekmore, whom he married in June 1970, and together they had two children, Kelly and Mickey.

Medich compiled a 124-109 record and logged

1,996⅔ innings with a 3.78 ERA in parts of 11 seasons. He was especially tough on Amos Otis (8-for-67, .119 batting average), Brooks Robinson (3-for-21, .143), and George Scott (9-for-51, .176); and had trouble with Lyman Bostock (13-for-27, .481), Boog Powell (12-for-27, .444), and Rod Carew (21-for-49, .429).

Medich's transition to full-time medicine was not as easy as expected. "I had an opportunity to be a team doctor but didn't want to do it," explained Medich. "Team doctors kind of get abused. It's a tough enough job without having divided loyalties."[30]

About a year after his retirement from baseball, Medich made national headlines as a resident in orthopedic surgery at Children's Hospital in Pittsburgh when he was arrested in November 1983 for writing illegal prescriptions. Medich revealed to the media that he had been addicted to painkillers and muscle relaxers stemming from his elbow and shoulder pain and the stress of a pennant race during his last season in baseball.[31] "You never really know when you've crossed the line, when you're using it or it's using you," said Medich about his addiction, which ultimately led to his admission to a treatment facility. "I think I came to realize that I really had a problem after I quit playing."[32] In March 1984 he plead guilty to charges and was given a two-year suspended sentence and fined but his medical license was not revoked.

Medich went on to a long career as a respected orthopedic surgeon with a private practice in the greater Pittsburgh area. He never fully overcame his demons with dependency. In 2001, he was charged with and convicted on a similar offense, and given nine years' probation.

As of 2018, Doc Medich still resided near Pittsburgh.

SOURCES

In addition to the sources cited in the Notes, the author also accessed Retrosheet.org, Baseball-Reference.com, SABR.org, The Sporting News archive via Paper of Record, and the player's file from the Baseball Hall of Fame in Cooperstown, New York.

NOTES

1 Phil Musick, "Medich Loose, Ready," *Pittsburgh Post-Gazette*, March 9, 1977: 18.

2 Nicole Crowder, "Part I. Life and Slow Death of a Former Pennsylvania Steel Town," *Washington Post*, November 4, 2015. washingtonpost.com/news/in-sight/wp/2015/11/04/the-former-steel-town-that-dimmed-its-light-to-help-pittsburg-shine/?utm_term=.19f008572472.

3 Russ Franke, "Panthers' Senior Pack of 21 Hates to See It All End Now," *Pittsburgh Press*, November 20, 1969: 49.

4 Baseball statistics from junior year are from "Panther 9 Will Play 33 games," *Pittsburgh Post-Gazette*, March 11, 1970: 22; statistics from senior year are from "Two Panthers on Star Nine," *Pittsburgh Post-Gazette*, June 10, 1970: 25.

5 Jim Ogle, "Doc Medich Could Cure Yankee Mound Aches," *The Sporting News*, April 14, 1973: 19.

6 Jim O'Brien, "Doc Medich: He's Good Medicine for the Yankees," *Baseball Digest*, February 1975: 72.

7 Murray Chass, "Medich Pitching Way To M.D, Learns As Yankees Are Beaten," *New York Times*, March 25, 1973: 237.

8 Steve Wulf, "How I Spent My Summer Vacation," *Sports Illustrated*, June 29, 1981.

9 Charley Feeney, "Playing Games," *Pittsburgh Post-Gazette*, September 2, 1972: 8.

10 Deane McGowen, "Yanks Beat Mets, 2-1, on Rookie's Pitching and a Homer by Ellis," *New York Times*, August 25, 1972: 23.

11 Don Anderson, Doc Medich and Pennant Trauma," *New York Times*, October 1, 1974: 49.

12 Ogle, "Doc Medich Could Cure Yankee Mound Aches."

13 Bill Christine, "Medich Chief Surgeon in Cutting Down Brewers Bats," *Pittsburgh Post-Gazette*, June 12, 1974: 26.

14 Joe Durso, "Medich Misses No-Hitter in 9th As Yanks Vanquish Royals, 6-2," *New York Times*, July 21, 1974: 177.

15 Gerald Eskenazi, "Brewers Lose on Medich's 5-Hitter," *New York Times*, September 5, 1974: 47.

16 Murray Chass, "Medich and Lyle Are Critical of Yankee Poor Performance," *New York Times*, August 26, 1975: 25.

17 United Press International, "Doc Medic Registers Big 'Save,'" *Pittsburgh Press*, July 18, 1978: 35.

18 David Fink," Doc Takes Bow, Waves to Folks," *Pittsburgh Post-Gazette*, April 17, 1976: 6.

19 Charley Feeney, "Too Much Nibbling by Doc," *Pittsburgh Post-Gazette*, April 30, 1976: 11.

20 Charley Feeney, "Bucs Count on Medic to Step Up Win Pace," *The Sporting News*, July 24, 1976: 11.

21 Vito Stellino, "Doc Medich Prescribes Loyalty Shot for Pirates," *Pittsburgh Post-Gazette*, March 22, 1977:10.

22 Scott Zucker, "First Hitters, Now Patients Get Medich Treatment," *USA Today Baseball Weekly*, August 12, 1997.

23 Ibid.

24 Randy Galloway, "Halt Dealing, Hunter Begs Rangers Boss Corbett," *The Sporting News*, April 22, 1978: 26.

25 Randy Galloway, "Doc Gives Puny Texas First Aid," *The Sporting News*, July 5 1980: 33.

26 Associated Press, "Royals Take First in West Away from California," *Odessa* (Texas) *American*, August 31, 1979: 10.

27 Galloway, "Doc Gives Puny Texas First Aid."

28 Tom Flaherty, "Medich Joins Brewers; It's Last Place to First Place," *The Sporting News*, August 23, 1982: 23.

29 Zucker.

30 Ibid.

31 Jim Gallagher " 'Doc' Medich to Face RX Charges," *Pittsburgh Post-Gazette*, November 15, 1983: 8.

32 Danny Robbins, "Medich Works on a Comeback," *Los Angeles Times*, March 18, 1984.

PAUL MOLITOR

By Daniel R. Levitt and Doug Skipper

Clad in the uniform of his hometown team, Paul Molitor stood on third base after he collected the 3,000th hit of his major-league career. The first player ever to reach the milestone with a triple, Molitor enjoyed a number of memorable moments in a Minnesota Twins uniform through the final three seasons of his 21-year Hall of Fame career. Just the 21st player ever to reach the magical mark, he was the second from St. Paul, Minnesota. Dave Winfield, who like Molitor had emerged from the sandlots of St. Paul to star for the University of Minnesota Golden Gophers, had achieved the milestone three years to the day earlier, also in the uniform of the Twins in the twilight of a Hall of Fame career.

Molitor's path to third base that September evening in 1996 took many turns. Hamstrung by a series of devastating injuries early in his career as an infielder with the Milwaukee Brewers, Molitor developed a reputation for fragility, and it appeared that his career was cursed as seasons were cut short. But the soft-spoken right-handed hitter from St. Paul persevered to achieve milestones of durability as a designated hitter for the Toronto Blue Jays and the Twins. In 21 seasons, he collected 3,319 hits in 2,683 major-league games, belted 234 homers, scored 1,782 runs, and drove in 1,307. A seven-time American League All-Star with a smooth swing, above-average speed, and outstanding base-running skills, he finished his career with a .306 batting average and became just the fifth player in major-league baseball history to collect 3,000 hits and 500 stolen bases.

A fixture atop the Milwaukee lineup for 15 years as one of baseball's best-ever leadoff hitters, Paul Molitor was nicknamed the "Ignitor" for the spark he generated—a nickname he never really warmed to. "Aside from its not even being spelled right," Molitor quipped, "it's a terrible nickname. I never once entered a room and my friends said, 'Hey, it's the Ignitor!'"[1] Still, as the leadoff hitter in the Brewers' batting order for a decade and a half, Molitor ignited rallies for Harvey's Wallbangers, the 1982 team that he and close friend Robin Yount led to Milwaukee's only American League pennant and World Series appearance. "I think he's one of the best baserunners — not for speed but for instincts — in the game ever," his one-time manager Tom Trebelhorn marveled.[2] As to his overall impact, "In Milwaukee, It's God, Robin Yount, and Paul Molitor," Brewers teammate Dave Engle once observed.

Called Paulie or Mollie by friends, Molitor later replaced Winfield as the designated hitter in the middle of Toronto's lineup in 1993. As Winfield had done in 1992, Molitor helped lead the Blue Jays to a World Series championship. Known as a clutch hitter, Molitor appeared in five postseason playoffs, including the two World Series, and batted .368. "Paulie had a way about him where if you gave him a chance, he could always beat you," Hall of Fame manager Sparky Anderson gushed. "He's what I call a winning player, like Joe Morgan. They're just winners."[3] And while one needs to take this statistic with some skepticism due to all the confounding factors involved, it is interesting to note that during his career Molitor's teams were 1382-1268 (.522) with him in the lineup and 281-349 (.446) when he was out.[4]

A player representative for much of his career, Molitor was at the center of several well-publicized contract negotiations. He won a battle with cocaine abuse during the injury-ravaged early part of his career, overcame the negative publicity that surrounded his mention in the trial of a prominent drug dealer, and delivered persuasive anti-substance-abuse messages to young people later in his career. Popular in both Milwaukee and Minnesota, Molitor remained close to baseball after his active career ended in 1998. After the 2014 season he was named manager of the woeful Minnesota Twins and spent four years at the helm, including one wild card appearance.

Paul Leo Molitor was born on August 22, 1956, in St. Paul, Minnesota, to Kathleen and Richard Molitor, an accountant with the Burlington Northern Railroad. Paul was the fifth of their eight children, six girls and two boys. When Molitor began playing organized baseball he lived near Grand Avenue and Pascal Street. Even as a seven-year-old, Molitor began earning recognition as a great baseball player and athlete. When he was about eight, the family moved to a large three-story Victorian home at the corner of Portland Avenue and Oxford Street. A big Minnesota Twins fan, Molitor remembered having his father toss balls high against a fence while he tried to jump up and pretend to be Twins outfielder Bob Allison robbing "a batter" of a home run. When he finally reached the majors, Molitor chose uniform number 4, Allison's number on the Twins, although not just because it was Allison's.[5]

In his new neighborhood Molitor began playing baseball at the nearby Oxford playground, celebrated for the recent play of another future Hall of Famer five years his senior, Dave Winfield. The youngster quickly took to baseball and dreamed of a major-league career — in his senior yearbook Molitor declared his ambition: "to play pro baseball and work with people."[6] Molitor's skill quickly became apparent, and he played in several organized youth leagues, most notably for Attucks-Brooks American Legion Post 606. In the youth leagues, he occasionally competed against another future big-league star, St. Paul native Jack Morris. As a youngster, Molitor suffered a number of fluke injuries, presaging his early career in the majors. When he was about eight, he fell out of a tree; a couple of years later he injured his foot while riding his bike barefoot.[7]

As a teenager Molitor was given a baseball autographed by Babe Ruth. The ball made enough of an impression that when Molitor reached the majors he began collecting baseballs autographed by Hall of Famers and potential Hall of Famers as souvenirs of his time in the game. Molitor would typically get his autographs at old-timers events, and by the 1990s he was up to 40 to 45 balls.[8]

Molitor attended Cretin High School (now coeducational Cretin-Derham Hall), a Catholic-military prep school that is legendary for its athletics. One of the best athletes in the school's storied history, Molitor lettered in soccer, basketball, and baseball in his sophomore, junior, and senior seasons from 1972 to 1974 and won titles in each sport. He was named all-state in both baseball and basketball.[9] In baseball he played for legendary baseball coach Bill Peterson, who also coached Molitor in American Legion ball.

Molitor missed much of his senior baseball season with mononucleosis. He was just recovering in time for the state tournament and received guarded permission from the doctor to play. One of Bill Peterson's favorite Molitor stories came from that state tournament. In the middle innings against a tough opponent, Cretin was trailing 2-1. Molitor came to the plate with the bases loaded and worked the count to 3-0. Peterson gave his star the take sign. The pitch came in over Molitor's head, but he swung anyway. Fortunately for Molitor, he tomahawked the ball for a grand slam and escaped his coach's wrath.[10]

After his senior prep season in 1974, the St. Louis Cardinals drafted Molitor in the 28th round. As a low draft pick, Molitor would have been considered a long shot to make the majors, and accordingly the Cardinals offered a signing bonus of only $4,000.[11] Despite not having any college scholarship offers that strongly appealed to him, Molitor held out for $8,000 from St. Louis.[12] Fortunately, as he weighed his options, University of Minnesota baseball coach Dick Siebert offered him a scholarship.[13]

At Minnesota it quickly became apparent that Molitor was going to be something special. As a freshman in 1975 the 6-foot Molitor weighed 170 pounds, and Siebert eventually installed him as his starting second baseman. Molitor lived up to his billing, hitting .375 and missing the All-Big-Ten first team by one vote.[14] Siebert called him "the most exciting player I have ever coached."[15] Molitor recalled Siebert's dedication to the basics: "Dick was a stickler for fundamentals, and when you practice for two months indoors during the wintertime, you get pretty good at them."[16]

The next year Siebert moved Molitor to shortstop, and Molitor responded with his best collegiate season. In Big Ten play, Molitor hit .406, third in the league, and finished second in home runs and fourth in runs batted in. For his season, Molitor was named to the All-Big-Ten first team and a first team All-American, only the seventh Gopher to receive such an honor. The team finished 36-9, earning a berth in the National Collegiate Athletic Association's (NCAA) Rocky Mountain Regional tournament. The Gophers started slowly and were later eliminated from the double-elimination tournament by top-ranked Arizona State. Later that summer, while playing in the Western Collegiate League, Molitor suffered a fractured jaw, ending his summer season.[17]

Molitor started his junior season slowly, which coach Siebert attributed to "pressing with so many

Paul Molitor played the first 15 seasons of his Hall of Fame career (1978-1992) with the Brewers, during which time he led the AL in runs three times, including in 1982 with 136. He retired in 1998 with 3,319 hits and a .306 batting average.

major-league scouts following him."[18] He soon recovered and turned in a fine junior season, if slightly below his phenomenal sophomore performance. He hit .325 with six home runs and 20 stolen bases and repeated as an All-Big-Ten first-teamer. The team finished 39-12 and again qualified for the NCAA postseason. Playing in the Mideast Regional at home at Bierman Field, the Gophers won three games to qualify for the College World Series, their fifth and most recent appearance as of 2008. The team lost two of three games, the final to eventual champion Arizona State, and finished sixth.

Eligible again for the draft after his junior season, Molitor was taken by the Milwaukee Brewers in the first round, third overall. Brewer scout Dee Fondy signed Molitor for an $80,000 bonus.[19] At the time of his jump to professional ball, Molitor held several University of Minnesota batting records, most since broken given today's longer season. For his play at Minnesota, the university retired his number 11. He was also awarded the university's highest commendation, the Distinguished Service Award.[20]

After the draft the Brewers invited their new phenom to Milwaukee County Stadium for the VIP treatment. While wearing a suit that was "way too big, I'm totally geekish," Molitor met some of the players in the dugout. At one point he was sitting next to shortstop Robin Yount, only 22 years old but already in his fourth year as a starter. Veteran third baseman Sal Bando stopped by and threw Yount an outfielder's glove, telling him, "Well, I guess this will be your last year at shortstop, kid." Molitor remembered acute embarrassment at the whole proceeding and just wanting to get away.[21]

Molitor was not quite ready to push Yount to the outfield. After his visit, the Brewers farmed the 20-year-old to Burlington (Iowa), their Class A team in the Midwest League. The Bees were 28-42 over the season's first half, but with Molitor on board for the second, manager Denis Menke's club posted a 43-26 record. In 64 games, the youngster from St. Paul stung the ball at a .346 clip, smacked eight homers, and drove in 50 runs to earn Midwest League Most Valuable Player and Prospect of the Year honors. In the playoffs the Bees buzzed Cedar Rapids (Iowa) in the first round and then met Waterloo (Iowa), the regular-season champions, in the finals. Burlington turned back Waterloo, two games to none, to capture the league championship.[22]

His solid half-season earned Molitor a trip to the Brewers' spring training in Chandler, Arizona. New manager George Bamberger and general manager Harry Dalton had inherited a Milwaukee squad that finished sixth among the seven teams in the American League East Division in 1977, ahead of only the expansion Toronto Blue Jays and 33 games behind the world champion Yankees. The Brewers intended to farm the St. Paul native to Spokane in the Pacific Coast League for additional seasoning. Yount, however, was unavailable to start the season due to an injured foot and his threats to become a professional golfer. In response, Bamberger named Molitor his starting shortstop and leadoff hitter despite only a half-season of minor-league experience, in Class A at that.

The Ignitor made his major-league debut on Opening Day, Friday, April 7, 1978, at County Stadium. He grounded out in his first at-bat, then singled to left and drove in a run against Baltimore's Mike Flanagan in the second inning in an 11-3 win. A day later, he hit his first home run, a three-run shot off Joe Kerrigan, singled twice, and drove in five runs in Milwaukee's 16-3 win over Baltimore. On the season's third day, he collected three more hits.

When Yount returned to reclaim the shortstop spot, Bamberger moved Molitor to second base. He continued to hit and boasted a .332 average in mid-June. Bamberger immediately took to his new second baseman. "He had tremendous instincts and you could see right away he was a talented athlete." Bamberger said. "Not only physically but mentally, too. He played the game like he had been up here for years."[23] But Molitor batted just .183 in the season's final month and Bamberger theorized that he was tired: "I don't think he was used to playing that much baseball. As hard as he played, and as little pro ball as he had played, he got tired, I think. His bat slowed down."[24] Nevertheless, Molitor finished with a .273 average and 30 stolen bases to earn *The Sporting News* Rookie of the Year honors. While the Brewers didn't challenge either the Yankees or the Red Sox in 1978, they did improve from 67 victories to 93 under Bamberger.

The Brewers took another step forward in 1979, when they won 95 games to finish second in the American League East behind the Baltimore Orioles. Molitor, too, improved on his previous season: he played in 140 games, hit .322 (sixth in the league), and stole 33 bases. The Brewers front office felt that in Molitor and Yount they had assembled a solid middle infield. "You say to yourself, they don't have just physical ability, they have the right kind of attitude. They enjoy the game. They give 100 percent," remarked general manager Harry Dalton, adding, "And you know, barring unfortunate happenings, you just look forward and say, 'I've got the middle set for quite a while.'"[25] After the season Molitor and his agent, Ron Simon, capitalized on that attitude and negotiated a $210,000 contract, one they liked so well that Simon needed to remind Molitor to keep a "poker face" at the negotiation.[26]

He started the 1980 season much the same way. But on June 6, batting .358, Molitor pulled a muscle in his rib cage and was forced out of the lineup for six weeks. Elected to the American League All-Star team for the first time, Molitor attended the game in Los Angeles though he didn't play. To fill in while he recovered, the Brewers installed Fond du Lac, Wisconsin, native Jim Gantner, who would become one of Molitor's close friends, at second base. While he was laid up, Molitor's cocaine use, begun recently under peer pressure and out of frustration with his injuries, slipped out of control.[27] Anxious to rejoin his teammates, he may have returned before he was ready, and his average slipped to .304 by season's end.

Molitor's heavy drug use continued into the offseason, and on Christmas Day 1980 reached its climax. When he failed to turn up at his parents' home on Christmas morning, they began to worry. His fiancée, Linda, knew Molitor was at Simon's — his agent was out of town in Florida — and went over to rouse him for the party. The door was locked, and she received no response to her banging on the door. It turned out that Molitor had hosted a wild cocaine-heavy party the night before and was still passed out. After this sorry episode Linda threatened to leave Molitor, and Molitor himself recognized the depths to which he had fallen. Molitor had been raised Catholic and attended Catholic school, but "kind of got away from it." At the University of Minnesota he had "[undergone] a religious transformation" in the words of reporter Tim Wendel and became a devout Christian.

Molitor resolved to quit the drug and credited his success to his faith. "I believe that God answered my prayers," Molitor maintained, "and gave me the strength to fight the addiction and finally to stop using cocaine."[28]

The 1981 season was one the most frustrating of Molitor's career. New manager Bob "Buck" Rodgers, who had split time at the Brewers helm with Bamberger in 1980 due to the latter's heart condition, was now officially in charge after Bamberger's retirement. Molitor had grown close to his first manager, and Bamberger's exit saddened him. Over the 1980-81 offseason Dalton and Rodgers decided to keep Gantner at second and move Molitor to center field. This shift forced veteran star center fielder Gorman Thomas to right field, a move resented by the big slugger. To help Molitor adjust to his new position, the Brewers brought in millionaire businessman and outfield guru Sam Suplizio to help with his fielding. (Suplizio had been an outfielder in the Yankee system in the mid-1950s before a broken arm prematurely ended his career. After baseball Suplizio went on to a successful career in banking and business and became a key player in the Colorado Republican Party. Suplizio never lost his love of baseball and stayed close to his friend Harry Dalton, often helping him with scouting or as a minor-league instructor.) Suplizio took outfield defense very seriously and traveled with a series of manuals on outfield play. The Brewers hoped that with an intense private tutorial, in three weeks or so, Suplizio could make Molitor into a competent major-league outfielder. "Paul has the potential to be great," his tutor remarked. "It will take hard work all spring. He will make mistakes. I hope he doesn't get discouraged when he does make them. Knowing Paul, I'm not worried about that." Suplizio added a forecast: "He should start feeling confident about a third or fourth of the way into the season. That position isn't a snap to learn, but there's no doubt he'll do it and do it very well."[29]

As the 1981 season opened Molitor struggled in the outfield but seemed to be catching on quickly. Manager Rodgers, emotionally vested in the decision, probably overstated a bit when he later remarked of Molitor, "He was already better than the average center fielder. He was as good overall as [Chicago's] Chet Lemon."[30] At the plate, Molitor hit the first grand slam of his career on April 22, but his season was cut short on May 3 in Anaheim when he suffered an ankle injury trying to beat out a grounder. While he was injured the major-league baseball players went on strike; when they returned, it was decided to split the season into two halves. Molitor returned to the Brewers' lineup on August 12 and produced just adequately over the remainder of the season. For the last four games of the season Rodgers adjusted his positional experiment and moved Molitor to right and Thomas — who had played center field during Molitor's absence — back to his natural position. The team edged the Tigers to win the East Division second-half race and the right to meet the first-half champion New York Yankees in the divisional playoff series. Molitor collected five hits in the series against the Bronx Bombers and hit a home run to win Game Three, but New York won the series three games to two. Molitor's overall performance for the season was the worst of his career for any year in which he collected substantial playing time.

Rodgers decided to move Molitor again in 1982, this time to third base, and Molitor was getting frustrated. "Last year they told me I was the center fielder of the future. Now I'm the third baseman of the future,"[31] he deadpanned. "If [closer] Rollie Fingers retires in a few years, I might be the relief pitcher of the future." To ease his concerns, Molitor received some comfort from Brewers owner Bud Selig, who told him it would be the last change — a curious involvement by an owner in the on-field decision-making.

The team started the season slowly, and, with the Brewers floundering in fifth place on June 2, Dalton replaced Rodgers with Harvey Kuenn. Energized, Harvey's Wallbangers posted a 25-11 record before the All-Star Game and grabbed a share of first place in the East Division. The Brewers battled Baltimore down the stretch, and won the division title with a 95-67-1 record on the season's final day when Yount homered twice and veteran right-hander Don Sutton stopped the Baltimore Orioles. In an injury-free year, Molitor played in 160 games, led the league with 136 runs scored, stole 41 bases, and collected 201 hits, third in the league behind teammates Yount (210) and first-baseman Cecil Cooper (205). He was positioned to lead the Brewers into their first League Championship Series.

The American League West champion California Angels quickly gained the advantage when they jumped out to wins in the first two games, at Anaheim, despite Molitor's inside-the-park home run in Game Two. The Brewers bounced back when the best-of-five series moved to Milwaukee, and they won the next three games at home. Molitor homered again, this time hitting one over the fence at County Stadium. For the series, Molitor keyed the Brewers offense by slugging .684, scoring four runs and driving in five.

Milwaukee opened the 1982 World Series at Busch Stadium, home of the National League champion St. Louis Cardinals. In the first game, Molitor set a fall classic record with five hits, all singles, to lead the Brewers to a 10-0 win. Cardinals manager Whitey Herzog was surprisingly dismissive of Molitor's feat: "I ain't runnin' down Molitor. . . . he's a heck of a ballplayer, but he had only one line drive. He had three infield singles and a broken-bat bloop. Nothin' you can do to stop things like that."[32] After the Cards won the next two games, Milwaukee captured Games Four and Five in Milwaukee. But a fourth win proved elusive. Back home at Busch, the Cardinals won Game Six 13-1. Molitor, who hit .355 for the Series, collected two hits in Game Seven, but the Cardinals won 6-3 behind Joaquin Andujar and Bruce Sutter.

After their 1982 season, the Brewers suffered a letdown in 1983. Molitor, who signed a five-year $5.1 million contract before the season, injured his wrist swinging a bat in May. With the sore wrist, Molitor struggled through the worst slump of his career, a 2-for-41 stretch in which he went hitless in the last 25 at-bats.[33] Near the end of the slump,

Molitor missed 10 games as he rested his wrist. He batted .270 in 152 games, and the team fell to fifth.

During the season, Molitor's old cocaine dealer, Tony Peters, was arrested. Molitor and his attorney negotiated immunity from prosecution and a commitment that, in exchange for answering all the investigators' questions, he would not be called to testify at the trial unless absolutely necessary. In the end, Molitor was not forced to testify when Peters went to trial, and he avoided punishment from the baseball authorities as well, but his name and those of four other players came out in public early in the 1984 season at the trial.

In the spring of 1984, Molitor was diagnosed with a slight tear in the medial collateral ligament in his right [throwing] elbow. He opened the season limited to designated-hitter duties and in late April tried a few games at third base. The elbow, however, was growing increasingly sensitive, and with Molitor hitting just .217 on May 1, the Brewers shut him down for season-ending Tommy John surgery. (Named after Tommy John, a pitcher who successfully resumed his career after this surgery, the procedure consists of replacing a ligament in the elbow with a tendon from elsewhere in the body.) Milwaukee, just two years removed from a World Series appearance, slid to last place in the American League East, 36½ games behind the Detroit Tigers. After the season, Molitor's wife, Linda, gave birth to the couple's daughter, Blaire.

Bamberger returned to the Brewers' helm for the 1985 season, and he returned Molitor to third base and the leadoff position in the batting order. Bamberger was concerned about Molitor's elbow early in the season and tried to play him no more than four games in row in the field.[35] The elbow responded well, however, and Bamberger played Molitor at third base in 135 games. On July 2, Molitor doubled and scored the winning run against Boston for his 1,000th hit. Shortly thereafter, he played in the All-Star Game in Minneapolis with fellow St. Paul natives Dave Winfield and Jack Morris. His season appeared to be relatively injury-free until the end of August, when he missed two weeks with a sprained ankle.

Molitor suffered through another injury-plagued season in 1986. He tore his hamstring on May 9 charging a bunt in Anaheim. He hit a home run when he returned on May 30 but played in just three games before he aggravated the injury and went back on the disabled list. Molitor returned on June 17 for two games before again tearing his hamstring chasing a fly ball while playing left field.[36] He came back on July 9 as the designated hitter; later that month the team moved him back to third, and Molitor played the rest of the season relatively injury-free. In one of the best games of his career, on August 19, Molitor led the Brewers to a 5-3 win in Cleveland by slugging two home runs and two doubles. He finished the year with a .281 batting average in 105 games and unexceptional on-base and slugging averages. At this point in his career Molitor's star had begun to dim a little: he was now 30 years old, three years removed from playing more than 140 games in a season and four years removed from hitting .300.

Milwaukee started the 1987 season red-hot, tying the modern major-league record with 13 straight wins from the opening bell. Molitor helped key the streak by batting .395 in the first 20 games, 18 of them Brewers wins. Unfortunately, the injury bug struck once more when he was caught in a rundown between third and home and again tore his hamstring. Out four weeks, he came back, but then missed games with groin and elbow injuries before re-injuring his hamstring.

When Molitor returned to the lineup on July 16 at home against California he had one hit, a double in four at-bats. Now limited to designated-hitter duties, over the next couple of weeks as Molitor consistently rapped out hits, he began attracting attention for his consecutive-game hitting streak. Joe DiMaggio's 56-game hitting streak has long been one of the most venerated streaks in sports, and even getting within shouting distance of this mark attracts enormous attention. As the pressure on Molitor mounted, he tried to keep the streak in perspective. "When you start a streak like this you're preparing for the end, anyway," Molitor said as the streak reached 34 games. "Initially I'll be disappointed. It's a unique opportunity to have a streak go on like this. But it shouldn't take me long to get over it. It won't be like the world came out from under me."[37] In Milwaukee on August 23, Molitor went 1-for-4 against Kansas City to raise the hitting streak to 38 games and pass Tommy Holmes for the seventh-longest streak in major-league history.

Three nights later Molitor was at home against Cleveland and going for his 40th consecutive game with a hit, which would tie Ty Cobb for sixth on the all-time list. Hitless in his first four at-bats, Molitor was on deck in the 10th inning when Rick Manning singled home the winning run. The fans were unnaturally subdued as the winning run crossed the plate, and Molitor joked about putting his hands up in the air: "People thought I was telling Mike [Felder] to score without sliding. What I was really doing was telling him to go back to third."[38] He also remembered the response from the fans: "When I headed for the dugout, the crowd got on its feet and gave me an ovation. That was probably the most emotional moment of the streak for me."[39] Molitor's 39-game hitting streak was one of the longest in baseball history. Only Joe DiMaggio, Pete Rose, George Sisler, and Ty Cobb crafted longer streaks in modern baseball; Willie Keeler and Bill Dahlen did so in the 1890s.

Buoyed by the streak, Molitor turned in his best season statistically. He batted .353, second in the American League to Wade Boggs. He led the league in doubles with 41 and runs scored with 114, an astounding accomplishment considering he played in only 118 games. He also stole a career-high 45 bases and during the streak became the 33rd major leaguer to steal second, third, and home in the same inning. His on-base percentage of .438 and slugging average of .566 were by far the highest of his career; his on-base percentage plus slugging average (OPS) of 1.003 was the league's second best. For his accomplishments, Molitor finished fifth in the American League Most Valuable Player Award voting and received the league's Joe Cronin Award for significant achievement and the Hutch Award as Comeback Player of the Year.[40]

After offseason arthroscopic surgery on his elbow, Molitor signed a two-year, $2.8 million contract, laden with bonuses based on games played.[41] Relatively healthy, the Ignitor started the 1988 season as a designated hitter but soon reclaimed his spot at third. Molitor was named the starting American League second baseman in the All-Star Game, despite appearing in only one game at the position. At the end of the 1987 season, Molitor had been moved over to second base briefly, and that was where he was placed on the ballot for 1988. Star second baseman Julio Franco was bitter over Molitor's starting berth: "The guy's played only one game at second and he deserves to go more than me?"[42] For the season, despite a nagging hamstring problem, sore wrist, and aching elbow, Molitor earned his playing time bonus by appearing in 154 games.

Molitor began the 1989 season on the disabled list with a dislocated finger, but he recovered quickly and joined the team in mid-April. He remained healthy throughout the remainder of the season, and again received his performance bonus when he played in 155 games. In another strong season, despite one of the longest slumps of his career after the All-Star break, Molitor hit .315 with 27 steals. A regular at third base through the bulk of the season, he was switched to second near its conclusion by manager Tom Trebelhorn. The Brewers had two young shortstop prospects, Bill Spiers and Gary Sheffield, and Trebelhorn wanted to get them both into the lineup, one at short, the other at third.

Before the 1990 season, Molitor reached an agreement with the Brewers for a three-year, $9.1 million contract, then one of the largest in baseball, and along with his friend Yount, the second $3 million-plus salary on the club. Only one other team, the Oakland Athletics, had two $3 million-a-year players, and some questioned the Brewers' wisdom on account of Molitor's injury history. In fact, 1990 did become one of Molitor's more frustrating seasons. Heading into spring training the Brewers' infield was completely unsettled. Molitor, Sheffield, Spiers, Gantner, and Dale Sveum, the starting shortstop in 1987 and 1988, were all vying for three positions (second, third, and short). Unfortunately for the Brewers, as the injury bug bit, the Brewers actually found themselves with too few alternatives, not too many.

The 33-year-old Molitor was bothered by a sore shoulder in spring training, then fractured his thumb. He missed a month, and when he returned Trebelhorn put him at second to reduce the strain on his shoulder.[43] In mid-June, Molitor suffered a fractured finger when he caught his hand in the glove of Cleveland's Brook Jacoby and missed another six weeks.[44] He returned at the end of July but was unable to throw because of the sore shoulder. Trebelhorn shifted him to first base, which riled regular first baseman Greg Brock and triggered his agent complaining to Dalton.[45] Brock's unhappiness only added to an already restless clubhouse — Sheffield, for example, wanted to be a shortstop, not a third baseman — and the struggling team dropped to sixth place after a .500 finish the year before. Molitor hit .285 in only 103 games, and his 1990 season ended prematurely when he collided with Jim Gantner in the final week. Already slated for shoulder surgery, he underwent a separate surgery on his forearm to repair the injury.

Molitor returned to full-time duty in 1991 but, no longer able to throw, was now limited to designated hitter and first base. For some reason Molitor flourished as a designated hitter — his position during the 39-game hitting streak — and over the remainder of his career he had some of his best seasons despite his advanced age (he turned 35 in August). On May 15 in Minnesota, Molitor hit for the cycle, and later in the year he singled off Bret Saberhagen for his 2,000th hit. Overall, belying his injury reputation, Molitor played in 158 games and led the league in plate appearances and at-bats. He performed well in all those opportunities: he batted .325 with a new career-high 216 hits, led the league with 133 runs scored, tied for the league lead in triples with 13, and finished eighth in OPS at .888.

Milwaukee brought in manager Phil Garner for 1992, and in late May the new skipper moved Molitor out of his familiar leadoff spot to third in the Brewers' batting order. Molitor thrived in his new role. He batted .320 and drove in 89 runs, was named to the American League All-Star team, and led Milwaukee to a second-place finish in the American League East Division, the best by the Brewers in a decade. But the Brewers faced a difficult decision at the end of the season. Molitor, who had turned 36 in August, was a free agent, and Milwaukee's ownership, which now behaved like a so-called small-market franchise, did not feel comfortable paying his market value.

Courted by the Red Sox and Angels, Molitor instead signed a three-year, $13 million contract with the world-champion Toronto Blue Jays on December 7. [46] Back in Milwaukee, his former teammates lamented the loss of Molitor and the economics of the national pastime. "I think it stinks," Yount said. "I think it's a sad day when one of the best players in the American League wants to stay in a city with a team he's been a part of for a long time, and the organization can't afford to keep him. I'm going to sit down here and weigh out what should be done and how badly I really want to come back, knowing that a lot of the Milwaukee Brewers have left now."[47] His other close friend on the club, Gantner, reflected, "If Paul Molitor leaving the Brewers doesn't show that the small markets are in trouble, nothing does."[48]

While his teammates mourned, Molitor moved on with some trepidation but ready to embrace his new opportunity. He moved his family to Toronto and showed up at spring training ahead of schedule. Molitor, who opted to wear number 19 on his Toronto uniform in honor of Yount, joined a veteran team that had won the World Series the year before. He was slated to replace a St. Paul native, 1992 designated-hitter Dave Winfield, in the Blue Jays lineup (Winfield had moved on to the Twins), and join another hometown product, pitcher Jack Morris.

Molitor quickly endeared himself to the fans north of the border. In May, he hit .374 and earned American League Player of the Month honors. In July, Blue Jays manager Clarence "Cito" Gaston, the American League field boss for the All-Star Game by virtue of the World Series appearance, selected Molitor for the A. L. squad. The Ignitor validated Gaston's confidence in his abilities by hitting .361 after the break, and he finished second in the league batting race behind teammate John Olerud. Molitor also drove in 111, scored 121 runs, and led the league with 211 hits.

In late September, Molitor returned to Milwaukee in triumph and hit a home run in Toronto's division-clinching 2-0 win at County Stadium. The next morning, Molitor awoke to find the *Milwaukee Journal* printing excerpts from agent Ron Simon's titillating book recounting Molitor's drug abuse and detailing his contract negotiations.[49]

Molitor was able to set aside the resulting uproar for the postseason. In the American League Championship Series opener in Chicago he collected four hits, including a two-run homer, in Toronto's win, then followed up with two more hits in Game Two as the Blue Jays won again. Chicago captured the next two games, in Toronto, before the Jays won Game Five at Skydome and Game Six in Chicago. In the latter Molitor's ninth-inning triple plated a couple of insurance runs in a 6-3 victory. For the series Molitor hit .391 and drove in a team-high five runs.

Set to appear in his second World Series, Molitor became the center of speculation. The Phillies and Jays split the two opening games in Toronto, and the question of the hour was how Cito Gaston would use Molitor in Philadelphia, the National League city, where he was unable to employ a designated hitter. In a gutsy decision, against the Phillies' left-handed pitcher Danny Jackson, Gaston benched left-handed-hitting John Olerud, the league batting champion, in favor of Molitor, who had played just 23 regular-season games at first base. The move paid off. Molitor, the third hitter in Toronto's order, drove in two runs with a triple in the first inning and scored on Joe Carter's sacrifice fly. He later slugged a solo home run and a single in a 10-3 win.

For Games Four and Five Gaston decided to risk Molitor's weak throwing arm at third base in place of the light-hitting Ed Sprague. Gaston felt he could run this risk because the Phillies were mostly a left-handed-hitting team. As it turned out, Molitor threw over to first base only three times in the two games, and all the throws were on target.[50] Game Four itself was a slugfest. The Jays outlasted the Phillies 15-14 in the longest nine-inning and highest-scoring game in World Series history. A day later, Philadelphia's Curt Schilling shut out Toronto to send the Series back to Skydome.

Game Six was a classic. Molitor tripled, drove in the game's first run, and scored on a sacrifice fly by Carter. In the fifth inning, to the chant of "MVP, MVP" (for Most Valuable Player) from Skydome fans, Molitor slammed a solo home run that gave Toronto a 5-1 advantage.[51] But the Phillies battled back to take a 6-5 lead into the bottom of the ninth. Toronto's Rickey Henderson walked to open the last half of that inning, and, one out later, Molitor smacked a hard line-drive single to center. With two on against Phillies closer Mitch Williams, Carter stepped in and pounded a line drive down the left-field line. The screaming liner slammed into the left-field bleachers. Molitor, leaping high, scored the winning run in front of Carter. When it was over Molitor let out a wave of emotion and wept on the field, later saying, "I'm not ashamed or embarrassed to admit that."[52]

In the six-game series, Molitor collected 12 hits in 24 at-bats, including two doubles, two triples, and two home runs. He scored 10 runs and drove in eight and was named the World Series Most Valuable Player. "In Canada, when you say PM they think of prime minister, but now they might start thinking Paul Molitor!" color analyst Tim McCarver quipped during the TV broadcast. Molitor almost achieved the rare feat of winning the MVP trophy for both the World Series and the regular season, for which the writers voted him second in the MVP balloting.

Winfield had parted ways with the Jays after one season and a World Series title, but Molitor, with two years remaining on his contract, stayed in Toronto. Once the 1994 season began Molitor again turned in a stellar, injury-free year. On July 5 in Minnesota he hit the second grand slam of his career. Overall, he led Toronto with a .341 batting average, the sixth best mark in the league, and in runs, hits, total bases, doubles, and stolen bases. But Toronto finished the strike-shortened season under .500. Molitor continued to put his reputation for fragility behind him as he led the league in games played with 115. He was one of several players, including Baltimore's Cal Ripken Jr., who appeared in all of their teams' games during the season, but the Jays played one more contest than any other team in the league. Molitor made just five appearances in the field, all at first base.

In 1995 Molitor appeared in 130 games, strictly as a designated hitter. The highlight of his season was August 26 and 27 when he put together eight hits in eight at-bats with back-to-back four-hit games. Including the 28th, he reached base on ten consecutive plate appearances. But overall Molitor turned in one of his worst seasons, and at the age of 39 his game appeared to be slipping.

His three-year contract now up, Molitor became a free agent at the end of the season. He considered remaining in Toronto or returning to either Milwaukee or Minnesota. In the end he decided on Minnesota, and on December 5, 1995, he signed with the Twins for $2.025 million. Molitor started quickly; his early-season exploits including scoring five runs and driving in five in an April 24-11 win over the Tigers. Later he put together a five-hit game against Toronto in a 6-4, 11-innning win.

On September 16, 1996, at Kansas City's Kauffman Stadium, Molitor singled in the first inning, the 2,999th hit of his major-league career. In the fifth inning, he hit a drive to right field off Jose Rosado and ended up on third base to become the first major leaguer to register a triple for his 3,000th hit. "I don't know much about that young man [Rosado], but I know he did not try to avoid being the one who gave up my 3,000th hit," Molitor said. "I know he shook off a couple of signs and threw fastballs—saying, 'If you're going to get it, you're going to get it.'"[53] George Brett and Molitor's friend Robin Yount were among those on hand to see him join them in the 3,000 hit club. The milestone hit came three years to the day after Winfield had collected his 3,000th hit, also for the Minnesota Twins, and the two became the first two players from the same hometown to accomplish the feat.

Molitor, the fourth oldest player in the league, appeared in a career high 161 of Minnesota's 162 games for manager Tom Kelly. He batted .341, third in the American League behind Alex Rodriguez and Frank Thomas. He led the league in hits with 225 — becoming the oldest player to ever lead the league in hits[54] — drove in a career high 113 runs, and scored 99.

After the season Molitor chose to remain in Minnesota and signed a two-year contract with the Twins for a substantial pay increase in recognition that his skills had not yet eroded. Unfortunately the injury bug bit again early in the season. Molitor returned to the disabled list for the first time since 1990 after he sprained his left wrist and strained his abdominal muscle in a home-plate collision on April 13 with Kansas City's Mike Macfarlane.[55] He rebounded to have a pretty good season, including five hits in a game against Oakland. He wound up the year hitting .305 with 10 home runs and 89 runs batted in. Molitor returned to the Twins in 1998 for his final season. Just two weeks shy of his 42nd birthday, on August 8 against Baltimore, he turned the five-hit trick again and stole his 500th base.

In retirement, honors poured his way. On June 11, 1999, Molitor returned to County Stadium, where the team retired the number 4 uniform he had worn for 15 years as a Brewer. That summer, he ranked number 99 on *The Sporting News's* list of the 100 Greatest Baseball Players and was a finalist for Major League Baseball's All-Century Team.

Although Molitor knew he wanted to remain in baseball after retirement, he turned down an opportunity to join Milwaukee's front-office or field staff — his first year off he just wanted to enjoy life. To keep his hand in the game Molitor worked part-time with the Twins broadcast team; he also golfed and went to Bruce Springsteen concerts around the world.[56] With his transition year out of the way, Molitor joined the Twins as bench coach for the 2000 season — principally to help with baserunning and the mental approach to hitting — with the expectation of eventually becoming a big-league manager. He turned down an offer from the Toronto Blue Jays to become a roving minor-league hitting instructor and de facto heir apparent to manager Jim Fregosi. The Blue Jays had been after Molitor for some time; prior to the 1998 season they had offered him the manager's position in either a standard or player-manager role. At the time Molitor turned the Blue Jays down to finish his playing career at home in Minnesota and because he thought he might need more seasoning before becoming a major-league manager.[57]

After the 2000 season, Toronto again offered Molitor the managerial position, which he again declined. He did not want to uproot his wife and high-school-age daughter; furthermore, veteran Twins manager Tom Kelly had just signed a one-year extension, and Molitor was likely next in line.[58] So he remained with the Twins as bench coach for the 2001 season. As expected, Kelly retired after the season, and Molitor and Ron Gardenhire, emerged as the finalists to be Minnesota's next manager. In early December, however, Molitor withdrew from consideration because of the uncertainty surrounding the potential contraction of the Twins. At the time Major League Baseball was actively negotiating to eliminate two major-league franchises, one of which was presumed to be the Twins. In the words of his agent, Ron Simon, Molitor "feels the situation's so unsettled that he'd rather not be involved with it right now."[59] While in Milwaukee, Molitor had become quite friendly with Brewers owner Bud Selig. Now baseball's commissioner, Selig had reportedly warned Molitor that contraction of the Minnesota franchise was likely.[60]

With the uncertainty of contraction and his daughter a senior in high school, Molitor elected to take the year off for some rest and relaxation.[61] Molitor missed baseball, however, and in 2003 he took a job with the Twins as a roving minor-league instructor. Seattle Mariners general manager Pat Gillick, who had recruited Molitor to Toronto back in 1993 and unsuccessfully chased him for other positions since his retirement, now targeted him to be Seattle's batting coach. This time Molitor accepted. One year was enough, however, and after the season the financially secure Molitor — he earned nearly $800,000 in 2004[62] — moved back to Minnesota to resume the less stressful job of a roving minor-league coach.

In semi-retirement Molitor's personal life became uncomfortably complex. In 2003 Molitor and his longtime wife, Linda, divorced. Molitor had fathered a son with Joanna Andreou a couple of years earlier and paid child support. While the Molitors were legally separated, Molitor fathered a daughter with another woman. In early 2004, Molitor married the child's mother, Destini, and he and his second wife have two children. Molitor's behavior and subsequent divorce from Linda caused such hard feelings that his ex-wife and daughter almost did not attend his Hall of Fame induction ceremony. His difficult personal life may have also contributed to his unwillingness to commit to a more prominent baseball job.[63]

On January 6, 2004, in his first year of eligibility, Molitor was elected to the Baseball Hall of Fame, garnering 85.2 percent of the possible votes. On July 25, before a crowd of 15,000 on a partly-sunny Sunday afternoon in Cooperstown, New York, Molitor and pitcher Dennis Eckersley were inducted into the Hall. A clearly emotional Molitor thanked the most important people in his life and talked about some highly personal issues, including his son, Joshua, and his drug use. He also reviewed his career and reminisced: "The baseball memories are great, but when you think about your career, the people memories are even better."[64]

After nine years as the Twins minor league baserunning and infield coordinator, Molitor decided to rejoin major league baseball in a more active capacity. In 2014 he accepted a job on the Twins major league field staff under manager Ron Gardenhire overseeing baserunning, bunting, infield instruction and positioning, plus assisting with in-game strategy.[65] Gardenhire was let go after season, the Twins fourth in a row with 70 or fewer wins, and the team embarked on an extensive manager search, led by GM Terry Ryan.

After a process Ryan dubbed, "our five-week ordeal," in November 2015 the Twins hired Molitor to manage the club on a three-year contract.[66] Many former teammates and coaches raved about his understanding of baseball. "He was as aware as player I ever saw," former manager Tom Trebelhorn recalled.[67] The other finalist for the job was reportedly Torey Lovullo, manager of the Arizona Diamondbacks as of 2019.[68] Molitor became only the third man in history (with Ted Williams and Ryne Sandberg) to get his first managerial opportunity after being elected to the Baseball Hall of Fame (excepting those with interim tags).

Despite the team's recent struggles, Molitor and Ryan both felt the club had some talent, and they were not in a rebuilding mode. "Things can change very dramatically at this level, very quickly… I want [players] to believe we can win now. I hope to set that tone right away."[69] He also offered some insights on his philosophy of managing, "Little mistakes left uncorrected lead to big mistakes. I firmly believe that. There's a right way to do things, and if you don't emphasize the fundamentals, you have to play that much better to overcome it. And we don't have that luxury." Later adding, "You watch a team like the San Antonio Spurs or the New England Patriots, these teams somehow are able to create a team-first atmosphere. When young players arrive, it's about 'Do I belong, can I stay, will I make a living?' Well you have to teach them that if you buy in to what we're doing collectively, if that becomes your focus, it's going to work out for you individually, too."[70] And in fact, Molitor delivered in 2015. The team jumped to 83 wins, and Molitor finished third in the AL Manager of the Year

Balloting and was named AL Manager of the Year by *The Sporting News*.

Unfortunately, 2016 was a disaster. The team lost a Minnesota record 103 games as several youngsters were either injured or failed to take the expected step forward, and the pitching disintegrated. Owner Jim Pohlad reorganized the front office, replacing longtime baseball man Ryan with Derek Falvey, a 33-year-old analytically-savvy wunderkind from the Cleveland Indians. And although Falvey had free rein to restructure the team as he saw fit, Pohlad let him know the one exception was that he needed to keep Molitor for at least one more season.[71] Both sides put a happy face on the marriage, but Falvey forced some changes on the coaching staff, and Molitor would have a much different relationship with the front office moving forward.

The team bounced back remarkably in 2017. Since 1901 only 14 of 143 teams had finished above .500 the season after losing at least 100 games. The Twins bucked this trend, winning 85 games and securing the second wild card slot. There were no real weak spots in the lineup, which could also boast some depth, and Molitor juggled a less-than-stellar pitching staff. For the team' and given a new three-year contract.

Once again, however, the Twins could not build on their momentum, backsliding to 78 and 84 in 2018, and the team bounced Molitor after four years at the helm. "It's about where our club is for the present and the future. This wasn't about our record this year." Falvey said. "We just felt a change in style with some of these younger players could be of benefit for us."[72] Minneapolis sportswriters speculated on other, more concrete, reasons: Falvey wanted to hire someone of his own choosing; the young players were not developing as quickly as hoped; and there was some friction between some of Molitor's holdover coaches and the new-school coaches.[73]

Tactically, Molitor issued intentional walks at a rate above the league average every season, leading the league in 2018. He also used the sacrifice bunt more than average and attempted relatively few steals of third. Over the last two years of his tenure, Molitor opened the game with the platoon advantage significantly more often than his peers.[74] As of 2019 Molitor was "enjoying some downtime," and considering what to do next in baseball.[75]

Throughout his career, Molitor earned recognition for his involvement with several charities and received a number of awards for his good works. For 1997 he was awarded the Lou Gehrig Award by Phi Delta Theta, Gehrig's fraternity at Columbia University, for "someone who best exemplifies the giving character" of Gehrig. Molitor was praised for sponsoring "a program which has allowed thousands of youngsters, senior citizens, and needy adults to attend big-league games, and [being] actively involved in fund raising to combat several diseases."[76] The next year Molitor received the Branch Rickey Award, given by the Rotary Club of Denver and selected by baseball notables and Rotary district governors to recognize baseball players who "exemplify the Rotary ideal of 'Service Above Self.'"[77] As of 2019 Molitor supported several charities including Starkey Hearing Foundation, Camp Heartland, Friends of St. Paul Baseball, and Salvation Army.[78]

For 21 seasons, Paul Molitor was a great player and a quiet leader. "When I first got to Milwaukee my locker was right next to Paulie's," remembered one-time teammate Cal Eldred. "He was an unbelievable teammate. Guys like him and Robin and Gumby [Jim Gantner] just went about their business every day. They didn't say a lot but when they did, everybody would listen."[79] Molitor achieved his dream, articulated many years earlier in his high-school yearbook, of playing pro baseball and working with people. And Molitor not only played professional baseball, but he became a star: 15 years in Milwaukee as one of the city's biggest celebrities, a world championship in Toronto, and a final few years in front of his hometown fans in Minnesota. Along the way he used his fame to work with people in his numerous charitable endeavors.

SOURCES

A version of this biography appeared in the book *Minnesotans in Baseball*, edited by Stew Thornley (Nodin, 2009).

NOTES

1 Richard Hoffer, "Career Move," *Sports Illustrated*, March 29, 1993: 45.
2 *The Sporting News*, March 6, 1989: 26.
3 *Seattle Times*, July 25, 2004.
4 Two websites, http://Retrosheet.org and http://Baseball-Reference.com, are essential for verifying and generating game and seasonal information.
5 Unless otherwise noted, the two main sources for Molitor's early life are Bill Koenig, *USA Today Baseball Weekly*, April 17-23, 1996, and Jim Souhan, *Minneapolis Star Tribune*, February 18, 1996.
6 Correspondence with Tony Leseman, Cretin-Derham Hall Development & Alumni/ae Officer, August 4, 2008.
7 Hoffer, op. cit.; Aschburner, Steve. "Strictly Business," *Inside Sports*, June 1994.
8 Rich Marazzi, "Batting the Breeze," *Sports Collectors Digest*, February 26, 1993: 190.
9 Correspondence with Tony Leseman, Cretin-Derham Hall Development & Alumni/ae Officer, August 4, 2008.
10 Koenig, op. cit.
11 Stewart Broomer and Paul Molitor. *Good Timing*, Toronto: ECW Press, 1994: 17.
12 *St. Paul Pioneer Press*, September 18, 1996.
13 *The Sporting News*, August 12, 1978: 3.
14 University of Minnesota press release, June 17, 1976.
15 1976 Minnesota Baseball.
16 *Minneapolis Star Tribune*, July 26, 2004.
17 *St. Paul Dispatch*, July 7, 1976.
18 *Minneapolis Tribune*, April 12, 1977.
19 W.C. Madden, *Baseball's First-Year Player Draft: Team by Team Through 1999*: 195.
20 *Minnesota Daily*, July 28, 2004; *Minnesota Daily*, February 3 and July 28, 1994.
21 Hoffer, op. cit.
22 C.C. Johnson Spink, *Official Baseball Guide for 1978*, The Sporting News; Johnson, Lloyd, and Miles Wolff. *Encyclopedia of Minor League Baseball*, 3rd Edition. Durham, N.C.: *Baseball America*, 2007: 579.
23 Tom Skibosh, "Paul Molitor: To Catch A Thief," *Milwaukee Scorebook*, 2nd Edition, 1979: 9.

24 *The Sporting News*, October 7, 1978: 27.
25 Mik Gonring, "Molitor & Yount: Opposites Really Do Attract," *Milwaukee Brewers Program*, June 1979: 50.
26 Simon, Ron. *The Game Behind the Game: Negotiating in the Big Leagues*. Stillwater, Minnesota: Voyageur Press:158.
27 *New York Times*, August 19 1985; Simon, op. cit.: 158.
28 Simon: 153-159.
29 Daniel Okrent, *Nine Innings*. New York: Houghton Mifflin, 1985: 68-69; *The Sporting News*, April 4, 1981.
30 Okrent, op. cit.: 70.
31 *The Sporting News*, February 13, 1982: 40.
32 *The Sporting News*, October 25, 1982: 14.
33 *The Sporting News*, June 27, 1983: 23; http://Baseball-Reference.com
34 Simon, op. cit.: 159-160.
35 *The Sporting News*, May 13, 1985: 24.
36 Broomer, op. cit.: 66.
37 *New York Times*, April 21, 1987.
38 *The Sporting News*, March 28, 1988: 8.
39 John Kuenster, "With 3,319 career hits, Paul Molitor merits Hall of Fame Status," *Baseball Digest*, February 2004.
40 Broomer, op. cit.: 89.
41 Broomer, op. cit.: 89.
42 *The Sporting News*, July 10, 1989: 13.
43 *The Sporting News*, May 14, 1990: 16
44 *The Sporting News*, July 2, 1990: 13.
45 *The Sporting News*, August 13, 1990: 10.
46 Simon, op. cit.: 182-183.
47 Broomer, op. cit.: 112.
48 Broomer, op. cit.: 112.
49 Broomer, op. cit.: 143-145.
50 *The Sporting News*, November 1, 1993: 17.
51 Broomer, op. cit.: 176.
52 Tom Verducci, "The Complete Player." *Sports Illustrated*, November 1, 1993: 28.
53 *Minneapolis Star Tribune*, September 17, 1996.
54 Tim Kurkjian, "No Asterisk Necessary," *Sports Illustrated*, September 9, 1996: 76.
55 *The Sporting News*, April 28, 1997: 37.
56 *Minneapolis Star Tribune*, April 30, 1999, November 24, 1999.
57 *The Sporting News*, November 10, 1997: 42; November 17, 1997: 51; November 16, 1998: 59; December 6, 1999: 74.
58 *The Sporting News*, October 23, 2000: 59.
59 Associated Press, http://espn.go.com/mlb/news/2001/1203/1289316.html.
60 *The Sporting News*, April 29, 2002: 32.
61 *Milwaukee Journal Sentinel*, August 13, 2002.
62 *Toronto Sun*, September 16, 2005.
63 Internet Movie Database, http://www.imdb.com; *Minneapolis Star Tribune*, February 15, 2004, October 13, 2003, November 20, 2005; *Toronto Sun*, September 16, 2005.
64 *Minneapolis Star Tribune*, July 26, 2004.
65 2018 Minnesota Twins Media Guide: 14.
66 Phil Miller, "Here to Win," *Minneapolis Star Tribune*, November 5, 2014.
67 Phil Miller, "A Mind for Managing," *Minneapolis Star Tribune*, February 22, 2015.
68 Phil Miller, "Twins Offer Molitor Managerial Reins," *Minneapolis Star Tribune*, November 2, 2014.
69 Phil Miller, "Here to Win," *Minneapolis Star Tribune*, November 5, 2014.
70 Phil Miller, "A Mind for Managing," *Minneapolis Star Tribune*, February 22, 2015.
71 Phil Miller, "Falvey More Than Happy to Keep Molitor at the Helm," *Minneapolis Star Tribune*, November 8, 2016.
72 Phil Miller, "Class Dismissed," *Minneapolis Star Tribune*, October 3, 2018.
73 Jim Souhan, "Falvey, Levine Offer Reasons That Leave a Lot of Guesswork," *Minneapolis Star Tribune*, October 3, 2018; LaVelle E. Neal III, "Living in a Future Without Molitor," *Minneapolis Star Tribune*, October 3, 2018.
74 Baseball-reference.com; *Bill James Handbook*, ACTA Publications, 2016-2019 editions.
75 LaVelle E. Neal III, "Molitor Also Staying Close to Home," *Minneapolis Star Tribune*, November 13, 2018.
76 *New York Times*, February 13, 1998.
77 *The Rotarian*, April 1999.
78 "Alumni Support These Causes and Charities," www.mlb.com/twins/community/player-charities
79 *Milwaukee Journal Sentinel*, July 24, 2004.

DON MONEY

By Steve Kuehl

Any list of the greatest players ever to don a Milwaukee Brewers uniform has to include Don Money. He is a four-time All-Star and a Brewers' Walk of Fame member who holds major-league records as a third baseman. Money was an infield specialist who amassed a .975 fielding percentage over 16 seasons from 1968 to 1983, including .968 at the hot corner, where he played about two-thirds of his games. Money ranks 15th in career fielding percentage at third base. In the batter's box, he batted .261, drove in 729 runs, and had a career WAR of 36.3.

Donald Wayne Money was born on June 7, 1947, in Washington, DC. His family moved to what is now known as Cherry Hill, New Jersey, when he was just a few weeks old. Money was the third of four children born to Robert Jarrett and Frances Estelle (Greenfield) Money. Robert was from New Jersey, and Frances was from Washington, and the family moved back and forth between the two because of his father's work. Money said he inherited his work ethic from his parents.[1] Robert was a carpenter and railroad worker; Frances looked after the house and the children. Money recalled working in the family garden with his brothers when they were children; Robert had them do manual labor to teach them the meaning of hard work.

Money had two older brothers, Robert Jr. and Kenneth, and one younger brother, Joseph. All were good ballplayers. Robert Jr. was a pitcher in high school and had a tryout with the Phillies at old Connie Mack Stadium after which he was asked to come back for a second tryout. He decided to skip the tryout, which happened to be on a hot summer day, to go swimming to with his friends. He spent over 40 years in the refrigeration business. Kenneth suffered a broken leg that ended his baseball career. Joseph played baseball in high school but was thrown off the team a couple of times and decided not to play ball his senior year.

Money's baseball career started when he was 7 years old playing Little League and he never missed a year through Babe Ruth, Pony League, high school, American Legion, the minors, and the majors until he retired when he was 37 years old. Money said Legion baseball was different in southern Maryland at the time; players came from any age group and most were in their mid-20s; some were even in their 40s.

Money graduated from La Plata (Maryland) High School in 1965. He had set school records for batting average (.512), hits, doubles, and home runs in one season and most home runs during his varsity career (12). On opening day of his junior year, Money hit three home runs and a triple. As a pitcher, the right-hander went 5-1 his senior year with a 1.08 ERA. As hobbies, Money played golf and pool. The football coach asked Money if he wanted to play wide receiver, but Robert wouldn't sign the permission slip. Growing up, Mickey Mantle and Willie Mays were Money's heroes, though Harmon Killebrew, playing for the Washington Senators, was also a favorite.

The story behind Money's major-league signing involves two Pittsburgh Pirates scouts, Joe Consoli and Syd Thrift. Thrift was hailed by *The Sporting News* as one of the best teachers in baseball and worked with such players as Rickey Henderson, Frank White, Al Oliver, and Bobby Bonilla.[2] Consoli worked with players like John Smiley and Tim Drummond. In 1965, when Money was 17 years old, his high-school coach, Dick Stone, got Consoli to come see Money play and Thrift worked Money out at the local field. Money was invited to a tryout in Salem, Virginia, where a teammate had to drive him because his mother wouldn't. Money was one of 35 players asked back the next day. Again Money was asked back, this time for tryouts in Fort Belvoir, Virginia. (This time his mother drove him.) Money was asked to work out at second base, and he recalled watching what others were doing at second base so he could mimic them. After the tryouts Money was asked to sign with the Pirates that day. He couldn't because his parents weren't there and he was underage. By the time his parents returned, the scouts were gone. On June 20, 1965, Consoli attended one of Money's American Legion games and recalled, "… (A)t the fifth inning, Don's father called me over behind the dugout. The boy was there and when I pulled out the contract, Mr. Money put his hand on it and said: There is one stipulation — I don't want Don to get any money. I don't even want him to know how much salary he'll be getting. All I want to know is do you think he has a chance to be a big leaguer?"[3] After the game, Money signed the contract on the hood of Robert's 1960 Buick.

After being signed, the 18-year-old Money was off to play for the Salem (Virginia) Rebels, a Pirates farm team in the rookie-level Appalachian League. The Rebels were crowned league champions in 1965 with a record of 43-27 under their manager, George DeTore. Money played in 66 of the games and batted .241 with 6 home runs. Playing every game at shortstop, Money was named to the league all-star team.

After the season Money enlisted in the Marine Corps Reserve in Pittsburgh. He was on active duty one weekend a month and two weeks in the summer for eight years. Money said the Marine Corps made a difference in his playing. "I guess it helped me a lot because I hit .310 at Raleigh (in 1967). Maybe I grew a little. Anyway, I felt stronger and more confident."[4]

After Salem the Pirates advanced Money to Clinton (Iowa) of the Class A Midwest League. Money played in every game, 75 at shortstop and 51 at third base. He batted .236; fielding, not hitting, was Money's strength that season.

Arguably, the best of Money's four minor-league seasons came in 1967 for the Raleigh Pirates of the Class A Carolina League. Playing shortstop in 135 games for the pennant-winning team, Money was named an all-star and the league MVP after batting .310 with 16 home runs, 86 RBIs, and a league-leading 37 doubles. His manager, Joe Morgan, was effusive in his praise: "This kid worked harder than anybody we had. He threw in batting practice every day, fielded extra groundballs and still played. I'll bet he threw a thousand pitches and caught as many grounders this year. He's the type that makes you a winner."[5] After the season Money played for the Pirates in the Florida Instructional League, batted .336, and was picked as the best player in the league by managers and scouts.

On the evening of December 15, 1967, Money was listening to the radio when he heard that he was being traded to the Phillies with Harold Clem, Bill Laxton, and Woodie Fryman for future Hall of Fame pitcher Jim Bunning. At the time, the Pirates were looking to compete so trading some prospects to the Phillies made sense even though Bunning was nearing the end of his career. Pittsburgh had Gene Alley at shortstop, so Money liked being traded to a team for which he could compete right away. "Actually, I'm very pleased," he said. "I think I have a better chance of playing with the Phils."[6] Philadelphia owner Bob Carpenter said Money was key to the trade: "We would not have made the deal if Pittsburgh turned it down on Money."[7]

Phillies manager Gene Mauch said, "I like his bat. He has short, quick strokes. In the field he has it all, although his speed is only average. Phil Rizzuto was not fast, but he was quick. Marty Marion couldn't run, but he was quick. Pee Wee Reese was faster than the other two and they were the top shortstops of my day as a player. Who knows? Maybe Money will be in their class someday."[8]

On April 10, 1968, the 6-foot-1, 170-pound, 20-year-old Money made his major-league debut, against the Los Angeles Dodgers. He hit a double in three at-bats with two RBIs. After playing in four games, Money was optioned to Triple-A San Diego (Pacific Coast League). In 127 games for the Padres, he batted .303 and was voted the PCL's all-star shortstop and voted its best defensive infielder in a poll of managers and fans. Money was also named San Diego's most popular player.

Recalled to the Phillies in 1969, Money played four seasons for Philadelphia. He was selected as the Topps Major League Rookie All-Star shortstop in 1969. Money continued to live in Vineland and commuted to Philadelphia. He and Larry Hisle helped lower the average age of the veteran team. His 1969 season was thoroughly unimpressive (.229 in 127 games). Money said it was hard to play in your hometown because you can't get away from baseball; even when you go to the grocery store, people walk up to you and ask why the team isn't playing well. The 1970 season was better: .295 with 14 home runs, and Money was named the New Jersey Athlete of the Year.

In 1971 Money felt really good, and he hit the first home run in new Veterans Stadium, on April 10, Opening Day. But the Phillies' hitting coach, Wally Moses, tried to get the pull-hitting Money to go the other way, and his batting average plunged to .223 in 1971 and .222 in 1972. Money said being shuffled from third base to left field and then to second base did not help matters. Through all of this, he never complained. It didn't help that future Hall of Famer Mike Schmidt was an emerging rookie third baseman for the Phillies. On October 31, 1972, Money was traded by the Phillies with Bill Champion and John Vukovich to the Milwaukee Brewers for Earl Stephenson, Ken Brett, Ken Sanders, and Jim Lonborg. Money said the trade worked out well for both teams: The Phillies wanted pitching help and the Brewers wanted help in the infield.

The Brewers, coming to Milwaukee from an expansion team in Seattle in 1970, were a young team, and Money automatically found a connection: He grew with the team. Money went back to being a pull hitter and took 15 minutes of extra batting practice before each game. The manager wanted Money to practice pulling pitches to the metal bleachers out in left field, even though that was foul territory. It worked, and Money hit the ball better. In 1973 his batting average rose to .284. Money recalled seeing the baseball as big a beach ball. Manager Del Crandall credited Money as being a reason for the Brewers' improvement from 65 victories in 1972 to 74 in 1973. "Don is really starting to produce with the bat," Crandall said. "He's swinging with authority and has been consistent. We couldn't ask any more of the trade than we have received."[9] Money also led American League third basemen with a .971 fielding percentage that year.

The 1974 season was bittersweet for Money. He set a major-league record for third basemen with 86 consecutive errorless games and the fewest errors (5) in one season; the records still stood in 2018. Money had a record-high .9894 fielding percentage that was bettered by Tony Fernandez (.9910) in 1994. The bitter part came when he wasn't selected to the American League All-Star team until the last minute as a reserve by manager Dick Williams. (He didn't play in the game.) Also, Brooks Robinson was chosen over Money for the third baseman Gold Glove, an award that Robinson won every year from 1960 to 1975 for the Baltimore Orioles. Having the best all-around season of his career, Money and thousands of fans were disappointed. Money's new nickname became "Brooks," after Robinson, but he was never able to win a Gold Glove.

The 1975 season was another disappointment for Money because of a string of injuries. He still managed to hit .277 in 109 games. During the offseason, negotiations between the Brewers and the New York Mets began. Rumors had Rusty Staub coming to the Brewers for Money, but the trade never happened. After the season surgery was needed to repair scar tissue from a previous hernia operation.[10]

In 1976 Money got off to his best start since 1970. He was being used more as a DH and finished the season hitting .267 in 117 games. That year Money was selected to his second All-Star team. (He was hitless in one at-bat.)

In 1977 Money was moved to second base after the third-base job was given to newly acquired Sal Bando. Several teams tried to get Money, but he was not traded. Playing in 152 games, he batted .279 and had personal highs in home runs (25) and RBIs (83). Selected as a reserve to his third All-Star team, Money was injured and was replaced on the squad by the Brewers' Jim Slaton. Money played 23 games in the outfield because Sixto Lezcano was on the disabled list.

In 1978 Money made his final All-Star team. He batted a career-best .293, hit 14 home runs, and drove in 54 runs with over 500 plate appearances in over 100 games for the last time in his career. During the season Money played every position in the infield: 19 games at first base, 36 at second base, 25 at third base, and two at shortstop. He was a designated hitter in 15 games.

In the remainder of his career, Money was plagued by injuries. In the second week of the 1980 season, he suffered a knee injury and was out of the lineup for a month. He also missed games because of a rib cage injury and underwent surgery for torn cartilage. In 1981 he only played in 60 games (56 back at third base) as the Brewers made it to the postseason.

The 1982 season was Money's most memorable.

A four-time All-Star infielder for the Brewers in the 1970s, 35-year-old Don Money saw most of his action as a DH in 1982, belting 16 home runs and slugging a career-best .531 in 275 at-bats.

He said the team was not jelling at the start until manager Harvey Kuenn took over for Buck Rodgers. The team steadily improved, and the comradery was better than ever. The team was full of good players and great friends who hung out off the field. Money played in the most games (96) since his All-Star season in 1978, batting .284 with 16 home runs. The Brewers finished the season 95-67 and faced the St. Louis Cardinals in the World Series. The Cardinals won the Series in seven games, but Money was happy to finally get to have a World Series plate appearance. (Don Jr. was a batboy during the Series.)

Money's final season of major-league baseball came in 1983, when he played in 43 games and batted .149, mainly as a DH. Ted Simmons was the primary DH for the Brewers, so Money could see the writing on the wall.

When Milwaukee offered Money a small contract to stay with the team in 1984, he decided to take his talents to Japan. The Brewers released him on January 17, 1984. The Osaka Kintetsu Buffaloes in the Japan Pacific League were his final team. Money batted .260 with 8 home runs in 29 games played over a three-month span. But things were far from ideal. Money had brought his family with him to Japan, and there were a lot of off-field issues. He said he had a bad interpreter who didn't allow him to have truthful conversations with his manager, Isami Okamoto. The family's apartment was not as nice as the one promised to him, and he was paid once a month in the tunnel of the ballpark. Money said the last straw came when the team told him that he wasn't playing well because his family was distracting him. He decided that his baseball career was over, and the next day the family boarded a flight home.

After coaching at Sacred Heart High School in Vineland, New Jersey, for five years, Money became the manager of the Class A Beloit Snappers, a Milwaukee farm team in the Midwest League, in 1998. His old teammate Cecil Cooper was now the Brewers' minor-league director, and Cooper offered him the position. After managing the Snappers from 1998 to 2004 and taking the team to the playoff finals in 2003, Money managed the Double-A Huntsville Stars (Southern League) from 2005 to 2008. In 2007 Money was named the Southern League Manager of the Year after taking the Stars to the finals in 2006 and 2007. From 2009 to 2011, Money managed the Nashville Sounds, the Brewers' Triple-A affiliate in the Pacific Coast League. In 2012 he was the hitting coach for the Helena Brewers, an Advanced Rookie affiliate of the Brewers in the Pioneer League. Finally, for half of 2012 and from 2013 to 2015, Money was a special instructor for the Brewers. This position entailed traveling to the Brewers' farm teams for 10 to 12 days at a time. Money worked with young talent and prepared them for the big leagues. This position was also welcomed by Money because he got to spend more time at home with his family.

In 1969 Money had married his wife, Sharon, whom he had known for several years while growing up. Together they had two children, Don Jr. (born in 1970) and Shannon (1971). Don Jr. has three children, Kelsey, Don, and Shelby who is currently a collegiate hockey goalie. Shannon has three children, Alexis, Buddy, and Cooper. Buddy, a third baseman, was selected in the fifth round of the 2017 first-year player draft by the Arizona Diamondbacks. As of 2018 Money also had two great-grandchildren, Everleigh and Emma, both daughters of Kelsey. Don and Sharon lived in Vineland.

In 2005, Money was elected to the Brewers' Walk of Fame with Harvey Kuenn. The four-time All-Star said that it was the "greatest honor of all," and added that it meant even more entering with Kuenn, who was a great friend. The Walk of Fame was established in 2001 with the opening of Miller Park. It is on the plaza area outside the ballpark near the statues of Hall of Famers Hank Aaron, Robin Yount, former Commissioner Bud Selig, and Bob Uecker. Each inductee is honored with a granite-shaped home plate set in the ground.[11] The Brewers consider the Walk of Fame the equivalent of a team hall of fame. As of 2018 it had 19 members.

In 2014 Money was elected to the Brewers' Wall of Honor, which is outside the ballpark and was created to commemorate Brewers players who have made a significant contribution to the team. The inaugural class of 2014 consisted of 58 members.

SOURCES

In addition to the sources cited in the Notes, the author also accessed Baseball-Almanac.com, Baseball-reference.com, and the Don Money player file at the National Baseball Hall of Fame Library.

NOTES

1 Unless otherwise noted, all quotations from Money are from the author's interview with him on March 14, 2018.

2 [Where does The Sporting News say this?]

3 Ray Kelly, "Scout Says Money May Be Phils' Shortstop in '68," *Philadelphia Evening Bulletin*, December 19, 1967.

4 Ed Rumill, "Money 'Best Young Infield Prospect,'" *Christian Science Monitor*, March 14, 1968.

5 Joseph C. DeLuca, "Don Money – "Mr. Steady," 1988. [is there a publication name?]

6 Bill Robinson, "Philadelphia Hopes Money Was Enough for Ace Bunning," *St. Petersburg Independent*, March 6, 1968.

7 Arthur Daley, "It's Only Money," *New York Times*, March 19, 1968.

8 Ibid.

9 DeLuca.

10 Ibid.

11 www.mlb.com/brewers/ballpark/attractions/walk-of-fame.

CHARLIE MOORE

By Phillip Bolda

Charlie Moore played in the major leagues for 15 seasons, spending the first 14 with the Milwaukee Brewers and finishing up with a short stint with the Toronto Blue Jays. He is remembered as a key member the young Brewers teams that reached the American League playoffs in 1981 and the World Series in 1982.

Charles William Moore Jr. was born on June 21, 1953, in Birmingham, Alabama, the son of a former minor-league baseball player. Charles Sr., pitched from 1949 to 1952, ending his career with the Evansville Braves of the Three-I League. He "hurt his elbow"[1] and abruptly ended his career before his son was born. Because of his own injury he urged his son to become a catcher

Charlie Jr. had planned to attend Auburn University on a football scholarship after playing quarterback for Minor High School in Birmingham, but was drafted by the Brewers in the fifth round of the June 1971 amateur draft. "Dad preferred that I play baseball," Moore said. "But he would have been happy with any decision I made."[2]

Moore spent barely two years in the minors. Although his versatility was seen an asset from the start, he was used almost exclusively behind the plate in the minors.

Moore played 1,334 games in the majors, all but 51 of them for the Brewers. He played most of them behind the plate and then fascinated many baseball fans by switching from catcher to right field in 1982.

He proved to be a competent outfielder, with 13 assists in his first year at the position, leading all right fielders in 1982 with six double plays and a .992 fielding percentage. He made a critical throw to third base to catch the California Angels' Reggie Jackson as he tried to take two bases on a single in the fifth game of American League Championship Series.

After a September call-up for eight games in 1973, Moore was never sent back down. He made his major-league debut on September 8, 1973, during a 15-1 loss to the Yankees. Moore joined 21-year-old Darrell Porter, the Brewers' first pick in the 1970 draft, and the presence of two promising young catchers allowed the team to trade Ellie Rodriguez to the California Angels.

Despite his rapid rise and acknowledged athletic abilities, Moore's catching skills were still raw. "Our whole idea was to make him into an adequate catcher. That's all we were hoping for," said manager Buck Rodgers said years later. "We wanted to get his bat into the lineup for 80 or 85 games. He can do so much offensively — hit with men on, steal a base, go from first to third. He's probably the fastest catcher in the major leagues. But Charlie's done more than we hoped. He's become better than adequate. He's become an asset behind the plate."³

As the backup to Porter, Moore played 72 games in 1974 (batting .245) and 73 games in 1975 (batting .290). In the winter of 1975 he joined fellow Brewers Jim Slaton and Kevin Kobel on the Dominican winter league champion Santiago team. "Moore played winter ball and improved tremendously," said Brewers general manager Jim Baumer.⁴

Moore caught through August 1975, then played left field through May 1976, moved there to cover for injuries in the outfield. "Then, too, there is the fact that Charlie is hitting the ball," said manager Del Crandall. "He has some speed and is an aggressive player."⁵

The Brewers resisted trade offers for their pair of young catchers. Moore worked out at second base in the instructional league after the 1975 season. They were surprised by his outstanding play there as well as at catcher, third base, and right field.

In 1976 Moore batted a disappointing .191 with 3 home runs and 16 RBIs in 87 games, suffering through several minor injuries. New Brewers manager Alex Grammas benched him, sending him back to backing up Porter. Despite his difficulties, on October 3 at Milwaukee County Stadium, he was part of a historic moment as the last runner batted in by Hank Aaron, crossing the plate on Aaron's sixth-inning single in the Brewers' 5-2 loss to the Detroit Tigers.

The Brewers finished a disappointing 66-95 in 1976. Grammas had replaced Crandall as manager in 1976 with a reputation of being a better motivator of players, but his first season was rancorous and led to the exit of some veteran players. Porter was included in a trade to the Kansas City Royals with the promise that Moore was ready to become the full-time catcher, backed up by Larry Haney. Brewers pitcher Bill Travers opined after the deal, "Porter probably had more potential, but Charlie Moore called a better game. He mixed his calls a lot more. Darrell might have been afraid to call for my forkball when I had a good one going because he thought it would bounce off his glove."⁶

After backing up All-Star Ted Simmons in 1981, Charlie Moore moved from behind the plate to the outfield in 1982. He started all 12 games of the '82 postseason as the right fielder, going 15-for-39 (.385).

After the 1976 season, Moore once again played winter ball, this time alongside Brewers teammates Jim Gantner and Tim Johnson with the Zulia club in Venezuela. As the team gathered for spring training in 1977, Moore was rewarded with a new two-year contract.

"You know when they asked me to sign at the end of last year," said Moore, "I told them I'd wait and see what happens. If they had kept Darrell, I would have asked to be traded or played out my option."⁷

The 1977 season was disappointing for the Brewers and unsettling for Moore, and cost Grammas his job. Moore caught in 137 games (116 as the starting catcher) and batted .248, an improvement over the previous year but far below expectations. On his way out the door, Grammas suggested that a change might be needed behind the plate, and Moore said he had the feeling "that I'm available for trade."⁸ He said he was happy in Milwaukee, but he was not interested in going back to being a backup catcher.

He returned in 1978 to find that he was one of seven catchers on the Brewers spring-training roster. Harry Dalton, the new general manager, identified newly signed free agent Ray Fosse as number one. Besides Fosse, Moore had to contend with the others Dalton had assembled — Buck Martinez, Andy Etchebarren, Larry Haney, Ned Yost, and Ron Jacobs.

But Fosse's time with the Brewers virtually ended during spring training when he tripped in a hole while running down the first-base line and injured his right leg. Reconstruction of a knee ligament forced him to miss the entire season.

Buck Martinez emerged as the starter, but in 1978 Moore hit better in a reserve role and new manager George Bamberger brought the team new magic as Bambi's Bombers. The team finished third in a tough division with 93-69 record. Moore caught 95 games and began a successful professional relationship with newly arrived left-handed pitcher Mike Caldwell.

Although Moore was never identified as Caldwell's personal catcher, they always seemed to form a battery in their years with the Brewers. They started 28 times together in 1978, Caldwell's first year with the team, even though Moore had only 74 starts at catcher. In 1979 Moore caught 89 games and Caldwell was the starter in 30 of them. And in 29 of Moore's 77 starts at catcher in 1980, Caldwell was the starting pitcher.[9]

In 1979 Moore, after signing another multiyear contract, shared considerable time behind the plate with Buck Martinez, with a few appearances by Fosse. His playing time and productivity had steadily increased, as he appeared in 138 games in 1977 (batting .248), 96 games in 1978 (batting .269), and 111 games in both 1979 and 1980 (batting .300 and .291). In 1979, he and Martinez were both hitting for high average with Moore peaking at .377 at midseason.

"A lot of people ask me, 'Who is your number-one catcher?'" manager George Bamberger said in 1980. "I don't have a number-one catcher. They are both number one."[10] Moore recovered from knee surgery for torn ligaments in the offseason and again shared time with Martinez in 1980. Remarkably, batting ninth on October 1, 1980, in a Brewers 10-7 win over the California Angels, he hit for the cycle and had two stolen bases in the same game.

Then GM Dalton made a deal for Ted Simmons (along with relief ace Rollie Fingers) before the 1981 season in a trade thought to establish the team firmly as a contender. Moore's response endeared him to the Brewers fans: "I had always done what the organization told me to do. Whatever I can do to help the team win, that's what I try to do, in whatever role they want me to play."[11] During the strike-shortened 1981 season, Moore played in 48 games, batting a career-high .301. In addition to 34 games behind the plate, he also appeared in the outfield and as designated hitter. And he played right field in the playoffs against the Yankees.

During the 1981 season the Brewers signed Moore to a new five-year contract that made him one of the highest-paid catchers in the majors. He had been eligible for free agency at the end of the season, the players strike was looming, and he faced an uncertain future backing up Simmons. Columnist Peter Gammons gave credit to Moore: "How many players can catch, play two outfield positions and third base, hit one-two in the order, run and hit .300? He's more valuable than his physical skills which is why he is getting paid the way he is."[12]

Even the new contract did not seem to be a guarantee of playing time, and there were reports that the Moore had asked to be traded, but by the end of spring training was assured that he had a clear shot at earning the starting job in right field. Moving him to the outfield in 1982 was a surprise to some, who expected Paul Molitor to finally find a permanent role there for the Brewers. Instead, Molitor eased Don Money into sharing time at designated hitter, and took over at third base.

The transition was not easy, and some joked that Moore seemed to be playing right field in self-defense. In spring training in 1982, he complained about his playing time. He suffered a muscle tear in his rib cage, preventing him from taking the field. "I was supposed to be given a shot in right field," he said, "but as of now I've hardly played there."[13]

Mark Brouhard was actually thought to be the right fielder at the end of spring training. Moore found himself platooning with Marshall Edwards and stressing at the plate. After hitting .283 in April, he slumped to .203 in May and .200 in June. Despite a boost to a .324 average in July, he got only 59 at-bats in August and hit .169.

In mid-August, Dalton and manager Harvey Kuenn met with Moore. "They told me they knew I was pressing, struggling, putting too much pressure on myself," said Moore in October. "They said, 'You have nothing to prove to us. You've done it in the past. You're part of the club. We know you can play. Don't worry about anything.' That was the turning point. That helped me a lot. It took a lot off my mind."[14]

Moore ended the season with a .254 average but was strong in September, hitting .308. Along with Robin Yount and Molitor, Moore showed speed on defense and the bases. By the end of the season he considered himself a right fielder. "People assume we're like nine lumberjacks dragging our bats up there, and we take three swings trying to hit the ball out of the ballpark," said Ted Simmons of the Brewers' glory years. "We have our guys — Molitor, Yount, Moore and Jim Gantner — who can do a lot of interesting things."[15]

While national television commentators debated his shift to the outfield during the 1982 playoffs and World Series, Moore was 6-for-13 (.462) in the American League Championship Series against the California Angels. Moore then hit .346 (9-for-26) with three doubles and two RBIs in the 1982 World Series, which the Brewers lost to the St Louis Cardinals in seven games.

Moore had perhaps his best season in 1983 when he had 605 plate appearances, by far the most in his career. Even after Simmons's catching days virtually ended that season, Moore did not take a regular role behind the plate until 1985. He continue to play in right field during the next two seasons; in 1983 he played in a career-high 151 games, batting .284, but in 1984 he played in just 70 games while batting .234. He became part of a right-field platoon with Dion James, and went on the disabled list for the first time in his major-league career. By midseason James was playing everyday.

During his final two seasons with Milwaukee, Moore returned to catching, playing in 105 games and batting .232 in 1985, largely because of an injury to starter Bill Schroeder, and playing in 80 games and batting .260 in 1986.

In November 1986 Moore became a free agent. The Brewers had put him on the field for the ninth inning of the last home game of season so that he could get one final at-bat with the team. He was now among the rare players to have spent more than a decade with one team. Although Dalton advised him to pursue free agency, the Brewers offered him a one-year contract, but with a significant pay cut. Moore called the offer "disgusting and insulting."[16]

Writer Peter Gammons recounted Moore's frustration as his career ended as a Type-B free agent during the collusion era of 1987. No team had been willing to give up a first-round draft choice for a 33-year-old catcher. Gammons wrote, "Former Brewers catcher Charlie Moore knew that no major league team would sign him until after the June draft, when no compensation would be needed. So he hooked up with the San Jose Bees. The airplane ticket the Bees sent him put him the middle seat between two enormous women. After renting a car and driving to his first workout, he took the field and was immediately hit in the knee by a line drive. Informed that there was no trainer around, Moore drove to a 7-Eleven and bought five bags of ice for his knee. When he returned to the car, the battery was dead."[17]

Moore eventually joined the Toronto Blue Jays. As a backup catcher for Ernie Whitt, he appeared in 51 games with the Blue Jays, batting .215 with one home run and seven RBIs. Toronto released him in November, bringing his career to a close.

In March 1988 Moore was one of the pallbearers — along with Gorman Thomas, Pete Vuckovich,

Robin Yount, Paul Molitor, and Jim Gantner — at the funeral of the Brewers' inspirational manager in 1982, Harvey Kuenn. Fans noted that Yount, Molitor, and Gantner were the only remaining players from the 1982 team on the Brewers spring-training roster.[18]

Moore and his wife, Lynn, lived in the Milwaukee suburb of Greendale in his playing days with the Brewers, but returned to Alabama with their three sons. For more than 15 years, Moore worked as a sales representative for a fastener company in Birmingham. His father and other members of his family were close by.

Fans warmly welcomed Moore when the 1982 team returned to Milwaukee in 2002 for a 20th-anniversary reunion.

In 2014 Moore was one of 58 Brewers inducted as a member of the Wall of Honor in Miller Park. He was one of three members of the All-Time Alabama Baseball Team in the group, along with Hank Aaron and Don Sutton. The Wall of Honor is open to Brewers who had at least 2,000 plate appearances, at least 1,000 innings pitched or 250 pitching appearances, won a major award, managed a pennant winner, earned induction into the Baseball Hall of Fame, or been honored with a statue outside Miller Park.[19]

SOURCES

In addition to the works cited in the Notes, the author also consulted BaseballReference.com, Retrosheet.org, and the following:

Okrent, Dan. *Nine Innings* (New York: Houghton Mifflin Company, 1985).

Schroeder, Bill, and Drew Olson, *If These Walls Could Talk: Milwaukee Brewers* (Chicago: Triumph Books, 2016).

NOTES

1 "Moore Follows His Father in Solid Triplets Debut," *The Sporting News*, August 4, 1973: 40.

2 Ibid.

3 "Face of the Franchise: 1983," *Brew Crew Ball*, September 9, 2013, brewcrewball.com/2013/9/9/4710890/face-of-the-franchise-1983.

4 Lou Chapman "Pressure to Be Name of Brewer Game," *The Sporting News*, March 8, 1975: 22.

5 Lou Chapman, "Moore Doing His Catching as Brewers' New Outfielder," *The Sporting News*, September 27, 1975: 19.

6 Lou Chapman, "Scott's Exit to Aid Brewers – Travers," *The Sporting News*, January 29, 1977: 33.

7 Lou Chapman, "Mitt Post Delights Brewers Moore," *The Sporting News*, March 19, 1977: 40.

8 Lou Chapman, "Brewers Tap Vet Fosse to Help Young Hurlers," *The Sporting News*, December 29, 1977: 57/62.

9 Michael Mavrogiannis, "Excruciating Baseball Lists – Personal Catchers," members.tripod.com/bb_catchers/catchers/perscatch.htm.

10 Tom Flaherty, "Buck Is Settling in with Brewers," *The Sporting News*, July 5, 1980: 21.

11 *Brew Crew Ball*.

12 Peter Gammons, "Goryl and Fregosi? Typical Fall Guys," *The Sporting News*, June 13, 1981: 16.

13 UPI Archives, "Milwaukee Brewers Reserve Catcher Charlie Moore, Who Had Complained...," March 25, 1982.

14 Tom Flaherty, "Moore Earning Brewer Praise," *The Sporting News*, October 4, 1982: 25.

15 Doug Feldman, *Whitey Herzog Builds a Winner: The St. Louis Cardinals 1978-1982* (Jefferson, North Carolina: McFarland, 2018), 191.

16 Associated Press, "Charlie Moore, Brewers Part Ways," *Green Bay Press-Gazette*, December 8, 1986: B-10.

17 Peter Gammons, "Peter Gammon's Midseason Baseball Report," *Sports Illustrated*, July 20, 1987.

18 UPI Archives, "Former Milwaukee Brewers Manager Harvey Kuenn Was Remembered Thursday," March 3, 1988.

19 Mark Inabinett, "Three State Baseball Greats Part of New Milwaukee Brewers Wall of Honor," AL.com, June 14, 2014. al.com/sports/index.ssf/2014/06/three_state_baseball_greats_pa.html.

BEN OGLIVIE

By Jay Hurd

Benjamin Ambrosio (Palmer) Oglivie was born in Colòn, Panama, on Friday, February 11, 1949. He was born into a Panama which offered certain privilege and opportunity, fed by the construction, completion, and use of the Panama Canal. Additionally, the post-World War II era affirmed a sense of optimism. Prior to 1949, the founders of the Panamanian Republic had passed legislation which provided for universal public education. This led to a very high literacy rate for all Panamanians over the age of 10 and encouraged talented, educated Panamanian youths to attend college abroad. These students were expected to return to Panama to foster strong political and cultural progress in a country long plagued by unrest and ignorance. By 1935, a University of Panama had evolved from newly created colleges and institutes. Ben Oglivie, unaware, of course, that he was born into a Panama where education and personal development were priorities, would attend schools, study music, ponder philosophy, play soccer, and hone a baseball talent.

Colòn and Panama had not always been a land of opportunity and relative optimism; nor would this sense prevail throughout Ben's young life. First explored by Columbus and Balboa in the early 16th century, the potential of the land which would become known as Central America — and specifically the land which would be called Colòn, Panama — could not be overlooked. However, malaria, yellow fever, poisonous reptiles, torrential rains, and a literally toxic atmosphere earned the region its "pest hole of the Universe" sobriquet.

As centuries passed and explorers grew bolder, the governments of numerous countries — including Spain, Colombia, France, the United Kingdom, and the United States — pressed to create a link, across the region, from the Atlantic Ocean to the Pacific Ocean. The first such connection would not occur until the 1840s to 1850s when the American, William Henry Aspinwall, led construction of the Panamanian Railroad. The California Gold Rush of 1849 spurred construction and successful completion of the railroad. The impact of this enterprise was great — not only did it create and support commercial enterprise, but also its construction demanded a large labor force. This labor force grew out of an immigrant population, including those of Afro-Antillean heritage (descendants of African slaves and people of the West Indies). It in this important immigrant subculture that Ben Oglivie finds his ancestry.

In the late 18th to early 19th centuries, also employing a substantial immigrant work force, the French would attempt to create the second significant connection — a sea level canal —

between the Atlantic and Pacific. The French did not succeed. However, the failure of the French did inspire a treaty between Colombia and the United States, leading to the construction of the Panama Canal. The treaty, the management of disease, and a strong work force changed Panama, and not all for the good. The Canal brought prosperity to the region, but it could not eliminate the political and social dissatisfaction which ultimately fostered violent riots. An unstable government, in addition to the untimely death of his father, led Ben Oglivie and his family to the United States, New York City, and Major League Baseball.

In 1967, 53 years after the *S.S. Ancon* became the first ship to pass, officially, through the Panama Canal, from Colòn (on the Atlantic) to Panama City (on the Pacific), Ben Oglivie left Panama for New York City. Ben's father, a ship oiler, had died and his family chose an assumed prosperity in the United States over a life of poverty and uncertainty in Panama. His older sister, one of six brothers and sisters, already living in The Bronx welcomed him and the family.

In The Bronx, Ben attended Theodore Roosevelt High School (somewhat ironic given President Theodore Roosevelt's influence in construction of the Panama Canal). Ben's transition to life in the United States was aided by his intelligence, education, and athletic abilities. Consistent with his desire for education and personal development, he "thought the best way to learn the language [English] was to read a lot of books. Big books, not funny books."[1] In 1967, Major League Baseball was not yet an option. After graduation from high school, he planned to study electrical engineering at Bronx Community College. This plan shifted when, in 1968, his baseball skills were noticed by "a bird dog named Al Harper."[2] Harper contacted Francis "Bots" Nekola, a Red Sox scout who had signed Carl Yastrzemski 10 years earlier, and suggested he have a look at Ben. Nekola watched Ben, met with the Oglivie family — "… the most wonderful family… "[3] and proceeded to press Haywood Sullivan, then Personnel Director for the Boston Red Sox, to

After co-leading the AL with 41 home runs in 1980, Ben Oglivie smashed 34 homers in 1982. The Panama-born Oglivie was a three-time All-Star and hit 235 round-trippers in his 16-year big-league career (1971-1986).

sign him. Ben Oglivie was drafted by the Boston Red Sox in the 11th round of the June 1968 free agent draft.

Consistent with much of baseball's history and mythology, to pinpoint precisely how and when baseball was first played in Panama is not probable. It is believed that baseball may have been introduced in Panama as early as 1855 when Americans, working on the Panamanian Railroad, played baseball. It is known that baseball became more popular in Panama during the early 1900s; and, by 1945, the Professional Baseball League of Panama was organized. Humberto Robinson (also of Afro-Antillean descent) and Hector Lopez are identified as the first Panamanians to be signed, in 1955, by major-league clubs. Ben Oglivie was one of the first 15 Panamanian ball players to reach the major leagues.

Ben, who threw left and batted left, stood 6'2" and weighed 170 pounds, began his professional career with the Jamestown (NY) Falcons of the New York-Penn League. In Jamestown, Ben shared first base responsibility with Cecil Cooper (also signed in 1968). Cecil Cooper thought that Ben was the new batboy — "He was that small."[4] Ben would not return to the minor leagues until 1989 when, at age 40, he attempted a return to the big leagues. His career with the Boston Red Sox ran from September 1971 to October 1973. In 1969, Oglivie shifted from first base to the outfield with the Greenville (SC) Red Sox of the Western Carolinas League. He was sent to the Winter Haven (FL) Red Sox of the Florida State League late that season having batted .317, with a .463 slugging percentage in 106 games. The 1970 season saw Ben with the Pawtucket (RI) Red Sox of the AA Eastern League. He did not hit well, batting only .233, but he played well enough to be sent, in 1971, to the AAA International League Louisville (KY) Colonels. With the Colonels, Ben batted .304, slugging .498; this earned him a September 1971 call-up by the parent team in Boston

According to Larry Doby, who had managed Ben in the Venezuelan league during the winter of 1972, Ben "does all five things… he can hit, run, field, throw and hit for power…"[5]

Doby expected Oglivie to be a star in the major leagues. Red Sox management did not necessarily agree.

He played in 14 games for the Sox in 1971 and was invited to report to spring training in Winter Haven in 1972. Four games into the spring season, Ben was sent to Hahnemann Hospital in Brighton, MA to be examined for a possible heart condition. After three days of cardiograms and other tests, he was given a "clean bill of health" and returned to spring training. Although he played with the Boston club during the regular season in 1972, he was not an everyday player, completing the season with a .241 average in 94 games.

In 1973, Ben again joined the Sox in Winter Haven for spring training. He performed very well, but another right fielder, Dwight Evans, was likely to be named the starter in April. Eddie Kasko, Red Sox manager, said of Ben that he "has tremendous value coming off the bench. But I want to give Evans a good shot." Ben had batted .362 in Winter Haven (highest average for the Sox in spring training that year), but Dwight Evans won the job as starter in right field.

Ben played in only 58 games in 1973, with sporadic starts. In May 1973, he hit at a .441 pace and started in place of the slumping Evans. In spite of this performance, Sox management felt Ben was, at best, a platoon player; his ungainly play — sporting long arms and skinny legs — in the outfield, which had earned him the nickname Spiderman, did not help. In September 1973, in one of his final plate appearances, Ben hit the gamewinning home run, in the 12th inning, off Jim Palmer of the Baltimore Orioles. Anti-climactically, in October 1973, Ben was traded to the Detroit Tigers for an aging Dick McAuliffe.

For Ben Oglivie, coming to the Red Sox when he did, baseball was "a sometime thing" — the Sox outfield of Carl Yastrzemski, Reggie Smith, and Dwight Evans certainly reduced his playing time. Eddie Kasko suggested that Ben might see more at-bats with the introduction of the designated hitter rule in 1972, but this was not to be. To some, Ben did not play with enough passion. In his June 8, 1981 article for *Sports Illustrated*, Steve Wulf states:

"Ironically, Oglivie was trapped in one of baseball's subtle prejudices. Latin American ballplayers are expected to be hot-tempered; if they're not, it must mean they don't care. 'People think Rod Carew is lazy,' says Oglivie. 'I look at him and see great intensity.'"[6]

Demonstrating propensity for thinking things through and yearning to understand, Ben said: "When I first came up, I was just happy to be there.

I figured I'd just wait my turn. My turn never came. I'd play two games, and then I was back on the bench again. I couldn't comprehend that."[7]

Ben Oglivie was, apparently, the only player the Sox were willing to trade for Dick McAuliffe. Ben began his playing time with the Tigers in 1974, at the age of 25.

Ben spent four seasons with the Tigers, 1974-1977; each season brought more playing time, but management would make no guarantees for a regular starting role. Tigers management regarded his fielding weak. As noted in Steve Wulf's article, Ben philosophically remarked:

"My weakness was not fielding. My weakness was not playing. And, personally, I think the author of the platoon system was a guy who couldn't hit lefthanders. But after a while you begin to believe these guys who are supposed to be the authorities. For a time I really believed that I couldn't field and I couldn't hit lefties."

While newspapers included reports that "Ben Oglivie virtually guaranteed himself a starting job for next year [1975] with his performances during the final two months [of the 1974 season],"[8] lack of playing frustrated and confused Ben. However, as noted in the *Baseball: The Biographic Encyclopedia*, Ben was an "intelligent, bookish man who read philosophy, he attended four colleges and studied Zen Buddhism because, he said, it merges into one with sports. He would let the game come to him."

In 1977, Ben — still uncertain regarding his role with the Tigers — became a focus not for his playing, but for his not playing, and for his unique approach to life. With the Tigers, Ben became known as "Banana Man" after third base coach, Joe Schultz, watched Ben eat one banana after another during a road trip. Ben became neither bitter nor angry about such a nickname or his lack of playing time — he said "that is not my style." Rather, he was able to focus on philosophy as a means to a "better perspective" on life, and on playing time. Ben had four seasons with the Tigers; and, although showing improvement each year — manager Ralph Houk noted he had "never seen a guy improve as much as he has, at his age"[9] — another trade came his way. His career with the Tigers ended after the 1977 season with an overall batting average of .276, a slugging percentage of .439, and 45 home runs. He would take his increasing power, and improved fielding to the Milwaukee Brewers, having been traded for pitchers Jim Slaton and Rich Folkers.

At age 29, Ben began his first of nine seasons with the Brewers in 1978. Immediately, Ben worked with Frank Howard, then a coach, to improve his unorthodox (Spiderman) fielding — "Day in and day out he'd hit fly balls to me in the outfield."[10] He began work with Nautilus equipment to increase his strength. As his play improved, his personal life became more serene. Cecil Cooper, now a teammate in Milwaukee, introduced him to attorney Tony Pennacchia, who would walk him through a divorce from his first wife. That same season, Ben met his second wife, Tammy Hunsinger, in Mesa, Arizona, near the Brewers spring training facility. Attorney Pennacchia said that Ben's "marriage to Tammy turned his career around. I think Ben was finally able to find peace with himself."[11]

In 1978, Ben led the Brewers in batting with a .303 average. However, his overall play remained, according to Brewers management, suspect. Had it not been for a teammate's misfortune, Ben may very well have been, again, a platoon player. Early in the 1979 season, veteran outfielder Larry Hisle suffered a torn rotator cuff; opportunity had come Ben's way. Hisle, "honored to have him [Ben] as a teammate"[12] graciously accepted this turn of events and saw Ben take over as the regular left fielder. In 1979, manager Buck Rodgers regarded Ben's only fault to be his inability to slide — this could be seen as praise to a player who had been, at best, a platoon fielder and pinch hitter.

In 1980, Ben started the first 9 games of the season, a circumstance which thrilled him; he had never started that many games consecutively. Demonstrating power at the plate, speed, and skill in the outfield and on the base paths, and a continuous introspection, 1980 would be the best of his 16 seasons in the major leagues. That season Ben earned yet another nickname — "philosopher-home run king."[13] He hit 41 home runs that year, had 118 RBIs, hit .304 overall, and had a .563 slugging percentage.

While Ben and Reggie Jackson, of the New York Yankees, both hit 41 home runs that season, Ben was the first foreign-born player to win a home run crown in the major leagues. This was also a season in which Gorman Thomas, Cecil Cooper, and Ben Oglivie each had more than 100 RBIs. Cooper, who hit .352 that season, said that "I've never seen a season like Benji [another nickname] had."[14] This was also the season Ben would grow his first moustache, noting the changing times, and he said it would likely take an 0-for-30 string to make him shave it.

Ben had come into his own with the Milwaukee Brewers — he was an everyday player, a "complete ballplayer". He was a three-time American League All-Star (1980, 1982, and 1983), a home run leader (1980), and a Silver Slugger Award winner (1980). He was an important component of his team in 1981 when the Brewers competed in the AL Division Series (lost series, 3-2) and in 1982 when the Brewers went to the World Series (lost series 4-3). Although he would not duplicate his All-Star seasons, he would finish his AL career with the Brewers.

Ben completed his nine-year career with the Brewers after the 1986 season when he hit a mere five home runs and batted .283. Desiring to remain in baseball, he played two seasons, 1987 and 1988, with the Osaka Kintetsu Buffaloes of the Japan Pacific League. In his two seasons in Japan, he hit 46 home runs (24 in 1987, 22 in 1988) and maintained .300 average. In 1989, at age 40, Ben returned to the United States and signed a minor-league contract with the El Paso Diablos, a Milwaukee Brewers affiliate, of the Texas League. However, a return to the Major Leagues, as a player, was not meant to be. A knee injury limited him to only two games with the Diablos and he finished his stint with 10 plate appearances, and three hits, one of which was a home run.

Ben continued to play baseball with the Winter Haven Super Sox of the short-lived Senior Professional Baseball Association. This team included Cecil Cooper, Ferguson Jenkins, Bernie Carbo, Butch Hobson, and Bill Lee, who was also the club's manager. However, Ben's time with this team was brief, as the Super Sox ceased operations after its first season.

Oglivie stayed away from baseball for only a few years, as he returned to the Brewers organization to work as a hitting coach with Class-A and Class-AA ball. He developed coaching skills and was named, in 1995, hitting coach for the Calgary Cannons (Alberta, Canada) of the Pacific Coast League. His career as hitting coach continued in 1999 with the Hickory Crawdads (NC) of the South Atlantic League. After a season as hitting coach with the major-league San Diego Padres in 2000, Ben returned to coaching for minor-league teams, including: Idaho Falls (ID) Padres (2001), Eugene (OR) Emeralds (2003-2005), Vero Beach (FL) Devil Rays (2007), Montgomery (AL) Biscuits (2008), and the Gulf Coast (FL) Rays (2009). And, in 2010, now age 61, Ben Oglivie was named hitting coach of the Detroit Tigers' Class A affiliate West Michigan Whitecaps.

Benjamin Ambrosio (Palmer) Oglivie, a.k.a. Gentle Ben, Benji, Spiderman, Banana Man, Philosopher-Home Run King, is a study in baseball and philosophy. His quiet and cerebral manner, his sometimes unpredictable play in the outfield, his healthy eating habits, his quick wrists and powerful swing all make up the man. Some of Ben's teammates noted that 24 hours was inadequate for all that he wanted to accomplish. Some, like Mark "The Bird" Fidrych, thought Oglivie "was crazy". One morning, during spring training with the Tigers, Fidrych awoke to the sound of philosophy "spouting"[15] from Ben's tape recorder.

In addition to working diligently to improve his game, he found time to feed his thirst for knowledge by attending four different colleges — in New York, Bronx Community College; in Boston, Northeastern University; in Detroit, Wayne State

University; and in Milwaukee, the University of Wisconsin. In his book, *The Wrong Stuff*, Bill Lee, a teammate with the Red Sox, remembers Ben:

"He was a tall, wiry left handed hitter with all kinds of power and good speed in the outfield. Ben faked a lot of people out. They heard he was from Colon, Panama, and assumed he would have difficulty speaking English. So on first meeting they would talk to him very slowly and in a loud voice, using many hand gestures. It was a riot, because the first thing I noticed about him was his ability to complete the "New York Times" crossword puzzle in about five minutes. He did not have an accent, but he was the brightest guy on the club and had hardly any trouble understanding anybody who didn't stick his hand in Ben's face while they spoke."

In another interview, Bill Lee suggests that Ben "should have become a GM."[16]

Ben played 16 years in the major leagues, played in 1,754 games, and in 5,913 at-bats achieved a total of 235 home runs, a .273 average, and a .450 slugging percentage. At age 17, he had lost his father and left a country which had been struggling with political unrest. He had been traded twice because team management regarded him as a good player off the bench. He often hit very well in spring training, only to be told he did not have a starting job. He was seen as dispassionate in his play. Despite setbacks, using his favorite philosophers — Plato, Jean Jacques Rousseau, Henry David Thoreau, and Bruce Lee — as guides, Ben waited for the game to come to him, and it did.

SOURCES

Baseball Almanac. http://www.baseball-almanac.com/

BaseballLibrary.com. http://www.baseballlibrary.com/homepage/

Baseball-Reference.com. http://www.baseball-reference.com/

History of Colòn, Panama. http://www.coloncity.com/history1.html

Fitzgerald, Ray. "Ben Oglivie Finds Stardom in Another Uniform." *Baseball Digest*, September 1980, 39: no.9. [online] http://books.google.com/books

Maisel, Ivan. 22 *Brewers*. SI Vault. 1985 [online]. http://sportsillustrated.cnn.com/vault/article/magazine/MAG1119345/index...

The New York Times. Sports People: Baseball: Oglivie in Class AA.

The Silver People Heritage Foundation. http://thesilverpeopleheritage.wordpress.com/

Wulf, Steve. *Swingo, Ergo Su: So Ben Oglivie, the philosopher-home run king of baseball, seems to be saying with his bat.* SI Vault. http://sportsillustrated.cnn.com/vault/article/magazine/MAG1124537/index.htm. 1981 .

Ben Oglivie. Folder: Newspaper Clippings. A. Bartlett Giamatti Research Center. National Baseball Hall of Fame and Museum. Cooperstown, NY.

Lee, Bill with Dick Lally. *The Wrong Stuff*. (New York: The Viking Press, 1984).

Okrent, Daniel. *Nine Innings*. (New York: McGraw-Hill Book Company, 1985).

Palmer, Peter and Gary Gillette, ed. *The 2006 ESPN Baseball Encyclopedia*. (New York: Sterling Publishing Co., Inc., 2006).

Pietrusza, David, Matthew Silverman, and Michael Gershman. *Baseball: The Biographical Encyclopedia*. (Kingston, NY: Total/Sports Illustrated, 2000).

Wolf, Rick et al. *The Baseball Encyclopedia*. 8th ed. (New York: MacMillan Publishing Company, 1990).

NOTES

1. Steve Wulf, "Swingo, Ergo Sum," *Sports Illustrated*, SI Vault http://sportsillustrated.cnn.com/vault/article/magazine/MAG1124537/index.htm. 1981.
2. Ibid.
3. Ibid.
4. Ibid.
5. Ben Oglivie. Folder: Newspaper Clippings. A. Bartlett Giamatti Research Center. National Baseball Hall of Fame and Museum
6. Wulf.
7. Ben Oglivie. Folder.
8. Ibid.
9. Ibid.
10. Ibid.
11. Wulf.
12. Ben Oglivie. Folder.
13. Wulf.
14. Ben Oglivie. Folder.
15. Ibid.
16. Baseball Almanac. http://www.baseball-almanac.com/.

ROB PICCIOLO

By John Gabcik

Rob Picciolo sat in the Milwaukee Brewers dugout in the early summer of 1982, watching Robin Yount and Jim Gantner execute another double play. The smooth coordination of the two fielders told Picciolo what he already knew: Barring an injury, he wouldn't be needed in the Brewers' middle infield any time soon.

Picciolo (pronounced \PEACH-uh-lo\) had been traded to the Brewers by his original team, the Oakland Athletics, in his sixth major-league season. As a rookie in 1977, Picciolo had been the A's everyday shortstop, but year by year his time on the field had eroded, down to 195 plate appearances in 1981. Now, with the Brewers, he would be an insurance policy, along with fellow sub Eddie Romero, for Yount and Gantner. Otherwise, Picciolo was an adept utility player who could carry a glove to most any position on the field, and perform without embarrassment. Picciolo's patience and willingness to study the game he loved were the qualities that would blend him into a skillful coach and mentor in the future.

"People think it's hard playing behind Robin, but it's really not," Picciolo told Bob Verdi of the *Chicago Tribune*. "It would be a lot harder if I were playing behind somebody who wasn't as talented or wasn't as devoted. I wouldn't say I'm in awe of Robin. I just totally respect the man."[1] So Picciolo sat, waited, watched — and learned.

Robert Michael Picciolo was born to Angelo and Rose Marie (Paone) Picciolo on February 4, 1953, in Santa Monica, California. The couple had one other child, Bruce, who was two years older than Robert. Angelo was a veteran of World War II who went to work for the Hyatt Regency hotel system after the service. Robert (Rob) attended Westchester High School, where he was all-league in baseball, batting .403, and also played basketball. Graduating from Westchester, he moved on to Santa Monica Junior College, where again he played both varsity sports. He became the first Santa Monica College baseball player to be named Athlete of the Year in 1973, batting .323 as a sophomore.[2]

Major-league franchises were very interested in Picciolo and his skills as a second baseman, but he proved to be an elusive target to sign. He was drafted by the San Francisco Giants in the second round of the amateur draft on January 10, 1973, but did not sign. He was drafted again on June 5 in the fourth round of the secondary draft, this time by the Kansas City Royals; he did not sign, but opted to continue his education at Pepperdine University in Malibu, California.

Pepperdine, under Coach Wayne Wright, had had a losing season in 1973, but Picciolo and his teammates brought success to the Waves the following year. The team had a 37-10 record, was the West Coast Athletic Conference champion, and beat Southern Cal, 4-2, in an NCAA District 8 playoff game before faltering. Wright had moved Picciolo from second base to shortstop; he led the team in doubles, stolen bases, and sacrifice flies, and was named to the All-District team. In 1982 Picciolo was named to the Pepperdine Athletic Hall of Fame.

In June of 1974, the Detroit Tigers made Picciolo the sixth pick of the first round — but he still no didn't sign as he continued his studies at Pepperdine into his senior year.

Finally, on January 9, 1975, the Oakland Athletics signed Picciolo in the first round of the January secondary draft. The Athletics had just won their third consecutive World Series, but all was not well with the franchise. Players like Reggie Jackson, Sal Bando, Joe Rudi, and Catfish Hunter were demanding pay increases to match their success, and not getting them. Athletics owner Charlie Finley was disinclined to throw his money around, and his franchise coffers were not as deep as you might expect. Despite their success, Oakland's star players had done little to endear themselves to the community, and the A's attendance barely reached a million once in the three championship seasons. Finley was either trading or not re-signing his players, opening the door to Picciolo and his fellow prospects.

Along with the obligations of his baseball contract, Picciolo was able to complete his education at Pepperdine, graduating that June with a bachelor's degree in journalism. That spring (1975), Picciolo reported to the Birmingham Barons of the Double-A Southern League, where he was the regular shortstop throughout the year, batting .277 with little power, but some ability to steal a base; he was named to the Southern League All-Star team at the end of the season. The next season the Athletics moved him up to manager Harry Bright's Tucson Toros of the Triple-A Pacific Coast League. Again, he would be the team's everyday shortstop, replacing veteran Tommy Sandt, who had joined the St. Louis Cardinals organization. Picciolo's batting average rose to .298; as at Birmingham, a promising trend. On November 1, 1976, longtime Oakland star shortstop Bert Campaneris was granted free agency; it was time for Picciolo to graduate to the majors. His initial salary was $20,000.[3]

That same winter, on January 29, 1977, Picciolo married Debra Gelderman, also a Pepperdine graduate. The couple had two sons, Breton, born in 1983 and Dustin (1986), both of whom became future Pepperdine graduates.

Picciolo at 6-feet-2 and 180 pounds, made his major-league debut on April 9, 1977, in Oakland as the starting shortstop against the Minnesota Twins; the Athletics won, 7-4, Picciolo going hitless in four at-bats. Two days later, on April 11, he beat out an infield single to California Angels shortstop Bobby Grich for his first major-league hit; Nolan Ryan was the pitcher. Then, on April 15, Picciolo hit his first major-league home run, a fifth-inning solo shot off Paul Thormodsgard of the Minnesota Twins. The milestone that was more of a challenge was the first walk: Picciolo had 45 plate appearances without a base on balls before drawing a pass from White Sox pitcher Francisco Barrios on April 22.[4]

Charlie Finley liked to have nicknames for his players, perhaps because, like his gold-and-green uniforms, they gave his team color — and sold a few seats — without increasing Charlie's expenses. So Charlie decided Picciolo should be nicknamed Peach, perhaps hypnotizing fans into thinking of his shortstop in the same terms as Ty Cobb (the Georgia Peach) — a real stretch of the imagination.[5] The similarity to Cobb never materialized, but the name stuck.

Picciolo went on to start at shortstop in 137 of the Athletics' games that 1977 season, usually batting ninth in the order. The team started out with Jack McKeon as its manager, and did well for the first few weeks of the season; the new faces, Picciolo included, were surprising winners. But then reality dawned, the team started to lose, and McKeon was fired with a 26-27 record. Bobby Winkles became the manager, and the A's slipped to a seventh-place

Acquired in an early-season trade with the Oakland A's, infielder Rob Picciolo made just 23 plate appearances for the Brewers in 1982, though he scored seven runs. He batted .234 in parts of nine big-league seasons (1977-1985).

relegated to the bench, a utility infielder. The end result was that Picciolo rarely started a game, and was often pinch-hit for when he did. He finished the year with 98 plate appearances and a .226 batting average, also spending a portion of the season demoted to Triple-A Vancouver. The Athletics continued to stumble about, firing Winkles, and bringing McKeon back to manage.

Oakland opened 1979 with yet another managing change as Jim Marshall was hired to run the team. The A's lack of success would worsen as players became disenchanted, plagued by injuries and lack of fan support; any hope for a winning season was killed by a 5-24 record in June. Picciolo's career was given fresh air when Guerrero became susceptible to injury and dissatisfaction with his contract.[6] He had opportunities to take the place of Guerrero or others who were hurt, or whose eagerness to play was dampened by the team's losing attitude; he made the most of his chance that August.

Picciolo started 27 of the team's 29 games in August, playing shortstop, and also logging time at second and third. He batted .362 for the month, going 34-for-94, with eight multi-hit games. By the end of August, his batting average had climbed 45 points to .279. The Athletics had had their best month in a disastrous season, going 14-15, finishing with a 54-108 record. Picciolo had demonstrated his value. His .253 average at the end of the season was well under the league average of .270, but acceptable for the bottom of the batting order. And his versatility on defense was showing the league that he would be a valuable component on most rosters.

When Marshall stated in a postseason interview that Guerrero was still the team's shortstop, Picciolo disagreed with this decision. Referring to his 1979 performance, the usually unassuming Picciolo said, "This time I made use of the opportunity when it came. I showed I can do the job. I think I should be considered the No. 1 shortstop next spring."[7]

On the day before the A's opened their 1980 spring training, Finley fired Marshall and brought

finish, going 63-98 for the season. Picciolo's batting average stayed below .200, approaching the end of the season. A relatively robust 31-for-122 (.254) September raised his average; on the last day of the season, he went 3-for-5 against the Texas Rangers to reach .200 even.

In the spring of 1978 the Athletics sloughed off their remaining star from the championship teams — pitcher Vida Blue — to the San Francisco Giants in exchange for seven players, one of whom was shortstop Mario Guerrero. Guerrero had more major-league experience than Picciolo, and a batting average in the .270 range, and so Picciolo was in Billy Martin as manager; the results were impressive. The offense led by Rickey Henderson and Tony Armas, along with a determined five-man pitching rotation that completed 94 games, made the Athletics winners; they finished second in the American League West with an 83-79 record. Picciolo lost his shortstop's position back to Guerrero, who had regained his enthusiasm, but Martin switched Picciolo to second, where he got the majority of starts for the first three months of the season. "Billy is the manager. I'm happy he thinks I'm good enough to make the transition," Picciolo remarked.[8] Eventually, Picciolo shared time with Dave McKay, another light-hitting utilityman, but saw steady playing time throughout the year.

Over his career, Picciolo's reluctance to accept a base on balls had gained notoriety. In 1980, he had almost pulled off a totally walk-free season. Orioles manager Earl Weaver had cracked at midseason, "He must be leading the league in "off-base percentage."[9] On October 2, in Chicago, Picciolo faced Richard Dotson of the White Sox and drew his first walk of the season. In a spirit of good humor, the game was stopped, and the ball presented to Picciolo. The next batter, Rickey Henderson, made Dotson pay dearly, hitting a two-run homer into the upper deck in left. Picciolo walked again on October 5, the last game of the 1980 season.[10]

If Picciolo had a patsy in the American League, it was the White Sox. Over his career, the White Sox had walked Picciolo 10 times, giving him the only intentional base on balls in his nine-year career. A *Chicago Tribune* column once stated that the "book" on Picciolo was that he could not resist a slider into the dirt, but White Sox pitchers must not have heeded the advice.[11]

In 1981 Picciolo saw a reduction in plate appearances, from 281 down to 195, but a noticeable split in batting against left-handed pitchers. Overall, he had a .268 average, but against left-handers he batted a formidable .338. His OPS of .687 was the highest of his career. Much of the reduction in plate appearances was due to the Athletics' addition of Fred Stanley from the New York Yankees.[12]

The Athletics, under Martin, reached the playoffs, then swept the Kansas City Royals, three games to none, in the American League Division Series. Picciolo started the second game, hitting a single in three at-bats. Picciolo then started the first game of the Championship Series against the New York Yankees, again collecting a single; the Yankees won the series, three games to none.

As the 1982 season began, Picciolo was getting some starts, along with Stanley and Jimmy Sexton — but he was hitting a weak .224 in 52 plate appearances. Picciolo was traded by the Athletics to the Milwaukee Brewers on May 14, 1982; the Athletics received minor-league first baseman Johnny Evans and pitcher Mike Warren. Billy Martin respected Picciolo's value to the A's, and was upset: "I'm not happy about this one bit; I liked Picciolo so much. …"[13] The Brewers were looking for insurance to protect their World Series aspirations against the loss of one of their position players. "It became evident when Robin Yount got hurt that we needed another infielder. We wanted to get the best one available. We've always liked the way Picciolo played," said Brewers manager Buck Rodgers."[14] Picciolo had a pair of sure hands for multiple field positions, and he had developed as a threat to left-handed pitchers.

Two weeks after Picciolo became a Brewer, Rodgers was fired and replaced by Harvey Kuenn. For two seasons, Picciolo was treated the way any important insurance policy would be: kept in a safe place and, hopefully, not needed. Picciolo played in 36 games over the two-year period, making nine starts. Most often he was a late-game defensive change. He pinch-hit, pinch-ran, played shortstop, second, and third, and even got into a game at first base. He came to the plate a total of 53 times. Although he did not appear in a postseason game, his team got to the World Series, and he was an important element in the dugout and clubhouse.

After the 1983 season, Picciolo was released by the Brewers. Returning to West Coast, he signed a contract with the California Angels. The Angels were fifth in their division in 1983, and were opening 1984 with a talented rookie, Dick Schofield, as their new shortstop. Picciolo, a utilityman once again, was to back up Schofield, and plug other holes that emerged for manager John McNamara. Picciolo saw more action than he had with the Brewers, playing short, second, and third, even a game in the outfield; but his results at the plate were diminishing, a .202 batting average and no walks. Again he was released, then signed on February 5, 1985, by his original team, the Athletics, managed by Jackie Moore.

Picciolo had few opportunities to play for the A's until third baseman Carney Lansford fractured his wrist on a hit-by-pitch in late July, whereupon Picciolo became the best alternative off the bench. But the opportunity didn't work out. Picciolo's second game in Lansford's place found him grounding into an inning-ending double play with the bases loaded, stopping a sixth-inning rally, and then committing an error in the seventh that resulted in three unearned runs. The A's lost the game to the Brewers, 4-3.

In a postgame interview, Picciolo did not go easy on himself: "I hurt the club. It's just a shame it happened tonight because it makes Carney's injury look even worse. Exactly what I didn't want to happen, happened."[15] Shortly thereafter, the A's put Picciolo on the disabled list with a stomach ulcer; he did not play again until September 1. Picciolo appeared in games throughout September, but was never again penciled into the starting lineup. At the end of the season, he retired as a player; he had a .234 lifetime batting average with 17 home runs and 25 bases on balls.

Picciolo joined the San Diego Padres organization as a minor-league manager, directing the Spokane Indians of the Northwest League (Rookie; short-season Class A) for two seasons. After a 39-35 record in 1986, he led the Indians to the league championship with a 54-22 record; he was named Northwest League Manager of the Year. The Padres then reassigned him as a roving field instructor for two years before bringing him up to the Padres staff.

In June of 1990, Picciolo was made the Padres' first-base coach at midseason under new manager Greg Riddoch. Padres general manager Jim McIlvaine had asked Riddoch to retain one coach from the preceding regime in order to maintain continuity; Riddoch chose Picciolo. An unnamed Padres infielder remarked: "I can't believe how good he is. I've been in this game for a while, and he's the best I've seen."[16]

Picciolo was then the Padres' bench coach from 1993 to 2002, then third-base coach from 2003 to 2005. The Padres changed managers twice more during Picciolo's years, going to Jim Riggelman at the end of 1992, then to Bruce Bochy in 1995. He was fired after 20 seasons with the Padres.

Picciolo then signed with the California Angels to be the franchise's roving infield coordinator, a position he held for five years. On November 10, 2010, Picciolo was promoted by the Angels to become their bench coach, replacing Ron Roenicke, who had been hired by the Milwaukee Brewers as their manager. Picciolo remained in this position for three years under manager Mike Scioscia, but when California had a losing season in 2013, only their second in 10 years, the Angels opted to retain Scioscia, but fired both Picciolo and hitting coach Jim Eppard. Scioscia summed up the club's thinking: "You're not going to find a guy who works as hard as Rob, but it's time for Dino (Ebel) to move to the bench. We're just looking for a different dynamic. …"[17]

At this point, Picciolo retired from baseball. He had played for eight major-league managers over nine seasons, coached for four others over 23 seasons, and been a teammate or mentor to eight Hall of Famers. As a student of baseball, his portfolio was full.

Picciolo died on January 4, 2018; the cause of death was not disclosed. The night before his death, he was reported to be out and about in downtown San Diego, feeding the homeless.[18]

SOURCES

In addition to the sources cited in the Notes, the author also consulted Baseball-Reference.com and Retrosheet.org. I also greatly appreciate the assistance of Vanessa Weaver of the Los Angeles Angels organization, who provided information from Angels media guides.

NOTES

1 Bob Verdi, "Yount Reluctantly Accepts Hero's Role," *Chicago Tribune*, October 18, 1982: 61.

2 *Los Angeles Times*, June 24, 1973: 347.

3 *The Sporting News*, April 23, 1977: 29.

4 This was not an aberration for Picciolo: During his two full seasons at Birmingham and Tucson, he had drawn 37 walks in 1,127 plate appearances.

5 Articles written about Picciolo early in his career often referred to him as "Pic"; perhaps the writers were mixing up the pronunciation of the name with that of Brian Piccolo, the Chicago Bears running back who died of cancer in 1970, and about whom the movie Brian's Song was made.

6 Tom Weir, "Guerrero Just Sits and Sulks on A's Bench," *The Sporting News*, September 8, 1979: 61.

7 Tom Weir, "Picciolo Galled by No. 2 Rating," *The Sporting News*, November 17, 1979: 56.

8 Tom Weir, "Billy's First Report Card – All A's," *The Sporting News*, March 22, 1980: 43.

9 Peter Gammons, "A.L. Beat," *The Sporting News*, June 28, 1980: 23.

10 Robert Markus, "Sox Victory Over A's Is Full of Firsts," *Chicago Tribune*, October 3, 1980: 60.

11 "Notes," *Chicago Tribune*, September 24, 1980: 64.

12 The A's traded pitcher Mike Morgan to the Yankees to acquire Stanley.

13 Kit Stier, "A.L. West," *The Sporting News*, May 24, 1982: 26.

14 Tom Flaherty, "A.L. East," *The Sporting News*, May 31, 1982: 26.

15 Kit Stier, "Lansford's Wrist Toughest Casualty," *The Sporting News*, August 12, 1985: 22.

16 Bob Nightengale,"Coaching Staff Sports New Lineup," *Los Angeles Times*, April 5, 1991: 371.

17 Mike DiGiovanna, "Angels Shake Things Up, but Not at Top," *Los Angeles Times*, October 9, 2013: 27.

18 Jeff Sanders, "Longtime Padres Coach Picciolo Dies; Just Loved the Game of Baseball," sandiegouniontribune.com/sports/padres/sd-sp-long-time-padres-coach-rob-picciolo-dies-at-64-20180103-story-html, accessed February 22, 2018.

CHUCK PORTER

By Mike Huber and Bill Mortell

In the *Who Gave It Up?* category of baseball trivia, ballplayers are known for certain batting accomplishments, but the opposing pitchers who served up those opportunities are sometimes not remembered. Milwaukee Brewers fans can probably remember Robin Yount's 3,000th career hit, but can they recall who gave up the hit? Many baseball trivia buffs know that Los Angeles Dodgers southpaw Al Downing gave up Hank Aaron's historic 715th home run on April 8, 1974, at Atlanta Stadium, while Hammerin' Hank was still playing for the Atlanta Braves. The great Aaron played his final two seasons in Milwaukee and hit his record-setting (and final) 755th home run at County Stadium. Who was the pitcher?[1]

Milwaukee's Chuck Porter fits into this *Who Gave It Up?* category. The longest official game in major-league history took place on May 9, 1984, between the Brewers and the Chicago White Sox. The two teams battled to a tie for 24 complete innings before Chicago won the contest in the bottom of the 25th with a walk-off home run by Harold Baines. Who gave it up? Chuck Porter.

Charles William "Chuck" Porter III was born on January 12, 1955, in Baltimore, the third child and only son of Charles William "Bud" Porter Jr. and Elizabeth (Snyder) Porter.[2] The Porters lived just north of Baltimore, and their ancestors had been in America about 100 years, having immigrated to Maryland from the Bavarian village of Donnersdorf in 1860. Chuck attended Perry Hall Senior High School and played baseball and football. He earned all-state baseball honors and was named team captain his senior year. His success earned him the 28th-round draft pick of his hometown Baltimore Orioles,[3] but he chose not to sign. He was one of four Marylanders drafted by Baltimore in the regular phase. Instead, the 6-foot-3 right-handed pitcher decided to attend Clemson University.

While pitching for the Clemson Tigers in college, Porter was primarily a starter. In his freshman campaign, he pitched in 11 games with seven starts, finishing with a 4-2 record and a 2.58 earned-run average. He doubled his win total in his sophomore season, then enjoyed national success as a junior. He pitched 119 innings in 14 starts, striking out 75 and allowing 29 earned runs. His 12-0 record, 2.19 ERA, and 1.92 strikeout-to-walk ratio were the primary reasons Porter was named 1976 Atlantic Coast Conference Player of the Year. Clemson played in the 1976 College World Series (the first to two consecutive trips). Porter entered the 1976 free-agent draft and was selected in the seventh round by the California Angels. The Angels assigned him to Quad Cities of the Class A Midwest League. Porter pitched 101 innings for the second-place team and won five games.

Porter posted a 20-2 record in 1977, pitching for both Salinas of the Class A California League and El Paso of the Double-A Texas League. He had his only professional at-bats in 1977, while playing for Salinas.[4] In three times at the plate, Porter had one hit (a solo home run!), and he finished his professional career with a .333 batting average and 1.333 slugging percentage. Porter's batterymate at Salinas was catcher Joe Maddon, who went on to manage the Angels, Rays, and Cubs.

The next season saw Porter split time between El Paso and Triple-A Salt Lake City (Pacific Coast League). The 23-year-old struggled in Salt Lake City, posting a record of 0-5 and allowing 29 runs in 24 innings, but he was 10-5 in El Paso. In 1979 Porter stayed in Salt Lake City, making 31 appearances. He pitched 137 innings but only two complete games, and had a 5-9 record.

While in the Angels' farm system, Porter developed tendinitis in his pitching arm. The Angels released him during spring training, on March 31, 1980. He signed with the Brewers as a free agent on May 16, beginning the season with Burlington (Iowa) of the Midwest League. By June he had moved up to Holyoke (Massachusetts) of the Double-A Eastern League. Fran Sypek of the *Springfield Union* wrote, "He's a reclamation project… cast adrift by one organization, but given a second baseball life by another. That's the Chuck Porter story and judging by his recent success, the Holyoke Millers have themselves quite a find."[5] By the end of July Porter was 4-0 with the Millers. His wife, Eileen, recalled the situation: "It was discouraging that California gave up on Chuck after his arm operation. We had to face his not making it then. He called around, but when no one was interested, he asked the accounting firm he was working for part-time for a full-time job and I started looking for a full-time job."[6] Fortunately for the Porters, the Brewers answered the call.

After being promoted to Triple-A Vancouver to start the 1981 season, Porter joined the Brewers on

Chuck Porter was a September call-up with the Brewers in 1982 and appeared in three games. In parts of five big-league seasons, all with the Brewers (1981-1985), he split his 26 decisions.

September 1, 1981, and made his major-league debut on September 14. Wearing number 43, he pitched in three games for the Brewers at the end of the 1981 season, allowing six hits and two earned runs in 4⅓ innings.

In 1982 Porter was once again assigned to Vancouver after spring training. And once again, in September, he was pitching in Milwaukee. He made three appearances out of the bullpen, pitching in both ends of a crucial doubleheader against the Orioles. Unfortunately for him and his family, his mother, Elizabeth, died on May 1, 1982 and did not get to see him pitch at the major-league level. As the

1982 season ended, the second-place Birds swept the twin bill from the Brewers, cutting their lead to one game with one game to play. Baltimore won the 162nd game of the season against Milwaukee as well, as Porter watched from the bullpen. On Sunday, October 3, the Brewers exploded for 10 runs against Jim Palmer and the Orioles, clinching the East Division title and sending them to the League Championship Series against the California Angels. Porter did not play in the postseason. He was a spectator as the St. Louis Cardinals beat the Brewers in a seven-game World Series.

After Milwaukee's magical season ended, Porter decided to play winter ball in Puerto Rico, to be able to "come to camp and be in good shape and ready to go."[7] It worked. The young right-hander made the 25-man roster. Although not considered a power pitcher, Porter consistently threw his fastball at 86 mph and the experience in Puerto Rico established him "as a genuine major leaguer at age 28."[8] He told reporters, "Now the ball's in my own hand. I got the break. Now it's up to me to out there and do the best I can."[9]

In the *1983 Milwaukee Brewers Media Guide*, directly under Porter's information is a small fact box titled "The Long and Short of Things." It describes both the shortest game by time in Brewers history (May 6, 1972, which lasted only 1 hour, 31 minutes) and the longest by innings (six days later on May 12, 1972 — a 22-inning affair that lasted 5 hours and 47 minutes).[10] How could the sports information team know to associate Porter with Milwaukee's longest game to date?

The Brewers called up Porter from Vancouver on May 2, 1983. He pitched in 25 games and finished the season with a record of 7-9 and a 4.50 earned-run average. A highlight came on August 6, when he pitched his first shutout, a 3-0 win over the Toronto Blue Jays. Porter scattered six singles and struck out three in pitching his fourth complete game. He told The Sporting News, "I decided to take it one inning at a time. The fact that it was a close game kept me going. I had to bear down because every pitch and every hitter was important."[11]

Porter anticipated starting the 1984 season back with Vancouver. When spring training came around, he wasn't sure where he should rent an apartment, in Vancouver or Milwaukee. He said, "I didn't consider myself a long shot, but at the same time, I didn't have the ball club made."[12] Said *The Sporting News*, "if all the [Brewers] veterans were healthy, there wouldn't be any room for the youngsters." Those veterans included Bob Gibson (not the Hall of Famer), Tom Candiotti, and Jaime Cocanower. Yet Porter made the trip to Milwaukee for the start of the season. He made four short relief appearances before starting on April 28 at Yankee Stadium. He scattered five hits in six scoreless innings as the Brewers bested the Yankees, 8-0. Porter then dueled New York's Phil Niekro on May 4 in Milwaukee, matching the future Hall of Famer with shutout pitching for eight innings. In the bottom of the eighth, the Brewers manufactured a run on an error, a walk, a hit batsman, and a sacrifice fly and won the contest, 1-0. Rollie Fingers came on for his fourth save, preserving Porter's victory.

Porter's next appearance was the historic game between the White Sox and Brewers. The night game at Comiskey Park was tied 3-3 after nine innings, and it was still tied by the same score after 17 innings, when umpires suspended play due to curfew. Both teams came back the next day and continued play. Milwaukee started fast, with runners at first and third and only one out in the opening frame, but Cecil Cooper grounded into a double play to end the threat. Porter started the bottom of the 18th, and he was the only Brewers hurler for the next seven-plus innings. Porter faced 36 batters, striking out five but allowing 11 hits. Each team scored three times in the 21st inning, and the game continued on. The White Sox rallied in the 23rd, but Dave Stegman was ruled out at third on a coach's interference call, and the game continued. The longest game in major-league history ended in the 25th inning. After Porter struck out Stegman on an attempted bunt, the White Sox' Baines blasted the 753rd pitch of the game out of the park, giving Chicago a walk-off 7-6 win.

Porter won his next three starts, lowering his ERA to 1.75. He reinjured his elbow midway through the 1984 season. He pitched 2⅔ innings on July 20 against the Oakland Athletics, allowing four runs on five hits and a walk. He had surgery on August 2 to repair a torn ligament in his right elbow and was finished for the season.[13] He missed almost all of the 1985 season as well, appearing in six games in September and October, pitching 13⅔ innings with only one start. Porter appeared in his final major-league game on October 6, 1985, working four innings and yielding four hits.

Porter spent the offseason pitching in the Puerto Rico League. By January 1986 he had made six starts and posted a 2.08 ERA, pitching his first complete game five weeks into the season. He was "happy with that game. Not because of the one-hitter. I finally pitched a complete game — started and finished it myself."[14]

The right-hander was still part of the Milwaukee system in 1986, but he never made it back to County Stadium, instead pitching again in Vancouver. On September 30, 1986, the Brewers released the 31-year-old Porter, and he hung up his glove.

In 10 minor-league seasons, Porter compiled a record of 70-61. He pitched 48 complete games and had six shutouts. At the big-league level, in parts of five major-league seasons Porter pitched 237 innings in 54 games with 34 starts. His 13-13 career record included seven complete games, one shutout, and an earned-run average of 4.14. He struck out 136 batters.

Four months after his baseball career was finished, Porter, his wife, Eileen, and their sons, Bryan and Christopher, moved back to Perry Hall, Maryland, and bought the family house where he grew up. Chuck and his wife started Porter Landscaping, which "has provided landscaping services for the Baltimore Metro area and surrounding counties since 1989."[15]

SOURCES

In addition to the sources mentioned in the Notes, the author consulted Chuck Porter's file from the Giamatti Research Center at the National Baseball Hall of Fame and Museum; baseball-reference.com; and retrosheet.org.

NOTES

1. Robin Yount hit an infield single off Cleveland's Jose Mesa in a home game on September 9, 1992, for his 3,000th base hit. California Angels pitcher Dick Drago delivered Hank Aaron's final career home run on July 20, 1976.
2. Chuck had a sister, Linda, who died at a year old in 1949, and another sister, three years older.
3. Porter was selected by Baltimore in the 28th round of the free-agent draft on June 5, 1973.
4. Porter did have one plate appearance with the Salt Lake City Gulls in 1979, drawing a walk, giving him an on-base percentage for the season of 1.000.
5. Fran Sypek, "Porter's Fourth Win … Millers Bop Brisox," *Springfield* (Massachusetts) *Union*, July 27, 1980: 3.
6. *Springfield Union*, August 17, 1980: 66.
7. Undated newspaper clipping from Porter's file at the Giamatti Research Center at the National Baseball Hall of Fame and Museum. Posted to the file on August 7, 1983.
8. Ibid.
9. Ibid.
10. *1983 Milwaukee Brewers Media Guide*, 34.
11. Newspaper clipping posted to Porter's HOF file on August 7, 1983.
12. Ibid.
13. "Baseball Notes," *Arizona Republic* (Phoenix), July 24, 1984: 79.
14. "Brewers," *The Sporting News*, January 27, 1986: 41.
15. porterlandscaping.com/. Accessed January 2018.

ED ROMERO

By Bill Nowlin

Milwaukee Brewers scout Felix Delgado "found [Ed Romero] playing in the mountains of Puerto Rico two years ago." Romero was 17 at the time. "After one workout, the Brewers signed … Romero, along with four others."[1]

Edgardo Ralph (Rivera) Romero, born on December 9, 1957, in Santurce, Puerto Rico, was indeed signed at 17, in 1975 as an amateur free agent. His family was a supportive one. Father Rafael A. Romero was a civil engineer who worked mostly on housing construction projects. "He loved the game of baseball and had played semipro baseball himself. He was with me all the way in my career, and a very proud father to have his son playing in the big leagues. My mother Flor Maria was very supportive as well; she was a housewife who took care of us, all the school stuff, etc. They attended every game I played at every level until I was signed as a pro. Even after that, they visited me in the States when I was in the minor leagues, and traveled to see me in the big leagues after that."[2]

Ed had an older brother, Rafael, who also played some baseball. He is a civil engineer in Puerto Rico who had worked with Chevron and Texaco. His sister Alexis, also older, worked as a secretary with a number of companies, later marring and opening up a resort on Puerto Rico's west coast.

Ed's first assignment was to Class A, the 1976 Burlington (Iowa) Bees in the Midwest League, and he was a rough talent. He played in 129 games, but hit for only a .219 batting average, though his .304 on-base percentage showed some plate discipline. He committed 41 errors in the field, in 647 changes, a .937 fielding percentage.

Romero started 1977 with Holyoke (Eastern League) and, in late July, got an unexpected break. Both Robin Yount (pulled thigh muscle) and Don Money (back spasms) were unable to play effectively and utility infielder Tim Johnson went on the DL with a groin pull.

The Brewers called up Romero. He was asleep in his room in Holyoke when manager Matt Galante awoke him, saying, "Pack your suitcase. You're going to the big leagues."[3] He couldn't believe it, but he was on his way.

Romero was a right-handed infielder listed at 5-feet-11 and 165 pounds. His debut game, on July 16, saw him go 0-for-2 against the Baltimore Orioles, but he worked two bases on balls in the game. The next day, he singled three times in four at-bats and the third single (in the bottom of the eighth) drove in pinch-runner Jim Wohlford with what proved the winning run in a 3-2 win for the Brewers at County Stadium. All three singles had been off O's starter Dennis Martinez, who bore the loss.

Romero played in eight more games in July, and then — with enough Brewers back in playing condition — was returned to Holyoke. He had hit 7-for-25, and walked four times (.280 BA, .379 OBP.) He felt it was easier to hit pitching in the majors than in the minor leagues. "Down there you don't know where the next pitch is going to be, up here or down there, way wide. But here every pitch they throw is in the strike zone. You can hit it better."[4] He hit .258 for the season with Holyoke, and matched his 41 errors from the year before.

In 1978 Romero played in the Pacific Coast League at Triple-A Spokane, mostly at shortstop. He hit better (.280, with 52 RBIs) and picked up his fielding percentage just a bit. It was Vancouver in 1979 (the Brewers had switched PCL affiliations), with his fielding definitely improved (.960), though his batting tailed off a bit to .260.

Romero returned to the majors in 1980, when he got another opportunity after Larry Hisle was placed on the 15-day disabled list. He got to the Brewers in time to play in the June 6 game (and was 2-for-3 with three RBIs his first game back, with a two-run double and a bases-loaded walk). That June 6 game was an emotional one because it was also the first game of the year for manager George Bamberger, who had suffered a heart attack in spring training and undergone quintuple-bypass surgery. The Brewers won the game, 8-4, and Bamberger said, "You always want to win the first one because you know you're on the board then. Romero did great. That's what makes this ballclub great — its depth. We got a lot of guys hurt, but a guy like Romero comes in tonight and picks us up."[5]

Romero got into 50 games in Vancouver and hit .273 while he appeared in 42 games for Milwaukee, hitting .260. He made 12 errors in 174 chances with the Brewers, mostly at second base.

Eddie Romero forged a very successful career as a utility infielder for the next decade, into the 1990 season, playing shortstop (288 games), second base (192), and third base (176), with 32 games in the outfield, 13 at first base, and 14 as a designated hitter. He was with the Brewers in eight seasons and the Boston Red Sox in four, and played a number of games for both Detroit and Atlanta.

Romero made the postseason three times, the first time being in 1981 with Milwaukee. He had played in 44 games, driven in 10 runs, and scored 6. He hit .198. The Brewers played the New York Yankees in a best-of-five American League Division Series, and lost in five. Romero played in only the fifth and deciding game. He singled to left field with one out in the top of the third and came around to score, giving Milwaukee a 2-0 lead. The Yankees came from behind and won the game. Romero struck out his next time up and then was removed for pinch-hitter Don Money, who flied out.

Romero played in 52 games in 1982, batting .250, but driving in only seven runs (he scored 18), and then 59 games in 1983, with a .317 batting average (the best of his career), with 18 RBIs. A 1982 column by Tom Flaherty quoted Romero on the difficulty of utility work: "It can be tough. I've always been used to playing every day. In the minor leagues, everywhere I played, I played every day. It's a hard adjustment. There's no way you can afford to get down when you're not playing. If you do that, then when you get the chance, you might not do the job."[6] Manager Harvey Kuenn said, "I think he's one of the best utility players in the league. Anybody who can play three positions as well as he can is a big asset. And he's not an out at the player, either."[7]

In 1984, with Paul Molitor out for the season, Romero was effectively Milwaukee's first-string third baseman, playing in 116 games and batting .252 with a career-high 31 RBIs. Nonetheless, he still thought of himself as primarily a shortstop. Manager Rene Lachemann thought Romero could be a regular for a number of teams, but prized his versatility for the Brewers. He too believed Romero the best utilityman in the majors. Romero put in about 15 minutes of infield work at each base, to be ready for wherever he might be needed. GM Harry Dalton said, "I can't say he's untouchable because he's a utility player," but made it pretty clear how very much he valued Romero.[8]

In 1985, with Molitor back at third base, Romero was back to his utility role, but he got into 88 games. He hit .251 and drove in 21 runs.

After the season was over, the Brewers traded Romero to the Boston Red Sox on December 11 for pitcher Mark Clear, primed to be popular, according to acerbic *Boston Globe* columnist Dan Shaughnessy, if for no other reason than that the Sox had replaced the "universally loathed Mark Clear." Rene Lachemann was with the Red Sox, too, as their third-base coach in 1986. Romero knew he was penciled in for the same utility role, saying, "I do the best I can, but if nobody gives you a chance to play every day, you've got to be a good utility player. If I ever get a chance to play, I feel I could play every day. My lifetime average is .257, and that's not bad when you realize that you can go three weeks or a month without playing. That's tough. Just one year I'd like the chance to play every day."[9]

Romero committed three errors in eight games, and knew he was pressing. "I'm hurting myself and the team by trying too hard to prove myself," he said in the early going. Manager John McNamara said, "He'll settle down. I'm not worried about him. He's been a pretty steady player in this league for six years."[10] Anyone who plays in 100 ballgames for a pennant-winning team during the course of one season is making a real contribution. Romero played in an even 100 games for the 1986 Boston Red Sox, mostly at shortstop, 75 games, with another 18 at third base. He made only 12 errors, but hit just .210. He pinch-ran a number of times, scoring 41 runs and driving in 23.

The Red Sox made it all the way to Game Seven of the 1986 World Series before folding to the Mets. Romero played in four postseason games, but only briefly — the first three times as a pinch-runner, though he stayed in the game each time as a defensive replacement. In Game Seven of the World Series, he came in to play shortstop in the bottom of the eighth, with the Mets ahead, 6-5. They scored twice more, the one ball hit to him converted to an out. Romero was the first batter for Boston in the

Ed Romero fashioned a 12-year career as a versatile backup infielder, capable of playing shortstop, second base, and third base. In 1982 he batted .250 on 36 hits for the Brewers.

top of the ninth and fouled out to first baseman Keith Hernandez. He'd had two previous plate appearances in the postseason, making an out both times as well.

Romero played only two innings in 1987 spring training, but Marty Barrett hurt his wrist the first week of the regular season, and Romero got more of a chance to play on a regular basis. Then Glenn Hoffman got hurt. Playing more regularly, Romero even put together a 15-game hitting streak from April into May, and in mid-May he was told the shortstop position was his.[11] He was batting over

.300 much of the season, and even after cooling off in August (where he lost a few weeks of playing time) and September, he still finished batting .272. He'd played in 88 games, though remarkably he drove in only 14 runs all season long. He'd played almost the same number of games at third base, second, and short, and even eight at first base. He started to become reconciled to the role of utility infielder: "I really don't want to be jumping around. I just want to play four or five more years. After eight years in the big leagues, it's going to be difficult to become a starter. If I didn't get it this year, I'm not going to get it."[12] When he wasn't in the lineup, he often volunteered to throw batting practice.

After the 1987 season, a few days before he could have declared free agency, Romero got some extra security — a two-year contract with the Red Sox guaranteeing him $900,000.[13] Romero wasn't getting a starting role out of it, though. Fair or not, manager McNamara already had him pigeonholed: "He can't play every day."[14]

Romero's playing time was sharply reduced in 1988, in part due to a right knee problem that led to a lengthy stint on the DL in June and July, but the team got to the postseason again. There was the annual lament again about not getting the chance to prove himself as a regular. He didn't understand why he kept hearing he wasn't an everyday player. "I'm a utility player because that's the only thing I've gotten a chance to be. You can't say someone can't do something until they get the chance."[15] He played in only two June games and three in July, and just 31 games in all. Many of the appearances were late in games, on defense. Romero hit .240 and drove in five runs. The Red Sox faced off against Oakland in the ALCS. In Game One Boston went into the bottom of the ninth down by one run, 2-1. With two outs, Jody Reed doubled and Rich Gedman drew a walk. Manager Joe Morgan (who had taken over for John McNamara in midseason) put in the faster Romero as a pinch-runner for Gedman in hopes that Wade Boggs could drive in both the tying and the winning runs, but Boggs struck out. It was Romero's only appearance in the 1988 postseason.

Romero had more playing time in 1989, but chafed a bit under Joe Morgan, and his frustration at being consigned to the utility role boiled over when he was removed in the middle of an at-bat in a June 11 game against the Yankees. The Red Sox had just come from behind and scored five runs in the top of the eighth to tie the score, 7-7. There was a runner on first base with two outs. Romero ran the count to 3-and-0, when Yankees skipper Dallas Green decided to change pitchers. Once he did, Morgan decided to change batters and send up Rich Gedman. Romero exploded, throwing a Gatorade cooler onto the field. "I don't want to play for that man," Romero said of Morgan. He shows me no respect. I just want to go somewhere else and play."[16] Asked what was wrong with their relationship, Romero said, "Everything."[17] GM Lou Gorman said he wasn't going to be fined, but that Romero had it explained to him that no other teams had been asking about him, that no one had brought his name up.[18]

Morgan did, however, keep using Romero for the next couple of months, though Romero had been batting just .233 at the time. Finally, on August 5, after Marty Barrett was reactivated, the Red Sox released Romero. He was hitting .212 in 46 games, with six RBIs and only three errors in 161 chances. "I wasn't treated fairly here at all," Romero said after cleaning out his locker. "It's a relief to be getting away from here."[19] Seven days later, after clearing waivers, he signed as a free agent with the Atlanta Braves.

Romero was, of course, speaking out of frustration. "I just wanted a chance to play every day," he said many years later. "When the media asked me about it, I was very honest, never disrespecting anyone."[20]

Romero was 5-for-19 with a solo homer in seven games with the Braves when his old team — the Milwaukee Brewers — suddenly suffered a spate of injuries that cost them several infielders and caused them to seek out the veteran Romero. On August 23 the Braves agreed to trade him for a player to be named later; Jay Aldrich was that player. In 52 chances, Romero made just one error; he hit .200 with three RBIs. The Brewers granted him free agency in mid-November.

On January 15 Romero signed with the Detroit Tigers. He played with them until the Tigers released him on July 15. He'd gotten into 32 games and batted .229. He made just one error in 57 chances.

Romero's final major-league stats show a career fielding percentage of .967 and a .247 batting average. He had driven in 155 runs and scored 218. And he had plugged a number of holes for his various teams in the course of the 730 games over the 12 years he'd played in the big leagues.

There was a brief return to minor-league ball in 1991, with the Las Vegas Stars (Pacific Coast League), and Romero hit .284 in 28 games. Las Vegas was a Padres affiliate, and the Padres kept him on for five years as manager of their Class-A teams (a different team each year — Spokane, Waterloo, Springfield, Clinton, and Memphis) and one year working as infield coordinator. He also worked managing seven seasons in winter ball in Puerto Rico. The Brewers then hired Romero as a minor-league manager and instructor, working in El Paso, Huntsville (where his team won the Southern League championship in 2001), and Indianapolis. In 2007 he became their minor-league infield coordinator, and in 2008 manager Cecil Cooper hired him to become the third-base coach for the Houston Astros. He served as the bench coach for the Astros in 2009.

It was back to managing in the minors in 2010, in Greeneville, Tennessee, with assignments in 2011 and 2012 as manager of the Gulf Coast League Astros. Romero managed the New York-Penn League's Tri-City Valley Cats, of Troy, New York, an Astros affiliate, from 2013 through 2015.

"I'm happily married to a wonderful woman," he wrote on the last day of 2015. "Ivonne Romero, my high school sweetheart."[21] The two met at the Colegio Bautista de Carolina high school. The married on Christmas Day in 1977 and celebrated their 38th anniversary on Christmas 2015.

Ivonne and Ed Romero have two children. Ariana Kay Romero is a registered nurse working for an orthopedic doctor in West Palm Beach, Florida. Son Eddie Romero Jr. has also forged a life in baseball. In 2006 Eddie Jr. was named as an assistant in international and professional scouting for the Red Sox.[22] Within a few years, he was the team's Latin American coordinator, and by 2012 he had become the team's director of international scouting. In October 2015 he was promoted to vice president, international scouting.

Asked at the start of 2016 how he feels looking back on his first 40-plus years in baseball, Ed Senior said, "After 40 yrs in professional baseball I thank the Lord for a wonderful and successful career as a player and as an instructor."[23]

SOURCES

In addition to the sources noted in this biography, the author also accessed Romero's player file from the National Baseball Hall of Fame, the Encyclopedia of Minor League Baseball, Retrosheet.org, Baseball-Reference.com, and the SABR Minor Leagues Database, accessed online at Baseball-Reference.com. Thanks to Ed Romero for assistance in completing this biography.

NOTES

1 Lou Chapman, "Teen-Age Romero Eases Brewer Infield Woe," The Sporting News, August 6, 1977: 29. Ed Romero said of Delgado, "Felix had a good reputation as one of the best scouts in Latin America. A high number of players he signed made it to the major leagues." Ed Romero email to author on December 31, 2015.

2 Ed Romero email to author on December 31, 2015.

3 Chapman.

4 Chapman.

5 Associated Press, June 8, 1980.

6 Tom Flaherty, "Romero a Handy Sub for Brewers," The Sporting News, July 12, 1982: 38.

7 Ibid.

8 Tom Flaherty, "Romero May Be Top A.L. Utility Player," The Sporting News, July 16, 1984: 41.

9 Dan Shaughnessy, "No Substitute for Romero," Boston Globe, April 5, 1986.

10 Pete Farley, "Romero Pressing in New Role," Brockton Enterprise, April 19, 1985.

11 Steve Fainaru, "Longshot Romero Wins at Shortstop," *Hartford Courant*, May 12, 1987: D4.

12 Paul Jarvey, "Romero's Utility a Futility," *Worcester Telegram*, July 24, 1987: 17B.

13 Joe Giuliotti, "Romero Signs Two-Year, $900,000 Pact with Sox," *Boston Herald*, November 10, 1987: 99.

14 Stave Fainaru, "Romero's Role Is Clear: He's a Utility Player," *Hartford Courant*, May 5, 1988: B7.

15 David Cataneo, "Romero Reserved About Backup Role," *Boston Herald*, May 19, 1988: 103.

16 Joe Giuliotti, "Romero Blasts Morgan," *Boston Herald*, June 12, 1989: 74.

17 Steve Fainaru, "Romero Throws Tantrum, Asks to Be Dealt," *Boston Globe*, June 12, 1989: 38.

18 Joe Giuliotti, "No Fine, No Trade, No Interest," *Boston Herald*, June 13, 1989: 36. The Globe's Larry Whiteside wrote a little later that Gorman left it up to Morgan to impose any fine, that there was one, but the amount was not specified.

19 Pete Farley, "Bitter Romero Is Released," *Brockton Enterprise*, August 6, 1989: D1.

20 Ed Romero email to author, January 2, 2016.

21 Ed Romero email to author on December 31, 2015.

22 Nick Cafardo, "Wallace Sidelined With Hip Infection," *Boston Globe*, February 9, 2006: C1.

23 Ed Romero email to author, January 2, 2016.

TED SIMMONS

By Gregory H. Wolf

He was an eight-time All-Star, batted .300-plus seven times, and upon his retirement after the 1988 season, held the major-league record for hits (2,472) and doubles (483) by a catcher, to go along with 248 home runs and 1,389 RBIs. In December 2019, 25 years after receiving only 3.7% of the vote in his first year of eligibility for baseball's Hall of Fame and being dropped from the ballot, he was elected by the Modern Baseball Era Committee to be enshrined in Cooperstown.[1] His name was Ted Simmons.

Ted Lyle Simmons was born on August 9, 1949, in Highland Park, Michigan, the last of four children of William "Bill" Finis and Bonnie Sue (Webb) Simmons. He grew up in Southfield, a suburb on Detroit's northwest side, where his father's job as a trainer for harness-racing horses afforded the family a stable middle-class, no-frills lifestyle. An athletic youngster, the right-handed-throwing, yet natural left-handed-hitting Ted began playing organized Little League ball by the time he was 9 years old at East Southfield school. His two brothers played an instrumental role in shaping his development. Jim, 15 years older than Ted, encouraged his sibling to begin switch-hitting by the age of 13 ["(He'd) whistle Wiffle Balls at me from 30 feet away," remembered Simmons[2]]; while brother Ned also spent hours practicing the fundamentals of the game with him.

The teenage Ted emerged at Southfield High School as one of the best all-around athletes in the Detroit metropolitan area. Standing about 6-feet-1 and weighing 175 pounds, Ted was quick, sinewy strong, and agile, athletic traits that enabled him to excel on the hardwood court and especially the gridiron, where he was a star halfback. He scored 14 and 15 touchdowns in his junior and senior seasons respectively, and was named to the Detroit-Area All-Star team and Third Team All-State in his final season.[3] He was heavily recruited and purportedly received scholarship offers to play football at the University of Michigan, The Ohio State University, Purdue University, and the University of Colorado, among others. Baseball, however, was his passion. His baseball and football coach, Ed Bryant, called him the "best athlete I have ever seen."[4] Big-league scouts were hot on Simmons's trail by the time he was a high-school junior. Especially interested was scout Louis D'Annunzio of the hometown Tigers, for whom he worked out as a 16-year-old in 1966 in Tiger Stadium and participated in summer clinics. After his junior year, Simmons helped lead the A&B Brokers to the title in the Class D Detroit Amateur Baseball Federation[5] and then to the National Amateur Baseball Federation Championship.[6] Local sportswriter Hal Schram noted that the switch-hitting catcher drew 8 to 10 scouts every time he played in his senior year, when he batted .490.[7]

Widely anticipated to be a first-round selection in 1967, the still 17-year-old made it known that he'd prefer to fulfill his dream of playing baseball than signing a letter of intent to play baseball at the University of Michigan; however, he also expected a hefty bonus from a big-league team. Just days before he graduated, Simmons was chosen by the St. Louis Cardinals on scout Mo Mozzali's recommendation with their first pick, and 10th overall, in the first round. According to St. Louis sportswriter Neal Russo, Simmons was initially disappointed that the Redbirds chose him because they already had 25-year-old All-Star Tim McCarver behind the plate, but a $50,000 bonus helped influence his decision to sign a few days later.[8]

"When I came to the rookie camp in Sarasota, I was 17, hot, and cocky," recalled Simmons of beginning his professional career with the Cardinals' rookie-level Gulf Coast League in mid-July.[9] The brash youngster was introduced to the "Cardinal Way" by longtime minor-league instructor George Kissell, who "helped me grow up," said Simmons, and he learned not just the fundamentals from the Redbirds lifer, but also "the ethical part of the game."[10] Simmons spent the bulk of the summer with Cedar Rapids in the Class-A Midwest League, where he hit .269 in 47 games. He also picked up the habit of smoking, which he continued for the rest of his career. "We took long bus rides. ... (T)here was a lot of time on your hands with nothing to do," he once offered as explanation.[11]

Simmons attended college at the University of Michigan in the offseason and his school requirements limited him to only a few days of spring training in the Cardinals' minor-league camp in 1968. Back in Class A, Simmons tore up the California League with Modesto, leading the circuit with a .331 batting average and 119 RBIs, and was named the league's MVP. In September he was back in Ann Arbor taking classes, but joined the big-league club on four weekends. He made his major-league debut on September 21, starting as catcher, and singling in his second at-bat against Claude Osteen of the Dodgers in Los Angeles.

One of the most overlooked hitters of his generation, Ted Simmons was an eight-time All-Star, batted .300-plus seven times, and knocked in at least 90 runs in eight seasons. In 1982 he belted 23 round-trippers and two more in the World Series.

After another abbreviated spring camp, Simmons was on the fast track to the majors and was assigned to Tulsa in the Triple-A American Association in 1969. As expected, he excelled with the bat, hitting .317 with 16 home runs and 88 RBIs and was named catcher on the Topps-American Association Triple-A All-Star Team. It was a different story while donning the tools of ignorance. "I was awkward," admitted Simmons.[12] He credited a minor-league coach and former Cardinals player from the 1930s, Mike Ryba for helping him develop footwork, proper shifting, balance, and throwing techniques, but it was an arduous learning experience. Simmons made the most of another late-season look-see with the Redbirds. In his first start, on September 18 in St. Louis, Simmons laced a two-out run-scoring single to drive in Curt Flood for a dramatic 8-7 victory over the Pittsburgh Pirates. He provided the fireworks again two weeks later, belting a two-out triple to drive in Joe Torre for another walk-off victory, 6-5, against the Philadelphia Phillies.

After two consecutive pennants, the Cardinals dropped to fourth place in the NL East in the first year of divisional play, 1969, prompting GM Bing Devine to execute a blockbuster trade. He shipped McCarver, Flood, reliever Joe Hoerner, and journeyman Byron Browne to the Phillies for enigmatic and disgruntled star Richie Allen, Cookie Rojas, and Jerry Johnson in a transaction that altered the baseball landscape forever. [Flood refused to report the Phillies and subsequently challenged the legality of baseball's reserve clause]. To make room for Allen, the Cardinals planned to move former catcher and regular first sacker in 1969 Joe Torre to third base and the veteran agreed to hone his skills at the Florida Instructional League that fall; however, the Cardinals' master plan fell apart when Simmons was called for a six-month tour in the Army Reserve beginning in December.

Praised by GM Devine as "the most promising young (player) we've got," Simmons missed all of spring training and was discharged in early May.[13] He celebrated his freedom by marrying his high-school sweetheart, Maryanne Ellison, an art student at the University of Michigan, on his way to Triple-A Tulsa to get in shape. Simmons hit .373 in 51 at-bats and was promoted to the Cardinals at the end of the month. With the Cardinals struggling to play .500 ball, Simmons made his first start on May 30, and never looked back. On June 7 he belted the first of 248 career home runs, connecting off the San Diego Padres' Roberto Rodriguez for a two-run shot in the Cardinals' 10-7 victory at Busch Stadium. It was one of Simmons's three hits to give him 10 in 18 at-bats in his last five games. "I finally feel I belong here," he exclaimed. "I feel confident at the plate now."[14] But the transition to a full-time big-league spot was anything but smooth for Simmons. While the Cardinals (76-86) finished in fourth place with their worst record since 1959, Simmons seemed overwhelmed by big-league pitchers. His batting average plunged to .226 on September 16 before he caught fire, going 15-for-45 over his last 13 games to finish with a .243 average, but slugged an anemic .317 with three homers. Just 20 years old, he struggled at times behind the plate, allowing 15 passed balls (second-most in the NL) in just 74 games. "When I came up … I didn't have time to know what a catcher does," said Simmons.[15] Thrust into the starting position without a chance to apprentice behind a veteran, Simmons needed help, and the Cardinals provided it with former Redbird All-Star catcher Hal Smith, who served as Simmons's personal tutor, instructing him on basic fundamentals, strengthening his arm on throws to first and second, and developing better balance and agility.[16]

In 1971 Simmons finally participated in his first full spring training, in St. Petersburg. GM Devine preached patience with the 21-year-old and thought the club could "make allowances for his inexperience."[17] In addition to Simmons's defensive learning curve, there were also questions whether he could hit big-league pitching. He himself wondered if he should continue switch-hitting, given his feeble .167 batting average as a right-hander (compared with .269 batting left-handed). "I almost quit," he said. "[Hitting coach] Kenny Boyer and Red Schoendienst saw something in my swing and told me that I'd eventually come [around]."[18] He worked with Boyer and also Bob Kennedy (director of minor-league operations) to improve the strength of his left hand, which controls the bat when hitting right-handed. His regimen over the next several seasons paid off handsomely, though he admitted that he "put less control and more aggression" into his swing from the right side.

Obsessively driven to improve all aspects of his game, Simmons emerged as one of baseball's biggest early-season surprises in 1971. He started 16 of the first 17 games of the season, batted .396 and drew 10 walks. "By not crouching too much, I'm able to open up more," said Simmons about his carry-over success from the previous campaign. "I'm not tying myself up at the plate."[20] He finished the campaign with a .304 batting average and 77 RBIs, both of which were second-best among catchers in the majors behind the Pittsburgh Pirates' Manny Sanguillen. Led by Simmons and '71 NL MVP Torre, the Cardinals made a run at the eventual NL East champion Pirates, coming as close as 3½ games on August 15, but finished runner-up. The day before, Simmons called Bob Gibson's first and only big-league no-hitter, an 11-0 shellacking of the Bucs at Three Rivers Stadium; Simmons belted four hits and scored three times, culminating a torrid nine-game streak when he collected 17 hits in 38 at-bats.

Labor strife racked baseball in 1972 and in no city was the tension between players and management more pronounced than in St. Louis — and Ted Simmons was in the middle of it. While Curt Flood waited for his case to be heard by the US Supreme Court, five Cardinals refused to sign contracts in an ugly standoff that played out over the summer in the newspapers, as team owner Gussie Busch became increasingly disillusioned with player salary demands and what he considered insubordination. The first casualty was Steve Carlton, a 20-game winner in '71, who was shipped to the Phillies on February 25; four others, Torre, Simmons, 14-game winner Jerry Reuss, and utilityman Bob Burda reported to camp. While Torre eventually signed a lucrative two-year deal, Devine invoked the renewal clause on the other three players. "Signed may not be the word," said a statement issued by a Cardinals spokesman, "but they are under contract."[21] Reuss and Burda were ultimately traded, leaving Simmons the last man standing. And he kept standing. This was transpiring as the Major League Baseball Players Association, led by Marvin Miller, voted to strike less than a week before Opening Day. In the first work stoppage in big-league history, 86 games over 13 days were canceled and not made up. When the season started, Simmons was widely described as the first known player to play without signing a contract.[22] While Busch dug in ("Let 'em strike," he said famously, "I won't give then one more cent."[23]), Simmons articulated his principled stance. "I'm not a crusader," he said. "I don't even have a lawyer. All I want is more money."[24] He freely admitted that the Cardinals had treated him well and even offered him a raise of $7,500 to $25,000; however, he wanted $35,000 and later reduced his demand to $30,000, but Busch and Devine stood pat. In the meantime, the season started, but save for a hot streak in June and early July, the Cardinals (75-81) were a lackluster fourth-place team. Their biggest offensive weapon was Simmons, who set a team record for home runs (16), RBIs (96), and hits (180) as a catcher, and batted .303. As the summer wore on and Simmons refused to accept the Cardinals' contract offer, St. Louis sportswriter Bob Broeg noted that "sympathy is with Simmons" as the Cardinals endured a public-relations nightmare.[25] When the Supreme Court rejected Flood's case for free agency on June 19, widespread speculation emerged that Simmons would sue baseball. One day before Simmons was to participate in his first All-Star Game (he was chosen as a backup and did not see action), he signed a two-year deal reported to be for $70,000 on July 24.[26] Devine attempted to save face by claiming that Busch had wanted the club to operate within the spirit of President Nixon's wage-price guidelines, and had waited until the US Pay Board announced that professional athletes were exempt from wage control before they addressed Simmons's demands.[27]

Simmons's 10 full seasons with the Cardinals (1971-1980) read like a broken record: He was regularly the team's most dangerous offensive weapon, leading it in home runs five times (and the runner-up three times) while the team finished last or next to last in the league in round-trippers six times; he led the Cardinals in RBIs seven times (runner-up two times), batted .300-plus six times and earned six All-Star berths.

Described by teammate Joe Torre as "about as strong a human as I've ever seen," Simmons was remarkably durable.[28] He caught an average of 135 games per season over that 10-year stretch, more than any catcher in the big leagues, and led the NL in games played as a catcher three times.

Simmons's reputation as one of the best catchers of his generation has suffered because he played at the same time as three of the most prolific and most beloved catchers in baseball history: Johnny Bench, Carlton Fisk, and Thurman Munson (and a fourth beginning in 1975, Gary Carter). Nonetheless, during that 10-year stretch, Simmons collected more hits (1,631) than anyone in baseball except for Rod Carew, Pete Rose, Al Oliver, and Steve Garvey; drove in more runs (902) than anyone but Reggie Jackson, Bench, and Tony Perez. He hit for a higher average (.301) than any of the aforementioned catchers and finished second in round-trippers (169) among them, though well behind Bench's 269.

Two factors have contributed to Simmons's relative inconspicuousness compared with those players. He was never able to shed the impression that he was average or even below average defensively. He led the NL in passed balls three times, including a record-tying 28 in 1975 (which was still tied as of 2019 for the most since the beginning of the twentieth century) and finished second four times. He allowed the most stolen bases four times and was runner-up two more times.[29] SABR member Bill Deane has suggested that such "counting statistics" misrepresent Simmons defensively, and offered a detailed analysis that Simmons was a slightly better than average defensive catcher.[30] In an exhaustive essay focusing on modern sabermetric analysis, Chris Bodig argues that Simmons was indeed a below-average defensive catcher, ranking 65th of 70 catchers with at least 4,800 plate appearances and at least 50% of their games played as catcher.[31]

"It takes a long time for a catcher to get established," said Simmons's former teammate Tim McCarver in an interview with Ron Fimrite of Sports Illustrated, published in 1978. "We're a different breed. But Teddy is thinking like a catcher now, and that's what it takes. He has everything else. He's the toughest guy behind the plate since John Roseboro, and he has terrific stamina. Sometimes I think the Cardinals are trying to kill him, catching him in all those games in that St. Louis heat. If they caught him 130 games instead of 150, he'd hit .360."[32]

Secondly, unlike Bench, Munson, and Fisk, who combined to play for eight pennant winners and four World Series champions in that stretch (1971-1980), Simmons toiled for Cardinals teams that were generally average clubs. The Redbirds finished as high as second place three times (all within Simmons's first four seasons) and also finished with a losing record four times.

As the funky '70s heated up, free-spirited Simmons began to wear his hair longer and gradually acquired the moniker Simba for his collar-length mane of brown hair. Simmons was also called Sleepy for his laid-back, droopy-eyed appearance. Notwithstanding that easygoing, nonchalant façade, Simmons was an intense, alert competitor with a killer instinct and occasional combative temper, who often spoke of the emotional toll that losing and slumping had on his life and even family. "Winning. Winning. That's what I want. I've done all the things except one," he said as a Cardinal.[33] Sportswriter Dick Wagner of the St. Louis Globe-Democrat opined in an exposé from 1980 that Simmons didn't "fit the glamorous and golden image of a pro athlete" and never cared much for what others thought about him.[34] According to Wagner, Simmons was a free-thinker who preferred leather jackets, boots, and motorcycles over coats and ties. "Most of what comes out of his mouth you will never hear from most players who perhaps are not capable of or willing to rise above the jock stereotype," wrote Wagner.

Simmons's best chance for the postseason with the Cardinals occurred in 1973 and 1974. After the Redbirds hit an NL-low 70 home runs in 1972, the club decided to install an artificial outfield fence that reduced center-field and power-alley depth by 10 feet and the height of the wall from 10½ feet to 8 feet in order to increase offense.[35] The effect was negligible: The team finished last in the majors in home runs (75) and below the major-league average in scoring and hitting. The Redbirds got off to a horrendous start, lost 12 of their first 13 games, and were 8-23 on May 14. Simmons too slumped, batting .194 on May 11; both heated up, but the season seemed to be feast or famine. Over a 19-game stretch from June 25 to July 12, Simmons hit .387 (29-for-75) and knocked in 18 runs. Ten days later, the Cardinals moved into an unlikely tie with the Chicago Cubs for first place after Simmons hit an eighth-inning two-run single and then scored the winning run in a 5-4 victory over the Dodgers. The Cardinals withstood an eight-game losing streak in August, but held onto first place until September 12 when only three games separated the Pirates, Cardinals, Expos, Mets, and Cubs in an abnormally weak NL East. Praised for his "high degree of maturity and tolerance to pain," the 23-year-old Simmons surged down the stretch when the club needed him most.[36] From August 24 to the end of the season, he was one of the hottest hitters in baseball, batting .384 (56-for-146), but his teammates bottomed out, at one point losing 13 of 17 in September to fall four games off the lead in the final week, and eventually finished runner-up despite a .500 record. Simmons finished with a .310 batting average and cemented his reputation as one of the best switch-hitters in baseball (batting .310 left-handed and .311 right-handed). For the second straight season he finished fourth in the NL in hits (192) and third in doubles (36), and once again led the NL in defensive games by a catcher (153). He received the J.G. Spink Award as the St. Louis Baseball Man of the Year for the second consecutive year.[37]

In 1974 the Cardinals battled for the East crown, leading the division by as many as three games and never trailing by more than 3½. Simmons commenced the campaign with a 15-game hitting streak (he had a career-best 19-game streak the previous year and again in 1975), but the Motor City native was uncharacteristically inconsistent with the bat. On May 15 he broke his season-long homerless drought by spanking two round-trippers in one game for the first time in his career and driving in four runs in a 10-1 win over the Mets at Busch Stadium. Two days later he knocked in four runs against the Cubs in a 9-8 win in St. Louis, en route to winning the NL Player of the Week honor for the first of two times that season.[38] From June through August he hit just .234, but the Redbird offense was sparked by a trio of .300-hitting outfielders, offseason acquisition Reggie Smith, Bake McBride, and 35-year-old Lou Brock, who swiped a record-setting 118 bases. Heating up down the stretch, Simmons's 13th-inning sacrifice fly gave the Cardinals a 2-1 win over the Pirates on September 17 and extended their division lead to 2½ games. The team lost five of its next eight games; Simmons was instrumental in all three wins, spanking a decisive three-run home run in one, lacing a walk-off single in another, and whacking an RBI double to begin the scoring in the 11th inning in a wacky 13-12 win over the Pirates on September 25. Tied with the Pirates with two games to play, the Cardinals lost to the Montreal Expos, 3-2, in Canada, when Gibson yielded a soul-crushing two-run home run to Mike Jorgensen. The Redbirds finished 1½ games behind the Bucs and did not seriously challenge for the NL East crown until 1982. Though his batting average slipped to .272, Simmons belted 20 home runs for the first of six times in his career, knocked in 103 runs, and remained one of the hitters most difficult to strike out in baseball, whiffing just 35 times in 662 plate appearances.

While the Cardinals were in the doldrums in the next six seasons (1975 to 1980), fielding three losing teams and not finishing higher than third. Simmons was a model of consistency and emerged as a vocal team leader. In 1975 he established career highs in batting average (.332, second-best in the NL) and hits (193), knocked in 100 runs, and finished sixth in MVP balloting. He was named the *The Sporting News* N.L. All-Star catcher for three consecutive campaigns (1977-1979), averaging 23 round-trippers and 87 RBIs. Duplicating his feat from 1972-1974, he was also named to the NL All-Star team three straight seasons (1977-1979), once as a starter, in 1978 when he collected his first hit in seven at-bats in the midsummer classic. En route to another Simmons-eque season (21-98-.303) in 1980, the 30-year-old catcher set a new record for most home runs as a switch-hitter in the NL, breaking Pete Rose's record of 155.

Simmons's 13-year stint with the Cardinals came to an unexpected end during baseball's winter meetings in 1980, but the writing was already on the wall during Whitey Herzog's 2½-month stint as interim skipper before moving into the front office as GM in August. Wanting to rebuild the team based on defense and speed, Herzog signed as a free agent three-time All-Star Darrell Porter, who had been his catcher when he managed the Kansas City Royals. Objecting to a possible move to first base that would push All-Star, Gold Glove winner, and former MVP Keith Hernandez to the outfield, Simmons was the odd man out. Just five days after Porter's signing, the Cardinals executed one of the biggest blockbuster deals in club history, sending Simmons, perennial All-Star reliever Rollie Fingers (whom they had also acquired during the winter meetings in a stunning 12-player trade with the San Diego Padres), and right-hander Pete Vuckovich, coming off two straight seasons with 222-plus innings pitched, to the Milwaukee Brewers in exchange for workhorse right-hander Lary Sorensen, right fielder Sixto Lezcano, and two prospects, pitcher Dave LaPoint and outfielder David Green. Sportswriters tried to portray the trade as a rift between Simmons and Herzog, but the catcher flatly denied any controversy. Simmons had some leverage, though, as a 10-5 man (10 years in the majors and the last five with the same club) and had to agree to the trade, which he did when the Brewers paid him an estimated $750,000 to accept the deal. Herzog was vilified in the St. Louis press for jettisoning the fan favorite Simmons in a trade that seemed like a salary dump while receiving relatively little for three established players.

"It's like a chance to start all over again," said Simmons about the trade. "A new league, new town, training in Phoenix for the first time."[39] The Brewers (86-76), coming off a third-place finish, were expected to challenge the Baltimore Orioles and New York Yankees for the AL East crown. GM Harry Dalton considered Simmons an "unknown factor" in the competitive division, but anticipated that he'd strengthen an already explosive offense.[40] The Brew Crew had led the majors with 203 home runs in 1980, paced by Ben Oglivie's 41 homers, which tied Reggie Jackson for the AL lead, and the '79 home-run champ, Gorman Thomas, who blasted 38 in 1980. "I feel like I belong in the American League," gushed Simmons after blasting a two-run shot against the Cleveland Indians on April 12 in his second game as a Brewer. "I got my first hit, a long ball."[41] The 31-year-old catcher's transition to the junior circuit, however, was anything but smooth. Bothered by a sore shoulder, Simmons struggled at the plate, batting as low as .190 on June 2. Ten days later, the players union went on strike in protest of several issues, chief of which was free-agent compensation. Known for his players'-first attitude, Simmons served as the team's player representative to the union. After the cancellation of 713 games (38% of the season), play resumed on August 9 with owners having split the season into two halves. After a retroactive third-place finish (31-25) in the first half, the Brewers were declared AL East Division winners (31-22) in the second half, thus earning their first playoff berth in franchise history. Simmons (14 home runs, 61 RBIs) finished with the second lowest batting average (.216) among qualifiers though he earned his seventh All-Star selection. After losses to the Yankees in the first two games of the ALDS at home, the Brewers took Game Three, 5-3, at Yankee Stadium, behind Simmons's two run-home home run and RBI double, but the Yankees took the series in five games.

Simmons experienced his most frustrating and torturous season in 1982. Despite a monstrous game against the Minnesota Twins on May 2, matching his career high with two home runs for the seventh of eight times and six RBIs (achieved twice previously), Simmons began the campaign in a prolonged slump. By the end of May he was batting just .217, eliciting regular boos from Brewers faithful at County Stadium. Struggling to play .500 ball, the Brewers fired manager Buck Rodgers on June 2, leading to an acrimonious departure. Rodgers blamed two clubhouse "cancers" for the club's problems. Though he didn't mention names, it was widely understood that he meant Simmons, whose perceived defensive liabilities, offensive meltdown, and outspoken personality grated on the former backstop, and pitcher Mike Caldwell.[42] Simmons responded by closing himself off from the press and not granting any interviews for the remainder of the season, and never publicly addressed the matter, stating only, "The whole thing was about my integrity."[43]

The entire clubhouse atmosphere changed when longtime Brewers minor-league coach Harvey Kuenn was named skipper. His famous epithet, "Have some fun," relaxed the players.[44] They won 30 of their next 41 games, moving into a sole possession of first place on July 15; and extended their lead to a season-high 6½ games on August 27. Simmons heated up, too, collecting 16 hits in his last 35 at-bats and knocking in 11 runs in 9 games to push his batting average to .273 at the end of August. Leading the division by four games with five more to play, the Brewers lost four straight, the latter three to the Orioles, with whom they fell into a tie in an epic season-ending four-game series in Baltimore. In the winner-take-all game on Sunday, October 3, the Brewers bats exploded for 10 runs and four home runs, including two by Robin Yount, cementing his eventual MVP award, and one by Simmons, who finished with 23 home runs and 97 RBIs. "It was a very difficult time," said Simmons, emphatically ending his self-imposed silence and reflecting on the turbulent season. "I figured the only way out of it was to win."[45]

After losing two straight to the California Angels in the ALCS, the Brewers won three in a row at County Stadium to advance to their first World Series. It was a contrast in styles: Harvey's Wallbangers, the major-league leaders in home runs (216) and runs scored (891), vs. Whitey Ball, a reincarnation of the Deadball Era game, stressing speed, stolen bases, small ball, and defense. The Brewers exploded for 10 runs in a Game One shutout on October 12 at Busch Stadium, which erupted in cheers each time their former favorite son, Simmons, came to bat. In the fifth, Simmons belted a solo shot off Bob Forsch. "I was geared to take the gamble that they would throw me a fastball down, and it was right there," he said.[46] Simmons hit another solo shot in Game Two, but collected only one more hit in the final five games as the Cardinals won Game Seven in the Gateway City.

In 1983 Simmons split his time behind the plate and as the DH and responded by batting .308, knocking in a career-best 108 runs, and earning his final All-Star section while the Brewers won 87 games yet finished in fifth place in the division. On June 12 Simmons doubled in the 10th inning against the Yankees in County Stadium to reach to reach the 2,000-hit plateau. He parlayed his successful season into a lucrative three-year/$3 million contract.

The wear and tear of catching of 1,700-plus games caught up to Simmons quickly. His batting average dipped to .221 and he hit just four round-trippers in 497 at-bats in 1984 despite not donning the tools of ignorance. He rebounded slightly in 1985 (12-76-.273) as a DH and first baseman as the Brewers (71-91) bottomed out with a sixth-place finish.

Traded to the Atlanta Braves in March 1986, Simmons spent his final three seasons playing sparingly behind the plate and at first and third base. A graybeard on a struggling young team, Simmons was a de-facto playing coach, helping players adjust to the major leagues.

After 2,456 games, the 38-year-old Simmons retired after the 1988 season, but he did not stay away from baseball long. As he had for almost his entire playing career, he returned in the offseason to St. Louis, where he resided with his wife, Maryanne, and their two children. He accepted a job as the Cardinals' director of players personnel and thus commenced a three-decade career as a baseball executive. In 1992 he was named GM of the Pittsburgh Pirates, won the NL East crown in his first season, then presided over a grueling transitional period that saw the club lose reigning MVP Barry Bonds and former Cy Young Award winner Doug Drabek to free agency. A three-pack-a day cigarette smoker, Simmons suffered a heart attack on June 8, 1993, and resigned less than two weeks later after just 16 months on the job to concentrate on his health.[47]

Simmons returned to baseball again in 1993, taking a less strenuous position with the Cleveland Indians as a special-assignment scout. During his stint in that capacity, the Indians rose from perennial also-rans to one of the best teams in the AL, winning the pennant in 1995 and 1997. In late 1997 Simmons was hired by the San Diego Padres to serve as vice president of scouting and player development, a position he held until 2007.

Simmons was back in a baseball uniform in 2008, as bench coach for the Milwaukee Brewers, and served in the same capacity for the Padres in 2009-2010. In 2011 Simmons was hired by the Seattle Mariners as senior adviser to Seattle Mariners GM Jack Zduriencik, and remained in that post through the 2015 campaign.

Simmons was unquestionably one of the most productive hitting catchers in terms of cumulative as well as peak performance in major-league history. Upon retirement, he ranked eighth all-time in games caught (1,771; and ranked 16th as of the end of 2019); his 2,472 hits ranked second all-time as of 2019 behind Hall of Famer Ivan Rodriguez; and his 1,389 RBIs rank second to Yogi Berra, as of 2019. He hit .300-plus seven times, knocked in at least 90 runs eight times, and finished in the top 10 in each category five times from 1971 to 1980; six times in doubles, and three times in total hits.

Despite those statistics, Simmons received just 3.7% of the votes in his first year of eligibility for enshrinement in baseball's Hall of Fame in Cooperstown, New York, in 1994, and was consequently purged from the list for failing to receive the required 5% of the votes. He was later included on two other "second chance" ballots; on the Veterans Committee in 2011, and the Expansion Era in 2014. In 2015 Simmons received a measure of atonement when the Cardinals inducted him into their Hall of Fame. He was also inducted into the Missouri Sports Hall of Fame (2005); the St. Louis Sports Hall of Fame (2010), and the Michigan Sports Hall of Fame (2012).

Simmons's chances to be elected to the Baseball Hall of Fame greatly improved when he was added in 2017 to the ballot of 10 "Modern Baseball Era" players which the 16-member Veterans Committee decided. In his first year of eligibility Simmons received 11 votes, one vote shy of the required 75% for election, while Alan Trammell and Jack Morris were elected. Simmons's 25-year wait for the Hall of Fame finally ended in December 2019. During baseball's winter meetings, it was announced that Simmons received 13 of 16 votes by the committee and was thus elected to the Baseball Hall of Fame, to be enshrined in a ceremony in July 2020. "There's never too long a time to wait if you finally make the leap," Simmons told *St. Louis Post-Dispatch* sportswriter Rick Hummel upon learning that the news. "And today I finally did."[48]

As of 2019, Simmons still resided in suburban St. Louis with his wife, Maryanne.

SOURCES

In addition to the sources cited in the Notes, the author also accessed Retrosheet.org, Baseball-Reference.com, the SABR Minor Leagues Database, accessed online at Baseball-Reference.com, SABR.org, The Sporting News archive via Paper of Record, Simmons's Hall of Fame file, the online archives via Newspaper.com, and Ancestry.com.

NOTES

1. AP, "Marvin Miller and Ted Simmons Elected to Baseball Hall of Fame," *New York Times*, December 8, 2019. Simmons received 13 of the 16 votes cast; 12 were required for election by the Modern Era Committee.

2. Neal Russo, "Plate Specialist," Everyday Magazine, *St. Louis Post-Dispatch*, September 14, 1971: 1.

3. Hal Schram, "1966 Free Press Detroit-Area All-Star Team," *Detroit Free Press*, November 19, 1966: 14.

4. Hal Schram, "Meet a Prep Superstar," *Detroit Free Press*, September 22, 1966: 1D.

5. "Tigers Draftee Star," *Detroit Free Press*, August 8, 1966: 39.

6. Schram, "Meet a Prep Superstar."

7. Hal Schram, "Southfield Draws All Baseball Scouts," *Detroit Free Press*, May 10, 1967: 4-D; stats from Hal McCoy, "$$ or College? Prep Catcher Awaits Call," *Detroit Free Press*, August 6, 1967: 4D.

8. Neal Russo, "Cards Pick a Winner – Workhorse Simmons," *The Sporting News*, April 27, 1974: 3.

9. John Ferguson, "Cards' Blue-Ribbon Prospect: Tulsa's Catcher Ted Simmons," *The Sporting News*, July 5, 1969: 35.

10. Ibid.

11. Dick Wagner, "This Man Isn't What He Looks," *St. Louis Globe-Democrat*, January 28, 1980: 6B.

12. Neal Russo, "No Easy Rest for N.L. Hitters With Simmons Awake," *The Sporting News*, June 27, 1970: 23.

13. Bob Broeg, "Shannon Is Out 'Most of Year,'" *St. Louis Post-Dispatch*, March 18, 1970: 3E.

14. "Simmons Ready to Unpack Bags," *St. Louis Post-Dispatch*, June 8, 1970: 3C.

15. Jim Smith, "The Best Hitting Catcher in National League History," *Baseball Quarterly*, Winter 1977: 40.

16. "Hal Smith Joins Cards as Ted Simmons' Tutor," *The Sporting News*, July 4, 1970: 12.

17. Bob Broeg, "Devine Flying Home on a Limb," *St. Louis Post-Dispatch*, March 26, 1971: 1B.

18. Smith.

19. Rick Hummel, "Simmons Became a Record Holder – And Didn't Know It," *St. Louis Post-Dispatch*, August 3, 1980: 1H.

20. Nealvt Russo, "Simmons' Bat a Pleasant Surprise to Cards," *The Sporting News*, May 22, 1971: 15.

21. Joseph Durso, "Cards Invoke Reserve Clause on Two," *New York Times*, March 8, 1972.

22. Bob Broeg, "Puppet Kuhn Can't Pull Strings to Untangle Ted, Cards," *St. Louis Post-Dispatch*, June 27: 1972: 2C.

23. Ira Berkow, "Simmons Case: Cause Without a Rebel," *Poughkeepsie Journal*, July 22, 1972: 13.

24. Ibid.

25. Bob Broeg, "The Simmons Case: A Touchy Issue," *The Sporting News*, July 8, 1972: 4.

26. Dick Kaegel, "Simmons Is 'Relieved' With 2-Year Pact," *St. Louis Post-Dispatch*, July 25, 1972: 1C.

27. Ibid.

28. Russo, "Cards Pick a Winner – Workhorse Simmons."

29. Earl Williams of the Atlanta Braves had 28 passed balls in 1972.

30. Bill Deane, "Simmons Deserves Better Break in Hall of Fame Balloting," *Baseball Magazine*, October, 1995: 13.

31. Chris Bodig, "Will Ted Simmons Ever Make the Hall of Fame," *Cooperstown Cred*, August 9, 2018. cooperstowncred.com/will-ted-simmons-ever-make-hall-fame/.

32. Ron Fimrite, "He's Some Piece of Work," *Sports Illustrated*, June 5, 1978. si.com/vault/1978/06/05/822710/hes-some-piece-of-work-cardinals-catcher-ted-simmons-is-a-collector-of-antiques-and-an-art-museum-trustee-but-none-of-his-old-treasures-is-as-masterfully-wrought-as-his-game.

33. Smith.

34. Wagner.

35. Bob Broeg, "Contrasting Cards' Reactions to Shorter Fences at Busch," *The Sporting News*, March 17, 1973: 36.

36. Bob Broeg, "'Losing Drives Me Crazy,' Says Simmons," *St. Louis Post-Dispatch*, March 20, 1973: 2B.

37. Simmons shared the award with teammate Lou Brock and St. Louis native Ken Holtzman, pitcher for the Oakland A's.

38. Simmons won the award for the week of May 13-19 by going 13-for-24 with three home runs, 10 RBIs, and 9 runs; and then again for the week of September 2-8 with 10 hits in 22 at-bats, 5 doubles, 5 RBIs, and 5 runs.

39. Associated Press, "No Manager at Brewers Open Camp," *Manitowoc* (Wisconsin) *Herald-Times*, March 1, 1981: 6.

40. Tom Flaherty, "Murder in Milwaukee," *The Sporting News*, April 11, 1981: 3.

41. Tom Flaherty, "Slaton Wins It," *Milwaukee Journal*, April 13, 1981: 13.

42. Steve Aschburner, "Simmons Talks Again," *Milwaukee Journal*, October 4, 1982: 3.

43. Ibid.

44. Tom Flaherty, "Brewers Harvey, a Blast," *The Sporting News*, August 9, 1982: 3.

45. Aschburner.

46. Dale Hofmann, "A Happy Homecoming for Simmons," *Milwaukee Sentinel*, October 13, 1983: part 2, 1.

47. Paul Meyer, "Players Stunned by Simmons' Decisions, but Wish Him Well," *Pittsburgh Post-Gazette*, June 21, 1993: B-3.

48. Rick Hummel, "After 25 years Cardinals catcher Simmons 'makes the leap' to Hall of Fame," *St. Louis Post-Dispatch*, December 9, 2019.

BOB SKUBE

By Clayton Trutor

Bob Skube was an outfielder, first baseman, and pinch-hitter who played in 16 games for the Milwaukee Brewers during the 1982 and the 1983 seasons. He batted and threw left-handed. In 32 plate appearances, Skube batted .250 and had nine RBIs, all in the 1983 season. In the late 1970s and early 1980s, Skube was one of the top power-hitting prospects in Milwaukee's farm system, but a series of knee injuries derailed his playing career. He became a highly respected hitting coach and occasional manager in the Brewers, Texas Rangers, and San Diego Padres organizations.

Robert Jacob Skube Jr. was born on October 8, 1957, in Northridge, California, the son of Robert and Margaret Skube, both originally from Colorado. Robert Sr. served in the US Navy during World War II and settled his family in Simi Valley, a half-hour east of Northridge in Southern California's San Fernando Valley, and worked as a salesman.[1] The younger Skube starred for the Simi Valley Pioneers High School baseball team, a powerhouse program in Southern California that has in subsequent years produced several other major leaguers, including Scott Radinsky, Bryan Anderson, and pitching brothers Jered Weaver and Jeff Weaver. In 1975 Skube led the Pioneers to the championship of the Coastal Canyon League, one of Southern California's most competitive high-school baseball conferences. Skube was also a standout running back on Simi Valley High's football team.[2]

The Atlanta Braves selected Skube in the fifth round of the June 1975 amateur draft. He chose instead to stay close to home, accepting a scholarship offer at the University of Southern California. Skube was a three-year starter in center field for Rod Dedeaux's Trojans teams of the 1970s. Skube played for the 1978 USC team that won the College World Series, defeating Arizona State in the finals.[3]

Skube improved his hitting each year at USC, progressing from .265 in his freshman year to .315 by his senior year. In his senior year Skube led the Trojans with 13 home runs and drove in 42 runs. This performance earned Skube USC's Most Improved Player Award in 1979.[4]

In 1979 the Milwaukee Brewers selected Skube in the 13th round of the amateur draft. After signing, the lefty spent the summer with the Burlington (Iowa) Bees of the low Class A Midwest League. Skube was the standout on a team that posted a 53-83 record. Splitting his time between first base and the outfield, he hit for a team-high .294 batting average with 9 home runs and 45 RBIs. He had a one-game call-up to the Stockton Ports of the California League, the Brewers' top Class A affiliate. He spent the 1980 season with Stockton, batting .291 with 19 home runs and 81 RBIs, and earning the

A September call-up in 1982, Bob Skube singled in hist first major-league at-bat.

Eddie Mulligan Award as the top newcomer in the league.[5]

Skube moved up to Double A for the 1981 season, playing for the El Paso Diablos of the Texas League. Playing for future Kansas City Royals manager (1997-2002) Tony Muser, Skube batted .284 with 15 home runs and 59 RBIs.

A solid performance in spring training in 1982 earned him a spot on the Brewers' 40-man roster and advancement to the Vancouver Canadians of the Triple-A Pacific Coast League. After batting .279 with 13 home runs and 61 RBIs, Skube got a September call-up to manager Harvey Kuenn's AL East-leading Milwaukee Brewers.[6]

Skube played sparingly for Harvey's Wallbangers, the power-hitting team that withstood a furious charge from the Baltimore Orioles in late September and early October to win the franchise's first AL East Division title. Skube played in four games, three as a pinch-hitter and once as a defensive replacement in the outfield. He was 2-for-3 at the plate.[7]

Skube made his major-league debut on September 17, 1982, in a 14-0 laugher against the New York Yankees. Skube entered the game in the eighth inning, pinch-hitting for designated hitter Roy Howell. The rookie singled to right field off Lynn McGlothen with two outs. He was left at first when Charlie Moore flied out to end the inning. He got his other hit on the 26th while pinch-hitting for second baseman Ed Romero in the eighth inning of a 5-2 home loss to the Orioles. The hit came off perennial All-Star Dennis Martinez. After moving to third on a sacrifice and single, Skube was thrown out at the plate by Baltimore center fielder John Shelby trying to score on Cecil Cooper's fly out.[8]

Skube was not on the Brewers' roster for the American League Championship Series, which Milwaukee won 3 games to 2 against the California Angels, or the World Series, which Milwaukee lost in seven games to the St. Louis Cardinals. Out of spring training in 1983, Skube was named to the Brewers' Opening Day roster, but was optioned to Vancouver on June 5 after getting into only 12 games.[9]

Those 12 games were Skube's last in the major leagues. One of his five hits was a bases-loaded, two-out triple off the Texas Rangers' Mike Smithson in the sixth inning of a 6-3 Brewers victory on May 8.

Skube played in 40 games for the Vancouver Canadians in 1983, batting just .209. Bone chips in both of his knees were causing him debilitating pain. On July 31 he had arthroscopic surgery on both knees, bringing his 1983 campaign to an end.[10]

Skube began 1984 with Double-A El Paso. In 56 games, the lefty showed a genuine return to form, batting .312 with 6 home runs and 41 RBIs. At midseason, the Brewers promoted him back to Vancouver, where he hit .267 in 61 games with 9 home runs and 40 RBIs. Skube returned to Vancouver for the 1985 season, but struggled to a .232 batting average in 89 games. The Brewers released him in February 1986.

After his playing days ended, Skube became a minor-league hitting coach and manager, working in the Brewers, Rangers, and Padres organizations.

SOURCES

In addition to the sources cited in the Notes, the author also consulted BaseballAlmanac.com, Baseball-Reference.com, and various newspapers.

NOTES

1 "Robert and Margaret Skube," Findagrave.com, 2003. Accessed on January 10, 2018: findagrave.com/memorial/36517358; Margaret Skube obituary, *Arizona Republic* (Phoenix), August 18, 2003: 62.

2 "Simi Valley Pioneers Wall of Fame," PioneerBaseball.Biz. 2017. Accessed on January 10, 2018: pioneerbaseball.biz/copy-of-coaches; "Valley Football Roundup," *Valley News* (Los Angeles), November 4, 1973: 37.

3 "USC Trojans 2012 Baseball Media Guide," University of Southern California Athletic Department, 2012. Accessed on January 10, 2018:grfx.cstv.com/photos/schools/usc/sports/m-basebl/auto_pdf/2011-12/misc_non_event/2012_USC_Baseball_Media_Guide.pdf.

4 Ibid.

5 "Awards," California League History, 2016. Accessed on January 10, 2018: californialeaguehistory.com/awards.

6 "Scoreboard," *Boston Globe*, September 8, 1982: 30.

7 Leigh Montville, "They're a Bunch of Swingers," *Boston Globe*, October 6, 1982: 1.

8 Joseph Durso, "Orioles Cut Lead to 2," *New York Times*, September 27, 1982: C1.

9 "Transactions," *Boston Globe*, June 6, 1983: 34.

10 Tom Flaherty, "Will Skube Do? No, Probably Not," *Milwaukee Journal*, March 19, 1984: 3.

JIM SLATON

By Isaac Buttke

Everyone knows about John Smoltz's dominance as both a starter and as a reliever. Same with Dennis Eckersley. Little do people know they were hardly the first people to be widely praised at both spots in the pitching staff. Though he started his career as a highly touted starting-pitcher prospect, Jim Slaton eventually moved to the bullpen and proved to be a major cog in the Milwaukee Brewers' bullpen for their 1982 World Series push. Based on his early successes, Slaton had many people thinking he would be as good as Smoltz would ever become, if not better. Brewers broadcaster Merle Harmon stated early on, "I don't want to exaggerate, but [fellow Brewer pitcher] (Bill) Parsons and (Jim) Slaton have a chance to be superstars."[1] Slaton even garnered a comparison to an all-time-great hurler. Former Brewers general manager Frank Lane said, "Slaton reminds me a lot of Tom Seaver in the way he works."[2] Things may not have panned out as well as Harmon and Lane had hoped, but Slaton certainly played a major role for the Brewers throughout his career.

James Michael Slaton was born on June 19, 1950, in Long Beach, California. He was the younger of two children, both sons. His family moved a couple of hours north by the time he got into high school, enrolling him at Antelope Valley High School in Lancaster, California. While there, Jim played both football and baseball. However, he decided to focus on baseball upon going to Antelope Valley College, just up the road.

His stay at the local college was brief, though. He entered the major-league first-year player draft while he was still 18 years old and was selected in the 15th round by the Seattle Pilots, 357th overall. Slaton was hardly the headliner of the team's selections; Gorman Thomas had been made the Pilots' first pick, 14 rounds earlier. This draft also featured the likes of Hall of Famers Bert Blyleven and Dave Winfield.

In his first year of professional baseball, Slaton hit the ground running. In 149 innings split between the rotation and the bullpen of multiple low-level Pilots affiliates, he produced a 3.02 ERA and 1.16 WHIP. He even fired seven complete games, collected two saves, and tossed a one-hitter during his time with Class-A Clinton (Midwest League). It appeared the Pilots had stolen a diamond in the rough in the 15th round of the draft before folding and moving to Milwaukee.

Slaton's second season began auspiciously as well. He threw complete games in his first two starts, allowing four runs (three earned) while striking out 15 batters. His season was cut short immediately after the second start, however. It wasn't due to injury. As many players before him had done, Slaton left professional baseball for the summer months to serve in the Army National Guard.[3]

Because of the time he missed during the regular season, the Brewers sent the young right-hander to the Puerto Rican Winter League. He joined the Mayaguez squad (featuring Mike Cuellar, Mike Wegener, and Bill Parsons) partway through the campaign and collected a victory in his first appearance.[4]

Slaton's unusual path took another turn for the better, as the Brewers liked what they saw in Puerto Rico and 1971 spring training enough to give him a major-league roster spot without his ever having thrown a pitch above Class A. Manager Dave Bristol defended the decision with his own take on the righty:

"He first caught my eye in the Arizona Instructional League. I knew he had good stuff and we sent him to play winter ball in Puerto Rico. He improved there and, when spring training ended, we thought enough of him to bring him along. Sure he's young, but he's got a good arm and he's coachable."[5]

Pitching coach Wes Stock also had good things to say about Slaton after spring training:

"He kept improving and improving. Each time out, he looked better. He's a good kid and he's smart. He's got a good arm and you have to tell him something only once and he's got it."[6]

To many, Slaton's emergence was a complete surprise. Not only did the 20-year-old have few minor-league innings to his name, but the military service in his second season made his leap to the majors all the more improbable. "I never threw a ball while I was in the service," the youngster said.[7] Slaton seemed surprised when the Brewers gave him a roster spot. "I had a good spring, but I didn't know that I was coming north with the club until two days before the camp broke," he said.[8]

That isn't to say Slaton didn't have his warts. Stock commented, "His only problem was a tendency to drop his elbow on his curveball. When he does that, it comes in like a lollypop."[9] Slaton said he wanted to add another pitch to his repertoire:

"My fastball is pretty good and so is my curve. Now I'd like to develop a changeup."[10]

Regardless of the high praise and shortcomings noted by himself and his coaching staff, Slaton had an overall solid rookie season for Milwaukee "Kiddie Korps." He achieved a 10-8 record with a 3.78 ERA, five complete games and four shutouts in 147⅔ innings pitched. This had him in the conversation for the Rookie of the Year Award,[11] which was won by Chris Chambliss of the Cleveland Indians.

Some hitters suggested something else was helping Slaton succeed in his first season. Wrote Jerome Holtzman in *The Sporting News*, "The hitters are saying that Jim Slaton, the Milwaukee bullpen ace, not only knows how to load 'em up, but also has a sharp belt buckle."[12] Despite these claims, virtually no evidence backed them up and nothing came of the issue in the coming years.

Slaton could've used a competitive edge when 1972 rolled around. He was sought by numerous teams during the offseason, but the Brewers as early as October 1971 had him slotted into the next season's rotation.[13] Wes Stock said in May 1972, "His curveball has improved almost 100 percent, and that alone should make him a better pitcher."[14] Slaton was one of the few pitchers used in Milwaukee's three-man rotation for the start of the season.[15]

However, the wheels fell off early on. The heavy usage in the season's first month took a toll on the young right-hander, as he stumbled to a 5.52 ERA without a single complete game (a travesty at that time). After his early-season struggles, manager Del Crandall decided to use him only as a spot starter for a bit[16] before finally relegating him to the minors in June.[17] It was only after this demotion that Slaton finally admitted that he had been dealing with a sore arm throughout the first half of the season.[18]

During his time back with the Brewers' minor-league affiliate in Evansville, Slaton showed vast improvement from his time in the majors. He produced a 2.92 ERA in 16 starts and threw a no-hitter (which he almost predicted would happen before the game began.[19]) Frank Lane suggested that his success in the minors could earn him a trip back to the majors, but the Brewers did not bring him back before the end of the season.[20]

Despite this, Slaton's strong finish with Evansville and an All-Star Game nod in the Puerto Rican Winter League[21] had him slotted for a rotation spot with the Brewers in 1973.[22] Those plans were put on hold before the season began, however, when Slaton suffered a chipped bone in his right wrist in a car accident in Puerto Rico.[23] He missed a fair amount of exhibition action during spring training, but he returned in early April with four shutout innings against the Angels,[24] leading pitching coach Bob Shaw to comment, "I don't think we'll have to worry about his wrist."[25] Shaw's words held true, as Slaton enjoyed a healthy season of 38 starts in which he produced a 3.71 ERA and threw 13 complete games. (At least one writer suggested that he could've won even more games with more offensive support.[26])

Slaton's strong performance raised expectations greatly for 1974. General manager Jim Wilson went as far as to say, "Slaton could be our best pitcher in 1974."[27] Milwaukee sportswriter Lou Chapman considered the right-hander a threat to win 20 games.[28] Slaton had trouble meeting this lofty bar, though; he struggled right out of the gate and was moved to the bullpen in mid-June to try to reclaim his 1973 form.[29] He pitched well as a reliever, prompting the Brewers to place him back in the rotation by the season's end.[30] Slaton got hot at the end of the season allowing only one earned run in a stretch of four starts,[31] but for the Brewers it was too late; the team was already near the cellar of the division by the time he figured things out. This seemed to be the story of Slaton's early career. Lou Chapman wrote, "[Slaton] sprouts quickly in the spring, languishes on the vine in midseason and then blooms like a 20-game winner in the season's late stages."[32]

To attempt to break this curse, Slaton went to the Dominican Winter League for more work. Perhaps it was the lesser competition, or perhaps it was the fact that his former pitching coach Al Widmar was coaching him in the Caribbean, but Slaton pitched well during his time in the Dominican.[33] He won his first four decisions and drew praise from new Brewers general manager Jim Baumer, who watched him pitch in the Dominican Republic.[34] "Slaton could be our best pitcher this year," Baumer said. "With the addition of Henry Aaron and our run-scoring ability, there's no reason why Jim finally couldn't become a 20-game winner."[35] First baseman Mike Hegan, who was Slaton's teammate in the Dominican, said Slaton had "the best stuff of any pitcher on our staff."[36]

So it came as little surprise that the Brewers were considering Slaton for 1975's Opening Day start. A month before spring training started, manager Del Crandall decided to tell everyone what he thought the lineup would look like, including his first starter of the season. "I would think Jim Slaton would be the choice [to start Opening Day] depending on how Ed Sprague and Jim Colborn have progressed after knee operations in the fall," he commented.[37]

Slaton did get his first Opening Day start that season, but lost to Luis Tiant and the Boston Red Sox, lasting just 2⅔ innings. His struggles continued throughout the first half, leading to yet another relegation to the bullpen in mid-May.[38] He returned to the rotation later in the month when Crandall decided to use a five-man rotation. "The starters have not been consistent in going the distance," he stated, "so we feel an extra day of rest will help."[39] The Milwaukee skipper felt confident in bringing Slaton back from the bullpen because he "had good stuff but wasn't winning" during the early portion of the season.[40]

Perhaps Crandall's move was just what Slaton needed. He turned things around in his return to the rotation thanks in part to a set of motivational cassette tapes. Slaton explained the difference the tapes made in an interview with *The Sporting News*: "The new course doesn't let me get down too much. It also helps with my confidence, although I never really gave up on myself. I'm throwing the same way now that I did earlier in the year. Only now the ball is being hit at somebody instead of going through."[41]

This only helped for a bit, though. Slaton slumped at the end of the season, dropping his last eight decisions of the season. He acknowledged earlier in the summer suffering from arm fatigue,[42] but it really took its toll at the end of the season. Lou Chapman didn't find the revelation overly surprising, as by his count, Slaton had thrown over 600 innings between the prior season, winter ball, spring training and the current season.[43] As a result, Slaton decided to take the winter off for the most part after posting a 4.52 ERA with an 11-18 record.

The Brewers still had faith that Slaton could become a 20-game winner,[44] but when 1976 rolled around, it seemed as if the hurler had even more faith in himself than the team did. Shortly before spring training was scheduled to start, the right-hander was one of the Brewer veterans holding out for more money. Slaton hired an agent to help him during the contract negotiations.[45] General manager Jim Baumer, a bit upset, invoked major-league baseball's renewal clause and attempted to sign some of the veterans at a 20 percent pay cut.[46] Slaton avoided this issue by signing with the team over the phone before many of the other players.[47]

With the contract negotiations out of the way, Slaton could get back to focusing on baseball. New manager Alex Grammas had some things he wanted to tweak on his right-hander:

"Jim Slaton has got to be considered as one of our starters, but he's got to be straightened around. With an arm like his, there's no reason why he can't be a consistent winner. We're going to have [pitching coach] Cal McLish work with him. Sometimes it's only a little thing that needs to be changed to restore confidence and make a winner."[48]

For the second consecutive year, Slaton was awarded the Opening Day start, and this one went much differently than the previous season's. Slaton outperformed Jim "Catfish" Hunter with a shutout of the New York Yankees. He followed that performance up with a shutout victory over the Detroit Tigers. Strong starts similar to these over the first half helped Slaton win American League Player of the Week honors in mid-April and collect 10 wins before the All-Star break.

What changed for the 26-year-old? According to Baumer, he was simply putting his pitches in the strike zone. "He's throwing a lot more strikes," Baumer said. "He's changing speeds more and is ahead of hitters."[49] Third baseman Don Money thought the mental aspect was what made things click for Slaton. "It looks like he's pitching instead of throwing," Money said. "He's using his noggin."[50]

McLish's take may be the most convincing. The coach focused on rhythm and tempo with the Brewers hurlers all spring, and it seemed to be paying off with Slaton. "No matter what sport you play, even if it's shuffleboard, you've got to have tempo," McLish said. "The feel from the last pitch stays with you. … You keep your rhythm more if you set a tempo."[51] He also had Slaton change the grip on his fastball to gain more movement, which Slaton said contributed to "the best start of [his] career."[52]

This stellar start didn't translate to the second half of the season. Slaton struggled to get run support down the stretch, leading to a number of hard-luck losses. The last straw perhaps was a 2-1 loss to the Athletics on August 10. He threw a complete game and allowed only one earned run. The decisive second run came on a throwing error by Brewers second baseman Gary Sutherland. A reporter after the game told Slaton, "Tough way to lose a well-pitched game." Slaton responded, "Heck, it's been happening for five years now. This game is so frustrating. I'm pitching better than I ever have in my career, and I'm going to have to struggle to win 15 games."[53] Slaton finished the season with a 3.44 ERA to go with a 14-15 record.

The 1977 season seemed like a duplicate of 1976 for Slaton. After inking a two-year contract with the Brewers during the offseason,[54] he started off the season well. He pitched a shutout in his season debut after missing a bit of time with the flu.[55] But he didn't get much run support the rest of the way, as he stumbled into the trade deadline with a 4-6 record despite a 2.86 ERA. The coaches of the All-Star team disregarded the deceptive losing record and named Slaton to the American League squad when Don Money was injured and couldn't play in the midsummer classic. This wound up being Slaton's only All-Star Game, though he didn't pitch in the game.

The Brewers' struggles continued into the second half, and Slaton was less than pleased, saying, "It's pretty depressing losing all year. You go out there and want to win, but it seems like someone's waiting for something to go wrong. ... I like it here, the fans are great. But we just lose every year. If I'm a losing pitcher, I'd like to find out before my career is over."[56]

That last comment made many believe that Slaton was a sure bet to be traded during the offseason. Sure enough, the Brewers found a trade partner in the Detroit Tigers. On December 9, 1977, the right-hander was sent with pitcher Rich Folkers to Detroit in exchange for outfielder Ben Oglivie. Slaton was going from a sixth-place team to a fourth-place team in the same division. With only one year left until free agency, he made it clear that he would only be a Tiger for one season. He insisted it wasn't anything against the city or the people, but he had aspirations of getting paid more and possibly playing close to home in California. "I told [Tigers general manager Jim Campbell] it didn't matter what he offered, I didn't plan to sign," Slaton said. "It just doesn't make sense for me to sign."[57]

Slaton maintained some connections with the Brewers during his time across Lake Michigan. When the Brewers came to town in early June, Milwaukee catcher Charlie Moore stayed with Slaton and his family during the series.[58] He then homered off Slaton in a 7-2 Brewers victory.

All in all, 1978 was a good year for Slaton. He didn't produce another year's worth of All-Star-caliber numbers, but he won a career-high 17 games and fired 11 complete games while posting a 4.12 ERA. Nothing spectacular, but it positioned him as one of the top pitchers in the "mostly unattractive" 1979 free-agent class.[59]

At the time, free agency worked a bit differently. Instead of all players being able to talk with any team, baseball held a Free Agent Re-Entry Draft. Teams would pick the players they wished to bid on, and the players would be limited to signing with those teams. Slaton was selected by 14 teams in the re-entry draft, including the Angels, Giants and A's from California. The Brewers and Tigers both bid on him as well despite knowing he wanted to head west.[60]

What seemed to be a token draft pick by Milwaukee wound up being significantly more. Slaton seemed insistent on moving west and then told the Tigers he would let them match any offers he received.[61] In the end he agreed to a six-year, $1.46 million contract with the Brewers.[62]

Slaton proved to be well worth the money, as he produced a 3.63 ERA and a 15-9 record in 1979. The biggest difference during Slaton's return trip to Milwaukee was his control. Manager George Bamberger preached control to his pitchers, and when Slaton arrived, the skipper simply commanded him, "Relax, throw the ball over home plate."[63] The right-hander did just that, cutting his walks by 31 from the year before.

Being on a winning team was also doing wonders for Slaton. "If you do give up a few runs early in the game, this is the type of team that can come back," he said. "The type of team that the Brewers have had a lot to do with my decision to sign. They score a lot of runs."[64]

In 1980 Slaton felt benevolent enough with his new money to set up a scholarship fund at his alma mater Antelope Valley College.[65] Things fell apart shortly thereafter.

Slaton was tasked with pitching on the road against the Toronto Blue Jays in mid-April. The temperature at first pitch was 26 degrees Fahrenheit, and Slaton was hit for four runs in three innings. He came out of the outing with what was dubbed at the time as shoulder soreness.[66] He was placed on the disabled list after discovering he had injured his rotator cuff and wound up missing the remainder of the season.[67]

There was some hope that Slaton could return

A durable workhorse in the 1970s, Jim Slaton averaged 13 wins and 243 innings pitched over a seven-year stretch (1973-1979). He went 10-6 as a valuable swingman in 1982 for the Brewers and posted a 151-158 slate and logged 2,683⅔ innings in 16 seasons (1971-1986).

before the end of the season, but the Brewers opted to play things safely by having him throw in the Arizona Instructional League. "There was no pain," he said.[68] He was hitting 91 mph on the radar gun, about where he normally pitched. He continued throwing all winter in order to keep his shoulder loose and even managed to add velocity to his fastball by spring training.[69] "So far, everything has really come along," Slaton commented. "I just hope I haven't peaked too early because right now my arm feels as strong as it ever has."[70]

Contrary to his hopes, Slaton's numbers suggest he did peak too early. The 31-year-old's ERA for the season rose to 4.37 and he failed to throw a complete game. By the end of the season he was pitching out of the bullpen, where he found a good amount of success. He pitched in four of the team's five American League Division Series games against the Yankees, hurling a total of six innings and allowing only a pair of runs in the series finale. After this strong showing, it came as no surprise that the team was going to move him into a full-time relief role for the 1982 campaign.[71] Slaton was a bit sour about the planned move to the relief corps, but he warmed up to it before the 1982 season began. "I wouldn't object to that at all," he said. "If they think that's where I'm best suited, that's fine."[72]

That was indeed what the team thought was best, and it was actually a very shrewd move by the organization. Slaton wound up collecting six saves during the season due to a pair of injuries to incumbent closer Rollie Fingers.[73] He made a handful of spot starts when Pete Vuckovich was hurt,[74] though instances like this that required Slaton to warm up unexpectedly revealed a bit about how he took to bullpen life. On one occasion, he was forced into action while munching on a Snickers bar. Another time, he almost choked on a handful of sunflower seeds when he was told he was entering the game in the second inning.[75]

Even with his next assignment varying as much as it did, the right-hander still seemed to like the move to being a reliever. "It's turned out I've made a very important contribution," Slaton said of his role in the Milwaukee bullpen. "I really enjoyed pitching in short relief when Rollie was hurt."[76] His pleasure showed up in his end-of-season stat line, as the 3.29 ERA he went on to produce wound up being the best of his career.

This strong showing made him an integral part of the Brewers' pennant chase. In the American League Championship Series, against the California Angels, Slaton threw 4⅔ innings in two games, allowing just one earned run on three hits and a walk. He continued his stellar play in the World

Series, notching 2⅔ innings and collecting a win in relief against the St. Louis Cardinals without allowing a run. Overall, Slaton posted a 1.23 ERA during the 1982 postseason.

In 1983 Slaton mustered just a 4.33 ERA exclusively out of the bullpen, though he managed to win 14 games in relief. The Brewers shopped the right-hander again during the offseason, though it wasn't an easy process. As a 10-5 rights player, Slaton could veto a trade. With this leverage, the righty said he would accept a trade only if he was granted a three-year extension.[77] After much deliberation, on December 20, 1983, Milwaukee struck a deal with a team Slaton had wanted to be with for a long time: the California Angels. The 33-year-old was sent to Southern California in exchange for outfielder Bobby Clark.[78]

Because of a rash of injuries in their rotation, the Angels intended to use Slaton temporarily as a starter.[79] The injuries failed to subside, keeping Slaton in the fray longer than his performance warranted. He wound up spending much of his time with the Angels as a starter and stumbled to a 4.87 ERA.

This wasn't to say Slaton's veteran presence wasn't felt among his teammates, especially when it came to humor. Slaton appeared to be a bit of a prankster, as is evidenced by his antics during spring training in 1986. According to Stan Isle of *The Sporting News*, Slaton was suspected of pranking fellow hurler Kirk McCaskill by cutting his toothpaste tube in half, shortening the bristles on his toothbrush and snipping his shoelaces.[80]

Slaton apparently got his funnybone from his father. During his tumultuous 1986 campaign, Slaton's brother Frank decided to not eat food that required chewing until Slaton won his fifth game of the season after being stuck on four victories for so long. Frank wound up losing 16 pounds. His father knew better than to take part in the hunger strike. "I love my son, but I'm not crazy," the elder Slaton said.[81]

Although he seemed to be loose, Slaton's performance continued to decline. He was banished from the rotation for the final time in late June and was released soon thereafter. The Detroit Tigers took a flier on him and scooped him up in mid-July,[82] but his middling performance in their bullpen led to his release after the season. He played one season in the Senior Professional Baseball Association with the Fort Myers Sun Sox.

Thus ended Slaton's playing career. He finished his time in pro baseball with 1,191 strikeouts, 151 wins, 14 saves, and over 2,600 innings to his credit. He moved on to be a pitching coach or a bullpen coach in the Oakland Athletics, Chicago Cubs, Seattle Mariners, and Los Angeles Dodgers organizations. He may not have matched the achievements of dual-role pitchers like John Smoltz or Dennis Eckersley, but Slaton wound up having a big impact on multiple teams throughout his career as both a starter and as a reliever. Who knows? With a little more luck, his stellar bullpen work in 1982 might have brought the Brewers their first championship.

SOURCES

In addition to the sources cited in the Notes, the author consulted Baseball-Reference.com and the Milwaukee Journal-Sentinel.

NOTES

1 Jack Craig, "sporTView," *The Sporting News*, August 7, 1971: 21.
2 Larry Whiteside, "Ken Sanders: Brewer Bullpen Jewel," *The Sporting News*, February 26, 1972: 44.
3 Miguel Frau, "Wegener Pitches No-Hitter in Puerto Rico," *The Sporting News*, December 12, 1970: 63.
4 Ibid.
5 Larry Whiteside, "Slaton Gives Brewer Mound All-Right Label," *The Sporting News*, May 1, 1971: 20.
6 Ibid.
7 Ibid.
8 Ibid.
9 Ibid.
10 Ibid.
11 Joe McGuff, "Fast-Rising Royals Eye Top Awards," *The Sporting News*, October 2, 1971: 24.

12 Jerome Holtzman, "When Luke Bunted, It Was a Surprise," *The Sporting News*, October 2, 1971: 16.

13 Larry Whiteside, "Lane Polishing Up Brewers' Trading Wares," *The Sporting News*, October 16, 1971: 19; Larry Whiteside, "All That's Left of Original Brewers Is Burp," *The Sporting News*, November 6, 1971: 47; Larry Whiteside, "Brewers' Deal Closes Gap Between Lane and Bristol," *The Sporting News*, October 30, 1971: 23.

14 Larry Whiteside, "Brewers' Slaton Shy on Experience, Long on Hill Ability," *The Sporting News*, May 6, 1972: 28.

15 Larry Whiteside, "Brewers Cheering Revival by Lonborg," *The Sporting News*, June 10, 1972: 21.

16 Larry Whiteside, "Crandall's Commandment: Have Fun," *The Sporting News*, June 24, 1972: 13.

17 Larry Whiteside, "Steady Stephenson a Beaut in Brewer Bullpen," *The Sporting News*, July 1, 1972: 17.

18 Larry Whiteside, "Lane Still Sees Brewer Beams as Sun Sinks Slowly in West," *The Sporting News*, September 2, 1972: 19.

19 Dave Mullen, "Slaton's 'Shutout' Becomes a No-Hitter," *The Sporting News*, August 19, 1972: 36.

20 Whiteside, "Lane Still Sees Brewer Beams as Sun Sinks Slowly in West."

21 Miguel Frau, "Imports Win in Puerto Rico," *The Sporting News*, January 20, 1973: 47.

22 Larry Whiteside, "Slaton Expected to Be Among Brewer Starters," *The Sporting News*, December 9, 1972: 47.

23 Larry Whiteside, "Vet Short: Is He Miracle Material for Milwaukee?" *The Sporting News*, February 10, 1973: 44.

24 Larry Whiteside, "Brewers' Briggs a Confident Clouter," *The Sporting News*, April 7, 1973: 32.

25 Ibid.

26 Lou Chapman, "Brewers See Slaton With 20 Wins in '74," *The Sporting News*, December 29, 1973: 38.

27 Ibid.

28 Ibid.

29 Lou Chapman, "June Means It's Swoon Time for the Hit-Starved Brewers," *The Sporting News*, July 6, 1974: 22.

30 Lou Chapman, "Briggs, Money Sparkle Despite Brewer Tailspin," *The Sporting News*, July 20, 1974: 17.

31 Lou Chapman, "Thomas and Lezcano Brighten Brewers' Future," *The Sporting News*, September 28, 1974: 9.

32 Lou Chapman, "Slaton's Brewer Slogan – Come Alive in '75," *The Sporting News*, January 18, 1975: 53.

33 Ibid.

34 Ibid.

35 Ibid.

36 Ibid.

37 Lou Chapman, "Brewers Name Coluccio to Lead Off," *The Sporting News*, February 22, 1975: 43.

38 Lou Chapman, "A Three-Man Bullpen Bolsters Fast-Moving Brewers," *The Sporting News*, June 7, 1975: 12.

39 "A.L. Flashes," *The Sporting News*, June 14, 1975: 22.

40 Lou Chapman, "Thomas Removing Doubts as Brewer Bomber," *The Sporting News*, July 5, 1975: 13.

41 Lou Chapman, "Motivation Course Rescues Brewer Slaton," *The Sporting News*, July 12, 1975: 14.

42 Ibid.

43 Lou Chapman, "Moore Doing His Catching as Brewers' New Outfielder," *The Sporting News*, September 27, 1975: 19.

44 Lou Chapman, "Too Much Brewer Youth? Wait Until Next Year," The Sporting News, October 25, 1975: 21.

45 Lou Chapman, "Brewer Regulars Take Their Time About Signing," *The Sporting News*, March 13, 1976: 42.

46 Lou Chapman, "Colborn Fuming Over Brewers' Offer," *The Sporting News*, March 27, 1976: 43.

47 Ibid.

48 Lou Chapman, "Grammas Calm Despite Training Delay," *The Sporting News*, March 20, 1976: 39.

49 Lou Chapman, "Tradeable Slaton Now a Brewer Untouchable," *The Sporting News*, May 1, 1976: 25.

50 Ibid.

51 Ibid.

52 Ibid.

53 "Slaton Airs Frustrations," *The Sporting News*, September 4, 1976: 26.

54 Lou Chapman, "Porter, Colborn Could See Brewer Deal in the Works," *The Sporting News*, December 18, 1976: 48.

55 "A.L. Flashes," *The Sporting News*, April 30, 1977: 23.

56 Lou Chapman, "Brewers Players Gripe. ... They're 'Sick of Losing,'" *The Sporting News*, September 24, 1977: 16.

57 Jim Hawkins, "'I'm Yours for One Year,' Slaton Tells Tigers," *The Sporting News*, February 11, 1978: 38.

58 Mike Gonring, "Slight Pause Mighty Refreshing to Castro," *The Sporting News*, July 8, 1978: 14.

59 Murray Chass, "Rose, Age Top Features On 58-Man Re-Entry List," *The Sporting News*, September 30, 1978: 6.

60 Jack Lang, "How They Were – or Weren't – Picked," *The Sporting News*, November 18, 1978: 37.

61 Jim Hawkins, "Slaton Promises Tigers a Chance," *The Sporting News*, November 25, 1978: 49.

62 Murray Chass, "10 Free Agent Signings Hit $15 Million Jackpot," *The Sporting News*, March 3, 1979: 13.

63 Mike Gonring, "Slaton Quiets Doubters with Brewer Victories," *The Sporting News*, May 19, 1979: 18.

64 Ibid.

65 Stan Isle, "Fans' Dollar Checks Help Amarillo Pay Rent," *The Sporting News*, May 3, 1980: 17.

66 Peter Gammons, "A's, Jays in First; Players in Fog," *The Sporting News*, May 31, 1980: 23.

67 Tom Flaherty, "Brewers' Slaton: 'I Know I'm Going to Pitch Again,'" *The Sporting News*, August 30, 1980: 21.

68 TomFlaherty, "Slaton Passes Key Arm Test," *The Sporting News*, November 8, 1980: 51.

69 Tom Flaherty, "Slaton Soars Off the Mark on His Comeback Journey," *The Sporting News*, March 21, 1981: 42.

70 Ibid.

71 Tom Flaherty, "Slaton Is Slated for Long Relief," *The Sporting News*, December 19, 1981: 48, 51.

72 Ibid.

73 Tom Flaherty, "Fingers' Injury Gives Brewers a Scare," *The Sporting News*, April 3, 1982: 36; Tom Flaherty, "Yost an Unlikely Brewers Hero," *The Sporting News*, October 11, 1982: 33.

74 Peter Gammons, "Agents Fear Free-Agent Brushoff," The Sporting News, August 2, 1982: 19.

75 Tom Flaherty, "Slaton Makes Hay as a Middle Man," *The Sporting News*, August 2, 1982: 20.

76 Ibid.

77 Tom Flaherty, "Clark Provides Depth in Outfield," *The Sporting News*, January 2, 1984: 38.

78 Ibid.

79 Tom Singer, "Reggie, John Ease McNamara's Worries," *The Sporting News*, April 2, 1984: 19.

80 Stan Isle, "Clubhouse Prankster," *The Sporting News*, March 24, 1986: 41.

81 Bob McCoy, "Father Knows Best," *The Sporting News*, July 14, 1986: 10.

82 "Detroit," *The Sporting News*, August 4, 1986: 22.

DON SUTTON

By Gregory H. Wolf

I never wanted to be a superstar, or the highest paid player," said Don Sutton. "[A]ll I wanted was to be appreciated for the fact that I was consistent, dependable, and you could count on me."[1] By that measure, Sutton achieved his goal and more, as few pitchers in baseball history were as reliable, and as healthy, for as long as the right-hander. During his 23-year major-league career (1966-1988), Sutton logged as least 200 innings in 20 of his first 21 seasons, a remarkable stretch interrupted only by the strike-shortened campaign of 1981; and fanned at least 100 batters in 21 straight seasons, a feat subsequently duplicated only by Nolan Ryan Greg Maddux, and Roger Clemens. As of 2019 Sutton ranked tied for 14th in victories (324), 10th in shutouts (58), seventh in innings pitched (5,282⅓) and strikeouts (3,574), and third in games started (756) in major-league history; and given the trends in baseball, his positions seem permanently fixed. Despite those gaudy "counting statistics" that deservedly secured his enshrinement in the Hall of Fame, Sutton wasn't flashy or overpowering and was rarely mentioned among the best pitchers of his era. He received votes for the Cy Young Award in only five separate seasons, all of which came during a five-year period (1972-1976), when he finished in the top five in the NL; and he won 20 or more games in a season just once. Sutton never put together a career-defining season with eye-popping statistics, like his contemporaries, from Sandy Koufax, Tom Seaver, and Bob Gibson, to Jim Palmer, Gaylord Perry, and Ryan; and never authored a no-hitter. More than anything, Sutton was a relentless, fierce, yet enigmatic competitor; to his detractors, he was a compiler and more concerned for himself than his team. "Baseball was a job for me," said the hurler bluntly. "It was not an emotional experience. It was a job that I wanted to keep getting better and better at."[2]

Donald Howard Sutton was born on April 2, 1945, in Clio, Alabama, a small rural farming community in Barbour County in the southeastern part of the state. His parents, Charlie Howard and Lillian (McKnight) Sutton, were just 18 and 15 years old respectively at the time of Don's birth, and subsequently welcomed two more children into the world, Ron and Glenda.[3] The elder Sutton was a sharecropper and eventually relocated his family around 1950 to Molino, in the Florida panhandle, about 25 miles north of Pensacola, where he also worked seasonally in construction. During his baseball career, Don often cited his parents as role models, and it's easy to understand why. They instilled in him uncompromising determination, an unyielding work ethic, and a devout religious conviction, qualities that defined his professional baseball career, too.

Despite his grade-school education, Howard Sutton was self-made man, eventually received his high-school equivalency degree in his 40s, and became a concrete specialist. The Suttons were strict Evangelical Christians who expected their children to follow a righteous path, but also pull their weight by holding down part-time jobs and earning money for their clothes and spending money.

"All I ever wanted to be was a pitcher growing up," said Sutton. "If you asked me where I wanted to play, I'd have said in the middle of the diamond. Whose diamond, I don't care."[4] Those words characterized Sutton's approach to baseball from the time he started playing in pastures and local sandlots to Little League through 24 years of professional baseball. Pitching was always more important for Sutton than the team whose jersey he wore. Abandoning any pretense of playing other positions by the age of 11 to concentrate exclusively on pitching, Sutton fell under the tutelage of his sixth-grade teacher, Henry Roper, who had hurled in the New York Giants organization. Roper taught the pre-teen Sutton how to throw a curveball and tutored him in the basics of mechanics and delivery. "I learned to throw a curve by raising my index finger," remembered Sutton, "and digging the tip into the ball."[5]

Sutton played football, basketball, and baseball at Tate High School, but vacated the hardwood and gridiron after his sophomore year to focus on pitching. Growing up more than 700 miles from the nearest big-league city (St. Louis), Sutton was a self-described New York Yankees fan, who devoured games on his transistor radio. He idolized three pitchers, Dick Donovan for his intensity, Camilo Pascual for his knee-buckling curve, and Whitey Ford for his strategy.[6] Modeling his game on his trio of heroes, the 6-foot-1, yet lanky and thin Sutton posted a 21-7 slate in his three varsity seasons at Tate.[7] In his junior year (1962), he led the Aggies to the Class A state championship, tossing a 13-inning complete-game two-hitter with 11 strikeouts to defeat West Palm Beach Forest Hill in the finals.[8]

Disappointed that he received no professional offers despite his prep success, Sutton pursued his passion. Following graduation in 1963, he was a Connie Mack All-Star, and then enrolled at Gulf Coast Community College in Panama City, Florida.[9] That spring he posted a 5-4 slate while fanning 130 in 90 innings, earning an invitation to play for Sioux Falls in the highly competitive, amateur Basin League, which featured some of the best collegiate players in the country.[10] Even more important than his 5-5 record and 118 punchouts in 90 frames was the national exposure Sutton achieved. His summer baseball season concluded with his participation with the Wyoming (Michigan) Colts in the National Baseball Congress Tournament in Wichita, Kansas. Sutton (3-1) was named to the all-tournament team, which also included Seaver, star of the champion Alaska Panhandlers.

By the end of the summer, Sutton had a major decision to make. His bona fides established, Sutton had attracted scouts from at least nine major-league teams. He was especially impressed with Los Angeles Dodger scouts Leon Hamilton, Monty Basgall, and Burt Wells, their honesty and humble attitudes, and the club's long and distinguished tradition of grooming top-notch hurlers. They also informed Sutton that baseball's inaugural amateur draft would take place the following year, and that he might be able to assert more control over the financial aspects of his signing if he returned to school for another year. In the end the choice was an easy one: Sutton eschewed higher offers and signed with the Dodgers for an estimated $15,000 bonus and stipends for college, in September 1964.[11]

Sutton reported to the Dodgers' minor-league spring camp in Vero Beach, Florida, in spring 1965. Just 19 years old, he quickly emerged as the best prospect in the Dodgers system, eventually packing on some weight to 185. He debuted with Santa Barbara in the Class-A California League, retiring 19 of the first 20 batters he faced in his first game, en route to a complete-game five-hit victory.[12] Two months later, he was the circuit's top twirler (8-1, 1.50), and earned a bump to Albuquerque in the

One of the most durable and consistent hurlers in major-league history, Hall of Famer Don Sutton won 324 games, tied with Nolan Ryan for 14th most, and logged 5,282⅓ innings (seventh most) in 23 seasons (1966-1988).

Double-A Texas League. Another auspicious debut, a complete-game, eight-inning three-hitter with 13 strikeouts in the first game of a doubleheader, led to a 15-6 record, culminating with the league championship. Sutton recalled that his first year in pro ball introduced him to two skippers who profoundly impacted his career: his first manager, former Dodgers catcher Norm Sherry, who helped him relax and enjoy the game; and Roy Hartsfield, a stern tactician and student of the game.

Sutton reported to skipper Walter Alston and his first spring training with the Dodgers in 1966. Coming off a dramatic World Series title in seven games over the Minnesota Twins, the club was without Koufax and Don Drysdale, both of whom were holding out. Sutton assumed he'd be demoted once the aces reported [which they did in mid-March] and got into game shape; however, he quickly proved he was big-league-ready. He tossed seven innings of seven-hit ball, yielding three runs, but just two earned and fanned seven in his debut, a 4-2 loss to the Houston Astros on April 14 in Los Angeles. Four days later, he avenged that loss, holding the Astros to three runs in eight frames to notch his first victory, 6-3, in the Astrodome. On May 11 he blanked the Philadelphia Phillies in Connie Mack Stadium to record his first shutout, drawing raves from Phillies star Johnny Callison, who called him the best rookie since Juan Marichal.[13] Dodgers VP Fresco Thompson praised Sutton for his "great natural talent" and his calm demeanor, noting that the rookie was "completely composed, both on and off the diamond."[14] With the Dodgers in a tight three-team pennant race with the Pittsburgh Pirates and San Francisco Giants, "Little D" (as the LA press liked to call Sutton in a nod to Big D Drysdale) pulled a muscle in his right forearm on September 5, endangering the team's pennant aspirations.[15] Plagued by arm pain, Sutton made only four more starts, logging just 14⅓ innings, for the rest of the season, but the Dodgers picked up the slack, moved into first place on September 11 and secured the pennant on the last day of the season. The Dodgers were swept by the Baltimore Orioles in the World Series. Sutton did not play because of his injury, which also prevented him from joining the club on its subsequent goodwill junket and baseball trip to Japan.[16] Despite the injury, the 21-year-old's rookie season was a resounding success. He split his 24 decisions, posted a 2.99 ERA in 225⅔ innings, and fanned 209, seventh most in the NL; however, his excellent control, walking just 52, garnered the most praise from players and coaches.

Noted for his command, Sutton's pitching arsenal consisted of five pitches. He initially relied early in his career on his fastball with good movement and a curve, one of baseball's best benders, which he threw on any count. He eventually added a slider, screwball, and a changeup that improved as he matured. He threw all the pitches with the same delivery and motion, like a fastball, varying only the grip for each pitch, which he hid effectively behind his hip.[17] "My pitching philosophy didn't change from the time I was a kid," quipped Sutton. "I believed in changing speeds, throwing strikes and throwing a curveball for a strike when behind in the count."[18] Never overpowering, despite striking out at least 200 batters in a season five times in his first eight campaigns, Sutton relied on technique, precision, strategy, and his pinpoint accuracy for his success. He challenged hitters up in the strike zone and was prone to the gopher ball, but kept batters guessing. "He emits an air of professionalism," said Burt Hooton about his Dodgers teammate (1975-1980). "He is the same whether he getting his tail kicked or tearing up the joint."[19] Opponents routinely claimed Sutton doctored pitches, scuffing them, which led to umpires checking him for sandpaper or other defilers, though nothing was ever found. Like Gaylord Perry, noted for his occasional wet one, Sutton exploited the opponents' charges of cheating, effectively creating a phantom pitch for them to worry about.

Sutton's progress over the next four seasons (1967-1970) was sporadic as the Dodgers organization underwent changes, including Koufax's retirement after the 1966 season, the end of GM Buzzie Bavasi's era (1950-1968), and the beginning of Al Campanis's tenure. The offensively-challenged Dodgers dropped to 73-89 in 1967, their worst season since 1944, then 76-86 in 1968, marking the first time the club had posted consecutive losing seasons since 1933-1938. Like his team, Sutton slumped; his ERA spiked to 3.95 (fourth highest in the NL) in his sophomore season. The front office entertained ideas of trading the hurler for a much-needed bat in the offseason, which Sutton spent fulfilling military obligation in the US Army Reserve, serving as a private at Fort Gordon, Georgia.[20] Discharged in mid-March, Sutton reported to camp late, struggled, and began the season with Triple-A Spokane (Pacific Coast League) to get in shape. In the "Year of the Pitcher," when the NL batted a collective .243 and teams scored just 3.43 runs per game, Sutton started off slowly and was ultimately demoted to the bullpen after a second consecutive sluggish start, on June 20. Perhaps feeling more empowered in his third season, Sutton was livid, and displayed the sharp tongue that would characterize his career, barking, "Because I'm owned by this team, I'll have to do what I am told or I'm out of baseball."[21] Sutton was too good to rust in the pen, though, and after a five-week exile, returned to the rotation in late July and put together a strong stretch over the final two months of the season (7-7, 2.06 ERA in 109 innings) to finish with his second consecutive 11-15 record, and a 2.60 ERA.

Shortly after the conclusion of the 1968 season, Sutton married Patricia A. Luther, a local Southern Californian whom he had met the previous year.[22] They had two sons, Daron, born in 1969, and Staci, four years later.

The Dodgers entered a new phase of prolonged success beginning in 1969 when major-league baseball expanded to 24 teams, finishing with an 85-77 slate and in fourth place in the newly formed NL West in the first season of realignment. On a staff featuring 20-game winners Claude Osteen and Bill Singer, Sutton was often overlooked. On May 1 he tossed the first of his five career one-hitters, yielding only a one-out eighth-inning double to Jim Davenport to beat the Giants at Candlestick Park, as part of his streak of 27⅓ consecutive scoreless innings, the second longest in the NL that season.[23] Sutton compiled what proved to be his career highs in starts (41) and innings (293⅓), yet produced a losing record for the third straight season (17-18) and an ERA (3.47), when adjusted to consider ballpark factors, was higher than league average.[24] In 1970 the Dodgers finished in a distant second place behind the Big Red Machine of Cincinnati, while Sutton fashioned another similar season, including a worse than league-average adjusted ERA. The highlight of his 15 victories was a stellar 10-inning, five-hit shutout with a career-best 12 punchouts (achieved six times) on July 17 at Dodger Stadium against the New York Mets and Seaver, who hurled nine scoreless on two days' rest after having started and hurled three scoreless innings in the All-Star Game.

After five seasons in the majors, Sutton proved to be a dependable workhorse, logging more innings than any NL hurler except bluebloods Fergie Jenkins, Gibson, Marichal, Perry, and teammate Osteen, yet the Alabaman was far from a star. Sutton had a losing record (66-73) and his ERA (3.45) when adjusted was worse than league average.[25] All of that changed beginning in 1971, when Sutton put together the first of seven consecutive stellar seasons, which coincided with the Dodgers' re-emergence as one of the NL's perennially top teams.

In 1971 the Dodgers engaged the Giants in an exciting pennant race that heated up in September, when Sutton emerged as an ace. However, he had started off the season poorly, and fell to 1-5 (with a 4.60 ERA) on May 22, dropping his career slate to 67-78. Dejected, suffering a crisis of confidence, and plagued by a sore elbow, he consulted an orthopedic doctor, but perhaps more importantly worked with pitching coach Red Adams to refine his mechanics. He switched to a more over-the-top delivery, rather from the three-quarters position, which put stress on his elbow.[26] That change led to Sutton's best season thus far (17-12 and the NL's fifth-lowest ERA, 2.54), highlighted by going 5-1 in his seven starts in September, fanning 57 in 57 innings, walking just seven while posting a 1.74 ERA. With the Dodgers needing a victory and a Giants loss on the last day of the season to force a playoff, Sutton got the start and displayed his humor when he arrived at the park on September 30 with his hand wrapped in gauze, informing teammates and coaches that he had had an accident cooking.[27] The 52,684 in Dodgers Stadium sat quietly as Sutton tossed a six-hitter to beat the Astros, 2-1, emitting their loudest groan in the eighth when it was announced the Marichal and the Giants defeated the hapless San Diego Padres, 5-1.

The 27-year-old Sutton considered 1972 his "best" and "most consistent year," helping the Dodgers to the NL's best team ERA (2.78), but that couldn't overcome a sluggish offense, resulting in a distant second-place finish to the Reds.[28] Named Opening Day starter for the first of seven consecutive seasons, Sutton began his seventh big-league season by winning his first eight decisions, extending his winning streak to 11 games. Included was a stretch of 30⅔ consecutive scoreless innings, 10 of which resulted in a tough-luck no-decision against the Expos in Montreal despite yielding only one hit. He was named to his first All-Star squad, tossing two scoreless frames and fanning two in the NL's 4-3 win in 10 innings. He concluded the season with a sense of déjà vu, winning his last five decisions in September, highlighted by three consecutive shutouts as part of a career-best streak of 36 consecutive scoreless innings, the longest such streak in the NL that season. The second of those whitewashings, an 11-inning three-hitter with 11 punchouts against the Giants at Dodgers Stadium on September 22, was the 100th victory of his career. Arguably the best game of his career, too, it was his career-longest pitching outing, subsequently matched twice, though both resulted in no-decisions. Despite missing several starts due to the first players strike in baseball history, from April 1 to 13, canceling 86 games, Sutton finished with a 19-9 slate, set career highs in complete games (18) and an NL-leading nine shutouts (which as of 2019 was still the Dodgers record for right-handers). He also led the NL in WHIP (0.913) for the first of four times in his career and fewest hits per nine innings (6.1), and finished tied with four others for fifth place in the Cy Young Award which the Phillies Steve Carlton (27 wins) won by garnering all 24 first-place votes.

Sutton posted similar numbers in 1973 (18-10, 2.42 ERA), but the Dodgers finished in second place for the fourth consecutive season. The tide turned in 1974, by which time a cadre of prospects from the club's deep farm system, such as infielders Steve Garvey (who was named NL MVP in '74), Davey Lopes, Bill Russell, and Ron Cey, had gained much-needed experience on the big-league level. Added to the mix were two offseason acquisitions, Jimmy Wynn (32 HRs, 108 RBIs) and rubber-armed, enigmatic reliever Mike Marshall (who set a big-league record by hurling in 106 games and won the Cy Young Award); as well as hard thrower Andy Messersmith (staff-best 20 wins), acquired from the California Angels two years earlier. Sutton got off to a hot start, pitched a shutout on Opening Day and then added two consecutive blankings, including a one-hitter, to improve his record to 6-2 on May 14, before the bottom suddenly and completely unexpectedly fell out. Sutton fell into a deep slump, going more than two months without winning a start and posting a miserable 5.64 ERA in 14 starts from May 19 through July 20. Remarkably, the Dodgers maintained their first-place standing. Critics claimed the 29-year-old was suddenly washed up, had lost his heater (which was never overwhelming to begin with, topping out at 88 or 89 MPH, according to Sutton[29]); or was tipping his pitches; or maybe hiding an injury. Through it all, Smoky Alston stuck with his longtime hurler. In the era before teams employed mental skills coaches and psychologists, Sutton recognized that baseball was much more than a clash of talents. "[M]ost of us have similar abilities," he said. "The differences are mental and emotional and the big thing is mental preparation. That's where everything starts: the poise, the confidence, the concentration."[30] Sutton also believed his struggles resulted from his mental situation, and not from what his detractors charged. Willing to try anything to end his slump, Sutton contacted LA hypnotist Arthur Ellen, who had helped former teammate Maury Wills, in late June. "I only saw him once," said Sutton, who also revealed his initial skepticism because of his Christian Fundamentalist beliefs. "[B]ut after that I knew I could have a good time doing my job. ... I credit Ellen for giving me back my ability to relax and pitch to my potential."[31] Sutton's slump didn't magically end after the first visit, but when it did, he transformed into one of baseball's best hurlers, going 13-1 with a 2.17 ERA in his last 17 starts. The Dodgers withstood a serious challenge from the Reds in September and took their first NL West crown, in the 161st game of the season, on October 1 in Houston. Fittingly Sutton started the game and hurled five shutout innings before yielding to relievers, to pick up his 19th victory of the season in the NL-most 40th start and secure the Dodgers' first postseason berth since his rookie campaign nine years earlier.

With the best record in baseball (102-60), the Dodgers were overwhelming favorites against the Pirates (88-74) in the NLCS. In Game One in the Steel City, Sutton shut out the Bucs on four hits, fanning six. Longtime LA sportswriter Jim Murray called it a "masterpiece," adding that Sutton is the "most underrated pitcher in the league."[32] Four days later, in Tinsel Town, Sutton stamped the Dodgers ticket to the fall classic by a performance almost as good as his first, holding the Pirates to three hits in eight innings to pick up the win in a 12-1 laugher. Widely predicted to capture their first title since 1965, the Dodgers met their match against the rough-and-tumble Oakland A's, in search of their third straight World Series championship. Sutton yielded just five hits in eight strong innings to win Game Two, 3-2, in LA, to even the Series, but that victory proved to be the Dodgers only one against their postseason-experienced adversaries. The A's took the next three, including Game Five, which Sutton started. (He was removed for a pinch-hitter in the sixth, with the Dodgers trailing 2-0.)

The Dodgers' hold on the NL West crown was short-lived as the Big Red Machine ran roughshod over the entire league in 1975 and 1976 to capture consecutive pennants and then became the first NL team to win consecutive World Series since the New York Giants in 1921-1922. Donning what became his signature man-permed, curly hair, Sutton produced a typical Suttonesque season, going 16-13 in '75, leading the NL in WHIP and strikeout-to-walk ratio for the first of three times in his career; he also hurled two scoreless innings in the All-Star Game. In 1976 he won 21 games (3.06 ERA), which included the most dominant stretch in his big-league career, going 14-1 with a

1.62 ERA from July 7 to September 27. He finished a distant third in voting for the Cy Young Award, behind winner Randy Jones (22-14, 2.74) of the Padres and the Mets' Jerry Koosman (21-10, 2.69). With four games remaining in the '76 season, 64-year-old Alston, feeling pressure from the front office, retired, ending his 23-year tenure as the Dodgers' skipper.

Alston's retirement marked a turning point in Sutton's career, and especially with his relationship with the Dodgers. "Alston was the most secure, best man that I have ever met," said Sutton, who appreciated how his skipper confronted problems behind closed doors instead of airing dirty laundry to the press.[33] Furthermore, Alston's quiet demeanor mirrored Sutton's own introverted personality in some respects, and they formed a mutual trust, indeed respect, for one another.

Sutton was unimpressed when longtime Dodgers coach and scout Tommy Lasorda, who had served as interim skipper for the final four games of the '76 season, was named permanent skipper in 1977. According to Ron Fimrite's feature on Sutton in *Sports Illustrated* in 1982, Sutton mentioned to reporters that spring that he had wanted his former catcher Jeff Torborg as the club's new manager, but knew it had been a foregone conclusion that Lasorda would land that job. The Dodgers' senior member, Sutton was "not an ally" of the new manager, and disdained his "show-biz approach."[34] Lasorda's rah-rah style clashed mightily with Sutton's staid, conservative, indeed introverted approach. The stage was set for some explosives in La-La Land, and Sutton was well beyond the point in his career that he would back down. Years after retiring, Sutton reflected on his relationship with Lasorda, and commented, "One regret I have is that Tommy and I never took a day, just the two of us, and sat down and explained our personalities to each other."[35]

Sutton had a complex personality, to say the least. "Don's the kind of guy you either like or you don't," quipped longtime Dodgers teammate Bill Russell.[36] Reserved with his emotions, Sutton could be icy, blunt, and matter-of-fact with his criticism of teammates. "I am much more comfortable dealing internally with ideas than I am externally with people," said Sutton, who gave the impression of being aloof, disinterested, stubborn, impatient, or cocky; some players objected to his religious convictions, leading to a standoffish attitude.[37] "I don't know that anybody here [with the Dodgers] was ever that close to Don," said Ron Cey.[38] Fimrite might have captured the intricacies and apparent contradictions of Sutton's personality best, opining that the hurler "masks his seriousness about life and obsession with perfection with a blithe manner that the uninitiated might confuse with flippancy. He protects the vulnerable underside of his nature with the quickest wit in baseball."[39] On the other hand, Sutton never forgot his Alabama roots, poor upbringing, or religious grounding, referring to himself as "nothing more than a semipolished hick."[40] His brutal honesty and willingness to speak his mind led occasionally to combustible confrontations in a clubhouse filled with highly competitive, yet easily insulted athletes.

Lasorda led the Dodgers to consecutive NL pennants in 1977 and 1978, losing to the New York Yankees in the World Series each season. Sutton put up similar numbers in both campaigns, going 14-8 and 15-11 and logging about 240 innings; however, the tone of the seasons was drastically different. In the former, Sutton blazed through the first half of the season and was chosen to start his first All-Star Game. The 32-year-old tossed three scoreless innings and earned the victory in the NL's 7-5 triumph at Yankee Stadium. It was his last of four All-Star appearances, during which he yielded just five hits and no runs in eight frames. The Dodgers featured big bats with a quartet of sluggers with at least 30 home runs (Dusty Baker, Cey, Garvey, and Reggie Smith) and the majors' best pitching staff, which led the baseball with a 3.22 team ERA, behind five starters who logged at least 212 innings (Sutton, Hooton, Tommy John, Rick Rhoden, and Doug Rau). After John, who led the staff with 20 wins, was hit hard in the opening-game loss to the

Phillies in the NLCS, Sutton came to the rescue in Game Two, tossing a complete-game 7-1 victory. Lasorda took no chances in the highly anticipated World Series with the Yankees, sending the club's longtime stalwart to the mound in Game One in Yankee Stadium. Sutton fulfilled a lifelong dream of pitching in the "House that Ruth Built" in the fall classic, but wasn't overcome with emotions. "I approach play with more emotion than I do work," he quipped. I approach work analytically and logistically, not emotionally. It's a day at the office."[41] Sutton went seven strong innings and was relieved in the top of the eighth after yielding the go-ahead run, 3-2. The Dodgers tied the game in the ninth before losing in the 12th. Called on again in Game Five with the Bombers on the verge of their first title since 1962, Sutton calmly dispatched the Yankees, 10-4, tossing a complete game to win his fifth consecutive postseason decision. The next day, however, Reggie Jackson spanked home runs on three consecutive pitches, and Yankees were back on the top of the baseball world.

Lasorda wanted the Dodgers to project his cheerleader disposition and Hollywood feel-good family vibes, but Sutton never bled Dodger blue. "I never considered the Dodgers family," he quipped in businesslike fashion. "I only have one family."[42] Behind the Dodgers' façade, animosity was stirring, especially between the skipper and Sutton, who Lasorda apparently felt never was in his corner, but also between some of the players. And it wasn't in Sutton's DNA to placate his teammates. The situation came to a head when Sutton was interviewed by sportswriter Thomas Boswell of the *Washington Post*. The hurler expressed his frustration that the baseball world seemed infatuated with "Steve Garvey, the All-American boy"; and bluntly called Smith the club's best player the last two years, noting that he doesn't get the attention because he doesn't "smile all the time" and tells the truth, much like Sutton himself, which alienated people.[43] Garvey confronted Sutton in front of his locker before a game at Shea Stadium in New York on August 20 and a brawl ensued. Sportswriter Milton Richman described it as "concentrated fury amounting to an almost homicidal desire to tear one another apart."[44] Players and coaches finally separated the two who emerged with scratches on their face and a red eye for Garvey, the result on a finger poke.[45] That ugly episode aside, the Dodgers weren't belting each other like the early 1970s A's or even the champion Yankees. The Dodgers continued to roll, and once again led the NL in home runs and lowest team ERA in 1978. Their postseason results repeated the script from the previous year: They defeated the Phillies in four games in the NLCS and lost to the Yankees in six in the World Series. One major difference was Sutton, who was clobbered in all three of his postseason starts. Charged with the loss in each, he surrendered 17 runs (14 earned) and 24 hits in 17⅔ innings.

Over the next two seasons Sutton chipped away at Dodgers pitching records as the club slumped to a sub-.500-seaon in 1979 and then squandered a September lead to finish runner-up to the Houston Astros in 1980. En route to a 12-15 slate in '79, Sutton labored through eight innings, yielding nine hits and four runs (three earned) against the Reds at Riverfront Stadium on May 20 to record his 210th victory, thus breaking Drysdale's cherished mark. The following season, the 35-year-old pitched his best and most consistent ball in five years, posting a 13-5 slate, leading the majors in ERA (2.20) and WHIP (0.989), and ranking second in the NL by allowing just 6.9 hits per nine innings.

Granted free agency after the 1980 season, Sutton signed a four-year pact with the Astros. "It was kind of exciting," he said about the challenge of a new team. "I think I reached a stage with the Dodgers where they really didn't appreciate what I was delivering for them, and I didn't appreciate how nice it was to play there."[46] Sutton left his mark on the Dodgers, setting team records for wins (233), starts (533), innings pitched (3,816⅓), strikeouts (2,696), and shutouts (52), all of which still stood as of 2019.

After 15 years of stability in Dodger blue, Sutton was often on the move in his last eight seasons (1981-1988), playing for four different teams, plus the Dodgers again, and was involved in two late-season trades to clubs needing an extra arm for a postseason push. Sutton's stint with the Astros lasted less than two full seasons, yet they were packed with drama — and not the positive kind. A strike by the players and their union led to the first work stoppage in baseball since 1972 and wiped out approximately one-third of the season. Teaming with another graybeard, Nolan Ryan, Sutton (11-9) fortified baseball's best staff, and led the NL once again in WHIP (1.015). With the Astros just a victory away from clinching the second-half championship (as part of a convoluted attempt to generate interest and extend the postseason), Sutton was hit on the right knee by a pitch from the Dodgers Jerry Reuss at Dodger Stadium on October 2.[47] The result was a fracture and Sutton missed the Division Series, which the Astros lost to the Dodgers.

In the offseason, Sutton gave an interview to longtime *Los Angeles Times* sportswriter Ross Newhan that turned himself into a persona non grata in Houston.[48] Sutton recounted a conversation with Astros GM Al Rosen, expressing his desire to finish his career on the West Coast in order to be with his family, who remained in the LA area, and business interests, and had no desire to live in Texas, though he didn't consider his signing to be a mistake. Once Houston papers picked up the story, Sutton and Rosen, who had prematurely ended his career to spend more time with his family, began verbally sparring, with Sutton apparently going so far as to suggest that he would return a signing bonus in order to be freed from his contract.[49] Sutton was booed loudly by Astros fan in his first start of the season, but the catcalls about a spoiled millionaire soon morphed into cheers when Sutton rolled off seven straight victories after losing his season debut. Sutton (13-8, 3.00 ERA) was back in form, but the Astros struggled, playing under .500 ball. In a salary dump at the trading deadline, the Astros sent the 37-year-old to the Milwaukee Brewers on August 30 for Kevin Bass, Frank DiPino, and Mike Madden.

Landing in the middle of an exciting divisional race, the old graybeard immediately shored up the Brewers' pitching corps, which had been led by Pete Vuckovich and Mike Caldwell, but was without reigning AL Cy Young Award and MVP winner Rollie Fingers, out with an arm injury. The Brewers were a raucous, home-run-smashing team, tabbed Harvey's Wallbangers in honor of skipper Harvey Kuenn, and featured eventual AL 1982 MVP Robin Yount, Cecil Cooper, Gorman Thomas, Ben Oglivie, and Paul Molitor. Sutton went the distance in his first start, losing 4-2 to the Cleveland Indians in the second game of a twin bill on September 2 at County Stadium, then blanked the Detroit Tigers on seven hits for his first AL victory five days later. The outcome of the division crown rested on the last series of the season, with the second-place Orioles in Baltimore. The Brewers lost the first three games, outscored 26-7, creating a tie in the standings and setting up a winner-take-all finale on October 3. In the most important regular-season game of his life, Sutton was at his best, tossing eight strong innings, yielding just two runs, as the Wallbangers bashed their way to a 10-2 victory and the West crown.

The Brewers' struggles returned in the ALCS against the California Angels, who took the first two games of the best-of-five series in the Southern California sun. In another win-or-go-home game, Sutton went 7⅔ innings, yielding all three of his runs in the eighth, but emerged victorious, 5-3, in a courageous outing. "We were shut down for seven innings by one of the cleverest pitchers of the last 15 years," quipped Angels skipper Gene Mauch. "He's capable of taking the straight out of the ball without defacing it. Our players didn't say a word about it. They know what the man is capable of doing with finger dexterity."[15] Reggie Jackson, who faced Sutton in the 1977 and 1978 World Series, agreed. "I've never seen him better. He had control of four pitches. He beat me fair and square. I didn't have one good swing."[51]

The 1982 World Series featured a clash of styles: The Brewers' long ball vs. the St. Louis Cardinals' speed and small ball. In a back-and-forth Series, with plenty of unexpected twists, Sutton fared poorly in both of his starts, both of which took place in the Gateway City, yielding a combined 12 hits and 11 runs (9 earned) in just 10⅓ innings, picking up the loss in Game Six. The Redbirds won the final two contests of the Series to capture their first title since 1967.

In his two full seasons with the Brewers, Sutton went 22-25 while the Brewers finished in fifth and then the cellar of the AL East. Nonetheless Sutton had fond memories and experiences of Beer City, perhaps feeling at home in a gritty, battle-tested, and workmanlike town that reminded him of his own personality. "Milwaukee was the greatest place I ever played," he cooed, praising the locals as sincere, genuine, and authentic. "It's a blue-collar lifestyle and work ethic that is very simple. There's no pretentiousness. I loved pitching in County Stadium."[52]

In December 1984 Sutton was traded to the Oakland A's in a multiplayer transaction. Just 20 victories shy of 300 to begin his 19th season, the 40-year-old proved to be the staff's most effective hurler, notching 13 victories before the A's sent him in a post-trade-deadline waiver deal to the Angels, who were battling the Kansas City Royals for the West crown. Sutton won his first two starts for the Halos, who eventually faded down the stretch, losing eight of their final 13 to finish runner-up to the Royals by one game.

In a quest for what he considered his "inevitable" 300th victory, Sutton began the 1986 campaign with the Angels so poorly that many skeptics wondered if he could win five more games.[53] He lost his first three decisions and posted a staggering 9.12 ERA in his first five starts before winning a game. Number 299 came in dramatic fashion on June 9 when he faced 306-game winner Tom Seaver of the Chicago White Sox and emerged victorious, spinning a two-hitter at Comiskey Park to record what proved to be the final shutout of his career. Nine days later, in front of more than 37,000 raucous fans at the Big A, Anaheim Stadium, the self-described "mechanic" and "unspectacular grinder" became the 19th pitcher in major-league history to win 300 games. Praising Sutton as a "working class hero,"

LA sportswriter Mike Penner wrote that the right-hander "did it his way, shunning the bright lights and sticking to a nose-to-the-grindstone work ethic," in a performance that mirrored the pitcher's personality: a distance-going three-hit, 5-1 win. Yet another historic matchup occurred 10 days later in Anaheim, when Sutton faced a 304-game winner, knuckleballer Phil Niekro of the Indians. The matchup marked the first time 300-game winners had faced one another since Tim Keefe and Pud Galvin on July 21, 1892. Fittingly, Sutton and Niekro pitched to a draw, saddled with no-decisions, though the Alabaman won the statistics contest, going seven strong innings and yielding three runs, while a wild Niekro logged a wobbly 6⅓ innings, also surrendering three runs, but 10 hits and seven walks. Sutton finished his fairy-tale-like season with a 15-11 slate while the Angels cruised to the West title. In the ALCS against the highly favored Boston Red Sox, Sutton got the call in Game Four, dueling eventual 1986 Cy Young Award winner Roger Clemens to a draw, throwing four-hit, one-run ball over 6⅓ innings in an Angels victory in 11 innings in Anaheim. Sutton's second appearance of the series was in Game Seven, in Boston, when he relieved John Candelaria in the fourth, trailing 7-0, tossing 3⅓ innings of mop-up duty, yielding one run.

After a rough season with the Angels in 1987 (11-11, 4.70 ERA) and missing the 200-inning mark for the first time in his career (191⅔) excluding the strike-shortened season, Sutton came full circle in 1988, signing with the Dodgers for his 23rd season. It was obvious that the 43-year-old had no more gas in the tank as he labored through 16 starts, landed on the disabled list with a sprained elbow, for the first and only time in his career, and was released on August 10.[54] "It was a mistake," admitted Sutton about his return. "It ended up being a depressing way to end my relationship with the Dodgers."[55]

Sutton retired with a 324-256 record, plus six more victories in the postseason, and a 3.26 ERA; his adjusted ERA was 108, or 8% better than league average. He also threw 58 shutouts, 10th most in big-league history; among pitchers who began their career after 1920, only Warren Spahn, Ryan, Seaver, and Bert Blyleven tossed more. Sutton also tossed at least nine scoreless innings on seven other occasions for which he received a no-decision. Never a threat at the plate, Sutton batted a paltry .144 and did not hit a home run in 1,354 lifetime at-bats.

Not expected to be a first-ballot Hall of Famer, Sutton garnered 56.8% in his initial year of eligibility, in 1994 [75% was required for enshrinement]. His totals steadily rose and in 1998 he was elected to the Hall of Fame with 81.6% of the votes, and was the only player elected by the baseball writers that year. [Larry Doby, who integrated the American League in 1947 with the Cleveland Indians, was elected by the Veterans Committee]. The news came after an anxious period in Sutton's life. In November 1996, his daughter with his second wife, Mary, was born four months premature, though gradually she became stronger and was discharged from Piedmont Hospital in Atlanta in March.[56] Sutton's Hall of Fame plaque depicts him with a Dodgers cap; the Dodgers retired his number 20 in 1998.

Sutton made a smooth transition into broadcasting immediately after retiring from baseball. He had begun laying the foundations for his career behind the microphone as early as 1969 when he served as a disc jockey at a radio station in Burbank in the offseason, and had been a television sports commentator periodically in the next decade. After broadcasting Dodgers games in 1989, he began a long and distinguished career doing play-by-play and analysis with the Atlanta Braves in 1990 until 2006. He returned to the club in 2009, after a two-year stint with the Washington Nationals, and as of 2019 called Braves games. In 2015 the Braves inducted Sutton into their Hall of Fame. "Don has been an integral part of the Braves family for decades, and is most deserving of this honor," said Braves President John Schuerholz. "Generations of Braves fans have been wowed by his knowledge and charmed by his ability to bring life to the broadcast. He is undoubtedly beloved throughout Braves Country."[57]

SOURCES

In addition to the sources cited in the Notes, the author also accessed Retrosheet.org, Baseball-Reference.com, the SABR Minor Leagues Database, accessed online at Baseball-Reference.com, SABR.org, *The Sporting News* archive via Paper of Record, the player's Hall of Fame file, the on-line archives via Newspaper.com, and Ancestry.com.

NOTES

1. Robert S Weider, 'Don Sutton: An Unsung Achiever among Mound Elite," *Baseball Digest*, September 1985: 35.
2. Bill Ballew, "Sutton Eyes Hall after Successful Career," *Sports Collectors Digest*, February 1, 1991: 102.
3. "Don and Patti Sutton Were Striking Out Till They Got Help – And Now They're Safe at Home," *People*, April 5, 1982: 90.
4. Ballew: 102.
5. Ron Fimrite, "'God May Be a Football Fan'," *Sports Illustrated*, July 12, 1982: 71.
6. Kevin Huard, "SCD Interviews 300-Game Winner Don Sutton," *Sports Collectors Digest*, February 1, 1991: 105.
7. Ronnie Joyce, "Former Aggie, Sutton Sign Dodger Contract," *Pensacola News-Journal*, September 13, 1964: 37.
8. Bill Kirby, "Northeast Wins Class AA Title," *Tampa Tribune*, June 15, 1962: C1. Sutton faced Harry Dahl, who also went the distance, fanning 16. Dahl later signed with the Los Angeles Dodgers, on the recommendation of scout Leon Hamilton, in June 1964, presaging Sutton's signing by about three months. See "Dahl Signs with Dodgers for 'Substantial' Bonus," Palm Beach Post-Times, June 7, 1964: D1. He went 15-15 in two seasons in the minors.
9. "Connie Mack All-Star Team," *Pensacola News-Journal*, July 31, 1963: 2.
10. All statistics from Sutton's junior-college, Basin League, and NBC participation are from Ronnie Joyce.
11. Frank Finch, "Scouts' Sales Talk Landed Don Sutton." *Los Angeles Times*, July 7, 1966: III: 4.
12. Associated Press, "Santa Barbara Rookie Pitcher Impresses in Cal League Opener," *Reno News-Gazette*, April 15, 1965: 13.
13. Ray Kelly, "Freshman Hurler Earned Starter's Diploma," *Philadelphia Bulletin*, May 12, 1965.
14. Bob Hunter, "L.A.'s New Big D Sutton Death to Foes," *The Sporting News*, May 14, 1966: 3.
15. Frank Finch, "Sutton Hurt as Dodgers Whip Giants," *Los Angeles Times*, September 6, 1966: III, 1.
16. "Don Sutton Skips Trip to Rest Arm," *Los Angeles Times*, October 12, 1966: III, 1.
17. Weider: 32.
18. Huard: 104.
19. Fimrite: 68.

20 Wilt Browning, "Grenade Explodes Sutton's Confidence," *Atlanta Constitution*, December 6, 1967: 2-D.

21 George Lederer, "Sutton Saves Win, but Hates Work," *Independent Press-Telegram* (Long Beach, California), June 23, 1968: S-2.

22 "Don and Patti Sutton Were Striking Out Till They Got Help – And Now They're Safe At Home."

23 Sutton streak of 27⅓ innings (April 23 to May 6) was second to the Chicago Cubs Ken Holtzman's 33⅔ from May 6 to 24.

24 Sutton's adjusted earned-run average (ERA+) in 1969 was 96; league average is 100.

25 His five-year adjusted ERA was 95.

26 Bob Hunter, "No. 20-Win Button in Sutton's Goal," *The Sporting News*, May 13, 1972: 3.

27 Ron Rapoport, "Dodgers Miss Despite Final Triumph," *Los Angeles Times*, October 1, 1971: III, 7.

28 Ballew: 102.

29 Weider: 31.

30 "N.L. Flashes," *The Sporting News*, June 22, 1974: 22.

31 Ross Newhan, "Sutton: 1974 Was Entrancing," *Los Angeles Times*, January 16, 1975: III, 1.

32 Jim Murray, "Sutton's Masterpiece Gets the Quiet Awe It Deserves," *Los Angeles Times*, October 6, 1974: III, 1.

33 Ballew: 101.

34 Fimrite: 72.

35 Ross Newhan, "Little D's Big Day," *Los Angeles Times*, July 26, 1998.

36 Fimrite: 75.

37 Weider: 32.

38 Fimrite: 75.

39 Fimrite: 67.

40 Ibid.

41 United Press Internaional, "Win or Lose, Dodgers' Sutton WILL Have Fun!" *Valley News* (Van Nuys, California), October 11, 1977: 12.

42 Fimrite: 73.

43 An excerpt of Thomas Boswell's article from the Washington Post was reprinted in "Morning Briefings," *Los Angeles Times*, August 18, 1978: III, 2.

44 "Morning Briefings," *Los Angeles Times*, August 23, 1978: III, 2.

45 The entire episode and its aftermath were recounted by Scott Ostler, "Suddenly, the Hugging Turns to Punching," *Los Angeles Times*, August 21, 1978: III, 2.

46 Ballew: 102.

47 Mark Heisler, "Astros Lose Sutton, Game," *Los Angeles Times*, October 3, 1981: III, 1.

48 Ross Newhan, "Sutton Talks of Coming Home," *Los Angeles Times*, February 18, 1982: III, 4.

49 Fimrite: 79

50 Ross Newhan, "Sutton Utilizes Twilight Zone to Stall Angels." *Los Angeles Times*, October 9, 1982: III, 1

51 Ibid.

52 Ballew: 102.

53 Mike Penner, "Sutton Is on the Button – 300th Is a 3-Hitter," *Los Angeles Times*, June 19, 1986: III, 1.

54 Sam McManis, "Dodgers Hand Sutton His Walking Papers," *Los Angeles Times*, August 11, 1988: III, 1.

55 Balfour.

56 Jill Lieber, "Baby's Struggle Preoccupies Suttons," *USA Today*, January 5, 1998.

57 Phil W. Hudson, "Braves to Induct Legendary Broadcaster Don Sutton into Hall of Fame," *Atlanta Business Chronicle*, April 20, 2015.

GORMAN THOMAS

By Dennis D. Degenhardt

He was the first amateur player selected by his expansion franchise and became its first home-run champion, alas, when the parent team was in a different city. In his major-league debut, he dropped the first ball hit to him for an error and got his first hit, a triple, in his second at-bat. Nine days later, he hit his first home run, off a future Hall of Famer. Gorman Thomas became one of the franchise's all-time fan favorites.

James Gorman Thomas III was born in Charleston, South Carolina, on December 12, 1950, to James Gorman Thomas Jr. and Gladys (Altman) Thomas. He had a brother, Gary, and a sister, Deborah. His father was a World War II veteran, and a postal worker who retired as a postmaster. He also preceded Thomas in professional baseball, having signed with the New York Yankees.[1] Gladys was a homemaker and active in her church.

Gorman' interest in baseball started early, in Little League baseball. He went on to the Pony League, the Colt League, and American Legion ball, making the all-star teams in each of the 11 years he played at those levels. His Pony and Colt League teams won state championships.[2]

At Cardinal Newman High School in Columbia, South Carolina, Thomas earned 14 letters in baseball, football, basketball, and track[3] and led the basketball team to three titles.[4] After his family moved to Charleston, Thomas enrolled in James Island High School for his senior year and led the football team to a 15-0 championship season.[5] Turning to baseball, he pitched and played shortstop with scouts in attendance noting his power potential.[6] Hitting .430, he was first-team All-Conference at shortstop and was named a High School All-American.[7]

On June 5, 1969, Thomas became the first player drafted by the expansion Seattle Pilots[8] in the amateur draft.[9] Forgoing a football scholarship with Florida State University,[10] he joined the Billings Mustangs in the rookie Pioneer League, batting .296 in 41 games with 26 errors at shortstop. As he told Mario Ziino in 2013, "I played the position like a hockey goalie. It was like I was fending off slap shots."[11]

After the season, the Pilots went bankrupt and re-emerged in 1970 as the Milwaukee Brewers. Thomas spent the 1970 and 1971 in the Class-A Midwest League. Playing for Clinton (Iowa) in 1970, he struggled, batting .212 and making 28 errors in 85 games. At Danville (Illinois) in 1971 he moved to the outfield, and both his hitting and fielding improved and he hit a league-record 31 home runs. (He also led the league with 170 strikeouts in 121 games.) Promoted to Double-A San Antonio in 1972, he won another home run title, swatting 26, while his 171 strikeouts also topped the league.

A few weeks into 1973 spring training, Brewers manager Del Crandall named the young slugger his starting right fielder.[14] His major-league debut, on Opening Day at Baltimore's Memorial Stadium, started poorly: He dropped the first ball hit to him for an error. He tripled[15] in his second at-bat. In the first game of an April 15 doubleheader at County Stadium, Thomas smashed his first home run, in the bottom of the ninth inning off Jim Palmer, forcing extra innings in a Brewers 11-inning 3-2 victory. But on July 2 with only 27 hits, and a slash line of .213/.281/.307 including 52 strikeouts, the struggling outfielder was demoted to Triple-A Evansville, missing a $6,500 progress bonus by two days.[16] Thomas was recalled when rosters expanded in September and was 2-for-28, including his second home run, but batted only .187 overall.

Thomas returned to the minors in 1974 with Sacramento of the Triple-A Pacific Coast League. Playing in Hughes Stadium, which had with a very short left-field wall,[17] he hit 51 homers, batted .297, and set a PCL strikeout record, fanning 175 times.

Thomas was considered a flake.[18] He was out of minor-league options but the club was reluctant to part with him because of his power potential. Crandall considered him "excess baggage"[19] but the club decided to keep him on the 1975 roster. Thomas rode the pines as an occasional defensive replacement until Crandall decided to platoon him in center because "[h]e had a good attitude and worked hard."[20] Thomas started strong but was removed from the starting lineup when he went into a severe slump.[21] Thomas hit only .179 in 240 at-bats with 84 strikeouts.

Again in 1976 Thomas began the season on the bench, until the starting center fielder Sixto Lezcano faltered and new manager Alex Grammas, saying, "I just think he has too much talent to sit around,"[22] put him in the lineup. When the Brewers acquired another center fielder, Von Joshua[23] on June 2 he returned to his bench role until early August, when Grammas shuffled his outfield, inserting Thomas in center for every game until he injured his left shoulder making a diving catch on August 30 and his season was over. It was Thomas's second consecutive season with a sub-.200 batting average (.198).

After spring training in 1977 the Brewers gave up on Thomas, demoting him to Triple-A Spokane. General manager Jim Baumer explained: "Lack of contact. He's had that problem all his life." Thomas considered it a "blessing in disguise," saying, "A good season with Spokane could give me another chance."[24] Thus motivated, he had his best year so far. He topped .300 for the first (and only) time with 36 home runs and 114 RBIs. His second chance came true on October 25 when he was dealt to the Texas Rangers to complete an August trade. Also in October, Thomas and Debbie Hansen of Milwaukee were married, "putting his life in some order."[25]

The Brewers purchased Thomas's contract from the Rangers on February 8, 1978, stirring speculation that the transaction had been prearranged to free a roster spot for the Rangers in a pennant race and find a way for the Brewers to keep their slugger. All parties denied the speculation.[26] But 30 years later, MLB.com reported that Milwaukee's Baumer had asked his Texas colleague for a favor. Texas GM Dan O'Brien recalled, "It was purely a friendship deal." The Rangers hid the slugger on their roster so the Brewers could bring him back, circumventing the option rules.[27]

Harry Dalton, hired from the Angels to be the Brewers GM after a front-office cleanout,[28] named George Bamberger, Baltimore's pitching coach, as the Brewers' manager. Bamberger wanted Thomas to be his center fielder. All the manager asked him was hit .250, to which Thomas replied, "I can hit better."[29] The prodigal slugger credited Spokane manager, John Felske for working with him daily and batting him fifth every day, building his confidence.[30] Thomas said he had learned a valuable lesson from Felske: "Don't try to hit taters on every swing."[31] Fortunately for Thomas, Bamberger preferred a strikeout over a double play. The more relaxed slugger had a big season, challenging for the home-run lead into August. He batted .246 with 32 homers and 86 RBIs. The free swinger still struck

Noted for his Fu Manchu 'stache, Stormin' Gorman Thomas twice led the AL in home runs with the Brewers: 45 in 1979 and 39 in 1982 (tied with Reggie Jackson). He belted 268 round-trippers in parts of 13 major-league seasons (1973-1976, 1978-1986).

out 133 times but drew 73 walks for a respectable .351 on-base average. And the Brewers had their first winning season, 93-69, finishing third.

Thomas's nickname, Stormin' Gorman, was given to him by Brewers coach Frank Howard. Asked why, Thomas said, "When a guy who is 6-feet-8 and 300 pounds gives you a nickname, you don't ask why."[32]

Thomas batted cleanup for much of the 1979 season, again hitting for power while fanning often but not concerned. "Strikeouts are overrated," he said. "Even batting average is overrated. The only thing that means anything is RBIs. That means you've done something to help your club win the game."[33] Bamberger wouldn't pinch-hit for him saying, "You never know when he's going to hit one out and he bears down more with men on base."[34] He had dry spells (2-for-38 and 0-for-24) and hot streaks like June's 14-game hitting streak, slugging five homers with 20 RBIs and August's six homers in seven games. Thomas was proud of his one consistent trait: strong, hard-nosed defense. He had 435 outfield putouts in 1979. He was knocked out of games four times during the season after running into walls.[35] He led the AL with 45 home runs; his 37th round-tripper, on September 2, set a franchise record. Bamberger considered benching Thomas on the season's last day when he was one strikeout shy of the league record. The free swinger replied, "No way, I sat on the bench too long."[36] In the eighth inning, a called third strike tied Dave Nicholson's 1963 American League record of 175.[37] For the season, Thomas slashed .244/.356/.539 and finished seventh in the AL MVP balloting. His 123 RBIs and 98 walks were also franchise records. What changed? Said Dalton: "It's hard for management to be tolerant of a player and give him total commitment when the player doesn't bring 100 percent of himself to the park." And Thomas agreed: "I used to be terrible, I'd stay out all night, then turn around and hunt or play golf all day."[38] The Brewers finished second in the AL East with a 95-66 record.[39]

Going into the 1980 season, Thomas and the Brewers anticipated a pennant after finishing third and then second. Bamberger was out until midseason after having a heart attack during spring training, and was replaced by third-base coach, Buck Rodgers. Through most of May, Thomas was hitting below .200 with only eight home runs and 49 strikeouts, and bouncing around the batting order. When Bamberger returned on June 6, he returned Thomas to the cleanup spot and the slugger responded with a hitting streak. On July 2 he belted his 17th homer and became the Brewers' all-time leader with 116.[40] He was a fan favorite, blue-collar like the hard-working Milwaukeans, whom he appreciated because "They know when to cheer and they know when to boo. And they know when to drink beer. They do it all of the time."[41] In a *Sporting News* poll of players and media for an all-hustle-team, Thomas was one of the three AL outfielders selected. "He knows every wall in the league" and plays hurt, said the paper. True to form, the gamer played in all 162 games in 1980, swatted 38 homers, had 105 RBIs, and led both leagues with 170 strikeouts. For the Brewers, though it was a disappointing year: They slipped to third place with 86 victories.

The offseason involved thorny contract negotiations with Thomas, who was potentially a free agent after 1981. In January, the Thomases welcomed their first child, daughter Kelly. In March, he signed a five-year contract for $3 million. But baseball and Thomas faced challenges in 1981. Bamberger retired and Rodgers, who succeeded him, was uncertain who would be his cleanup hitter. He also asked Thomas to move to right field to make room for Paul Molitor in center. By the end of spring, training, the proud defender questioned the moves: "I think I proved myself playing center field, offensively and defensively. So why make the change? Why not move Molitor to right field and leave me in center."[43] He told Peter Gammons, who considered Thomas the most underrated center fielder in the league, "I'm two steps quicker in center field than I was in right. In center, I don't have to think, I just react."[44] Thomas started strong and with oft-injured Molitor on the disabled list, he played more in center and was leading the AL with 15 homers on June 12, when the players walked out for the first midseason strike in major-league history.

A settlement was reached on July 31 with the season's second half resuming on August 10 with another level of playoffs added with each half's division winners meeting in the first round. After a disappointing third-place finish when the strike began, it was a new opportunity for the Brewers. Thomas was chosen for his only All-Star Game,[45] played on August 9, popping out as a pinch-hitter. He was thrilled with being selected. "I really enjoyed this," he said. "I waited a long time. I would have liked to have gotten another chance to hit, but that's not the way the game is set up. I was happy to get one at-bat."[46]

Thomas played center more in the second half with Molitor's continuing injury problems, becoming permanent in September. Although his second-half production fell off, his sacrifice fly on October 3 against Detroit proved to be the game-winner and clinched the Brewers' first trip to the postseason. Asked after the game if the title meant less due to the split season, he replied, "They can say what they want. I'm going to the playoffs. That's all I care."[47] Thomas's power numbers slipped that season but the .259 batting average was his best in the majors. His 85 strikeouts were only fourth in the AL and he never led that futile category again.

Facing the New York Yankees[48] in the Division Series, The Brewers lost Games One and Two at home as Thomas went hitless with five strikeouts. They tied the series in New York, winning Games Three and Four. Thomas hit a solo home run in Game Five but the Yankees won the game and the series. Thomas was 2-for-18 with nine K's in the series.

Thomas was anxious for the 1982 season[49] and a return to the playoffs, knowing he was the starting center fielder with the Molitor experiment over. He didn't hit his first homer until May 1 and was part of the team's May slump when the Brewers lost 14 of 20 and fell to fifth place. He injured his shoulder in late May and missed five games. While he was out, Dalton replaced Rodgers with hitting coach Harvey Kuenn, saying "[T]he chemistry had gone sour and the performance level of the team was not up to the expectations we have with the talent here."[50] Kuenn's philosophy was different: "I like the club to be loose, have a laugh. Go out and play the game and have fun."[51] The free-spirited Thomas welcomed the new philosophy, saying, "Everyone is loose. Just go out and have a good time."[52] Thomas got hot, topping the league with 22 home runs by the All-Star break. He was named AL Player of the Week for the week of August 9 after hitting five home runs to retake the AL lead with 32.[53] Injuring his elbow throwing to the infield for a double play on September 5, Thomas doubled over in pain but continued playing, holding the arm stiff and close to his body. After the game, he visited the team physician in a great deal of pain; he had reaggravated an earlier injury suffered making a diving catch.[54] He received a cortisone shot and after taking just one day off, he did not miss a game the rest of the season. But Thomas struggled after the injury, going, seven consecutive September games without a home run and finished the final week's stretch run without a homer or RBI. (He still shared the AL homer title with Reggie Jackson and had 100-plus RBIs for the third season in a row.) The season went down to the wire with the Brewers winning their first division title in the season finale. Thomas was excited about playing, saying, "Damn, this is why I love this game. Down to the last moment. I love it."[55]

Entering the AL Championship Series, Thomas was in a 0-for-16 slump that ended immediately when he homered in his first at-bat against the California Angels. That was his only long ball in 46 postseason plate appearances and his only hit in the ALCS. He injured his right knee with an awkward slide in Game Four and was limping badly before Sunday's decisive contest, but the gamer started, then watched the dramatic seventh-inning rally from the bench after grimacing in pain grounding out to end the sixth inning. The Brewers victory propelled them into their first World Series in 25 years.[56]

The World Series opened in St. Louis and Thomas was a doubtful starter after the ALCS injury. The resilient trouper wanted to play, saying, "It's no better than 50 percent. But I've got to play. You don't play 168 games and take a day off."[57] Playing center field in all seven games, he had minimal impact. In Game Three, with the Series tied, a record County Stadium crowd of 56,556[58] saw his seventh-inning single end a 1-for-23 slump; in the ninth inning he was robbed of a home run by St. Louis center fielder Willie McGee's leaping catch as the Cardinals won. With the Brewers trailing 5-1 after six innings in Game Four, Thomas's single drove in the final two runs in a six-run seventh-inning rally for a 7-5 victory, tying the Series. That game-winning hit and RBI were his last in the Series; he was hitless in the final three games. The Brewers took a 3-2 Series lead and needed only one victory to win the Series in St. Louis but they ran out of steam and lost the Series in seven games. Thomas ended Game Seven and the Series by striking out with two men on base. In 26 at-bats, he had just three singles and three RBIs.

During the offseason, Thomas finished eighth in the MVP vote and was selected to *The Sporting News* 1982 American League All-Star Team.[59] The Brewers shopped Thomas at the winter meetings; Dalton was a proponent of the Branch Rickey theory "It's better to unload an aging player one year too early than one year too late."[60] But there were no takers. The slugger had arthroscopic knee surgery to clean up the injury that affected his World Series performance. Also, son Justin was born on January 9.

Thomas's 10th major-league season, 1983, had a new challenge: a June trade to Cleveland. He had been below .200 most of the season. (His third home run of the campaign, on May 6, was his 200th.) All changed on June 6 when Dalton swapped starting center fielders and pitchers with Cleveland, obtaining Rick Manning for Thomas. Thomas was devastated. "I hate to even think about leaving Milwaukee" he said. "Milwaukee's my home. I love the people."[61] The feeling was mutual with fans bombarding the Brewers switchboard and talk shows with their shock and disappointment. As fate would have it, he returned as an Indian 18 days later with nearly 135,000 ecstatic fans welcoming their hero home for a weekend series. He received a standing ovation leaving the dugout for batting practice and when his picture appeared on the scoreboard. The center-field bleacher fans shouted repeatedly "Gorman" when he went to his position.[62] There were signs and posters everywhere. And the fans were relieved that their struggling Brewers swept the series with Thomas going 1-for-10, the one hit a solo homer. He played with aches and pains and struggled, batting mostly in the low .200s and ending with 17 homers in 106 games with Cleveland. As a player traded in the middle of a contract, Thomas exercised his right to demand a trade and was dealt to the Seattle Mariners on December 7.[63]

Drafted by a Seattle team, Thomas finally played for one in 1984. He was reunited with his new skipper, Del Crandall, who considered him excess baggage in 1975. Diagnosed with a torn right rotator cuff during spring training, Thomas was determined to play through the pain: "Let's take two aspirins and go get 'em."[64] After his arm went numb following a diving catch on May 15,[65] he finally succumbed to the pain going on the DL. A complete tear of the rotator cuff was discovered during surgery on June 8 with doctors unsure if he would play again. His season was over after 35 games with one homer and 13 RBIs.

Determined to come back, Thomas reported to spring training in 1986 without a glove per doctor's instructions to make sure he didn't even think about picking up a ball.[66] The comeback was accomplished: He was the Mariners' DH in 135 games, batting cleanup, and playing nearly every day. His first homers, three, including a grand slam, came in the third game of the season, driving in six runs. In Milwaukee in July, he smashed two home runs and was cheered by his fans twice, leaving the dugout to tip his cap. He got a standing ovation the next day after another home run.[67] As he had done throughout his career, he was hot with homer binges and cold with hitless streaks. The 1985 American League Comeback Player of the Year batted only .215 but hit 32 home runs.

Thomas received a 1986 contract offer with a 20 percent cut in pay,[68] which he rejected; eventually he reluctantly agreed to a $650,000 nonguaranteed contract because the club wasn't sure the repaired shoulder would hold up.[69] He started the season batting .289 and slugging .578, then slowly cooled off, striking out almost daily. Thomas lost playing time when Dick Williams became manager on May 9 and he was released on June 25. "We weren't getting any production from Gorman so he became expendable," Williams said. "We want to go with younger players."[70] The highest-paid Mariner in team history wasn't producing with only 10 homers and 26 RBIs. On July 16, he was signed by the Brewers after they lost 14 of 19 games and fell to last place in the AL East; they needed a strong bat to DH and back up first base. He was home again, playing for George Bamberger, who gave him his big chance. On his second day back, batting cleanup, he was the DH in the first game of a doubleheader. He played first base in game two and hit a home run. It was his first time in the field since the shoulder surgery. As in Seattle, he started hitting well and then struggled. After batting fourth for a month, he dropped in the order and played less. Hoping to hit 20 or more homers when he rejoined the Brewers, he finished with only six and 10 RBIs and batted only .179.

At age 35, Thomas's career ended when the Brewers released him on October 16. He retired as the Brewers' career home run leader with 208. Striking out 1,339 times in his 13-year career, he looked more like a twenty-first-century all-or-nothing hitter. He made Milwaukee baseball fun during his five-year peak when he hit more home runs than anyone and missed four consecutive titles by four homers.[71] He was a free spirit who gave everything between the lines, never finding a wall he couldn't run into which probably prematurely ended his career. He was a flake, a free spirit, and a folk hero in Milwaukee.

Thomas did have a life after baseball. His initial venture was a neighborhood bar on the south side of Milwaukee for several years in the mid-'80s with his best friend and fellow Brewer Pete Vuckovich named Stormin and Vukes. Going through a messy divorce in 1987, he made mistakes including two drunk-driving arrests with a 10-day jail sentence. Instead of serving the jail time, he left for his hometown, Charleston, South Carolina, where he owned a bar, Stormin Gorman's, and golfed daily. He returned to Wisconsin in 1994 to serve the jail time and was hired by the Brewers, who wanted to help him get his life in order. He scouted and did personal appearances. In 1995, he moved back to Milwaukee with the Brewers opening Gorman's Grill at County Stadium and then Gorman's Corner when the team moved to Miller Park. He got involved in their community outreach and attended Brewers fantasy camps.[72] He was inducted into both the South Carolina and Wisconsin Athletic Halls of Fame as well as the Brewers Wall of Fame. He married Susie Wiggins and as of 2019 the couple resided in the Milwaukee area.

SOURCES

In addition to the sources cited in the Notes, the author also accessed Retrosheet.org, Baseball-Reference.com, the SABR Minor Leagues Database, accessed online at Baseball-Reference.com, SABR.org, The Sporting News archive via Paper of Record, the player's Hall of Fame file, the online archives via Newspaper.com, and Ancestry.com.

ACKNOWLEDGMENT

Special thanks to SABR member Bill Mortell of Maryland whose knowledge of Ancestry.com and research skills have proven invaluable in finding information on Gorman Thomas.

NOTES

1. National Baseball Hall of Fame, Gorman Thomas File, 1974; Jerome Holtzman, "Thomas Is Still Indomitable." *Chicago Tribune*, July 4, 1985.
2. Hall of Fame file.
3. Mario Ziino, "Test Pilot, Gorman Thomas Was the Franchise's First Pick." *Brewers Game Day*, Issue 22, 2013.
4. Hall of Fame file.
5. Hall of Fame file.
6. Ziino.
7. Hall of Fame file.
8. Thomas signed his first professional contract with Bob Clements, Jack Sanford, and Bobby Mattick.
9. Other noted players selected before Thomas included first pick Jeff Burroughs, J.R. Richard, Alan Bannister, Terry McDermott, Don Stanhouse, and Don Gullett.
10. Ziino.
11. Ibid.
12. "Class A Leagues," *The Sporting News*, September 18, 1971: 45.
13. Larry Whiteside, "New Delivery in Parsons Message," *The Sporting News*, March 31, 1973: 42.
14. Although a triple was his first hit, he had only 13 in the major leagues.
15. Slash line: batting average/on-base percentage/slugging average.
16. "A.A. Atoms," *The Sporting News*, July 21, 1973: 38.
17. The left-field wall was only 233 feet from home plate, less than the 250-foot minimum. It was a one-year concession to return a franchise to Sacramento playing in a football stadium. The club was required to move the wall back after the season.
18. Thomas reported to camp with orange hair, a failed attempt at dyeing it blond. He was a free spirit and prankster always looking for ways to have fun while not appearing serious about the game.
19. Lou Chapman, "Thomas Removing Doubts as Brewer Bomber," *The Sporting News*, July 5, 1975: 13.
20. Ibid.
21. On July 27 and 28 at Boston, Thomas became the third player to strike out in eight consecutive at-bats, following Rick Monday in 1970 and Wayne Twitchell in 1973. "Baseball," *The Sporting News*, September 10, 1990: 14.
22. Lou Chapman, "'Let's Deal' Moan Folding Brewers," *The Sporting News*, June 12, 1976: 12.
23. "Brewers Obtain Giants' Joshua." *Milwaukee Sentinel*, June 3, 1976, Part 2, 1.
24. "Coast Toasties," *The Sporting News*, May 14, 1977: 36.
25. Mike Gonring, "Thomas Set to Erase Brewers Doubts," *The Sporting News*, March 11, 1978: 46.
26. Ibid.
27. Jamey Newberg, "Swapping Stories: The Gorman Thomas trades of 1977 and 1978." *Newberg Report*, MLB.com/blogs, August 16, 2007.
28. Dalton was hired after what is known in Milwaukee as the Saturday night massacre, when team owner Bud Selig fired GM Baumann, anager Grammas and director of player development Al Widmar. Lou Chapman, "Brewers Purge Puts Dalton in Charge," *The Sporting News*, December 3, 1977: 58.
29. Bob Nold, "Thomas Hitting Home Runs in Majors Now," *Akron Beacon Journal*, June 21, 1978: 4.
30. Ibid.
31. Dick Young, "Young Ideas," *The Sporting News*, May 6, 1978: 14.
32. Bill Schroeder, *If These Walls Could Talk: Milwaukee Brewers* (Chicago: Triumph Books, 2016), 76-77
33. Mike Gonring, "Brewers Reap RBI Harvest on Thomas's Bat," *The Sporting News*, July 21, 1979: 39.
34. Anthony Cotton, "Gorman Is Always Stormin'," *Sports Illustrated*, September 9, 1979: 90.

35 Ibid.

36 "Thomas Shares AL Whiff Mark," *The Sporting News*, October 20, 1979: 28.

37 Ibid.

38 Cotton.

39 The Brewers drew 1.9 million fans, the largest Milwaukee attendance since the Braves had 1,971,101 in 1958, their second consecutive World Series season.

40 Don Kausler Jr., "Yount Leads Brewers' HR Parade," *Milwaukee Sentinel*, July 2, 1980: Part 2, 1.

41 "Insiders Say," *The Sporting News*, May 31, 1980: 6.

42 Joe Goddard, "They're Doing the Hustle," *The Sporting News*, October 4, 1980: 3.

43 "Bunts and Boots," *The Sporting News*, April 11, 1981: 46.

44 Peter Gammons, "Goryl and Fregosi? Typical Fall Guys!," *The Sporting News*, June 13, 1981: 16.

45 Joining Thomas Were Teammates Rollie Fingers and Ted Simmons.

46 "Wage Dispute Unresolved," *Milwaukee Journal*, August 10, 1981: Part 2, 5.

47 "Quote, Unquote," *Milwaukee Journal*, October 4, 1981: 9.

48 The Milwaukee fans saw a familiar postseason foe, the New York Yankees, whom the previous County Stadium tenants, the Braves, had faced in the 1957 and 1958 World Series.

49 Although the Brewers were anxious to start the season, the April 6 home opener and the rest of the series were called off after an 8.7-inch snowstorm blanketed the ballpark. The team flew to Houston to work out for three days and then opened in Toronto on Friday.

50 Vic Feuerherd, "Rogers Fired, Kuehn at Helm," *Milwaukee Sentinel*, June 3, 1982: 1.

51 Tom Flaherty, "Crises Nothing New for Kuehn," *The Sporting News*, June 21, 1982: 14.

52 Ibid.

53 Tom Flaherty, "Edwards Success Keyed to Patience," *The Sporting News*, August 30, 1982: 26.

54 Vic Feuerherd, "Thomas Key Hit Pain to Angels," *Milwaukee Sentinel*, September 6, 1982: Part 2, 1.

55 Vic Feuerherd, "Kuehn Had No Doubt." *Milwaukee Sentinel*, October 4, 1982: Part 2, 5.

56 ALS Game Five remains the best, most electric game this author ever attended along with his then 7-year-old son, Derek.

57 Vic Feuerherd, "Thomas, Oglivie Not 100%," *Milwaukee Sentinel*, October 12, 1982: Part 2, 1.

58 They would have record attendance on three consecutive days with 56,560 on Saturday and 56,562 on Sunday.

59 "In the A.L.: Right Makes Might," *The Sporting News*, November 8, 1982: 28.

60 Dick Young, "Moffett – Players Deal Too Cozy," *The Sporting News*, December 27, 1982: 7.

61 "Gorman Leaves 'Em Mourning," *The Sporting News*, June 20, 1983: 16

62 Terry Pluto, "Brewer Fans Love Thomas," *Cleveland Plain Dealer*, June 25, 1983: 1-D.

63 Manning remained with the Brewers, retiring after the 1987 season, one year after Thomas.

64 Bill Plaschke, "Thomas Accepts Shoulder Surgery," *The Sporting News*, May 28, 1984: 20.

65 Ibid.

66 Thomas's doctor eventually allowed light throwing during the season. He was happy to play again, but he would only DH for Seattle.

67 Bill Plaschke, "'Gormbo' Heats Up With Homer Binge," *The Sporting News*, August 12, 1985: 22.

68 "A.L. West," *The Sporting News*, January 13, 1986: 38.

69 "A.L. West," *The Sporting News*, February 3, 1986: 40.

70 "Mariners' Thomas Swept from Roster," *Boca Raton* (Florida) *News*, June 26, 1986: 3D.

71 Thomas won the home-run titles in 1979 and 1982, missing the 1980 title by three homers and by one in 1981.

72 This author had the pleasure of talking smack daily with Stormin' Gorman at the '82 Brewer Players Fantasy camp in 2005.

PETE VUCKOVICH

By Rory Costello

Pete Vuckovich was a menacing figure. He was big: 6-feet-4 and 220 pounds (or more). He glowered over a Fu Manchu mustache and often had a few days' growth elsewhere to go with his long, unkempt hair. While pitching, he had "a streak of calculated weirdness."[1] Rasputin comparisons arose, and he encouraged them, applauding the Mad Monk's "extreme mental energy and intense concentration."[2] To those who knew him, Vuckovich was funny and friendly — but his on-field demeanor was just right for his small yet memorable role as the unpleasant, tobacco-spitting "Clu Haywood" in the 1989 cult classic *Major League*.

As a player, the combative Vuckovich combined mound psychology with a very wide repertoire. It made the righty effective for several years in the late 1970s and early '80s. With the Milwaukee Brewers, he led the American League in winning percentage in both 1981 and 1982. He won the AL Cy Young Award in 1982, helping the Brewers to the pennant.

Arm problems then curtailed Vuckovich's career. He pitched in just three games in 1983 and missed all of '84. He retired as a player after spring training 1987. Vuckovich soon came back to baseball, though, as a color commentator for Brewers telecasts. He went on to serve the Pittsburgh Pirates, Seattle Mariners, and Arizona Diamondbacks in various capacities for more than 20 years.

Peter Dennis Vuckovich was born on October 27, 1952, in Johnstown, Pennsylvania. "Having a life at all was his biggest victory — actually a series of victories," said St. Louis sportswriter Mike Eisenbath. "He had many brushes with death. Vuke was born with the umbilical cord wrapped around his neck; he suffered undiagnosed appendicitis that led to peritonitis when he was 1½; he had a benign tumor removed from his head a year later."[3]

The close calls didn't end there. As a high-school sophomore, complications from his appendicitis episode led to emergency surgery. "I almost cashed it in right there," he said in 1982. At age 21, he drove over an 80-foot embankment at 105 miles per hour. The car rolled over several times, yet somehow he walked out of it. After that he was installing a 15,000-volt reactor, which shorted. "Six more inches and I'd have been fried like a piece of bacon."[4]

Vuckovich's parents were both of Serbian descent. His father was Lazo Vuckovich, a steel-mill worker. His mother, Bosiljka (née Gjurich), was a homemaker known for her baked goods, especially orehnjača, or Serbian nut roll. They were fondly known as "Laze" and "Bossie" or "Bosa" — but they also went by the Americanized names Louis and Betty. Pete was the only boy among five children. His sisters were named Dianne, Karyn, Melanie, and Maryann.[5]

Vuckovich's childhood baseball heroes were Roberto Clemente, Bob Gibson, and Juan Marichal.[6] He was later compared to "The Dominican Dandy" for using varied arm angles. Pete knew he wanted to be a pitcher when he was 8 years old.[7] He inherited some ability from his father, a noted pitcher in fast softball circles around Johnstown. He was largely a self-made player, though, because "Dad was too busy earning a living in the steel mills."[8]

At Conemaugh Valley High School in Johnstown, Vuckovich stood out in three sports, also including football (as a receiver) and basketball (as a forward).[9] The school's baseball field was later named in his honor.

After graduating in 1970, Vuckovich turned down football scholarships from Navy, Pitt, Michigan State, and other major schools. Instead, he attended Clarion State College in northwestern Pennsylvania — mainly because his wife-to-be, Anna Kuzak, was going there.[10]

Staying in school also kept Vuckovich out of the Vietnam War. Of this, he later remarked, "I've taken a lot of guff along the way but that's politics and I don't want to get into politics."[11] He aimed to become a schoolteacher.[12]

Though Vuckovich had mainly been a pitcher in high school, he had filled in across the infield, so he told Clarion baseball coach Joe Knowles that he could play anywhere but catcher. "Maybe I shouldn't have said that," Vuckovich recalled, "but I was cocky back then. Coach Knowles said I'd play second base — the position I had probably the least experience with." However, he proved more valuable as a pitcher.[13] He was All-Conference in the Pennsylvania State Athletics Conference from 1972 through 1974 and an NAIA All-American in 1974.[14]

While in high school and college, Vuckovich also played with the All American Amateur Baseball Association. Johnstown has hosted the AAABA's annual tournament since 1945. Vuckovich became the first player from his hometown to appear in that tourney for four consecutive years (1969-72).

On the recommendation of scout Fred Shaffer, the Chicago White Sox selected Vuckovich in the third round of the June 1974 amateur draft.[15] He split that summer between Appleton (Class-A Midwest League) and Knoxville (Double-A Southern League).

Vuckovich then jumped to Triple A in 1975. With Denver of the American Association, he went 11-4 with a 4.34 ERA in 19 games. That May he thanked White Sox pitching coach Johnny Sain, saying, "He taught me all my breaking pitches in spring training — I mean everything — curve, slider, how to make the fastball sink, how to throw a changeup."[16]

Vuckovich got his first call to the majors that August, appearing twice before going back to Denver as Terry Forster came off the disabled list. As he later told it, Chicago manager Chuck Tanner had scouted him, liked what he'd seen, and said, "You're coming with me." To Tanner's great surprise, Vuckovich said that he didn't want to go, but explained that he wanted to be with Denver because he thought the Bears could win the Triple-A championship. Tanner agreed to send Vuckovich back for the league playoffs, which Denver lost in six games.[17] Vuckovich returned to the big club in September and got into two more games. He would not hurl again in the minors until 1986.

Also in 1975, Vuckovich married Anna. They had three sons: Lazo (like his grandfather, also known as Louis), Peter, and Damian.[18] Pete Jr. was also drafted by the White Sox out of Clarion (48th round, 2004) but injury cut his career short. In 2017, he became a scout for the Brewers.[19]

Vuckovich pitched in Puerto Rico for the Ponce Leones during the winter of 1975-76 and "showed well."[20] His manager was Ken Boyer, later his skipper with St. Louis. "Ken's the man who got me thinking like a big leaguer," Vuckovich later remarked. "He said to give it my best and not to let the little things bother me. He taught me the importance of concentration."[21]

For the White Sox in 1976, Vuckovich started seven times in 33 appearances, posting marks of 7-4, 4.65. He later took a swipe at manager Paul Richards (who'd succeeded Tanner) about how he was used. "I'll tell you what [Richards] knew about pitching. He made me a reliever, and he made Goose Gossage a starter."[22]

The AL added two new franchises — Seattle and the Toronto Blue Jays — for the 1977 season. In November 1976, the Blue Jays took Vuckovich as the 19th pick in the expansion draft. "To be truthful," he said the next year, "I didn't think that much about whether or not I would be protected. If I got drafted, I figured it was because somebody wanted me and I'd still be in the big leagues."[23]

Five years later, though, he thought differently. "It was a stupid decision for the White Sox to make. I had a pretty good idea even at 23, and I cared a lot. But I suppose it was all business for them. Maybe they spent $50,000 developing me, and they got $150,000 for me in the draft [actually $175,000]. So, they made $100,000 off the whole thing."[24] The team did run on a shoestring budget under Bill Veeck's ownership then.

Vuckovich was the first player to report to spring training for the Blue Jays. Manager Roy Hartsfield promptly told him, "We will not have any long hair or beards. Mustaches on the upper lip are OK, but that's all." Vuckovich, who said he'd had a mustache since he was 17, was already sporting his Fu Manchu.[25]

Vuckovich remained a swingman for Toronto, going 7-7, starting eight times in 53 games with a team-leading 3.47 ERA. He recorded the franchise's first save (on the frigid Opening Day at Exhibition Stadium) and its first shutout (as he outdueled Jim Palmer in Baltimore on June 26). However, that was his only season with the Jays. In December, he and a player to be named later (John Scott) went to the St. Louis Cardinals for Victor Cruz and Tom Underwood. Two days later, the Cardinals dealt away another pitcher known for his Fu Manchu and ferocity: Al Hrabosky. Earlier in 1977, "The Mad Hungarian" had clashed with manager Vern Rapp and owner Gussie Busch over Rapp's ban on facial hair.

St. Louis beat writer Neal Russo called Vuckovich a good prospect after the trade.[26] He was right. During his first season with the Cardinals, Vuckovich posted a 12-12 record, but his ERA was a career-best 2.54, third in the National League behind Craig Swan and Steve Rogers. He was a reliever to begin the year, but Ken Boyer — who'd replaced Rapp as manager in April — put him in the rotation in early June.

Vuckovich blossomed immediately as a starter. In late July, Cardinals pitching coach Claude Osteen — who'd helped Vuke as a teammate in 1975 — said, "He's a master at changing speeds, and he does it with total command of three or four basic pitches, with quite a few variations of each kind of pitch. He's deceptive, too."[27]

On August 8, after a complete-game win over the Philadelphia Phillies, Vuckovich credited much of his success to his ability to remain calm and collected under pressure. That game report noted the "sometimes strange behavior" that inspired another nickname — "Vuke the Spook" — and that he worked more quickly than most pitchers.[28] A few weeks later, the great Bob Gibson — also noted for his brisk pace — said, "I've watched him on television and like his tenacity and the rapidity with which he works. He's already found that the quicker you pitch, the more your defense is likely to be on its toes to make the good plays behind you."[29]

Vuckovich remained a capable starter for the Cardinals in 1979-80, winning 27, losing 19, and posting a 3.50 ERA. Mike Eisenbath cited Vuckovich's variety of pitches and arm slots — and, in particular, his fiercely competitive nature. Vuke later said, "I really hate hitters. They're goofy. They're trying to get me, to ruin my career, so I hate them. That's the way it has to be — them or me. I want it to be me."[30] Yet his free spirit was also visible as he belly-flopped through puddles in the outfield and hung an "out to lunch" sign over his locker.[31]

On December 12, 1980, St. Louis and Milwaukee — who would face each other in the 1982 World Series — swung a seven-player deal. The Cardinals traded Rollie Fingers, Ted Simmons, and Vuckovich for pitchers Dave LaPoint and Lary Sorensen, outfielder Sixto Lezcano, and another outfielder, touted prospect David Green. It started off in October with an even-up swap proposal from St. Louis: Vuckovich for Sorensen.[32] But it developed into a blockbuster, with many moving parts before everything fell into place. In the final analysis, both sides benefited.[33]

Vuckovich could be droll. When asked why he thought Cardinals manager/general manager Whitey Herzog traded him, he replied, "Whitey wanted to build a team on speed and I never really ran that well."[34]

In Milwaukee, Vuckovich struggled early in 1981 but turned his season around after coach Cal McLish suggested using a no-windup delivery even with no one on base.[35] Vuke went on to lead the AL with 14 wins during the strike-interrupted season; he lost just four. He came in fourth in the AL Cy Young Award voting — the winner was Fingers.

The Brewers also made it to the postseason for the first time. They faced the New York Yankees in the AL Division Series, and Vuckovich appeared in two games. He started and won Game Four, allowing one unearned run in five innings. In Game Five at Yankee Stadium, he faced the Yankees' final batter; New York eventually won the pennant.

The 1982 Brewers were called "Harvey's Wallbangers" because manager Harvey Kuenn had such a potent batting order. Yet they wouldn't have won the AL pennant without respectable pitching. The team ERA of 3.98 was sixth in the AL, but not far behind the league-best 3.80. There were no dominant starters — but they got the job done.

Vuckovich led the staff with 18 wins against 6 losses. He was in hot water often — his WHIP in 1982 was 1.5. Yet more often than not, he got himself out of the jams; his ERA was just 3.34. "He gets further behind, works deeper in counts, throws more pitches and generally contradicts more canons of pitching with more success than anybody else in baseball," said sportswriter Tom Boswell.[36]

Interesting observations of Vuckovich in '82 come from Daniel Okrent's book *Nine Innings*, which focused on a game between the Brewers and Baltimore Orioles on June 10 of that season.

For example, "If considered looniness won ball games, the eccentric Vuckovich would forever be a success." Okrent also noted the hurler's habits of crossing his eyes as he stared in for the sign and (while holding runners on) "twitching his head rapidly ... again and again, as if he had a violent tic." Catcher Simmons, Vuckovich's closest friend on the team, thought it helped the pitcher as much as his strange delivery did.[37]

Center fielder Gorman Thomas (who looked like a brother to Vuke) expanded. "You could look past the goofy hair and the growth on the face. He'd go out there and pitch with two different brands of shoes on. He'd have Puma on one foot and Adidas on the other. It was almost like he was semi-clownish. Yet he knew what he was doing and he'd get other people to focus more on his mannerisms than on what they're supposed to be doing."[38]

Beneath the quirky trappings, though, Vuckovich's intensity was unrivaled. Thomas added, "I don't think I ever saw anybody who would be so competitive when it was time to pitch. It's hard to stay 100 percent, 100 miles per hour, 24 hours a day. But when it was Pete's day to pitch, it was more than tunnel vision. It was straw vision. That's how finely tuned he was. He was that way every time I saw him pitch."[39]

Vuckovich started twice in the 1982 ALCS against the California Angels. In Game Two, he gave up four runs in an eight-inning complete game, losing to Bruce Kison, who went all the way. In Game Five, he allowed three runs in 6⅓ innings and left the game as the pitcher of record on the losing side. But the Brewers took the lead with two in the seventh and held on to win the pennant.

Vuckovich also started twice in the World Series. In Game Three, he allowed six runs (four earned) in 8⅔ innings and took the loss. In Game Seven, he took a 3-1 lead into the sixth inning but put the tying runs on base and was pulled. The bullpen couldn't hold the lead, and though Vuckovich got no decision, the Cardinals won the championship.

Vuke had been pitching while hurt.[40] As Roger Angell later wrote, he was "in great pain during the final stages of the pennant race. ... In late

In his first season with the Brewers, Pete Vuckovich tied for the major-league lead with 14 wins in the strike-shortened 1981 season. The following year he won 18 and was named the AL Cy Young Award winner for the pennant-winning Brewers.

September, two days after receiving a cortisone shot in his shoulder, he somehow went 11 full innings against the Red Sox, throwing 173 pitches, and won the game."[41] After his first outing against St. Louis, Vuckovich was stoic: "I get paid to take the ball when they give it to me, and I get paid to give it back when they ask for it."[42] When he retired, he said that he carried on because the pennant race would have been a bad time to "walk."[43]

A few weeks later, the Cy Young Award was announced. Five pitchers got first-place votes, but Vuckovich got 14 of the 28 and outdistanced runner-up Jim Palmer. "I feel great about it, but I can't take full credit for it," he said. "I just happen to be lucky enough to be out there on the days the team's playing well enough to be a winner."[44]

Indeed, "He Doesn't Look Pretty, but He Wins," proclaimed *Baseball Digest*'s cover story in May 1983. By the time it appeared, though, Vuckovich was on the disabled list. In March, an arthrogram revealed a tear in his rotator cuff. He put the downtime to good use, though, gaining his first experience as a cable TV commentator for the Brewers. He also filled in for Bob Uecker on the radio when Ueck was calling games for ABC-TV.[45]

Vuckovich started throwing gingerly on the sidelines in May.[46] His progress continued, and he made it back at the end of August. He pitched well in his first two starts, going five innings in each and surprising Simmons with his velocity. In the third, however, he was hit hard and pulled a hamstring. The Brewers kept him sidelined after that for fear that he might reinjure his arm.[47]

Before the 1984 season, Vuckovich was cautiously optimistic after a busy offseason continuing his exercise program. However, he wasn't ready for Opening Day because of pain from a bone spur in his right shoulder.[48] The resulting surgery included muscle repair as well as removal of the spur. It kept him out for the whole season. Yet again, he wasn't idle — he charted pitches, worked the radar gun, and studied hitters' tendencies. This too laid the foundation for his future career.[49]

Vuckovich was back in action in 1985 but was largely ineffective in 22 starts (6-10, 5.51). A shoulder strain landed him on the DL in May and June, and he underwent surgery for a large calcium deposit and another small bone spur in mid-September. That November, he became a free agent after refusing a minor-league assignment.[50]

Milwaukee invited Vuckovich to spring training in 1986 as a nonroster player. At the end of camp, he announced his retirement and went to work for the Brewers as a scout and minor-league instructor. In August, however, he wanted to see if he could still pitch. He joined Milwaukee's Triple-A club in Vancouver.[51] He did well (2-1, 1.26 in six games) and got back to the majors in September, going 2-4, 3.06 in six starts.

Vuckovich was a nonroster invitee again in 1987, but he retired for good on April 1, saying, "I'm a realist. I have an awareness of myself."[52] He finished with a lifetime record in the majors of 93-69 and an ERA of 3.66. Charlie O'Brien, who caught Vuckovich during that last spring training, summed up his career nicely. "He had a great feel for pitching. ... [T]he word that comes to mind is guile. ... He marched to his own drummer. ... He liked a cold beer and a good time, and he liked to play baseball. He was willing to do whatever it took to win."[53]

Vuckovich, who then lived in the Milwaukee suburb of Hales Corners, tended bar at "Stormin' and Vuke's," the joint he co-owned with Gorman Thomas.[54] He was also involved in local civic affairs. At the opening of the Samson Jewish Community Center in Whitefish Bay in September 1987, he helped teach youngsters how to play baseball along with Sal Bando and Bill Castro.[55]

Major League was filmed at Milwaukee's County Stadium in the summer of 1988. The project — like many Hollywood movie properties — had been in gestation for years. But when it finally got the green light, the cast included many inspired choices, and Vuckovich was one of them. Originally he was to play opposing closer Duke Simpson, but writer/director David S. Ward liked Vuckovich's look so much that he was given a slightly bigger role. Vuke then brought in his old Brewers teammate Willie Mueller to take over as Simpson.[56]

The new part was well suited to Vuckovich's image. In April 1989, shortly after the film was released, *Sports Illustrated* wrote, "Former Brewers pitcher and dirtball Pete Vuckovich plays Yankee slugger and dirtball Clu Haywood." The article quoted Bob Uecker's line as announcer Harry Doyle: "He [Haywood] leads the majors in most offensive categories, including nose hair."[57] A 2016 article described the character as "awesomely gross," noting that his "favorite pastime, apart from hitting dingers, is to call rookies Hayes and Vaughn 'meat' whenever he gets the chance."[58]

Vuckovich made another juicy little contribution to the film. In one scene, Haywood approaches the plate and says to catcher Jake Taylor (played by Tom Berenger): 'How's your wife and my kids?' The line wasn't in Ward's script; he told Vuckovich to improvise something that major-leaguers would say. What's more, "Stormin' and Vuke's" was a regular off-hours hangout for the cast and crew while they were on location in Milwaukee.[59]

Vuckovich was an analyst on Brewers telecasts from 1989 through 1991. Then Ted Simmons, whom the Pirates had hired as GM in February 1992, invited his old friend and batterymate to join the Pittsburgh organization. It was ideal because no big-league franchise was closer to family in Johnstown. Vuke stayed with the Bucs for 20 seasons, through 2011. He was first a roving pitching instructor (1992-93) and then special assistant to GM Cam Bonifay (1994-95). In 1996 he was promoted to assistant GM/director of player personnel.[60]

Shortly after the '96 season ended, the Pirates made Vuckovich the big club's pitching coach, a longstanding goal of his. He replaced Ray Miller because "the club didn't feel Miller's methods were resulting in progress. Vuckovich will coach attitude and mental approach as much as mechanics." A subsequent report noted that he would "spend a lot of time getting to know young players, trying to determine the best way to tap their talents."[61]

Vuckovich held that position for four seasons (1997-2000). When the Pirates hired Lloyd McClendon as manager, he and Bonifay turned over the coaching staff.[62] As a result, bullpen coach Spin Williams moved up and Vuke returned to the front office. He continued to work as special assistant to Bonifay, and later to David Littlefield, then Neal Huntington.

Vuckovich joined the Mariners as a special assistant to GM Jack Zduriencik before the 2012 season. His job included much travel, scouting amateurs and pros, as well as visiting with minor-league teams. Zduriencik, who'd been scouting director for the Pirates from 1991 through 1993, respected his old colleague's baseball mind. In November 2013, Vuckovich was a candidate for pitching coach with the Phillies, but he removed his name from consideration.[63] The job went to his former Milwaukee teammate Bob McClure.

Seattle fired Zduriencik in August 2015, and that October Vuckovich was part of the ensuing organizational purge.[64] A few months later, he became a roving scout for the Diamondbacks. When asked what brings a scout the most satisfaction, Vuckovich said, "Being right on a player. ... That's what you strive to do."[65]

In late 2017, Pete and Annie Vuckovich still called Johnstown home. "It's where I grew up, and where my wife and I met. Even when I was playing, in the offseason we always came home to Johnstown," he said just before taking the Diamondbacks job. Vuckovich is a member of the Sports Halls of Fame of Cambria County, Clarion University, the AAABA, Western Pennsylvania, and Pennsylvania. He remained happy and confident at work. "Baseball has been my whole life. It's what I know, and I know it better than most."[66]

SOURCES

Cambria County Sports Hall of Fame (ccshof.org/member/pete-vuckovich/).

Official website of the AAABA Tournament (aaabajohnstown.org/).

Findagrave.com.

Betty Vuckovich funeral announcement (hindmanfuneralhomes.com/obituary/betty-bosa-j-vuckovich/).

Newspapers.com.

NOTES

1 Daniel Okrent, *Nine Innings* (Boston: Houghton Mifflin Company, 1985), 237.

2 Neal Russo, "Vuckovich: Unusual Man With Some Evil Pitches," *St. Louis Post-Dispatch*, July 25, 1978: 36.

3 Mike Eisenbath, *The Cardinals Encyclopedia* (Philadelphia: Temple University Press, 1999), 300.

4 Bob Verdi, "Close Calls All Go Vuckovich's Way," *Chicago Tribune*, March 18, 1982. Tom Boswell, "Brewers' Vuckovich Becomes Off-the-Wall Force on the Mound," *Washington Post*, October 13, 1982.

5 David L. Porter, editor, *Biographical Dictionary of American Sports*, Volume 2, Q-Z (Westport, Connecticut: Greenwood Press, 2000), 1607. The Vuckovich parents' Serbian nicknames are visible on the pictures of their shared grave marker at findagrave.com. There are various references to Lazo Vuckovich as "Louis," including his 2005 obituary in the *Johnstown Tribune-Democrat*. The Biographical Dictionary of Sports entry gives Bossie's Americanized name as "Betty Jane." See also Betty Vuckovich funeral announcement.

6 "Life Inside the Diamond," Clarion University website, January 4, 2016.

7 Rick Hummel, "Birds V-Sign Stands for Vuke and Victory," *The Sporting News*, May 3, 1980: 13.

8 Neal Russo, "'Gimme the Ball, Often,' Vuckovich Tells Cards," *The Sporting News*, February 25, 1978: 54.

9 "Mariners Name Pete Vuckovich Special Assistant to the General Manager," MLB.com, September 16, 2011. Football position comes from *Indiana* (Pennsylvania) *Gazette*, accessed via Newspapers.com. Basketball position comes from email to Rory Costello from Mike Mastovich of the *Johnstown Tribune-Democrat*, October 5, 2017.

10 Bob Broeg, "McBride Deal Wins Belated OK," *St. Louis Post-Dispatch*, September 3, 1978: 76.

11 Hummel, "Birds V-Sign Stands for Vuke and Victory."

12 Verdi, "Close Calls All Go Vuckovich's Way."

13 "Life Inside the Diamond."

14 "Mariners Name Pete Vuckovich Special Assistant to the General Manager."

15 Russo, "'Gimme the Ball, Often,' Vuckovich Tells Cards."

16 "Pitcher Credits Sain," *The Sporting News*, May 17, 1975: 38.

17 "Life Inside the Diamond."

18 Porter, op. cit., 1608. Front-office biographies, Pittsburgh Pirates, MLB.com. Date unknown, but could range from 2008 to 2011.

19 Pete Vuckovich Jr. profile on LinkedIn.com.

20 Jerome Holtzman, "Dent, Downing Only Chisox Certain of Regular Berths," *The Sporting News*, March 6, 1976: 11.

21 Russo, "'Gimme the Ball, Often,' Vuckovich Tells Cards."

22 Okrent, *Nine Innings*, 207. The original source of this quote is uncertain.

23 Neil MacCarl, "Shear Locks, Jays Order Vuckovich," *The Sporting News*, March 12, 1977: 43.

24 Verdi, "Close Calls All Go Vuckovich's Way."

25 MacCarl, "Shear Locks, Jays Order Vuckovich," 46.

26 Neal Russo, "Devine Gives Royal Look to New Card Hand," *The Sporting News*, December 24, 1977: 59.

27 Neal Russo, "Brother Vuckovich a Wheelhorse for Cards," *The Sporting News*, August 5, 1978: 20.

28 "Cards Spook Phillies," *Pittsburgh Press*, August 9, 1978: 56.

29 Broeg, "McBride Deal Wins Belated OK."

30 Eisenbath, op. cit., loc. cit. Original source of quote: "The Pete Vuckovich Story Is Filed Under 'Sci-Fi,'" *St. Louis Post-Dispatch*, February 8, 1983: 30.

31 Hummel, "Birds V-Sign Stands for Vuke and Victory."

32 Okrent, *Nine Innings*, 206.

33 Dave Anderson, "Trade That Brewed the 6-Pack Series," *New York Times*, October 12, 1982.

34 Boswell, "Brewers' Vuckovich Becomes Off-the-Wall Force on the Mound."

35 Tom Flaherty, "Vuckovich Brewers' Big Bargain," *The Sporting News*, June 27, 1981: 25.

36 Boswell, "Brewers' Vuckovich Becomes Off-the-Wall Force on the Mound."

37 Okrent, *Nine Innings*, 71, 237.

38 Mike Mastovich, "From AAABA to Cy Young, Vuckovich Made His Pitch," *Johnstown Tribune-Democrat*, August 5, 2007.

39 Mike Mastovich, "Competitiveness, Talent Took Vuckovich to the Top of Baseball," *Johnstown Tribune-Democrat*, October 8, 2016.

40 Tom Flaherty, "Vuke Shares Credit With Teammates," *The Sporting News*, November 15, 1982: 53.

41 Roger Angell, "The Arms Talks," *The New Yorker*, May 4, 1987.

42 Stan Hochman, "Life in the Fast Lane Doesn't Faze Vuckovich," *Philadelphia Daily News*, October 15, 1982.

43 Mike Mastovich, "Vuckovich Honored: Area Ex-Big-Leaguer to Take Spot With Pennsylvania's Best," *Johnstown Tribune-Democrat*, October 23, 2008.

44 "Vuckovich Says He's Happy," Associated Press, November 4, 1982.

45 Peter Gammons, "Brewers' First Three Rank with Best," *The Sporting News*, May 2, 1983: 14.

46 Tom Flaherty, "Outlook Bleak for Vuckovich," *The Sporting News*, March 28, 1983: 42. Flaherty, "Simmons Hits .300 Jackpot," *The Sporting News*, May 23, 1983: 22.

47 Tom Flaherty, "Vuckovich's Return Impresses Brewers," *The Sporting News*, September 19, 1983: 14; Flaherty, "Job in Jeopardy, but Kuenn's Secure," *The Sporting News*, October 3, 1983: 17.

48 Tom Flaherty, "Vuckovich Is Cautiously Optimistic," *The Sporting News*, February 27, 1984: 36. Flaherty, "Hurts Hamper Molitor, Vucko," *The Sporting News*, April 9, 1984: 15.

49 Mastovich, "Vuckovich honored: Area Ex-Big-Leaguer to Take Spot With Pennsylvania's Best."

50 Tom Flaherty, "As Vuckovich Exits, Porter Returns," *The Sporting News*, September 23, 1985: 20; Flaherty, "Yount Will Return to Center Field," *The Sporting News*, December 2, 1985: 48.

51 "A.L. Notebook: Brewers," *The Sporting News*, August 11, 1986: 17.

52 Tom Flaherty, "Facing the Inevitable," *The Sporting News*, April 13, 1987: 16.

53 Charlie O'Brien and Doug Wedge, *The Cy Young Catcher* (College Station, Texas: Texas A&M University Press: 2015), 18-19.

54 "Brewers' First Loss of Season Fails to Dampen Fan Enthusiasm," United Press International, April 22, 1987.

55 "Thousands Celebrate Opening of Sampson [sic] JCC," *Wisconsin Jewish Chronicle*, September 25, 1987: 3.

56 Jonathan Knight, *The Making of "Major League,"* (Cleveland: Gray & Company, 2015), exact page number unavailable online.

57 Steve Wulf, "Too Bush for the Bigs," *Sports Illustrated*, April 17, 1989. This article spelled the character's first name as "Klu," as have other sources over the years.

58 Danny Kelly, "'Major League' Is Baseball," *The Ringer*, July 22, 2016.

59 Knight, op. cit. Mike Oz, "'Major League' Turns 25 – Here Are 15 Things You Didn't Know About the Movie," Yahoo! Sports, April 7, 2014. Chris Nashawaty, "A League of Its Own," *Sports Illustrated*, July 4, 2011.

60 "Mariners Name Pete Vuckovich Special Assistant to the General Manager." Mike Mastovich, "Johnstown native Pete Vuckovich Starts New Baseball Chapter as Diamondbacks Scout," *Johnstown Tribune-Democrat*, January 6, 2016.

61 John Mehno, "Pittsburgh Pirates," *The Sporting News*, October 21, 1996, 20. Mehno, "Pittsburgh Pirates," *The Sporting News*, November 11, 1996: 37.

62 John Mehno, "Pittsburgh," *The Sporting News*, November 6, 2000.

63 Jim Salisbury, "Phils Feel Rejection in Pitching Coach Search," NBC Sports Philadelphia, November 11, 2013.

64 "Sources: Mariners' Front Office Overhaul Begins With Four Changes," Foxsports.com, October 5, 2015.

65 Mastovich, "Johnstown Native Pete Vuckovich Starts New Baseball Chapter As Diamondbacks Scout."

66 "Life Inside the Diamond."

NED YOST

By Ken Carrano

A major-league ballplayer gets called a lot of things during his career, and a manager probably more so. In the case of Edgar Frederick Yost III, some of those things include taxidermist, catcher, grinder, idiot, app developer, survivor, twitter hashtag (#yosted), clothier, pot scrubber, and hunter. Oh, and one more thing — World Series champion manager.

Ned Yost was born on August 19, 1954, in Eureka, California, the son of Edgar Yost Jr. and Lael (Prindle) Yost. The Yost's divorced while Ned was in elementary school. Yost's father played football at Santa Rosa Junior College where he was named a Little All-American.[1] His mother was a homemaker. In May 1971, when Yost was a junior in high school, his father, a tanker-truck driver for the Arco petroleum company, was killed when a car cut his truck off. "Right after you get drafted, and then you work your way up, the first day you make it in the big leagues, you're thinking, 'Man, I wish he could have seen this,'" Yost said in 2014. "And then in '82, when we made it to the World Series (as a player with Milwaukee), it was, 'Man, I wish he could have seen this.'"[2]

Around the time of his father's death, Yost's family had moved to Dublin, California, where Yost joined the high-school baseball team, with little to no effect. "I went a whole year in high school without getting a hit, 0-36 my sophomore year."[3] Yost would improve, thanks to a summer job. "I went to work at Kentucky Fried Chicken. I was a pot scrubber. I'd sit there and scrub pots all summer long and my arms got strong."[4] Yost's improved strength translated to the field as he earned all-league status as a senior, but didn't translate to any college scholarship offers, so he decided to walk on at Chabot Junior College in Hayward, California.

Chabot had produced several major-league players, including Dick Tidrow and Von Joshua, but coach Gene Wellman didn't think too much of Yost's chances after he was drafted seventh by the New York Mets in the first round of 1974 June Secondary Phase Draft. After deciding to sign with the Mets, Wellman told Yost to take care of himself for the next week. Wellman then told him why a just a week — "Because that's how long you're going to last, son. You're going to be back on the first bus. You think you're a professional player? You ain't going to make it. Good luck. See you later."[5]

Yost went to Batavia of the New York-Penn League in the summer of 1974 to try to prove Wellman wrong. He played in 44 games and hit .252, splitting time behind the plate and struggling with his defense, allowing six passed balls and 11 errors. Still, his performance gained him promotion to Wausau of the Midwest League for the 1975 season. Yost's hitting was more challenged at the higher level; he hit only .192 while handing most of the catching duties for the Mets' Single-A club. In spite of these troubles, Yost advanced to Double-A ball in 1976, with the Jackson (Mississippi) Mets of the Texas League. In Jackson, Yost improved his defense enough to catch most of the team's games even though he hit only .199 in 83 games.

While with Jackson Yost opened a taxidermy studio during the offseason, behind his uncle's bowling alley. "And that was my winter job. We'd go deer hunting and we'd do taxidermy in the back of the bowling alley back there. It was a lot of fun."[6] Yost would list taxidermy as his current occupation on the National Baseball Hall of Fame questionnaire that players complete when they make the major leagues.

The 1977 season changed the direction of Yost's life. After a great start with Jackson, he was promoted to Tidewater of the Triple-A International League. He continued his good play, hitting 12 home runs in 60 games while batting .291. Once the season ended, he married the former Deborah Ann Ferrell in September 1977. And finally, the Milwaukee Brewers acquired Yost in the Rule 5 draft during the winter meetings. Yost performed well with the Brewers' Triple-A affiliates in Spokane (1978) and Vancouver (1979), earning an invitation to the Brewers 1980 spring-training camp. Yost had confidence that he would make the major-league roster, whatever it would take, telling Brewers coach Larry Haney, "I'll warm up the pitchers, I'll wash the uniforms. I'll scrub out the clubhouse; anything."[7]

Yost made the team as the Brewers' third catcher behind Charlie Moore and Buck Martinez, and made his major-league debut on April 12, 1980, in the first game of a doubleheader against Boston. "We were blowing them out big, 14-0, 15-1, something like that, in the seventh inning and they put me in," Yost recalled. "The first hitter was Carl Yastrzemski. I remember just staring at his face, thinking that I can't believe this is happening."[8] After three appearances without a hit, Yost was sent back to Vancouver in May. His performance there (.309/2/41) earned him a trip back to Milwaukee in September. In his first at-bat back in the big leagues, Yost got his first major-league hit, off Albert Williams in a 15-2 drubbing of the Brewers at the hands of the Minnesota Twins. Yost wound up the season hitting .161 without a home run or RBI.

In December 1980 the Brewers acquired Ted Simmons from the St. Louis Cardinals, seemingly burying Yost deep in the Brewers roster. However, the Brewers traded Martinez in May, and Moore spent time on the disabled list and in the outfield, giving Yost an opportunity to learn from the experienced Simmons. Simmons wanted to pass on what he had learned in the majors, and found Yost a willing, if not skeptical, student. Simmons told Yost that he would have something for him every day to learn. Yost thought, "Yeah, right. And then for the next two and a half years, Simmons had something for me every day."[9] Yost got only 30 plate appearances in 1981 but experienced postseason baseball for the first time as the Brewers won the second half of the strike-shortened 1981 season, losing the Division Series to the New York Yankees.

Yost served as Simmons's primary backup behind the plate during the Brewers' 1982 campaign that took them to Game Seven of the World Series. Yost saw limited action, playing in 40 games with 107 plate appearances. He hit only one home run during the season, but it was one of the most important homers in the Brewers' season. They had taken over first place at the end of July and led the Baltimore Orioles in the AL East by three games with six to play going into their game at Boston on September 29. Yost entered the game in the bottom of the eighth and came up with two on and two out in the top of the ninth inning after Cecil Cooper was intentionally walked. Yost's home run gave the Brewers the 6-3 win and a four-game lead with five games to go over the Orioles. He was so sure he wouldn't be playing on the road trip that he had not packed a bat for the road trip, using Moore's bat to hit the game-winner. "It's a dream come true. You think about it, then you saw 'Naw. That would never happen.'"[10] The Brewers lost their next four, allowing the Orioles to tie for the division lead going into the last game of the season, in Baltimore. Milwaukee defeated the Orioles in game 162 to win the division flag. Yost did not play in the League Championship Series against the California Angels, and walked in his only appearance (in Game Six) of the World Series against the Cardinals.

The home run against Boston was the pinnacle of Yost's playing days. In 1983 he started 57 games behind the plate for the Brewers, 30 more than in 1982. He added six home runs in 1983, but his average dropped to .224 and he continued to struggle throwing runners out, nailing only 8 of 65 would be stealers for a 12 percent rate (the league average was 33 percent). The Brewers decided to move on from Yost, trading him to the Texas Rangers for veteran catcher Jim Sundberg.

Rangers manager Doug Rader thought Yost would be his starter for the 1984 season. "I believe Yost will be a top catcher," Rader said. "But because of the situation in Milwaukee — where Ted Simmons had a lock on the job — he has not been able to prove it. He will get that opportunity with the Rangers."[11] For his part, Yost was excited about the chance to be a number-one catcher. "I'm happy as heck about it," Yost said. "From everything I've heard, I think it's going to be fun."[12] Yost was the Opening Day catcher in 1984, but did not take advantage of the opportunity, hitting only .182 in 80 games. His hitting woes and continued difficulty with baserunners saw him lose time to Donnie Scott, and in April of 1985 he was released by the Rangers, catching on later that month with Montreal, who sent him to their Indianapolis affiliate for the season. Yost's numbers came up a bit at the Triple-A level, and he was called up to Montreal to finish the season and his major-league career. Yost signed with the Braves organization, where he bounced between Triple-A Richmond and Double-A Greenville for the next two seasons.

Knowing his playing days were over, Yost wondered what his next move would be when the Braves asked if he would work with the young players on their minor-league team in Sumter, South Carolina. He wound up being appointed manager in Sumter, and worked with some of the Braves that would go on to success at the major-league level, including Ryan Klesko, Ron Gant, and Mark Wohlers. After three years working in the South Atlantic League, Yost was again promoted to the big leagues, this time as the bullpen coach in Atlanta. "I was in the right place at the right time," he said. "It was just pure luck."[13] Phil Niekro had been the bullpen coach and was named the manager at Richmond, opening up the bullpen-coach job for Yost, working for manager Bobby Cox.

Yost joined Atlanta at the start of one of the most remarkable team runs in sports history. In every year Yost with the Braves (save the strike-shortened 1994 season), they won the National League East title. Yost spent eight years in the Braves bullpen and then moved to the third-base coach's box in 1999. Bobby Dews, who had been the third-base coach, was moved to the bullpen by Cox after the 1998 season.

Yost didn't spend all of his time in Atlanta studying box scores. In May 1993 he opened a clothing store, Major League Image, whose customers were helped to match their wardrobes using a dress-by-the-numbers strategy. The store had evolved from a computer program that Yost and local retailer Mac McLemore had developed. Yost used the system himself — "Hey, my wife can't travel with me everywhere," Yost once joked.[14] He also spent time outdoors with friends, including NASCAR legend Dale Earnhardt. The two were introduced by a mutual friend, Jody Davis. "We hit it off. Hunted together every year," said Yost.[15] Yost even worked on Earnhardt's pit crew during the 1994 baseball strike. Earnhardt was a huge Braves fan, and often pestered Yost to help him get into the Braves dugout so he could help manage. Earnhardt died in a crash near the end of the Daytona 500 in 2001. "There'd be times when we'd have an exciting play on the field and I'd think, 'Boy, I bet that fired Dale up.' I'm gonna miss knowing he's there watching us do our thing. There's a lot to miss when a man like him's not around anymore."¹⁶ Yost began to wear uniform number 3 as a tribute to Earnhardt after his death.

The Brewers were looking for a new manager after the 2002 season. Jerry Royster had been fired after leading the team to a 106-loss season that saw attendance at Miller Park drop by nearly a million. The Brewers had looked at a number of candidates, and had offered the job to Ken Macha, who turned them down to take the Oakland A's open position. Brewers general manager Doug Melvin had not considered Yost until Yost's agent, Alan Hendricks, spoke with him. Melvin also spoke with Cox and Braves general manager John Schuerholz and gave Yost an interview. After he made the hire, Melvin said that Yost's "work ethic, energy and enthusiasm" set him apart from the other candidates.¹⁷ Brewers fans would have been expected to wonder if a guy with no major-league managerial experience was ready for this job, but Yost believed that he was. "I don't have any apprehension about being a major-league manager," he said. "I don't have much experience managing but I've been around a Hall of Fame manager (Cox) for 11 years."¹⁸

The 2003 Brewers showed improvement in Yost's first year, improving to 68-94. Melvin was pleased with the team's improved play. "I guarantee you he talked our team into 15 or 20 wins last year just by telling the players they were better than they actually were. They believed him and went out and did it," Melvin said.¹⁹ The Brewers continued to improve under Yost, and their record of 81-81 in 2005 was the first time since 1992 that the team did not have a losing record. After a slight step back in 2006, the Brewers rebuild was in full form for the 2007 season. They started the season 16-9 in April and by mid-May had an eight-game lead in a weak National League Central Division. They kept the lead until mid-August when a five-game losing streak knocked them to second place. The Brewers stayed in the hunt and moved into a tie for first on September 18. But the heat of the pennant race seemed to take its toll on Yost and the players. Yost was ejected from three games during a four-game stretch and served a one-game suspension on September 27 for retaliation in a game against the Cardinals. Yost was defiant, stating, "What happened in the past doesn't really concern me right now, but to answer your question, no, I wouldn't do a thing differently."²⁰ GM Melvin supported Yost, but admitted, "This is a situation we haven't been in before, and it's a situation Ned hasn't been in before as a manager. We handle all these things together as a team."²¹ Brewers fans had been filling the sports airwaves and message boards looking for Yost's removal after the team lost an 8½-game lead in June, but Brewers owner Mark Attanasio confirmed Yost's status when he said, "Ned is fine."²²

The 2008 version of the Brewers played better than they did in 2007 but found the division race more challenging with the improved play of the Chicago Cubs. Still, the Brewers were in the hunt for the playoffs after going 20-7 in August, finishing the month with a record of 80-56 and a 5½-game lead for the wild card over the Philadelphia Phillies. A poor homestand to start September saw the wild-card lead shrink to four games with a key four-game set coming in Philadelphia. The series was a disaster for the Brewers, who lost all four games and their wild-card lead. Attanasio and Melvin had seen enough after the Phillies series, and decided to fire Yost with 12 games left in the season. "When we talked to (Ned), he didn't have all of the answers to what's gone on the last two weeks," Melvin said.²³ Yost said he did not see the move coming, stating, "The timing of it surprised me. It's the nature of the business, but it's gotten a little strange. Two bad weeks (and you get fired)."²⁴ Yost's bench coach, Dale Sveum, took over the team, and while the results improved only slightly (7-5 over the final 12 games), it was enough for the Brewers to end their postseason drought and claim the wild card. The Brewers were eliminated by the Phillies (who had overcome the New York Mets to win the NL East) three games to one in the Division Series.

Yost spent 2009 on his 210-acre farm in Georgia but was not out of baseball long. In early

2010, Kansas City Royals general manager Dayton Moore hired him as a special assistant to baseball operations. Many saw it as an insurance policy for the Royals, whose manager, Trey Hillman, had taken a lot of criticism after a 97-loss season in 2009. "That's not the motive," said Moore. The motive is hiring good people to impact the organization. Trey was as much on board bringing in Ned as I was."[25] It didn't take long for the insurance policy to be cashed in, as Moore fired Hillman on May 12, 2010, and replaced him with Yost. "Ned has been through what we're going through (in terms of building a club). He has a lot of similarities to Trey, actually as far as their energy and relationship skills with people."[26] Yost later said that managing in the big leagues is mostly about three things: You must manage the personalities of the players, the games, and the media. Thinking he did okay with the first two while in Milwaukee, he decided that he wouldn't read, listen, or watch any coverage of the Royals. Some of the decisions he would make as the Royals returned to respectability would challenge this.

The Royals whom Yost inherited were in many ways like the Brewers in 2003, or even the Braves in 1991. After an 83-win season in 2003, they had three straight 100-loss seasons. Hillman was able to get them out of the AL Central cellar in 2008 with a 75-87 campaign. A promising 18-11 start in 2009 fell apart as the Royals crashed to a 65-97 final record in 2009, setting the table for Hillman's demise. But the poor record translated into high draft choices, and Moore and his staff made some good choices in these years, including first-round picks Alex Gordon (2005), Mike Moustakas (2007), and Eric Hosmer (2008). This infusion of young talent and a manager experienced in growing young talent led to improvements in the standings, from 67 wins in 2010 (Yost was 55-72) to 71 in 2011 and 72 (and a third-place finish in the division) in 2012.

Offseason moves to add pitchers James Shields and Wade Davis lifted expectations for the 2013 season, and *The Sporting News* predicted a second-place finish for the Royals and Manager of

Though he'll forever be known as the skipper of the 2015 World Series Champion Kansas City Royals, Ned Yost was also a catcher in parts of six seasons in the majors (1980-1985), the first four of those with the Brewers.

the Year honors for Yost. Yost shrugged off the pressure of these expectations, saying, "There's pressure with everything that you do, there really is, whether it's expectation and pressure. But there are so many variables. You can't get too carried away, because there are a lot of things that have got to happen right."[27] The season got off to a fair start, but by the end of May the Royals were 22-30 and in last in the division again. Speculation began to rise regarding Yost's job security, but Moore came to his defense, stating that Yost "was the least of the club's problems."[28] The team responded to Moore's defense of their skipper, going 64-46 the rest of the season to finish in third place with a winning record for the first time since 2003 and a contract extension for Yost, setting up several very exciting years of baseball in Kansas City.

Yost realized by the start of the 2014 season that the strict boundaries he had learned from Cox in Atlanta needed to be adjusted for the player of today. "I've gotten much better results than just coming in and trying to be the tough guy," he said. "The authoritarian. Yelling, screaming. That doesn't work with kids nowadays."[29] Billy Butler noticed the change in Yost. "He's been easier to talk to," Butler said.[30]

The Royals got off to another slow start in 2014, and in early June were three games under .500, bringing up discussion of Yost's job again. But just as in 2013, the young Royals found their form in the summer. They stayed in race for the division crown as well as the wild card. They could not catch the Detroit Tigers for the AL Central, but clinched a spot in the wild-card game after beating the Chicago White Sox on September 26.

The wild-card game cemented Yost's growing reputation as a manager who would manage his way, and not how convention would have him manage. In the top of the sixth inning, the Royals clung to a 3-2 lead, but starter Shields put the first two hitters on. Convention said that Yost should bring in Kelvin Herrera, as he usually did in the seventh inning, but instead he chose Yordano Ventura, a starter who had pitched two days earlier. Ventura promptly gave up a three-run home run and the lead. Fans in Kansas City had taken to Twitter to express their displeasure in similar Yost moves with the hashtag/verb #yosted, describing what happens when a choice goes horribly wrong. When Yost pulled Ventura three hitters later for Herrera, the Royals fans gave Yost rousing disapproval of the moves. "I'd never in my life heard anything like it,'" said broadcaster Ryan Lefebvre.[31] "It didn't bother me. I still felt like we were going to win the game. I had no doubt that we would," Yost said.[32] They did, coming from behind with three runs in the eight and one in the ninth to tie, and then with two runs in the 12th after the A's scored one in the top of the frame. So inspired were the Royals after this multiple come-from-behind win that they swept the Los Angeles Angels in the Division Series and then the Baltimore Orioles in the AL Championship Series.

Suddenly the guy who couldn't handle the pressure of pennant race in Milwaukee and had nearly thrown away the Royals' first playoff appearance since 1985 became the first manager in history to start a postseason 8-0. "I've been called a dunce (*Wall Street Journal*), an idiot (*Chicago Tribune*) and everything else. It just doesn't bother me. I'm really comfortable with who I am. I know who I am," said Yost after the season.[33] The Royals faced Yost's favorite team growing up, the San Francisco Giants, in the World Series and came as close as you could to winning, leaving the tying run on third base in the bottom of the ninth inning in Game Seven. Yost spent time during the offseason doing exactly what one would never think he would do — develop an app for iPhone and Android. Ned Yost's Baseball Academics was launched at the American Baseball Coaches Association conference, where it won best in show. "It just teaches kids to think, teaches them to think quick and where to properly throw the ball. Even college coaches said, 'I would make my kids do that,'" Yost said.[34]

The 2015 Royals would not leave anything to chance. Avoiding the slow start that plagued the previous two seasons, they jumped out to a 15-7 record by the end of April, took over the Central Division lead for good on June 9, and won the division by a comfortable 12 games. Yost became the Royals' all-time winning manager on June 18 with his 411th victory. The Division Series against the Houston Astros went the distance, but trade-deadline pickup Johnny Cueto pitched a gem to win the series for the Royals. The Toronto Blue Jays were the opponent in the ALCS, and were dispatched in six games, leaving the Royals in the World Series in consecutive years for the first time. In the 1985 Series, the Royals had to battle back from a 3-1 deficit to claim the title. The 2015 Royals avoided this drama, winning the Series over the New York Mets in five games when they scored two runs in the top of the ninth inning to tie Game Five, then five more in the 12th to win the series.

Yost and the Royals perhaps used up all of their magic in their 2015 run to the title and could not replicate it in 2016. This version of the Royals briefly flirted with first place in May but fell to third in the division with a record of 81-81. The 2017 version was no better, finishing with an 80-82 record. Perhaps the most excitement that 2017 provided Yost nearly cost him his life. On November 4, while in a tree stand on his property in Georgia, Yost fell 20 feet when the stand collapsed as he was trying to attach a safety strap. He broke his pelvis and severed his iliac artery. The trauma doctor told him that he was lucky to be alive, as this type of injury has a 25 to 30 percent mortality rate. "I had my cell phone in my pocket, which was my key to the whole thing and being in a spot on my farm that had service was key," Yost said.[35]

After two mediocre seasons, the Royals decided to rebuild in 2018, and their record fell to 58-104, their second-worst performance in franchise history. Moore hired former Cardinals manager Mike Matheny as a special adviser in November 2018, perhaps as another insurance policy, especially with Yost under contract for only one more season. The 2019 season was more of the same, with the Royals posting a 59-103 record. On September 25, 2019, Yost announced his retirement. Yost may have preferred to simply walk away at the end of the season, but he wanted to thank the Royals fans. "That's what's really important to me," he said at his retirement ceremony on September 27. "I've thoroughly enjoyed my 10 years here, and I've got a world of memories from them 10 years, but what makes them special is you," Yost said gesturing to the crowd.[36] He retired as the winningest manager in Royals history (746-839), and the second-winningest manager in Brewers history (457-502). His 1,203 total wins as a manager rank him 45th in major league baseball history as of the end of the 2019 season.

In May 1983, after hitting home runs in consecutive games in Oakland, Yost saw his old coach Wellman for the first time since he left Chabot. "I was dead wrong about you," Yost recalled him saying. "The one thing I didn't take into account is that you can't keep a good man down."[37] Yost has been called many things during his career, some not fit for print. But he helped build one of the great teams in baseball history, then transformed two small-market losers into winners. Perhaps the best thing said about Yost came from a man who both hired and fired him, Doug Melvin: "He took a franchise that had not been to the playoffs in 25 years, built it up and got it to the playoffs. Then he took a franchise in Kansas City that hadn't been to the playoffs in 30 years and did the same thing. I don't care what anyone says about him. How many managers have done that?"[38]

SOURCES

In addition to the sources listed in the Notes, the author accessed Retrosheet.org and Baseball-Reference.com.

NOTES

1. Vahe Gregorian, "Ned Yost Has Been Making 'Most of What He Has' Since Growing Up a Giants Fan," *Kansas City Star*, October 20, 2014, kansascity.com/sports/spt-columns-blogs/vahe-gregorian/article3185608.html.
2. Ibid.
3. Dick Kaegel, "Yost Recalls Hitless Season in High School," MLB.com, April 22, 2014 mlb.com/royals/news/royals-manager-ned-yost-recalls-hitless-season-in-high-school/c-72993074.
4. Gregorian.
5. Ibid
6. Chris Fickett, "Yes, Royals Manager Ned Yost Was a Taxidermist," *Kansas City Star*, October 27, 2015.
7. Tom Flaherty, "Kid Yost Mentally Ready, So Are Brewers," *The Sporting News*, April 26, 1980: 18.
8. Chuck Greenwood, "'82 World Series Yost's Career Highlight," *Sports Collectors Digest*, July 18, 1997: 60
9. Gregorian.
10. Tom Flaherty, "AL East Notes – Yost an Unlikely Brewers Hero," *The Sporting News*, October 11, 1982: 33.

11 Jim Reeves, "Deals for Ward, Yost Please Rader," *The Sporting News*, December 19, 1983: 42.

12 Jim Reeves, "Yost Promises Plenty of Hustle," The Sporting News, December 26, 1983: 47.

13 Greenwood.

14 I.J. Rosenberg, "Getting Dressed by the Numbers," *Atlanta Journal-Constitution*, February 18, 1993: E2.

15 Bruce Schoenfeld, "How Ned Yost Made the Kansas City Royals Unstoppable," *New York Times Magazine*, October 1, 2015.

16 Steve Hummer, "When NASCAR Lost an Icon, Yost and Others Lost a Friend," *Atlanta Journal-Constitution*, February 20, 2001: F5.

17 Michael Cunningham, "Yost Gets Two Years to Show Brewers He's the Man for the Job," *Milwaukee Journal Sentinel*, October 30, 2002: 1C.

18 Drew Olson, "Yost Looks to Catch On in Milwaukee," *Milwaukee Journal Sentinel*, October 29 2002.

19 Tom Haudricourt, "Yost Offers Brewers a Fresh Approach," *Milwaukee Journal Sentinel*, February 22, 2004.

20 Gary D'Amato, "Tumultous Week Finally Ends for Yost," *Milwaukee Journal Sentinel*, September 29, 2007: C1.

21 Ibid.

22 Rick Braun, "Players Not Surprised Yost Returning," *Milwaukee Journal Sentinel*, September 27, 2007: C5.

23 Tom Haudricourt, "Brewers Fire Manager Yost," *Milwaukee Journal Sentinel*, September 15, 2008.

24 Ibid.

25 Sam Mellinger, "Royals Hire Ex-Brewers Manager Yost as Special Advisor," *Kansas City Star*, January 13, 2010.

26 Bob Dutton, "Royals Fire Hillman, Select Yost as Replacement," *Kansas City Star*, May 13, 2010.

27 Pete Grathoff, "Ned Yost, Manager of the Year," *Kansas City Star*, February 6, 2013.

28 Bob Dutton, "Royals' Yost Says He 'Doesn't Listen' to Speculation Regarding His Job Security," *Kansas City Star*, May 29, 2013.

29 Andy McCullough, "Royals Manager Ned Yost Loosens the Reins as He Adjusts to a New Generation of Players," *Kansas City Star*, March 1, 2014.

30 Ibid.

31 Schoenfeld.

32 Ibid.

33 Joe Strauss, Royals' Yost Shrugs Off the Critics," *St. Louis Post Dispatch*, December 9, 2014.

34 Pete Grathoff, "Royals Manager Ned Yost Developed App to Teach Baseball Strategy," *Kansas City Star*, February 4, 2015.

35 Pete Grathoff and Rustin Dodd, "Royals Manager Ned Yost Says He Nearly Died as a Result of Fall from Tree," *Kansas City Star*, November 13, 2017.

36 Lynn Worthy, "Royals Ned Yost Thankful for 10-year Ride," *Kansas City Star*, September 27, 2019

37 Gregorian.

38 Schoenfeld.

ROBIN YOUNT

By Gregory H. Wolf

If any player could be called Mr. Brewer it is Robin Yount. He played his entire 20-year major-league career with the Milwaukee Brewers, debuting as an 18-year-old shortstop in 1974, and helped reinvigorate and reenergize a fan base that been reeling since the Braves abandoned Milwaukee for Atlanta in 1966. Yount led the Brewers to their first AL pennant, in 1982, and that season became the first Brewer to be named league MVP. Two years later he underwent career-threatening shoulder and arm surgeries, switched positions to center field, and was named MVP again, in 1989. The 17th member of the exclusive 3,000-hit club, Yount was elected to the Baseball Hall of Fame in his first year of eligibility.

Yount endeared himself to Brewers fans and teammates because of his all-out hustle, humble nature, and team-first attitude. "Part of the reason I played as hard as I did," he said years after retiring, "was because I didn't want to embarrass myself. If you're fearless, sometimes you get careless, and that's when mistakes happened."[1] Yount never changed that style, even when he was nearing the end of his career. "He runs out every groundball to the pitcher as hard as he can," said teammate B.J. Surhoff about the 34-year-old in 1990. "He is the best baserunner in baseball, he plays hitters perfectly, he's an incredible clutch hitter, he gives himself for the team at all personal costs. When you play with him, you realize that he plays the game on the edge."[2]

At 6-feet tall and just 165 pounds, Yount certainly did not have the physical build of a power hitter, yet was surprisingly muscular and quick, both with the bat and on his feet. He developed surprising power as he matured, spanking 20-plus home runs in a season on four occasions. He was a natural spray hitter and took advantage of the powers alleys to collect doubles, hitting at least 40 in four seasons, and 30-plus eight times, and triples, racking up double figures four times. Yount had a closed stance and gripped the bat in an unorthodox style; instead of lining up the knuckles of his forefingers and and pinky on the bat as most right-handed hitters do, his hands were slightly twisted, the left hand clockwise and the right hand counterclockwise. "Nobody else looks quite like Robin Yount in the batter's box," observed sportswriter Gary D'Amato. "He has a distinctive stance; his right foot drawn back, left heel off the ground, left toe pointed in, crouched low."[3]

"My swing was certainly not the prettiest thing I've ever seen, even though it worked for me," Yount told *ESPN The Magazine*. "I had very few mechanical thoughts. ... I was strictly a reaction hitter. I would let the ball get as deep on me as I could, try to recognize it as early as I could, and … I tried to hit it as hard as I possibly could."[4] Said knuckleballer Charlie Hough of Yount, "He doesn't have the type of swing you would teach. It's a very unorthodox style. He actually looks like he's tied up, but just when you think you have him beat, he gets the bat head out there for a single or double down the line."[5]

Milwaukee sportswriter Tom Flaherty described Yount as "the most modest superstar in sports."[6] Shy, quiet, and unassuming by nature, Yount was a club leader who led by example and deed, and not by a rah-rah attitude. He kept his teammates loose with his relaxed approach and humor, and willingly let them take the spotlight. "Publicity? I don't especially like it," he quipped as an 18-year-old rookie, "but I understand there is a need for it in baseball."[7] As he developed into star and MVP, reporters always flocked to him for interviews, but Yount was never good with sound bites. About the 1982 World Series and his record-setting hitting, he retorted, "If there is a drawback, I suppose it would be all the exposure."[8]

Robin R. Yount was born on September 16, 1955, in Danville, Illinois, just over the state line from where his parents, Phil and Marion Yount, lived in Covington, Indiana. Within a year of Robin's birth, the elder Yount relocated the family, which also included his older brothers Jim and Larry, to the affluent community of Woodland Hills, in the San Fernando Valley about 25 miles northwest of Los Angeles. An aerospace engineer, he began a job with Rocketdyne, a division of Rockwell International.[9]

A precocious youngster, Robin was always small for his age, yet a gifted athlete with myriad interests. By the age of nine, he began golfing and two years later was racing motorcycles, two passions that remained constant throughout his life. At Taft High School he played basketball and football, though he abandoned them after his sophomore year to concentrate on baseball. He initially pursued it with a certain nonchalance, unlike his brother Larry, five years older, who was an acclaimed pitcher and was selected by the Houston Astros in the fifth round of the 1968 amateur draft. Robin's attitude to baseball became more serious in the summer of 1972, after his junior year, when he moved to Oklahoma City to live with his brother, who was playing for the 89ers of the Triple-A American Association. "That exposed me to the professional life," explained Yount years later. "I lived it — went to the park early, hit, took grounders, hung around the clubhouse, hung out with the guys."[10] Aided by a noticeable growth spurt, the 6-foot, slightly-built yet sinewy 165-pound Yount emerged as a star in his senior year. That spring dozens of scouts followed the hard-hitting shortstop, who with a stellar .455 batting average led his team to the West Valley League championship.[11] He was named the league's Co-MVP, as well as All-Los Angeles City Player of Year.[12] Just days after graduating, the 17-year-old Yount was selected by the Milwaukee Brewers, on scout Gordon Goldsberry's recommendation, with the third overall pick in the 1973 amateur draft, after the top selections, pitcher David Clyde and catcher John Stearns.[13] Two decades later, the longtime veteran talent evaluator Goldsberry still considered Yount "the best athlete I've ever been associated with."[14] Yount withdrew his letter of intent to play baseball at Arizona State University[15] and signed with the Brewers, accepting an estimated $75,000 bonus.[16]

The Brewers assigned Yount to the Newark (New York) Co-Pilots in the short-season Single-A New York-Penn League. The club was atrocious, winning just 15 of 70 games, but Yount was its bright spot, batting .285, earning All-Star honors at shortstop and being named the league's player most likely to reach the majors.

Yount was invited as a nonroster player to the Brewers spring training in Sun City, Arizona, in 1974. The club was coming off its fourth consecutive miserable season in Milwaukee since relocating from Seattle and changing its name from the Pilots after its inaugural season in 1969. Skipper Del Crandall initially gave little thought to Yount making the club, not just because he had only 64

THE 1982 MILWAUKEE BREWERS

Arguably the most popular player in Brewers history, Robin Yount debuted in 1974 as an 18-year-old shortstop. A lifelong Brewer, Yount was a two-time AL MVP and collected 3,142 hits in 20 seasons (1974-1993). He was elected to the Baseball Hall of Fame in 1999, in his first year of eligibility.

All-Star catcher. "Others, like Robin, have the ability always to concentrate on what's coming up next."[17] Unfazed by Yount's smooth transition to the speed and cerebral aspects of game was Goldsberry, noting, "One reason Robin adapted to the major leagues at age 18 was that he had been exposed to professional ball by Larry. Robin had worked out with Triple-A players and had seen that he could do all the things they could do."[18] As the Brewers' roster was gradually trimmed during camp, Robin was briefly reunited with Larry who was traded to the club on March 30. While Larry was ultimately cut, Robin was named the starting shortstop and debuted as the majors' youngest player on April 5 against the Boston Red Sox at County Stadium. Surprisingly relaxed, Yount claimed he felt no pressure to perform. "I had nothing to lose," he said years later. "If I didn't play well, they would send me back to the minor leagues which was probably where I belonged anyway."[19] Batting ninth, Yount drew a walk off Luis Tiant in his first at-bat and flied out to left field in his other plate appearance before he was lifted for pinch-hitter Felipe Alou. Hitless in his first 10 at-bats, Yount singled off Baltimore's Dave McNally on April 12 in Milwaukee for his first hit. The next day he went from goat to hero in a matter of minutes. His error on Bobby Grich's grounder enabled the Orioles to tie the game, 2-2, in the top of the eighth. Moments later, Yount led off the bottom of the frame by smashing his first home run, off starter Ross Grimsley, to give the Brewers the lead and eventual victory, 3-2. Yount seemed overwhelmed by big-league pitching early in the season, with his batting average under .200 through May 11; however, he proved his mettle, collecting 18 hits in 49 at-bats (.367 average) from May 12 through May 31 to secure his position on the field, which he didn't relinquish for the next 20 years. "I don't think about how scared I should be because I'm in the major leagues at 18," Yount told sportswriter Pat Jordan for his *Sports Illustrated* feature in 1974. "I just go out and play. When I'm at bat I concentrate on hitting the ball, and when I'm in the field I concentrate on

games of A-ball under his belt; but also because Yount had made 18 errors in those games, plus the shortstop spot seemed to be secure on club with Tim Johnson making 135 starts in his rookie season in 1973. But Yount proved that he was no ordinary 18-year-old big-league wannabe. He impressed the staff as much with his physical prowess as with his mental toughness. "Some people are always worrying about what just happened, and that makes them unprepared for what happens next," quipped Crandall, himself a former 11-time picking it up."[20] By early August, Yount's mobility was becoming compromised by tendinitis in his feet, a malady that ultimately shelved his season after August 17. Praised by Brewers beat reporter Lou Chapman as "display[ing] the poise and ability of a Marty Marion," Yount's totals (3 HRs, 26 RBIs, .250 batting average, .276 on-base percentage, and .346 slugging average) belied what his future foretold.[21]

Cast into national spotlight as a teenager, hailed as the next superstar, and dubbed "the Kid," Yount handled the psychological pressure to perform and the demands of the press. "I can't worry about how old I am," he said, deflecting questions about his age. "There are too many other things to think about."[22] Some of that pressure subsided in 1975, when the Brewers acquired Henry Aaron from the Atlanta Braves. Yount got off to a hot start, batting .386 and slugging .649 to be named the AL Player of the Month in April, but a severely sprained ankle on the artificial turf in Kansas City sidelined him for two weeks in May, and he never regained that form. In an era when shortstops weren't expected to produce offensively, Yount exceeded expectations (8-52-.267) and played in 147 games to finish with 256 games played as a teenager, which ranked second in major-league history, behind the Chicago Cubs' Phil Cavarretta's 277 (1934-1936).[23]

Yount was praised for his range at shortstop and his strong arm. "He's got [Mark] Belanger's lateral rhythm," said Chicago White Sox coach Al Monchak, comparing Yount to the Orioles fielding whiz. "He's always in control of his body. He moves backward after flies better than any young player I've ever seen."[24] Nonetheless, Yount was still learning the position and suffered a setback in '75, committing the most errors (44) of any player in baseball; consequently, he participated in the Brewers' Arizona Fall Instructional League.

In 1976 Yount revealed his fiercely independent streak, foreshadowing a bigger confrontation two years later. Empowered by arbitrator Peter Seitz's ruling that major-league players could become free agents by playing out their option, Yount threatened to play the entire season without a contract to test his market value, though he did report to spring training on time.[25] He eventually signed a two-year pact in late April.[26] Durable, he played all but three innings the entire season, improved his defense (committing 13 fewer errors), and batted in the .280s through July before slumping in July and August to finish with a lackluster .252 average and just a .301 slugging average. By the end of the 1977 season, however, Yount could lay legitimate claim to be the best all-around shortstop in the AL. Emerging offensively, he collected 174 hits and batted .288, both of which ranked second behind Cecil Cooper on the team.

After four years in the big leagues, Yount was sick of losing and playing for an uncompetitive team, which had averaged 92.5 losses per season since his arrival. Even before the 1977 campaign concluded, Brewers players seemed in open revolt against skipper Alex Grammas. "It's depressing, day in and day, out," said Cooper about the losing.[27] Yount, whose contract was to expire at the end of the season, said, "I can't say that I've enjoyed baseball that much. It's not as much fun as it should be."[28] The cornerstone and future of the team, Yount considered the players' attitude to be part of the problem and made it known that he'd like to see the Brewers make substantial on-the-field improvements and commit to winning if he were to sign with the club again. Team owner and President Bud Selig made wholesale changes in the offseason, including hiring Harry Dalton as new GM and George Bamberger as manager, and also signed free agent Larry Hisle, the reigning AL RBI leader, and acquired Ben Oglivie in a trade.

Optimism abounded when the Brewers spring training opened in 1978, with Selig claiming the squad was the best club in franchise history.[29] Before camp concluded, Yount was on the DL, away from the team, and actively contemplating retirement. For the second time in three years, he had reported to camp without a contract. He was still unsigned by mid-March, and trade rumors swirled. Adding to the mental stress of his contract situation, Yount was struggling on the diamond, plagued by painful tendinitis in his feet, a recurring problem since his rookie year, and a sore right elbow, hampering his throwing. On March 28 he was placed on the DL, and soon thereafter abruptly left the team.[30] Frustrated mentally and physically, Yount contemplated quitting baseball to became a pro golfer. Reactions from sportswriters were diverse: Some criticized Yount for being impetuous and selfish, holding the Brewers hostage with his indecisiveness; while some like Bob Wolf of the *Milwaukee Journal* were sympathetic at a time when athletes were often portrayed as a spoiled millionaires, opining that Yount is "an unusual young man, one who supposedly is more interested in contentment than money."[31] Looking back on this this period in his life, Yount commented to Robert Creamer, "I'm not very introspective, but I guess I was at an age, 20, 21, 22, when people wonder what they're going to do with their lives. I suppose I was beginning to wonder if playing baseball was what I wanted to do. I think now it might have been a part of growing up. I was very fortunate. Bud Selig was very patient with me. It's as though he said, 'Give the young man all the time he needs to straighten this out.'"[32]

The 1978 season opened without Yount, his future with the club still cloudy. His absence paved the way for another wunderkind, 21-year-old shortstop Paul Molitor, a nonroster invitee to camp, who like Yount had only 64 games in single-A ball. Molitor had been reassigned during camp, but Yount's injury and then self-induced exile forced the club to recall the player who was the Brewers starting shortstop on Opening Day. After conversations with Dalton and Selig, Yount returned to the club in May, though he remained unsigned. Not yet ready to play the field and needing extra time to get his arm back in shape, Yount debuted on May 6 by pinch-hitting, then started his first game at shortstop on May 15 (in the club's 31st game of the season), shifting Molitor to second base. Yount seemed rejuvenated, batting .315 (17-for-54) in his first 14 starts, as the club went 9-5 to move over .500. The Brewers seemed to fulfill Selig's prediction, stringing together 10 straight victories to move 10 games over .500 on June 17, though in fourth place in the power-packed AL East. During that stretch, Yount hit the first of his 10 career walk-off home runs, sending the first pitch from the Toronto Blue Jays' Tom Murphy over the wall to give the Brewers a 5-4 victory, after which his "teammates acted as it were the World Series," quipped Lou Chapman in the *Milwaukee Sentinel*, emptying from the dugout.[33] "I enjoy playing with this club more than I ever had," said an elated Yount after his heroics.[34] By the end of the month, Yount came to terms with the Brewers, signing a five-year deal, reportedly for in excess of $2.3 million, a hefty increase from his $80,000 salary.[35] The contract, negotiated by his brother Larry, who had become a successful real-estate developer, definitively ended the incessant trade speculation buzzing around Yount since his return to the team. It was a new era in Brewers baseball, characterized by a dazzling offense that led the majors with 173 homers, featuring Hisle (34-115-.290) and Gorman Thomas (32-86-.246), and five other players with at least 13 round-trippers. On September 6 Yount added his name to the home-run bonanza by spanking two for the first of 14 times in his career, victimizing the Blue Jays at Exhibition Stadium, highlighting a 4-for-4 performance with 5 RBIs in a 7-0 shellacking. It was part of the most productive stretch in his career thus far, batting .356 and slugging .546 over 41 games (July 26 to September 7). Despite missing almost one-fifth of the season, Yount had his most productive campaign at the plate (9-71-.293). The Brewers set a team record with 93 wins, finishing in third place, 6½ games behind the New York Yankees.

In 1979 Yount married Michele Edelstein, whom he knew in high school. They welcomed four children into the world in the 1980s, Melissa, Amy, Dustin, and Jenna. He fiercely guarded his family's privacy and shielded them from media attention. A born competitor, Yount enjoyed living on the edge. "I didn't play for the love of baseball," he quipped, "I played for the love of competition." He had various offseason pursuits, some of which probably made the Brewers' front office cringe.[36] Throughout his baseball career, he raced motorcycles on off-road courses, all-terrain vehicles, and go-carts. He later dabbled in auto racing, once crashing a car in the late 1980s. "I had just bought a new race car, a Sports 2000," Yount told sportswriter Peter Gammons. "One of the first times I raced it, I took a corner wrong at about 120 and flipped. As I was lying there upside down, I thought, this must not be for me. A brand-new car, and look what I did to it."[37] Yount also fished, hunted, skied, and continued to play golf.

The 23-year-old Yount began his sixth big-league season in 1979 looking for consistency. After a seeming breakout season in 1978, he had regressed the following year, batting .267, with a .308 on-base percentage, while slugging just .371, the second lowest totals among regulars on the club, though all three statistics matched his career averages to that point (.270, .308, and .364). His rising star seemed to have been eclipsed by Molitor, who hit .322 in his sophomore season, and Thomas (who led the AL with 45 home runs). The Brewers bashers, dubbed Bambi's Bombers in honor of their skipper, George Bamberger, slugged their way to a team-record 95 wins in 1979, the second-best record in the AL, but finished a distant runner-up to the 102-win Orioles.

In the best physical shape of his life, Yount got off to a hot start in 1980 en route to one of the most productive seasons for a shortstop in big-league history. He collected 22 hits in 52 at-bats in a 13-game stretch, from April 12 to April 27, to raise his average to .400. "People would say that I had 'potential,'" said Yount," but they never understood that I needed to learn to play the game after a half-season in the minors. It is different when you're learning in the majors, because everyone sees you, and there isn't any room for patience. For me, it's a matter of consistency."[38] On May 4 at Comiskey Park in Chicago, he smashed his first career grand slam in the Brewers' 11-1 laugher. Yount appeared stronger and more determined. After hitting just 34 home runs in his first six seasons, he walloped his 10th of the campaign on June 14 to set a new personal best. He batted almost exclusively all season long in the two-hole, which afforded him better pitches and more protection; his power numbers soared and his new-found offensive prowess gained him more exposure He was finally selected to his first All-Star Game, as a backup to the starter, weak-hitting Bucky Dent of the Yankees. [Yount went 0-for-2]. On August 16 Yount went 3-for-5 with two doubles, a home run, and four RBIs. It's hard to imagine in a sport as obsessed with statistics as baseball, but lost completely on sportswriters at the time was that Yount's second hit, a double off Sandy Wihtol in the 10-5 drubbing of the Indians at Cleveland Stadium, was the 1,000th base hit of his career, making him the sixth youngest player to reach that milestone, after Ty Cobb, Mel Ott, and Al Kaline, Freddie Lindstrom, and Buddy Lewis. Bambi's Bashers once again led the majors in home runs, but were sunk by 10 losses in 11 games in the second half of August and ultimately finished in third place (86-76), while their intradivisonal rivals, the 103-win Yankees and 100-win Orioles, produced the two best records in baseball. Competing in the tough AL East did no team favors in the pre-wild-card era. In a phenomenal campaign, Yount joined Ernie Banks as the only shortstops in big-league history to collect 80 or more extra-base hits in a season, and became the first AL shortstop to compile more than 300 total bases since 1965 AL MVP Zoilo Versalles of the Minnesota Twins.[39] Yount set Brewers records for runs scored (ranking 2nd in the AL with 121) and doubles (a major-league-most 49), while batting .293, slugging .519, and hitting 23 home runs.

Yount's encore to his phenomenal season seemed like a resounding failure with three weeks to go in the 1981 season, one of the most forgettable in big-league history, yet most memorable in Brewers lore. A strike by the players union (the Major League Baseball Players Association) canceled about one-third of the season, leading owners to divide the season into halves with the "winners" playing one another in a newly established divisional series in order to generate interest for the postseason. The Brewers finished in third in the first half (31-25), and were fading in the second half, having lost five of eight games to fall to third place, 20-16, three games behind the Detroit Tigers on September 14. Just 3½ games separated the top five teams. Yount's batting average at the time was just .251 with a paltry .295 on-base-percentage and a .389 slugging percentage.

Defying the odds, the Brewers got hot and their pesky shortstop was in the middle of the club's unlikely march to the first postseason berth in its 13-year history. With the Brewers trailing the Tigers, 6-5, on September 25 in the first game of a pivotal three-game series in Detroit, Yount "salvaged a pennant race," exclaimed sportswriter Tom Flaherty in the *Milwaukee Journal*, smashing a dramatic three-run home run off starter Jack Morris to give the Brewers an 8-6 lead.[40] The victory pulled the Brewers, piloted by Buck Rodgers, to within a half-game of the Red Sox and Tigers; a loss would have dropped them 2½ back.[41] After splitting the next four games, the Brewers pulled into first place with the Tigers on September 30 with a resounding 10-5 victory over the Red Sox at County Stadium. "The team has gradually grown up," quipped Yount, who led the way with four hits and three runs. "Experience and doing pretty well in pressure situations have given us confidence."[42] The spotlight was set on the final series of the season, a winner-take-all three-game set against the Tigers in Milwaukee. Yount once again supplied the offensive power, going 3-for-4, giving him nine hits in his last 13 at-bats, and knocking in two runs in a thunderous 8-2 shellacking. "I'm not trying to do anything different," said Yount of his offensive explosion after his season-long struggles. "When you're hitting good, you don't think that much."[43] With the Brewers trailing 1-0 in the eighth inning the following night, Yount's all-out hustle on a routine sacrifice bunt led to the winning run and the second-half championship. After Molitor led off with a walk, Yount laid down a perfect bunt to first baseman Ron Jackson. According to Flaherty, Jackson looked to second, but was unable to make the throw with the speedy Molitor; that delay was costly.[44] By the time he threw to shortstop Lou Whitaker covering first, Yount was safe. Four batters later, Yount scored what proved to be the winning run, 2-1, on Thomas's sacrifice fly. It was the conclusion of the most exciting eight-game stretch thus far in Brewers history, and Yount led the way, collecting 15 hits in 33 at-bats and scoring nine runs, more than compensating for his otherwise disappointing offensive numbers (10-49-.273).

The Brewers faced the Yankees in the ALDS, which surprisingly unfolded as a battle of pitchers instead of sluggers, featuring just 32 combined runs (13 by the Brewers) in the five-game series. The Brewers lost the first two contests at home, then won the next two at Yankee Stadium, to set up another do-or-die game. Yount collected three hits but the Yankees emerged victorious, 7-3. The Brewers batted just .222 collectively, while Yount led the club with six hits and four runs.

The Brewers got off to another sluggish start in 1982, dropping into the AL East cellar on May 31. The next day Rodgers was fired and replaced with Harvey Kuenn. Whereas Rodgers was a nervous type, pacing in the dugout, the 51-year-old Kuenn, who had had a leg amputated two years earlier, was laid back with his atmosphere-changing "Have some fun" mantra.[45] The players immediately responded to Kuenn's style, posting a 30-11 record under his guidance, and moved into first place. Harvey's Wallbangers, the power-packed lineup that crushed a major-league-most 216 home runs, were born, featuring the Fu Manchu-wearing Gorman Thomas, who tied for the AL-lead with 39 home runs; Ben Oglivie, who smashed 34; the criminally underrated Cecil Cooper (32-121-.313); and Molitor with a major-league-most 136 runs scored; however, no one put on a show like Yount.

Unlike his team, Yount started off the 1982 season red-hot, rapping three hits on Opening Day, and had collected 13 hits in 29 at-bats in his first nine games. While the Brewers clawed their way into contention, trading the top spot in a fierce back-and-forth battle against the Red Sox with the Orioles lurking behind, the 26-year-old Californian surged over a 28-game stretch (June 30 to July 31), batting .410 on 48 hits, including 8 home runs, 24 RBIs, and 32 runs, and was named the AL Player of the Month for July. He became the second Brewer to be selected to consecutive All-Star Games (joining Don Money, 1976-1977), earning the start and going 0-for-3. It appeared as though the Brewers might run away with the crown, hold a commanding 6½-game lead over the Red Sox on August 27. While the Wallbangers played inconsistently in September, the Orioles surged, at one point winning 30 of 40 games. The two powerhouses played each other seven times in the final 10 games, and as in the previous season, Yount's bat was decisive. In the first of those games, on September 24 in Milwaukee, Yount's two home runs and career-best six RBIs propelled the Brewers to a 15-6 thumping. But the Brewers lost the next two to the Orioles and held a precarious one-game lead on October 1 on the eve of a season-defining four-game series in Baltimore to close the season. Skipper Earl Weaver's bunch slaughtered the Brewers in the first three games, outscoring them 26-7, setting up a dramatic winner-take-all-game on the last day of the season. Yount cracked a first-inning home for the first run of the game and another solo shot in the third, marking the seventh time in the season that he hit two round-trippers in one game. He also added a triple, his career-best 12th, in an electric 3-for-4 performance with four runs scored as Harvey's Wallbangers strolled to a convincing 10-2 victory. "If there were skeptics around who didn't believe that Robin Yount was the most valuable player in the American League,"[46] wrote Flaherty in the *Journal*, "they changed their minds." Yount was a star on a team filled with them, concluding one of the best seasons for a shortstop in baseball history: He became first shortstop to lead the AL in total bases (367) and slugging percentage (.578); only the Chicago Cubs' Banks and Pittsburgh Pirates' Honus Wanger had ever accomplished that feat. Yount also paced the circuit with 210 hits and 46 doubles, while clubbing 29 home runs and driving in 114 runs. Yount lost the batting title by one point to the Royals' Willie Wilson (.332 to .331) in an episode that produced some controversy when skipper Dick Howser sat Wilson on the final day of the season to protect the title.[47] "He's the best all-around shortstop I've ever seen," opined Kuenn, himself a former 10-time All-Star, about Yount.[48] Yount received 27 of 28 first-place votes to become the first Brewer to win the league's MVP Award. He also won his first and only Gold Glove Award, a year after leading the AL in fielding percentage at short.

The Brewers captured their first pennant after a stunning comeback against the California Angels in the ALCS. After losing the first two games in Anaheim, Kuenn's crew won the next three in Milwaukee. Yount managed only four hits in 16 at-bats without an RBI.

The 1982 World Series featured a contrast in styles: Harvey's Wallbangers vs. Whitey Ball, the St. Louis Cardinals' version of small ball and speed, espoused by their skipper Whitey Herzog. The Brewers flipped the script in Game One, relying on 13 singles and just one home run to crush the Redbirds, 10-0, in the Gateway City, led by Molitor's five hits and Yount's four. Quiet in Games Two and Three, the Brewers exploded for six runs in the seventh inning of Game Four, including Yount's checked-swing, bases-loaded two-run single, to win, 7-5, and tied the Series.[49] In front of 56,562 screaming fans in Game Five, the third consecutive record-breaking crowd at County Stadium, Yount once again provided the fireworks, becoming the first player in World Series history to record two four-hit games in the same World Series. His home run in the seventh brought a lusty chant of "MVP!" from the crowd, in the Brewers 6-4 victory. A win away from the first world championship for Milwaukee since the Braves won the title in 1957 (they relocated to Atlanta after the 1965 season), the Brewers lost the final two games in St. Louis. Yount went 1-for-8 in those two contests, finishing with a Series-high 12 hits, as well as a team-best six runs and six RBIs (tied with Cooper).

The end came abruptly for Harvey's Wallbangers, though it was not immediately evident in

1983. Widely expected to win another pennant, the 1983 Brewers were racked by injuries, losing their reigning Cy Young Award winner, 18-game winner Pete Vuckovich, for all but three starts, 1980 Cy Young recipient Rollie Fingers, whose forearm injury forced him to mis the entire '82 postseason and all of '83; while Oglivie and Thomas missed significant portions of the season and combined for just 18 home runs, down from 73 the year before. The Brewers struggled to play .500 ball through the first half of the season, then went on a roll, winning 24 of 33. On August 11 Yount went 2-for-4 with two RBIs in the Brewers' 6-4 win over the Blue Jays to catapult the Brewers into first place, one game ahead of the Tigers, Yankees, and Orioles. The emotional leader of the team, however, was suffering, plagued by lower back pain since at least the All-Star Game (his third and final), which had forced to him to the bench for several games and into a designated hitter role for a few more. On August 22 he blasted a walk-off solo home run, his first round-tripper in five weeks, in the bottom of the 10th inning to give the Brewers a 3-2 victory, their seventh in eight games, and keep them on top of the East by a half-game. Two days later, he had another walk-off hit, a clutch single with the bases loaded in the 14th against the Angels, but that proved to be one of the last highlights for the Brewers. Two days later, they began their collapse, losing 18 of 24, including 10 in a row, and finished in fifth place. Their 87 wins marked the club's sixth consecutive winning season, which they have not matched as of 2020. Despite back pain, eventually diagnosed as a ruptured disc which would have far-reaching implications in his career, Yount (17-80-.308) finished with a .503 slugging percentage; scored 102 runs, hit 42 doubles; and led the AL with 10 triples. According to one modern metric established well after he retired, Yount was once again the league's most valuable offensive player, following up his 9.9 oWAR with 7.6 in '83, though he finished 18th in the MVP voting.[50]

A turning point for Yount came in 1984 when a series of injuries threatened to derail his career. Two years after winning the pennant, the Brewers finished with the worst record in the AL, (followed by two successive sixth-place finishes in 1985 and 1986). Injuries, aging players, and an unproductive farm system had decimated the club. Just 28 years old, Yount began his 11th big-league season in 1984 still feeling the lingering effects of lower back pain that had zapped his power in the second half of 1983, hitting just four home runs in his final 67 games. By mid-July he began having pain in his right arm and shoulder, making it difficult to throw to first, and was ultimately shifted to DH for most of the final month of the season. A rare bright spot on an awful team, Yount led the club in almost every offensive category, including 16 home runs, as the Brewers hit the fewest in the league, and 105 runs scored.

A month after the conclusion of the regular season, Yount underwent arthroscopic surgery to remove bone spurs in his shoulder and shore up tendons, and was expected to be ready for spring training in 1985. He reported on time, but his shoulder pain remained, making it impossible to play shortstop. Skipper George Bamberger, who had replaced Rene Lachman after one season, moved his inspirational team leader to left field, a position Yount hadn't played since Little League. "It's difficult just getting used to the ball. The angle is different," said Yount, who didn't complain about the move, though that didn't make it easier. "It's a different game. I don't know if I'd call it boring. There's a lot of standing around, but there's plenty for me to think about because I still have to learn the position."[51] A naturally gifted and instinctive athlete, Yount was moved to center field in July to take advantage of his speed, but runners exploited his weak arm, which was limited by pain and required cortisone shots. "The year just became one of those wasted seasons," said Yount. "Eventually I realized that something had to be done to clean up the shoulder."[52] Yount's season ended on September 1 and he underwent his second shoulder surgery in less than 10 months to remove bone spurs and calcium deposits.[53]

Frustrated and concerned, Yount wondered if he'd ever be pain-free or play baseball again after his second invasive procedure. He had already resigned himself to the idea that he would never play shortstop again — and never did, not even an inning — after his last start on September 7, 1984. "If the operation didn't work, I would have said, 'It's been nice,'" and would have gone on to other things," explained Yount the following year. "I love baseball and wanted to keep playing. But I was prepared to leave. I didn't see myself as a DH."[54]

A 13-year veteran at the age of 30, Yount revived his career as a full-time center fielder in 1986. He was pain-free for the first time in almost three years, and it showed at the plate. He didn't have the power as before, hitting just nine home runs, but he made solid contact, batting a robust .312 (sixth best in the league) mainly from his accustomed two-spot. He made a seamless adjustment to center field, leading all AL outfielders in fielding percentage (.997). "He's a manager's dream," said Bamberger. "Never complains, never wants to sit out, just shows up every day and plays."[55] Propelled by 12 hits in his previous six games, Yount became the seventh youngest player in big-league history (following Cobb, Rogers Hornsby, Ott, Aaron, Joe Medwick, and Jimmie Foxx) to collect 2,000 hits when he singled against the Indians at County Stadium on September 6. "Robin has never changed in all the years I've known him," said coach Larry Haney. "I've only seen a couple of players in my 19 years in the game that I haven't seen dog it at least once, Robin's one of them."[56]

Beginning in 1987, Yount enjoyed the most productive three-year stretch in his career, culminating with his second MVP award in 1989 as a 33-year-old in his 16th season. He played in 480 of 486 games, collected at least 190 hits each season, and twice knocked in at least 100 runs. On April 15, 1987, Yount made arguably the most memorable defensive play in his career, diving to snag a flyball from the Orioles Eddie Murray to preserve Juan Nieves's no-hitter, the first in franchise history, as part of the Brewers' major-league record-tying 13 consecutive wins to start the season.[57] After an early-season lead in the division, the Brewers lost 12 straight, falling well off the front-running Tigers and Blue Jays, and finished in third place (91-71).[58] In 1988 the Brewers played below .500 before ending the season on a torrid 22-9 streak, to finish in third place again, two games behind the Red Sox.

The Brewers finished with an 81-81 record and in fourth place in 1989, which unfolded as a magical year for Yount. Five days after collecting his 2,500th hit in a 3-for-5 performance with a home run and five RBIs in the Brewers' 10-2 drubbing of the Yankees in New York, Yount was feted at County Stadium on Robin Yount Day on July 7. "The attention, I don't need it," quipped Yount in his typical modest fashion. "I'm just a human being with the ability to play baseball. I'm nothing special."[59] In his first at-bat against the Orioles, Yount delighted the County Stadium faithful by hitting a homer. Always appreciative of the support he received from fans, Yount brushed off his accomplishments. "You can't play the game without recognition, but statistics just aren't what make me go," he said. "I enjoy the competition."[60] And competing he was. The day after his career-longest 19-game hitting streak ended, Yount raked the 200th home run of his career and 13th of the season in the Brewers' 6-1 victory over the Indians in Milwaukee on July 31. That blast put an exclamation point on an especially productive month (40-for-101, 22 runs, 5 home runs, 24 RBIs in 26 games) garnering him the AL Player of the Month Award. In a surprisingly weak division, the Brewers moved to within a half-game of the first-place Orioles on August 20, but struggled thereafter, finishing with a .500 record and in fourth place. Praised by sportswriter Dennis Punzel for "almost singlehandedly [leading] the Brewers from the depth of despair into contention," Yount became the first player in AL history to be named MVP who did not play for a winning team and just the third player in major-league history to win MVP awards at different positions (following Hank Greenberg and Stan Musial).[61] In a tight four-man vote in a year with no truly dominating player in the AL, Yount collected eight of the 28 first-place votes. Judged by one modern metric (WAR), sportswriters made the right decision as Yount (21-103-.318) led the AL in offensive WAR for the third time in his career (7.3) and ranked in the top five of many offensive categories, including third in slugging percentage (.511) and second in total bases (314).

Declared a free agent after the season, Yount expressed his desire to play for a winner and consequently tested his market value. His brother Larry handled negotiations with several teams, including the Angels, Dodgers, Cubs, Royals, and Blue Jays, but in the end, the decision was easy. Yount re-signed with the Brewers, inking a three-year deal in mid-December for reportedly $9.6 million, making him the highest-paid player in baseball in 1990 ($3.2 million). "Bud Selig was a big part of the reason for staying," Yount told sportswriter Peter Gammons. "Milwaukee's been a big part of the reason I've had some success. It's small, without a ton of media attention, and it's easier to play there than in a big media town. It's a family city. I can go to the park, play, come home, and be with my family. The kids are very happy in our neighborhood."[62]

In his final four seasons (1990-1993), Yount experienced a pronounced decline in production while the Brewers competed for the division crown just once. During this stretch, Yount batted between .247 and .264, slugged as high as .390, and had a .330 cumulative on-base percentage; however, he remained healthy, averaging 141 games per season. "I've been just good enough to keep my name in the lineup — never too good and never too bad," Yount told Los Angeles sportswriter Ross Newhan in September 1992, as he approached his monumental 3,000th hit. "It's a game of streaks, but my strength … is consistency."[63] On September 9 in front of a capacity crowd of 47,589 at County Stadium, Yount stepped into the batter's box against the Indians reliever Jose Mesa. The Brewers legendary radio announcer Bob Uecker made the call, "One strike on him. Back against Mesa, who is working from the windup. The 0-and-1 pitch. Swings and there it is! A base hit into right-center. He's done it! Three thousand for Robin!"[64] At 36 years of age, Yount became the third youngest (after Cobb and Aaron) and the 17th player to reach the coveted milestone.

Yount signed a one-year contract to return for his 20th and final season with the Brewers, in 1993. His Hall of Fame bona fides were secure: 2,856 games, 3,142 hits, 1,632 runs, 583 doubles, 126 triples, and 251 home runs. He batted .285, slugged .430, and had a .342 on-base percentage. Remarkably consistent, Yount produced a .288/.347/.435 line at home in County Stadium; and .283/.338/.425 on the road; against right-handed pitching (.285/.337/.430) and against southpaws (.286/.354/.429). Yount's importance to the Brewers, his loyalty to the team and its fan base, however, transcended his statistics. "Robin is what the Brewers stand for," said Bud Selig. "He's perfect for this franchise. He's a great player, but also a great person."[65]

In one of the most widely anticipated Hall of Fame elections with three other extremely popular and sure-bet Hall of Fame players, Nolan Ryan, George Brett, and Carlton Fisk, also in their first year of eligibility, there was some doubt whether Yount would receive the required 75% of the vote. He did (77.5%) and joined Brett (98.2%), and Ryan (98.8%) as the triumphant trio of the class of 1999. (Fisk received 66.4% of the vote, and was elected the following year with 79.6%.)

As he was during his playing career, Yount kept a low profile after hanging up his spikes. He resided with his family in the Phoenix area, where he had lived in the offseason for much of his playing career. Yount never lost his desire to compete and continued riding motorcycles and racing cars. He also coached some Little League ball; his son Dustin was chosen by the Baltimore Orioles in the ninth round of the 2001 amateur draft. (He played eight seasons, rising as high as Double A.)

The most famous player in Brewers history, Yount maintained a close relationship to the club.

By 1996 he was back at spring training with the Brewers, serving as an assistant, helping players with hitting and throwing batting practice. Though he harbored no intention to manage, Yount felt the tug to put on a major-league uniform and the ideal situation arose. In 2002 he joined the defending World Series champion Arizona Diamondbacks, serving as skipper Bob Brenly's first-base coach for two seasons. In two separate seasons Yount was back in a Brewers uniform as bench coach: in 2006 on Ned Yost's staff and in 2008 with Yost and Dale Sveum, both of whom were former teammates of his. After that he continued to work with the Brewers during spring training and act as an ambassador of sorts for Brewers baseball.

In 2012 Yount was part of an ownership group, which included Bob Uecker, for the expansion Lakeshore Chinooks, an amateur collegiate team in Mequon, Wisconsin, of the Northwoods summer league.

As of 2019, Michele and Robin Yount resided in both greater Milwaukee and the Phoenix area.

SOURCES

In addition to the sources cited in the Notes, the author also accessed Retrosheet.org, Baseball-Reference.com, the SABR Minor Leagues Database, accessed online at Baseball-Reference.com, SABR.org, *The Sporting News* archive via Paper of Record, the player's Hall of Fame file, the online archives via Newspaper.com, and Ancestry.com.

NOTES

1. Peter Gammons, "3 of a Kind," *ESPN The Magazine*, February 2, 1989: 94.
2. Peter Gammons, "Forever a Kid," *Sports Illustrated*, April 30, 1990. si.com/vault/1990/04/30/121905/forever-a-kid-robin-yount-has-mvp-talents-worth-millions-but-revels-in-high-risk-fun-with-very-big-toys.
3. Gary D'Amato, "Yount's Slashing Swing Not Class, but It Works," *Milwaukee Journal*, September 11, 1989: 4.
4. Gammons, "3 of a Kind," 98.
5. Joe Bierig and Bruce Levine, "Robin, the Boyish Wonder," *The Sporting News*, July 27, 1992: 11.
6. Tom Flaherty, "Dead? No! Champions? Yes," *Milwaukee Journal*, October 4, 1982: 22.
7. Milton Richman, UPI, " 'The Kid' Robin Yount Not Worried About Age," *The World* (Coos Bay, Oregon), May 14, 1974: 16,
8. Dale Hofmann, "Winning, Not Record, Counts – Yount," *Milwaukee Sentinel*, October 11, 1982: III, 1.
9. Robert W. Creamer, "This Robin's a Rare Bird," *Sports Illustrated*, September 27, 1982. si.com/vault/1982/09/27/625002/this-robin-is-a-rare-bird.
10. Peter Gammons, "Forever a Kid."
11. "Taft's Chamberlain, Yount Share Award in West Valley," *Van Nuys (California) News*, June 15, 1973: 62.
12. "Taft's 'Finest' Robin Yount Named 1973 City Baseball Player of the Year," *Valley News*, June 19, 1973: 46.
13. The 1973 draft proved to be historic, producing three Hall of Famers: Robin Yount; third-round pick Eddie Murray (Baltimore Orioles) and Dave Winfield, chosen after Yount, with the fourth pick in the first round by the San Diego Padres. Only two other drafts (as of 2019) produced at least three Hall of Fame players 1971 (George Brett, Jim Rice, and Mike Schmidt) and 1985 (Randy Johnson, Barry Larkin, and John Smoltz).
14. Gammons, "Forever a Kid."
15. "Texas Pitcher First Pick," *Los Angeles Times*, June 6, 1973: III, 7.
16. Susan Shemanske, "Yount: a Winner All the Way," *The Journal Times* (Racine, Wisconsin), September 1, 1992: journaltimes.com/sports/yount-a-winner-all-the-way/article_45612bbb-26c2-592d-9279-9ec3d9c2a7ba.html.
17. Pat Jordan, "Years Ahead of His Time," *Sports Illustrated*, July 29, 1974. si.com/vault/1974/07/29/616164/years-ahead-of-his-time.
18. Gammons, "Forever a Kid."
19. Tom Flaherty, "The Kid. Yount's Love for the Game Never Grows Old," *Milwaukee Journal*, September 11, 1982: 6.
20. Jordan.
21. Lou Chapman, "Brewers Get Glad Tiding; Yount's Foot Good as New," *The Sporting News*, December 7, 1974: 58.
22. Richman.
23. Prior to Cavarretta, Mel Ott held the record of 241 set from 1926-1928 with the New York Giants.
24. Jordan.
25. Associated Press, "Robin Considers Playing Out His Option," *Lacrosse (Wisconsin) Tribune*, March 12, 1976: 8.
26. Associated Press, "Yount Signs," *Daily Tribune* (Wisconsin Rapids, Wisconsin), April 21, 1976: 8.
27. Lou Chapman. "Brewers Players Gripe ... They're Sick of Losing," *The Sporting News*, September 24, 1977: 16.
28. Ibid.
29. Lou Chapman, "'78 Brewers Best in Club History, Selig Says," *The Sporting News*, February 4, 1978: 54.
30. Associated Press, "Yount Put on Disabled List," *Stevens Point (Wisconsin) Journal*, April 3, 1981: 13.

31. Matthew J. Prigge, When Robin Yount Almost Quit," *Shepherd Express* (Milwaukee), December 14, 2015. shepherdexpress.com/sports/brew-crew-confidential/robin-yount-almost-quit/.
32. Creamer.
33. Lou Chapman, "Yount's Homer Caps Big Day," *Milwaukee Sentinel*, June 12, 1978: III, 1.
34. Ibid.
35. Murray Chass, "Suddenly Millionaires Are a Dime a Dozen," *The Sporting News*, March 10, 1979: 31.
36. Gammons, "3 of a Kind," 98.
37. Gammons, "Forever a Kid."
38. Peter Gammons, "Yount, Mature at 24, Reaching Potential," *The Sporting News*, April 26, 1980: 12.
39. Since Versalles' feat, as of 2018 only one shortstop in the majors had exceeded 300 total bases in a season before Yount did it: The St. Louis Cardinals Garry Templeton had 308 in 1979.
40. Tom Flaherty, "Brewers Still in Contention, Thanks to Yount," *Milwaukee Sentinel*, September 26, 1981: 1.
41. After games of September 25, the Red Sox and Tigers were both 26-18; Brewers 26-19; the Orioles 1½ back at 24-19.
42. Bob Wolf, "Yount's Hits Spark Drive," *Milwaukee Journal*, October 1, 1982: 4.
43. Don Kausler Jr., "Brewers Need One More Win," October 3, 1981: II, 1.
44. Tom Flaherty, "Celebration! Brewers Win Title," *Milwaukee Journal*, October 4, 1981: 21.
45. Tom Flaherty, "Brewers Having a Blast," *The Sporting News*, August 9, 1982: 3.
46. Tom Flaherty, "Dead? No! Champions? Yes."
47. Howser's decision to bench Wilson on the last day of the season was just the tip of the iceberg in a smoldering controversy. When news reached Kansas City that Yount had gone 3-for-4 and was about to come to the plate in the ninth, Howser contrived to stop action in his game against the Oakland A's and had even been in contact with A's manager Billy Martin for help. Howser hurriedly called Wilson to get ready to pinch-hit while Martin visited the mound to stall, even though his hurler Dave Beard, was not in trouble. It proved for naught as Yount was hit by a pitch, leaving him at .331, a point behind Wilson, who returned to the bench. See "Yount Almost Gets a Batting Title," *Milwaukee Journal*, October 4, 1982: 22
48. Kevin Horrigan, "Cards Analyze Loss: 'That's Baseball,'" *St. Louis Post-Dispatch*, October 17, 1982: 1F.
49. Ibid.
50. WAR: Wins Above Replacement is an attempt by the sabermetric community to quantify a player's contributions in the total number of wins he provides in comparison to a replacement player.
51. Tom Flaherty, "Yount Playing Left Like an Old Pro," *The Sporting News*, April 15, 1986: 18.
52. Paul Attner, "Robin Rebounds with a Flourish," *The Sporting News*, June 2, 1985: 8.
53. Ken Picking, "Yount to stay in center," *Wausau* (Wisconsin) *Daily News*, September 4, 1985: 7.
54. Attner.
55. Ibid.
56. "Yount Singles for Hit No. 2,000," *Milwaukee Journal*, September 7, 1986: 9C.
57. The Atlanta Braves opened the 1982 season with 13 victories.
58. The Brewers started the season with 13 straight and were 20-3 before losing 12 straight games and 18 of 20, after which they played about .500 ball the remainder of the season.
59. Gary Reinmuth, "Yount Not Counting Hits," Chicago Tribune, July 13, 1989: B1.
60. Ibid.
61. Dennis Punzel, "Yount's Play Recalls '82 Season," *Capital Times* (Madison, Wisconsin), August 1, 1989: 13.
62. Gammons, "Forever a Kid."
63. Ross Newhan, "Hitting His Stride," *Los Angeles Times*, September 9, 1992: C1.
64. "How Bob Uecker Called No. 3,000," *Milwaukee Journal*, September 10, 1992: C5.
65. Attner.

BOB UECKER

By Eric Aron

When Bob Uecker was sent down to the minor leagues in 1961 after breaking camp with the Milwaukee Braves, manager Charlie Dressen told him, "There is no room in baseball for a clown."[1] Dressen could not have been more wrong. While no one would dispute that professional baseball is a business, Bob Uecker has spent more than a half-century in the game reminding us that the national pastime should also be about fun. "Mr. Baseball," as he is known to both casual and diehard baseball fans alike, has been a player, broadcaster, coach, actor, all-around ambassador for the game, and, yes, comedian. Beloved for his self-deprecating humor, he would be the first person to make fun of his rather unremarkable playing career, particularly his offensive statistics. "Uke," *Sports Illustrated*'s William Taaffe once said, "is the man who made mediocrity famous".[2]

In six seasons (1962-67) as a major-league catcher (almost all of it as a backup), Uecker batted exactly .200. In 297 games (217 starts) he got 146 hits, hit 14 home runs, and drove in 74 runs. "Anybody with ability can play in the big leagues. … But to be able to trick people year in and year out the way I did, I think that was a much greater feat," he once said.[3] In truth, he was a solid defensive catcher, with a career fielding percentage of .981. He played for the Milwaukee/Atlanta Braves, St. Louis Cardinals, and Philadelphia Phillies. In the Cardinals' world-championship season of 1964, he was the backup to Tim McCarver. He did not play in the World Series. In 2003 he was honored by the Baseball Hall of Fame with the Ford C. Frick Award, presented annually to a broadcaster.

The first Milwaukee native to be both signed and traded by the Braves, Uecker joked that the highlight of his major-league career was when he "walked with the bases loaded to drive in the winning run in an intersquad game in spring training."[4] Another time he said of his career highlights, "I had two. I got an intentional walk from Sandy Koufax (He also hit a home run; both came on July 24, 1965, at Dodger Stadium), and I got out of a rundown against the Mets."[5] On being intentionally walked by Koufax, he joked, "I was pretty proud of that until I heard that the commissioner wrote Koufax a letter telling him the next time something like that happened, he'd be fined for damaging the image of the game."[6]

Robert George Uecker was born on January 26, 1935, in Milwaukee, Wisconsin, although he jokes to the contrary: "My mother and father were on an oleo margarine run to Chicago back in 1934, because we couldn't get colored margarine in Milwaukee. On the way home, my mother was with child. Me. And the pains started, and my dad pulled

Bob Uecker received the Ford C. Frick Award from the Baseball Hall of Fame in 2003 in recognition of his broadcasting career, which began in 1971 as the Milwaukee Brewers radio play-by-announcer.

off into an exit area, and that's where the event took place. … There were three truck drivers there. One guy was carrying butter, one guy had frankfurters, and the other guy was a retired baseball scout who told my folks that I probably had a chance to play somewhere down the line."[7]

Parents Gus and Sue Uecker were Swiss immigrants who came to Wisconsin in the 1920s. Gus was a tool and die maker. He played soccer in his native Switzerland. "That's where I got my talent," Uecker said.[8] Even during the Great Depression, Gus was able to support his wife, son, and two daughters, earning $3 to $4 a day working on cars.[9] Uecker called his father a great family man who never let him down. He said, "In the minors, when I was making $250 a month and the money ran out, he was there."[10] Gus had a circulation problem in his legs. The conditioned worsened over the years, and by the end of the 1962 season, his legs had to be amputated. He died a few years later.

Uecker attended a technical high school in Milwaukee, where he played baseball and basketball. He would ride his bike eight blocks to Borchert Field, home of the minor-league Milwaukee Brewers, where he would see his idols Alvin Dark, Johnny Logan, Heinz Becker, and Danny Murtaugh play. He made his baseball team as a pitcher after a scout saw how hard he could throw. The story goes that at the age of 18, he became a catcher when a teammate handed over his gear to him, asking if he could do any better.[11] In his joking fashion he gave a different version of his switch: "My first game, my parents and everybody was there, my friends, and the manager came out to take me out of the game. I didn't want to come out because I was embarrassed. I said, 'Let me face this guy one more time, because I struck him out the first time I faced him.' He said, 'I know, but it's the same inning. I've got to get you out of here.' And that was my move to catching."[12]

Uecker didn't finish high school and in 1954, at the age of 20, he enlisted in the Army. He hoped to avoid going overseas by playing military baseball with soldiers who had played in the minors or in college. At the time he had done neither, so he made up a college and lied. He claimed he had played at Marquette, given that it was a college in his native Milwaukee. "Marquette didn't have a team, but they never checked," he said.[13] He played at Fort Leonard Wood in Missouri, and later at Fort Belvoir, Virginia, where he teamed with shortstop and future Cardinals teammate Dick Groat.

Coming out of the service, he signed with his hometown Braves in 1956 for $3,000. "I could have signed with the Phillies or the Pirates. The Yankees were also interested at that time."[14] He bounced around the minors for six years, playing for Braves affiliates at all levels and showing decent batting ability and some power. In 1956, his first year, he played for two teams in Class C, Eau Claire (Northern League) and Boise (Pioneer League). Between the two clubs he hit 19 home runs. Appearing in 53 games for Boise, he also had a .312 average. With Eau Claire, Evansville and Wichita in 1957 he hit 15 homers. He kept moving up the ladder, and with Boise and Atlanta (Southern Association) in 1958, he hit 22 home runs. In 1959 he played for Jacksonville and Wichita, and in 1960 he was with Triple-A Louisville and Indianapolis. He spent 1961 with just one team, Louisville, where he hit .309 with 14 home runs, and began the next season with the Brewers.

Uecker made his major-league debut on April 13, 1962, grounding out as a pinch-hitter against the Los Angeles Dodgers' Don Drysdale at Dodger Stadium. His hometown debut came on April 19 at Milwaukee's County Stadium. Facing the San Francisco Giants and Juan Marichal, he was the starting catcher, going 0-3 with two strikeouts and a walk. His first major-league hit came on May 3 at Connie Mack Stadium in Philadelphia. He replaced Joe Torre and singled to left off Art Mahaffey.

After a season of backing up Torre and Del Crandall, Uecker finished the 1962 season on a high note. On September 29 he caught Warren Spahn in the left-hander's 327th victory, which broke Eddie Plank's record for the most victories by a left-hander. Uecker went 3-for-4 with three singles, driving in two runs in the 7-3 triumph over the Pittsburgh Pirates in Milwaukee. The next day was the last day of the season. Uecker caught again, and his hit first major-league home run, off Pittsburgh's Diomedes Olivo. Uecker got into 33 games that season and hit .250. He started the 1963 season with the Brewers but got into only nine games as the third-string catcher before being sent down in June to Triple-A Denver, where he batted .283 in 52 games.

While Milwaukee manager Bobby Bragan always liked Uecker defensively, catchers Joe Torre and Ed Bailey made him expendable, and on April 9, 1964, he was traded to the St. Louis Cardinals for two minor leaguers, catcher Jimmie Coker and outfielder Gary Kolb. During his two years in St. Louis, Uecker was used sparingly. Neither manager Johnny Keane nor his successor, Red Schoendienst, stuck with him very long. He was pulled if he wasn't hitting well and generally played only when another catcher was injured or a late-game substitution was made. The primary receiver Uecker backed up during those years was Tim McCarver. Uecker had just 106 at-bats and hit .198 in the World Series season, but McCarver (who also made a successful second career as a broadcaster) praised him for helping to keep the World Series team loose. He said, "If Bob Uecker had not been on the Cardinals, then it's questionable whether we could have beaten the Yankees."[15]

The 1964 National League pennant race was one of the closest and most exciting of all time. After going 21-8 in September, the 93-69 Cardinals finished just one game ahead of both the Phillies and Reds, who along with the Giants were all alive going into the season's final weekend. Gene Mauch's Philadelphia team had a 6½-game lead with 12 games remaining, but blew the pennant by losing 10 straight. As for the NL champs, Uecker called them "the loosiest, goosiest team ever to come from ten games behind to reach the World Series"[16]

McCarver played every inning of the World Series, hitting .478. "Sat my way through it," Uecker wrote. "Called it from the bullpen. Yankee fans threw garbage at us, and I picked it up and threw it back."[17] Bob did however contribute in his own way, through his usual antics. During pregame ceremonies before Game One in St. Louis, he found a neglected marching band tuba in the outfield. He picked it up and started shagging fly balls with pitcher Roger Craig.

McCarver broke his finger early in the 1965 exhibition season and Uecker was the Opening Day receiver, catching ace Bob Gibson against the Chicago Cubs. The game was the kind of contest Uecker would joke about while doing his post-career shtick. It was a 10-10 tie at Wrigley Field, which didn't have lights yet, and was called by the umpires after 11 innings on account of darkness. Uecker was injured in the sixth inning after slamming into a wall while attempting to catch a foul ball. He had been picked off trying to steal home the previous inning, apparently crossed up on coaching signs. Gibson had one of the worst outings of his career, going only 3⅓ innings and giving up five runs on six hits. (Future Hall of Famer Steve Carlton made his major-league debut in the game, walking the only batter he faced.)

Uecker hit .228 in 53 games and after the season he was traded to the Phillies with shortstop Groat and first baseman Bill White for catcher Pat Corrales, outfielder Alex Johnson, and pitcher Art Mahaffey. The 1966 season was the closest he came to being a primary catcher. He had 237 plate appearances, platooning with Clay Dalrymple, who had 404 plate appearances. Always quick to discuss his own futility, Uecker summed up his experiences as a hitter for the Phillies: "With Philadelphia, I'd be sitting on the bench and (manager) Gene Mauch would holler down "grab a bat, Bob, and stop this rally.""[18]

Uecker's favorite line about his time in Philadelphia was when he was once fined by a police officer for being intoxicated on the street. "They fined me $50 for being intoxicated and $400 for being on the Phillies."[19] "My managers didn't want me in the game. Heck, they didn't want me on the bench. Kids ask which club I played for. Nobody, but I sat for a lot."[20] Ironically, his best offensive season was in 1966. As a Phillie, he hit seven of his 14 career home runs while establishing a career high in hits with 43.

On June 6, 1967, Uecker was traded by the Philadelphia Phillies to the Atlanta Braves for utilityman Gene Oliver. The Braves wanted Uecker specifically to catch Phil Niekro's knuckleball. "I had caught (knuckleballers) Bob Tiefenauer in Milwaukee and Barney Schultz in St. Louis, so I had a basic idea of how to survive back behind the plate."[21] In 59 games he caught for the Phillies he had 25 passed balls, and led the National League with 27 overall. Two weeks after the trade he hit his only major-league grand slam, off Ron Herbel of San Francisco.

During 1968 spring training, Uecker and his Atlanta teammates Deron Johnson and Clete Boyer were involved in a nightclub fight in West Palm Beach, Florida, on March 21, 1968, at the Cock 'n Bull Restaurant. Uecker was struck on the head with a beer bottle and required 48 stitches to close the wound. On the field he re-aggravated an injury suffered in a motorcycle accident. He was released as a player and coach on April 2. His final major-league game had been on September 29, 1967.

Capitalizing on his gift as a storyteller, Uecker became a public-relations ambassador for the Braves. "I did stand-up, weird and ignorant stuff about my career — anything for a laugh," he said.[22] In 1969 Uecker's broadcasting career began with WSB-TV, on which he did television work with Ernie Johnson and Milo Hamilton. His career as a personality in television and movies took off after he did an opening act for Don Rickles at jazzman Al Hirt's Atlanta nightclub.[23] Beginning in 1970 Uecker made close to 100 appearances on Johnny Carson's *Tonight Show*, doing three to five shows a year.[24]

He said Carson was the first to refer to him as "Mr. Baseball." Carson "didn't know that much about baseball but as we went along he let me do whatever I wanted," Uecker recalled. "As a matter of fact, when I started doing the shows in New York, you get a script to follow and promote whatever you want to talk about. After about the tenth time I did the show Johnny said, 'Do you need this stuff?' and I said, 'No, I thought you did.' So from then on we pretty much just ad-libbed and went along and whatever he said I just jumped in and went along with it."[25] His on-air relationship with Carson concluded with Carson's retirement from late-night television in 1992.

As he continued his entertainment career, Uecker was lured back to his native Milwaukee by Brewers owner Bud Selig. The 1970 Brewers were in their inaugural season, a franchise purchased by Selig after the Seattle Pilots went bankrupt after their first season. Uecker initially signed with the Brewers as a scout before becoming the club's radio voice. "Worst scout I ever had," Selig said. "We sent him up to the Northern League, and the next thing I know (general manager) Frank Lane comes raging into my office asking what kind of scout I hired. The report was smeared with gravy and mashed potatoes."[26] "Yeah, I did scouting, if you could call it that," Uecker said. "For every guy, I wrote, 'Fringe major leaguer,' so in case he made it nobody could say, 'How'd you miss that guy?'"[27]

Clearly his talent lay behind the microphone, and on September 4, 1971, the Brewers announced that Uecker would broadcast games on TV and radio. "I've never signed a contract with the Brewers since I've been broadcasting and I never will," he said in 1999. "Whatever we agree on, we have a talk and a handshake, and I don't even think that I have had a handshake the last ten years."[28] On radio station WTMJ he first partnered with friend and colleague Merle Harmon. Tom Collins filled in as well. "Merle Harmon helped me from the start," Uecker wrote. "I'd never done (radio) baseball when I joined him in the booth, not unless you count my play-by-play into beer cups in the bullpen. Beer cups don't criticize, [but] people do. ... Merle and Tom Collins let me do color, then play-by-play, and saved me if I screwed up."[29]

While achieving quick fame as a buffoon on TV, Uecker slowly grew as a play-by-play announcer on radio. "It's amazing to think of now, given his ability, but Bob's problem then was in finding stuff to ad-lib," recalled Tom Collins. "He'd constantly repeat the count and the score, and swing his legs like a pendulum, and smoke cigarette after cigarette."[30] Uecker honed his craft with hard work. "I had everything to learn and I spent ten years learning it. ... I didn't try to wisecrack my way through it."[31] In a rare moments of seriousness, he said he never spoke badly of or criticized a player on the air, reasoning, "I know how hard this game is to play."[32] Uecker, who became the main play-by-play man in 1980, said he preferred radio over television: "You paint a picture in the mind. It's a kick to make baseball come alive to a guy hundreds of miles away who's never seen your home park."[33]

Uecker was serious behind the mike. The only time he let loose in the booth is in a blowout at Miller Park, said former broadcast partner Jim Powell (1996-2008). "It's a 9-1 game, that's when the buttons at home get pushed [off]. That's when everyone tunes in.... When it's 9-1, Bob becomes Uke. It's a lopsided game where he really gets going."[34]

While continuing his radio work with the Brewers in the '70s, Uecker went national and helped telecast play-by-play for ABC *Monday Night Baseball* from 1976 to 1982. During his tenure there, which included All-Star Games, League Championship Series, and World Series games, he teamed up in the booth with an initial crew of Bob Prince, Warner Wolf, and Howard Cosell. Cosell in particular had great chemistry with Uecker, playing the straight man while Bob was his comedic foil. Cosell once teased him on the air, saying that he didn't know what the word "truculent" meant. "Sure I do," Bob said one night in Minneapolis, "If you had a truck and I borrowed it, that would be a truck-u-lent." Cosell paused and said to the national audience, "Need I say any more?"[35]

Uecker co-hosted a variety of television shows in the 1970s and '80s, among them ABC's *The Superstars*, *Battle of the Network Stars*, and *Bob Uecker's Wacky World of Sports*. He also appeared in a number of commercials. The ones he is best remembered for were for Miller Beer, both starring himself and as part of the ex-jock Miller Lite All-Stars. In his first ad he appeared outside a tavern only to be locked out because a fan asks him if he is Bob Uecker. In a sequel, he gets into the bar by claiming that he is actually Yankees pitching legend Whitey Ford. "So I lied," he says as he looks into the camera.[36] A popular Ueckerism was born in another Miller ad when he thinks that management has given him the best seats in the ballpark. Ready to sit down close to behind home plate, he is escorted elsewhere by an usher while bragging, "I must be in the front rooow."37 He has in fact been placed way up in the nosebleed seats, as animated and excited as ever.

While his career as the radio voice of the Brewers continued, Mr. Baseball landed his first major acting gig in 1985. It was a new ABC sitcom about a family in suburban Pittsburgh. *Mr. Belvedere* was based on a 1949 Gwen Davenport novel, *Belvedere*, which first was made into films starring Clifton Webb. The small-screen version was similar in story to the Hollywood films. Christopher Hewitt played Lynn Belvedere, who was hired as a nursemaid for the family's three children. Uecker was the patriarch of the family, a sportswriter named George Owens. "A lot of his character was picked up from my own," Uecker said.38 To do the show, the Brewers granted him permission to shoot episodes in Hollywood in the late summer and early fall. He continued to make Miller Lite commercials and make appearances on the Tonight Show. He even hosted *Saturday Night Live* once, on October 13, 1984. *Mr. Belvedere* was by all accounts a successful show, running for six seasons from 1985 to 1990.

In 1989 Uecker's acting career reached new heights when he appeared in the comedy movie *Major League*, starring Tom Berenger, Wesley Snipes, and Charlie Sheen, with a plot about a woman who inherits the Cleveland Indians from her late husband. She wants to move the team to a warmer climate, yet the only way she can get out of a contract is by fielding a bad team with low attendance. The players foil her plans by making the playoffs. Uecker played the gregarious yet often inebriated team broadcaster Harry Doyle. Many of the film's scenes were shot in Milwaukee's County Stadium.

With the release of the film, Uecker made himself a household name while introducing him to a new generation of fans. The Harry Doyle line of "Juuuuuust a bit outside," which described a wild pitch, became a piece of baseball popular culture. It has become an oft-quoted phrase like "There's no crying in baseball" (*A League of Their Own*), or "Chicks dig the long ball" (a late 1990s Nike commercial with pitchers Tom Glavine and Greg Maddux). Uecker reprised his role as Harry Doyle in two sequels. He enjoyed making the first two movies, but as for *Major League 3: Back in the Minors*, he said, "Three stunk. ... It was on airplanes the day after we finished it."39 Upon the first *Major League*'s 20th anniversary in 2009, Uecker said, "It seems to be playing more now than when it originally came out. ... Every day I run into someone at the ballpark or on the street and they say, 'Hey, I saw you in that movie ... it was on again today.' I mean, I go into clubhouses all the time and these players today are playing it in clubhouses before the game." 40

At one point Uecker considered leaving broadcasting to concentrate full time on acting, doing commercials, making movies, and appearing on television. It was not helping that Milwaukee was fielding some consistently bad teams. Such an example was the 1984 Brewers, who finished last in the American League East, 36½ games behind the World Series champion Detroit Tigers. In the end he decided to stay put, declaring, "I could have left there a long time ago, but no matter what I do, I'm staying. All the television stuff, the movies, the sitcoms, the commercials, that's all fun. All I wanted to do is come back to Milwaukee every spring to do baseball."41

Over the years Uecker has called some of the biggest games in Brewers history. He was behind the mike on July 20, 1976, when former teammate Hank Aaron hit his 755th and final home run. He was there when the "Harvey's Wallbangers" Brewers clinched their first and only American League pennant in 1982 (The team switched to the National League's Central Division in 1998), and he called Juan Nieves' April 15, 1987, no-hitter, as of 2011 the only one in franchise history, and Robin Yount's 3,000th hit, on September 9, 1992.

In the 1990s, Uecker helped call the 1995 and 1997 World Series on NBC-TV alongside Bob Costas and Joe Morgan. In 2003 he received the prestigious Ford C. Frick Award for Broadcasters, denoted by a plaque at the Hall of Fame. Even in accepting the award he couldn't resist a few jokes. He thanked all the people he worked with in the booth over the years: "I remember working first with Milo Hamilton and Ernie Johnson. And I was all fired up about that, too, until I found out that my portion of the broadcast was being used to jam Radio Free Europe. And I picked up a microphone one day and it had no cord on it, so I was talking to nobody."[42]

He also didn't forget to thank his family for sticking with him over the years: "My family is here today (Uecker has been married and divorced twice with two daughters, Leann and Sue Ann, and two sons, Bobby Jr. and Steve).[43] My kids used to do things that aggravate me, too. I'd take them to the game and they'd want to come home with a different player. But my two boys are just like me. In their championship Little League game, one of them struck out three times and the other one had an error allowing the winning run to score. They lost the championship, and I couldn't have been more proud. I remember the people as we walked through the parking lot throwing eggs and rotten stuff at our car. What a beautiful day."

In addition to winning the Ford Frick Award, Uecker has been named Wisconsin Sportscaster of the Year five times by the National Sportscasters and Sportswriters Association. He was named to the Wisconsin Performing Artists Hall of Fame in 1993 and inducted into the Wisconsin Athletic Hall of Fame in 1998. He was elected into the National Radio Hall of Fame in 2001.

In 2006 Uecker's 50th year in professional baseball, the Brewers placed a number 50 in their "Ring of Honor," near the retired numbers of Hall of Famers Robin Yount and Paul Molitor. Three years later, on May 12, 2009, Uecker's name was also added to the Braves Wall of Honor inside Miller Park. In March 2010, in an honor likely no other major-league baseball player will ever claim, Uecker was inducted into the WWE Wrestling Federation's Hall of Fame for participating in *Wrestlemania III* and *IV* in the 1980s.

Finally, the words of his famous home-run call "Get up! Get up! Get outta here! Gone!'" were inscribed in the lights above Miller Park. Perhaps more fittingly, there are 106 obstructed-view seats in the upper terrace level above home plate that cost only $1 in honor of Uecker's Miller Lite "Front Row" commercial. As of 2011 he could still be heard calling Brewers games on WTMJ-AM radio with partner Cory Provus. "It's been great," he said in a 2005 ceremony marking 50 years in baseball, "I'd like to do this again 50 years from now when I get to 100. Wherever I am, dig me up. Bring me back here. A couple times around the warning track and take me back to the hole where you picked me up."[44]

SOURCES

Statistics and game information found through Baseball-Reference.com and Retrosheet.org.

NOTES

1 Bob Uecker and Mickey Herskowitz, *Catcher in the Wry: Outrageous but True Stories of Baseball* (New York: Jove Books, 1982), 25.

2 Curt Smith, *Voices of Summer: Ranking Baseball's 101 All-Time Best Announcers* (New York: Carroll and Graff Publishers, 2005), 269.

3 Uecker, op. cit., 4.

4 Curt Smith, *Voices of the Game: The Acclaimed Chronicle of Baseball Radio & Television Broadcasting From 1921-Present.* (New York: Simon & Schuster, 1992), 420.

4 Larry Stewart, "Just a Bit Outside the Bounds of Reality," The Inside Track Morning Briefing, *Los Angeles Times*, May 23, 2006.

5 "A Life Of Detours: Confessions of a Feather-Hitter," *Christian Science Monitor*, July 24, 1961.

6 Uecker, op. cit.: Introduction.

7 Smith, *Voices of Summer*: 266.

8 Uecker, *Catcher in the Wry*, 12.

9 Ibid.

10 Michael Hiestand, "Broadcaster spin years: Punchless former catcher casts out baseball's best punchlines," *USA Today*, October 14, 1997.

11 Adam McCalvy, "Brewers celebrate native son Uecker; 'Mr. Baseball' honored as Milwaukee's first home-grown player," MLB.com, May 12, 2009

12. (http://mlb.mlb.com/news/article.jspymd=20090512&content_id=4686608&vkey=news_mlb&fext=jsp&c_id=mlb&partnerId=rss_mlb)
13. Hiestand, "Broadcaster spin years." 14 Chuck Greenwood, "As Voice of the Brewers, Uecker 'Just Started Talking,'" *Sports Collectors Digest*, February 5, 1999.
15. Andrew Milner, *The St. James Encyclopedia of Popular Culture*, 2000.
16. Uecker, *Catcher in the Wry*, 31.
17. Richard Sandomir, "World Series, as told by Bob Uecker," *New York Times*, October 15, 1995.
18. "A Life of Detours," *Christian Science Monitor*.
19. Smith, *Voices of Summer*, 267.
20. Ibid.
21. Greenwood, "As Voice of the Brewers."
22. Peter Carlson, "They Locked Bob Uecker Out of the Bar, but they can't keep him out of the announcer's booth," *People*, September 18, 1983.
23. Smith, *Voices of Summer*, 411.
24. Greenwood, "As Voice of the Brewers."
25. Bob Costas Interview with Bob Uecker, MLB Network, September 28, 2010.
26. Richard Sandomir, "Bob Uecker Returns to the Booth." *New York Times*, August 13, 2010.
27. Ibid.
28. Greenwood, "As Voice of the Brewers."
29. Dan O'Donnell and Jay Sorgi, "Remembering Merle Harmon," NBC Milwaukee, May 18, 2009. http://www.todaystmj4.com/news/local/45359962.html
30. Smith, *Voices of the Game*, 412.
31. "They Locked Bob Uecker Out of the Bar," *People*. September 19, 1983.
32. Bob Costas Interview with Bob Uecker, MLB Network, September 28, 2010.
33. Curt Smith, *The Storytellers. From Mel Allen to Bob Costas: Sixty Years of Baseball Tales from the Broadcast Booth*. (New York: Macmillan, 1995), 267.
34. Shannon Ryan, "Finally, the Front Row: Baseball's Funnyman Gets a Seat in the Hall," *Philadelphia Inquirer*, July 23, 2003.
35. Uecker, *Catcher in the Wry*, 113.
36. Bob Uecker Miller Lite commercial, 1984. (http://www.youtube.com/watch?v=_Ql7m9LQULM&feature=related)
37. Smith, *Voices of Summer*, 269.
38. Lauren Simon, "Uecker To Star in new TV sit-com," *USA Today*, March 6, 1985.
39. Bob Costas Interview with Bob Uecker, MLB Network, September 28, 2010.
40. Ben Platt. "Popularity of 'Major League' remains: Classic Baseball Comedy Celebrates its 20th Anniversary." MLB.com, April 7, 2009. (http://mlb.mlb.com/news/article_entertainment.jsp?ymd=20090407&content_id=4147526&vkey=entertainment&fext=.jsp)
41. Michael Hunt, "Uecker Heading For Hall," *Milwaukee Journal-Sentinel*, March 14, 2003.
42. Bob Uecker Ford Frick Award presentation Speech, National Baseball Hall of Fame, July 27, 2003.
43. Ibid.
44. Drew Olson, "Uecker Celebrates Golden Anniversary," *Milwaukee Journal-Sentinel*, August 27, 2007.

BREWERS SHAKE OFF WINTER BLUES WITH OPENING DAY ONSLAUGHT

MILWAUKEE BREWERS 15, TORONTO BLUE JAYS 4
APRIL 9, 1982, AT EXHIBITION STADIUM, TORONTO

By Isaac Buttke

April 9 was Opening Day in 1982… at least, that's what it turned out to be for numerous teams in the Northern cities of the major leagues. Teams like the Milwaukee Brewers and the Toronto Blue Jays were unable to play their scheduled Opening Day contests on April 5 after waves of snow rushed through the area. This was no ordinary snowstorm, either. Accounts from Milwaukee County Stadium suggest that around 13 inches covered the field early in the week.[1] Hundreds of Brewers employees worked all day to try to get the blanket of snow off the field, but it was hopeless: Milwaukee wouldn't be able to host its scheduled home opener.[2]

Although winter's clutches enveloped the North, the fans' excitement couldn't be tempered by a blizzard twice as big. In the strike-interrupted 1981 season the team made its first postseason appearance, finishing first in the American League East Division despite inconsistent play from its regulars, then falling to the New York Yankees in the Division Series. Experts were picking the Brewers to fight for the American League East crown again in 1982 season.[3] Fans flocked to the box office ahead of the season, and there were predictions that the Brewers could draw two million.[4]

Despite these high hopes, many question marks remained. How would Paul Molitor fare in his first season at third base?[5] Could Cecil Cooper and Ben Oglivie bounce back after down seasons? Would Larry Hisle finally be healthy enough to make an impact for Milwaukee?[6] Was Rollie Fingers' preseason injury[7] going to jeopardize the team's playoff aspirations? Hindsight tells us many of these worries vanished, but at the time the questions added an element of uneasiness to the euphoria of a brand-new season.

In the days leading up to the new Opening Day, many Northern teams had to keep their players in playing shape in spite of the weather. Spring training helped to quell some of the concerns surrounding roster spots and injuries, but a few days off in the cold Wisconsin weather would likely be detrimental to the pennant hopefuls. The Brewers, with open-air Milwaukee County Stadium unprotected from the elements, attempted to find someplace else to train before traveling north of the border. The initial plan was to work out at either Carroll College, the University of Wisconsin-Milwaukee, or the University of Wisconsin-Oshkosh, but the club opted to seek a bigger venue.[8] Their first call was to Minnesota, asking to use the new Metrodome, but the White Sox and Blue Jays were already there.[9] Then they tried to book the Superdome in New Orleans, but the employees who assist with booking the venue were out of the office, and general manager Harry

Dalton said the woman who answered the phone "didn't seem real interested in helping us out."[10]

The team's saviors wound up being the Houston Astros. "[Astros general manager] Al Rosen said, 'Come on down, we'll take care of you,'" Dalton reported.[11] The Brewers took the first flight down to the Astrodome in Houston to play two intrasquad games in the indoor facility. They declined an offer to play the University of Houston so that manager Buck Rodgers could work out more players.[12] When all was said and done, Milwaukee's team had gotten a pair of extra spring-training days before finally getting to play their first regular-season game.

The delayed Opening Day game pitted Milwaukee ace Pete Vuckovich against Toronto hurler Mark Bomback. Fewer eyes were on the pitching matchup than on the Brewers' batting order. With Robin Yount's availability uncertain, Rodgers came up with two batting orders.[13] Yount had injured his hamstring at the tail end of spring training, and with a 41-degree game-time temperature in Toronto, his status was up in the air. Yount ended up playing, but he batted seventh, the same spot his replacement, Ed Romero, would have filled had Yount been deemed unfit to play.[14]

As things turned out, Yount played a big part in the game, but he was hardly the headliner. The Brewers scorched Bomback right out of the gate, with leadoff singles by Molitor and Charlie Moore, followed by a two-run double by Cooper and a two-run homer by Oglivie. Bomback retired only one batter and was yanked after giving up an RBI single to Mark Brouhard. Dale Murray, who relieved him, allowed an inherited runner to score on a sacrifice fly by Molitor. The Brewers wound up batting around and tallying six runs before the Blue Jays had a chance to bat.

Toronto fans were immediately restless. Boos rained out from the crowd of 30,216, then chants of "We want beer!" rang through the concourse. That was in response to the fact that Exhibition Stadium was the only major-league ballpark that didn't sell beer at concession stands. *Milwaukee Journal Sentinel* writer Vic Feuerherd suggested that this was a good thing for this particular day. "It's scary to think how the crowd might have reacted if they were liquored up," he wrote in his game recap.[15]

Vuckovich wasn't overly dominant, but he held the Blue Jays scoreless through three innings. He walked two, gave up two hits and struck out a pair in that span. The Brewers added another run in the fourth on a bases-loaded walk to Gorman Thomas. The Blue Jays finally struck back in the bottom of the inning. With two outs Vuckovich walked Jesse Barfield and Ernie Whitt hit a home run.

The Brewers turned things on again in the sixth inning. Jerry Garvin was pitching for Toronto, and after four straight hits and three runs, he was relieved by Jim Gott. With the score 10-2, the Brewers gave Yount and his balky hamstring a rest and lifted him for pinch-runner Romero after Yount's two-run double. Gott proceeded to walk the bases loaded and allow four more runs to score on a pair of errors and another two-run double by Cooper. When the dust settled at the end of the Milwaukee sixth, the scoreboard read Brewers 14, Blue Jays 2.

The Blue Jays tallied a pair in the bottom of the inning on RBI singles by Whitt and Damaso Garcia, but that was the end of their offense for the day. Oglivie added an RBI single in the eighth inning to bring the final tally to 15-4. Vuckovich picked up the win with a six-inning effort, allowing four runs on seven hits and three walks while striking out three. Bomback was tagged with the loss. Despite the two teams racking up 19 runs, the game took just 3 hours and 5 minutes to play.

The auspicious start was a foretaste of the magical season that awaited the Brewers in 1982. As for the Blue Jays… well, there was always next season.[16]

SOURCES

In addition to the sources cited in the Notes, the author also accessed Retrosheet.org, Baseball-Reference.com, and SABR.org.

NOTES

1 Vic Feuerherd, "Mother Nature 1, Brewers 0 in Opener," *Milwaukee Journal Sentinel*, April 6, 1982: Sports, 1.

2 Amy Diamond and Ernst-Ulrich Franzen, "Brewers Fly to Houston; Home Opener Is April 16," *Milwaukee Journal Sentinel*, April 7, 1982: 1.

3 Feuerherd, "Brewers, A's Likely to Meet for AL Title," *Milwaukee Journal Sentinel*, April 6, 1982: Sports, 5; Carl Clark Jr., "Writers Call for Rematch in Pennant Picks," *The Sporting News*, April 10, 1982: 16.

3 Bud Lea, "If Brewers Stay in Title Race, Attendance of 2 Million Likely," *Milwaukee Journal Sentinel*, April 6, 1982: Sports, 6.

4 Tom Flaherty, "Hisle and McClure Add to New Look," *The Sporting News*, April 10,1982: 38.

5 Ibid.

6 Flaherty, "Fingers' Injury Gives Brewers a Scare," *The Sporting News*, April 3, 1982: 36.

7 Feuerherd, "Mother Nature 1, Brewers 0 in Opener."

8 Flaherty, "Snowed-Out Brewers Head for Houston," *The Sporting News*, April 24, 1982: 28-29.

9 Ibid.

10 Ibid.

11 Ibid.

12 Feuerherd, "Brewers Whip Toronto, 15-4", Milwaukee Journal Sentinel, April 10, 1982: *Sports*, 1.

13 Ibid.

14 Ibid.

15 The 1982 Blue Jays (78-84) finished tied for last in the AL East Division. "Next year" (1983), they had an 89-73 record and finished in fourth place, two games ahead of the Brewers.

MOLITOR SLAMS THREE HOMERS FOR ONLY TIME IN CAREER

KANSAS CITY ROYALS 9, MILWAUKEE BREWERS 7
MAY 12, 1982, AT ROYALS STADIUM, KANSAS CITY

By Gregory H. Wolf

"**I'm not a home run hitter,**" said the Milwaukee Brewers' Paul Molitor after smashing three home runs.[1] He wasn't exaggerating either: Entering that historic game, the speedy line-drive hitter hatd cranked only 27 round-trippers in parts of five big-league seasons. Though he developed a stroke to belt a career high 22 in 1993 with the Toronto Blue Jays and finish with 234 homers in his 21-year career, he never had another game like this one. "I just happened to hit the ball where the wind was blowing," he said. "I've never had three in a game — not in sandlot, high school, minor leagues, anywhere."[2]

Skipper Buck Rodgers' Brew Crew was reeling heading into the final game of a three-game set with the Kansas City Royals at Royals Stadium. After losing a heartbreaker, 3-2, on Amos Otis's walk-off home run in the opener, the club was spanked 17-3 to drop to 16-12, third place in the AL East. Manager Dick Howser's squad (16-13) was also in third place (AL West) and looking to get on track, coming off its first losing record in the strike-shortened 1981 season since 1974.

The 17,788 spectators in Royals Stadium on a Wednesday evening were treated to another slugfest, albeit not quite as prodigious as the previous night's 32-hit, 20-run extravaganza.

Molitor jacked Dennis Leonard's second pitch into the left-field bleachers for a leadoff home run.[3] That sound must have been reassuring to Rodgers, who counted on Molitor to rebound after a subpar 1981 campaign when injuries limited him to just 46 starts in the field (all in the outfield, where he played for the first time in his big-league career) and 16 at DH. There was pressure on Molitor, too. After batting .322 in 1979 and .304 in 1980 and earning his first All-Star berth, as a second baseman, the 25-year-old was converted to yet another new position, third base, and had to prove that he could resurrect his stroke. That wasn't happening thus far in the '82 season, as Molitor entered the game batting .268 with one home run.

The Royals tied the game in the second on consecutive triples by Frank White and Greg Pryor off Brewers starter Randy Lerch, a 27-year-old southpaw, whose 3-1 slate (and inflated 5.33 ERA) improved his career record to 45-51 A versatile utilityman, Pryor had been acquired in the offseason as an insurance policy for oft-injured third sacker George Brett, who missed his fifth straight game with laceration on his knee.

The initial innings were like early rounds of a heavyweight boxing match with each team trading jabs and picking up a point here and there. The Brewers took the lead in the third on Cecil Cooper's two-out single, only to lose it in the bottom of the frame on Hal McRae's run-scoring double to plate John Wathan, who moments earlier had been picked off second but was safe when Lerch's throw sailed into center field. The Royals tacked on three more on in the fourth, keyed by Pryor's two-run double and Wathan's single to plate him.

The Royals's starter, 31-year-old Dennis Leonard, was a grinding workhorse, an overlooked yet vital piece of the club's success in the late 1970s and early 1980s. He was a three-time 20-game winner and won more games (120) than any other right-hander in baseball from 1975 to 1981; however, if he had one bugaboo, it was the long ball. He yielded two solo shots to begin the fifth, by Marshall Edwards and Molitor, marking the first time that the latter had connected for two in a big-league game.

Shoddy defense and weak pitching by relievers Dwight Bernard and Jim Slaton led to the Brewers' demise in the sixth as the Royals scored three times on just one hit to increase their lead to 8-4. Two walks, two stolen bases, and two throwing errors were the culprits; Willie Wilson's deep fly ball and McRae's two-out, two-run double were responsible for the tallies, all unearned.

The Brewers were made up of long-ball threats, like Gorman Thomas, who went on to capture his second AL home-run crown in '82 (tied with the California Angels' Reggie Jackson) and Ben Oglivie, the 1980 AL homer champ; however, their bats were quiet in this game, going a combined 1-for-8. Molitor did his best Gorman impression, minus the Fu Manchu, raking a single in the seventh to drive in a run and pulling the Brewers to within three, 8-5. Jim "Gumby" Ganter's grounder off reliever Dan Quisenberry with bases loaded should have been the last out of the eighth; instead, it was the second and drove in an unearned run. [Two batters earlier, Pryor had committed a throwing error on Ted Simmons's grounder.].

A day after Brewers starter Jerry Augustine was clobbered for 12 runs and 15 hits in just five innings, this game revealed the weakness of the club's relieving corps. Not trusting his wobbly bullpen, Rodgers called on starter Moose Haas, who had thrown two-run ball over 7⅔ innings in the first game of the series. The decision backfired. Moose yielded a leadoff single to Pryor, who subsequently scored on Wilson's single. The "shell-shocked Milwaukee pitching staff took it on the chin again," lamented Brewers beat reporter Vic Feuerherd.[4]

A three-run deficit was rarely worrisome to the Brewers, who ultimately led the majors with 216 home runs in 1982; however, it was a different story facing the game's best closer, the submarining Quisenberry, en route to leading the AL in saves for the second of five times in his career. Called to record an eight-out save, the Quiz was far from his best in this game, as Molitor connected for his third homer to make it 9-7. Quisenberry retired Yount, the eventual 1982 AL MVP, and Cooper to preserve the victory and end the game in 2 hours and 48 minutes.

Buck Rodgers was happy to see his squad get out of Kansas City. "The ballpark's been a pain to us, this team's been a pain to us," he said after losing the fourth straight game to the team in powder-blue uniforms. "I'm ready to get the hell out of here."[5]

As for Molitor, he had little to say after a 4-for-5, three-home-run performance with three runs and four RBIs in a loss. "The first one was a fastball up," he told the press. "In the fifth, I hit a pretty good pitch, slider down. The last one was a knuckleball up."[6]

The scrappy Molitor emerged as the Brew Crew's offensive catalyst in 1982. He led the majors with 136 runs scored and collected 201 hits for a .302 batting average

SOURCES

In addition to the sources cited in the Notes, the author also accessed Retrosheet.org, Baseball-Reference.com, Newspapers.com, and SABR.org.

NOTES

1. Associated Press, "KC Overcomes Molitor's Blasts," *Wisconsin State Journal* (Madison), May 13, 1982: 17.
2. Ibid.
3. AP, "3 Molitor HRs Not Enough," *Stevens Point* (Wisconsin) *Journal*, May 13, 1982: 19.
4. Vic Feuerherd, "Molitor's 3 Homers Can't Save Brewers," *Milwaukee Sentinel*, May 13, 1982: II, 1.
5. Ibid.
6. AP, "3 Molitor HRs Not Enough."

BEN OGLIVIE WALLOPS THREE HOMERS AS HARVEY'S WALLBANGERS ROLL

MILWAUKEE BREWERS 7, DETROIT TIGERS 5
JUNE 20, 1982, AT TIGER STADIUM, DETROIT

By Gregory H. Wolf

"**I haven't been swinging the bat real good**," admitted former home-run champ Ben Oglivie after breaking out of a 1-for-17 slump and just one homer in his last 41 at-bats by whacking three round-trippers. "I've been getting a lot of changeups. I give a lot of credit to my teammates for helping me make some adjustments."[1]

The Milwaukee Brewers were hitting on all cylinders, erasing the memories of the club's early-season funk that resulted in the firing of manager Buck Rodgers after 47 games. New skipper Harvey Kuenn took a losing club (23-24) and had guided them to 11 wins in their last 17 games (including a tie) to move into third place in the AL East. "There's a big change of attitude on this club," said Oglivie about the fresh start under Kuenn. "When that happens, I think you have a good chance to win some games. I think we're on a roll now."[2] A player's manager, Kuenn, himself a former 15-year big-leaguer, who led the AL in hits four times in the 1950s, kept his players relaxed and encouraged them to go for the fences. "We're playing one at a time," cautioned Kuenn.[3] Harvey's Wallbangers, so named for their long-ball ability, were born and teams were taking notice. The Brew Crew was looking to sweep a four-game series against the Detroit Tigers in the Motor City. Manager Sparky Anderson's club (36-25) was in a free fall, having lost their last six games and seven of eight to fall out of first place in the AL East, and trailed the Baltimore Orioles by two games.

Tiger Stadium, the Old Gray Lady at the intersection of Trumbull and Michigan Avenues, drew a robust crowd of 31,696 for a 12:35 start time on a beautiful summer Sunday in southeastern Michigan. The partisan crowd had ample reason to cheer in the first inning when the hometown Bengals exploded for four runs off Brewers starter Jim Slaton. A 32-year-old right-hander and longtime workhorse on poor Brewers teams in the 1970s, Slaton (4-1 thus far in '82 and 114-121 in his career) had been moved to bullpen and was making just his fourth start of the season. Kirk Gibson cranked his sixth home run of the season, a three-run blast with no outs, and Richie Hebner hit a two-out solo shot.

Two players with Detroit connections enjoyed their homecoming with productive afternoons. Ted Simmons, from suburban Southfield, who played college ball at the University of Michigan, doubled, and then was driven home when former Tiger Oglivie smacked a fastball from starter Jerry Ujdur over the wall. A 25-year-old right-hander, Ujdur was recalled at the beginning of the month and was making his third start of the season.

The long balls were far from over. Lance Parrish smacked a solo shot in the third to give the Tigers a 5-2 lead. With runners on the corners and two outs

With 34 home runs in 1982, Ben Oglivie formed the core of Harvey's Wallbangers with Gorman Thomas (39 homers), Cecil Cooper (32), Robin Yount (29), and Ted Simmons (23).

and the Tigers threatening to blow the game open, Kuenn pulled Slaton and called on Jerry Augustine to extinguish the fire.

A 29-year-old left-hander, Augustine had struggled mightily thus far in 1982 and was 0-2 with a 5.90 ERA, but he "looked like a different pitcher" in the game, gushed Brewers beat reporter Vic Feuerherd in the *Milwaukee Sentinel*.[4] Augustine silenced the Tigers' bats over the next 4⅓ innings, yielding just one hit and fanning three. He "kept working the inside corner with a varied assortment of fastballs and changeups," wrote Feuerherd.[5] Augustine's performance was not lost on Kuenn, still figuring out his bullpen. "He did a super job to keep us in the game," the skipper said.[6]

While Augustine was slinging zeroes, the Detroit connection was causing Sparky Anderson nightmares. It was a case of déjà vu in the fourth when Simmons singled and Oglivie sent Ujdur's changeup over the fence to pull the Brewers to within one run, 5-4. Two innings later Simmons got into the home-run derby, cranking his ninth of the season to tie the score, 5-5. Oglivie took aim at what sportswriter Brian Bragg of the *Detroit Free Press* called a "lousy fastball from Ujdur and rocketed one that "bounced off the stadium roof and back into the ballpark," according to Bragg.[7] All 11 runs of the game at this point were courtesy of home runs.

Oglivie's 15th blast of the season helped end Ujdur's day. The 33-year-old Panamanian slugger had paid his dues in developing into an All-Star and home-run threat. After clubbing 21 round-trippers as a 28-year-old in 1977 in his first season as primarily a starter with the Tigers, he was shipped to the Brewers. Two years later, he whacked 29 and then 41 in 1980 to tie Reggie Jackson for the AL lead in home runs. He had also hit three home runs once before, on July 8, 1979, also against the Tigers in Detroit. This time, however, he came to the plate with a chance to join a select group of players with four home runs in a game. After Cecil Cooper led off the eighth with a double, Anderson had no intention of letting Oglivie even sniff a strike and called for an intentional walk from reliever Dave Tobik. "I wasn't disappointed when they walked me," said Oglivie, probably disingenuously, but added, [w]hen you look at your lineup I figure it's an advantage to us for them to put another runner on."[8] Oglivie was right: Two batters later Roy Howell lined a single to drive in Cooper for the game's final run.

Despite the Brewers' inconsistent pitching thus far in '82, Kuenn had the luxury of calling on the reigning AL MVP and Cy Young Award winner at the end of the ballgame. Rollie Fingers hurled the last two frames, striking out the side in the ninth to preserve the 7-5 victory for Augustine and end the game in 2 hours and 34 minutes.

Postgame discussion concentrated not just on Oglivie's big day, but also on the Wallbangers' impressive bats. "I don't know how you're going to hold Milwaukee down right now," declared Anderson. "They are just swinging the bat so well."[9] Tigers catcher Lance Parrish described the Brew Crew's offense as "awesome" and gushed, "They've got five guys right in the middle of the lineup who are capable of 25 homers a year. If everybody in that lineup hits like they're capable of, they've got the best-hitting team in baseball."[10] Parrish wasn't exaggerating. The Brewers ultimately led the majors with 216 home runs in 1982, and those "five guys" were the reason: Robin Yount, the eventual AL MVP, hit 29, Cooper spanked 32, Ted Simmons hit 23, Oglivie walloped 34, and the number-six hitter, the Fu-Machu-wearing Gorman Thomas, led the club with 39.

Oglivie hit 235 home runs in his 16-year-major-league career, including three on three occasions. The last time occurred On May 14, 1983, in the Brewers' walk-off 8-7 victory over the Boston Red Sox at County Stadium.

SOURCES

In addition to the sources cited in the Notes, the author also accessed Retrosheet.org, Baseball-Reference.com, Newspapers.com, and SABR.org.

NOTES

1 Vic Feuerherd, "Oglivie Blasts Tigers with 3 Homers," *Milwaukee Sentinel*, June 21, 1982: II, 1.

2 Ibid.

3 Associated Press, "Oglivie's 3 HRs Key 5th Straight Win," *Stevens Point* (Wisconsin) *Journal*, June 21, 1982: 13.

4 Feuerherd.

5 Ibid.

6 Ibid.

7 Brian Bragg, "4-Run Lead Is No Help; Tigers Lose 7th in Row," *Detroit Free Press*, June 21, 1982: F1.

8 Feuerherd.

9 AP.

10 Bragg.

SUTTON TOSSES SHUTOUT FOR FIRST WIN IN AL TO KEEP BREWERS IN THE HUNT

MILWAUKEE BREWERS 4, DETROIT TIGERS 0
SEPTEMBER 8, 1982, AT COUNTY STADIUM

By Gregory H. Wolf

A contest pitting age versus youth produced a "scintillating pitching duel," gushed Motor City sportswriter Brian Bragg.[1] The Milwaukee Brewers' 37-year-old, 254-game winner, Don Sutton, recently acquired as a postseason insurance policy, and 23-year-old Detroit Tigers emerging star Dan Petry, with 40 career wins to his credit, tossed zeros for seven innings until Harvey's Wallbangers woke up and exploded for four runs in the eighth, leading to a benchmark victory in Sutton's 17-year-career. "I don't usually show much emotion," said the curly-haired, man-permed Sutton. "But it was a big game for the Milwaukee Brewers and my first victory in the American League. Tonight was very special."[2]

Skipper Harvey Kuenn's Brewers were marching to their first division title in their 14-year existence as they prepared for the second game of a three-game series against the Tigers to complete a 15-game homestand in Beer City. [The Brewers were declared second-half winners in the strike-shortened 1981 season and went to the postseason for the first time in franchise history.] The Wallbangers, so named for the club's slugging prowess, had the big leagues' best record (81-56), though they led the Baltimore Orioles by just three games in the highly competitive AL East. Sparky Anderson, in his fifth season as Tigers' pilot after nine immensely successful seasons with the Cincinnati Reds, had his club (71-65) in third place, nine games back in the division.

The Brewers pulled off one of the baseball's biggest trade-deadline deals when they acquired Sutton from the Houston Astros on August 30 for cash and Kevin Bass, Frank DiPino, and Mike Madden.[3] "I hadn't seen him in person since the 1960s," quipped Kuenn about Sutton.[4] Kuenn played against Sutton when the right-hander was a rookie with the Los Angeles Dodgers in 1966 and he himself was finishing his 15-year career. After 567 starts in the NL, Sutton went the distance in his first trip to the mound in the AL but lost, 4-2, to the Cleveland Indians in the second game of a twin bill on September 2. In his second start, he faced 14-game winner Petry, the Tigers' second option after staff ace Jack Morris.

On a pleasant late summer Tuesday evening, County Stadium drew a disappointing crowd of 11,709 spectators given the hometown Brewers' pennant ambitions. Because of a malfunctioning transformer, the large scoreboard in center field was not in use; however, for most of this game, the fans didn't need one to keep score. Sutton and Petry, who had missed his last start with lower-back stiffness, kept the game scoreless through seven innings. "I've never seen him with better stuff," raved

Acquired by the Brewers at the trading deadline in 1982, Don Sutton went 4-1 and won the AL East clincher.

complained Anderson. "Romero hits that same ball (at Tiger Stadium) and he's out. Easy."[7] But they weren't playing in the Old Gray Lady at the corner of Trumbull and Michigan Avenues. The Brewers then benefited from some Tigers inexperience. Starting in place of second baseman Lou Whitaker was regular third sacker Tom Brookens (Howard Johnson was at third), who admitted that he and Trammell should have discussed who'd be responsible for second base with the dangerous Paul Molitor at the plate. After fouling a pitch to right, Molitor hit what sportswriter Vic Feuerherd of the *Milwaukee Sentinel* described as a "dying quail," a short blooper to right field.[8] Kuenn had called for a hit-and-run; as soon Romero broke for second, so, too, did Brookens, who added, "I catch that ball easy if I'm playing normal."[9]

With runners on the corners, Robin Yount strode to the plate. Just 26 years old but already in his ninth big-league season, Yount entered the game leading the AL in slugging (.571) and was second in batting average (.327). "Without a doubt," declared Petry, "if the season ended today, he'd be the MVP. He has power. He hits for average."[10] Yount connected on a 1-and-2 count for his third hit of the game, sending a sharp grounder between third and short to drive in Romero with the first run of the evening. "It was a slider," said Petry. "I was trying to strike him out or get him to pop up."[11] Yount, who went on to win the AL MVP in '82, capturing 27 of 28 first-place votes, noted that the pitch was "up a little more than (Petry) wanted."[12]

At this critical juncture, Cecil Cooper dug in in the batter's box. Cooper had 100 RBIs, good for third in the AL, but was suffering from a severe cold and his eyes watered profusely. "His head felt as if it were trapped inside an elevator with eight loud-mouthed cigarette smokers," wrote Brewers beat reporter Steve Aschburner in his best mind-reading impression. "I think the ball Paulie hit messed (Petry) up," said Cooper. "And then Robin got a hit with two strikes. That starts him thinking about something else besides me." Cooper parked Petry's last pitch of the game in the right-field bleachers

Anderson about Petry, who yielded just three hits and a walk through seven.[5] Sutton had surrendered six hits (two each to three September call-ups, Howard Johnson, Glenn Wilson, and Mike Laga) and hadn't walked a batter. "I'm not that quick," said Sutton. "To be effective I have to throw strikes and change speeds. Tonight, I was as good as I've been all year at putting the ball where I wanted to."[6]

The Brewers caught a break in the eighth. With one out, Ed Romero hit a bounder to shortstop Alan Trammel, who dove for the ball, but missed it. "This concrete infield got (Petry) tonight," with his 28th home run of the season to give the Brewers a 4-0 lead. Ted Simmons greeted reliever Dave Rucker with a single and moved up a station on catcher Lance Parrish's passed ball, but was left stranded.

Undoubtedly more relaxed with a four-run lead, Sutton took the mound in the ninth. He surrendered his seventh and final hit, a two-out single to Jerry Turner, then finished the game in 2 hours and 25 minutes by recording his ninth strikeout. Normally reserved on the mound, Sutton pumped his fists as batterymate Ted Simmons clenched the ball and did a little dance at home plate before racing to and embracing his hurler in a bear hug.

Sutton's 255th victory was his first in the American League and his 56th shutout to tie Bob Gibson for ninth place all time. "I think I have the advantage over here because I have Ted as a catcher," gushed Sutton after the game, directing all of the credit to Simmons, in his second season with the Brewers after 13 with the St. Louis Cardinals. "Ted has seen me in the National League a long time, and he knows how I pitch. I just followed Ted. He did a god job of leading. I didn't change but one or two pitches. He does his homework."[14]

Sutton proved to be an invaluable acquisition for the Brewers' drive to their first postseason berth. On the last day of the season, Sutton pitched eight strong innings against the Orioles to notch the victory that gave the Brewers the division crown. After going 4-1 in seven starts with a 3.29 ERA in 54⅔ innings in September, Sutton won another start in the Brewers' best-of-five victory over the California Angels in the ALCS. His magic subsided in the World Series against the St. Louis Cardinals, who hit him hard in two starts, scoring 11 runs (nine earned) in 10⅓ innings and collaring him with one loss.

SOURCES

In addition to the sources cited in the Notes, the author also accessed Retrosheet.org, Baseball-Reference.com, Newspapers.com, and SABR.org.

NOTES

1   Brian Bragg, "Brewers Break Petry Spell, 4-0," *Detroit Free Press*, September 8, 1982: D1.

2   Tom Flaherty, "Sutton, and Simmons, Shut Out Tigers," *Milwaukee Journal*, September 8, 1982: Part 2, 9.

3   The three players sent to the Astros were initially classified as player-to-be-named-later on August 30, and were sent to the Astros on September 3.

4   Vic Feuerherd, "Sutton Is a Hit; So Are the Brewers," *Milwaukee Sentinel*, September 8, 1982: II, 1.

5   Ibid.

6   Ibid.

7   Bragg.

8   Feuerherd.

9   Bragg.

10 George Sauerberg, "Losing Hurler Heaps Praise on Yount After Clutch RBI," *Milwaukee Sentinel*, September 8, 1982: II, 1.

11 Ibid.

12 Ibid.

13 Steve Aschburner, "Cooper's Hit Is Nothing to Sniff At," *Milwaukee Journal*, September 8, 1982: II, 9.

14 Flaherty.

CALDWELL'S SHUTOUT AGAINST YANKEES EASES BREWERS' WORRIES

MILWAUKEE BREWERS 14, NEW YORK YANKEES 0
SEPTEMBER 17, 1982, AT COUNTY STADIUM

By Phillip Bolda

The New York Yankees had long been out of contention by Friday night, September 17, 1982. Their 14-0 loss at the hands of the Milwaukee Brewers that night signaled their statistical elimination from the race. Harvey's Wallbangers moved to a two-game lead over the Baltimore Orioles in the American League East Division, while the Yankees remained in fifth place.

The Brewers conquered the team that defeated them in the playoffs after the strike-shortened 1981 season, but the Orioles continued to hang tough in the race with 15 games left in the regular season. They had won 24 of their last 29 games, despite a 5-3 loss to the Cleveland Indians that night. It was the first time in nine days that the Brewers picked up a game in the standings over Baltimore.

The Brewers — and the 20,144 spectators at Milwaukee County Stadium — were clearly watching the scoreboard throughout the game. They were well aware that the previous weekend the Brewers had lost three of four games to the Yankees in New York. And the Brewers had lost seven of their 15 games since closer Rollie Fingers suffered a forearm injury on September 2. "Everyone was kind of down," said Brewers manager Harvey Kuenn after the Brewers routed the Yankees, "and I'm not talking about the players. I'm talking about other people."

"Don't worry about these guys," Kuenn said. "They'll come back."[1]

Brewers starter Mike Caldwell, who had built a reputation as a Yankee killer since joining the Brewers in 1978, pitched a three-hit shutout for the victory. It was the left-hander's 16th win in 1982, and his ninth in his last 10 decisions. He left the game with a 12-3 lifetime record against the Yankees.

Showers had fallen throughout the day, and along with a 62-degree temperature at game time, the weather kept the size of the crowd below expectations. The wet field caused a number of fielding miscues by the Yankees.

The game began poorly for the Yankees starter, Stefan Wever, making his first (and only) major-league appearance after a promotion from Double-A Nashville, where he had been named Pitcher of the Year in the Southern League. He had established himself as one of the top prospects in baseball in 1982 with a 16-6 record in 214 innings pitched, throwing 10 complete games and two shutouts with a 2.78 earned-run average.

In the first inning, Wever allowed a single to Paul Molitor followed by doubles by Robin Yount and Cecil Cooper. Ted Simmons then reached on an error by Yankees shortstop Andre Robertson before Wever was able to retire a batter — Ben

Oglivie, who flied to left. Then Gorman Thomas powered a home run, giving the Brewers a 5-0 lead before the Yankees came to bat.

"I had thrown (Thomas) four straight fastballs and had gotten him to swing at one of them," Wever said. "I tried to sneak another one by him. It started out low and away and then it rode into his power zone. You make a mistake in Double-A ball and you maybe are able to get away with it. Here Gorman Thomas can hit it 450 feet."[2]

At some point in Thomas's at-bat, Wever felt a twinge in his shoulder. Many years later the 6-foot-8-inch, 245-pound right-hander admitted he told no one. "There was no way I was coming out of that game," he said in a 2005 interview. "I'm not going to say, "Hey, take me out of my major-league debut" because I had a little twinge in my arm. I needed to show them I was tough."[3]

Wever's troubles continued through the next two innings. Jim Gantner walked to open the second. He was forced at second by Paul Molitor, who moved to second on Robin Yount's single and to third on a wild pitch. He scored on Cecil Cooper's sacrifice fly.

Things got even worse for Wever in the third. After striking out Ben Oglivie, he walked Thomas, who was out at second as Roy Howell reached on a fielder's choice. The powerful young pitcher then uncorked two wild pitches before Charlie Moore's run-scoring single pushed the Brewers' lead to 7-0. Wever's evening ended after he walked Gantner,

Reliever George Frazier walked Molitor and gave up a two-run single to Yount. Wever's line in 2⅔ innings pitched was six hits, nine runs (eight earned), three walks, two strikeouts, one home run, and three wild pitches. Yount had touched him for three hits and three RBIs over the first three innings of the game.

The Brewers added a 10th run in the sixth inning off Doyle Alexander as Molitor singled and scored on Simmons's sacrifice fly. In the seventh Alexander gave up four more runs: Yount hit his 24th homer, Molitor bashed an RBI triple, and Alexander allowed two runs on balks.

Caldwell never allowed the Yankees a real scoring threat, just three hits and a walk on 108 pitches. After a walk to Dave Winfield and a lineout by Lou Piniella in the second, he allowed a single to Steve Balboni but retired Barry Evans on a fielder's choice and Rick Cerone on a fly ball to left field. In the fourth Ken Griffey Sr. Singled but was erased when Winfield grounded into a double play. In the top of the eighth, with two outs and a 14-run Brewer lead, Cerone doubled but was stranded when Robertson grounded out to short.

Caldwell relished his role as the Yankee Killer to the point of including the phrase on baseballs he signed for fans. After joining the Brewers in a June 1977 trade with Cincinnati, he revived his career with the help of manager George Bamberger, who taught him to throw the "Staten Island Sinker" that writers and opponents often claimed was a doctored pitch. He shut out the Yankees three times in 1978 and five times in his career.

After the game Caldwell had no explanation for his success against New York, which had ousted the Brewers in the 1981 playoffs. "I don't know," he said sarcastically. "Tonight, I guess it was 14 runs and those five runs in the first that did it."[4]

"I kept the ball down and away from them," Caldwell said. "My sinker was away from them tonight. And when I did come right over the plate on my changeup, I was actually jamming them because they were looking for the ball down and away."[5]

The "little twinge" Wever felt in the first inning turned out, after two years of rehab and attempts to "pitch through it," to be a torn rotator cuff. A visit to Dr. James Andrews resulted in surgery for a fully torn rotator cuff and torn labrum. After the operation he pitched in 19 games over three years in the minors and ended his playing career in June 1985 at age 27.

Despite the rout, the Brewers still had substantial cause to worry. Before the game Rollie Fingers had attempted to throw from the mound for the first time since tearing a muscle in his right forearm. Fingers abandoned the session after 20 pitches from the mound, because of continued tightness in his throwing arm.

Kuenn was pessimistic, commenting, "I would say we are more or less resigned to the fact that he may not be back this year."[6]

SOURCES

In addition to the sources cited in the Notes, the author consulted the following sources:

Baseball-Reference.com.

Retrosheet.org.

Okrent, Dan. *Nine Innings* (New York: Houghton Mifflin Company, 1985).

Flaherty, Tom. "Kuenn Sneaks a Peek During Brewers Romp," *Milwaukee Journal*, September 18, 1982: 8.

Feuerherd, Vic. "Brewers Blast Yankees, 14-0," *Milwaukee Sentinel*, September 18, 1982: part 2, 1.

NOTES

1. Jane Gross, "Brewers Eliminate Yankees," *New York Times*, September 18, 1982.

2. Michael V. Uschan, "Even Mike Caldwell Can't Quite Figure Out His Mastery of the New York Yankees," UPI Archives, September 18 1982.

3. Doug Miller, "A Dream Unfulfilled; Onetime Prospect Looks Back at Brief Major League Career," MLB.com, September 9 2005. mlb.mlb.com/news/article_leftfield.jsp?ymd=20050912&content_id=1206578&vkey=leftfield&fext=.jsp

4. Uschan.

5. Vic Feuerherd, "Caldwell Peaking at Right Time," *Milwaukee Sentinel*, September 18 1982: part 2, 1.

6. Gross.

VUCKOVICH HURLS 11-INNING COMPLETE GAME AS BREWERS RALLY TO WIN

MILWAUKEE BREWERS 4, BOSTON RED SOX 3
SEPTEMBER 20, 1982, AT COUNTY STADIUM

By Joel Rippel

Pete Vuckovich's consistency contributed to his American League Cy Young Award season in 1982. Teammate Gorman Thomas had a consistent remark for Vuckovich after each of his victories that season. After Vuckovich went the distance in the Brewers' 4-3, 11-inning victory over the Boston Red Sox on September 20, Thomas uttered the same remark to Vuckovich for the 18th time that season: "You're the worst, Vukie. You're the worst."[1]

Despite that remark, Thomas had deep respect for Vuckovich. "He's the best," Thomas said. "I call him the worst, but he's the best. It's getting to the time of the year where you have to win. Vukie is one of the best I've ever seen in baseball. He's the kind every ballclub would like to have. Just give him the ball and he'll do everything he can to beat you." Thomas had just watched Vuckovich consistently pitch out of jams in the complete-game win over the Red Sox. The 6-foot-4 right-hander threw 162 pitches while allowing 11 hits, walking four and hitting a batter. But Vuckovich coaxed the Red Sox to hit into five double plays, tying a Brewers' team record.

The victory was Vuckovich's eighth consecutive win, which also tied a club record (held by Mike Caldwell and Vuckovich himself). It was the third time Vuckovich had won eight games in a row since he joined the Brewers for the 1981 season. The victory improved Vuckovich's record to 18-4 for the season and 32-8 since joining the Brewers. According to the *Milwaukee Journal*, "Vuckovich is not an ordinary pitcher. His performances might not be tidy, but they're usually successful."

But it hadn't been the easiest of wins. In fact, the Brewers were within one strike of a 3-2 loss before the heroics of two other consistent Brewers rescued them. Red Sox starter Dennis Eckersley took a 3-2 lead into the bottom of the ninth and quickly retired Cecil Cooper and Ted Simmons. Eckersley then got two strikes on Ben Oglivie, but then Oglivie connected with his next pitch for a game-tying home run. It was Oglivie's 31st home run of the season. "Before I got up at bat, after Teddy made the second out," Oglivie said, "I'll say, yes, I was trying to hit it out. … I know the percentages are very low in a situation like that. The chances are very slim. But with two outs, and no one on, I was thinking about a home run. Everyone in the park knew it."

Eckersley, who had thrown just 85 pitches before Oglivie's home run, didn't second-guess himself. "He's a low-ball hitter," Eckersley said. "And I get him out throwing high balls. I just threw what I normally throw. You might second-guess me, but I'd do it again. That ball just wasn't high enough."

Vuckovich retired the Red Sox in the 10th and 11th innings to give Thomas the opportunity to do what he had done consistently all season – provide the big RBI.

Robin Yount led off the bottom of the 11th with an infield single off Bob Stanley, who had entered the game in the 10th inning. Cooper followed with a single. Simmons moved the runners up with a sacrifice to bring Oglivie to the plate. The Red Sox intentionally walked him to load the bases.

Thomas, who had hit a solo home run in the second inning (his 38th home run of the season), then hit a sacrifice fly to score Yount with the winning run. "I was just trying to stay away from hitting into a double play," Thomas said. "You know what kind of pitcher Stanley is. He usually keeps the ball down."

The victory, Milwaukee's 90th of the season, was just the Brewers' fifth in 18 extra-inning games in 1982. Coming off a three-game sweep of the New York Yankees, the Brewers into the game with a two-game lead over the Baltimore Orioles in the AL East Division. The Orioles defeated the Detroit Tigers, 3-1, that night and remained two games behind with 12 games left in the regular season.

The AL East title wouldn't be decided until the final day of the regular season. The Brewers took a three-game lead over the Orioles into a season-ending four-game weekend series in Baltimore. But the Orioles swept a doubleheader (8-3 and 7-1) on Friday, October 1, then won 11-3 on Saturday to tie the Brewers for first place with one game remaining.

On Sunday, October 3, the Brewers won 10-2 to earn the AL East title with a 95-67 record.

NOTES

1   All quotations in this article are from the *Milwaukee Journal*, September 21, 1982.

HARVEY'S WALLBANGERS CLINCH DIVISION IN SEASON FINALE

MILWAUKEE BREWERS 10, BALTIMORE ORIOLES 2
OCTOBER 3, 1982, AT COUNTY STADIUM

By Lee Kluck

When Harry Dalton left the Cross Keys Inn down by the harbor in Baltimore on the morning of October 3, 1982, he knew that the Milwaukee Brewers were going to win him a division title. Why? Baltimore was his town. He had come of age in baseball there. He had raised a family there. He had won two world championships there and built the best run organization in baseball. Simply put, Baltimore was his town. Of course, nothing in baseball is that simple.

That day, on a sun-dappled field at Memorial Stadium in Baltimore, the Brewers and Birds played what amounted to a one-game playoff for the American League East title. Three days earlier, this had seemed inconceivable. When the series began on Friday, the Brewers, whom the national media and even Milwaukee fans had left for dead after some early-season struggles, needed to win only one game to secure the division title and a berth in the American League Championship Series. But the Orioles took the first three games of the series, outscoring the Brewers 26 to 7.

By Sunday, when they took the field in front of 51,642 screaming Orioles fans, Harvey's Wallbangers were tied with the Orioles, who seemed to have all the momentum. But the baseball adage of momentum being only as good as a team's next starting pitcher ran against the home team that day.

Jim Palmer, a 15-game winner and the ace of the Baltimore staff since the mid-1960s, surrendered one run in each of the first three innings, including two home runs by Brewers shortstop Robin Yount. Yount would end up collecting one more hit (a triple in the eighth), scoring four times, coming within less than a point of winning the AL batting title, and putting a cap on a possible MVP season.

Of course, Yount, who had a reputation as the consummate team player, did not want to talk about his own performance that day or about any possible individual accolades because of his season-long exploits. "The batting title was the last thing on my mind, there were more important things to think about," he said. Those important things were beating the Orioles and winning the division championship. The possibility of winning the MVP was not even in his purview: "If it were up to me, they wouldn't even have that award."[1]

While Yount was leading the offense, Don Sutton, whom Milwaukee had acquired late in the season to get a big-game pitcher, gave up just two runs and shut down the Orioles. As for how he managed to set the Brewers up for victory, Sutton gave credit to the fact that he had above-average control that day. "I'm not going to overpower anybody. I'm probably not going to be that over-impressive," he said. "But if I can keep 'em off stride, then that's the key for me to pitch."[2]

That did not mean that he sailed the whole day. Sutton gave up a home run to Glenn Gulliver in the third inning. In the fifth he worked out of a bases-loaded jam unscathed. Then, in the eighth, Sutton struggled and the O's looked set for a big inning. With one run in and two Orioles on base, Sutton got some help from his defense; leftfielder Ben Oglivie made a sliding catch into the leftfield sidewall. This killed the O's rally, and it was 5-2 Brewers.

At that point, the Brewers offense, which had gained the nickname Harvey's Wallbangers as the team got back into the pennant race, exploded. By the time the top of the ninth inning ended, the team had roughed up Dennis Martinez and former Cy Young Award winner Mike Flanagan for five runs to give the Brewers a 10-2 lead.

In the bottom of the ninth, fill-in closer Bob McClure (Rollie Fingers, the usual closer, was out with a shoulder injury) gave up two hits but got the final three outs, securing for the Brewers the division title and sending them on their way to victory over the California Angels in the ALCS.[3]

SOURCES

For this work, the author consulted various articles in the *Milwaukee Journal* and *Sentinel*, as well as *Nine Innings* by Daniel Okrent and the 2007 documentary "Harvey's Wallbangers," along with Retrosheet.org.

NOTES

1 For Yount's comments see Dale Hofmann, "Yount Is Just 'All World,' Says Teammate Sutton," *Milwaukee Sentinel*, October 4, 1982: 1.

2 Steve Aschburner, "Sutton Will Talk Forever," *Milwaukee Journal*, October 4, 1982: 22.

3 The 1981 season was abbreviated due to a player's strike, resulting in first and second half division winners. The Brewers won the second half division title.

BAYLOR CONCENTRATES, DRIVES IN FIVE

CALIFORNIA ANGELS 8, MILWAUKEE BREWERS 3
OCTOBER 5, 1982, AT ANAHEIM STADIUM

AMERICAN LEAGUE CHAMPIONSHIP SERIES, GAME ONE

By Ken Carrano

No one in baseball had a better view of Don Baylor's 1982 season than Reggie Jackson, who usually followed Baylor in the California Angels batting order. And what he saw were a couple of different Baylor. "He can get with it in the clutch," Jackson said. "Like Paul Newman in *Cool Hand Luke*: 'He gets his mind right when he has to.'"[1] "It's obvious I don't concentrate when there aren't men on base," Baylor said. "I am a completely different hitter with men on base. I do a lot more thinking when there are guys in scoring position. I look for pitches and I don't go for home runs. I just try to hit the ball hard and drive it somewhere."[2]

The American League Championship Series between the American League East champion Milwaukee Brewers and the West champion Angels promised to be a slugfest. "These are probably the two best offensive clubs in the American League. At least that's what everyone said coming out of spring training. It's pretty much held true over the course of the year," said Brewers Game One starter Mike Caldwell.[3] The numbers back this up. The Brewers and Angels were the top two teams in many AL stats, including runs per game (MIL 5.47 CAL 5.02). Jackson and the Brewers' Gorman Thomas led the American League with 39 home runs. AL MVP Robin Yount led the league in hits, doubles (tied with Hal McRae), and slugging. But these teams could pitch as well. The Angels were second in team ERA at 3.82, with the Brewers sixth at 3.98. Dale Hoffman of the *Milwaukee Sentinel* said "Call this the Snow White series. Two teams are looking into a mirror this week and wondering aloud who is the fairest in the American League."[4] The *Chicago Tribune*'s Jerome Holtzman called the series "The Battle of Muscle Beach."[5]

The Brewers could be excused for trying to catch their breath going into the series. Leading the second-place Orioles by three games with four to play in Baltimore, the Brew Crew lost the first three of the series by a combined 19 runs, only to win the season final and the division crown, 10-2. The Angels run-up was calm by comparison; they clinched the division with a 6-4 win over Texas on the next-to-last day of the season. The Angels started 39-year-old veteran Tommy John to face the Brewers. John, traded from the New York Yankees at the end of August went 4-2 in September to help the Angels win the division. With this start, John would be pitching in the playoffs for the fourth time in the last five seasons, for his third team.[6]

The sinkerballer did as expected in the top of the first, retiring all three Brewer hitters on infield grounders. His left-handed counterpart, Caldwell, coming off two losses to end the regular season, was not as fortunate. Brian Downing led off the

Angels' first with a single to center, and went to second on Caldwell's error. After a wild pitch and strikeout, Baylor hit a sacrifice fly to center field, and Downing had the Angels' first tally.

But the Brewers were not known as Harvey's Wallbangers because of their fondness for the cocktail.[7] Catcher Ted Simmons led off the second with a single to center, and Thomas hit the first home run of the series to give the Brewers a 2-1 lead. "It was kind of a sinker," Angels catcher Bob Boone said. Not the good kind.[8] John retired the Brewers in order after that, but gave up another run after consecutive singles by Paul Molitor and Yount brought up Cecil Cooper, whose fielder's-choice grounder plated Molitor in the third. But the veteran John knew how to call on experience. "It was a typical Tommy John performance," wrote a Los Angeles writer. "He was hit early, three runs in the first three innings, and then he shut the Brewers down the rest of the way. It's an old story, but he's an old pitcher."[9]

Brewers manager Harvey Kuenn was surprised by the Angels lineup. Angels skipper Gene Mauch bunched four right-handed hitters at the top of the order, followed by three left-handers. "It surprised me," admitted Kuenn. "You can do that when you've got left-handed hitters who can hit left-handed pitching."[10] Staked to a two-run lead, Caldwell found the difficulties that he had in his last two starts. Downing reached base to lead off the third with a walk, and Doug DeCinces singled to center, bringing up Bobby Grich, whose single scored Downing. Baylor then crushed a 386-foot triple off the right-center-field wall[11] that scored DeCinces and Grich, and when Jackson's groundout scored Baylor, the Angels had turned a two-run deficit into a two-run lead. Baylor knew he had to adjust his approach against Caldwell. "I said to myself, 'Tonight, if he pitches me outside, I'm going to the opposite field,'" said Baylor.[12]

Pitching again with the lead, John now settled in. "I'll tell you, pitching against the Brewers is a chore – as you saw in the first few innings. But once we got up, it took a lot of pressure off me,' John said after the game.[14] The Brewers put two on in the top of the fourth with two out, but John induced a fielder's-choice grounder from the ailing Jim Gantner, and the threat was ended. The Angels reduced the pressure on John further in the bottom of the fourth. A leadoff single by Boone ended Caldwell's day, and Molitor's error and a walk brought up Baylor again, this time with the bases loaded, facing Jim Slaton. Baylor stroked a single to left that scored Boone and DeCinces, and the lead increased to 7-3.

John was dominant the rest of the way, giving up only two-out hits in the fifth and eight innings, and hitting Charlie Moore with a pitch with two out in the ninth. "He pitched the same way tonight that he pitched six years ago," said Simmons. As long as his bionic arm holds up, he'll keep pitching that way." John's performance reminded Mauch of a Milwaukee legend, Hall of Famer Warren Spahn. "Once he got the humidity right and the wind right, he settled down and did the job," Mauch said after the game.[15]

Fred Lynn ended the scoring with a home run leading off the fifth inning. Baylor had a chance to set the record for RBIs in a game in the sixth when he came up with Grich on second after a double, but Slaton retired him when he snared a line drive at the mound before it could whiz into center field.[16] "It was special for me to see Donny do well," Grich said. We've played together for 14 of the past 15 years, and this might be our last week together."[17] Baylor's contract was up at the end of the 1982 season. Baylor's five RBIs tied the ALCS record set in 1969 by Paul Blair of the Orioles against the Minnesota Twins, and as of 2019 had been exceeded only once; by Johnny Damon of the Boston Red Sox in Game Seven of their 2004 ALCS series against the Yankees.

With the 8-3 loss, some may have wondered if the season-ending struggle the Brewers had with the Orioles may have been a contributing factor. The sentiment in the Brewers' clubhouse was mixed, though there were some thoughts that maybe an emotional letdown was to be expected. "I think we were pretty much emotionally drained," said Caldwell after the game. "I don't think we were as keyed up as we could have been, but that's no excuse" added Yount. "We just didn't play very good."[18] With the ALCS a best-of-five series in 1982, the Brewers would have to play better quickly to reach their first World Series.

SOURCES

In addition to the sources listed in the notes, the author accessed Retorsheet.org, Baseball-Reference.com, SABR's BioProject via SABR.org, *The Sporting News* archive via Paper of Record, the *New York Times* archives, and the *Chicago Tribune* and *Los Angeles Times* via newspapers.com.

NOTES

1 Malcom Moran, "Baylor Is a Success Despite Distractions," *New York Times*, October 6, 1982.

2 Ibid.

3 Tom Flaherty, "This Should Be a Hitter's Series," *Milwaukee Journal*, October 5, 1982.

4 Dale Hoffman, "AL Look-Alikes Face Off Tonight," *Milwaukee Sentinel*, October 5, 1982.

5 Jerome Holtzman, "Don Baylor's Five RBIs Rip Brewers," *Chicago Tribune*, October 6, 1982: 69.

6 Mike Littwin, "John Is Still Up to His Old Tricks," *Los Angeles Times*, October 6, 1982: 52.

7 en.wikipedia.org/wiki/Harvey_Wallbanger.

8 Littwin.

9 Littwin.

10 Holtzman.

11 Holtzman.

12 Holtzman.

13 Vic Feuerherd, "Brewers Lose, 8-3, to Angels," *Milwaukee Sentinel*, October 6, 1982.

14 Murray Chass, "Angels Capture Opener as Baylor Bats in 5 Runs," *New York Times*, October 6, 1982.

15 Holtzman.

16 Chass.

17 Chass.

18 Feuerherd, "Did Orioles Drain Brewers?" *Milwaukee Sentinel*, October 6, 1982.

KISON'S COMPLETE GAME SHUTS DOWN HARVEY'S WALLBANGERS

CALIFORNIA ANGELS 4, MILWAUKEE BREWERS 2
OCTOBER 6, 1982, AT ANAHEIM STADIUM

AMERICAN LEAGUE CHAMPIONSHIP SERIES, GAME TWO

By Gregory H. Wolf

He "pitches with such intensity that he ought to be declared a fire hazard," gushed sportswriter Mark Littwin after Bruce Kison's dominant five-hit complete-game victory, while California Angels teammate Reggie Jackson described him "as so mentally tough, he's a ball of fire."[1] Kison touted his coolness under pressure as a product of his postseason "experience" as a member of two Pittsburgh Pirates World Series championship teams. Cribbing how he mesmerized the vaunted Brewers sluggers with his slider, the hurler said, "I used it inside and outside and from different angles."[2] Kison was "a deceptive pitcher with that motion," declared Paul Molitor. "He had us chasing a lot of bad balls. We didn't give ourselves much of a chance."[3]

Skipper Harvey Kuenn's Brewers (95-67), known as Harvey's Wallbangers for their big-league-most 216 home runs in the regular season, were slumping and the timing couldn't have been worse. They lost six of their last nine regular-season games, but beat the Baltimore Orioles in the season's finale to capture their first AL East crown. The Angels (93-69), on the other hand, rolled into the ALCS having won 16 of 23 games, and took the first game, 8-3, behind a complete game by 39-year-old Tommy John, a September acquisition from the New York Yankees.

Scheduled to start the second game in Anaheim was Kison, a whip-like 6-foot-4, 175-pound right-hander, who might have seemed like a curious choice were it not for his noteworthy late-season success throughout his career. He had a 95-75 record in his 12-year big-league career, but was 28-10 in regular-season games in September and October. He also sported a 4-1 record with a 2.01 ERA in the playoffs, all with the Pirates. Since signing with the Angels before the 1980 season, Kison had been plagued by injuries, notched only four wins in his first two campaigns with the club, and underwent potentially career-threatening operations on his wrist and elbow. Kison started out strong in '82, going 6-3 before suffering a bruised knee on a line drive back to the mound by the Texas Rangers' Johnny Grubb on June 22. He returned a week later, but things got testy with his skipper, the notoriously hotheaded Gene Mauch, who claimed the hurler was still hurt. Whether that was the case or if Kison was in Mauch's doghouse, the result was an "inexcusable 82-game residency in the bullpen," opined Angels beat reporter Ross Newhan in the *Los Angeles Times*.[4] "I would have liked to have had more innings," quipped Kison, "but personal feelings are overrated."[5] With the Halos clawing for the crown, Kison moved back into the rotation on September 14, blanked the Chicago White Sox on seven hits, and sported an impressive 1.67 ERA in 32⅓ innings in his last four starts.

On the mound for the Brewers was their staff ace, Fu-Machu-wearing Pete Vuckovich, the '82 Cy Young Award recipient with an 18-6 record. After hurling an 11-inning complete-game victory against the Boston Red Sox on September 20, big Vuck had been shelled in his last two starts, surrendering 10 earned runs in 11 innings. Rumors swirled that he had an injured right wing, but Kuenn cautioned everyone that it was just a "tired arm."[6] Vuckovich was 5-0 lifetime against the Angels, including 3-0 in '82.

Anaheim Stadium, the Big A, was packed with 64,179 spectators on a gorgeous early fall Wednesday afternoon. The Brewers swung for the fences, but so too did the Angels, finishing with 186 round-trippers, second in the majors behind the Wallbangers; however, the Halos also employed small-ball tactics, and this game featured both strategies.

The Angels struck first when they loaded the bases in the second with one out. Fred Lynn led off with a bloop single and caught a break when center fielder Gorman Thomas "broke back," noted Newhan, and had no play on the ball.[7] Doug DeCinces doubled with one out and Bobby Grich was hit by a pitch. After Tim Foli, Kison's teammate on the '79 "We Are Family" Pirates, lined a single for the first run, Bob Boone surprised the Brewers by laying down a squeeze bunt for another run.

The defensive play of the game occurred in the third inning, though at the time its importance to the game's outcome was not yet known. The Brewers' Charlie Moore led off with a single and moved up a station on Jim Gantner's grounder. Molitor singled up the middle, but shortstop Tim Foli made a spectacular diving stop to save a run. "There's no question in my mind that [Moore] scores because he's breaking with contact," lamented Molitor. "That leaves us with the tying run on first with Robin and Cecil coming up."[8] Kison retired Robin Yount, the '82 AL MVP, and Cecil Cooper to end the threat.

In the bottom of the frame, Reggie Jackson made his presence felt by smashing a home run well over the 404-foot marker in center field. It "caromed off the canvas batter's eye," reported Newhan, to give the Angels a 3-0 lead. The blast was Mr. October's 18th in the postseason, tying him with Mickey Mantle for the most in baseball history, though Mantle's home runs were all in the World Series. "Reggie's hit came on a fastball right down the chute," said Vuckovich. "I know he was looking for it and I got it up a little more than I wanted."[9]

It was back to small ball in the fourth for the Halos. After DeCinces and Grich led off the frame with a walk and single, respectively, Foli's bunt moved them into scoring position. Boone followed with a sacrifice fly to plate the Angels' fourth and final run of the game. Sportswriter Pat Donovan called Boone's 0-for-1 game with two RBIs the "most misleading hitless game in the history" of the postseason.[10] "It's the kind of thing you obviously take a lot of pride in," noted Boone about his two run-scoring sacrifices. "We enjoy playing that kind of ball, bat control. It's my strong suit offensively."[11]

The Angels were leading 4-0 with two out in the fifth and Moore on first when Molitor came to bat. A dangerous offensive catalyst who led the majors with 136 runs scored, Molitor was a speedy, slappy hitter, who also swiped 41 bags. He sent a sinking liner to center field. Instead of playing it safe and taking the ball on the hop, four-time Gold Glove winner Fred Lynn made an ill-advised dive for the ball. He missed it and the ball rolled to the wall, enabling Molitor to circle the bases for a two-run inside-the-park home run and give the Brewers a new lease on life. "I can't compromise the way I play," said Lynn, who also noted that the outfield grass was chewed up from a Los Angeles Rams football game. "If I have a chance to dive and make a catch or run into a wall, I'll do it and think about the consequences later."[12]

Molitor's hit proved to be the last one of the game as both pitchers showed their mettle. While Vuckovich yielded three walks, Kison set down 13 straight batters and ended the pitching duel in 2 hours and 6 minutes.

Kison's five-hit gem with eight strikeouts and no walks gave the Angels what appeared to be an insurmountable two-games-to-none lead in the best-of-five ALCS. No team at the time had ever come back to win an LCS after losing the first two games. "If people don't believe in us by now," said scheduled Game Three starter Geoff Zahn, who led the Angels with 18 wins, "they won't believe in us no matter what happens."[13] Fred Lynn, coming off his eighth of nine consecutive All-Star berths, harbored no doubts who'd emerge victorious: "When you look at the super pitching we've been getting and the way we've been playing for the last month, I think it is a tall order for any team to win three games in a row from us."[14]

The ace in the hole for the Brewers was two graybeards. One was Harvey Kuenn, who kept his players loose; the other was 37-year-old Don Sutton, a September acquisition from the Houston Astros, tabbed to start Game Three when the series moved to Milwaukee. The Brewers were in a do-or-die position in the last game of the season and it was Sutton who tossed eight strong innings to clinch the AL East crown. "We've lost six of our last seven games," stated Molitor unequivocally, "but on a positive note we're still only three games from the World Series."[15] And then the future Hall of Famer laid it all on the table: "I really feel confident we can come back and win three straight."[16]

SOURCES

In addition to the sources cited in the Notes, the author also accessed Retrosheet.org, Baseball-Reference.com, Newspapers.com, and SABR.org.

NOTES

1   Mark Littwin, "Kison Realized It's Serious When Leaves Start to Turn," *Los Angeles Times*, October 7, 1982: III, 1.

2   Dale Hofmann, "Kison May Be Angels New Mr. October," *Milwaukee Sentinel*, October 7, 1982: II, 1.

3   Vic Feuerherd, "Angels Grab 2-0 Series Lead," Milwaukee Sentinel, October 7, 1982: II, 1.

4   Ross Newhan, "Kison and Angels Have Right Stuff, 2-0 Playoff Lead," *Los Angeles Times*, October 7, 1982: II, 1.

5   Littwin.

6   Feuerherd.

7   Newhan.

8   Feuerherd.

9   Ibid.

10 Pete Donovan, "Angels' Second Bananas Are Stealing Playoff Show," *Los Angeles Times*, October 7, 1982: III, 8.

11 Ibid.

12 Newhan. The Los Angeles Rams played their home games in Anaheim Stadium from 1980 to 1994. They played a home game on September 19, 1982, after which the NFL players went on strike.

13 Newhan.

14 Ibid.

15 Feuerherd.

16 Joe Karius, "Needed: Another Miracle," *Milwaukee Sentinel*," October 7, 1982: II, 1.

SUTTON HURLS A GEM

MILWAUKEE BREWERS 5, CALIFORNIA ANGELS 3
OCTOBER 8, 1982, AT COUNTY STADIUM

AMERICAN LEAGUE CHAMPIONSHIP SERIES, GAME THREE

By Rick Schabowski

On Friday, October 8, on a beautiful afternoon in front of a Milwaukee County Stadium crowd of 50,135, for the second time in six days, Don Sutton took the mound for the Brewers in Game Three of the American League Championship Series. With the Brewers down two games to none to the California Angels and facing elimination from the postseason, Sutton came through with another victory as the Brewers defeated the California Angels, 5-3, to stay alive in the series.

Sutton had been acquired from the Houston Astros in a pennant-drive trade on the August 30 trade deadline in exchange for highly regarded Brewers prospects Kevin Bass, Frank DiPino, and Mike Madden. Sutton posted a 4-1, 3.29 record for the Brewers in September, with one of the wins a closing day, 10-2 win at Baltimore that clinched the American League East Division championship.

The Angels starter was lefty Geoff Zahn, who had also had a great 1982 season, posting an 18-8 record with a 3.73 ERA. His performance earned him a spot on *The Sporting News* AL All-Star Team.

After 3½ scoreless innings, the Brewers took the lead in the bottom of the fourth. Robin Yount, who would later be voted the American League's Most Valuable Player, led off the inning with a walk and scored on a double by Cecil Cooper. Ted Simmons followed with a single up the middle, moving Cooper to third base. Cooper scored on a sacrifice fly by Gorman Thomas. Smart baserunning by Simmons helped the Brewers score the third run of the inning. Ben Oglivie grounded a single through the infield to right field, but Simmons didn't stop at second and with a head-first slide, he beat Reggie Jackson's throw to third base. Don Money's sacrifice fly to left scored Simmons, giving the Brewers a 3-0 lead. This rally sent Zahn to the showers and he was replaced by Bobby Witt.

Simmons, no speedster on the bases, said of his gutsy base-running decision, "There's no question I'm going to third on that play. When you have a left-handed pull hitter up and the right fielder has to play him deep, it doesn't matter who's out there. You have to take the gamble. When someone hits it on the ground like Benji did, the right fielder has to run a long way to get the ball. Eight of 10 times make the gamble or at least take it."[1]

Angels third baseman Doug DeCinces suffered a broken nose in the top of the seventh after fouling off a pitch that bounced and hit him in the face. He dropped to his knees and slammed down his batting helmet. "Nobody had to tell me. This is the sixth time I've broken it, starting with a high school basketball game," DeCinces said. "I knew right away and I had to vent my frustration because this is no time to get hurt."[2] In spite of the injury, DeCinces played the remainder of the game, grounding out to third base to end the eighth inning. He also played in Games Four and Five, going 3-for-4 in Game Five.

The Brewers stretched their lead to 5-0 in the bottom of the seventh with a two-out, two-run home run by Paul Molitor off Witt. After the home run, Yount walked and Angels manager Gene Mauch replaced Witt with Andy Hassler, who ended the inning by striking out Cecil Cooper.

After the game Molitor said of his round-tripper, "I was just looking to make contact. I think (Witt) got it up higher than he wanted. It was right over the middle of the plate. I knew I made good contact, but I wasn't sure it was out with the wind blowing in. It wasn't until I was at second that I realized it was out."[3]

Bob Boone led off the top of the eighth inning with a fly ball to deep left field. Ogilvie had the ball played perfectly. He reached the fence, jumped to make the catch, and had the ball taken away by a spectator who reached over the fence and caught the ball. Umpire Larry Barnett signaled a home run. (After the game Barnett said, "For me, the fan was behind the fence and touched the ball."[4]) Ben Ogilvie disagreed with Barnett's home-run call, saying, "I think the ball was playable, and I think I would have caught it if I had the opportunity. It should have been an automatic out. The fan had his hand extended over the fence. Without a doubt, I would have caught it. It was already arcing into my glove."[5]

Sutton was showing signs of tiring. After Brian Downing made the first out of the eighth, Rod Carew singled. Reggie Jackson struck out, but back-to-back doubles by by Fred Lynn and Don Baylor made the score 5-3. Pete Ladd, who was the Brewers closer after a season-ending injury to Rollie Fingers, came in and retired Doug DeCinces on a groundout to end the inning. After the Brewers went down quickly in the eighth, Ladd retired the Angels in order in the ninth inning, striking out the last two batters he faced.

Sutton pitched 7⅔ innings and scattered eight hits while striking out nine. Angels manager Mauch praised Sutton's performance, calling him "one of the cleverest pitchers of the last 15 years," and adding, "He's capable of taking the straight out of the ball without defacing it. Our players didn't say a word about it. They know what the man is capable of doing with finger dexterity."[6] Reggie Jackson agreed with his manager. "I've never seen him better," he said of Sutton. "He had control of four pitches. He beat me fair and square. I didn't have one good swing."[7]

The Angels had been so confident of wrapping up the series in this game that they asked their traveling secretary, Frank Sims, to get a charter flight ready for after the game Friday rather than wait until the next day. He made the arrangement, but the Brewers changed things.

Ladd was happy to extend the Brewers' postseason run as it would delay his reporting to his offseason job as a prison guard in Tucson, Arizona.

Sutton obviously was pleased with the outcome. "I'm logical enough to know if we don't win today, we don't get to play tomorrow," he said. "That didn't change my approach to it. As I've said before, it's fun to play when it's on the line. It was on the line, and I was going to go out and enjoy myself. It didn't mean that I was going to do well or do poorly. It just meant I would much rather be someplace playing than some place watching."[8]

SOURCES

Baseball-Reference.com/boxes/MIL/MIL198210080.shtml

Retrosheet.org/boxesetc/1982/B10080MIL1982.htm

Paper of Record

NOTES

1. Vic Feuerherd, "Stayin' Alive: AL Playoff Moves to Game 4 Thanks to Two Brewers Hurlers," *Milwaukee Sentinel*, October 9, 1982: pt. 2, 1.
2. Ross Newhan, "DeCinces Knows All About Broken Noses; It's His 6th," *Los Angeles Times*, October 9, 1982: pt. 1, 1.
3. Feuerherd.
4. Ross Newhan, "Sutton Utilizes Twilight Zone to Stall Angels," *Los Angeles Times*, October 9, 1982: pt. 3, 1.
5. Murray Chass, "Brewers Set Back Angels and Trail by 2 Games to 1," *New York Times*, October 9, 1982: 19.
6. Newhan, "Sutton Utilizes Twilight Zone to Stall Angels."
7. Ibid.
8. Tom Flaherty, "Like a Good Neighbor ... Sutton Is There," *Milwaukee Journal*, October 9, 1982: pt. 2, 10.

HARVEY'S WALLBANGERS HAVE A NEW MEMBER

MILWAUKEE BREWERS 9, CALIFORNIA ANGELS 5
OCTOBER 9, 1982, AT COUNTY STADIUM

AMERICAN LEAGUE CHAMPIONSHIP SERIES, GAME FOUR

By Gregg Hoffmann

Mark Brouhard was a moon-faced reserve outfielder with some power and limited playing time for the Brewers in 1982.

But in Game Four of the American League Championship Series against the California Angels, Brouhard was a hero. He drove in three runs with a single, double, and a home run, and scored an ALCS-record four runs.

During the game, Brouhard got demands for two curtain calls from a packed County Stadium.[1]

"I knew the only way I'd get to start in this series was if someone got hurt," Brouhard told the *Milwaukee Journal*. "I sure didn't want that to happen."

But it did happen when regular left fielder Ben Oglivie bruised his ribs in Game Three trying to catch a double off the bat of Fred Lynn.[3] Brouhard suddenly was asked to be the Game Four starter.

"There's no doubt I was nervous," he said. "When you haven't played for four weeks, there's not much you can do but look up and say a little prayer to the Lord and do the best job you can do."[4]

The Lord answered Brouhard's prayers and the prayers of thousands of Brewers fans with the 9-5 win that evened the series at two games each.

Brouhard wasn't the only hero in the rain-plagued contest (a total of 2 hours 15 minutes in delays, including a 1 hour 40 minute delay of the start of the game).[5]

Moose Haas, who had started only two games since Don Sutton was obtained from the Houston Astros, held the Angels in check for 5⅔ innings. The Angels were hitless in the sixth inning, when rain held up the game for 19 minutes.

"I was thinking if they ended the ballgame, I'd be in the record books with an asterisk for pitching a five-inning no-hitter in the playoffs," Haas said. "But I knew we were going to play nine no matter how long it took. They told us we were going to get in a full game."[6]

The Brewers battered California starter Tommy John. Brouhard singled home Ted Simmons with the first run of the game in the second inning. Don Money, who was on first base, headed for third base on the single, and California center fielder Lynn's throw hit Money and bounced to the railing.

Money scored on the play, and Angels third baseman Doug DeCinces threw wildly to the plate in a futile attempt to get Money. The wild throw allowed Brouhard to also score for a 3-0 lead.

"You want to try to go from first to third in that situation," Money said. "You think that the ball's going to slow down in the damp grass. I lined myself up with the throw. It hit me in the shoulder, and we ended up getting more runs out of it. Maybe if I don't go, we only get one run that inning."[7]

John, pitching on three days' rest, uncharacteristically walked five and threw three wild pitches in 3⅓ innings.

"I could never find the groove," said John, who had a 6-2 record in the playoffs going into the game. "I was missing, missing, missing. I could have had three days' rest or a month's rest and it wouldn't have made a difference.

"I got behind and got hard-headed. I don't like to groove it against the Brewers, and so I kept getting behind. Maybe I didn't give myself enough credit for having the good stuff everyone said I did."[8]

The Brewers followed their three-run rally in the second with another three-run rally in the fourth off Goltz. John issued two walks (one intentional) and threw two wild pitches, the latter of which resulted in Brewers' fourth run. Jim Gantner drove in Brouhard with a single, which broke his 0-for-11 streak in the playoffs. Paul Molitor's groundout drove in Charlie Moore to make it 6-0.

The Angels finally got on the board in the sixth when Lynn doubled home Reggie Jackson. Gantner drove in Brouhard in the bottom of the frame to put the Brewers up 7-1. "I'm just happy that when I did get hits, it meant something," Gantner said of his two hits in the game. "The crowd really helped. It's great. It gets you pumped up. Playing in front of your home crowd definitely gives you a lift."[9]

Haas tired in the eighth inning and gave up a grand slam to Don Baylor that made the score 7-5. "We were right there at 7-5," Baylor said. "Our pitching wasn't up to it today. We were riding the wave when we first got here. Now they are."[10]

If reliever Rollie Fingers had been available, 7-5 would have looked like a lock to many Brewers fans. But the future Hall of Famer was injured, so Jim Slaton relieved Haas in the eighth. He retired the last five Angels. Brouhard provided some insurance with his homer in the bottom of the eighth.

"We've all had to step up to fill in for Rollie," Slaton said. "I just went out there and tried to get outs."[11]

Fittingly, the final out was recorded by Brouhard, who made a running catch of Brian Downing's fly ball.

"I think I turned the easiest play of the day into a hard one," Brouhard said of the catch.[12] Nobody was complaining, not after the overall day Brouhard had.

There was plenty of second-guessing after the game. Why did California manager Gene Mauch go with John on short rest? Why didn't he pinch-hit in certain spots? For example, Mauch allowed Tim Foli and Bob Boone to bat in the eighth against Slaton, even though they were a combined 4-for-26.

"I had no qualms about pitching Tommy on three days' rest," Mauch said. "Some people thought I was hoping for a rainout so he had an extra day, but I was actually hoping we wouldn't. My attitude all along was that I wanted him to pitch today, and he felt the same way. The man told me that's the way he thinks he's best. It isn't typical of him to have control trouble, but the amount of rest he had between starts had nothing to do with it. There isn't enough room left for me to second-guess myself. It's all taken up."[13]

Milwaukee manager Harvey Kuenn did not second-guess Mauch. Instead, he praised his team for coming back to even the series after being down 2-0. "This team has had what it takes in big games all season," Kuenn said. "They've been at their best when their backs are against the wall."[14]

The win in Game Four set up the dramatic Game Five, won by the Brewers, 4-3, on Cecil Cooper's two-run single.

Simmons, one of the team leaders, previewed Game Five after the win in Game Four.

"Last Sunday, Baltimore had the same thing going," Simmons said, referring to the final regular-season series against the Orioles, in which the Brewers clinched the division title. "Win one game. Tomorrow will be the same game. We've both got the same at stake. Last week, on Baltimore, it was like they were stealin' our season. Well now, we're trying to steal California's, and they're trying to steal ours."[15]

SOURCES

In addition to the sources cited in the Notes, the author accessed Retrosheet.org, Baseball-Reference.com, SABR.org, and *The Sporting News* archive via Paper of Record.

NOTES

1. Tom Flaherty, "Brewers Win, Force Showdown," *Milwaukee Journal*, October 10, 1982: 1.
2. Ibid.
3. Flaherty: 2.
4. Gregg Hoffmann, interview with Mark Brouhard after game, October 9, 1982.
5. Michael Bauman, "Haas Does the Job," *Milwaukee Journal*, October 10, 1982: 3.
6. Gregg Hoffmann, interview with Moose Haas after game.
7. Gregg Hoffmann, interview with Don Money after game.
8. Ross Newhan, "The Ghosts of '64 Haunt Mauch, and Series Is Tied," *Los Angeles Times*, October 10, 1982: Part III, 10.
9. Gregg Hoffmann, interview with Jim Gantner after game.
10. Pete Donovan, "Now Angels Can't Shrug Off a Loss," *Los Angeles Times*, October 10, 1982: Part III, 11.
11. Gregg Hoffmann, interview with Jim Slaton after game.
12. Flaherty: 2.
13. Bob Wolf, "…And John Doesn't," *Milwaukee Journal*, October 10, 1982: 3.
14. Gregg Hoffmann, interview with Harvey Kuenn after game.
15. Steve Aschburner, "A Tale of Two Sundays," *Milwaukee Journal*, October 10, 1982: 3.

CECIL COOPER'S TWO-RUN SINGLE IN 7TH PROPELS BREWERS TO VICTORY

MILWAUKEE BREWERS 4, CALIFORNIA ANGELS 3
OCTOBER 10, 1982, AT COUNTY STADIUM

AMERICAN LEAGUE CHAMPIONSHIP SERIES, GAME FIVE

By Frederick C. Bush

Game Five of the 1982 American League Championship Series on Sunday, October 10, 1982, was the most important contest fans at Milwaukee County Stadium had been treated to since its former occupants, the Braves, fell to the New York Yankees, 6-2, in Game Seven of the 1958 World Series. While the Brewers had made the postseason for the first time in strike-shortened 1981 after winning the second-half AL East Division title, they had been eliminated in the first round. This time around, the Brewers aimed to earn the franchise's first trip to the World Series in front of 54,968 rabid hometown fans.

The first four games in the best-of-five ALCS against the California Angels had brought a feeling of déjà vu. The previous year, the New York Yankees had taken a commanding series lead by winning the first two games in Milwaukee only to have the Brewers return the favor by winning Games Three and Four in New York. Three consecutive victories at Yankee Stadium had been too tall an order, however, and the Yankees had vanquished the Brew Crew in Game Five. Against California, Milwaukee again faced a 2-0 deficit as the Angels won both games in Anaheim. Experience kept the team from panicking, though, as manager Harvey Kuenn tried to explain after Game Two: "We've had the walls behind our backs before. I mean, you'd have to say our backs are behind the wall."[1] With their backs against the wall, the Brewers stormed back to tie the series and, though no team in 13 years of ALCS history had overcome a 2-0 deficit to win, they were confident that this year would be different.

Pete Vuckovich, the eventual 1982 AL Cy Young Award winner, faced a rematch against Bruce Kison, who had outdueled him in the Angels' 4-2 victory in Game Two. Vuckovich's shot at redemption got off to an inauspicious start as leadoff batter Brian Downing stroked his fourth pitch to right field for a double. After Rod Carew flied out, third baseman Paul Molitor made a diving catch of Reggie Jackson's liner, but his wild throw to second hit Downing in the back, allowing him to advance to third. Hot-hitting Fred Lynn drove in Downing with a single that gave the Angels a quick 1-0 lead, with Lynn advancing to second as left fielder Ben Oglivie committed the Brewers' second error of the inning. Vuckovich limited the damage by retiring Don Baylor (10 RBIs in the first four games) on a grounder for the final out.

In the bottom of the first, a chorus of "Anything You Can Do" would have been appropriate for the two teams, although the number of errors committed in the inning demonstrated that things were not always being done better. First, Molitor matched Downing's feat when he led off with a double of his own, after which he advanced to third on a Robin Yount groundout. Next, Cecil Cooper reached base safely when Angels third baseman Doug DeCinces joined the parade of errors with a poor throw to first. And finally, a Ted Simmons sacrifice fly scored Molitor to tie the game.

The Angels recaptured the lead in the third when Lynn singled again, scoring Boone and putting California back up, 2-1. Oglivie appeared moonstruck by Lynn's hits on this day as he misplayed the ball for his second error of the game, allowing Lynn to advance to second. But in another instance of déjà vu, Vuckovich escaped further trouble by inducing a Baylor pop fly to get out of the inning.

Boone extended the Angels' lead to 3-1 with an RBI single that scored DeCinces in the top of the fourth, but Oglivie got that run back with a solo home run off Kison in the bottom of the frame. Oglivie's homer was his only offensive contribution to the ALCS and was one of the few times that "Harvey's Wallbangers" had made an appearance. The team's nickname was an affectionate reference to both Harvey Kuenn, who had taken over as manager in the season's 48th game, as well as to the .279 team batting average and 216 home runs they had amassed in the regular season. The ALCS, however, was a different story as the Brewers struggled with the bats, finishing with a meager .219 team batting average. As Game Five progressed, with their hitters continuing to struggle and the Angels clinging to a 3-2 lead, time appeared to be running out on Milwaukee's season.

A key play in the top of the fifth kept the Brewers' hopes alive as right fielder Charlie Moore gunned down Reggie Jackson, who was attempting to advance from first to third on yet another Lynn single. Lest anyone underestimate the significance of Moore's outfield assist, Vuckovich later affirmed, "'Munchkin' throwing out Reggie was really important. If he doesn't make that play, only God knows how many runs they would have scored."[2]

In the bottom of the seventh, the stage was set for Cooper – who next to Oglivie was the "Wallbanger" in the worst slump – to become one of the heroes of the series. Cooper had registered a .313-32-121 batting line with 205 hits in the regular season but had entered Game Five at .125-0-2. Now Angels reliever Luis Sanchez, who had replaced Kison in the bottom of the sixth inning, found himself facing Cooper in a two-out, bases-loaded situation. After the game, Cooper acknowledged, "If somebody asked where Cecil Cooper had been during the playoffs, it would have been a fair question."[3] As it turned out, Cooper was in the right place at the right time in Game Five as he slapped a single to left field that scored Moore and Jim Gantner for a 4-3 Brewers lead. After Gantner dove across home plate with what turned out to be the winning run, he found himself in Moore's joyous embrace. "All I remember is I went down on my knees. I grabbed him and hugged him," Moore recalled.[4]

The game was not yet over, though, and center fielder Marshall Edwards, who had replaced a hobbled Gorman Thomas in the top of the seventh, turned in the Brewers' second defensive gem with a leaping catch at the wall in the eighth inning that robbed Baylor of a hit. ABC television announcer Keith Jackson exclaimed, "If Gorman Thomas is in center field, that's off the wall for extra bases!"[5]

Edwards's catch stunted any potential Angels rally, and after that bit of excitement, the Brewers took care of business. Bob McClure, who had entered the game in the seventh, earned the win, while Pete Ladd registered his second save of the series by retiring the side in the ninth following a Jackson single off McClure. As soon as Yount threw out Carew at first for the final out, fans streamed onto the field to initiate a celebration that spread through the entire city of Milwaukee, "show[ing] that, even with a gap of a quarter-century, it had not forgotten how to celebrate a baseball pennant."[6]

After the game, Fred Lynn, who had batted .611 with 11 hits and 5 RBIs, was named the series MVP, a rare honor for a player on the losing team and one that riled Kuenn, who said, "Fred Lynn got the MVP? Not in my book. It should have gone to Ladd."[7] Ladd, who had retired all 10 batters he faced in the series, conceded, "Freddie deserved the MVP. But what we got is a chance to go to the World Series. And we deserved that."[8]

Ladd was right. Nothing, including an MVP snub, could overshadow the Milwaukee Brewers' accomplishments: They had earned their first trip to the World Series after becoming the first team to overcome a 2-0 deficit in an ALCS that also was the first such series to be played between two of the major leagues' 1960s expansion teams. Brewers owner Bud Selig praised his team's effort and declared, "You gotta love 'em. I love 'em like my own family."[9] Indeed, fans throughout Wisconsin and much of the rest of the nation did love "Harvey's Wallbangers," the 1982 American League Champion Milwaukee Brewers.

SOURCES

Baseball-Reference.com.

Essential Games of the Milwaukee Brewers.

Milwaukee Journal.

Milwaukee Sentinel.

The Sporting News.

NOTES

1. Dave Nightingale, "Second-Liners Rally Brewers," *The Sporting News*, October 18, 1982, 24, 26.

2. Vic Feuerherd, "Brewers win first AL title," *Milwaukee Sentinel*, October 11, 1982.

3. Dave Nightingale, "Demons Return to Haunt Mauch," *The Sporting News*, October 18, 1982, 26.

3. Tom Flaherty, "Yes! Yes! A pennant!" *Milwaukee Journal*, October 11, 1982.

4. *Essential Games of the Milwaukee Brewers*, "1982 ALCS Game 5 Pennant Clincher" (A&E Home Video, 2012), DVD.

5. "Go Brewers Go!" *Milwaukee Sentinel*, October 11, 1982.

6. "Second-Liners Rally Brewers."

7. Ibid.

8. Joe Karius, "Selig's longest day ends in victory celebration," *Milwaukee Sentinel*, October 11, 1982.

"WHITEYBALL" IN THE SHADOW OF THE GATEWAY ARCH
THE 1982 ST. LOUIS CARDINALS

By Russ Lake

On September 27, 1982, pregame showers in Montreal held up the contest between the St. Louis Cardinals and the Expos. The "Magic Number" for the Redbirds to win their first-ever National League East Division was two. Radio announcer Jack Buck remembered several unpleasant "north-of-the-border" events involving his beloved team. The last two St. Louis managers were relieved of their duties in Montreal. The 1981 players strike prompted Commissioner Bowie Kuhn to authorize a split-season playoff format. The Cardinals, with the best overall record in the NL East, remained on the postseason sidelines after finishing second, initially to Philadelphia and later to Montreal.[1]

St. Louis lit the scoreboard with a four-run first inning. Up one with two on, Willie McGee's two-out sinking liner skipped to the wall after it eluded center fielder Andre Dawson. Dane Iorg and Darrell Porter scored while the speedy McGee circled the bases for an inside-the-park home run.[2] In the ninth, the Redbirds held a two-run margin with closer Bruce Sutter on the hill vying for his 36th save. The Cubs had defeated the second-place Phillies, so except for the shouting, the division race was over.

Dawson lined to center, and Al Oliver grounded out. Gary Carter stepped in, and Buck made the long-awaited call that pronounced St. Louis the champs, "The pitch. A groundball to third, Oberkfell has it. Throws. That's it. The Cardinals have won it by the score of 4-2. And that one is for Mr. Busch, for Butch Yatkeman, for Ken Boyer, and for all the Cardinal fans who have been so loyal this year."[3] The team eventually ended the regular season 92-70 for their best finish since 1968.

Prosperity improved for the St. Louis Cardinals after they hired Whitey Herzog as manager on June 8, 1980. The 48-year-old "White Rat" turned down an initial one-year offer because of past difficulties negotiating his annual agreements with Kansas City. Busch and his lawyer quickly approved a three-year deal.[4] Herzog replaced Ken Boyer with St. Louis in last place in the NL East with an 18-34 mark.[5] He joined his new team in Atlanta the next evening, and began to see examples of what cost Boyer his job. After a short time, he reported to Busch that it was the first time he had ever been scared to walk through his own clubhouse. Redbirds GM John Claiborne was fired, and later Herzog, on a plea from Busch, accepted the front-office position. Herzog would be the guy to remove players and add talent. Busch agreed that Herzog could return as manager after the "housecleaning" was completed.[6]

The 81-year-old Busch wanted one more world championship, and was stunned by Herzog's report that the Cardinals were in no position to win anything with the "sorry bunch" of players on the roster; or with much of the minor-league assemblage. Busch asked to be kept informed and gave Herzog carte blanche to construct a team to his preference.[7] On a suggestion from former Cardinals GM Bing Devine, Herzog frequently visited Busch at his home over some Budweiser to talk baseball.[8]

The Cardinals had All-Star talents in catcher Ted Simmons, first baseman Keith Hernandez, and shortstop Garry Templeton. Simmons was an exciting switch-hitter, but lacked the "pitcher-handling" and defensive abilities required by a backstop. Hernandez was a proven leader in offense and defense, and shared the 1979 NL MVP. The brash-talking, switch-hitting Templeton batted with "hard-nosed" authority, but could be a challenge on the defensive and hustling lines.

In the offseason, Herzog first pursued a catcher, and set sights on Kansas City's Darrell Porter. Joe McDonald, the former New York Mets GM, was made an assistant, and they got Porter (who was on his honeymoon cruise) to agree to a five-year deal. The plan was to shift Simmons to first with Hernandez moving to left. Hernandez said the outfield was fine with him, and Simmons (through his agent) agreed to his position relocation. With that rework seemingly done, Herzog chased after a needed closer. The first big deal of the winter meetings was made with San Diego's Jack McKeon to acquire relief ace Rollie Fingers, catcher Gene Tenace, southpaw Bob Shirley, and minor-leaguer Bob Geren for young catcher Terry Kennedy and five other roster denizens whom Herzog felt he could do without.[9] "I'll be back tomorrow," Herzog promised the media.[10]

Former Cy Young Award winner Sutter was the reliever Herzog coveted, but getting Chicago Cubs GM Bob Kennedy (whose son the Cardinals had just traded) to support such a transaction proved cumbersome. Kennedy wanted first baseman-outfielder Leon Durham and infielders Tommy Herr and Ty Waller. Herzog wanted to keep Durham and Herr, so he offered third baseman Kenny Reitz. After relenting on Herr, Kennedy asserted,

"No Durham, no Sutter." As pieces came together, Herzog learned that Reitz had a no-trade clause. St. Louis bought this out for $50,000 to complete the bartering. Finally, Herzog had Sutter and his split-finger fastball. Fingers insisted that he would be fine in the same bullpen, but after Herzog offered game-situation scenarios, Fingers felt he would be better off with another team.[11]

A problem surfaced a day later when Simmons balked about playing first, and told his agent to inform Herzog that he had changed his mind. Herzog liked Simmons, but was upset about this reversal since he now had to deal with another significant roster shakeup. The Oakland A's and Milwaukee Brewers were the only teams willing to talk about Simmons and his large no-trade contract. Simmons vetoed Oakland because it was too far away. A multiplayer package was compiled, but Brewers GM Harry Dalton froze once Herzog requested Milwaukee's top prospect, outfielder David Green. Simmons requested $750,000 for his no-trade to be purchased, so Milwaukee started to withdraw from the proposal. Suddenly, George Steinbrenner informed Herzog that the Yankees wanted to acquire Simmons, and it did not matter how much the buyout would be.[12]

Dalton reconsidered and asked Herzog how much the Cardinals would be willing to pay on Simmons's buyout. Herzog retorted, "Not one red cent. Either you take him or we'll ship him to someone else." Since he did not want Simmons moved to a rival, Dalton requested extra time, and then an extension of the Cardinals' deadline. After lengthy front-office discussion, Milwaukee agreed to swap Green, outfielder Sixto Lezcano, and pitchers Lary Sorensen and Dave LaPoint for Simmons, Fingers, and pitcher Pete Vuckovich.[13] While the transactions with San Diego and Chicago had St. Louis fans chirping positively, the trade of Simmons had them proclaiming that it was one swap too many.[14]

Meanwhile, there were 22 candidates to consider for the St. Louis manager's position. One applicant told Herzog that he had never played baseball, but did not see why that made any difference. Herzog wrote him back and said he would keep him in mind. Gene Mauch and Joe Altobelli were viewed as front-runners, but went elsewhere.[15] Herzog later announced that he would return as the Redbirds' pilot since he had orchestrated the roster overhaul.[16]

The media-coined term Whiteyball started taking shape during 1981 spring training in St. Petersburg, Florida. Herzog appointed longtime Cardinals minor-league coach George Kissell to implement ways for St. Louis baserunners to get a better break from third base. Kissell accepted the task and applied his longtime "Cardinal Way" philosophy. Kissell preached to his plebes, "Tell me and I'll forget. Show me and I'll remember. Involve me and I'll understand."[17] Coach Red Schoendienst categorized Whiteyball as good fundamental baseball that worked with productive outs. "It was getting a guy on first, stealing second, moving to third on a groundout, and scoring on a fly ball," explained Schoendienst.[18] Herzog tabbed Chuck Hiller to be his third-base coach. Hiller had served Herzog in the same capacity during prior managerial locations.

The Cardinals opened the 1981 season with a 5-2 loss to the World Series champion Philadelphia Phillies. Many of the Redbirds faithful had already painted a large target on the back of Porter, and the new catcher did not help his cause by grounding into a rally-killing double play while going hitless. Also, on the first ball fielded by Ken Oberkfell at third, his throw sailed high over the reach of Hernandez. Conversely, Sutter entered the next afternoon to notch a save with three frames of relief.

Porter, who had left the Royals for alcohol and drug treatment in 1980, was hitting .176 with nine RBIs when he was shelved on May 18 with a right-shoulder rotator cuff injury. Cardinals surgeon Stan London consulted with Dr. Frank Jobe in Los Angeles on a diagnosis, but the prognosis appeared unfavorable.[19] An anticipated players strike started on June 12 with the Cardinals in second place, 1½ games behind the Phillies. Just before play halted, switch-hitting center fielder Tony Scott was traded to Houston for Joaquin Andujar. Herzog directed pitching coach Hub Kittle to bring Andujar out of a delivery funk the high-strung hurler had been in for the past year and a half.[20]

After the strike was settled in early August, the Cardinals started the "second season" winning five of their first six. However, a concern was festering in the clubhouse and it came to an unfortunate head at Busch Stadium. On August 26 Templeton was nursing a sore knee and complained about having to play in a rain-delayed afternoon contest following a night game. Herzog explained to his shortstop that the team was in a pennant race, and that Templeton would be in the lineup whether he liked it or not. Templeton took his brooding to the field, and failed to run to first on a dropped third strike. The small Ladies Day gathering started booing and resumed their taunts as Templeton returned to his position.[21] Templeton responded with an obscene gesture and received a warning from the umpires.[22]

In the top of the fourth with St. Louis trailing San Francisco, 2-0, Templeton saluted the hecklings with another indecency. Plate umpire Bruce Froemming ejected Templeton, and he stalked off the field.[23] At the mound, he grabbed his crotch as the catcalls increased. When the volatile infielder neared the dugout, a furious Herzog reached up and yanked Templeton down the steps before players got between the two combatants.[24] A comeback 9-4 win did not appease the locals after they witnessed or learned of the ballfield drama. Herzog later said, "I'm not proud about what I did. But I had to do it. No player is going to show up the fans."[25]

Templeton was suspended and fined $5,000. Days later he was hospitalized for depression and a chemical imbalance and requested a change of baseball scenery.[26] He returned on September 15, batted .369 through the end of the season, and played pretty well, according to Herzog. However, the damage was done. Templeton had upset the fans, his teammates, and Mr. Busch — who told Herzog to trade the moody talent.[27] On the plus side, Andujar finished 6-1, and Porter returned with a healthy shoulder and drove in 23 runs. Nonetheless, the Cardinals lost out on the divisional playoff berth by a half-game and missed postseason play for the 13th consecutive season.

Herzog was voted UPI's Executive of the Year before thoughts of a new shortstop for the next season could percolate. He executed a pair of offseason transactions that ultimately made heads turn. October brought a deal dubbed negligible when it involved southpaw Bob Sykes going to the Yankees for Double-A switch-hitting outfielder Willie McGee. In November, starting pitchers Silvio Martinez and Sorensen were sent to Cleveland via a three-team trade that brought Philadelphia outfielder Lonnie Smith to St. Louis. The speedy, right-handed-batting Smith was projected as the new center fielder.[28]

Herzog was earnestly looking for a shortstop to exchange Templeton for and found the pickings slim. After several veterans were eliminated, Herzog checked to see if San Diego's Ozzie Smith was available, but McKeon said that Smith was untouchable. Nonetheless, during the early part of the winter meetings, McKeon asked Herzog if he was still interested in Ozzie. Herzog was confused, but the San Diego GM explained that the Padres were miffed at Smith's agent. A package involving six players was orchestrated with Templeton, Lezcano, and minor-league pitcher Luis DeLeon going to San Diego for Smith and pitchers Steve Mura and Al Olmsted.[29]

However, Ozzie Smith had a no-trade clause and zero desire to leave sunny California, and did not want to be swapped to St. Louis. Reading about the apparent stonewall, "Cardinals Nation" disdained Smith's two Gold Gloves, and focused on the career offensive yield of Templeton's .305 outpacing Smith's .231. A public campaign to rescind the deal was forged, but quickly flamed out. Herzog could see all sides of the matter, and the clubhouse climate he desired prompted him to fly to San Diego and meet with Smith about what Herzog was trying to accomplish. Herzog told Smith and his agent that if one year in St. Louis did not work out, then Ozzie could be a free agent after the season.[30]

Ozzie Smith finally agreed to the trade and Herzog looked back over 18 months of roster manipulation. The starting lineup from June 1980 had Hernandez, Oberkfell, and George Hendrick still in St. Louis, while the only starting pitcher remaining was Bob Forsch. Herzog had added speed, subtracted difficult personalities, and upgraded pitching, catching, and defense. He felt the guys currently on the roster could play together and win games. It also became time for Herzog to move away from the GM position to concentrate on piloting his crew toward the postseason.[31]

The 1982 campaign started in Houston on April 6 with the Cardinals blasting the Astros, 14-3. Everyone in the starting lineup collected at least one hit, and it was the most runs scored by the franchise on Opening Day since 1928. After three straight losses, St. Louis followed with 12 consecutive wins. Second baseman Herr commented, "We just go out and play with confidence every day. To me, that's the sign of a good club."[32] The 12 successive victories were the team's longest winning streak since 1943, but this particular feat was overshadowed by the Atlanta Braves, who opened the season with 13 wins.[33]

Green's hamstring injury in early May brought McGee from Triple A, and he rapidly became a popular fixture in center field. A May 30 walk-off 6-5 win over San Diego was noteworthy after St. Louis rallied for three runs in the ninth to force extra innings. However, the Padres answered with a pair in the 10th to go up 5-3. In the Cardinals' half with two out and nobody on, the Redbirds pulled a stunner. Down a run, super-sub Mike Ramsey singled home Lonnie Smith with the tying run. After a hit batsman, Iorg knocked home the winner. As Ramsey scored, all Jack Buck could exclaim was, "Unbelievable!"[34]

St. Louis moved four games up on Montreal after a hard-fought 3-2 walk-off on June 15. A new fan-appreciation measurement had morphed at Busch Stadium when standing ovations held up contests after Ozzie Smith made another spectacular play. Displaying fire and flamboyance on the mound, Andujar, described himself as "One Tough

Dominican" while being monitored by Herzog and Kittle. At the All-Star break, Lonnie Smith was batting .306 with 70 runs scored and 41 stolen bases.

The Cardinals slumped from late July into August and found themselves trailing the Phillies by three games. A 7-1 road trip to New York and Pittsburgh vaulted the Redbirds back into first place. On August 22, a steamy afternoon against San Francisco ended astonishingly when third-string catcher Glenn Brummer took it upon himself to steal home with the bases loaded, two outs, and a two-strike count in the 12th. The Giants argued heatedly with plate umpire Dave Pallone, to no avail.[35]

Philadelphia mounted another charge and moved a half-game ahead of St. Louis on September 13. The next evening at Veterans Stadium, Sutter relieved rookie starter John Stuper with two on and one out in the bottom of the eighth. The Cardinals were leading 2-0, and an infield hit by Gary Matthews jammed the bases. Sutter took a deep breath, went into his stretch, and got Mike Schmidt to ground into a 1-2-3 double play.[36] The bearded closer retired the Phillies in the ninth and moved St. Louis back to the top. By winning 11 of their next 14 games, the Cardinals secured the NL East Division title, and were in the postseason for the first time since 1968.

Skippered by former Cardinal Joe Torre, the NL West champion Atlanta Braves came to St. Louis to begin a best-of-five National League Championship Series on October 6. Torre had ex-Redbirds Bob Gibson and Dal Maxvill on his coaching staff. During the regular season, the Braves earned a 7-5 advantage over the Cardinals. Phil Niekro had St. Louis down 1-0 after 4½ innings before heavy rain washed out the game.

The next evening Forsch fired a 7-0 shutout while defeating Pascual Perez with a five-run sixth inning. Rain shrouded the Midwest the next day to push Game Two off 24 hours. Atlanta called on the 43-year-old Niekro again, and the ageless knuckleballer controlled a 3-1 lead after five. The Cardinals plated single tallies in the sixth and eighth to set the stage for the bottom of the ninth. Oberkfell lined a one-out drive just past the reach of center fielder Brett Butler to send Green home with the walk-off 4-3 winner.

With two postponements stretching the NLCS, the teams flew to Atlanta with no day off before Game Three. On October 10 the Cardinals rocked Rick Camp with four second-inning runs and breezed behind Andujar and Sutter for a 6-2 NL pennant-clincher. During the series sweep, Porter and Ozzie Smith both hit .556. Porter also walked five times, and was named the MVP of the NLCS. It was the 13th pennant for the franchise.

The World Series opened in St. Louis on October 12 with the Cardinals facing the powerful Milwaukee Brewers. Managed by Harvey Kuenn, his Wallbangers clouted 216 home runs to the Cardinals' 67, and plated over 200 more runs than the Redbirds did in the regular season. More than a light rain dampened the Series opener as Milwaukee jumped on St. Louis early and often during a 10-0 thumping. Left-hander Mike Caldwell allowed just three hits, while the first two Brewers, Paul Molitor (5 hits) and Robin Yount (4), amassed three times that figure as part of a 17-hit attack. Herzog said the only good thing about the evening was that they did not have to play a doubleheader.[37]

In Game Two Simmons proved that you can go home again when he blasted his second homer of the series to give Milwaukee a 3-0 third-inning cushion against Stuper. The Cardinals plated a pair off Don Sutton in the bottom half, but Cecil Cooper nicked Jim Kaat for an RBI single in the fifth. Porter put St. Louis fans on their feet by dropping a two-out two-run double down the left-field line to tie things, 4-4. Steve Braun coaxed a controversial bases-loaded walk from Pete Ladd in the eighth inning to account for the 5-4 finish tying the Series at a game each.[38]

Game Three became the Willie McGee show. First, the rookie center fielder made a leaping catch at the wall on Molitor's first-inning drive. With the game scoreless in the fifth, McGee blasted a three-run homer off Vuckovich. In the seventh, after Lonnie Smith tripled and scored on a throwing error, McGee went deep again to make the score 5-0. In the bottom half, Andujar took a painful comebacker to his right leg and was carried off. The advantage was 6-2 with Sutter pitching in the ninth. With one on and no outs, Gorman Thomas knocked an offering high and deep to the left-center alley. McGee raced over and soared high at the fence to backhand the drive.[39] Sutter retired the next two, and the Cardinals were up two games to one.

In Game Four, St. Louis had struck for three runs by the third frame with two scoring on Herr's deep sacrifice fly. Former Brewers southpaw LaPoint was cruising, 5-1, with one out in the seventh when he dropped an easy toss covering first.[40] The harmless-looking miscue opened the floodgates as Milwaukee plated six runs on five hits off four hurlers to take a 7-5 lead, and tie the Series at two games each.

The Cardinals figured out how to hit Caldwell in Game Five, but they could not outscore the Brewers during a tough 6-4 loss. Fifteen safeties by St. Louis could not produce enough tallies as they stranded 12. Yount homered among his four hits and was serenaded with MVP chants by the Milwaukee fans. The Redbirds headed back home trailing three games to two.

With precipitation definitely in the St. Louis forecast for Game Six, Stuper was phenomenal, hurling a complete game through separate weather delays totaling over two hours. Cardinals bats thundered throughout a stormy night as Porter and Hernandez each ripped two-run homers, while Iorg collected three hits. Coupled with Sutton and Doc Medich being roughed up, the Brewers committed four errors during the 13-1 blowout to even the Series at three wins apiece.

On a cold and crisp October 20, Game Seven moved into the spotlight with Andujar and Vuckovich squaring off for the title. St. Louis mustered a short-lived 1-0 lead until Ben Ogilvie parked a long home run to open the fifth inning. Milwaukee seemingly took command during the sixth, scoring two runs on three hits, Andujar's error, and

a sacrifice fly to go up 3-1. With one down in the bottom half, the "Smith Brothers" rallied the Cardinals. Ozzie punched a single to left, and Lonnie scorched a double into the left-field corner.[41] Lefty Bob McClure relieved and walked pinch-hitter Tenace, with Ramsey coming in to pinch-run.

Hernandez laced a game-tying two-run single to right-center with Ramsey diving safely into third. Hendrick directed a single to right to plate Ramsey for a 4-3 lead. With one out in the seventh, Milwaukee's lefty-swinging Roy Howell lofted a drive to left. Lonnie Smith turned the catchable fly ball into a twisted-running "lucky stab" for a "heart-stopping" second out. After Charlie Moore singled, Jim Gantner was retired when Andujar threw him out at first. Unexpectedly, Andujar and Gantner exchanged verbal barbs near the baseline. As the benches began to stir, plate umpire Lee Weyer wrapped up Andujar, and instructed Kittle to accompany the fiery competitor to the dugout.[42]

Sutter, who was hit hard in County Stadium, retired Milwaukee in order in the eighth. The Cardinals added important insurance runs in their half with two-out RBI singles off Caldwell by Porter and Braun to increase their advantage to 6-3. In the ninth, Sutter got Simmons and Ogilvie to ground out before fanning Thomas for the final out. Porter ripped off his mask and flung it high as he ran to embrace Sutter before the rest of the Redbirds and thousands of fans joined the celebration.[43]

In an unusual twist of ironies, Darrell Porter, the Brewers' top draft pick in 1970, was selected the World Series MVP. August Busch Jr., who kept the Cardinals' franchise from moving to Milwaukee in 1953 after his brewery purchased the team, accepted the World Series championship trophy.[44] The championship was the ninth in Cardinals history. Porter happily reflected, "Ever since I was a Little Leaguer, I wanted to be on a world championship team. And now my dreams have come true."[45]

SOURCES

In addition to the sources cited in the Notes, the author accessed Retrosheet.org, Baseball-Reference.com, Baseball-Almanac.com, Newspapers.com, and SABR.org/bioproj.

NOTES

1 With no games that were missed due to the players strike from June 12 to August 10 to be made up; the Cardinals (59-43) and the Cincinnati Reds (66-42), with the best won-lost records for the full season in the NL, did not qualify for the playoffs.

2 Video, *The Saint Louis Cardinals, The Movie* (St. Louis National Baseball Club, 1985).

3 Video, *The Saint Louis Cardinals*. During his end-of-game call, Jack Buck paid homage to August A. Busch for his 30th season of team ownership; Butch Yatkeman, the well-liked Cardinals clubhouse man, who was retiring in 1982 after 59 years of service; Ken Boyer, captain of the Cardinals, 1964 MVP, and former St. Louis manager, who succumbed to lung cancer on September 7, 1982; The St. Louis fans who made the '82 Busch Stadium turnstiles click a then franchise-high 2,111,906 times.

4 Whitey Herzog and Kevin Horrigan, *White Rat, A Life in Baseball* (New York: Harper & Row, 1987), 115-116.

5 Boyer skippered the 1980 Cardinals to an 18-33 record before he was fired by GM John Claiborne on June 8, 1980, between games of a doubleheader. Third-base coach Jack Krol (0-1) piloted St. Louis during their loss in the nightcap.

6 Herzog and Horrigan, 119-120.

7 Herzog and Horrigan, 117-118.

8 Jack Buck with Rob Rains and Bob Broeg, *Jack Buck: That's a Winner!* (Champaign, Illinois: Sports Publishing, 1997), 174.

9 Herzog and Horrigan, 124-127.

10 Bill Conlin, "While Rivals Snoozed, Herzog Pulled Heists," *The Sporting News*, December 27, 1980: 46.

11 Herzog and Horrigan, 127-128.

12 Herzog and Horrigan, 129-131.

13 Ibid.

14 Rick Hummel, "Fans Give Whitey a Heat Treatment," The Sporting News, January 3, 1981: 52.

15 Hummel, "22 Candidates in Cards Derby," *The Sporting News*, October 25, 1980: 35; Dick Young, "Young Ideas," *The Sporting News*, September 27, 1980: 16.

16 Rob Rains, *The St. Louis Cardinals, The 100th Anniversary History* (New York: St. Martin's Press, 1992), 241.

17 Derrick Goold, "Now in Book Form: The Cardinal Way," *St. Louis Post-Dispatch*, May 18, 2012: stltoday.com, accessed August 18, 2018.

18 Red Schoendienst with Rob Rains, *Red, A Baseball Life* (Champaign, Illinois: Sports Publishing, 1998), 181.

19 Rick Hummel, "Rincon Injury Shakes Redbird Roost," *The Sporting News*, May 30, 1981: 41.

20 Herzog and Horrigan, 134.

21 Herzog and Horrigan, 135-136.

22 Rick Hummel, "Templeton Gets Psychiatric Help," *The Sporting News*, September 12, 1981: 39, 53.

23 Ibid.

24 Herzog and Horrigan, 136.

25 Hummel, "Templeton Gets Psychiatric Help."

26 Herzog and Horrigan, 136.

27 Ibid.

28 Herzog and Horrigan, 139.

29 Herzog and Horrigan, 137-138.

30 Herzog and Horrigan, 138.

31 Herzog and Horrigan, 139-140.

32 Rick Hummel, "Cards Halted by Carlton," *St. Louis Post-Dispatch*, April 26, 1982: 26.

33 Ibid.

34 Video, *The Saint Louis Cardinals, The Movie*.

35 Ibid.

36 Ibid.

37 Dick Kaegel, "A Contrast in Styles," *The Sporting News*, October 25, 1982: 3.

38 Ibid.

39 Ibid.

40 Ibid.

41 Video, *The Saint Louis Cardinals, The Movie*.

41 Youtube.com, *1982 World Series – Game 7*, accessed August 30, 2018.

42 Youtube.com, *1982 World Series – Game 7*.

43 Gregory H. Wolf, ed., *Sportsman's Park in St. Louis* (Phoenix: Society for American Baseball Research, 2017), 55.

44 "Porter Delivers the Goods," *The Sporting News*, November 1, 1982: 28.

MIKE CALDWELL TOSSES 3-HITTER AS BREW CREW DEMOLISHES REDBIRDS IN SERIES OPENER

MILWAUKEE BREWERS 10, ST. LOUIS CARDINALS 0
OCTOBER 12, 1982, AT BUSCH STADIUM, ST. LOUIS

THE WORLD SERIES, GAME ONE

By Gregory H. Wolf

It was an eagerly anticipated matchup between opposite styles of play: Harvey's Wallbangers and Whiteyball. Skipper Harvey Kuenn's Milwaukee Brewers who led the majors in home runs (216), runs scored (891), and slugging (.455) against manager Whitey Herzog's St. Louis Cardinals who paced the NL in stolen bases (200) and fielding (.981), while hitting the fewest round-trippers (67) the big leagues. The result of Game One of the fall classic was a "whale of a skunking," opined Gateway City sportswriter Bob Broeg;[1] while Herzog himself quipped that it was a "good, old-fashioned butt-kicking"[2] as the Brew Crew played small ball, pounding out 17 hits, but only four for extra bases, to pummel the Cards, 10-0, in the most lopsided shutout in the World Series since the New York Yankees beat the Pittsburgh Pirates 12-0 in Game Six in 1960. The Brewers "did what the Cardinals are known for," noted Redbirds beat reporter Rick Hummel, "bouncing balls off the artificial turf, plugging the gaps in the outfield and running like the wind."[3]

The AL-pennant-winning Brewers boasted the best record in baseball (95-67), but needed the final game of the season to capture the East crown after losing seven of 11 games. Their struggles continued in the ALCS, in which they lost the first two to the California Angels before taking the next three to advance to their first World Series. After more than a decade of irrelevance, the NL East champion Cardinals produced the best slate (92-70) in the senior circuit, advancing to the postseason for the first time since the glory days of Bob Gibson and Lou Brock in 1968. A blockbuster trade between the two clubs after the 1980 season enabled each team to end years of mediocrity. The Cardinals sent reliever Rollie Fingers and pitcher Pete Vuckovich (both of whom subsequently won Cy Young Awards in 1981 and '82, respectively), and perennial All-Star catcher Ted Simmons to the Brewers in exchange for pitchers Lary Sorensen and Dave LaPoint and outfielders Sixto Lezcano and David Green. The Cardinals afterward flipped LaPoint and Lezcano as parts of separate trades after the '81 campaign to acquire Lonnie Smith and Ozzie Smith, each earning All-Star berths in '82.

On a clear, crisp Tuesday evening with temperatures in the high 60s, Busch Stadium was rocking with 53,723 rabid fans. Many prognosticators wondered if the Brewers could adjust from their grass field at County Stadium to the Redbirds' fast artificial turf. The Brew Crew came out swinging against Bob Forsch, longtime staff workhorse and former 20-game winner who had tossed a nifty three-hit shutout in his last outing, in the opener of the Cardinals' three-game sweep of the Atlanta

Braves in the NLCS. In a fear-inspiring lineup, AL MVP Robin Yount (29-114-.331) sliced a one-out single followed by Cecil Cooper's (32-121-.313) walk. Two batters later, Ben Oglivie (34-102-.244) hit a routine hopper to Gold Glove first baseman Keith Hernandez. "I just booted it," admitted the former NL MVP, and Yount scored.[4] Gorman Thomas (39-112-.245) followed with a hard-hit smash that shortstop Ozzie Smith stopped on the outfield turf, but not in time to make a throw to first while Cooper tallied the second run. Forsch tossed 39 pitches in the first inning and looked taxed. The Brewers Express kept rolling. After two more singles in the second didn't produce any runs, Charlie Moore scored the third run when he led off the fourth with a double and raced home on Paul Molitor's bloop single over Ozzie's head.

The game marked the return of Simba to St. Louis. Still widely popular and an offseason resident in the Mound City, Ted Simmons (23-97-.269) gave his hometown fans something to cheer in the fifth inning of an otherwise disappointing game, at least for them. Simmons has a "picture-perfect left-handed swing," poetically waxed Redbirds scribe Kevin Horrigan, and sent "the ball screaming on a low arc through the St. Louis night to crash seconds later against the concrete façade above the home-run line down the left-field line" to give the Brewers a 4-0 lead.[5] "I'm a good fastball hitter," said Simmons, "so I expected a lot of slow stuff."[6] Forsch fed him a heater and the result was a no-doubter one pitch after a monstrous blast had curved foul.

Milwaukee's relentless lineup scraped together two more in the sixth with two outs. Yount's two-out bloop double plated Jim Gantner and Molitor (both of whom had singled) to end Forsch's evening. "Forsch seemed to be trying to steer the ball," said longtime Cardinals instructor George Kissell "[H]e tried to pinpoint his pitches too much."[7] He was replaced by Jim Kaat, who at age 43 became the second oldest pitcher to appear in a World Series game, following Jack Quinn of the Philadelphia Athletics in 1930.

With the game well out of reach, the Brewers added four more runs, all with two outs, in the ninth. Key hits were Don Money's RBI single, Gantner's two-run triple, and Molitor's World Series-record fifth hit (and fifth consecutive single) driving in the final run.[8] Suffering from tendinitis in his right elbow over the last six weeks,[9] Molitor led the majors with 136 runs scored, joined teammates Cooper and Yount in collecting at least 200 hits in the regular season and thrived in relative anonymity on a team with big personalities and sluggers.

As impressive as the Brewers batters were, starting pitcher Mike Caldwell was even better. The 33-year-old left-hander, who overcame serious arm injuries early in his career to post a 79-48 record over the last five seasons with the Brewers, including a 17-13 slate in '82, had been struggling. In his last three starts, including a disastrous one in the ALCS, Caldwell had been clobbered for 32 hits and surrendered 16 earned runs in just 18 innings. "At times he has tried to overthrow," said pitching coach Pat Dobson. "When he does that, he gets the ball up in the strike zone and they hit it."[10] Nonetheless, Mr. Warmth, as teammates called him ironically for his ornery and competitive personality, demanded the ball in the club's maiden World Series contest. "I don't hate batters," he snapped. "I just hate everybody on the other team. Once they cross the white line, to hell with them."[11]

A control pitcher who relied on changing speeds on his assortment of sliders, sinkers, and screwballs, Caldwell had also long been suspected of throwing spitters. That reputation and pinpoint location flummoxed Redbird batters the entire game. He went the distance, yielding just three hits, two of which were infield singles. Said an exasperated Keith Hernandez, who went 0-for-4, "He might have been throwing me screwballs, but I never saw a screwball drop like that."[12] Cardinals DH and catcher Gene Tenace suggested that batters gave a psychological edge to pitchers if they requested umpires to check for wet ones; instead he credited Caldwell's command performance. "He got the ball where he wanted it and he had good motion on his offspeed pitches. He kept the ball down."[13] Caldwell adamantly rejected any charge of using an illegal substance, "Nope — nothing but natural sinkers tonight and I've got the blister to prove it," he retorted.[14]

Supported by his teammates' run barrage, Caldwell yielded only one hit — a second-inning double by Darrell Porter — through seven innings. In the eighth Porter and Ken Oberkfell connected for scratch singles, but they were sandwiched around the defensive play of the game. Right fielder Charlie Moore, a converted catcher, raced back to the warning track to snare David Green's potential run-scoring extra-base hit. Caldwell breezed through a 1-2-3 ninth to end the game in 2 hours and 30 minutes.

"That's as good as you'll ever see Mike Caldwell," opined Simmons. "He was throwing the groundball. He had a great slider, and he was changing speeds on his sinker."[15] Caldwell tossed only 100 pitches (66 for strikes), fanned three, and walked one.

"It ain't that bad," said Broeg of the Cardinals' humiliating loss in their first World Series game since the Detroit Tigers' Mickey Lolich outdueled Gibson in Game Seven of the '68 fall classic.[16] And Broeg was right. In a seesaw series, the Cardinals overcame a three-games-to-two deficit, returning to St. Louis to win the final two games at Busch Stadium and secure their first title since 1967 and ninth in franchise history.

SOURCES

In addition to the sources cited in the Notes, the author also accessed Retrosheet.org, Baseball-Reference.com, Newspapers.com, and SABR.org.

NOTES

1 Bob Broeg, "Cards Bounced Back Before," *St. Louis Post-Dispatch*, October 13, 1982: 1B.

2 Rick Hummel, "Brew-haha. Cardinals Embarrassed," *St. Louis Post-Dispatch*, October 13, 1982: 1A.

3 Ibid.

4 Joseph Durso, "Brewers 10, Cardinals 0," *New York Times*, October 13, 1982: B7.

5 Kevin Horrigan, "'Simba' Comes Home in Rousing Triumph," *St. Louis Post-Dispatch*, October 13, 1982: 1A.

6 Durso.

7 Neal Russo, "Hernandez: It's Not the Heat, It's Humidity," *St. Louis Post-Dispatch*, October 13, 1982: 1B.

8 Molitor (five hits) and Yount (four hits) marked the first time since 1946 that more than one player had at least four hits in a World Series Game. It had happened last in Game Four when four players had four each: Enos Slaughter, Whitey Kurowski, and Joe Garagiola of the Cardinals and Wally Moses of the Red Sox in the Redbirds' 12-3 victory at Fenway Park.

9 Arnold Irish, "Molitor Surprised by Record," *St. Louis Post-Dispatch*, October 13, 1982: 1B.

10 Murray Chass, "Molitor Defensive About His Offense," *New York Times*, October 13, 1982: B7.

11 Mike Smith, "Brewers 'Mr. Warmth' Proves Too Hot for Cards to Handle," *St. Louis Post-Dispatch*, October 13, 1982: 1B.

12 Russo.

13 Ibid.

14 Smith.

15 Vic Feuerherd, "Caldwell Decks Cards," *Milwaukee Sentinel*, October 13, 1982: II, 1.

16 Broeg.

ROOKIE RELIEVER WALKS IN WINNING RUN

ST. LOUIS CARDINALS 5, MILWAUKEE BREWERS 4
OCTOBER 13, 1982, AT BUSCH STADIUM, ST. LOUIS

THE WORLD SERIES, GAME TWO

By Dennis D. Degenhardt

After administering the worst home-team defeat ever in a World Series opener,[1] the Brewers began Game Two against the St. Louis Cardinals at Busch Stadium looking for a sweep and a commanding lead to take home to Milwaukee. The Cardinals, who had won the World Series five of the last six times they won Game Two, were hoping for a split.[2]

The Brewers started future Hall of Famer Don Sutton, who had been obtained at the trading deadline from the Houston Astros and was 4-1 with the Brewers (17-9 overall). He was starting his seventh World Series game. Opposing the 17-year veteran was 25-year-old Cardinals rookie John Stuper, who had a 9-7 record in 21 starts. Both had pitched in League Championship Series victories, Sutton earning the win over the California Angels in ALCS Game Three and Stupor getting a no-decision in NLCS Game Two against Atlanta.

Seldom is there suspense with the first batter but after setting the World Series record with five hits in Game One, Brewers leadoff hitter Paul Molitor had a chance to tie Goose Goslin's 1924 record, tied by Thurman Munson in 1976 with six consecutive World Series hits.[3] He grounded out to third, but with two hits in the game, he tied four players with seven hits in consecutive World Series games.[4]

The Brewers struck first, scoring a run on Charlie Moore's two-out double in the second. They added two more runs in the third, highlighted by a solo home run by former Cardinal Ted Simmons, who had been obtained in a blockbuster December 1980 trade.[5] It was his second homer of the Series and the natives started to get restless, booing at 8:11 P.M. when Ben Oglivie singled. (Coincidentally, at the same time the message board had a Red Cross ad regarding first-aid instructions.[6]) It was starting to look like a repeat of the previous night's shelling, the Brewers up 3-0 and the Cardinals scoreless through 11 innings. As the Cardinals' catcher, Darrell Porter, exclaimed, "At first, I thought we were going to die. It felt like we were losing a little momentum on the bench."[7]

The Redbirds finally got on the board in the third after Willie McGee reached on a fielder's choice. Playing Cardinal baseball, he then stole second base and scored on Tommy Herr's two-out double. They added another run on Ken Oberkfell's single to right driving in Herr, and it was 3-2, Brewers.

In the top of fifth, Robin Yount's leadoff double knocked rookie Stuper out of the game. He was replaced by a 24-year veteran, 43-year-old southpaw Jim Kaat, to pitch to left-handed-swinging Cecil Cooper. Cooper's RBI single drove in Yount. After

Kaat retired two hitters, reliever Doug Bair entered the game and struck out slugger Gorman Thomas. It wasn't looking good for St. Louis, trailing 4-2 with Sutton allowing just three hits so far.

The visitors were retired in the top of the sixth inning without a baserunner for the only time in the game. That would not be the case for the home team, which tied the game in the bottom of the inning. After Herr struck out, Oberkfell singled and stole second base. Sutton then walked cleanup hitter George Hendrick on four straight balls after getting out in front with two strikes. Next up was former Brewer Darrell Porter whom the Brewers had traded to Kansas City in December 1976. Porter played well for Cardinals manager Whitey Herzog when they were together with the Royals and St. Louis signed him as a free agent to replace Simmons. The NLCS MVP already grounded out twice on sliders. When Sutton hung another slider, Porter doubled to left field, driving in both runners and tying the game, 4-4. Sutton later said he had made a mistake, getting the ball up, and Porter agreed, saying, "I know Sutton has great control and that he can hit the corners on you. That may be the first ball I hit down the line in left field in three years."[8] Sutton acknowledged Porter's at-bat while returning to the dugout after the inning, telling him, "Nice piece of hitting."[9]

The Brewers threatened in the seventh with Cooper's two-out double bringing in St. Louis's closer extraordinaire, Bruce Sutter. Because Simmons had caught Sutter and was familiar with his split-finger fastball, the Cardinals played it safe and gave him an intentional walk. Sutter said later, "It was pretty much my decision to walk Simmons. Simmons got me twice with home runs when I was with the Cubs and he was with the Cardinals, so it was an easy decision. It was only logical to pitch to somebody who didn't know me."[10] The move worked as Oglivie grounded out, ending the inning. With Sutton tiring, Bob McClure relieved to start the seventh inning and held the Cardinals scoreless.

Remaining in the game to start the eighth, McClure walked the first batter, Keith Hernandez.

The game began to unravel when McClure failed to cover first base on Hendrick's double-play grounder to first. Hendrick was safe and he advanced to second on Porter's single. With Cardinals at first and second, Brewers manager Harvey Kuenn brought in his temporary closer, rookie Pete Ladd, who had two big saves in the ALCS. (Regular Brewers closer Rollie Fingers, the reigning AL MVP and Cy Young Award winner, had not pitched since September 2 after suffering a torn muscle in his right forearm. Although on the active World Series roster, Fingers was unable to pitch in Game Two after throwing batting practice the previous day because of stiffness caused by inactivity.[11])

With the uncertainty surrounding Fingers' availability and effectiveness as well as a rookie closer, the pundits gave St. Louis the edge with the better bullpen. Would that be the difference? Yes. The first batter Ladd faced, outfielder Lonnie Smith, worked the count to 3-and-2. He thought his sixth pitch hit the outside corner for strike three and many of the 53,723 in Busch Stadium, Kuenn, and even Smith agreed as he headed back to the dugout.[12] But home-plate umpire Bill Haller called it a ball, and the bases were loaded. The call got to Ladd, who said later, "It rattled me. It shouldn't have. I saw Smith heading back to the dugout on that pitch."[13]

Up stepped pinch-hitter Steve Braun, an 11-year veteran used mostly for pinch-hitting with only 17 hits and 4 RBIs in 58 games that season, and playing in his first World Series. "My thought as I came out of the dugout was, 'Hell, I'm in the World Series,'" Braun said. "And then I was thinking how my family was there and I had to get that run in somehow."[14] Ladd walked Braun on four pitches, none close to the strike zone, and the lead run scored. Braun commented, "I'll take the walk."[15] Ladd commented, "I guess I tried to go a little beyond myself on the next hitter."[16] It was the Cardinals' first lead, in the game and the Series.

With his team trailing for the first time in the Series, the Brewers ignitor, Molitor, led off the ninth and reached on a bunt down the first-base line. Kuenn called for a hit-and-run to get him into scoring position but Yount, a good low-ball hitter, swung and missed at a high pitch and Molitor was caught stealing on a perfect throw by Porter. Said Molitor, "I didn't get a real good jump and the pitch he threw Robin was not a good pitch to hit. It was the only high pitch he threw."[17] The play was criticized by many but Detroit Tigers manager Sparky Anderson, working on the national radio broadcast, said, "That's the greatest move [by a manager] so far in the Series, and I don't think there'll be a greater one for the rest of the Series. If Yount gets a pitch he can handle better and puts the ball into right field, Harvey has men at first and third, none out and the ball game is his."[18] That was their last chance and the Cardinals held on, winning 5-4, after Sutter got Yount on a groundball to shortstop and Cooper on a flyball to center. In the battle of the bullpens, the better pen made the difference.

The World Series was tied, each team with one victory and heading to Milwaukee. Asked about splitting the two games, manager Kuenn said, "Of course, we would have liked to have won two, but I'm not worried. We'll just go home and take them one at a time there."[19] Cecil Cooper was asked if the loss was the end of the world and the first baseman, replied, "Oh no. It's just the beginning. This gives our fans a chance to see us three more times."[20]

NOTES

1. Dennis Hannon and Ellen Futterman, "Cardinals Fans Dismiss Brewers' Victory as Mere Nuisance," *St. Louis Post Dispatch*, October 13, 1982: 10B.
2. Bob Broeg, "Winning Game Two a Part Of Cards' Series Tradition," *St. Louis Post Dispatch*, October 14, 1982. The six years they won Game Two were 1926, 1931, 1942, 1943, 1944, and 1946, losing only in 1943 to the New York Yankees. Of the six times they lost Game Two, they won the Series three times.
3. "Game Two Notes," *The Sporting News*, October 25, 1982: 17.
4. "Molitor's Hits Tie a World Series Record," *Milwaukee Journal*, October 14, 1982: Part 3, 2. The other four players were Frank Isbell in 1906, Fred Lindstrom in 1924, Monte Irvin in 1951, and Thurman Munson in 1976.
5. In their biggest trade ever, as of 2019, the Brewers on December 12, 1980, acquired closer Rollie Fingers, starter Pete Vuckovich (both won Cy Young Awards with the Brewers), and catcher Ted Simmons for outfielder Sixto Lezcano, pitcher Lary Sorenson, and minor leaguers David Green and Dave LaPoint, who had part-time roles in St. Louis in 1982.
6. Broeg.
7. Tom Flaherty, "Cards Walk On by the Brewers," *Milwaukee Journal*, October 14, 1982: Part 3, 1.
8. Vic Feuerherd, "Cards Walk by Brewers," *Milwaukee Sentinel*, October 14, 1982: Part 2, 1.
9. Tom Flaherty, "Sutton Stop," *Milwaukee Journal*, October 14, 1982: Part 3, 4.
10. Bob Wolf, "All 'What-Ifs' Point to Fingers, *Milwaukee Journal*, October 14, 1982: Part 3, 1.
11. Vic Feuerherd, "It Wasn't Time to Use Fingers," *Milwaukee Sentinel*, October 14, 1982: Part 2, 4.
12. Feuerherd, "Cards Walk by Brewers."
13. Ibid.
14. Dale Hoffman, "Sorry, Brewers, but Sutter Will Be Sutter," *Milwaukee Sentinel*, October 14, 1982: Part 2, 1.
15. Ibid.
16. Feuerherd, "Cards Walk by Brewers."
17. "Sparky Supports Harvey's Move," *Milwaukee Journal*, October 14, 1982: Part 3, 2.
18. Ibid.
19. Feuerherd, "Cards Walk by Brewers."
20. Flaherty, "Cards Walk On by the Brewers."

WILLIE MCGEE'S TWO HOMERS SINK BREWERS

ST. LOUIS CARDINALS 6, MILWAUKEE BREWERS 2
OCTOBER 15, 1982, AT COUNTY STADIUM

THE WORLD SERIES, GAME THREE

By Stew Thornley

Game Three of the 1982 World Series was the first Series game in Milwaukee since 1958. It was the first World Series for the Milwaukee Brewers, who had entered the league in 1969 as the Seattle Pilots, and the 13th World Series for their opponents, the St. Louis Cardinals.

Milwaukee had a heavy-hitting lineup that had led the majors in runs scored in 1982 and became known as Harvey's Wallbangers, after manager Harvey Kuenn.

Kuenn was a former All-Star who still maintained his crusty look with a chaw of tobacco in his left cheek. He was a tough man who had endured heart-bypass surgery in 1976 and later had a leg amputated because of a blood clot.

Kuenn had been a coach for the Brewers starting in 1971. He managed the club for its final game in 1975 and took over again in early June 1982, succeeding Buck Rodgers with Milwaukee near the bottom of the standings.

The Brewers came back and were tied for first with the Orioles in the AL East as the two teams met in Baltimore in the final game of the regular season. Milwaukee beat the Orioles to take the division title and then, after losing the first two games of the American League Championship Series to the California Angels, won the next three to go to the World Series. Kuenn got a telegram from a sore loser in California, saying he hoped termites would eat his artificial leg.[1]

The World Series opened in St. Louis, and the Brewers took the first game as Paul Molitor set a Series record with five hits.

The Cardinals took Game Two, the winning run forced in on back-to-back walks in the bottom of the eighth. The plate umpire, Bill Haller, took some heat for his tight strike zone, and in Milwaukee fans heckled him and held up anti-Haller signs. Years later, Haller was asked about the guff he received and answered, "I deserved it. It was one of the worst games I ever worked."[2]

A County Stadium record crowd of 56,556 came for the third game. Many were too young to remember the last World Series game in the city, and those of all ages were excited. In the early innings, the fans jumped in anticipation on every batted ball, especially when Molitor opened the last of the first with a long drive to center.

Willie McGee, who had come up to the Cardinals in May and finished third as the National League's Rookie of the Year balloting, drifted back to the fence, waited, leaped, and hauled in the drive, interrupting the enthusiasm of the crowd.

In the top of the second, George Hendrick reached first in a strange way. He hit a chopper that came down behind third base. As Molitor

Aerial view of County Stadium during the 1982 season. The ballpark hosted World Series games for the Milwaukee Braves in 1957 and 1958 and for the Brewers in 1982.

fielded the ball, third-base umpire Jim Evans threw his hands in the air before bringing them down toward fair territory. The signal confused everyone. First-base umpire Dave Phillips, thinking Evans had called the ball foul, put up his arms as Molitor sailed a throw to first. Cecil Cooper stretched for the throw and may have come off the bag.

Evans and Phillips huddled with plate umpire John Kibler and ruled Hendrick safe, bringing Kuenn out of the dugout. After being told that Cooper had been pulled off the base by the throw, Kuenn asked his first baseman if that was true.

Cooper said he didn't know but added, "He said 'foul ball' over there," pointing to Evans. Hendrick, standing on first base, lightened the mood by saying, "It was [my] blazing speed that did it, I tell you."

Kuenn replied, "Hey, George, I know better than that."[3]

The official scoring panel credited Hendrick with a single, which was the only St. Louis hit until the fifth, when Lonnie Smith doubled.[4] After Dane Iorg reached on an error, McGee homered to right to give St. Louis a 3-0 lead.

The Cardinals added another run in the seventh when McGee came up again, this time with a man on third. He dealt with some chin music from Pete Vuckovich but hung in and hit the next pitch over the fence in right to make the score 5-0.

McGee, who hit only four home runs during the regular season, had upped his postseason total to three. He had homered during the National League Championship Series and also had a triple that could have been an inside-the-park home run had he been watching third-base coach Chuck Hiller and seen Hiller waving him home.

On the mound, the Cardinals' Joaquin Andujar was cruising. He had given up only two hits and a walk entering the last of the seventh. With one out Ted Simmons hit a hard one-hopper that smashed into Andujar's right knee. The pitcher fell to the ground in pain and had to be carried off the field.

The injury didn't affect the outcome of this game but may have had an impact on subsequent games. Jim Kaat relieved and got an out before giving up a single. Doug Bair came in and walked pinch-hitter Don Money. This caused St. Louis manager Whitey Herzog to call for fireman Bruce Sutter, who had also entered the previous game in the seventh inning.

Sutter got the final out of the inning but in the eighth gave up a two-run homer to Cooper.

St. Louis added a run for a 6-2 lead in the top of the ninth, but in the bottom of the inning Ben Oglivie led off by reaching base on an error. Gorman Thomas then sent a fly to deep center. McGee raced back, jumped, and made a backhanded catch, probably robbing Thomas of a two-run homer.

Willie McGee, the sensational rookie, had done it all – leaping catches in the first and last innings and two home runs in between – to put the Cardinals back in front in the World Series, two games to one. McGee didn't go long again, but by the time the Series was over, he had hit more home runs in the postseason than the rest of his teammates combined.

NOTES

1. "Game 3 Notes," *The Sporting News*, October 25, 1982, 19.
2. Haller made his comments while speaking at the convention of the Society for American Baseball Research in St. Louis on July 28, 2007. He also said, "You should never read the paper when you're in the crapper," although it wasn't clear what point he was trying to make with this observation.
3. 1982 Milwaukee-St. Louis World Series highlights, produced by Major League Baseball Properties, Inc.
4. The official scorers were Jack Herman of the *St. Louis Globe-Democrat*, Dave Nightingale of *The Sporting News*, and Dick Young of the *New York Post*. Sources: *The Sporting News Official Baseball Guide*, 1983, and Bill Shannon, *Official Scoring in the Big Leagues: A Primer for Baseball Fans* (New York: Sports Museum Press, 2005), 40.

HARVEY'S WALLBANGERS EXPLODE

MILWAUKEE BREWERS 7, ST. LOUIS CARDINALS 5
OCTOBER 16, 1982, AT COUNTY STADIUM

THE WORLD SERIES, GAME FOUR

By Stew Thornley

Gorman Thomas was a slugging star for the Milwaukee Brewers in 1982. He led the Brewers with 39 homers and drove in 112 runs. However, in the postseason, Gorman was no longer Stormin'. He had only 2 hits in 11 at-bats (along with two walks) in the first three games of the World Series. In the League Championship Series, he had been even worse — one hit in 15 at-bats in addition to two walks. His struggles extended back to the final week and a half of the regular season. Since September 21, Thomas had only 7 hits in 67 at-bats and had driven in only 7 runs in 20 games.

The heat was on, and Thomas was hearing the displeasure of the fans as the Brewers, trailing in the World Series two games to one to the St. Louis Cardinals, took the field for Game Four. The Cardinals scored a run in the first and padded the lead the next inning. With Willie McGee on third and Ozzie Smith on second with one out, Tom Herr sent Thomas back with a long fly to center. Thomas backpedaled and caught the ball, as his momentum carried him back to the warning track. As he planted to throw, his gimpy right knee went out from under him, and he fell to the ground. McGee had tagged at third and was scoring easily. From second, Smith took off and ran hard. He gave a glance back and then picked up his third-base coach, Chuck Hiller, who was waving him home. Smith never slowed and slid home ahead of Robin Yount's relay. The two-run sacrifice fly gave St. Louis a 3-0 lead.

In the fourth the Brewers put two on with one out when Thomas came up. He fouled out to catcher Darrell Porter, and Milwaukee came up empty in the inning.

The Brewers trailed 5-1 when Thomas came up to start the bottom of the seventh. Another foul out to Porter brought him more serenading (and not the good kind). However, Thomas would get another chance — in the same inning.

Milwaukee was only eight outs away from falling behind by two games in the Series. Ben Oglivie hit a grounder to first that took a high hop. Keith Hernandez leaped to bring it in and flipped to pitcher Dave LaPoint covering. LaPoint dropped the ball. Don Money singled, but LaPoint got Charlie Moore to pop out. The final out of the inning, though, took a long time. Jim Gantner doubled to score Oglivie and finish the day for LaPoint. As Whitey Herzog went to the mound, the fans derisively chanted, "We Want Sutter!" Bruce Sutter was the Cardinals' relief ace; however, the night before he was tagged for two runs in 2⅓ innings. It was the second game in a row that Herzog had called on Sutter in the seventh inning, and the skipper said he wanted to wait until at least two out in the eighth before using him again.[1]

So instead, Doug Bair relieved and walked Paul Molitor to load the bases. Bair came in with a high pitch to Robin Yount, who tried to hold up on his swing. Yount was unsuccessful but liked the result. The ball shot off his bat into right field, bringing in two runs and sending Molitor to third. Jim Kaat was next to the mound. Cecil Cooper hit a hard shot off the glove of third baseman Ken Oberkfell for a single as Molitor scored the tying run. Ted Simmons was up when Kaat delivered a wild pitch, advancing the runners to second and third. With the count now 2-and-1 on Simmons, Herzog brought in Jeff Lahti and had him complete an intentional walk to Simmons (with the walk charged to Kaat).

The Brewers had batted around, and the next hitter was Thomas. Regardless of his recent struggles and whatever lack of confidence the fans had in him, Thomas drilled a single to left-center to score Yount and Cooper. Six runs in the inning — all unearned to the team — put Milwaukee ahead 7-5.

St. Louis made one last run at catching up, putting runners at first and third with one out in the eighth. But Bob McClure relieved starter Jim Slaton, got Willie McGee to ground into an inning-ending double play, and then retired the side in order in the ninth.

The Brewers had evened the World Series.

NOTES

1 Rick Hummel. "Error Opens Floodgates, Birds Drown, 7-5," *St. Louis Post-Dispatch*, October 17, 1982, 1.

ROBIN YOUNT COLLECTS FOUR HITS, MIKE CALDWELL NOTCHES SECOND VICTORY AS BREWERS WIN TO TAKE 3-2 ADVANTAGE IN WORLD SERIES

MILWAUKEE BREWERS 6, ST. LOUIS CARDINALS 4
OCTOBER 17, 1982, AT COUNTY STADIUM

THE WORLD SERIES, GAME FIVE

By Stew Thornley

Throughout the three World Series games in Milwaukee in 1982, the fans chanted "MVP!" for the Brewers' shortstop, Robin Yount, who was awarded the American League Most Valuable Player after the season. The chants increased in intensity in Game Five and became even more robust each time Yount came to the plate.

Yount had four hits in the Series opener, a 10-0 win at St. Louis, although he was overshadowed by teammate Paul Molitor's five hits.

The winning pitcher in Game One was Mike Caldwell, who shut down the Cardinals with a three-hitter. Caldwell was back on the mound in Game Five, and he came out on top again although it was more the result of Yount's performance with the bat and his fielders' work with their gloves.

Yount singled in the first inning and came around to score the first run of the game. St. Louis tied the game in the third, but in the bottom of the inning Yount doubled to move Molitor to third. Molitor came home on an infield out to put the Brewers on top again. In the fifth Milwaukee added another run, and Yount came up with another hit.

St. Louis scored to close to within a run in the seventh, but Yount soon got the cushion back with his fourth hit, this one a home run to right off St. Louis starter Bob Forsch. As he rounded the bases the "MVP!" chants reached a crescendo. Yount became the first player to get four hits in a game twice in the same World Series.

Milwaukee held the lead through most of the game, and Caldwell got his second win of the Series despite allowing 14 hits in 8⅓ innings. He was able to space the hits enough to keep mostly goose eggs on the scoreboard, but he needed some slick fielding to help him out:

- With one out in the top of the first, Lonnie Smith tried stealing third, but Ted Simmons's throw was in a perfect spot for Molitor to put the tag on Smith.
- With two out in the top of the third and Keith Hernandez on second with the potential go-ahead run, second baseman Jim Gantner dove to his right to prevent George Hendrick's sharp grounder from getting through. Although Hendrick reached first with a single on the play, Gantner's effort kept Hernandez from scoring.
- With the Cardinals down 2-1 in the fourth, they had Ken Oberkfell on second and Tom Herr on first. On a chopper hit by Ozzie Smith, Molitor leapt, corralled the ball, stepped on third to force Oberkfell, and threw to a stretched-out Cooper at first to complete the inning-ending double play.

THE 1982 MILWAUKEE BREWERS

Robin Yount became the first player in World Series history to collect at least four hits in a game twice in the same series, accomplishing the feat in Game One and Game Five.

- After giving Bruce Sutter a day off for a much-needed rest, St. Louis manager Whitey Herzog brought in his fireman in the bottom of the eighth even though the Cardinals were down 4-2. Sutter was even less effective than in his last outing — when he gave up two runs in 2⅓ innings in Game Three — and the Brewers pushed their lead to 6-2. They needed the insurance runs because Caldwell gave up three hits, bringing his total for the game to 14, in the ninth. With one out, Bob McClure came in to protect the lead for the second day in a row. He gave up a single to put the tying run on base but got the final two batters to finish a 6-4 win and put Milwaukee ahead three games to two as the World Series shifted back to St. Louis.

As had happened after the Brewers' win the day before, people took to the street in downtown Milwaukee to celebrate — or just to drink and be rowdy. The Milwaukee Sentinel estimated the crowd after Game Five at 20,000 and reported, "As the night wore on, the crowd grew more intoxicated and police reported 10 fist fights and a [sic] unspecified number of arrests. Besides the fistfights, some in the crowd broke beer bottles and limbs from saplings along Wisconsin Ave."[1]

Back at the ballpark, fans swarmed the field, despite a scoreboard message reminding them that left fielder Ben Oglivie had been injured because of fans storming the field in the postgame celebration a week before when the Brewers won the American League Championship Series.

The fans got all they could in this celebration — a good thing because it was the final postseason game ever played at County Stadium and, through 2019, the last game won by the Brewers in the World Series.

- Charlie Moore dove and made a diving backhanded catch in right-center to rob Lonnie Smith of an extra-base hit to start the fifth.
- In the seventh the Cardinals already had a run across, cutting the Brewers' lead to 3-2, and had runners on first and second with two out. Darrell Porter hit a bouncer toward the hole on the right side. Cooper sprawled to snag the ball and, from the ground, threw to Caldwell covering first to end the inning.

NOTES

1 "Some Incidents Mar Downtown Victory Parade," *Milwaukee Sentinel*, October 18, 1982.

STUPER WAS STUPEFYING IN COMPLETE-GAME WIN TO FORCE GAME SEVEN

ST. LOUIS CARDINALS 13, MILWAUKEE BREWERS 1
OCTOBER 19, 1982, AT BUSCH STADIUM, ST. LOUIS

THE WORLD SERIES, GAME SIX

By Gregory H. Wolf

Described as a "dazzling performance," by sportswriter Joseph Durso, St. Louis Cardinals rookie John Stuper overcame two rain delays to toss a complete-game four-hitter, beat the Milwaukee Brewers, 13-1, and force Game Seven of the World Series.[1] "For him to pitch nine innings was one of the most impressive performances I've ever see under the circumstances," quipped veteran Jim Kaat about his teammate.[2] "Considering the circumstances and the importance of it," admitted the hurler himself, "this is the best game of my life."[3]

After losing the last two games to the Brewers on the road, skipper Whitey Herzog's Redbirds returned to the Gateway City in a do-or-die situation. He called on Stuper for another youth-vs.-age matchup against 258-game winner Don Sutton and a rematch of Game Two starters. The Cardinals won that game, 5-4, though neither hurler looked good with Stuper yielding four runs in four innings and Sutton the same in six frames. Acquired in 1979 in a trade with the Pittsburgh Pirates, Stuper had been a long-shot project. "When we got him, he was a strong well-conditioned kid but was throwing down from the side," said pitching coach Hub Kittle. "Gradually we changed his mechanics, and when he came over the top, the ball began to jump."[4] Stuper moved through the Cardinals farm system, struggled in his first taste of Triple-A ball in 1981, posting a 6-14 record and 4.92 ERA with the Springfield (Illinois) Cardinals. A 7-1 slate, including five complete games in eight starts, and a 1.46 ERA with Louisville in 1982 earned the 25-year-old western Pennsylvanian a promotion to the big stage in late May. He proved his mettle, going 9-7 (with a robust 3.36 ERA) and logging 136⅔ innings. Sutton, a trading-deadline acquisition from the Houston Astros, gave manager Harvey Kuenn's Brew Crew a psychological boost for the September stretch run and bolstered the staff, winning four times, including the AL East Division Series winner in the last game of the season.

Busch Stadium was packed with 53,723 fervent, red-clad Cardinals fans on a Thursday night, despite persistent dark skies and an ominous weather forecast including a tornado alert. Temperatures dropped more than 20 degrees, into the 40s, during the contest.

After both hurlers breezed through the first, Stuper looked shaky in the second. He surrendered a leadoff walk, then a single, but an inning-ending double play ended the threat. "During the first two innings," said Stuper, "I was more nervous than I've ever been in my entire life."[5] Another leadoff single and inning-ending twin killing defined the third, then Stuper went on a tear. "I was throwing strikes and getting ahead of batters," he said. "That's the name of the game."[6] With an array of fastballs, curves, and sliders, he held the Brewers hitless in the fourth through eighth innings and endured 2 hours and 39 minutes of rain delays while the Cardinals clubbed the Brewers into submission.

The thunder and lightning provided by Mother Nature to begin the second was duplicated by the Redbirds bats. Dane Iorg basted a double deep left field that caromed off Ben Oglivie's glove with two outs. Then "the impossible happened," lamented sportswriter Tom Flaherty of the *Milwaukee Sentinel*.[7] Shortstop Robin Yount let Willie McGee's routine grounder roll between his legs and Iorg scored. Tom Herr followed with a double off the right-field wall; Charlie Moore rifled a strike to catcher Ted Simmons, who should have erased a sliding McGee, but "tried to make the tag before he had the ball," noted the *Sentinel*'s Vic Feuerherd.[8] "We got a little disoriented with the errors early on," said Simmons.[9] The Brewers committed four errors in the game, two each by the "surest hands" on the team, noted Flaherty, Yount and second baseman Jim Gantner.[10]

After Lonnie Smith was thrown out trying to steal home on a bang-bang play to end the third (television replays suggested he was safe and Feuerherd opined that home-plate umpire Jim Evans missed the call),[11] the Cardinals tacked on three in the fourth. George Hendrick led off with a single and moved up a station on Sutton's balk. Herzog complained about Sutton's hesitation in his windup in Game Two and claimed, "He's been balking for years and getting away with it."[12] Darrell Porter made it 4-0 by walloping a round-tripper to deep right field. It was the first Redbird home run in the postseason by someone other than McGee (who had three); the Cardinals hit a big-league low 67 homers in the regular season, but did their best impression of Harvey's Wallbangers, the Brewers moniker owing to their major-league-high 216 homers. Iorg followed with a triple and scored the fifth run on Herr's perfectly placed squeeze bunt to the pitcher.

A misty downpour began as the Cardinals came to bat in the fifth. Lonnie Smith, who had injured the ring finger on his left hand in his attempted steal of home, led off with a single, and scored on Keith Hernandez's home run, his first in 32 games, to give the Cardinals a 7-0 lead and send Sutton to the showers. "I had good stuff," said the 17-year veteran, who eventually won 324 games, "but bad location."[13] Jim Slaton retired the only two batters he faced, sandwiched around a 26-minute rain delay.

The sixth was one of the longest innings in postseason history. Iorg led off with a double[14] off reliever Doc Medich, acquired from the Texas Rangers in August. Medich, a 10-year veteran, who had won 124 games, was forced to take one for the team, and it was brutal. He uncorked a wild pitch, then McGee's single plated Iorg. Torrential rains interrupted the game for 2 hours and 13 minutes. Once the cold front passed through and the temperature plummeted, the grounds crew frantically dried the turf, aided by a fleet of Zambonis. The real-life orthopedic surgeon Medich went back to the mound, and by the time the inning was over, he had yielded five hits and six runs (four earned), five hits, walked one, and tossed two wild pitches in what proved to be the last outing of his career. Hernandez laced a bases-loaded two-out single to drive in two runs, Hendrick followed with an RBI single, and another scored when Gantner muffed Porter's grounder.

Stuper kept loose during the second rain delay, unsure how long it would last. Trainer Gene Gieselmann applied heat packs to his right arm and eventually gave him at least three rubdowns. As Stuper began to warm up to take the mound for the first time in more than 2½ hours, Herzog also sent 43-year-old Kaat, who had made 62 appearances, to join him in the pen. According to Redbirds beat writer Rick Hummel of the *St. Louis Post-Dispatch*, Herzog claimed he would not have sent Stuper back out to finish the game after the second delay; however, the right-hander was working on a shut-out and "has all winter to sleep," quipped the old-school pilot.[15]

Admittedly "pumped up," Stuper breezed through the seventh and eighth.[16] The only blip was third baseman Ken Oberkfell's throwing error on Gorman Thomas's single in the eighth. "I wasn't throwing with great velocity but my ball was moving well," offered Stuper.[17]

After scoreless frames by Medich and Dwight Bernard, Stuper faced the Brewers in the ninth as the clock struck midnight and the game rolled over into Friday morning. He yielded his first hits in 5⅔ innings when Gantner and Paul Molitor led off with a double and single, respectively, and then a wild pitch scored Gantner. Stuper worked around a two-out walk to Ned Yost, and the ended the game at 12:21 A.M., exactly five hours after it had started, (though only 2 hours and 21 minutes officially) by retiring Oglivie on a fly ball to center, forcing a dramatic Game Seven.

"I made some good pitches tonight," said Stuper, who became the first Cardinals pitcher to toss a complete game in a World Series since Bob Gibson lost to Mickey Lolich, 4-1, in Game Seven of the 1968 fall classic. "The way I've been pitching all year is hard stuff — down — and hoping they hit it on the ground."[18] He finished with a four-hitter, struck out two and walked two, and threw 104 pitches, 66 of which were strikes.

Stupor's inspiring performance led to the winner-take-all game the next day. The Cardinals overcame a 3-1 deficit in the sixth by scoring five unanswered runs to capture their first title since 1967.

In 1983 Stuper went 12-11 with a 3.68 ERA in 198 innings, but suffered a series of arm injuries. He was out of baseball two years later, finishing with a 32-28 slate.

SOURCES

In addition to the sources cited in the Notes, the author also accessed Retrosheet.org, Baseball-Reference.com, Newspapers.com, and SABR.org.

NOTES

1. Joseph Durso, "Cardinals Defeat Brewers, 13-1, to Force 7th Game," *New York Times*, October 20, 1982: A1.
2. Rick Hummel, "Cards on Brink of World Series Title," *St. Louis Post-Dispatch*, October 20, 1982: 1.
3. Dave Anderson, "Stuper Calls Game 'Best' Performance," *New York Times*, October 20, 1982: B12.
4. Kevin Horrigan, "Stupendous: Rookie Puts Cards in Game 7," *St. Louis Post-Dispatch*, October 20, 1982: 7.
5. Ibid.
6. Arnold Irish, "Stuper's Effort Was Show-Stopper," *St. Louis Post-Dispatch*, October 20, 1982: 1C.
7. Tom Flaherty, "Stupor Puts the Brewers Bats in a Stupor," *Milwaukee Sentinel*, October 20, 1982: II, 1.
8. Vic Feuerherd, "Cards Swamp Brewers, 13-1," *Milwaukee Sentinel*, October 20, 1982: II, 1.
9. Hummel.
10. Flaherty.
11. See Feuerherd; Durso.
12. Durso.
13. Bob Wolf, "Sutton's Poor Location Leaves the Brewers Lost," *Milwaukee Sentinel*, October 20, 1982: II, 1.
14. Iorg's blow marked the first time a DH had collected three extra-base hits in a World Series game.
15. Hummel.
16. Anderson.
17. Ibid.
18. Tony Moton, "Cardinals Float to Seventh Game," *Dispatch* (Moline, Illinois), October 20, 1982: 33.

CARDINALS CAPTURE NINTH WORLD SERIES CHAMPIONSHIP

ST. LOUIS CARDINALS 6, MILWAUKEE BREWERS 3

OCTOBER 20, 1982, AT BUSCH STADIUM, ST. LOUIS

THE WORLD SERIES, GAME SEVEN

By Joseph Wancha

You hear the phrase "On paper, they are the best team in the league" all the time in professional and collegiate sports. Of course, the ready-made answer to that statement is that the outcomes of games or contests are not decided on paper.

This may have applied to the St. Louis Cardinals and the Milwaukee Brewers, who were the combatants in the 1982 World Series. The matchup might have looked like a mismatch to some who believed Milwaukee had the statistical advantage.

The Cardinals had only one batter who exceeded 100 RBIs in 1982 (George Hendrick, 104); only one who batted over .300 (Lonnie Smith, .307; Keith Hernandez was close at .299); and no player hit more than 20 home runs; Hendrick was top man with 19. Their offense was built on speed. Smith stole 68 bases and led the league in runs with 120. Tom Herr and Ozzie Smith each stole 25 bases and Willie McGee was right behind them with 24.

The St. Louis pitching staff was led by Joaquin Andujar (15-10, 2.47 ERA) and Bob Forsch (15-9, 3.48). Bruce Sutter led the National League with 36 saves.

By contrast, the Milwaukee Brewers were given the name Harvey's Wallbangers for both their hitting prowess and in a nod of respect to their manager, Harvey Kuenn. The Brew Crew had three players who swatted over 30 home runs and knocked in over 100 runs: Gorman Thomas (39 HRs, 112 RBIs), Ben Oglivie (34 HRs, 102 RBIs), and Cecil Cooper (32 HRs, 121 RBIs). Robin Yount just missed joining the trio as he belted 29 homers and drove in 114 runs. And the Brewers were not neophytes in the running game: Paul Molitor swiped 41 bases and led the league with 136 runs scored.

Milwaukee's pitching staff was anchored by right-hander Pete Vuckovich (18-6, 3.34 ERA), who after the season was voted the winner of the American League Cy Young Award. Mike Caldwell, a southpaw, also had a good year (17-13, 3.91 ERA).

Nicknamed the Suds Series because both cities were prominent in the brewing industry, the King of Beers (Budweiser) was going keg-to-keg with the Champagne of Bottled Beers (Miller). Fans in both metropolises "hopped" with excitement and could "barley" contain themselves. Especially fans in the Dairy State, whose Brewers were making their debut in the fall classic. Why, they could hardly "camembert." Yes, now that the Series was here, it was going to be a "gouda" day.

Milwaukee held a 3-2 advantage in the Series on the strength of two-run victories in Games Four and Five at County Stadium. Both teams returned to Busch Stadium for Game Six (and Game Seven if necessary). The Brewers were hoping to finish off the Cardinals while St. Louis was looking for some "home cooking" to extend the series to Game Seven.

In Game Six, the Cards blitzed their guests with a six-run sixth inning (which was also interrupted by a 2:13 rain delay). St. Louis was leading 7-0 at the time and went on to win 13-1 and force Game Seven.

The pitching matchup was a rematch of Game Three, with Andujar opposing Vuckovich. Andujar was the 6-2 winner in that game, as Sutter picked up his first save. Vuckovich surrendered six runs, four earned and the Brewers made three errors.

Busch Stadium was rollicking to a fever pitch for Game Seven, with a sold-out crowd of 53,723 disguised in a sea of cardinal red. St. Louis scored first, in the bottom of the fourth inning. McGee led off with a single and moved to third base when Herr singled to right field. After Ozzie Smith popped out, Lonnie Smith beat out a grounder to shortstop and McGee scored. St. Louis did not enjoy the advantage for long; Oglivie homered to right field leading off the fifth.

Milwaukee took the lead in the top of the sixth inning. Jim Gantner led off with a double to right-center field. He moved to third when Molitor laid down a bunt to the pitcher. Andujar's throw to first hit Molitor in the back and got past Herr, who was covering first base. Gantner scored and Molitor went to second base. Yount followed with a single to the right side of the infield to put runners at the corners, and Cooper's fly ball scored Molitor.

The Cardinals came right back in the bottom of the frame. With one out, Ozzie Smith singled to left field and Lonnie Smith doubled him to third. Bob McClure relieved Vuckovich. The chess match began as St. Louis skipper Whitey Herzog sent up right-handed-hitting Gene Tenace to hit for Ken Oberkfell against the lefty McClure. Tenace walked and Mike Ramsey ran for him. Hernandez took his place in the batter's box. "When I went up, it was in my mind to get a hit," said Hernandez. "I knew a sacrifice fly would only get one run home and leave us one run behind."[1] McClure who was a grade-school teammate of Hernandez in the San Francisco area, was looking for two outs, never mind just one. "I was looking for a double play," said McClure. "It didn't work out that way."[2]

Indeed. Hernandez singled to right-center to drive in two runs and tie the game, 3-3. Then Hendrick singled home Ramsey with the go-ahead run. The Cardinals led, 4-3. "I pride myself on being an RBI man," said Hernandez. "I'd better be if I'm hitting third."[3]

Andujar whiffed Thomas to lead off the seventh inning. It was his only strikeout of the game. He gave up a scratch single to Charlie Moore, but it did no damage. Sutter relieved Andujar in the top of the eighth and set the Brewers down in order. "Once (Andujar) got us to the seventh inning, we've got the best reliever in baseball," said Herzog. "We pay him an awful big amount of money. I figured we better use him."[4]

St. Louis add two insurance runs in the bottom of eighth inning. Lonnie Smith led off with a ground-rule double to right field. Ramsey struck out on a foul bunt. Hernandez walked, and Caldwell relieved Moose Haas. Darrell Porter followed with a single to right field to score Smith and send Hernandez to third base. Steve Braun's single to center scored Hernandez and the Cardinals led 6-3.

That was the final score: Sutter set Milwaukee down 1-2-3 in the ninth. Hundreds of fans stormed the field after the final out, as the scoreboard flashed "We Win." It was the ninth World Series championship in the storied history of the St. Louis Cardinals. Darrell Porter, who was the Most Valuable Player of the ALCS, was also named the Series' MVP. He was 8-for-28 with two doubles, one home run, and 5 RBIs. He threw out two of three would-be basestealers. Jim Kaat, in his 24th season, was a World Series champion for the first time.

"We just got beat by a better team," said Vuckovich." They deserve anything they got — and they got a ring from the World Series tonight. I felt like I let down my teammates, all Milwaukee. But tomorrow's another day and next year's another year."[5]

SOURCES

In addition to the sources mentioned in the Notes, the author consulted Baseball-Reference.com and Retrosheet.org.

NOTES

1 Kevin Horrigan, "Hernandez: Clutch Base Hits Came in Bunches," *St. Louis Post-Dispatch*, October 21, 1982: 3B.

2 Ed Wilks, "McClure: A Boyhood Pal of Hernandez," *St. Louis Post-Dispatch*, October 21, 1982: 3B.

3 Horrigan.

4 Rick Hummel, "Triumph … Sutter Puts on the Finishing Touches," *St. Louis Post Dispatch*, October 21, 1982: 1A.

5 Neal Russo, "Brewers Credit the Cardinals, and Vuckovich Takes the Blame," *St. Louis Post-Dispatch*, October 21, 1982: 7B.

THE PARADE

By Rick Schabowski

A person not knowing the final score and watching the homecoming reception for the Brewers after Game Seven of the 1982 World Series against the St. Louis Cardinals would have bet money that the Brewers had won. Despite the loss, Brewers fans gave the team a heroes' welcome when they returned to Milwaukee.

A crowd estimated at 100,000 filled both sides of Wisconsin Avenue from North Cass Street to 10th Street as their motorcade, with the players riding in vintage convertibles provided by local car dealer Wally Rank, was showered by confetti and greeted with loud cheers.

Brewers pitcher Jim Slaton recalled how he felt the day after the Brewers lost Game Seven. "I remember how down I was. My first feeling was that I didn't want to go. I think everybody was mentally drained. But to see the way the fans reacted around town was very gratifying and uplifting. I've been in a lot of places, just about every baseball town, and I can't think of any place better than Milwaukee was."[1]

Robin Yount shared Slaton's emotions. "I was still so mad that morning knowing we had to go to the ballpark and go through this parade. I really didn't want to do that. … But it ended up being a great thing."[2]

Brewers manager Harvey Kuenn commented about the huge turnout, "It's like my wife (Audrey) said on the ride to the park through that crowd on Wisconsin Avenue. She told me it was like we didn't lose, and that's the way I feel. We might have lost the game, but we were not losers."[3]

Team owner Bud Selig's thoughts were about the loyal Brewers fans: "I guess when I woke up this morning, I was the only disappointed man in town, and I have to qualify what I mean by disappointed. We had such a storybook year, there's no question about that. But through the last three innings of last night's game, I kept thinking about the fans here. I know how bad I felt, so I know how bad they must have felt. But when the car was stopped during the parade, a man came up to me and said, 'You just can't imagine the joy you have brought to this town.' And he's right. We did something for this city, and I can't explain how remarkable it is. It's just wonderful."

After the parade, the motorcade moved off Wisconsin Avenue and took I-94 westbound for County Stadium for a rally there. While in transit, semi-truck drivers acknowledged the team by sounding their horns, and some cars pulled onto the shoulder to watch.

Fifteen thousand fans were awaiting the Brewers at Milwaukee County Stadium for a rally that began at about 1:20 P.M. The only sour note came when the car carrying Dwight Bernard and Jerry

Augustine broke down on the right-field warning track and needed a tow.

All of the players rode in the vintage cars, but Robin Yount had another idea. When he arrived at County Stadium, he left the car he was riding in, ran to the dugout and toward the clubhouse. Yount talked about his means of transportation for his trip inside the stadium. "I rode this dirt bike through the streets of Milwaukee. It didn't even have license plates," he said. "I didn't care if I got pulled over. It just didn't matter. Nothing mattered at that time. I was kind of being a rebel or whatever. That motorcycle wasn't even street legal, but for whatever reason I had it in Milwaukee all year. It was just a dirt bike. It just happened out of the clear blue. It wasn't planned. It ended up being something that everybody remembered."[5]

Brewers owner Selig was surprised and concerned about Yount's motorcycle ride. "I almost died," Selig exclaimed. "Here comes this figure racing around like a madman, and it's Robin. I can still remember Vuckovich and Simmons saying, 'Don't worry. Your kid will be all right.' I'm up there ready to faint, but the crowd went wild. Nobody knew he was going to do it."[6]

Charlie Moore summed up his feelings about the great homecoming: "The whole thing was simply unbelievable. It helps take the sting out of the Series."[7]

Paul Molitor expressed the emotional roller-coaster of the last 24 hours. "Last night I said I was sorry because we weren't able to bring back a world championship for you, but today, you've paid us all back."[8]

NOTES

1. Tom Haudricourt, *Brewers Essentials: Everything You Need to Know to Be a Real Fan* (Chicago: Triumph Books, 2008), 62.
2. Haudricourt, 63.
3. Vic Feuerherd, "Cheers! Fans Let Brewers Know That Losing Series 'Doesn't Matter,'" *Milwaukee Sentinel*, October 22, 1982: 2-1.
4. Feuerherd: 2-8.
5. Haudricourt, 62.
6. Haudricourt, 64.
7. Feuerherd: 2-1.
8. Ibid.

BY THE NUMBERS
1982 MILWAUKEE BREWERS

By Dan Fields

REGULAR SEASON

1ST

Shortstop to lead the AL in slugging percentage: Robin Yount. His .578 mark led all major leaguers in 1982 and remained a Brewers single-season record until 1995.

2ND

Consecutive year in which both the AL MVP Award and Cy Young Award went to the Brewers. In 1982 Robin Yount was the MVP and Pete Vuckovich was the Cy Young winner. In 1981 Rollie Fingers won both awards.

2.67

Ratio of strikeouts to walks by Moose Haas, third highest in the AL.

3

Home runs by Paul Molitor on May 12 and Ben Oglivie on June 20.

3

Doubles by Don Money on May 15.

3

Consecutive home runs by Cecil Cooper, Don Money, and Gorman Thomas on May 28; by Robin Yount, Cecil Cooper, and Ben Oglivie on June 5; and by Cecil Cooper, Ted Simmons, and Ben Oglivie on September 12.

3

Shutouts by Mike Caldwell, tied for fourth in the AL.

3

Players with at least 30 home runs: Gorman Thomas (39, tied with Reggie Jackson of the California Angels for most in the majors), Ben Oglivie (34), and Cecil Cooper (32). Robin Yount just missed, with 29 home runs.

THE 1982 MILWAUKEE BREWERS

3

Players with at least 200 hits and 100 runs: Robin Yount (210 hits, most in the majors, and 129 runs), Cecil Cooper (205 hits and 104 runs), and Paul Molitor (201 hits and 136 runs, most in the majors). They were the only players in the AL with at least 200 hits. Molitor's run total was the most in the AL since 1949 and remains a Brewers single-season record through 2018.

3RD

Consecutive year in which Cecil Cooper won a Silver Slugger Award as first baseman with the Brewers.

3.34

ERA of Pete Vuckovich, tied for sixth lowest in the AL.

3.98

ERA of the 1982 Brewers, sixth lowest in the AL.

4

Runs scored by Charlie Moore on April 9, Robin Yount on June 13, Paul Molitor on September 17, and Robin Yount on October 3.

4

Walks drawn by Paul Molitor on April 9 and Gorman Thomas on September 14.

4

Home runs allowed by Mike Caldwell in the second game of a doubleheader on October 1.

4

Players with at least 100 RBIs: Cecil Cooper (121, second most in the majors), Robin Yount (114), Gorman Thomas (112), and Ben Oglivie (102). Ted Simmons was close behind, with 97.

4

Future Hall of Famers who played for the 1982 Brewers: Rollie Fingers, Paul Molitor, Don Sutton, and Robin Yount.

5

Home runs by the Brewers on June 5 and June 13.

5

Hits in five at-bats by Robin Yount on July 2. He had a double and four singles.

6

RBIs by Ted Simmons on May 2, Gorman Thomas on August 26, and Robin Yount on September 24.

6

Double plays turned by right fielder Charlie Moore, the most by any AL outfielder.

8

Consecutive games won by the Brewers from July 9 through July 18.

9

Consecutive games with an RBI by Cecil Cooper from June 21 through June 30.

11

Innings pitched by Pete Vuckovich on July 29 and September 20.

12

Earned runs allowed in five innings by Jerry Augustine on May 11. He gave up 15 hits and two walks.

12

Triples by Robin Yount, third most in the majors.

12

Complete games by Mike Caldwell, tied for fifth in the AL.

14-0

Score by which the Brewers beat the New York Yankees on September 17. Two days later, they beat the Yankees 14-1; the Brewers scored nine runs in the eighth inning.

15

Runs scored by the Brewers on April 9 and September 24.

17

Runs allowed on May 11 by the Brewers, who scored only three runs against the Kansas City Royals.

18

Wins by Pete Vuckovich, tied for second most in the AL. Mike Caldwell, with 17 wins, was tied for fifth most.

20-7

Record of the Brewers in June.

29

Saves by Rollie Fingers, third most in the AL.

32

Errors (29 as third baseman and 3 as shortstop) by Paul Molitor, most in the AL.

41

Stolen bases by Paul Molitor, fourth most in the AL.

45⅓

Consecutive innings without issuing a walk by Moose Haas from April 16 to May 15.

46

Doubles by Robin Yount, tied for most in the majors. Cecil Cooper had 38 doubles, tied for sixth in the AL.

48

Double plays turned as third baseman by Paul Molitor, most in the majors.

72-43

Record as manager in 1982 by Harvey Kuenn, who replaced Buck Rodgers on June 2, when the Brewers had a record of 23-24.

THE 1982 MILWAUKEE BREWERS

87

Extra-base hits by Robin Yount, most in the majors in 1982 and a mark that was not equaled by a Brewers player until 2007 by Prince Fielder. Cecil Cooper had 73 extra-base hits in 1982 (fifth in the majors), and Gorman Thomas had 69 (tied for sixth).

102

Walks issued by Pete Vuckovich, second most in the AL.

143

Strikeouts by Gorman Thomas, second most in the AL.

185

Double plays turned by the 1982 Brewers, most in the AL.

216

Home runs by the Brewers, most in the majors in 1982 and a Brewers single-season record until 2007.

258

Innings pitched by Mike Caldwell, fourth most in the AL.

277

Doubles by the Brewers in 1982, second most in the majors.

.279

Batting average of the Brewers in 1982, second highest in the majors.

300TH

Career save by Rollie Fingers, on August 21. He was the first major leaguer to reach this mark.

.331

Batting average of Robin Yount, tied for second highest in the majors. Cecil Cooper had a .313 average, fifth highest in the AL.

367

Total bases by Robin Yount, most in the majors in 1982 and a Brewers single-season record through 2018. Cecil Cooper had 345 total bases in 1982, the second most in the majors.

.455

Slugging percentage of the Brewers, highest in the majors in 1982 and a Brewers single-season record until 2007.

489

Assists by Robin Yount, most in the AL. He was the Gold Glove winner among AL shortstops.

666

At-bats by Paul Molitor, most in the majors in 1982 and a Brewers single-season record through 2018. Cecil Cooper had 654 at-bats in 1982, second most in the AL.

714

Strikeouts by Milwaukee batters in 1982, second lowest in the majors.

.750

Winning percentage of Pete Vuckovich, tied for best in the AL.

751

Plate appearances by Paul Molitor, most in the majors in 1982 and a Brewers single-season record until 1991.

.789

OPS of the Brewers in 1982, highest in the majors.

891

Runs scored by the Brewers, most in the majors in 1982 and a Brewers single-season record until 1996.

.957

OPS of Robin Yount, highest in the majors.

.992

Fielding percentage as right fielder by Charlie Moore, highest in the AL.

.995

Fielding percentage as catcher by Ted Simmons, highest in the majors.

.997

Fielding percentage as first baseman by Cecil Cooper, tied for best in the AL.

2,606

Total bases by the Brewers in 1982, most in the majors.

1,978,896

Regular-season attendance at County Stadium in 1982, a new team record.

THE 1982 MILWAUKEE BREWERS

LEAGUE CHAMPIONSHIP SERIES
MILWAUKEE BREWERS OVER CALIFORNIA ANGELS (3-2)

0

Batters who reached base out of 10 faced by Milwaukee reliever Pete Ladd during the series. Ladd had saves in Games One and Five.

1ST

Team to win a League Championship Series after trailing two games to none: the Brewers. In Game Five, the Brewers trailed the Angels after 6½ innings.

1ST

League Championship Series to feature two 1960s expansion teams.

4

Runs scored by Milwaukee left fielder Mark Brouhard (subbing for an injured Ben Oglivie) in Game Four. It would be the only postseason game of his major-league career.

.219

Batting average of the Brewers in the series, compared with .255 by the Angels.

.611

Batting average of series MVP Fred Lynn of the Angels, who had 11 hits in 18 at-bats.

WORLD SERIES
ST. LOUIS CARDINALS OVER MILWAUKEE BREWERS (4-3)

0-2

Record of reliever Bob McClure, who took the loss in Games Two and Seven. He had saves in Games Four and Five.

1ST

Player with two four-hit games in a single World Series: Robin Yount, in Games One and Five.

2ND

Player to be named MVP of a League Championship Series and the World Series in the same postseason: St. Louis catcher Darrell Porter. The first was Willie Stargell of the Pittsburgh Pirates, in 1979.

2-0

Record of Mike Caldwell, who pitched a three-hit shutout in Game One and gave up four runs in 8⅓ innings in Game Five.

5

Hits by Paul Molitor in Game One, a World Series record for a single game.

12

Hits by Robin Yount during the series, in 29 at-bats (.414). Paul Molitor had 11 hits in 31 at-bats (.355).

ROUND THE MAJORS IN 1982

0

No-hitters in major-league baseball in 1982, the first year since 1959 that this happened.

0

Home runs in 636 at-bats by Jerry Remy of the Boston Red Sox in 1982.

0-13

Record of Terry Felton of the Minnesota Twins in 1982. He finished his four-season career that year with a record of 0-16.

1ST

Major-league game played at the Hubert H. Humphrey Metrodome in Minneapolis, on April 6. The Twins lost to the Seattle Mariners 11-7 before a crowd of 52,279.

1ST

Career hits by Wade Boggs of the Red Sox (on April 26) and Tony Gwynn of the San Diego Padres (on July 19). Gwynn had 3,141 career hits, and Boggs had 3,010.

1ST

Game of 2,632 consecutive games played by Cal Ripken Jr. of the Baltimore Orioles, on May 30. The next game he missed was on September 20, 1998. Ripken had 28 home runs and 93 RBIs in 1982 and was named the AL Rookie of the Year.

1ST

All-Star Game to be played outside of the United States, in Montreal's Olympic Stadium on July 13. The NL won 4-1 to beat the AL for the 11th consecutive year. Dave Concepción of the Cincinnati Reds, who hit a two-run homer in the second inning, was named the game's MVP.

2

Different teams for which Joel Youngblood got a hit, in two different cites, on August 4. In a day game at Chicago's Wrigley Field, he was the starting center fielder for the New York Mets and went 1-for-2 with two RBIs. He was replaced in the fourth inning and informed that he had been traded to the Montreal Expos, who were playing that night at Philadelphia's Veterans Stadium. He entered the game as right fielder in the sixth inning and singled in the seventh.

2.40

ERA of Steve Rogers of the Expos, lowest in the majors. Rick Sutcliffe of the Cleveland Indians had the lowest ERA in the AL, 2.96.

3

Grand slams in one week (July 4 through 10) by Larry Parrish of the Texas Rangers. He was the third player to accomplish this, after Lou Gehrig of the Yankees in 1931 and Jim Northrup of the Detroit Tigers in 1968.

3

Home runs by Doug DeCinces of the Angels on August 3 and again on August 8.

3-26

Record of the Twins in May 1982.

4

Home runs in consecutive plate appearances by Larry Herndon of the Tigers on May 16 and 18.

4TH

Los Angeles Dodger in a row to be named NL Rookie of the Year: second baseman Steve Sax. He followed pitchers Rick Sutcliffe (1979), Steve Howe (1980), and Fernando Valenzuela (1981).

4TH

Consecutive year that Bruce Sutter led the NL in saves (with the Chicago Cubs in 1979 and 1980 and with the Cardinals in 1981 and 1982). His 36 saves in 1982 topped the majors.

4TH

NL Cy Young Award won by Steve Carlton of the Philadelphia Phillies. He was the first player with four Cy Young Awards. In 1982 he led the majors in wins (23), strikeouts (286), shutouts (six), and innings pitched (295⅔) and led the NL in games started (38) and complete games (19).

5

Stolen bases by Lonnie Smith of the Cardinals on September 4, to tie a modern-day NL record.

6

Hits in eight at-bats by Joe Lefebvre of the Padres in a 16-inning game against the Dodgers on September 13.

13

Consecutive games won by the Atlanta Braves to start the season, a modern-day major-league record. In 1884 the St. Louis Maroons of the Union Association won their first 20 games.

15

Consecutive games lost by the Mets from August 15 through August 31.

19

Wins by LaMarr Hoyt of the Chicago White Sox, most in the AL.

23RD

Consecutive season in which Jim Kaat of the Cardinals was credited with at least one win.

25 AND 7

Home runs at home and on the road, respectively, by Bob Horner of the Braves.

35

Saves by Dan Quisenberry of the Royals, most in the AL.

36

Stolen bases by John Wathan of the Royals, a record by a catcher.

37

Home runs by Dave Kingman of the Mets, the most in the NL, despite a batting average of .204.

78

Stolen bases by Tim Raines of the Expos, the most in the NL.

119TH

Stolen base of the season by Rickey Henderson of the Oakland Athletics on August 27, to break Lou Brock's 1974 record. Henderson would finish the season with 130 steals; he was also thrown out a record 42 times.

133

RBIs by Hal McRae of the Royals, the most in the majors in 1982 and a new record for designated hitters.

168⅓

Innings pitched in relief by Bob Stanley of the Red Sox, an AL record.

209

Strikeouts by Floyd Bannister of the Mariners, the most in the AL.

269⅓

Innings without allowing a home run by Greg Minton of the San Francisco Giants from September 6, 1978, to May 2, 1982.

.281/36/109

Batting average, home runs, and RBIs by NL MVP Dale Murphy of the Braves. He was tied with Al Oliver of the Expos for most RBIs in the NL. Murphy also won his first Gold Glove Award as an outfielder in 1982.

300TH

Career win by Gaylord Perry of the Mariners on May 6. He became the 15th player to accomplish the feat.

.332

Batting average of Willie Wilson of the Royals, highest in the majors. Al Oliver of the Expos led the NL with an average of .331.

475TH

And final home run by Willie Stargell, on July 21. He played his entire 21-year career with the Pirates.

479

Consecutive chances as second baseman without an error by Manny Trillo of the Phillies from April 8 to July 31. He broke the record of 458 that was set by Baltimore's Jerry Adair during the 1964 and 1965 seasons.

3,000TH

Career strikeout by Ferguson Jenkins of the Cubs, on May 25. He was the seventh player to reach this mark.

3,000TH

Career game by Pete Rose of the Phillies, on June 20. He was the fifth major leaguer to play this many games.

12,635TH

Career at-bat by Pete Rose on August 14, to break Hank Aaron's major-league record.

13,942ND

Career plate appearance by Pete Rose on August 18, to break another of Aaron's records.

3,608,881

Regular-season attendance at LA's Dodger Stadium in 1982, a new major-league record. The Angels set an AL record with an attendance of 2,807,360 at Anaheim Stadium.

SOURCES

Nemec, David, ed. *The Baseball Chronicle: Year-by-Year History of Major League Baseball* (Lincolnwood, Illinois: Publications International, 2003).

Society for American Baseball Research. *The SABR Baseball List and Record Book* (New York: Scribner, 2007).

Solomon, Burt. *The Baseball Timeline* (New York: DK Publishing, 2001).

Sugar, Burt Randolph, ed. *The Baseball Maniac's Almanac* (third edition) (New York: Skyhorse Publishing, 2012).

Baseball-Almanac.com.

Baseball-Reference.com.

Retrosheet.org.

ThisGreatGame.com/1982-baseball-history.html.

A HALL OF FAME ROSTER OF CONTRIBUTORS

Eric Aron has contributed a number of bios for the BioProject website and books. Originally hailing from Rye, New York, he now lives in Boston. Currently, he is a researcher and exhibit interpreter at the Edward M. Kennedy Institute for the United States Senate.

Bill Bishop is a lifelong resident of Michigan and an ardent fan of the Detroit Tigers. This fanaticism has been passed down to his two daughters, Amy and Pascale, and three grandchildren, Kevin, Drew, and Penny. Bill has been a member of SABR for twenty plus years, writing bios for two Detroit Tiger books, as well as the Deadball Stars of the AL and NL. Now retired from his job as safety engineer at DTE, he is pursuing his dream of attending a game in every major league stadium, with only three to go. He currently resides in Clarkston, Michigan with his wife, Nora.

Richard Bogovich, who lived in Wisconsin for 25 years, is the author of *Kid Nichols: A Biography of the Hall of Fame Pitcher*, about Madison's most noteworthy ballplayer. His previous book was *The Who: A Who's Who* and he has contributed chapters to numerous SABR books. He attended the Brewers' final game at County Stadium and Carlos Zambrano's no-hitter at Miller Park. He works for the Wendland Utz law firm in Rochester, Minnesota.

Phillip Bolda was born in Milwaukee and grew up within walking distance of Milwaukee County Stadium. A graduate of Ripon College, he spent his career on university campuses as a fundraiser and he now lives in Tempe, Arizona. He became a member of SABR in 1979 and he has become active in supporting the fundraising efforts of the organization.

Frederick C. "Rick" Bush has written articles for more than two dozen SABR publications as well as the Biography and Games Projects. He has also collaborated with Bill Nowlin to co-edit two SABR Negro Leagues books: *Bittersweet Goodbye*, about the 1948 Birmingham Black Barons and Homestead Grays, and *The Newark Eagles Take Flight*, which covered the 1946 Negro League champions. He and Bill are currently at work on a third volume, about the 1935 Pittsburgh Crawfords. Rick, his wife, Michelle, and their three sons — Michael, Andrew, and Daniel — live in the Houston metro area, and he teaches English at Wharton County Junior College in Sugar Land.

Isaac Buttke was born in Wausau, Wisconsin, and grew up an avid Brewers fan. During college, he wrote about baseball for sites such as RotoWire and Reviewing the Brew. He then graduated from the University of Wisconsin-Madison with a degree in marketing and international business. Upon graduation, he pursued his passion for baseball, initially working as an intern for the West Virginia Power before moving into his current position as a baseball operations video associate for the Los Angeles Dodgers. He hopes to continue working his way up in baseball operations with the ultimate goal of having a prominent role in a major-league front office.

A lifelong White Sox fan surrounded by Cubs fans in the northern suburbs of Chicago, **Ken Carrano** works as a chief financial officer for a large landscaping firm and as a soccer referee. Ken and his Brewers' fan wife, Ann, share two children, two golden retrievers, and a mutual distain for the blue side of Chicago.

Alan Cohen has been a SABR member since 2010. He serves as vice president-treasurer of the Connecticut Smoky Joe Wood Chapter and is datacaster (MiLB First Pitch stringer) for the Hartford Yard Goats, the Double-A affiliate of the Colorado Rockies. His biographies, game stories, and essays have appeared in more than 40 SABR publications. Since his first *Baseball Research Journal* article appeared in 2013, Alan has continued to expand his research into the Hearst Sandlot Classic (1946-1965), which launched the careers of 88 major-league players. He has four children and six grandchildren and resides in Connecticut with his wife, Frances, their cat, Morty, and their dog, Buddy.

Rory Costello has contributed to a variety of SABR book projects over the years. This one intrigued him because of the characters on the club. Rory lives in Brooklyn, New York, with his wife, Noriko, and son, Kai.

Dennis D. Degenhardt has been a proud SABR member since 1997, thanks to a Christmas gift from his wife, Linda. He is a retired 40-year credit-union executive who is doing what he wanted to do when he grew up, baseball research and writing. He has contributed to the SABR publications *From the Braves to the Brewers. Great Games and Exciting History at Milwaukee County Stadium* and *Bittersweet Goodbye, The Black Barons, The Grays, and the 1948 Negro League World Series*. In addition, he has been an active member serving as an officer in SABR's Ken Keltner Badger State Chapter since 2001.

Dan Fields has contributed to many SABR books. He is a senior manuscript editor at the *New England Journal of Medicine* and a longtime volunteer with the Grief Support Services program of Samaritans Inc. He lives in Framingham, Massachusetts, and can be reached at dfields820@gmail.com.

John Gabcik passed away in August 2019. He was born and raised in Chicago, and followed the White Sox since 1952. He wrote biographies and game stories for SABR, concentrating on underappreciated White Sox pitchers and other personalities. He also heled Retrosheet develop game play-by-play recreations.

Gordon J. Gattie is an engineer for the US Navy. His baseball research interests include ballparks, historical records, and statistical analysis. A SABR member since 1998, Gordon earned his Ph.D. from SUNY Buffalo, where he used baseball to investigate judgment performance in complex dynamic environments. Ever the optimist, he dreams of a Cleveland Indians-Washington Nationals World Series matchup. Lisa, his wonderful wife, who also enjoys baseball, and Morrigan, their yellow Labrador, enjoy traveling across the country to visit ballparks and other baseball-related sites. Gordon has contributed to multiple SABR publications and the Games Project.

Austin Gisriel planned to replace Brooks Robinson at third base for the Baltimore Orioles, and it was only a lack of talent that kept him from doing so. Gisriel is the author of *Fathers, Sons, & Holy Ghosts: Baseball as a Spiritual Experience* (2017), as well as *Boots Poffenberger: Hurler, Hero, Hell-Raiser* (2014). A former board member and webcaster for the New Market Rebels of the Valley Baseball League, Gisriel and his wife, Martha, are enjoying life in Winchester, Virginia. To learn more about this longtime Oriole fan, visit austingisriel.com

Gregg Hoffmann covered Wisconsin sports for more than 40 years, including the Brewers for 43 years. His media outlets included the *Kenosha News*, *USA Today*, *Baseball Weekly* and *The Sporting News*. He has authored seven books, including *Down in the Valley: The History of Milwaukee County Stadium* and *Immortalized in Bronze*, stories of Wisconsin Hall of Famers. Hoffmann is a senior lecturer emeritus in mass communications from UW-Milwaukee. He now lives in the Driftless Area of Wisconsin with his wife, Pauline.

Mike Huber grew up in Baltimore, near the same neighborhood as Milwaukee's Chuck Porter. Mike has been rooting for the Baltimore Orioles for over 50 years, and he joined SABR in 1996. He is the chair of SABR's Games Project Committee and he enjoys writing for both the Games Project and the BioProject.

Jay Hurd, a longtime member of the Society for American Baseball Research, is a contributor to the SABR Baseball Biography Project, serves as co-editor of the SABR Arts Committee journal, *Turnstyle*, presents on topics including the Negro Leagues, women in baseball, baseball literature for children and young adults, and baseball and the Blue Laws. Jay, a librarian, retired from Harvard University, where he worked as the preservation review librarian for Widener Library. He has also worked as a museum educator and interpreter at the Concord Museum, Concord, Massachusetts. A fan of the Boston Red Sox, he relocated from Medford, Massachusetts, to Bristol, Rhode Island, in 2016. His current research focus is baseball in Rhode Island.

Maxwell Kates is a CPA who lives and works in Toronto. Prior to joining SABR in 2001, he worked in sports radio in St. Catharines, Ontario. He has been a member of the Hanlan's Point (Toronto) Chapter steering committee for 12 years. His writing has appeared in *The National Pastime*, *The Globe and Mail*, the (Houston) *Pecan Park Eagle*, and, most recently, in *Baltimore Chop*. Speaking engagements have included the University of Toronto, the Limmud Conference, and the Canadian Baseball History Conference, along with SABR meetings and conventions in Seattle, Montreal, and Houston. His first SABR convention was in Milwaukee, which was also attended by a member of the 1982 Brewers, and that's Gorman Thomas.

Jimmy Keenan has been a SABR member since 2001. His grandfather, Jimmy Lyston, and four other family members were professional baseball players. A frequent contributor to SABR publications, Keenan is the author of the following books: *The Lystons: A Story of One Baltimore Family & Our National Pastime*; *The Life, Times and Tragic Death of Pitcher Win Mercer*; and *The Lyston Brothers: A Journey Through 19th Century Baseball*. Keenan is a 2010 inductee into the Oldtimers Baseball Association of Maryland's Hall of Fame and a 2012 inductee into the Baltimore's Boys of Summer Hall of Fame.

A prolific contributor to SABR's BioProject and its various publications, **Norm King** died in 2018. Through his writing and research we met many of the heroes of his youth, including Warren Cromartie, Steve Rogers, Bill Lee, and Hall of Fame Expos broadcaster Dave Van Horne. In 2016 SABR published *Au jeu/Play Ball: The 50 Greatest Games in the History of the Montreal Expos*, for which Norm served as senior editor and main writer. It was SABR's top-selling book of the year.

Lee Kluck is a historian from Stevens Point, Wisconsin. An avid baseball fan, he has contributed to various SABR projects, including books on Milwaukee County Stadium and the 1986 New York Mets. His next project is a biography of Harry Dalton, to published by the University of Nebraska Press. When he isn't writing or working for a major insurance company, Lee can be found cooking and binge-watching baking shows produced in the United Kingdom with his wife, Carla.

A lifelong Tigers fan, **Steven Kuehl** was born in Michigan's Upper Peninsula, but now resides in Wisconsin with his wife, Kathleen; son, Connor; and Labrador retrievers Lola and Oliver. He is an assistant professor of mathematics and department chair at Silver Lake College of the Holy Family in Manitowoc, Wisconsin. His article "The 20/30 Game Winner: An Endangered/Extinct Species" was published in the *Baseball Research Journal in 2013*. He has also worked on the SABR book projects *Tigers by the Tale: Fifty Great Games at the Corner of Michigan* and *Trumbull and From the Braves to the Brewers: Great Games and Exciting History at Milwaukee's County Stadium.*

Russ Lake lives in Champaign, Illinois, and is a retired college professor. The 1964 St. Louis Cardinals remain his favorite team, and he was distressed to see Sportsman's Park (aka Busch Stadium I) being demolished not long after he had attended the last game there on May 8, 1966. His wife, Carol, deserves an MVP award for watching all of a 13-inning ballgame in Cincinnati with Russ in 1971 — during their honeymoon. In 1994 he was an editor for David Halberstam's baseball book *October 1964*.

Len Levin is retired after many years as a newspaper editor in Rhode Island and Massachusetts. He is the copy editor for most SABR books and is one of the leaders of the SABR Games project. He is chairman of SABR's Lajoie-Start (Southern New England) Chapter. In season, he also edits the decisions of the Rhode Island Supreme Court.

Dan Levitt is the author of several baseball books and numerous essays. He is a longtime SABR member and a recipient of the Bob Davids Award and the Chadwick Award. His books have won the Larry Ritter Book Award, and the Sporting News-SABR Baseball Research Award, and have twice been finalists for the Seymour Medal.

Bill Mortell has been a SABR member since 1977. For 35 years he worked for the U.S. Department of Defense, from which he retired in 1987. A Chicago native, he lived in various cities in Japan (Kyoto, Nara, and Tokyo area) for 13 years and once saw both Frank and Brooks Robinson homer in the same Tokyo game against a Japanese all-star team. His current interests include family genealogy, and watching MLB, particularly Cubs and White Sox. He provides occasional research assistance to SABR members who are engaged in writing biographies on major-league players.

Rod Nelson is the chair of the SABR Scouts Committee and maintains the Who-Signed-Whom database, which is the foundation of the *Diamond Mines* exhibit on the Baseball Hall of Fame website. He was SABR's first research services manager (2006-2007) and the founder and moderator of the Baseball Necrology Yahoo group, as well as managing editor of the *Emerald Guide to Baseball* from its first edition in 2008 through 2014. He makes his home in Saint Clair Shores, Michigan.

Bill Nowlin is a Boston native and Red Sox fan, author, and editor of several dozen books (mostly on baseball). He has been a member of SABR's board of directors since 2004. His first SABR convention was the 2001 convention in Milwaukee. He was co-founder of the record label Rounder Records.

J.G. Preston is a writer and communications consultant in Santa Fe, New Mexico. He has contributed to several SABR publications and writes about baseball at prestonjg.wordpress.com/.

Carl Riechers worked at United Parcel Service in St. Louis during the 1982 World Series. Someone working in the sort aisle at the time was adding "GO CARDINALS" to every parcel heading to Milwaukee during the series. This "someone" would like all the Brewers fans to accept his sincere apologies for this inappropriate act.

Richard Riis is a writer, researcher, genealogist, and lifelong baseball maven. A former New Yorker, he now resides in Southern California, where he can finally stay awake to see the end of Yankees and Mets games on TV. He has contributed to SABR's BioProject and several SABR publications, and recently co-authored the autobiography of his close friend, former child actress Pamelyn Ferdin.

Joel Rippel, a Minnesota native and a graduate of the University of Minnesota, is the author or co-author of nine books on Minnesota sports history and has contributed to several SABR publications.

Rick Schabowski has been a SABR member since 1995. He is a retired machinist at the Harley Davidson Company, is currently serving as an industrial mathematics teacher at Waukesha Community Technical College and at the Wisconsin Regional Training Partnership in the Manufacturing Program, and is a certified manufacturing skills standards council instructor. He is president of the Ken Keltner Badger State Chapter of SABR, treasurer of the Milwaukee Braves Historical Association, and a member of the Hoop Historians and the Pro Football Research Association. He is the author of a book about the Milwaukee Bucks championship season, *From Coin Toss to Championship: 1971 The Year of the Milwaukee Bucks*. He lives in St. Francis, Wisconsin.

From an early age, **David E. Skelton** developed a lifelong love of baseball when the lights from Philadelphia's Connie Mack Stadium shone through his bedroom window. Long removed from Philly, he resides with his family in central Texas, where he is employed in the oil and gas industry. An avid collector, he joined SABR in 2012.

Doug Skipper joined SABR in 1982. A member and former president of the Halsey Hall (Minnesota) Chapter, Doug has written a number of biographies and Games Project summaries for SABR publications and websites. He is the chairperson of the Larry Ritter Award Committee and has been a committee member for several years. A native of Texas who grew up in Colorado, lived in Wyoming and North Dakota, and now Minnesota, Doug is an avid Red Sox fan. Doug and his wife, Kathy, have two daughters, MacKenzie and Shannon. He is a marketing research, customer-satisfaction and public-opinion consultant who reads and writes about baseball.

Stew Thornley has been a SABR member since 1979, and was the 2016 recipient of the Bob Davids Award. He is a former class clown.

Clayton Trutor is the chairman of the Vermont Chapter (Gardner-Waterman). He holds a Ph.D. in US history from Boston College and is an instructor at Norwich University in Northfield, Vermont. He has authored more than 25 player biographies and is the co-editor of *Overcoming Adversity: Baseball's Tony Conigliaro Award* (2017). He writes about college football for SB Nation and is currently writing a history of professional sports in Atlanta. You can follow him on Twitter: @ClaytonTrutor.

Dale Voiss grew up in southern Wisconsin and has followed the Brewers closely since their arrival in Wisconsin from Seattle in 1970. He has written several player biographies and other essays for the SABR BioProject. The divorced father of a 17-year-old daughter, Dale has lived in Madison, Wisconsin, since 1978.

Joseph Wancho lives in Brooklyn, Ohio, and is a lifelong Cleveland Indians fan. He has been a SABR member since 2005 and serves as the vice chair of SABR's Baseball Index Project Committee. He was the editor of *Pitching to the Pennant: The 1954 Cleveland Indians* (University of Nebraska Press, 2014) and *The Sleeping Giant Awakes: The 1995 Cleveland Indians* (SABR, 2019). He also authored *So You Think You're a Cleveland Indians Fan?* (Sports Publishing, 2018).

Gregory H. Wolf was born in Pittsburgh, but now resides in the Chicagoland area with his wife, Margaret, and daughter, Gabriela. A professor of German studies and holder of the Dennis and Jean Bauman Endowed Chair in the Humanities at North Central College in Naperville, Illinois, he has edited a dozen books for SABR. He is currently working on projects about Shibe Park in Philadelphia and Ebbets Field in Brooklyn. Since January 2017 he has been co-director of SABR's BioProject, which you can follow on Facebook and Twitter.

Mario Ziino is the director of sports publications at Delzer Lithograph Co., Waukesha, Wisconsin. He spent 25 years with the Milwaukee Brewers as the director of publications and assistant director of public relations, and has written about the Brewers for over 40 years. Mario edited and/or authored three Brewers publications: *Robin Yount — The Legend Lives On* (1992), *True Brew — A Quarter Century with the Milwaukee Brewers* (1994), and *Down in the Valley — The History of County Stadium* (2001). He co-produced two specialty videos: "On Deck for Cooperstown — Robin Yount" (1994) and "End of an Era" (2000). He also scripted Brewers ceremonial events, including Robin Yount's retirement (1994), the closing of County Stadium (2000), the opening of Miller Park (2001), the Miller Park Plaza statue dedications (2001, 2010 and 2012), and the Brewers Wall of Honor (2014 and 2015).

Friends of SABR

You can become a Friend of SABR by giving as little as $10 per month or by making a one-time gift of $1,000 or more. When you do so, you will be inducted into a community of passionate baseball fans dedicated to supporting SABR's work.

Friends of SABR receive the following benefits:
- ✓ Annual Friends of SABR Commemorative Lapel Pin
- ✓ Recognition in This Week in SABR, SABR.org, and the SABR Annual Report
- ✓ Access to the SABR Annual Convention VIP donor event
- ✓ Invitations to exclusive Friends of SABR events

SABR On-Deck Circle - $10/month, $30/month, $50/month
Get in the SABR On-Deck Circle, and help SABR become the essential community for the world of baseball. Your support will build capacity around all things SABR, including publications, website content, podcast development, and community growth.

A monthly gift is deducted from your bank account or charged to a credit card until you tell us to stop. No more email, mail, or phone reminders.

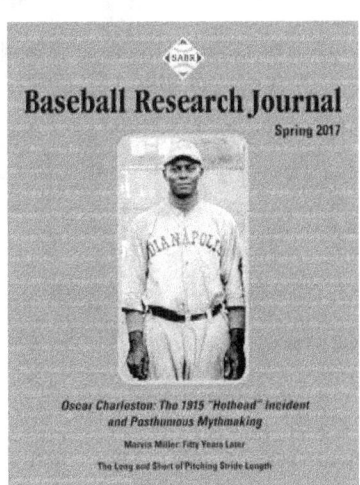
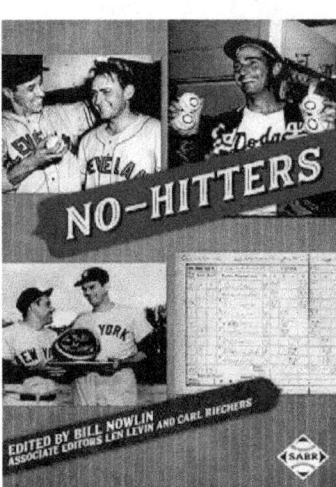

Join the SABR On-Deck Circle

Payment Info: _____Visa _____Mastercard

Name on Card: _____

Card #: _____

Exp. Date: _____ Security Code: _____

Signature: _____

- ○ $10/month
- ○ $30/month
- ○ $50/month
- ○ Other amount _____

Go to sabr.org/donate to make your gift online

New Books from SABR

Part of the mission of the Society for American Baseball Research has always been to disseminate member research. In addition to the *Baseball Research Journal*, SABR publishes books that include player biographies, historical game recaps, and statistical analysis. All SABR books are available in print and ebook formats. SABR members can access the entire SABR Digital Library for free and purchase print copies at significant member discounts of 40 to 50% off cover price.

JEFF BAGWELL IN CONNECTICUT:
A Consistent Lad in the Land of Steady Habits
This volume of articles, interviews, and essays by members of the Connecticut chapter of SABR chronicles the life and career of Connecticut's favorite baseball son, Hall-of-Famer Jeff Bagwell, with special attention on his high school and college years.
Edited by Karl Cicitto, Bill Nowlin, & Len Levin
$19.95 paperback (ISBN 978-1-943816-97-2)
$9.99 ebook (ISBN 978-1-943816-96-5)
7"x10", 246 pages, 45 photos

MET-ROSPECTIVES:
A Collection of the Greatest Games in New York Mets History
This book's 57 game stories—coinciding with the number of Mets years through 2018—are strictly for the eternal optimist. They include the team's very first victory in April 1962 at Forbes Field, Tom Seaver's "Imperfect Game" in July '69, the unforgettable Game Sixes in October '86, the "Grand Slam Single" in the 1999 NLCS, and concludes with the extra-innings heroics in September 2016 at Citi Field that helped ensure a wild-card berth.
edited by Brian Wright and Bill Nowlin
$14.95 paperback (ISBN 978-1-943816-87-3)
$9.99 ebook (ISBN 978-1-943816-86-6)
8.5"X11", 148 pages, 44 photos

1995 CLEVELAND INDIANS:
The Sleeping Giant Awakens
After almost 40 years of sub-500 baseball, the Sleeping Giant woke in 1995, the first season in the Indians spent in their new home of Jacob's Field. The biographies of all the players, coaches, and broadcasters from that year are here, sprinkled with personal perspectives, as well as game stories from key matchups during the 1995 season, information about Jacob's Field, and other essays.
Edited by Joseph Wancho
$19.95 paperback (ISBN 978-1-943816-95-8)
$9.99 ebook (ISBN 978-1-943816-94-1)
8.5"X11", 410 pages, 76 photos

CINCINNATI'S CROSLEY FIELD:
A Gem in the Queen City
This book evokes memories of Crosley Field through detailed summaries of more than 85 historic and monumental games played there, and 10 insightful feature essays about the history of the ballpark. Former Reds players Johnny Edwards and Art Shamsky share their memories of the park in introductions.
Edited by Gregory H. Wolf
$19.95 paperback (ISBN 978-1-943816-75-0)
$9.99 ebook (ISBN 978-1-943816-74-3)
8.5"X11", 320 pages, 43 photos

TIME FOR EXPANSION BASEBALL
The LA Angels and "new" Washington Senators ushered in MLB expansion in 1960, followed by the Houston Colt .45s and New York Mets. By 1998, 10 additional teams had launched: the Kansas City Royals, Seattle Pilots, Toronto Blue Jays, and Tampa Bay Devil Tays in the AL, and the Montreal Expos, San Diego Padres, Colorado Rockies, Florida Marlins, and Arizona Diamondbacks in the NL. *Time for Expansion Baseball* tells each team's origin and includes biographies of key players.
Edited by Maxwell Kates and Bill Nowlin
$24.95 paperback (ISBN 978-1-933599-89-7)
$9.99 ebook (ISBN 978-1-933599-88-0)
8.5"X11", 430 pages, 150 photos

MOMENTS OF JOY AND HEARTBREAK:
66 Significant Episodes in the History of the Pittsburgh Pirates
In this book we relive no-hitters, World Series-winning homers, and the last tripleheader ever played in major-league baseball. Famous Pirates like Honus Wagner and Roberto Clemente—and infamous ones like Dock Ellis—make their appearances, as well as recent stars like Andrew McCutcheon.
Edited by Jorge Iber and Bill Nowlin
$19.95 paperback (ISBN 978-1-943816-73-6)
$9.99 ebook (ISBN 978-1-943816-72-9)
8.5"X11", 208 pages, 36 photos

BASE BALL'S 19TH CENTURY "WINTER" MEETINGS 1857-1900
A look at the business meetings of base ball's earliest days (not all of which were in the winter). As John Thorn writes in his Foreword, "This monumental volume traces the development of the game from its birth as an organized institution to its very near suicide at the dawn of the next century."
Edited by Jeremy K. Hodges and Bill Nowlin
$29.95 paperback (ISBN 978-1-943816-91-0)
$9.99 ebook (ISBN978-1-943816-90-3)
8.5"x11", 390 pages, 50 photos

FROM SPRING TRAINING TO SCREEN TEST:
Baseball Players Turned Actors
SABR"s book of baseball's "matinee stars," a selection of those who crossed the lines between professional sports and popular entertainment. Included are the famous (Gene Autry, Joe DiMaggio, Jim Thorpe, Bernie Williams) and the forgotten (Al Gettel, Lou Stringer, Wally Hebert, Wally Hood), essays on baseball in TV shows and Coca-Cola commercials, and Jim Bouton's casting as "Jim Barton" in the *Ball Four* TV series.
Edited by Rob Edelman and Bill Nowlin
$19.95 paperback (ISBN 978-1-943816-71-2)
$9.99 ebook (ISBN 978-1-943816-70-5)
8.5"X11", 410 pages, 89 photos

To learn more about how to receive these publications for free or at member discount as a member of SABR, visit the website: sabr.org/join

www.ingramcontent.com/pod-product-compliance
Lightning Source LLC
Chambersburg PA
CBHW081352070526
44583CB00020B/2530